POWER & CHOICE

Eleventh Edition

POWER & CHOICE

An Introduction to Political Science

W. Phillips Shively

University of Minnesota

 **McGraw-Hill
Higher Education**

Boston   Burr Ridge, IL   Dubuque, IA   New York   San Francisco   St. Louis
Bangkok   Bogotá   Caracas   Kuala Lumpur   Lisbon   London   Madrid   Mexico City
Milan   Montreal   New Delhi   Santiago   Seoul   Singapore   Sydney   Taipei   Toronto

McGraw-Hill
Higher Education

Published by McGraw-Hill, an imprint of The McGraw-Hill Companies, Inc., 1221 Avenue of the Americas, New York, NY 10020. Copyright © 2008, 2007, 2005, 2003, 2001, 1999, 1997, 1995, 1993, 1991, 1987. All rights reserved. No part of this publication may be reproduced or distributed in any form or by any means, or stored in a database or retrieval system, without the prior written consent of The McGraw-Hill Companies, Inc., including, but not limited to, in any network or other electronic storage or transmission, or broadcast for distance learning.

This book is printed on acid-free paper.

2 3 4 5 6 7 8 9 0 DOC/DOC 0 9 8

ISBN: 978-0-07-340391-5

MHID: 0-07-340391-1

Editor in Chief: *Michael Ryan*
Publisher: *Lisa Moore*
Sponsoring Editor: *Mark L. Georgiev*
Marketing Manager: *Simon Heathcote*
Developmental Editor: *Larry Goldberg*
Production Editor: *Regina Ernst*
Production Service: *Laserwords Private Limited*
Manuscript Editor: *Leslie Ann Weber*
Design Manager: *Preston Thomas*
Cover Designer: *Preston Thomas*
Art Editor: *Sonia Brown*
Manager, Photo Research: *Brian J. Pecko*
Composition: *10/12 Minion by Laserwords Private Limited*
Printing: *PMS 1805, 45# New Era Matte, R. R. Donnelley & Sons/Crawfordsville, IN*

Cover: World sphere with an airplane circling in Queens, New York. © Dirk Anschutz/ Nonstock/JupiterImages

Library of Congress Cataloging-in-Publication Data

Shively, W. Phillips, 1942-
    Power and choice : an introduction to political science / W. Phillips Shively.—11th ed.
        p. cm.
    Rev. ed. of: Power & choice. 10th ed.
    Includes bibliographical references and index.
    ISBN-13: 978-0-07-340391-5 (alk. paper)
    ISBN-10: 0-07-340391-1 (alk. paper)
        1. Political science—Textbooks. I. Shively, W. Phillips, 1942- Power & choice. II. Title.
    JA66.S47 2008
    320—dc22

                                                                    2007038648

www.mhhe.com

To Ruth Phillips Shively
and
Arthur W. Shively

CONTENTS

PART III   ❧ THE CITIZEN AND THE REGIME 149

PART V   ❧ INTERNATIONAL POLITICS 395

EXAMPLES AND BOXED FEATURES

Examples

Boxed Features

PREFACE

This book provides a general, comparative introduction to the major concepts and themes of political science. For a number of years, I had taught a course that attempted to accomplish this aim, and that experience had shown me how badly we need a text that is conceptually alive and that engages students with concrete examples of analysis without losing them in a clutter of definitional minutiae. That is what I aimed for when I first wrote this book, and I've been most pleased at the response it has elicited.

The title of the book, *Power & Choice,* indicates a subsidiary theme that recurs at intervals. Politics may be seen as (1) the use of power or (2) the production of a public choice. Often one or the other is heavily emphasized in approaching the subject. Marxism emphasizes politics as the use of power, while pluralism and much formal modeling work emphasize the emergence of public choices. For our present purpose, I have defined politics as the use of power to make common decisions for a group of people, a definition that obviously demands that one hold both perspectives simultaneously. At various stages of my presentation, I note instances in which an emphasis on just one of the two halves of the definition may yield a distorted interpretation.

Behind this subsidiary theme lies a broader theme that remains largely implicit—that political analysis is best conducted eclectically, rather than being straitjacketed into a single approach. My own research is squarely in the "behavioral" realm, for instance, but I found as I was working on this book that necessities of exposition and understanding pulled me toward a greater emphasis on policy and institutions than I had originally intended. Similarly, the state as an organizer of politics thrust itself more to the fore than I had anticipated. Distinctions that provide useful boundaries for research proved unhelpful in my efforts to build an understanding of politics among students; I think this is a healthy sign.

Material in the book is presented topically rather than on a country-by-country basis; but in order to add the sort of detailed contextual grounding that students gain from a country presentation, I have included within each substantive chapter a couple of extended examples from countries that particularly display the conceptual material of that chapter. For instance, Chapter 3, which deals with the state, concludes with detailed sections on the establishment and maintenance of the Nigerian state and on the European Union. Similarly, Chapter 16, "Bureaucracy and the Public Sector," gives detailed treatment to France and a comparison of bureaucratic cultures in Europe and Africa.

✦ NEW TO THE ELEVENTH EDITION

Over the couple of decades since I first wrote this book, the world has proved to be a strange and wonderful place—even more than I realized at that time. The book has seen the joy and light of the young people who pulled down the Berlin Wall in 1989 and the darkness of the suicide attackers who destroyed the World Trade Center in 2001. As it has evolved across several editions during this time, very little that it started out with has remained unchanged. Its mood has also varied from time to time, but one thing that has been constant is my faith in people's capacity to shape their futures through politics.

In this eleventh edition there is, of course, a great deal of general updating. When a book deals with all the states of the world, a lot changes over even a couple of years. In revising the book this time, however, in addition to the normal requirements of updating I found that I was challenged (in a good way) by an exceptional set of reviewers, who led me to do an unusually extensive revision.

The most general revision in this edition is a considerable reorganization to improve flow for the reader. One aspect of this is a move of Chapter 7 (on legitimacy and political culture) to place it behind Chapter 8 (on regimes) and adjacent to other chapters on constituent aspects of the state. But I moved many sections around within chapters as well, added more explanatory captions to illustrations, and so on. Reviewers pointed out a number of these useful moves.

The main substantive subtraction that has occurred in this edition is that I have finally exorcised the Soviet Union as an example in all but a couple of places. It was a great example for many concepts, but it is too distant in the past. In some places I have instead added analysis of the Communist Party in China.

I have also dropped or reduced various sections in order to keep the length of the book about the same, while adding substantive treatment in many areas. New or added material includes:

- *Expanding the treatment of the "choice" side of "power and choice."*

- *Increasing coverage of religion and politics.*

- *Righting an ancient wrong. Chapter 2, on ideologies, emphasizes the ideologies that arose out of the industrial revolution, but I also try to offer a brief sense of the broader development of political philosophy. In the section on political philosophy in other eras, I have always felt I had not done justice to the Greeks. I hope I am now closer to giving them their due.*

- *Developing treatment of democracy as a range of possibilities, not as a single type.*

- *Adding monarchies and theocracies to the coverage of autocracy.*

- *Including a new example on Iran.*

- *Supplementing coverage of the Iraq constitution.*

- *Expanding the treatment of social movements.*

- *Adding a section on terrorism.*

✦ SUPPLEMENTS

For the Student

Student's Online Learning Center. This free Web-based student supplement features a variety of helpful resources, including interactive self-quizzes, news sources, bibliography, Web links, and other learning tools. Discover this material at www.mhhe.com/shively11.

For the Instructor

Instructor's Online Learning Center. This password-protected, Web-based supplement offers access to important instructor support materials and downloadable supplements. Visit www.mhhe.com/shively11 for a comprehensive Instructor's Manual, Test Bank, Computerized Test Bank, and PowerPoint lecture slides, as well as all the tools available to students.

✦ ACKNOWLEDGMENTS

I have been very pleased by the response to this book. It is a wonderful experience to run into people who have used it and feel that it has helped them. As noted previously, I am even more than usually grateful to the following reviewers of the eleventh edition, who will notice many of their suggestions incorporated: Victor Aikhionbare, Palm Beach Community College; Jorge Aragon, University of Florida at Gainesville; Michael J. G. Cain, St. Mary's College of Maryland; David Conradt, East Carolina University; Alper Dede, Central Michigan University; Melanie Kintz, Western Michigan University–Kalamazoo; Lynn M. Maurer, Southern Illinois University; and one reviewer who preferred to remain anonymous. And special thanks to John Shockley's class at Augsburg College in Minneapolis.

W. Phillips Shively

ABOUT THE AUTHOR

W. Phillips Shively is Professor of Political Science at the University of Minnesota, and has taught at the University of Oregon and Yale University. He has also served as Visiting Professor at the University of Oslo in Norway. His research, which has appeared in numerous books and articles, deals with the comparative study of elections, and he has written *The Craft of Political Research,* an introduction to research techniques. He has also had practical political experience as a lobbyist in Minnesota. His true love is birding.

PART I

The Idea of Politics

CHAPTER 1

POLITICS: SETTING THE STAGE

Everyone knows something about politics, and many people know a great deal about it. It is an interesting, amusing, and moving spectacle that ranks not too far behind professional sports in the public eye. Political scientists, however, *study* politics and *analyze* it. This involves doing pretty much the same sorts of things that other people do who follow politics: we read the newspapers and listen to press conferences, take part in political campaigns, and so on. However, we also do some things differently. We usually try to see both sides of any question and to keep our emotions in low key, because emotions can cloud judgment. We borrow deliberately from other disciplines—such as economics, history, sociology, psychology, and philosophy—to help us understand what is going on politically. Above all, as you will see later in this chapter, we try to be precise about the meanings of the words we use. Many words having to do with politics—such as *liberal, represent,* and even *politics*—are quite complex, but most people use them unthinkingly. Political scientists are careful to analyze the varied meanings of such words and to use them precisely, partly because it is important to know exactly what we mean by the words we use and partly because careful examination of a richly complex word may teach us a lot about the things it describes.

What do political scientists study? Over the years, we have seen work in which political scientists:

- Measure just how much it actually costs a country to lose a war
- Devise a new system of voting in primaries that might have led to a different set of candidates for most presidential elections
- Analyze and explain the various styles that members of the U.S. Congress adopt in dealing with their constituents
- Study the spread of welfare reforms across the states

- Show that the roots of successful government may go back to social institutions several centuries ago
- Show why most nations will ignore warnings about surprise military action by hostile nations
- Study why democracies almost never wage war on other democracies

These are the sorts of things political scientists do. In this book you will be introduced to the broad principles of what we have learned about politics, especially about the politics of democracies like the United States. I hope the study will sharpen and enrich the more general understanding of politics that you already have.

This first chapter, in particular, involves the precise definition of several words with which you are already somewhat familiar. We must examine these definitions because you should start your study with some basic terms in place. You may also find it intriguing to see complexity in words, such as *politics*, that have probably not struck you before as being particularly complicated.

✦ POLITICS

What is **politics?** What is it that makes an act political? Consider the following questions, all of which involve political circumstances. What do these have in common?

- How was Hitler able to take power through a series of supposedly democratic elections?
- Why does the U.S. Congress so often disagree with the president in framing energy policies?
- Why should workers sort letters the way their boss directs if they know a more efficient way?
- Why were southern blacks denied the vote and placed in segregated schools throughout the 1950s while at the same time their housing was not as segregated as that in the North?
- Should homosexuals be barred from the military?
- Should fascists be barred from teaching in the schools?
- Why does the United States have only two major political parties when most democracies have more?
- Should state and local governments have the right to force landholders to sell them land that is needed for public purposes?
- Was Harry Truman right to bomb Hiroshima and Nagasaki?
- Why do people so often feel guilty about not doing what their parents want them to do?

These questions deal with politics. The questions about bosses and parents may not have looked to you as if they belonged in this group, but their connection with politics should become clearer by the end of this chapter.

What is it that these questions have in common? There are two main things, and both have often been used as the defining characteristics of politics. First, all the questions involve the *making of a common decision for a group of people,* that is, a uniform decision applying in the same way to all members of the group. Second, all involve *the use of power* by one person or a group of people to affect the behavior of another person or group of people. Let us look at both of these in more detail.

✦ POLITICS AS THE MAKING OF COMMON DECISIONS

Any group of people must often make decisions that will apply to all of them in common, as a group. A family must decide where to live, what sorts of rules to set for children, how to balance a budget, and so on. A class in a college or university (including the instructor as part of the "class") must decide what reading material to require, how students are to be graded by the instructor, how bright the light should be in the classrooms. A country must decide where to locate parks, what allies to seek out in war, how to raise revenue by taxing its citizens, how to care for the helpless, and many other things. Each of these requires the setting of common policy for the group, a single decision that affects all members of the group.

Not all human actions, of course, involve the making of a common policy for a group. When one brother teases another, he is not making a family policy, nor is a family member who decides to write the great American novel. A student who decides to read extra material on one section of the course (or, perhaps, to skip a bit of the reading) is not making a policy of the class. A person's decision to build a new house is not part of any common national policy, although the country may have policies—on interest rates, the regulation of building, land use, zoning, and so on—that affect this person's decision. Ford Motor Company's decisions on new-car styling are not part of a common national policy.

Those actions that contribute to the making of a common policy for a group of people constitute politics, and questions about those policies and the making of those policies are political questions. The political/nonpolitical distinction is not always easy to draw. The example of the Ford Motor Company, above, is tricky because Ford is so large that its decisions verge on being common policy for the whole United States, even though the company has no formal role in the nation's government. In other words, one might argue that because the U.S. government tolerates the concentration of our automobile industry among a few giant corporations and because (as a result of this) the decisions of any one of the three bulk so large in American life, those decisions have a quasi-public character and are "sort of" political.

Another tricky aspect of the political/nonpolitical distinction is that it is also a matter of perspective. Ford's design decisions are not (except via Ford's quasi-public nature) political decisions for the *United States;* but they *are* political decisions for Ford's stockholders, managers, and workers, because they set a common policy for the company. A family's decision to build a house is not a political decision for the *country,* but it is a political decision for the *family* as a group inasmuch as it involves a common policy for the family. "Company politics" is involved in Ford's decision, and "family politics" is involved in the family's decision. Neither, however, is a national political decision. Society consists of groups within groups within groups. Ford Motor Company is a group within the United States, and a family may be a group within the larger group of those dependent on Ford. Politics exists within any of these groups whenever a decision that will apply to all the members of the group is made. Depending on which group you are thinking of, a given decision—the decision of the Clauski family to build a house— may be treated as either political or nonpolitical. The Clauski decision is political for the family as a group but not political for the country.

✤ POLITICS AS THE EXERCISE OF POWER

A second characteristic of politics, one that runs through the questions at the start of this chapter, is that politics always involves the exercise of *power* by one person or persons over another person or persons. **Power** is the ability of one person to cause another to do what the first wishes, by whatever means. Politics always involves this: one person causing others to do what that person wants either by forcing or convincing them to do so. Looking back at the questions, we note that Hitler rose to high office by convincing many Germans to vote for him; the U.S. Congress disagrees with the president so often about energy policy because the president does not have much power either to force or to convince Congress to go along with his wishes in that area; and so on. In such ways, each of these questions involves the power of one person or persons over others.

The two defining characteristics of politics, then, are that (1) politics always involves the making of common decisions for groups of people *and* (2) those decisions are made by some members of the group exercising power over other members of the group. Power can consist of a wide variety of tools that help one person affect the actions of another. Power may be stark, as when a police officer stops a demonstrator from marching up the street; or it may be subtle, as when a group of poor people, by their very misery, elicit positive governmental action on their behalf.

Power may be exercised as *coercion* when we force a person to do something he or she did not want to do, as *persuasion* when we convince someone that that is what she or he really wishes to do, or as the *construction of incentives* when we make the alternative so unattractive that only one reasonable option remains. The ability to exercise any of these forms of power may be based on all sorts of things— money, affection, physical strength, legal status (the power of a police officer to direct traffic, for instance), the possession of important information, a winning smile, strong allies, determination, desperation (which helped North Vietnam to defeat the United States in the 1970s), and many more. Any of these can help some people get other people to act as they wish.

It is not necessary to learn the specific bases of power listed. They are meant to provide a sense of the variety and complexity of power, not as an exhaustive list of its important sources. The point is that all politics involves the use of power, and such power may take varied forms.

Authority

One particularly important source of power is *authority,* which will be discussed in more detail in Chapter 7. A person (or a group of people) has authority if there is general agreement among those involved that she has the right to control certain decisions and that her decisions in those areas should be complied with. For instance, parents in families generally have the authority to decide when small children should go to bed and what they should eat. A professor in a college course has the authority to decide what is to be discussed in the class and how the students are to be tested. A government has the authority to decide where roads should be located and how people are to be taxed.

Authority is so pervasive and important because it is an efficient way to exercise power. It provides a "standard operating procedure" for power, in which a decision does not require any direct use of force, making of arguments, or construction of incentives. Authority allows smooth day-to-day decisions on many questions with minimal spinning of wheels. It leaves time and energy free to be devoted to questions where there is not a general consensus on the right to make decisions—in the case of government, for instance, whether the government has the authority to detain suspected terrorists indefinitely. If every action of government required a full justification from scratch, a question like that would get lost in the torrent of debates about everything else.

Implicit and Manifest Power

Power need not consist of any observable link at all between the people or groups involved. Scholars distinguish between **manifest power** and **implicit power.** Manifest power is based on an observable action by A that leads B to do what A wants. A police officer's signal that causes a driver to stop and wait is an example of manifest power. In the case of implicit power, B does what A desires not because of anything A says or does but because (1) B senses that A wants something done and (2) for any of a variety of reasons B wishes to do what A wants done. Many examples of implicit power are found in families, whose members are so attuned to one another that there is often no observable communication between members of the family who yet manage to "read" and comply with one another's wishes. A father may toss the car keys to his daughter on Saturday morning completely unprompted except by his knowledge of her habits and his desire to comply with her wishes. As she drives, the daughter may obey the 55-miles-per-hour speed limit because she knows that her parents feel strongly about it. In neither case is there any overt signal from one family member to the other.

A famous example of implicit power in a broader sphere of politics comes from the reign of King Henry II of England. The king had been involved in a series of disputes with Thomas à Becket, the Archbishop of Canterbury. Henry exclaimed one day, "Will no one rid me of this man?" Four of his knights overheard what the king said and proceeded to murder Becket. Historians still dispute whether the king really wished to have Becket killed.

What is most important and interesting about implicit power is that an observer would have a hard time deciding whether or not such power has been exercised in any particular instance. The source of implicit power may lie far away from its exercise. To understand why the daughter drives 55 miles per hour, for instance, we might have to

Politics as power: a child-soldier abducted and forced to fight. His shirt reads, in either bravado or pathos, "I fear old age more than death."

© AP/Wide World Photos.

look back to her early childhood, to observe the hugs and admonitions she received years before. Power can be analyzed easily in the case of one country telling another, "Cede the province Anemone to us or we'll invade you." It cannot be so easily analyzed if the resources on which it is based are varied and complex, as in the power of a defeated Iraq to draw economic aid from the United States, or if it is in whole or in part implicit, as in the king's muttered remark in the presence of his soldiers.

An Example of the Difficulty of Analyzing Power

Both because power is important to politics and because it is difficult to measure precisely how and when power is exercised, there are recurrent disputes within political science about how much power various groups have. A famous dispute of the 1950s and 1960s centered on American cities, about which the following question was asked: "Is there a small group of people [the "downtown people," the political bosses, or what have you] who run things in American cities?" This might seem to be a simple question, but it was difficult for political scientists to answer, and we still do not have a clear answer to it. In a broader form, the dispute has continued to this day.

The dispute started when, in a study of Atlanta, Georgia, Floyd Hunter attempted to answer the question by asking journalists, officials, business leaders, and others who the most important people in the city were.[1] When his varied sources named roughly the same set of leaders, he concluded that Atlanta was run by a small group of insiders.

In response, however, Robert Dahl observed that Hunter's respondents might all be mistaken, but mistaken in the same way; they might *think* that the downtown corporate elite ran Atlanta because that idea was part of the conventional wisdom about the city, but they might be wrong. That the downtown people had a reputation for power did not prove to Dahl's satisfaction that they really *had* power; rather, he said, we must actually see power being used. As a response to the earlier Atlanta study, he performed a new study of his own based on New Haven, Connecticut.[2] He chose a set of major issues that faced the community—education, urban renewal, and so on—and recorded who participated in making decisions on each type of issue. He was restricting himself to observable power; therefore, he had to ignore the possibility of implicit power. Other than that, his procedure was straightforward. He found that quite different groups of people were active on the different issues. Parents and "society people" were especially involved in education, for example, while downtown people were especially involved in urban renewal. He concluded that New Haven was not run by a single group of insiders but that all sorts of groups were involved, moving in and out of participation depending on what issue was up for decision.

Still a third position was then staked out in the dispute. Peter Bachrach and Morton S. Baratz criticized Dahl's study of New Haven, noting that it is not enough just to see who has been active in various kinds of decisions but that we must also investigate why particular issues get raised in the first place.[3] Perhaps the most important decision is the one that governs which issues will be brought before the public. For instance, during the period Dahl studied, New Haven did not consider any policies for taking over utilities and running them publicly, for breaking up the residential racial segregation of the city, or for cutting taxes. An ability to influence or control the public agenda in this way gives one great power over public policies. Who has this ability? Political leaders? The media? Teachers and professors? Bloggers? At this level, decisions may or may not be controlled by a small "power elite"; we simply cannot tell from a study designed as Dahl designed his.

To add a further complexity, a "third face of power" has been suggested by Peter Digeser, who draws on the work of Steven Lukes. Taking Bachrach and Baratz beyond the notion of an elite controlling the agenda of discussion about different groups' needs and wants, Digeser points out that the process they describe might consist of an elite controlling ideas and public opinion such that it does not even occur to some groups to want the things they should want: "Lukes contended that power could be exerted even if B consciously wants to do what A desires. Lukes claimed that if B acts contrary to her objective, real interests then power is being exercised."[4] In other words, an elite might exercise power not just by preventing discussion of proposals it does not want to see on the

---

[1]Floyd Hunter, *Community Power Structure* (Chapel Hill: University of North Carolina Press, 1953). Note that the politics of Atlanta today is very different from that which Hunter described in 1953. The most obvious difference is that Atlanta has now had black mayors for a number of years. The power structure Hunter described was all white.
[2]Robert Dahl, *Who Governs?* (New Haven: Yale University Press, 1961).
[3]Peter Bachrach and Morton S. Baratz, "The Two Faces of Power," *American Political Science Review* 56 (1962): 947–53.
[4]Peter Digeser, "The Fourth Face of Power," *Journal of Politics* 54 (November 1992), p. 980. References to Lukes and Gramsci are: Steven Lukes, *Power: A Radical View* (London: Macmillan, 1974); Antonio Gramsci, *Letters from Prison* (New York: Columbia University Press, 1994).

table, but by influencing what people want so that inconvenient proposals never occur to them in the first place. The test for Digeser (based on Lukes) is not whether people have proposals that never reach the table, but whether the things people want are contrary to their real interests. Such a disjunction between people's wants and their real interests, for Digeser, is the footprint of elite power. That is to say, the elite maintains its power by controlling communications and ideas, such that people do not want (do not realize they need) things that threaten the elite. Of course, this becomes remarkably difficult to analyze, because it requires us to identify what people really need as distinct from what they merely think they need. Academics, who have very distinctive values of our own, are not always in a good position to judge other people's "true" needs.

Notice how complex the question of power in American cities has become. Hunter gave us a very straightforward assessment of Atlanta. Dahl complicated the issue by pointing out that in New Haven different types of people had dominant power with respect to different kinds of issues. Bachrach and Baratz reminded us that we must also consider who controls which issues will even come up for discussion. And Digeser added the consideration that this control might operate at an unconscious level, in elite control of how people form their very desires. In the end, it is difficult to say anything general and conclusive about the concentration of power in our cities because it is difficult to study what might have been—what issues might have entered public discussion but did not. This series of studies illustrates clearly the inherent complexity of power.[5]

Although these studies certainly show that there are few blanket truths about power, one should not therefore conclude that power is impossible to study. Rather, an understanding of the complexity of power and the difficulty of measuring it can lead us to detailed examinations of very specific instances of power. In response to the Bachrach and Baratz article, for instance, several interesting studies appeared on the setting of agendas in American politics. These were a direct result of the argument that the most important power is that which decides what issues will be up for debate.

Politics and Power

Despite the complexity and elusiveness of power, we *can* say that all politics is based on some form of power and that its sources may be highly varied. For most questions about politics, it is not necessary to specify in detail exactly what sort of power is involved. It is always helpful to bear in mind that you are dealing with power of one sort or another; but that realization may often serve rather as a background or setting for your analysis. For instance, most of the questions posed at the opening of this chapter can be addressed without conducting precise analyses of the power relationships that form contexts for the questions.

Before we leave our consideration of power in politics, we might draw attention to the surprising universality of the use of power to determine common decisions for groups of people. People around the world vary remarkably little in physical strength and intelligence; they are also more or less equal in their basic talents. Yet millions of

---

[5]Digeser goes on to describe still another approach to power (this is his "fourth face")—that of Michel Foucault, who develops a rich but elusive concept in which our definition of ourselves and of our very interests results from others' exercise of power over us. That is, the elite can maintain hegemony not only over what people want, but also over how they define themselves. At this point, analysis becomes difficult—some would say it collapses—because nothing is anchored.

them will fear and obey another person whose intrinsic capacities are little superior to theirs.

It is understandable that this should be so within families because of the weakness and inexperience of children. The adult members of a family are stronger than the children, and it is perhaps natural that they should be able to control them. However, it is astounding that large numbers of adults will grant this sort of control over their own actions to a military officer, a member of Congress, a dictator, or a religious leader. How is it that political power is so universal and often so concentrated in small numbers of people?[6]

Simply posing the question in this way demonstrates once again that the bases of power must be varied and complex. Physical compulsion alone would not be sufficient to ensure the obedience that people all over the world give to their political leaders.

Politics as the Exercise of Choice

Though power is difficult to pin down in observations, conceptually it is rather simple: One person manages, by some means or another, to get another person to do (or not do) what the first one wants. We have seen above that identifying the "some means or another" can be difficult, but the concept itself is fairly simple.

When we look at "choice," however, we find that the concept itself is a bit hard to get our arms around. Just what do we mean by "choice"? When we view a political outcome as a matter of choice, we explain the outcome by the fact that it was needed, either by society as a whole or at least by some politically significant figures. That is, the result came about because, to a significant set of people (possibly all of the people) it *should* have happened. On the face of it, this sounds mystical. We know that causation must always work forward in time, but here we say that the need for something brought about the actions that would produce it!

The choice interpretation, however, is really a shorthand for many factors that led various people to act, all of which had to do with the fact that they felt the need to bring something about.

Thus, you will see in Chapter 3 that one explanation (the "choice" explanation) for why powerful governments developed in the fifteenth to eighteenth centuries in Europe was that modern large-scale commerce and industry arose in Europe at about that time, and powerful governments holding sway over broad territories were necessary if the commerce and industry were to operate efficiently. This does not mean that in some mystical way the need called forth the strong governments. Rather, kings could extend and deepen their power because large, significant groups in the society (merchants, factory owners) felt they would benefit from a strong king and supported him in extending his power. In other words, the need for strong governments brought them about—but not in some mystical way. Rather, many individual exercises of power brought about the "choice" outcome.

As another example, you will see in Chapter 14 that parliamentary government works most smoothly when prime ministers can control tightly how individual members vote. As a result—in a "choice" interpretation—most parliamentary systems have

---

[6]R. M. MacIver, *The Web of Government* (New York: Macmillan, 1967), chap. 1.

developed tightly disciplined parties. This does not mean that the need, in some mystical way, produced the disciplined parties. Rather, over a number of years and by trial and error, prime ministers found that their lives were easier if their political parties were tightly disciplined, and they devised all sorts of rewards and punishments to keep their party members in line.

In principle, each of these examples could have been reduced to a large number of relatively small individual power transactions. But, that would almost certainly have meant missing the forest for the trees. The central process running through all the individual power transactions was that patterns of behavior were being reshaped to meet the needs either of society as a whole or of significant and powerful parts of society. A "choice" interpretation captures that truth in a way that analyzing thousands of small power transactions could not.[7]

We see that "choice" actually involves "power," because it is through power events that the "choice" outcome is reached. The "choice" perspective has some advantages, however. First, as we have seen above, it is sometimes more efficient than power in helping us to see the "big picture." And second, it emphasizes the fact that politics meets needs. From a purely power perspective, the role of needs in shaping politics can easily be lost.

✦ POWER AND CHOICE

Politics, then, consists of the making of common decisions for a group through the use of power. Though the concept involves some complexity, it will usually be clear to everyone concerned whether a given action is or is not political in this sense. From the two parts of our definition there stem two basic ways of looking at the making of such common policies, and people often emphasize one or the other of these in evaluating any particular political action. In so doing, they may fail to consider how their viewpoint colors their conclusions. The two alternative viewpoints are as follows:

1. Political action may be interpreted as a way to work out rationally the best common solution to a common problem—or at least a way to work out a reasonable common solution. That is, politics consists of *public choice.* (Even though this perspective emphasizes the cooperative aspect of decisions, power will still be involved in the making of choices; if nothing else, the power to persuade will be involved; and of course some of the "public" will undoubtedly have had more power than others and will have tipped things in favor of their needs.)
2. Political action may be interpreted as a process through which some people are dominated by other people. That is, politics consists simply of the use of *power.* Here power is often thought of as power through coercion.

---

[7]A choice interpretation in political science is analogous to the statement of an evolutionary biologist that a certain tree has developed sweet fruit buds to reward and attract ants that will keep its leaves free of caterpillars. No one believes that the tree thinks this through in that way, of course! Rather, the end result is the culmination of millions of events of natural selection in the species over the years. The biologist's statement gives a true understanding that would be lost in an enumeration (even if that were possible) of all the selection events.

"Because this family isn't ready to hold democratic elections—that's why!"
Cartoon by Lee Lorenz. Published in *The New Yorker* April 19, 2004.

In other words, two people who observe the same political action from these op-posing viewpoints might have very different ideas of what is going on. For instance, a person operating from the "public choice" viewpoint might look at the large number of people who fail to vote in American presidential elections and conclude that this is a reasonably healthy situation, because if such a large number of people have chosen not to bother voting, they must be tolerably satisfied with things as they are. Someone else, operating from the "power" viewpoint, might look at that same large number of nonvoters and conclude that American elections are a sham, that they are meant to give the appearance of popular choice without providing the voter with significantly dif-ferent options (i.e., many voters do not bother to vote because their choices have been restricted).

Most often, *both* viewpoints are partly accurate. Politics generally involves con-sidering at least the broad needs of the group for whom policy is being made: Pure tyranny is rare and is difficult to maintain. At the same time, the making of common policy generally means that one part of a group will be dominating another part to at least some extent. In the previous presidential voting example, both characterizations probably have some truth to them.

It is good to bear these two perspectives in mind, because we may then be able to avoid misjudging a particular political situation as being all one or the other. For example, a college or university class is a group for which common policies must be made and in which a single person (the instructor) is formally charged with responsibility. Thus, the group's politics will largely consist of domination of the students by the instructor, based on the authority of her role as professor. However, the class is not solely or simply a system of domination because there are a number of informal mechanisms by which students participate in decision making, and these should not be overlooked. In short, the politics of a classroom also includes aspects of a rational working out of solutions to common problems. Such questions as the timing of tests, whether or not doors should be closed or the lights on, or the nature of special projects and examinations are often decided by the instructor in consultation with the students. In less direct ways, students—by their expressions of interest—often influence the content or pace of a class. (Never underestimate the effect of paper shuffling two minutes before the end of a class!) Thus, although the politics of a classroom consists primarily of domination, there is also some element of a common search for solutions to common problems. This might be overlooked if one were not alert to the two sides of politics.

An example of this problem is raised by Terry M. Moe, who argues that a popular theory (rational choice theory, which will be discussed in Chapter 5) emphasizes "choice" too much at the expense of "power." One of the things this body of theory is concerned with is the question of why institutions like Congress, the Presidency, bureaucracies, and the like are set up as they are. The theory emphasizes voluntary choice in setting up such institutions; it sees them as evolving as they have in order to solve problems of coordinating varied people's actions to get coherent policies. This is clearly a "choice" perspective, in that it explains the way institutions are set up by what is needed for coherent policy-making. But as Moe points out, while this benign view may be part of the story, institutions are also shaped by powerful political figures to get things they want. And, he argues, the absence of such a "power" perspective is a serious flaw in the theory.[8]

It is especially important to bear in mind these two points of view when we consider political actions about which we have strong feelings and about which we may expect to be prejudiced. Until the opening up of democratic elections in the Soviet Union, for instance, Americans tended to dismiss elections in communist countries as simple fraud, since voters were given a single candidate to vote for, with no electoral competition for their votes. However, there was also evident in those elections a surprising element of broad participation in a search for common action. For instance, even during the period of noncompetitive elections, with only a single candidate on the ballot, 28 percent of Soviet citizens reported that they had at one time or another attempted to persuade others to vote as they did; 19 percent had contacted a state or national government official about some problem.[9] "The weeks preceding the election see the formation of countless study circles, discussion groups, campaign meetings, door-to-door

---

[8]Terry M. Moe, "Power and Political Institutions," *Perspectives on Politics* 3 (June 2005), p. 214.
[9]Richard D. Little, "Mass Political Participation in the U.S. and the U.S.S.R.," *Comparative Political Studies* 8 (January 1976), p. 439.

canvassing, rallies, demonstrations and speeches."[10] There appears to have been something more to the Soviet Union's uncontested elections than we were able to see at the time.

Another example of emotions leading us to think of politics not as an interplay among power and choice, but just as one or the other, is furnished by Iraq at the time of the second Gulf War in 2003. The United States government focused so strongly on Saddam Hussein as a brutal dictator, ruling by the power of coercion, that they assumed victorious American troops would therefore be greeted by jubilant crowds of grateful Iraqis. In their intense dislike of Saddam Hussein, they forgot that although he did indeed maintain his regime by unspeakable violence, the basis of his rule was more complex than that. He was not only a brutal dictator, but at the same time a focus of national unity and nationalism; some parts of the country had been favored by his regime (though others had suffered); and he was seen as having maintained order in a potentially violent territory. The resulting mixed reaction to American troops—relief at the end of Saddam Hussein's oppression, but anger at the breakdown in security and the presence of a foreign army of occupation—caught the U.S. government by surprise, and left it unprepared for the rise of a crippling insurgency.

Bearing in mind that there is almost always more to any political choice than just the exercise of power, or just the provision of a collective choice, helps us to remain alert to more varied possibilities even when we know we are strongly prejudiced about a subject.

To sum up this section of the chapter: Politics consists of the making of a common decision for a group of people through the use of power. Any act of politics may be viewed from either of two perspectives, either as a search for an answer to common problems or as an act by which some members of a group impose their will on other members of the group. It is important to remember that generally both viewpoints have at least some validity. It is especially important to remember this when we might be prejudiced about the subject at hand, because keeping both viewpoints in mind can help us to avoid thinking about the subject in narrow, prejudiced ways. Power and choice, the two major themes by which we organize our views of politics, have provided the title of this book. They will recur in succeeding chapters as we examine various aspects of politics.

✦ POLITICS OF THE STATE

One thing that has probably seemed odd to you in this chapter, right from the set of questions on page 2, with its inclusion of family and workplace, is that some things we do not always think of as "politics" have been described under this heading. There is some variation in common usage of the word. Family, workplace, church, and so on are not often thought of as political places, though they are *sometimes* thought of in that way. When we refer to "office politics," "campus politics," and "church politics," we mean activities that fit under the definition of politics presented in this chapter: the use of power to make common decisions for groups of people.

---

[10]Ibid.

This broad use of the word *politics* fits the general definition presented in this chapter, but a much more common use of the word is narrower. If we say, "Frank went into politics," or "I'm fascinated by politics," we are not thinking of the family or corporation or church. In this sense of the word we are referring only to the kind of politics that has to do with government of the state.

State has a special meaning in political science. It is not the same thing as the states of the United States; instead, it is what we commonly call a country. The United States is a state in this sense, as are France, Russia, Algeria, Mexico, and so on. Political scientists prefer the word "state" to the more usual "country" because it is more precise. Except for the minor confusion of "states" in the United States, the word means just one thing. "Country," on the other hand, can mean a state like France or Canada; a region or type of place ("cattle country"); the opposite of urban ("I live in the country"); and so forth.

We will look at the state in more detail in Chapter 3, but for now it is enough to note that the state is a particular kind of social group. Over the last few centuries, people have focused increasingly on the state of which they are citizens, and the state has determined more of what goes on in our lives. Several centuries ago, most people were almost unaware of the state in which they lived; they noticed it only if the king's soldiers marched through their fields. At that time, many large geographic areas could hardly be said to have been organized as states at all. Gradually states have become more thoroughly organized and have demanded more from us. First, states became the prime focus of peace and war, maintaining peace within their borders and waging war with other states. Then, states also became the organizers of commerce and industry within their borders, regulating prices and the quality of products, constructing roads and canals, and so on. Only for the last several decades has the state generally been expected by its citizens to maintain stability in the economy, guarantee employment, and keep the value of currency stable. A couple of centuries ago, events in the economy were treated as "acts of God," and the state was not much involved in them, but today the state is generally held responsible for economic conditions. The responsibilities of the state continue to grow. In the future might the weather, now treated as an "act of God," become part of the responsibility of the state?

For better or worse, the state has become critically important to us, and its politics has taken on great importance. When we say "politics," we usually mean "politics of the state." Political science shares this general preoccupation with politics of the state. Though we will occasionally look at other sorts of politics in this book, most of our attention will be directed to the politics of the state. Remember the more general meaning of politics, however, and remember that in dealing with the state we will be looking at politics only in one of its forms, albeit its most important and most complex form.

✦ POLITICAL SCIENCE

Political science is the academic field that takes as its sole and general task the analysis of politics, especially the politics of the state. There has been continuing debate over how "scientific" political science should be. Some political scientists think that politics is so complex and involves such basic personal values that we should not try to pin it down to exact regularities. Rather, we should interpret each political event and idea more or less in and of itself, in a personal, subjective way. Such political scientists would model themselves upon historians, who interpret a particular sequence of events more or less in and of itself, seeking to retain the richness of its detail while making a general patterned interpretation of what process unfolded through the events. Or, upon anthropologists, who interpret a particular society and culture more or less in and of itself, seeking to retain the richness of its detail while making a general patterned interpretation of it.

Other political scientists think that their discipline should be more scientific, seeking out the basic essence of regularities across a whole set of events, even though this means sacrificing some of the rich detail with which each single event is laden. They think that the only way we will be able to explain and predict what happens in politics is to emphasize the underlying processes that a number of disparate events may have in common. These political scientists would model themselves on other social scientists such as economists, who analyze events simply as instances of general processes, which they treat in the abstract. Economists, for instance, prefer to deal at a general level with supply-and-demand theories rather than analyze specifically what happens in a given used car lot.

The first type of political scientists are sometimes called "interpretivists" (or often "qualitative"), the latter "behavioralists" (or "quantitative"). **Interpretive political scientists** are most likely to deal in historical and philosophical aspects of politics and to seek detailed, nonnumerical information on a few cases. **Behavioralists** lean more toward looking for broad patterns across cases and using statistical analyses of numerical information. They find numerical information especially attractive because it distills a set of complex details down into something very simple and basic—a number. Therefore, because behavioralists are looking for simple descriptions of basic processes, they see it as more useful to summarize party competition in many congressional districts with a single index number for each district than to try to digest masses of biography, newspaper accounts, and so on from a few congressional races.

This picture should not be seen as black and white. Political science does not consist of two warring camps, and most political scientists combine some element of "interpretivism" with some element of "behavioralism." However, there are different *degrees* of these among political scientists, which add greatly to the variety of materials available in the field.

Whatever their preferred way of gathering information about the political world, all political scientists tend, in their *thinking* about politics, to emphasize broad generalization and abstraction. Political scientists pursue generalization through *theory*.

A **theory** is a statement linking specific instances to broader principles. **Empirical theories** are theories describing how things work in the world we observe. They are usually explanatory; that is, they have to do with why things happen as they do. This means they consist of causal statements of the form "X causes Y." (For more on causation, see the discussion in the appendix, pp. 429–431.) An example of an empirical theory addressing one of the questions from page 2—why does the United States have only two major political parties—would be: "Single-member-district-plurality (SMDP) electoral systems, by disadvantaging small parties, tend to reduce the number of political parties to two; and since the United States has an SMDP electoral system, that tends to lead to a two-party system in the United States." You will meet the single-member-district-plurality electoral system in Chapter 10; for now, the point is that this is a *causal* statement (SMDP causes two-party systems) and it links the specific case (the United States, which has an SMDP electoral system) to a general principle.

Normative theories involve making a judgment about the world, not describing how it works. They address the question: "What should X be or do?" Again, these theories link specific cases to general principles. An example would be, "What sort of public health care plan should the United States have?" Normative theories would answer this question by applying general principles, such as "governments should intervene as little as possible in people's lives" or "societies are good to the extent that everyone has equal chances in life," to the specific policy question.

The important thing to note here is that both of our major kinds of theory—normative and empirical—are statements that deal with specific instances by linking them to general principles. Our relatively strong reliance on theory is what sets political scientists apart from others, especially historians, who also deal with politics as a subject. Theories are the building blocks of political science, and you will find them throughout this book.

For practical purposes of curriculum and organization, the field of political science in the United States is divided into subfields according to the subjects in which political scientists specialize. The major subfields are:

- *American political behavior:* The study of individuals and nongovernmental organizations involved in politics and of why they do what they do. Studies of public opinion, elections, interest groups, and political parties would fall under this heading.

- *American political institutions:* The study of national governmental bodies, the Congress, the presidency, the bureaucracy, and—in part—the courts.

- *American public law:* The study of legal reasoning and of why courts hand down the decisions they do.

- *American public policy:* The analysis of the product of politics, the kinds of policies that are laid down.

- *American state and local politics:* The study of all of these, but at the level of "states" (such as California or Minnesota) and localities rather than the country as a whole.

- *Comparative politics:* The study of all of these in any place but the United States. To lump together all aspects of politics outside of the United States is parochial, but that is what is usually done. Political scientists in other countries are as bad; Swedish political scientists have many subdivisions of the study of Sweden, as do the French for France, the Japanese for Japan, and so on.

- *International politics:* The study of politics between states—the making of common decisions for a group of states through wars, diplomacy, and so on.[11] "International politics" is the only subfield that does this; all of the other subfields listed previously deal with politics *within* states, not between them.

---

[11]International politics also includes other actors that operate beyond the state, such as the United Nations, international professional organizations, and humanitarian groups like Amnesty International. Such actors are growing in importance in international politics.

- *Political theory:* The history of ideas about politics, and critical discussion of political values.

This book reviews the general findings of political science but blends U.S. politics and "comparative politics," treating the politics of all parts of the world (including the United States) comparatively.

→ THE PLEASURES OF POLITICS

I have led you through some rather dry material in this chapter because it was necessary to start you off with clarity on a number of concepts. Frequently throughout this book you will find that we are working toward greater precision than is found in everyday language; this usually requires abstraction and may also seem a bit dry. I hope, however, that as we do this, you will remember—and I can communicate—what a fascinating and dramatic thing we are studying.

"The use of power to reach collective choices"—think what this phrase means. We are talking about struggles for the souls of nations. The "use of power" has meant Thoreau going to prison to protest the United States' invasion of Mexico; underground resistance by the Catholic Church and the Communist Party against Nazi occupation troops in the Second World War; students braving police dogs and murderous assaults to integrate American businesses and public facilities in the 1960s; Mikhail Gorbachev and Boris Yeltsin juggling political coalitions to create democracy in the Soviet Union, where it had never been seen before; indigenous people in the mountains of Mexico confronting the government and the army to assert their rights. "Collective choices" have included the invention of democracy as a way to accomplish government by the people; the development of public education, park systems, public health—and also such horrors as the Nazis' murder of millions of Jews and other "undesirables."

I try in this book to write dispassionately about politics, because it is easier to keep a clear head that way, but a love of politics lies behind all of it. I switched from an English Literature major to political science in the 1960s because I was excited by John Kennedy's call for public service. I have remained a news "junkie" and sometime participant in politics ever since. The things we will be analyzing in the pages that follow involve real people devoting their energies to things they want and things they believe in. While you will learn how to analyze what is happening in these events and to deal with the events dispassionately, I hope you will not forget the humanity that is moving through them.

KEY TERMS

politics	state	behavioralists
power	political science	theory
implicit power	interpretive political	empirical theories
manifest power	scientists	normative theories

FURTHER READING

Politics and Power

Dahl, Robert. *Modern Political Analysis.* 5th ed. New York: Prentice-Hall, 1990, chaps. 3 and 4.

Digeser, Peter. "The Fourth Face of Power." *Journal of Politics* 54 (November 1992) pp. 977–1007.

Jones, Bryan D., and Baumgartner, Frank R. *The Politics of Attention: How Government Prioritizes Problems.* Chicago: University of Chicago Press, 2005.

MacIver, R. M. *The Web of Government,* rev. ed. New York: Free Press, 1965.

"Power." In *The International Encyclopedia of the Social Sciences.* David L. Sills, editor. New York: Macmillan, 1968.

Political Science

Almond, Gabriel A. *A Discipline Divided: Schools and Sects in Political Science.* Newbury Park, CA: Sage, 1990.

Annual Review of Political Science (Palo Alto, CA: Annual Reviews, serial) is a series that presents each year a collection of essays in which leading scholars review research and theory in their areas of political science.

Fenno, Richard. *Home Style: House Members in Their Districts.* Boston: Little, Brown, 1978. (The appendix to this book provides a good argument for qualitative social science.)

Goodin, Robert E., and Klingemann, Hans-Dieter, eds. *A New Handbook of Political Science.* New York: Oxford University Press, 1997.

Lave, Charles A., and March, James G. *An Introduction to Models in the Social Sciences.* New York: Harper & Row, 1975. (Chapters 1–3 provide a good nontechnical argument for quantitative social science.)

Lichbach, Mark Irving, and Zuckerman, Alan S., eds. *Comparative Politics: Rationality, Culture, and Structure.* New York: Cambridge University Press, 1997.

"Political Science." In *The International Encyclopedia of the Social Sciences.*

Stepan, Alfred. *Arguing Comparative Politics.* New York: Oxford University Press, 2001.

Wahlke, John C. "Liberal Learning and the Political Science Major." *PS* 24 (March 1991), pp. 48–60.

 ## BROAD WEB SITES OF GENERAL USE IN POLITICAL SCIENCE

American Political Science Association Web site, with many links:
http://www.apsanet.org/

Canadian Politics on the Web:
http://www.nelson.com/nelson/polisci/canpol.html

Canadian Politics: A Net Station, myriad links maintained by the University of British Columbia library:
http://www.library.ubc.ca/poli/

The CIA's *World Factbook,* with assessments and data on every country of the world:

https://www.cia.gov/cia/publications/factbook/

The Library of Congress country studies:
http://lcweb2.loc.gov/frd/cs/cshome.html

The Center for the American Woman and Politics:
http://www.rci.rutgers.edu/~cawp/

Journalist Ron Gunzberger's grab bag of news, candidate biographies, and Web links:

http://www.politics1.com

BBC online news:
http://www.bbc.co.uk

The International Herald Tribune (an excellent newspaper):
http://www.iht.com

intute: social sciences. Links, articles, resources:
http://www.intute.ac.uk/social sciences/

A good page on political resources, based in Britain:
http://www.psr.keele.ac.uk/

CHAPTER 2

MODERN IDEOLOGIES AND POLITICAL PHILOSOPHY

Most people approach politics through an **ideology**—an organized set of related ideas that modify one another. For instance, one person may believe that everyone is basically selfish, that politicians are all crooks, that a citizen owes nothing to the state, that it is all right to cheat on one's taxes, that gun control is a bad thing because it keeps us from protecting ourselves, and so on. This is an ideology—a set of ideas about politics, all of which are related to one another and that modify and support each other. The belief that everyone is basically selfish helps provide a justification for the need to carry a gun, the wish to cheat on taxes helps make one comfortable in the belief that the citizen owes nothing to the state, and vice versa, and so on. Another person may believe that individual freedom is very important, that government should regulate people as little as possible, that the United States should try to protect any people whose government is oppressing them, and that the U.S. government should not tell people whether they may carry guns. This is also ideology, an organized set of ideas that modify and support each other. In this second example, the high value placed on individual freedom supports both a wish to protect human rights around the world and a reluctance to have the government regulate the ownership of guns.

Ideologies are useful to people, both for their own personal ease and satisfaction and for their public political activities. From the *personal* point of view, an ideology helps us to make sense reasonably easily and quickly of the varied political questions that come to our attention. In any given week, the newspaper will raise questions about the control or deregulation of oil prices, the busing of schoolchildren to improve racial balance, the level of support for retired people in the Social Security system, the size of the military budget, federal acquisition of land for parks and wildlife refuges, and so forth. If we had to consider each of these issues anew, we would have an awesome task. However, if we approach each from the standpoint of a general ideology that we have developed over time, the job is much simpler. Most issues will turn out to be instances of more general principles, and can quickly be settled by applying the principles.

The new issue may also modify our ideology, because an ideology is not graven in stone. For instance, devout Catholics who believe that the government should regulate people as little as possible may find themselves torn over the issue of legalized abortion and may modify some of their more general ideas about politics in light of the new issue. An ideology, then, while it is an organized set of ideas about politics that helps us to make sense of the myriad of political questions that face us, is not static. An ideology organizes ideas, but as it absorbs new ideas it itself evolves and is slowly modified.[1]

An ideology also has *public* uses. In politics, we are typically concerned to convince others that a policy we favor is the right one. We usually have personal reasons for favoring the policy (we may want taxes to be cut because we are wealthy, oppose gun control because we like to collect guns, or favor national health insurance because we are poor), but these personal reasons are not usually good *public* reasons. People distrust a self-interested argument. Also, arguing for a policy by giving one's personal reasons for it would not win many allies; only those who are also rich could be convinced by the argument "I'm wealthy, therefore I want to see taxes cut." In political argument, we usually try to attract as many allies as possible to our position, and so personal reasons will not make good arguments. *Ideologies,* however, can serve this purpose very well. The wealthy person who argues, "Government spending and taxation hamper individual initiative," may appeal to a great many people who for various reasons favor individual initiative.

Ideologies are developed and maintained because of their usefulness to individuals in responding to events and their utility in public political argument. This is not a conscious, cynical process in which we deliberately frame an ideology so as to enlist allies in some cause or another. Rather, we are all comfortable with ideology and generally, over time, work out ideologies that fit our particular needs. Too, ideologies are not simply the creation of those who hold them; they tend to take on a life of their own and guide their holders' political views in unanticipated ways. A business leader who feels that government should regulate as little as possible (for what we may think are obvious reasons) may find that this ideology also leads to positions—not particularly connected to self-interest—on the censorship of books in public libraries or the regulation of handguns.

An ideology helps us make sense out of politics for ourselves and gather allies for public argument. We develop our ideologies in such a way that they fit our needs and predispositions, reflecting what we want; but they also take on a life of their own and *guide* our decisions.

---

[1]See Pamela Johnston Conover and Stanley Feldman, "Belief System Organization in the American Electorate," in *The Electorate Reconsidered,* ed. John Pierce and John L. Sullivan (Beverly Hills, Calif.: Sage, 1980); Michael Billig, Susan Condor, Derek Edwards, Mike Gane, Daniel Middleton, and Alan Radley, *Ideological Dilemmas: A Social Psychology of Everyday Thinking* (Beverly Hills, Calif.: Sage, 1988); Teun A. Van Dijk, *Ideology: A Multi-Disciplinary Approach* (Beverly Hills, Calif.: Sage, 1998).

✦ AMERICAN IDEOLOGIES

All of us have some sort of ideology, in the sense that our various ideas about politics bear some sort of relationship one to another. However, not every ideology is equally neat and tidy, nor is every ideology worked out in equally full detail. Americans' ideologies tend to be more loosely organized than those of other peoples. In fact, Americans tend to admit exceptions and inconsistencies into their ideologies rather cheerfully.

Two main ideologies are found among Americans: **"American liberalism"** and **"American conservatism."** As we shall see, both of these ideologies are variants of a more general and well-worked-out ideology known as *liberalism* . "American liberalism" and "American conservatism" are simply differing versions that have sprung up in a predominantly liberal society. As you will see when we look at more established ideologies below, ideologies usually are determined by an intellectual structure—a core value or values, from which a number of disparate policy positions can be derived by deduction. For instance, you will see that the core value of liberalism in its general (not American) sense is that all individuals should be able to develop their capacities to the fullest; from this it is possible to deduce arguments for the defense of free speech, for democracy, for minimizing regulation, and so on. Since in America political thought was dominated from the start by a general liberalism in this sense, Americans did not sort themselves out politically by competing deductive systems. Rather, ideologies in America have evolved as rival coalitions operating within a common intellectual structure.

American liberalism, for instance, has developed as a rather loosely held sense of support for underdogs. As a result, concerns for economic equality are strong in American liberalism (the poor as underdogs), as is support for the interests of ethnic minorities, women, and gays. Support for environmental protection is also part of American liberalism. And so is support for a fairly radical defense of freedom of expression, as exemplified by the American Civil Liberties Union.

American conservatism has traditionally emphasized more the maintenance of an efficient, minimally regulated economy, which has involved opposition to governmental regulation of people's lives and of businesses, and fiscal prudence in the form of balanced budgets. In recent decades American conservatism has added to these concerns a desire to maintain common values of morality and spirituality, and opposition to legalized abortion.

American liberalism and American conservatism are not neat ideologies. It is hard to see, for instance, what logical connections exist among the various attitudes detailed. It frequently happens that an American political figure is "liberal" on some of these issues and "conservative" on others. American labor unions, for example, have generally been quite concerned about issues of equality but have not been equally concerned about an issue such as abortion rights. There are many other complexities as well. As one more example, American conservatives generally favor free trade but are also concerned about the repression of religion in China. This leaves them to grapple with the question of what sort of trade relations the United States should maintain with China.

Both ideologies are therefore mixtures, representing marriages of political convenience, and it is difficult to find internal coherence among the various parts of either one.

The two American ideologies have been shaped as coalitions largely by the American two-party system. As you will see in Chapter 10, the American system of elections forces Americans into a system of two large parties; small parties find it very difficult to establish themselves. As a result, Americans with a wide variety of ideas on different questions find themselves squeezed together into one or another of the two parties, along with a large number of people who may have different concerns. American ideologies are shaped by this process of squeezing into coalitions, rather than by an intellectualized process of deduction. One indication that this is what happens is the fact that some issues migrate between ideologies. It is probably the case, for instance, that at the time of the Supreme Court decision legalizing abortion, more American liberals than American conservatives opposed the decision. (Simply from historic patterns of immigration, there were more Irish, Italian, and Polish Catholics in the Democratic Party at that time than in the Republican Party.) Democratic Party gatherings at the time were often split about evenly on the issue. However, there was another part of the American liberal constellation of interests that could not easily coexist with a pro-life position—the feminist movement. The presence of both positions within American liberalism proved untenable. Over the ensuing decade or two, large numbers of those opposing abortion drifted away from American liberalism, until eventually abortion lodged on the right and became one of the defining issues separating the two ideologies.

Similarly, protection of the environment was at least as much an issue of American conservatives in the 1950s as it was of American liberals. As conflicts between businesses and environmental protection intensified in the 1960s and 1970s, environmentalism partially migrated to American liberalism, although there is still a significant minority of environmentalist conservatives. In this case, it was never entirely clear which way things would go: business interests associated with American conservatism experienced conflicts with environmentalism, but so did trade unions associated with American liberalism. Key issues do tend to sort themselves out to one side or the other, however, and this is just what happened to environmentalism.

Foreign policy issues are especially fluid. A cynic might say that American liberals trend internationalist when a Democrat is president, and isolationist when a Republican is president—and that American conservatives trend internationalist when a Republican is president and isolationist when faced with a Democrat. Thus Republicans opposed President Clinton's military intervention in former Yugoslavia, and spoke scathingly of his "nation-building." But after 2000, with a Republican president, it was the Democrats who opposed George Bush's interventions. Positions on foreign policy seem to flip freely back and forth between American liberalism and American conservatism.[2]

American ideologies may be untidy, but they still have real influence. American labor leaders have probably been more concerned than they might otherwise have been with freedom of expression because of this issue's association with the redistribution of income in American liberalism. Americans concerned about high taxes have probably picked up more concern than they might otherwise have had for questions of common values of morality because of the juxtaposition of these positions in American conservatism.

---

[2]Consistent with this interpretation of American ideologies, Paul Goren finds that American voters' party attachments shape their ideologies, rather than their ideologies determining which party they identify with. ("Party Identification and Core Values," *American Journal of Political Science* 49 (October 2005): 882–897.)

"I keep my core beliefs written on my palm for easy reference."

Over the last few decades, the intensity of ideological debate has strengthened markedly in the United States. I describe American ideologies as "hodgepodges," but they are still ideologies people care a lot about. The intensity of ideology today can be seen in the very strong reactions (positive and negative) to President George W. Bush in the 2000s; it can be seen in the contemporary sharp contestation over judicial appointments in the Senate, which in the 1960s and 1970s would have been almost pro forma; and it can be seen in the proliferation of ideologically based interest groups and think tanks.

It is not obvious why we should have come to feel so much more strongly about our "hodgepodge" ideologies in the 2000s than we did in earlier decades. In part, it may be because of new techniques and technology (direct mailings, focus groups, polling, e-mail) that have made it easier for ideologues to raise money and fire up their troops. In part, it may be because of the involvement of the newly active religious right, who have brought some of the emotion of religious belief into the political sphere. In part, it may be the addition to the political realm since 1973 of a new issue, abortion, which excites deep emotion and on which compromise is at best exceedingly difficult. In part, it may be the partisan realignment of the 1960s and 1970s in which the conservative South moved to the Republican Party, leaving the two parties more cleanly divided along ideological lines than they had been and thus adding the emotion of partisanship to conflicts over ideology. But in the end, it is also because these ideologies do articulate real conflicts between real groups in the population. They may be primarily coalitions rather than intellectual systems—less neat systems of ideas than the more general liberalism, conservatism, and socialism that I describe in the next sections. But as systems of conflict, they are just as real as those more tightly knit intellectual systems. At the end of the day, there are real differences between "American conservatives" and "American liberals."

→ LIBERALISM

The two American ideologies are actually variants of **liberalism,** one of the three great ideologies that developed in Europe in the eighteenth and nineteenth centuries. These ideologies—liberalism, conservatism, and socialism—have provided the framework for most political debate throughout the world since then.

To understand their development, we must remember that the medieval social order in Europe was one in which people were bound together in patterns of rather strict domination, with mutual responsibilities between those who were dominated and those who dominated them, between "top dogs" and "bottom dogs." Farmers often lived in a condition of near-slavery, subject to a local church official or a member of the nobility. A farmer paid heavy taxes to his local patron and had to provide him with specified periods of labor for road building, war, and so on. In many parts of Europe, the farmer was not allowed to leave his land and move elsewhere without the permission of his patron. Furthermore, farmers were required to offer the patron formal social respect and deference. In return, the patron was supposed to provide his farmers with protection and with help in times of illness or want. Such industry as existed was organized in guilds, which laid down strict rules as to how an item was to be manufactured, how many such items were to be produced, and what was to be charged for them. Trade in many items was subject to ancient rules: The king might have a monopoly on trade in a commodity such as salt, for instance, or a particular town might have the enduring right to receive all imports of some specific item. Jews were a pariah group, banned from many occupations and generally forbidden to own land. The Roman Catholic Church maintained a stern control over proper belief (a striking example of this occurred when, in 1616, the church forced the great astronomer Galileo to state, contrary to his true convictions, that he did not believe the earth orbited around the sun). To transport goods from one end of a country to another could be a complex affair in which the carrier of the goods was required to pay taxes, fees, and tributes to various local personages at all stages of the journey. Politics was the province of the king, the nobility, and the church.

For our present purposes, two things are important about these arrangements: (1) people were bound to each other in complex and cumbersome systems of domination; and (2) the arrangements were static, difficult to change. Ownership of the land, feudal privileges, the rights of the church, the political role of the king and nobility, the power of the guilds—all were granted in perpetuity and could only evolve slowly.

Onto this setting—faintly in the fifteenth and sixteenth centuries, in crescendo through the seventeenth and eighteenth centuries, and with a deafening crash in the nineteenth century—came modern large-scale commerce and industry. The new commercial and industrial leaders chafed under the static restrictions of medieval society. To carry on large-scale trade and manufacture, it was often necessary to move commodities over great distances; laborers had to be gathered at large factories, which often involved moving people from one end of the country to another; canals and roads had to be built, which would run through many different patrons' domains; prices and the nature of goods often had to be adjusted to reflect changing needs and technology; and science and invention had to be free to pursue truth wherever they found it, regardless of orthodoxy. These requirements collided with the organization of preindustrial medieval society. The new and increasingly powerful commercial and industrial elite cast about for ways to make society more fluid and manageable. One helpful solution, as we shall see in Chapter 3, was the invention of the modern state as a way to organize politics and government. Another was the appearance of liberalism.

Liberalism was not introduced by the commercial and industrial leaders themselves. Rather, it was invented by intellectuals who were moved by the general artistic and scientific restlessness of the age. However, it suited the new economic leaders, and they warmed to it. It gave them a view of politics that could make sense to them in light of their needs, and it allowed them to argue for their causes in ways that were less crass than simply saying, "We wish to limit the power of the nobility, the guilds, and the church because we want to make money."

Liberalism posits as the highest good of society *the ability of the members of that society to develop their individual capacities to the fullest extent.* That is, in a good society, all individuals should be able to develop their minds, musical talents, athletic abilities, or any other gift as much as possible. This requires, according to liberalism, that people be maximally responsible for their own actions, rather than having someone else do things for them or tell them what to do. It is only by acting and feeling the consequences of such action that we can develop our capacity to act.

This is the central assumption of liberalism, from which a number of consequences flow. For instance, in his essay *On Representative Government,* John Stuart Mill based his argument in favor of democratic government on liberal premises, as follows: The chief end of politics is to allow people to become responsible and mature. They can do this only if they take part in decisions affecting their own lives. Therefore, even though a wise and benevolent despot or monarch might make better decisions on behalf of the people than they could make for themselves, democracy would be better, because under it the people make their own decisions, mistakes and all. Therefore, some form of democracy is the best kind of government.

By the same sorts of argument, the following elements follow from the basic liberal premise; together, they constitute the liberal ideology:

- Democracy of some sort is the proper form of government.
- People should have full intellectual freedom, including freedom of speech, freedom of religion, and freedom of the press. (They should have responsibility for their own values, so that they will develop the ability to judge values.)
- Government should remain minimal and should regulate people's lives very little. (As few decisions as possible should be made *for* people, so that they learn to make decisions for themselves.)
- In particular, people should be free to regulate their own economic activity.
- Power of one person over another is a bad thing; hence, government should be organized to guard against abuses of power. (Again, one person should not make decisions for another.)

Liberalism flourished especially in Great Britain and its colonies, perhaps because Britain was the first country to industrialize. In Britain, liberal forces first gained control of the House of Commons and the cabinet in 1832; through the nineteenth century, political control of the country seesawed between liberals and conservatives.

John Stuart Mill and Liberalism

John Stuart Mill (1806–1873) was a major figure in liberal thought. His father, James Mill, an important figure in the history of British philosophy, educated young John himself, following an incredible regimen: John was reading Greek at age three, and by the time he reached maturity he probably knew more of science and literature than anyone else in Britain. He spent his adult years in a sinecure with the British East India Company, which allowed him plenty of time to write. His main contribution to liberal thought was to reconcile individual freedom with the general good of society, in a fairly tight logical system. Unusually for his time, John Stuart Mill was a strong feminist and advocated women's suffrage. Some believe the logic of liberalism pushed him to this conclusion, while others have ascribed it to the influence of his wife, Harriet Taylor Mill.

(See the section on "The Conservative Reaction" for a discussion of conservatism.) In the United States, the new Constitution of 1789, with its precautions against a concentration of power in any one part of the government and its guarantees of various individual freedoms, clearly signified the ascendance of liberalism. On the continent of Europe, liberalism was a potent force throughout the nineteenth century, but it was nowhere as strong as in Britain and its former colonies. Most Western European countries had established liberal constitutions by the end of World War I, but by that time liberalism was fading quickly.

With regard to the distinction between the "choice" and "power" perspectives, liberals will strongly favor a view of politics as choice. To liberals, power is a bad thing that should be limited as much as possible. Power allows some people to force choices on others, which flies directly in the face of liberal principles. To a liberal, politics should properly consist of public choices, in the making of which each person shares equally. As many choices as possible should be kept private. That is, the sphere of politics itself should be limited.

✦ THE CONSERVATIVE REACTION

When liberalism arose to challenge the existing social arrangements, the defenders of those arrangements needed an ideology to counteract the persuasive power of liberalism. **Conservatism** developed in response to this need.

Conservatism in the European sense is unfamiliar to Americans, because it is rather different from American conservatism. Defenders of existing arrangements in Europe pointed out quite properly that liberalism is an individualistic doctrine; that is, liberalism looks on society as consisting of the individuals constituting it. To liberals, the whole of society equals the sum of its component parts, so that a society is happiest when the total of individuals' happiness is greatest. This is implied in the basic premise of liberalism, that the goodness of a society is to be judged by the extent to which its members individually are able to develop their capacities.

In opposition to this, conservatism holds that societies and other groups of people are *more* than just the sums of their parts, that a group of people creates greater happiness through its existence and maintenance as a group than its members could individually produce for themselves. Liberalism, conservatives say, is a lonely and selfish philosophy whose ultimate result would be a group of people resolved to better themselves with no regard for the people around them.

Conservatives regard it as important that their society should have order and structure and that this structure should be stable enough to let people know where they stand with regard to each other. Most important, an ordered group develops and maintains religion and standards of morality. People gain greater happiness as members of a family, members of a church, and members of society than they could possibly gain individually. This is what conservatives see as the highest good of society: *the maintenance of ordered community and of common values.*

In such a society, it is silly to try to keep one person from doing things for another or to keep one individual from exercising power over another. The whole point of "community" is that people are important as members, not as individuals. What matters is how they fit into the web of mutual responsibilities.

The structure of the community should be relatively stable and predictable so that all may easily fit into their place in it; therefore, there is nothing wrong with assigning power to people by even such arbitrary devices as heredity if those people can be expected to use their power wisely. Patterns of domination that have evolved gradually should not be changed casually, because what has grown slowly is at least familiar to us and must have had some virtue to have lasted so long. Conservatism is an ideology that accepts and welcomes power; conservatives believe that appropriate arrangements for power will ensure good treatment for everyone.

It is obvious why this philosophy based on ordered community was useful to the aristocracy, the established church, and others who were trying to maintain their positions against the liberal challenge. However, ideologies take on a life of their own, and conservatism stresses another theme that might not otherwise have come so naturally to the defenders of the status quo: the responsibilities of power. Where liberalism is suspicious of power and seeks to limit it, conservatism sees power as binding and shaping its holder in good ways. Conservatives do not see a powerful monarch or president as one who is in a position to treat people capriciously. Rather, they see such an official as one who is in a position of awesome responsibility, with generally little choice as to courses of action. Conservatism stresses the responsibility of the powerful in a community to help the weak, a position opposed to the view of liberals that the weak should be given responsibility for their own affairs. European conservatives, because of this side of conservatism, have not been especially reluctant to help the poor or to develop the welfare state. In the late eighteenth century in Britain, under the conservative regime, there was already a system of guaranteed minimum income for anyone in Britain—a floor below which no one was to be allowed to fall. *Abolishing* this system, on the grounds that people should have responsibility for their own affairs, was one of the first tasks of the liberals when they took power in 1832. To take another example, when Otto von Bismarck, the conservative chancellor of Germany from 1871 to 1890, introduced the world's first

Edmund Burke and Conservatism

Edmund Burke (1729–1797) is perhaps the most important figure in the development of conservative thought, at least in Britain. He was born and educated in Dublin, Ireland, the son of a lawyer. Although he was a professional politician and a great orator in the House of Commons, he was too intellectual and independent to rise to a major position in his party. As a philosopher, he was not abstract and did not deal in logical systems. Rather, he drew pragmatically from experience. What was already a well-developed conservative ideology was sharpened for him by what he saw as the excesses of the French Revolution.

systems of unemployment insurance, workers' compensation, and social security, he had no apparent sense that he was doing something out of character.

Conservatism in this sense is unfamiliar to Americans. This is because, to the extent that the early immigrants had any ideas about politics at all, America was founded by liberals and populated largely by liberals. Most of the early settlers were trying to escape the rigidities of the old order in Europe. Also, our more fluid society has had few ordered systems of domination; conservatism, a defense of such systems, has therefore been largely irrelevant.[3]

In the last quarter of the twentieth century, however, one of our few ordered systems of domination came under liberal questioning, and something rather like conservatism arose as a defense. The feminist attempt to eliminate men's domination of women was often framed as a classic statement of liberal argument. Women should be free to take on all sorts of responsibility, feminists said, so that they could develop their capacities to the fullest. Protective laws (limiting the hours women may work, barring them from certain dangerous jobs, protecting them from combat in the armed forces, and so on) were wrong because in being protected from unpleasantness people were made weak and dependent. Feminists did not want women "put on a pedestal."

Opponents of feminism often responded in ways that were akin to conservatism. The traditional family is a good thing in its own right, they said. It is the family we should be thinking of, not the individuals who make it up. Families work better, children are raised better, everyone is in the end happier, if there is a clear structure of authority in the family rather than a situation in which each member is striving individually. This has clear echoes of European conservatism.

Conservatism was a strong force throughout Europe in the nineteenth and early twentieth centuries. With the massive changes brought by World War II and its aftermath, European conservatism changed. The nobility were generally destroyed or discredited, the church was in ferment, and most countries had introduced a sweeping expansion of taxation and social services, the "welfare state," to make people more

---

[3]Louis Hartz, *The Liberal Tradition in America* (New York: Harcourt Brace, 1955).

equal. After the huge destruction of the war, it was not always clear that there was a social order for conservatism to defend.

However, conservatism adapted fairly rapidly to these changed circumstances. Conservatives' traditional emphasis on the responsibility of the powerful to help the poor and weak, together with a willingness (in contrast to the position of liberals) to see power concentrated, made it fairly easy for conservatives to accept the welfare state. Also, conservatism welcomes active encouragement of religion by the state, whereas liberalism is suspicious of it; large numbers of Europeans after the war felt a need for a stability of values offered by religion, although among recent generations religious practice has now dropped off sharply. While liberalism declined in Europe throughout the twentieth century, conservatism has lived on healthily. Its adherents accepted the welfare state but urged that it be built in ways that were consistent with traditional moral values and that it should not lead to a leveling of society. In other words, conservatives felt that some structure should remain by which one part of society can lead the rest. In Britain, the Liberal Party declined during the 1920s and 1930s, but the Conservative Party remained as the chief opponent of the new Labour Party. When Labour introduced the welfare state in 1945, the Conservatives accepted it within a few years and went on to dominate British politics for the next forty years. On the continent of Europe, after the war, Christian Democratic parties arose in many countries; these adhered to an established church but were flexible and pragmatic with regard to taxes and social programs. They were especially strong in Italy and Germany, while a somewhat similar movement, the Gaullist movement, dominated French politics from 1958 to 1981. One can safely characterize the politics of most west European states since World War II as having consisted of a conflict between socialism (described in the section on "The Socialist Alternative") and a modified conservatism.

In the Third World, liberalism outside of Europe and North America has generally been weak (countries that are trying to develop their economies apparently find that they cannot afford to limit and restrain concentrations of power) and conservatism is rather strong. Traditional religious leaders and the aristocracy, as in Saudi Arabia and Iran, or new elites of business leaders, as in Japan or Brazil, can often maintain a strong political movement to keep the political leadership of the state in their hands. And frequently, the two groups join forces.

There is often a strong element of direction from the military in such movements as well, as in the series of conservative regimes in South Korea from 1952 to 1987. While not all military governments are conservative, there is often an affinity between military leaders and conservative political parties. Military organization requires an ordered structure of command in which certain members of the military direct the activities of other members. This is rather similar to the conservative view of society as a whole and may help to make military leaders comfortable with conservatism.[4]

A major exception to the general weakness of liberalism in the Third World (the poor states of the world) has appeared in recent years, as part of the worldwide rise

---

[4]However, see the more detailed discussion of military governments in Chapter 7.

of "neoliberalism" (see p. 37). This has involved reduced regulation by governments, privatization of government-run industries, and a general reliance on open markets for, economic decisions. This picks up on the *economic* aspects of liberalism but not necessarily on any others. Under this impetus, a number of states of the Third World have reduced governmental involvement in the economy, while not particularly "liberalizing" their societies in other ways.

About now, you might be asking, "Why are we looking at this ancient history? These are obviously things that were fought out a century or two ago. How about today's issues?" The answer is that the general frameworks of liberalism and conservatism (and the ideology dealt with in the next section, socialism) still live on in European and American societies, if somewhat subconsciously. In order to understand contemporary politics of these countries we must understand the foundational ideological traditions on which they are built.

Why is it that the United States is the only advanced industrial country in which gun ownership is only lightly regulated? Our overwhelmingly liberal tradition might have something to do with this.

Or, consider another example. Socialist parties in Scandinavia built pervasive, cradle-to-grave welfare states after the Second World War. (In Sweden at one point in the 1990s, 68 percent of all spending in the country was done by government programs.) In the last couple of decades, however, most of the Scandinavian countries have replaced their Socialist governments with center-right coalitions; as of this writing, only one of the five countries had a Socialist prime minister. But these non-socialist governments have continued to support the welfare state about as much as their Socialist predecessors did. Why is there essentially no opposition to the massive welfare states of Scandinavia? Could it be because liberalism (with its opposition to governmental involvement in people's lives) never took much of a hold there? Instead, conservatism provided the Scandinavian alternative to socialism, and conservatism does not have a problem with welfare states.

If you tried to explain American gun regulation or the Scandinavian welfare state without knowing the ideological background of politics in these countries, you would be reduced—*as most journalists and pundits seem to be today*—to saying, "Well, Americans are like that; they love guns," or "Oh, those Swedes!"

✦ THE SOCIALIST ALTERNATIVE

When liberalism first arose to challenge the established order, it drew considerable support from the "working class," the workers and their families who were beginning to congregate in the growing cities. Workers especially liked the assumption that all people were equal and should have an equal opportunity to develop their talents. They liked the liberal doctrine of democracy, which would recognize them as having full and equal citizenship rights. In 1848, a wave of attempted revolutions by liberals swept across the continent of Europe; in most of these, skilled workers played a leading part, along with shopkeepers and other small businessmen. In Britain, the leaders of most labor unions were active in the Liberal Party as late as 1900.

Karl Marx and Socialism

Karl Marx (1818–1883) was raised at first in Bonn, Germany, and later in Berlin. After graduating from the university, Marx and his close friend Friedrich Engels (1820–1895) worked as journalists. In 1848 they wrote the *Communist Manifesto* and, in the aftermath of unsuccessful liberal revolutions in Germany in that year, were forced to flee Germany. They settled in London, where Engels's family had connections and Engels could take care of Marx. Marx did not return to Germany until shortly before his death. In London he worked as a correspondent for the *New York Tribune* and wrote his massive, major work, *Das Kapital*. Marx combined a sweeping view of history with an astonishing appetite for the minutiae of economics. At its most basic level, his theory of politics, as of all other human activity, was that it is determined solely by economic processes and can be understood by economic analysis.

However, through the latter part of the nineteenth century, the enthusiasm of the working class for liberalism weakened. Liberalism implied not only that people should be politically equal but that they should be regulated and helped by the government as little as possible. Workers were in a weak position socially and economically, and they often found that they would like help from the government in ways that were inconsistent with liberalism. Governmental protection against unemployment and sickness, governmental regulation of working hours and of safety in the factories, governmental prohibition of child labor—these and similar wishes of labor were inconsistent with liberal principles. Naturally, compromises and accommodations could be reached within the movement, and labor was not left totally out in the cold, but the fact remained that labor often found that it had to buck the basic philosophy of the movement of which it was a part. When a new ideology appeared that was more congenial to labor, workers moved to it fairly readily. This ideology was **socialism**.

Socialism retained the assumption of liberalism that all persons deserve equal treatment by the state and should have equal opportunities to develop themselves; but unlike liberalism, it did not posit that people could develop individually, and it was not as suspicious as liberalism of the concentration of power and of positive action by the state. Karl Marx (1818–1883) was the greatest socialist writer, and all socialism since Marx has been heavily influenced by his views. Marx thought that society consisted not of individuals but of ***classes***. A class is a group of people who share the same relationship to the means of production and who therefore develop a distinctive view of themselves and of the world. Marx thought that the most important thing about us is our work, that this is what creates for us most of our view of the world; people who share similar work (a similar "relationship to the means of production") form the natural basis for a class. The aristocracy had been such a class, intellectuals were such a class, the industrialists were such a class, and now a new class—the working class—was appearing in Europe. To Marx, people did not develop themselves individually—in a vacuum, as it were—but of and through the class to which they belonged. According to this view, individuals do not form their own values, their own ideas about politics, their own sense of their needs; rather, they and the people they associate with form these things communally in ways that are difficult to specify. A person may contribute to these values and ideas, but so do the other members of his or her class. Each member draws much more from the class than any single member contributes to it.

For Marx, then, the basic unit of concern was the class. As he saw it, the working class was oppressed; it was made to give up its members' labor to feed the rich capitalist class. This was wrong, he said, because the working class were numerically much larger than the capitalist class and their oppression bred great misery. Therefore, the working class should take over control of the government and the government should take over industry, so that the workers, through their government, would control the industries in which they worked. This would ensure fair treatment for everyone.

The writings of Marx and other socialists derived their energy and moral force from the writers' awareness of the truly miserable conditions under which workers lived in the nineteenth century. Marx's friend and collaborator Friedrich Engels, in his study of the living conditions of English workers, quoted an Anglican priest's account in 1844 of conditions in his parish:

> It contains 1,400 houses, inhabited by 2,795 families, comprising a population of 12,000. The space within which this large amount of population are living is less than 400 yards square, and it is no uncommon thing for a man and his wife, with four or five children, and sometimes the grandfather and grandmother, to be found living in a room from ten to twelve feet square, and which serves them for eating and working in. . . . There is not one father of a family in ten throughout the entire district that possesses any clothes but his working dress, and that too commonly in the worst tattered condition; and with many this wretched clothing form their only covering at night, with nothing better than a bag of straw or shavings to lie upon.[5]

Engels goes on to describe his own investigation of the living conditions of the working class in the city of Manchester:

> One walks along a very rough path on the river bank, in between clothesposts and washing lines to reach a chaotic group of little, one-storied, one-roomed cabins. Most of them have earth floors, and working, living and sleeping all take place in the one room. In such a hole, barely six feet long and five feet wide, I saw two beds—and what beds and bedding!—which filled the room, except for the fireplace and the doorstep. Several of these huts, as far as I could see, were completely empty, although the door was open and the inhabitants were leaning against the door posts. In front of the doors filth and garbage abounded. I could not see the pavement, but from time to time, I felt it was there because my feet scraped it.[6]

Marx developed a theory of history arguing that a revolution of the working class was not only appropriate but inevitable. According to Marx's theory, all history has consisted of a successive unfolding of domination by one group, leading to revolution against that group, followed by domination by a new group (the group that had

---

[5]Friedrich Engels, *The Condition of the Working Class in England,* tr. by W. O. Henderson and W. H. Chaloner (Oxford, England: Basil Blackwell, 1958), pp. 35, 36.
[6]Ibid., p. 61.

Karl Marx, architect of socialist ideology.

© Hulton–Deutsch Collection/Corbis

led the successful revolution), leading to yet another revolution, and so on. Currently the capitalist class (which had earlier overturned the rule of the aristocracy) dominated the working class, but according to his theory the working class would eventually overturn them—either at the ballot box, or by revolution. This theory of history and revolution was powerfully attractive to workers. It told them that their unhappy plight was not their own fault as individuals but rather a condition imposed on them as a class by the working out of a broad historical process. Furthermore, it prophesied that they must, in the end, prevail over the capitalists because that is the way history works. Finally, it assured them that once they had prevailed, a brave new world would be created in which the cycle of revolutions was no longer necessary.

Socialism burst explosively on Europe. In 1850, there were only a few socialists on the continent. By the early 1900s, the Social Democratic Party was the largest party in Germany and was growing fast, and socialism was growing just as rapidly in other Western European countries.

✦ COMMUNISM AND SOCIALISM

In 1917, a key event occurred in the development of socialism when Lenin's Bolsheviks succeeded in seizing control of the Russian Empire and transformed it into a socialist state renamed the Union of Soviet Socialist Republics (U.S.S.R.). Marx and Engels had never fully settled whether they thought the working class should take control of the state peacefully through electoral victory or violently through revolution. Many socialists thought revolution was the only answer, while others believed deeply in democracy. Lenin's successful revolution galvanized those who wanted to take the route of revolution, and over the years after 1917 they tried to dominate the socialist movement. They argued that the one state that had now successfully become socialist, the U.S.S.R., should lead all socialists in the world. The attempt to commit socialism to a revolutionary strategy led to a split in the socialist movement in the 1920s. The revolutionists set themselves up as **Communist** parties, while the democratic socialists continued to call themselves Socialist or sometimes **Democratic Socialist** parties.

The split has endured, so that there are two branches of socialism, although outside of a few places such as Cuba, communism has been in broad retreat for the last couple of decades. Communists have generally held to a revolutionary strategy, although with the passage of time they have grown a good deal less emphatic about it. Socialists have been much more willing to settle for a portion of power within an only partially socialist system, and they have generally worked within a democratic framework. Socialists have also been more willing than communists to settle for partial improvements for workers, rather than holding out for a total change.

In the period after World War II, most of Eastern Europe was governed by communists, with military help from the U.S.S.R. By 1989, communism in Eastern Europe and the Soviet Union had become more a bureaucratic sink than a shining ideology, and over the next two years these communist regimes collapsed. The Eastern European states tend to look to democratic socialism, combined with free markets, as a model; the remnants of the Soviet Union have made stabs at economic change, but many have also been occupied with working out ethnic and nationalistic conflicts. In Western Europe, Socialists have participated strongly in government for many years, and Socialists took the lead in bringing the modern welfare state to Europe. Communism and socialism have been strong forces in the Third World. China, Cuba, Vietnam, and North Korea have more or less communist governments, while a number of Third World states have socialist governments.

✦ FASCISM

In the 1920s and 1930s, there arose a political movement, **fascism,** that did not hang together well as ideology, but was rather more a style of politics and a popular movement. Adolf Hitler in Germany, Benito Mussolini in Italy, and Francisco Franco in Spain established fascist regimes at this time. Fascists did not generally write elaborations of their theory, because among other things, they despised intellectualism and ideology. Accordingly, most analysts of fascism as an ideology have looked mainly at what fascists did. The essence of fascism seems to have been a rejection of most institutions of modern life, combined with a national rebirth focused on a charismatic, dictatorial leader. Fascists were antisocialist, generally anticapitalist, and (at least in Hitler's and Mussolini's cases) hostile to the church. They tended to glorify instead a mythical war-based society of the past—for Mussolini the ancient Roman Empire, for Hitler the Teutonic knights of the Middle Ages and Wagner's dreamy stories about the old Germanic gods.

Their political style was opportunist. All used violence and terror to advance their movements. Somewhat paradoxically—remember, they despised modern institutions—they were also "up to date" and presented themselves as forward-looking. Hitler was the first German politician to campaign from an airplane, for instance, and the design of fascist propaganda and rallies was often done in the modern-looking art deco style.

Fascism appealed particularly to those who felt left out in the modern age. In Spain and Italy, these were mostly the traditional elites, who felt threatened by modern industrial managers and by socialist workers. In Germany, the "left out" appear to have been mainly the middle class, small farmers, and shopkeepers. The uprooting of European civilization in the First World War helped prepare the ground as well, adding to the sense of loss among the disinherited of modern life.

The details of fascism actually varied a good deal from one place to another. The Nazi party of Germany attacked the existing social system, including the churches, more actively than most. It had a strong element of anti-Semitic racism that was not present in Italian or Spanish fascism and that ultimately led to the murder of millions of

Jews. Spanish fascism identified with conservative church leadership and supported the church. Italian fascism was marked by an attempt to reorganize the economy into "corporations"—guilds of employers and workers in each industry. Such variations in fascist policy again underscore that fascism was, and is, rather more a political style than a system of ideas.

The defeat of the fascist powers in World War II ended most organized fascism; but since then, when established sets of people have felt their positions threatened by modern change—especially by new racial or ethnic claims, or by immigration of new groups into the country—echoes of fascism have often been heard. The American Nazi party and white power movements, anti-immigrant movements in Europe, and so on, often involve a dramatic leader, violence, and a denial of modern change in ways that show kinship with the old fascist movements.

✦ IDEOLOGIES IN THE TWENTY-FIRST CENTURY

With the long period of general peace in Europe and among other industrialized states since World War II, some of the edge has worn off the conflict among the great modern ideologies. As modern society has become more firmly established, the old grievances do not seem to move people as strongly as they once did. With the decline of religion (at least in Europe) and with the poor economic performance of socialist states, there has been a resurgence of liberalism—but a liberalism modified by considerable governmental support for the weak.

Many leaders of parties, especially those that hold responsibility for the government of a state, have begun to modify their ideologies in light of practical experience. The most dramatic example of this was provided by the collapse of the communist regimes of Eastern Europe and Russia. Many states of this region have become liberal democracies, and all have abandoned their old, ideologically based communist systems.

Other leaders, too, have shown a more compromised blend of ideologies. Britain's Margaret Thatcher was for fifteen years the leader of the Conservative Party, which among other things had emphasized ties to the Anglican Church and the monarchy. However, her personal ideology combined these conservative elements with a set of very liberal economic policies calling for a great shrinkage of the state's role in the economy, marked by the privatization (sale to private owners) of many government enterprises. On the other side of the spectrum, some socialists such as Felipe Gonzalez, leader of Spain's Socialist Party, or Tony Blair, the Labour Party prime minister of Britain, so blended their socialism with concerns for efficiency and stable economic growth that it was scarcely recognizable as a doctrine of conflict between classes. Italy's former Communist Party, with even the word *Communist* now removed from its name, emerged in the mid-1990s as the Democratic Party of the Left, a left-of-center, democratic party—and is one of the leading parties of post–Cold War Italy.

However, ideological conflict is not dead in the twenty-first century. In Europe, new "green" parties have raised over the past few decades a set of issues that established leaders, accustomed to the old ideologies, found hard to absorb into their debates. These issues, labeled "postmaterial issues" by Ronald Inglehart, included feminism, protection of the environment, and open and spontaneous styles of life.[7] In part, they have been represented by totally new parties (among others, the Greens); in part, they have found their way into established Socialist parties where they often represented a minority voice. In Socialist parties, the new mood especially has produced interest in direct participation by workers in the management of their industries.[8] At the other end of the spectrum, anti-immigrant parties, such as France's National Front, have raised issues of race and nationalism that had been thought dead since the Second World War. Outside of Europe, militant Islam, with its claims for a religious state, has raised a qualitatively different kind of challenge in many states of North Africa, the Mideast, and South Asia. Faith-based politics, based on divine will, is intense and difficult to compromise. This has proved true of both militant Islam and the religious strand of American conservatism. We will explore the political impact of fundamentalist religion in more detail in the next section.

History, and the development of ideologies, does not stop. The great modern ideologies were a product of the tension between Europe's industrialization and the static institutions Europe had inherited from its feudal past. As that tension recedes, other sources of ideological development have come to the fore, in a sometimes confusing mix of forces and tensions: the practical economic experiences of the United States, Europe, and Japan; the increasing problem of degradation of the environment; the resurgence of militant Islam; the discovery of youth and women as classes, even though Marxist socialism saw classes as based solely on economic position; and the division of interests between rich and poor parts of the world.

Perhaps most notably, in a new mood of **neoliberalism,** many states have cut back on governmental regulation of the economy, privatized state-run businesses, made their central banks more independent of direction from the government, and opened business in their state to international competition by lowering trade barriers. In effect, these governments adopted the economic part of liberalism, though not necessarily the full ideology. (Many of these states established democracy at the same time, but some carried out "neoliberal" reforms without any of the other parts of liberalism; a good example is China, whose communist government maintains tight control over politics and speech but has hugely opened up the economy.)

The impetus for this neoliberal tide seems to be less ideology than a practical desire to operate economies more efficiently. It was heightened, for example, by the economic success of the United States in the 1990s, which was taken by many states as a model to be imitated. The tide was also encouraged by the International Monetary Fund and U.S. foreign policy, which generally tied economic help in times of crisis to reforms along neoliberal lines.

Neoliberalism has also been connected with the growth of "globalization," in which states can no longer control the flow of ideas or goods across their borders as well as they once could. Since it is increasingly difficult for a state to control its affairs

---

[7]Ronald Inglehart, *Culture Shift in Advanced Industrial Society* (Princeton, N.J.: Princeton University Press, 1990).
[8]See, for example, W. Rand Smith, "Toward 'Autogestion' in Socialist France? The Impact of Industrial Relations Reform," *West European Politics* 10 (January 1987), pp. 46–62.

by itself, it must be able to connect with the states around it. And the openness that this requires fosters "neoliberal" competition with businesses beyond the state's borders.

As you will see in other parts of this book, many of the main sources of political conflict and ideological ferment in the world today involve questions of national, ethnic, or religious identity, gender, and what to do about the increasingly shared international problems of economic development and the environment.

✦ RELIGION, POLITICS, AND POLITICAL PHILOSOPHY

Religion is an important part of politics and political philosophy, even though religious practice and belief have indeed diminished somewhat in the last few decades in Europe and America (see below, pp. 195–198). Two of the most intractable issues in American politics, for instance, are based on religious doctrine: abortion and gay marriage. And elsewhere, violent politics often has had its roots in religious differences: Catholics and Protestants in Northern Ireland; Sunni and Shiite Moslems in Iraq; anti-Western attacks by Moslems, especially Moslems living in Europe; to give a few examples.

Religions are belief systems, so they are in fact a kind of ideology. But they are set apart from other ideologies by their origin in divine inspiration. This makes them so different from other ideologies that it is only in a technical sense that we would call them "ideologies." Their divine core makes them more difficult to argue about, because one either does, or does not, believe in the divine basis of a religion. Two who share that belief may argue about important differences of interpretation within the religion, but a believer and a nonbeliever just have to agree to disagree. This is a very different discourse than what we usually think of as ideological argument.

How much religious discourse differs from other ideological discourse depends in part on how fundamentalist the believer is. Fundamentalist believers take it that every word of the God-given scripture, be it the Bible or the Qu'ran, is true because it came from God. Other believers, noting that in every religious book there are inevitable contradictions and ambiguities, see the documents of their faith as having a central core of principles, but as being interpretable as to exact prescriptions. These more interpretive believers may not compromise on the Golden Rule, for instance, but may consider God's words on homosexuality more open to discussion. Interpretive belief often leaves a good deal of room for blending with elements from other ideologies like liberalism, socialism, or conservatism, and so discourse about such belief is in the end somewhat more like other ideological discussion than is discussion based on fundamentalist belief. But to the extent that understandings of God's truth are part of the discussion, *any* religious discourse always has a special character.

Religion (like its modern cousin nationalism, which we will discuss in the next chapter) appears able to tap deep emotions of love and hate more easily than other ideologies, and this contributes to its immense impact on politics. Its place in politics comes partly from the fact that a religion is an **identity group**—a group of people who share an identity that they (and others) think defines them and sets them apart from others. Since politics often involves questions of various groups' power and rights, this involves religion in politics in a way that is different from other adherents of an ideology.

Yet a religion is also a belief system. In this aspect, religions function in politics much like other ideologies, though with the differences in discourse that I mentioned above.

These two aspects of religion can be easily confused. And, they may make it difficult to analyze the role of religion in politics, and how to respond to it. The political role of Islam is an excellent case in point. As a belief system, Islam emphasizes generosity and doing good to others. And historically, Islamic empires were notably tolerant of other religions. While it is true that many versions of Islam distinguish how believers and nonbelievers may be treated (wars may generally only be fought against nonbelievers, for instance), it is primarily a peaceful and generous religion.[9]

But in various parts of the world, Moslems are involved as an identity group in conflicts that have excited emotions deep enough to inspire acts of political violence even up to suicide attacks. In the Mideast, Moslems are confronted with the ongoing, identity-based conflict between Israel and the Palestinians. In other parts of Africa and Asia, however, that conflict has not in the past inspired as much emotion, and there we have not generally seen politics waged as intensely as in the Mideast.[10]

Moslem immigrants in Europe find themselves largely ghettoized and marginalized in society—without much access to jobs, citizenship, or a regular role in society. This has bred much alienation and bitterness and has spawned a good deal of violence: riots in France, terrorist attacks in Britain and Spain. The terrorist attack on the World Trade Center and the Pentagon on September 11, 2001, was organized by European Moslems.

In contrast, Moslem immigrants in the United States are relatively well integrated. (A surprising 59 percent of adult Moslems are college graduates, compared with only 29 percent of all adult Americans.[11]) And there has been virtually no terrorist activity or support from among Moslems living in the United States.

Depending on the situation, then, identity-based Moslem politics can vary widely. This contrasts with the effect of Islam as a belief system, which generally inclines its adherents toward very traditional values on abortion, homosexuality, and the family, and to generous programs for the poor, but does not vary so greatly from one region to another.

Islam as a belief system, the identity-based politics of Moslems in the Mideast, the different identity-based politics of European Moslems, and the still different situation of American Moslems—these get badly muddled in the public mind, and in governments' policies.

In the United States, identity-based religious politics based on Christianity is fairly low-key, but still has some resonance. While it has disappeared in the United States, the mutual hostility of Catholics and Protestants was still strong enough sixty years ago that it was a major factor in the 1960 Presidential election; many Republican Catholics switched that year to vote for John F. Kennedy, and many Protestant Democrats switched to vote against him. In the run-up to the 2008 Presidential election, significant

---

[9]It is, of course, very traditional in questions of sex and family.
[10]The advent of 24-hour news coverage, however, has made it more immediate and intense for Moslems everywhere than it used to be.
[11]Paul M. Barrett, "They're Muslims, and Yankees, Too," *BusinessWeek,* January 15, 2007, p. 1.

TABLE 2.1

Various Types of Born-Again Christians Compared

	Percent Regularly Feeling Divinely Inspired	Percent Believing Every Word of the Bible Is True	Percent Believing Abortion Can Never Be Justified	Percent Republican
Not born again	9%	20%	3%	22%
Nurtured in faith	12	54	8	46
Gradual experience	12	70	13	53
Profession of faith	14	73	16	61
Specific experience	21	85	20	74

Source: Adapted from Table 10.3 of Ted G. Jelen, Corwin E. Smidt, and Clyde Wilcox, "The Political Effects of the Born-Again Phenomenon," in David C. Leege and Lyman A. Kellstedt, *Rediscovering the Religious Factor in American Politics* (Armonk, N.Y.: M. E. Sharpe, 1993), p. 211.

numbers of voters told pollsters they could not support Mitt Romney for the Republican nomination because he was a Mormon.

By and large, though, the impact of religion on politics in the United States stems more from the differing belief systems of different religions that lead to differing policy choices and votes. For instance, in a study of evangelical Protestants (almost all of whom described themselves as "born-again Christians"), variations in the nature of the born-again experience had important political ramifications. The evangelical Protestants were sorted into a small group who said they were not born again; a group who said being born again was a result of being nurtured in Christ's Church throughout their life; a gradual experience that occurred over time; a condition that they enjoy by profession of faith in Jesus; or a specific, memorable "born-again" moment in their life. These groups varied by their views on both religion and politics, as seen in Table 2.1. Differences in belief systems produced varying political choices.

Religion mixes somewhat uneasily with other ideologies in a country like the United States, because the discourse of religion differs in significant ways from the discourse of other ideologies. But as it mingles and merges with other ideologies, it is a major factor in politics.

✦ POLITICAL PHILOSOPHY IN OTHER HISTORICAL ERAS

In all of these discussions of ideology, it should have been clear that ideologies develop in response to the dominant problems and dilemmas that people face at a given time. Liberalism, conservatism, and socialism all arose out of the changed world of the Industrial Revolution. But what sorts of concerns drove political thought and ideology over the long play of Western history before the challenge of industrialization?

The scope of this book does not allow space enough to deal fully with this rich history of political thought; I will just sketch some of the major strands for you here in order to place the presentations of this chapter in their broader context. I also hope this may whet your appetite to dig more deeply. Political philosophy of earlier eras is worth reading partly for its own sake, to see how intelligent people dealt with the problems they faced. But it also often applies, by analogy, to problems we face today. Thomas Hobbes, for example, struggled in the sixteenth century with the problem of what obligation and obedience he owed to the king of England. Today, we have kings only in a few countries, but we do have governments, and what obedience we owe to governments, whether deliberate disobedience of a government's laws is legitimate, and so on are live political questions.

The Greeks were the first great political philosophers, especially the Greeks of Athens a few centuries before the birth of Christ. These were a people who valued speech and argument highly, and incorporated debate and rhetoric into their daily, practical lives. From that tradition of debate there sprang an extraordinary burst of questioning and thought around 400 to 300 B.C., which eventually laid the basis for virtually all Western thought in all areas. The Greeks were especially concerned with how we know what we know, and how we can reason. They developed the basis for *rationalism,* a reliance on reason as the sole basis for truth, including religious truth. This in turn led to the development of mathematics, of esthetics as we know it, and of the natural sciences. In the realm of morality and politics, they were especially concerned with the nature of justice and with the question of what sort of constitution would produce the best political community. Plato (428–347 B.C.) was perhaps the greatest of the Athenian philosophers. In *The Republic,* he describes a utopian political community in which good, gifted people are selected as infants to be the leaders ("guardians") and are carefully trained (their reading censored, their minds honed by the study of mathematics) so that they will be able to rule wisely and autocratically and thus produce a just state. His was an ideal world, not likely to be accomplished in fact. It is reminiscent of modern conservatism.

While Plato sought for the ideal, Aristotle (384–322 B.C.), another great Athenian, restricted himself more to observations of the world around him. Aristotle thought that if people could be trusted to rule unselfishly, the best constitution was one in which a single person ruled; the next best was aristocracy, the rule of the few; and the least good was rule by a large number of people. In practice, however, people were selfish, and Aristotle argued that—because the perversion of the best leads to the worst—selfish rule by a single person was worse than selfish rule by a large number. Therefore, in the end he argued for something like democracy.

With their concerns about the proper role of citizens, about the nature of justice, and about what sort of constitution produces a good community and good people, the Greeks laid the foundation for Western political philosophy that followed. During the Roman Empire, relatively little was done in this area, the Romans rather tending to rely on what the Greeks had already done. With the coming of the Christian church in the first centuries after Christ, however, a new period of activity began. The development of a church that claimed allegiance from people all over Europe raised to the forefront the question of just what obligation people bore to their *earthly* rulers. If they were ruled by

Analytic Political Philosophy

Much work in the study of political philosophy is of the sort presented in this chapter—a history of the development of political ideas, with critical commentary on them. An alternative way of approaching the study draws its inspiration from the modern school of "analytic philosophy," which concerns itself especially with the meaning of words.

This approach, called "analytic political philosophy," does not primarily concern itself with the history of political ideas or with critical argument about them at a general level. Rather, its practitioners feel that they can contribute most to our understanding of politics by clarifying the language we use when we talk about politics. Certainly, a problem of muddled language lies behind many political arguments. The United States calls itself a "democracy," and so did the Soviet Union throughout the post–World War II period until its dissolution. The two meant quite different things by the word, but this was often forgotten in red-faced arguments along the lines of "We're a democracy!" "Are not!" "Are!" "Aren't!"

Some questions commonly dealt with by analytic political philosophers are, What is the state? (you will have a taste of the complexities of this question in Chapter 3) and, more important, What are our *obligations* to the state? What is the "public interest"? What should be considered "rights," as in "human rights"? What should be meant by "equality"? And so on.

One excellent example of work in the mode of analytic political philosophy is Hannah Pitkin's study, *The Concept of Representation,* in which the author examines the varied ways in which, over the last several centuries, the word *representation* has been used in order to make clear what general, central meaning it has.[12] A useful collection of analytic works is *Political Philosophy,* edited by Anthony Quinton.[13]

[12]Hannah Pitkin, *The Concept of Representation* (Berkeley: University of California Press, 1967).
[13]Anthony Quinton, ed., *Political Philosophy* (Oxford, England: Oxford University Press, 1967).

God in Christ, why should they do what their king told them to do? What should they do, for instance, if ordered by their king to do something that was a sin?

Much of the development of political philosophy for a thousand years or so centered on this question, and the answers shifted as the relative power of the church and of secular rulers waxed and waned. Early Christian writers, perhaps reflecting the weakness of the young church, claimed a rather modest role for the church in the affairs of this world. The greatest of these writers was Saint Augustine (354–430), who argued that government was made necessary by humanity's sinfulness and that only once we were without sin could we be ruled by God. To Augustine, government was a necessary evil (*made* necessary by evil), which at least produced internal order for sinful humanity.

As the church grew in power, popes sought to assert more authority over secular rulers. By the Middle Ages, Saint Thomas Aquinas (1225–1274) was asserting that the church was responsible for people's spiritual well-being and rulers were responsible for their physical well-being; since the spiritual was more important than the physical, however, rulers must be guided by the church whenever the church held that spiritual needs were involved.

The church was not without opposition in this thrust, of course, especially as it weakened in later centuries. A curious and famous response to it was that of Niccoló Machiavelli (1469–1527), who wished to help kings resist the church and wrote *The Prince*, a primer of how to be a successful king, to help them. In it he argued that a king should be ruthless and pragmatic, not swayed by sentiment or morality.

Toward the end of the Middle Ages, and as Europe entered the modern period, kings grew stronger and the church weakened. This became particularly clear during the Reformation, when the historic Catholic Church was replaced in much of northern Europe by local Protestant churches established by local kings. The pendulum of political philosophy swung back against the church, as in the writings of Martin Luther (1483–1546), who returned to Saint Augustine's doctrine that government is a necessity to which even faithful Christians should submit.

As kings became more powerful, questions of political philosophy shifted to what obligations people in general bore to *them*. This question was brought to a head in the English Civil War (1647–1649), in which a diverse group of opponents to the king succeeded in deposing him and set up a republic that lasted for a bit over a decade. This successful challenge to royal authority focused attention on the question of the duties owed to kings and eventually led to the development of liberalism, discussed previously.

One particularly important writer who participated in this debate was Thomas Hobbes (1588–1679), author of *Leviathan*, a strangely modern defense of authority. (Hobbes does not specify whether that authority must be vested in a king.) His argument is as follows: All people are selfish; in the absence of authority they will turn on each other, and life will be "solitary, poor, nasty, brutish, and short." To avoid this, people voluntarily band together into states and contract to give their rights to a sovereign, who will rule autocratically to provide peace and order for all. Hobbes's theory was intended primarily to justify the rule of kings, but it could be used to justify any sort of dictatorship. Of their free wills, by a cooperative decision, the people set up a power to dominate them for the common good.

With the questioning of royal authority at this time, the stage was set for the development of liberalism and of the other modern ideologies responding to liberalism; the bulk of this chapter has dealt with these ideologies. But while these ideologies have dominated political discourse in this century, they do not represent some kind of final stage of philosophical development. Ideologies are always rooted in the social challenges of their time, and at the beginning of the twenty-first century numerous new questions of political philosophy face us. Chief among these are a number of issues having to do with identity: feminist political theory, theories of politics based on a religion such as Islam, and theories of multiethnic politics. Emerging problems in the environment also stimulate philosophical discussion, especially regarding the question of what one generation owes the next.

The one sure thing is that as the new discourse develops, it will build on and absorb the old, just as liberalism, conservatism, and socialism did over the past couple of centuries.

KEY TERMS

ideology
American liberalism
American conservatism
liberalism

conservatism
socialism
classes
communism

democratic socialism
fascism
neoliberalism
identity group

FURTHER READING

Appleby, R. Scott. *The Ambivalence of the Sacred: Religion, Violence, and Reconciliation.* Lanham, MD: Rowman & Littlefield, 2000.

Arendt, Hannah. *The Origins of Totalitarianism.* New York: Harcourt Brace, 1951.

Ball, Terence, and Bellamy, Richard, eds. *The Cambridge History of Twentieth-Century Political Thought.* New York: Cambridge University Press, 2003.

Berlin, Isaiah. "Does Political Theory Still Exist?" In *Philosophy, Politics, and Society,* 2d series, ed. P. Laslett and W. G. Runciman. Oxford, England: Basil Blackwell, 1962.

Calhoun, Cheshire, ed. *Setting the Moral Compass: Essays by Women Philosophers.* New York: Oxford, 2003.

Cassels, Alan. *Fascism.* Arlington Heights, IL.: Harlan Davidson, 1985.

Dahl, Robert. *A Preface to Democratic Theory.* Chicago: University of Chicago Press, 1956.

Dryzek, John S. *Deliberative Democracy and Beyond: Liberals, Critics, Contestations.* New York: Oxford University Press, 2000.

Ebenstein, Alan, Ebenstein, William, and Fogelman, Edwin. *Today's Isms,* 11th ed. Upper Saddle River, NJ.: Prentice-Hall, 2001.

Euben, J. Peter. *Platonic Noise.* Princeton: Princeton University Press, 2003.

Gutmann, Amy, and Thompson, Dennis. *Why Deliberative Democracy?* Princeton: Princeton University Press, 2004.

Heywood, Andrew. *Political Ideologies: An Introduction,* 3rd ed. New York: Palgrave Macmillan, 2003.

Honig, Bonnie. *Democracy and the Foreigner.* Princeton: Princeton University Press, 2001.

Ignatieff, Michael. *The Lesser Evil: Political Ethics in an Age of Terror.* Princeton: Princeton University Press, 2004.

Leege, David C., and Kellstedt, Lyman A. *Rediscovering the Religious Factor in American Politics.* Armonk, NY: M.E. Sharpe, 1993.

Neiman, Susan. *Evil in Modern Thought.* Princeton: Princeton University Press, 2002.

Rawls, John. *Political Liberalism.* New York: Columbia University Press, 1993.

———. *A Theory of Justice.* Cambridge, MA.: Belknap, 1971.

Riker, William. *Liberalism Against Populism.* San Francisco: Freeman, 1982.

Shapiro, Ian. *The State of Democratic Theory.* Princeton, NJ: Princeton University Press, 2006.

Strauss, Leo. "What Is Political Philosophy?" *Journal of Politics* 19 (August 1957), pp. 343–68.

Wald, Kenneth D., and Calhoun-Brown, Allison. *Religion and Politics in the United States,* 5th ed. Lanham, MD: Rowman & Littlefield, 2007.

Wolff, Jonathan. *Why Read Marx Today?* New York: Oxford University Press, 2002.

Wolin, Sheldon S. *Politics and Vision: Continuity and Innovation in Western Political Thought,* revised and expanded ed. Princeton: Princeton University Press, 2004.

WEB SITES OF INTEREST

American political thought:
http://www.geocities.com/Heartland/Fields/9206/welcome.html

Libertarian Party home page:
http://www.lp.org/

Political Compass. An interactive Web site that helps you to examine your own ideology:
http://www.politicalcompass.org/

PART II

The State And Public Policy

CHAPTER 3

THE MODERN STATE

In this book, I will focus on the politics of the *state*—rather than on "office politics," politics in the family, and so on—simply because the state has come to play such a central role in modern politics.[1]

The extent to which the state has come to dominate our attention is evident even in the way we treat individuals. When we think about a person who comes from a different country, we are likely to think of him or her primarily in terms of this—to the exclusion of other characteristics that may actually have more to do with what the person is like. If you knew a Danish engineer named Ole, for instance, and were asked to say quickly, in one word, what Ole is, you would be likely to say "a Dane." The other likely answer would be "a man"; gender has not given way even to the state in the amount of attention we give it. Ole is an engineer, and that should say a lot about him; but not many people would choose that over his nationality as a label for him. He may be a Lutheran or a Jew, pious or apathetic, tall or short, a charmer or a clod; still, most people who know him would characterize him first as a Dane. This does not make much sense, because almost all the other things mentioned would have told you more about Ole's personality or person than does the fact that he is a Dane. It is a result not of logic but of our modern fixation on nationality and the state.

If you have ever lived abroad, you will have noticed this phenomenon in a particularly striking way. Most of us do not ordinarily think of ourselves in terms of the state to which we belong. However, let us reside in a different state, and suddenly our native state becomes a most important aspect of our identity. Canadians living in the United States or Europe begin to think of themselves much more as Canadians than they ever have before, Nigerians studying or working in the United States suddenly begin to think of themselves as Nigerians, Americans living in Europe or Asia suddenly feel themselves

---

[1] As noted in Chapter 1, the word *state* as used here does not refer to a place such as California or Pennsylvania. Rather, it means approximately what is often called a "country," such as Canada, Nigeria, or the United States of America.

to be vividly American, and so on. When everyone you meet responds to you as a Nigerian or an American, it is hard not to start feeling that way about yourself.

Our fixation on the state goes almost beyond what reason would dictate. We have seen that we could say more about Ole if we characterized him as tall or university educated than merely as a Dane. Another paradoxical result of our fixation on the state is that most people pay a good deal more attention to the central government, which is remote and inaccessible to them, than they do to their relatively more accessible local governments. In America, politics and attention to politics reach a peak every four-years at the election of a new president. This national event so seizes our attention that enrollment in political science courses at American universities generally follows a four-year cycle, rising 10 percent or so in a presidential election year! Americans turn out to vote in considerably larger numbers at presidential than at local elections.

One can reasonably argue that the policies of local government are just as important as the policies of the national government. It is true that foreign policy and issues of war or peace, the state of the national economy, and the broad issues of social policy—all the purview of the national government—are extremely important to people's lives. However, the policies of local government are also important. The public schools, the condition of the street in front of your house, the purity and taste of your drinking water, how you are treated by police officers—all these and more are decided by your local government. How odd, then, that most people pay so much more attention to their national than to their local government. This is just further evidence that our focus on the state and its operations goes beyond the demands of reason.

The people of the world have not always been so thoroughly organized into states. In the remainder of this chapter, we shall look at the history of how the modern system of states arose; we shall then consider the relationship between the modern state and "nationalism"; finally, we shall look at contemporary challenges to the state and emerging political forms that might serve as alternatives to the state.

✧ THE DEVELOPMENT OF THE MODERN STATE

The invention of this thing to which we pay so much attention, the state, is fairly recent. Six or seven hundred years ago, people did not think of themselves as belonging to a state or nation as we know it. Most people lived on subsistence farms, intimately concerned with the village in which they lived but not caring much about the world beyond. Armies sometimes raided the village, but it did not make much difference to the villagers whether the army was hired by the king of France, by the pope, or by the Inca king. Barbara Tuchman's picture of today's "France" as it existed in the fourteenth century depicts a geographic region carved into various political divisions that might be controlled by the English king or by the French and whose populations did not seem to care much which of these was their ruler.[2]

In the fourteenth and fifteenth centuries, as European kings began to claim greater powers and to tighten their control over large territories, these shifting political divisions began to coalesce into states. Even in Europe, however, it was not until the early nineteenth century that states were well established in the form we know.

Throughout the early period of state building in Europe, populations continued to be largely indifferent about the state to which they belonged. During the early stages of its formation, for example, the state of Prussia was spread in little smears and droplets all over the map of northern Europe (see Figure 3.1), and this did not especially concern the Prussians. Some of these regions had been acquired for the crown by royal marriages, others by settlements of war or debt, and the people living in them were transferred like property from one ruler to another.

If ordinary people did not care much about the state, the leaders and the educated elite also saw it more as a convenience than as something special. This was particularly true early in its formation, but to some extent it remained true even as late as the eighteenth century. At the beginning of the period of state building, most members of the elite, if they could write, wrote in Latin rather than in their local tongue. Although daring writers such as Dante were breaking out in their local languages by the fourteenth century, most writers still tended to think of themselves well into the seventeenth century as belonging primarily to a cosmopolitan, European literary world rather than to a local English, French, or Spanish community.

---

[2]Barbara W. Tuchman, *A Distant Mirror: The Calamitous Fourteenth Century* (New York: Knopf, 1978).

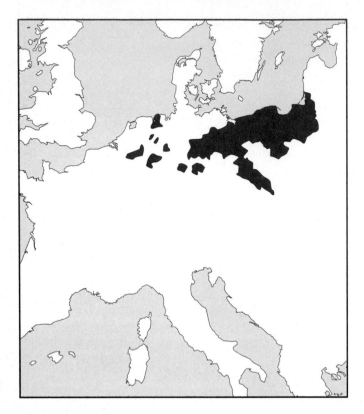

FIGURE 3.1   Prussia in 1789. As recently as this, a state did not need to be contiguous. Prussia splashes all across northern Europe.

The kings who were creating these new states often had family ties or other interests that took priority over their state. As late as 1714, a German line of kings whose members could not even speak English for the first generation came to power in England. Later, during World War I (after Britain and Germany had evolved into modern states), it would prove an embarrassment to the British royal house that the kaiser of Germany was their cousin—so much so that they changed their name from Hanover to Windsor.

Even military affairs were not as clearly divided by state through much of this period as they were at the end. Foreign mercenaries were an important part of most wars: Bands of English soldiers could be hired by the French king to fight the English, and vice versa. In the American Revolution, the king of England hired German troops (the Hessian soldiers) to do some of the fighting in America.

It was not until the early nineteenth century that the state as we know it could be seen—a relatively large territory with stable boundaries, whose people were bound together by intricate political ties and who thought of themselves distinctively in terms of the state to which they belonged.

The invention of modern states in Europe may be said to have been completed by Napoleon from 1800 to 1815. In France, he created one of the first recognizably modern states by joining the excitement and the passions of the French Revolution to an active and efficient bureaucracy and army. The resulting state was nearly invincible and succeeded in conquering most of Europe. Its power rested partly on the first European army whose members fought not only for what they themselves might gain but for their nation—*France.* The modern state had finally emerged. Even after Napoleon eventually overreached himself and was defeated, things could never be the same. He had demonstrated what could be accomplished by a full-fledged state, and the new or remaining states that emerged after 1815 tried, some eagerly and some with more hesitation, to emulate his method of organization.

Although the modern state had finally been invented in Europe and North America by the early nineteenth century, most other peoples of the world still lived under a variety of other arrangements. However, a great surge of European colonial expansion during the eighteenth and nineteenth centuries had divided the rest of the world into colonies organized somewhat as subsidiary states. When European power waned in the twentieth century as a result of two disastrous world wars, these colonies were able to break away and establish themselves as independent. Then their new leaders, almost all of whom had been educated in Europe, adopted the state as their own form of political organization. The modern state became the universal form of political organization.

You should not underestimate how novel this new way of organizing people's lives and efforts was. As Joel Migdal puts it (somewhat slyly):

> Unlike most premodern political structures, the state has aimed to impose uniform and ultimate conformity on social life within far-reaching (but still circumscribed) boundaries: Its leaders have sought obedience in even the most personal realms of social interaction, from whom one might sleep with to how one must bury the dead. Compliance to these sorts of social norms was not new, but the claims of a single centralized organization to enforce such norms over huge territorial expanses were novel almost everywhere they were made. And, indeed, one can point to real cases in which this kind of microregulation has been successfully achieved. Astonishingly, some states have been able to garner from people's yearly earnings a share equivalent to all their work performed through April or May or, sometimes, even June of that year and to sequester their children for 30 or so hours a week in a state institution. Premodern political leaders could not have imagined such audacious goals.[3]

✦ THE ORIGIN OF STATES: POWER, OR CHOICE?

What was it that led to the invention of the state over the last several centuries? Perhaps an exploration of this question will help us to better understand the nature of the state. There has long been a vigorous debate among scholars as to why states developed in

---

[3]Joel Migdal, "Studying the State," *Comparative Politics: Rationality, Culture, and Structure,* ed. Mark Irving Lichbach and Alan S. Zuckerman (Cambridge, England: Cambridge University Press, 1997), p. 209.

Europe.[4] However, one thing is clear: The modern state developed there along with the coming of industry and of complicated commercial arrangements. Large-scale industry and commerce could be carried on most easily among large populations whose members could be held together with minimal difficulty and who were willing to have their economic activities coordinated. If most economic activity consisted of subsistence farming, cottage weaving, coastal fishing from small boats, and so on, almost any form of political organization would do. However, as larger-scale, more complicated economic operations developed, something like the state offered important advantages.

With the development of the state, merchants and industrialists could draw on a large, uniformly treated population as their pool of laborers, and they could sell their products across a large market subject to a single set of laws. Goods could be transported readily, without being subject to special taxes or duties as they passed from one part of the state to another. On the greater scale made possible by the modern state, large factories and ships could be built, and these could be involved in complex nets of transactions. Industry and commerce thus benefited from the development of the state.

In this sense, then, modern industry and commerce *needed* something like the state, and this partly explains why it developed when it did. However, modern industry and commerce also made the state *possible* by providing the hardware, the technology, and above all the ease of communication by which a large, widespread population could be readily controlled by an army. Before the coming of modern communications, it was difficult for the government of a state of even moderate size to control the population with any exactness. As late as the early nineteenth century, it took a stagecoach three days to cross southern England. Under those circumstances, the government's control was necessarily loose. With the coming of the railroad and the telegraph in the nineteenth century, however, governments could keep an instantaneous check on what was happening throughout their realm and could move troops rapidly to any trouble spot. Add to these the development of gunpowder, cannons, and large warships, and we can see that by the nineteenth century, kings had acquired unprecedented power to provide uniform government across large territories.

We can see that the relationship between the modern state and modern commerce and industry can be interpreted in two ways. On the one hand, commerce and industry needed something like the state, and so the state was invented. It emerged because it was an appropriate choice. On the other hand, modern commerce and industry made it easier to control people and seize taxes from them, and so the state was able to develop. Governments were able to spread their power more widely. Probably both explanations carry part of the truth. These interpretations embody "choice," and "power," the two sides of politics introduced in Chapter 1. To the extent one believes that the state emerged because it was made necessary by the modern economy, its invention represents politics as choice. To the extent one believes that it developed because people could now be controlled more easily, it represents politics as power. Different scholars will lean more to one or another of

---

[4]This theme and the theme of the next paragraph are well developed in Tilly (1992). In general, recent studies of the establishment of states in early modern Europe have emphasized the new possibilities for coercion in the 1500s much more than the new needs of society, so I am something of an outlier in my interpretation above. Two other good examples are Perry Anderson, *Lineages of the Absolutist State* (London: N.L.B., 1974); and Thomas Ertman, *Birth of the Leviathan* (New York: Cambridge University Press, 1997).

The Marxist Theory of the State

In this chapter, the state has been interpreted partly as being made possible by modern military technology and communications and partly as required by modern commerce and industry. Another way of interpreting the rise of the state is offered by Marxist socialism. (See the fuller treatment of Marx and socialism offered in Chapter 2.)

Marx thought that modern society consisted of one class (the capitalists) dominating another (the workers). The workers had to be controlled because of the tensions caused by this domination, and for this the state was needed. The state keeps the workers under control partly by repression (the police) and partly by integrating them into the prevailing system by convincing them, in school and by other means, that their current situation is good.

Marx thought that eventually the workers would revolt and set up a socialist system in which one class would no longer dominate another. Then the state would have become unnecessary and would wither away through disuse.

This theory sees the state solely as an instrument of power and it does not analyze public choice. As you saw in Chapter 2, this is generally true of Marxist theory, which interprets politics solely as a matter of power.

Further readings in the Marxist theory of the state are Ernest Mandel, *Late Capitalism* (London: NLB, 1975), chap. 15; and V. I. Lenin, "State and Revolution," in *Sources in Twentieth-Century Political Thought*, ed. Henry Kariel (New York: Free Press, 1964).

these points of view. In extreme cases, such as that noted in the box headed "The Marxist Theory of the State," some may hold that one of the viewpoints explains everything; but to go wholly one way or another is probably a distortion.

→ THE STATE AS A DEVICE TO PROVIDE PUBLIC GOODS

Another explanation for why states might exist is offered by the problem of *public goods*. This is a basic problem for all human societies, and it turns out that the state is a good device for solving it. A **public good** is something that benefits all members of the community but that no one can be prevented from using; every member of the community can enjoy the benefits of it whether that person has helped pay for it or not. Some examples of public goods are national defense, medical research, the space program, and public health programs to control the spread of disease. It is impossible, for instance, for the United States to defend its borders without defending me where I live in Minnesota; therefore, if the United States provides defense at all, it cannot avoid defending me. Public goods like defense are benefits that cannot be turned on for some citizens and turned off for others.

Plenty of things that governments do, of course, are *not* public goods, since they could in principle be given selectively, only to those who would pay for them: highways, for instance, which could be set up as toll roads rather than being provided free to all from tax revenues; or education, which could be sold rather than being provided free to all children. The test of a public good is whether it is impossible to deny it to any member of the group; if a public good is available to any, it is available to all.

Thus, all members of the community benefit from public goods, whether or not they have helped pay for them—and this is what makes public goods a problem. An army, for instance, cannot defend just those people who have helped pay for it; it defends a territory and unavoidably defends everyone within that territory. Left to purely voluntary action, such public goods would be very difficult to finance. Each individual could quite sensibly think, "If I don't pay my share, the army will still be there, and I'll get all the benefits of it. Why should I pay? I'll let someone else do it." In other words, everyone would try to be a free rider on all the others. As a result, no one would pay to finance the army, there would be no army, and all would lose out.[5] States provide one way to prevent such paradoxical failures. Faced with the need for a public good, a state can decide not to rely on volunteers. Instead, it can force the people to pay taxes, and then use those taxes to provide the public good that all (or most) desire.

A good example of the painful dilemma of producing public goods through voluntary choices is familiar to anyone who watches public television in the United States. Every few months, everyone watching public television has to sit through excruciating sessions in which the station's staff run on in a staccato patter to try to encourage viewers to help pay the costs of running the station by becoming members. They appeal to guilt: "Only one in ten of you who watch this station is a member." They appeal to greed: "For the basic $35 membership, we offer this lovely ceramic mug, embossed with the logo of the station." Perhaps the most effective pitch was made a few years ago in Minnesota, when the Twin Cities station staff promised that if they reached their goal early, they would cut off the fund drive before its scheduled conclusion. Contributions flooded in!

Public television stations are caught in the classic bind of those who produce public goods. Since they broadcast on open bands, they cannot restrict watching their shows only to those who have contributed (as pay-per-view television providers can), and so they can offer no incentive to force anyone to contribute. As a result, only about one in ten viewers sends in a contribution. This is actually a fairly generous response, but it still makes life difficult for the station.[6]

The problem of providing public goods can only be solved by the use of power—not necessarily coercion, but power in some form: coercion, persuasion, shaming, and so on.[7] The state turns out to be a very effective way to organize power; not the only way, but a very effective way. And so, the problem of public goods, by providing an important reason to have states, serves as an additional explanation for why we see states so dominant today. Certain public goods are so important, especially the defense of territory, that they provide a powerful motivation to organize power in a way that allows coercion to be institutionalized—in other words, the state.[8] The state

---

[5]The basic statement on the problem of public goods and free riders in politics is Mancur Olson's *Logic of Collective Action*. See the box on page 285.

[6]Actually, about one-fourth of the operating costs of public television comes from government subsidies. But for the marginal dollar, which makes or breaks the station, public television relies on membership contributions.

[7]The public television station tries all of these except coercion, which of course is not available to it; it does not have the power to levy taxes or apply thumbscrews.

[8]One of the main reasons why the thirteen independent colonies resolved to unite into a single state, the "United States of America," appears to have been that they found it impossible to provide for the "common defense" as long as they were not organized in a single, unified state.

can solve the public goods problem of defense (or any other public good it decides to provide) by using its coercive power to gather money from the citizens in the form of taxes, and then using that money to provide for defense.

The problem of public goods will arise at various points throughout this book. We have discussed it here in relation to the state, but for any sort of collectivity—the state, a family, an interest group—providing public goods without everyone trying to be a free rider is a central problem of politics. When we look at interest groups, for instance, we will see that the lobbying function of an interest group is a public good; if a farmers' interest group succeeds in getting a tax break for farmers, all farmers will get the break whether they have contributed to the group or not. How to get potential members to contribute is a central problem of interest groups.

But for our purposes in this section, our conclusion is that the need for a vehicle to coerce the production of important public goods is yet another explanation for the existence of the modern state. Notice, by the way, that this is a "choice" explanation, not a "power" one: the existence of the state is explained by the need for a coercive mechanism to provide needed public goods.

✦ "STATE," "NATION," AND THE "NATION-STATE"

Up to this point the word *state* has not been defined precisely, although we have considered the modern state, its development, and its characteristics at some length.

We will now distinguish between **nation** and **state**. We often use these terms loosely as synonyms, along with the more common word *country*, and they are clearly related. As one example of the relationship between the two, we will later in this chapter label as "nationalism" a passionate identification with the state. In fact, in ordinary conversation, most people use the words *state, nation,* and *country* interchangeably.

However, *nation* and *state* have more precise meanings for political scientists. A nation is *a large group of people who are bound together, and recognize a similarity among themselves, because of a common culture; in particular, a common language seems important in creating nationhood.* Beyond language, many other factors may lead a group to identify in common as a nation. A shared history has apparently been important in welding what were originally diverse linguistic groups of immigrants into a single nationality in the United States. A shared religion blended speakers of various languages into a national identity in Israel. Various aspects of people's lives and circumstances may figure in their formation of a shared identity—but a shared language appears usually to be the most compelling of such bonds.

A state, on the other hand, is a *political unit that has ultimate **sovereignty**—that is, a political unit that has ultimate responsibility for the conduct of its own affairs.* France is a state, Brazil is a state, the United States of America is a state. The Jewish people do not make up a state, since they are not a political unit, but Israel is a state. General Motors and Exxon are not states, though they are large organizations. Chicago is not a state, although it is a political unit. It lacks sovereignty (the ultimate responsibility for the conduct of its own affairs) because another government, represented by the Supreme Court and the U.S. Army, has the right to intervene and force decisions on Chicago should that be necessary. A nation is a *cultural* and especially a linguistic grouping of people who feel that they belong together; a state is a *political* unit with sovereignty. Though we have this straight for our purposes, I must admit that the mixing of the terms in every-day use does cause confusion. Some of that confusion will be unavoidable in the rest of this book. The United Nations is an organization of states, for example, not of nations. We will still call it the United Nations, however, because that is what it calls itself!

One reason *state* and *nation* tend to commingle in common use is that leaders of states have almost universally tried to link the two in order to harness the emotional attachment of people to their nation and use that attachment to build support for the more abstract, legal entity—the state. If a state can coincide with a nation, then the state's leaders can more easily obtain acquiescence in the laws of the state and can build positive support in willingness to serve in the armed forces, pay taxes, and so on. It is striking and somewhat disturbing to see how much the modern state has been able in this way to enlist its people to its cause.

Figure 3.2 shows a linguistic map of Europe. Some apparent nations spread across the boundaries of states. For instance, the German language and culture spread well be-yond the boundaries of Germany. Austria, a large part of Switzerland, and a small part of Italy are German, and there are pockets of German population across Eastern Eu-rope. The Basques are spread across northwest Spain and southwest France. Switzerland encompasses a variety of linguistic groups that might qualify as nations.

Correspondence between nation and state is particularly loose in Africa and Asia. The boundaries of many African and Asian states are left over from the older colonial era, when they were drawn by the colonizing powers to suit their own convenience.[9] Thus, a crazy quilt of boundaries was superimposed on the land, with little regard for the culturally coherent groups of people living there. Once they regained their indepen-dence, of course, those people inherited these peculiar boundaries. The map of Nigeria in Figure 3.3 illustrates the loose correspondence between nation and state that exists in much of Africa today. In the Mideast, Turkey, Iraq, and Iran are home to parts of the Kurdish people, who are a minority in each of these countries and have made attempts to break away and form their own unified state. India includes fifteen official linguistic groups. Many other former colonies exhibit similar mismatches of state and nation.

With the modern importance of nationalism, we have come to think it a right of people, if they feel that they have a common nationality, to have a state to match that nationality. This "right" has become a constant source of political tension and conflict for two reasons. First, as just pointed out, many state boundaries do not coincide with the geographic distribution of nations. And second, the sense of nationhood is a subjec-tive thing. A "feeling" on the part of a group of people may be stimulated or laid to rest by persuasive leaders and is therefore liable to change. Even if state boundaries could ever at any one time be brought into a perfect fit with the distribution of nations, this benign situation could not last, because new nations would gradually be invented and some old ones would fade and be forgotten. The small black nationalist movement in the United States is just one example of an attempt to arouse a "nation" (the nation of blacks) among a people who had not generally thought of themselves as belonging to a separate nation.

---

[9]The correspondence between state and nation is reasonably close in South and Central America, for an unhappy reason: Here the native population was either exterminated, to be replaced by a reasonably coherent population of settlers from Europe, or over a period of centuries absorbed culturally in a *mestizo* blend of natives and Europeans.

FIGURE 3.2 Linguistic map of Europe: Note that languages tend to coincide with states' borders, but matchup is by no means perfect.

SOURCE: From Kingsbury, *An Atlas of European Affairs.* Copyright © 1964 by Praeger Publishers. Reproduced by permission of Greenwood Publishing Group, Inc., Westport, CT.

Another good example is Belgium, where the French- and Dutch-speaking regions of the state coexisted without much notice for a long time but then became agitated about their separate nationalities in the 1970s. Today they operate with such autonomy that they have almost become separate states within the state of Belgium.

A good example of how malleable national identity can be is offered in Figure 3.4, which shows the dramatic rise from 1969 to 1997 in the proportion of French-speaking residents of Quebec who thought of themselves as Quebecers, rather than as Canadians

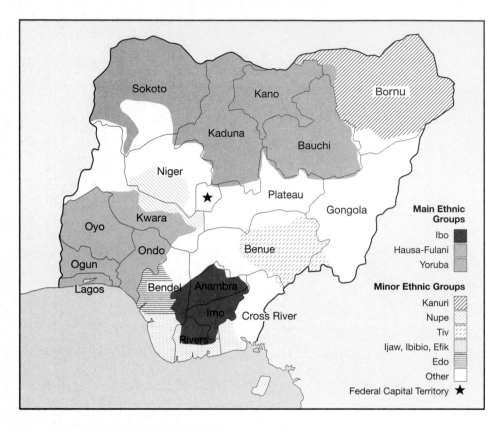

FIGURE 3.3   Ethnic map of Nigeria.

SOURCE: From the *Wilson Quarterly,* Winter 1980. Copyright © 1980 by the Woodrow Wilson International Center for Scholars.

or French Canadians. Over those three decades the percent thinking of themselves as Quebecers grew from about 20 percent to a bit over 60 percent.

At any given time, then, the system of states will not coincide with the system of nations. Points at which state and nation fail to coincide are likely to be hot spots politically; indeed, many of the most intense political struggles in the present era have resulted from such situations. The movement to separate Quebec from the rest of Canada; the war between East and West Pakistan, which resulted in the formation of a new state, Bangladesh; the Basque nationalist movement in Spain, which killed an estimated 31 people and injured 125, in 36 attacks from 1995 to 2003; the conflict between French- and Dutch-speaking Belgians; the activities of the Palestine Liberation Organization, which embodies the desire of Palestinians for a state of their own; the chronic unrest among Kurds in Iraq, Iran, and Turkey; the attempt by the region of Chechnya to secede from Russia; the bloody ethnic wars of the 1990s in Bosnia, Croatia, and Kosovo; the disastrous conflict between the Darfur region of Sudan and the central government of that state; and the difficulty of getting the three regions of Iraq to function together as

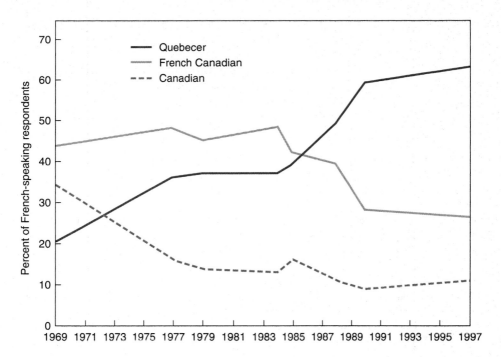

FIGURE 3.4   Collective identification among French-speaking Quebecers, 1970–1997.

SOURCE: Citizen Politics: Research and Theory of Canadian Political Behaviour, edited by Joanna Everitt and Brenda O'Neill. Copyright © Oxford University Press 2002. Reprinted by permission of Oxford University Press.

a state—these are only some of the hot political conflicts occasioned by a disparity between states' boundaries and peoples' sense of nationhood.[10]

One striking, and sometimes disturbing, reality about the modern state is the way it has been able to enlist its people in its cause. Citizens of a state generally identify themselves strongly with it and will defend it with passion. This passionate identification with a nation, or with a state riding on the coattails of nation, is called **nationalism,** and like any passion, it can make people either noble or base.[11] Some have performed great acts of courage and self-sacrifice under the influence of this sentiment, and others have carried out cowardly assassinations and brutal massacres under the same influence. Whether it makes people noble or ignoble, nationalism is undeniably convenient for governments. It predisposes a large and varied population to obey the single government of the state; and if the state is attacked from outside, nationalist passion makes the defending soldiers a more formidable force than they would otherwise be. Therefore, all governments try to encourage

---

[10]Source on Basque nationalist attacks: International Policy Institute for Counter-Terrorism (Israel), *www.ict.org.il.*

[11]An alternative word is *patriotism,* which is actually more directly associated with the state than *nationalism* (since it does not have any other referent, as *nationalism* has the nation). *Patriotism* has a bit of an old-fashioned ring to it, since it stems from the root *pater,* or "father"—embodying a sense of the state as the fatherland.

nationalism—not necessarily a hate of others, but at least a national pride—by holding parades, using national symbols such as the flag, presenting the state's history to schoolchildren, and so on.[12]

Benedict Anderson points out that nationalism (even though it is an "ism") is more akin in many ways to a religious identity than to an ideology like conservatism or socialism.[13] It obviously reaches deeply into people's psyches, because men and women have often been willing to die for their nation. Anderson argues that political ideologies, which mostly address the distribution of power and rewards among different groups of people, leave out an important part of people's lives—the deep, cyclical mysteries of death, procreation, birth, and a continuity that extends beyond our own lives. For many centuries, religion met these needs, and when religion began to decline in the latter part of the eighteenth century in Europe, nationalism arose (or was created) to take its place. Like religion, nationalism offers an identity that takes us beyond ourselves and builds something that lasts across generations.

We have always been ambivalent about nationalism. Consider the two sides presented in the following quotations. The first is Sir Walter Scott's celebration of it in his *Lay of the Last Minstrel:*

> *Breathes there the man, with soul so dead,*
> *Who never to himself hath said,*
> *This is my own, my native land!*
> *Whose heart hath ne'er within him burned,*
> *As home his footsteps he hath turned,*
> *From wandering on a foreign strand!*
> *[Such a man] concentered all in self,*
> *Living, shall forfeit fair renown,*
> *And, doubly dying, shall go down*
> *To the vile dust, from whence he sprung,*
> *Unwept, unhonoured, and unsung.*[14]

The second gives the view of a cynical spy, portrayed in a novel by Eric Ambler:

> Love of country! There's a curious phrase. Love of a particular patch of earth? Scarcely. Put a German down in a field in Northern France, tell him that it is Hannover, and he cannot contradict you. Love of fellow-countrymen? Surely not. A man will like some of them and dislike others. Love of the country's culture? The men who know most of their countries' cultures are usually the most intelligent and the least patriotic. Love of the country's government? But governments are usually disliked by the people they govern. Love of country, we see, is merely a sloppy mysticism based on ignorance and fear. It has its uses, of course. When a ruling class wishes a people to do something

---

[12]There is a large literature on what causes nationalism and how nationalist sentiments are maintained. See, for instance, Hugh Seton-Watson, *Nations and States: An Enquiry into the Origins of Nations and the Politics of Nationalism* (Boulder, CO.: Westview Press, 1977); Tom Nairn, *The Break-up of Britain* (London: Verso, 1977); E. J. Hobsbawm, *Nations and Nationalism Since 1780* (Cambridge, England: Cambridge University Press, 1990); Benedict Anderson, *Imagined Communities*, 2d ed. (London: Verso, 1991); and David Laitin, *Identity in Formation: The Russian-Speaking Populations in the Near Abroad* (Ithaca, NY.: Cornell University Press, 1998).

[13]Benedict Anderson, *Imagined Communities*, 2d ed. (London: Verso, 1991).

[14]Walter Scott, *The Lay of the Last Minstrel*, canto 6, 1807.

which that people does not want to do, it appeals to patriotism. And, of course, one of the things that people dislike most is allowing themselves to be killed.[15]

The idea of "nation" has been so adapted to modern states for their own use, especially to tap into the emotion of nationalism that is associated with it, that we often refer today simply to **nation-states.** This use recognizes that every state in the world tries to promote feelings of common nationhood among the people living within its boundaries. There is not a state in the world that is not to some degree a nation-state, and political scientists simply recognize that the basic units we deal with are a combination of state and nation. At the same time, it is good to keep the concepts "state" and "nation" clear because competing claims of nationhood continue to provide one of the strongest challenges to states.

While state leaders would like to enforce a one-to-one correspondence of state and nation, and while this is close enough to being the usual case that we generally use the term *nation-state* to describe the basic political unit, nations do not always or necessarily coincide with the political boundaries of states.

→ STATE-BUILDING

Most of the European states with which I introduced this chapter developed rather slowly, some over a few centuries. The process of establishing a state may have seemed rather natural in these examples, even if I did try to emphasize the use of power by those who constructed the state. But states do not just "happen." A state is a structure of rules and institutions, and a set of expectations by people as to how collective actions will be performed. Constructing a state from scratch, or **state-building,** is a complicated thing.

This may not be so evident in the European examples, but it is obvious when we look at current examples in which someone has tried to build or transform a state. One of the most dramatic current examples is Iraq, where the victorious United States forces eliminated almost all aspects of the regime of Saddam Hussein and set to work to build a new state apparatus untainted by any association with his old Ba'athist Party. This proved to be a very difficult job, as rivalries between the three main ethnic/religious groups in Iraq prevented any easy marshalling of the whole society in a new state structure. Even building the skeleton of the state—the police and military—proved difficult.

Many other new or reconstructed states have faced similar problems—Japan after the Second World War, Russia after the fall of the Communist Party in 1991, newly freed colonies since the 1960s, Iraq in the last few years. Some of these efforts have simply failed, and the regions have descended into what we call **failed states,** geographic entities with no effective central state apparatus, but controlled by various warlords and gangs in loose and fluid relationships with one another. Failed states are rare, but Somalia is a good example, as was Afghanistan in the 1990s. More often, states under construction stumble between varying forms of government for what may be a fairly long time, unless a strong leadership group (the original movement for independence,

---

[15]Eric Ambler, *Journey into Fear* (New York: Knopf, 1943; rpt. Bantam), p. 166.

for instance, in the case of a former colony; the United States occupation forces, in the case of Japan after World War II) is able to establish a firm direction from the start.

✣ GOVERNMENT AND THE STATE

Who is the state? In the section on "'State,' 'Nation,' and the 'Nation-State,'" I referred to "the state" acting in various ways; for example, I wrote, "One striking, and sometimes disturbing, reality about the modern state is the way it has been able to enlist its people in its cause." Who is acting here? If the people are the state, what does it mean to say that they enlist themselves to their cause? We defined the state above as a geographical unit of people who have the legal right to make and enforce rules within their boundaries. This definition implies that the state can be thought of in two ways:

- as everyone living in a given territory (the idea of the nation-state, for instance, emphasizes this usage), or
- the governing apparatus that makes and enforces rules.

In the latter vein, when we say "Egypt called for new peace talks in the Mideast," we do not mean that all 78 million Egyptians issued this call; it was the government of Egypt that did so. When we are referring to the *actions* of a state, it is the **government** we are talking about, because it is the government that acts for a state. This legal right to make and enforce rules is such a central part of our basic definition of *state* that for many purposes, we simply equate the repository of that right (the government) with the state itself; when we use the word in this way, by *state* we mean the government and bureaucracy.

Thus, the *government* is a key part of the state. The government of a state is a group of people who have the ultimate authority to act on behalf of the state. (See Chapter 8 for a definition of *authority;* essentially, authority means that the government is regarded by the people of the state as the appropriate group of people to make decisions for the state and act on its behalf.) The government is a unique group in the state; only that group has the right to make decisions that everyone in the state has a duty to accept and obey. When we speak of a state acting—as in the previous example, or as in "South Korea asked the International Monetary Fund for help in its current crisis"—it is the government to which we refer.

An influential current of thought in political science has sensitized us to the fact that governments and their bureaucracies are often self-starters in questions of policy— that they actively develop problems and seek solutions to them, rather than waiting for the population to come to them with problems. To understand politics properly, according to this current of thought, we must think of the government and bureaucracy itself as a participant and claimant in politics, rather than as a passive adjudicator over a political process that comes from outside it; this is often referred to as the theory of the **autonomous state.**[16] The idea is that the state often participates autonomously in political conflict and decision making.

---

[16]P. B. Evans, D. Rueschmeyer, and Theda Skocpol, eds., *Bringing the State Back In* (Cambridge, England: Cambridge University Press, 1985).

There is a creative ambiguity here, because this theory requires us to speak of the government and the bureaucracy as the "state," while treating them as autonomous of the rest of what we also call "state." In effect, we use *state* to mean both a territory and its people as well as the government that acts on behalf of those people. This should not be too difficult. In other circumstances, for instance, we are used to saying "the White House" to signify both a building and the presidency that is headquartered in that building. Recognizing the creative ambiguity of our usage helps us address an inherent vagueness in our notion that the "state" acts—that it does things. In the example of the state "enlisting its people to its cause," for example, the actions of the state in fostering nationalism come largely from government and bureaucracy (in outlawing burning of the flag, for instance) but also to some extent from a broader group including television announcers, religious leaders, teachers, and writers (as in the quotation from Sir Walter Scott). The theory of the autonomous state helps sensitize us to this problem, but it cannot answer it finally, because there is an inherent ambiguity in whom we mean when we refer to the state as acting.

Another good thing about the theory of the autonomous state is that it emphasizes for us that the government and bureaucracy may often participate in politics directly, as claimants on their own behalf.[17] Especially in new states where diverse populations have been thrown together into a state and where there is little consensus about proper directions to take, the state apparatus may be forced to (or find itself free to) govern in an authoritarian way.[18] Under these circumstances, free from the constraint of shared traditions and norms, governments may pursue policies benefiting their own personal or class interests in a fairly direct way, which adds to the problems of the new state. This is part of what is going on in the example of Nigeria at the end of this chapter. Two other examples would be the Philippine government's charge that Ferdinand Marcos stole several billion dollars from the government during the period of his rule, and the protected business interests of the family of President Suharto that came to light in the financial crisis of Indonesia in 1997.[19] Some governments have even savaged the people of their state to further their own ends. Between 1975 and 1979, the government of Cambodia killed about 3 million people (out of a population of 9 million) in its effort to establish a new socialist society. From 1991 to 1994, Haiti's military government encouraged systematic terrorizing of the democratic opposition by troops and thugs. And most recently, the government of Sudan has turned loose terror to subdue the Darfur tribe in its western region.

Thinking of the government (and associated bureaucracy, media, public institutions, etc.) as "the state" is also useful because it allows us to draw a distinction between "state" and "society." As we have seen, the state is a set of legal arrangements involving sovereignty and embodied in a government. However, the people of the state have a *society* of personal, social, and economic interactions that is partially independent of the

---

[17]This is especially relevant to the discussion of "pluralism" in Chapter 12, and to the discussion of institutional interest groups in that chapter.

[18]Here is another nice contrasting example of alternative "choice" and "power" interpretations of a political situation. In this sentence, I was uncertain whether to characterize the government as "forced" to govern in an authoritarian way (which would suggest that they were seeking the best public outcome and that circumstances forced them into authoritarian rule: a choice perspective) or to characterize them as "free" to govern in an authoritarian way (which would suggest that they were self-seeking and took advantage of the chance that was available to them to initiate authoritarian rule: a power perspective).

[19]In 2003 the Philippines Supreme Court awarded the government $650 million in Marcos' Swiss bank accounts, all that could be found of his fortune.

people's organization into a state. For instance, from 1989 to 1993, Czechoslovakia was organized as a single state. In 1993, it split into two states: the Slovak Republic and the Czech Republic. Before and after the split, the people of Czechoslovakia were involved in families, friendships, clubs, and economic arrangements (jobs, investments, etc.) that were only indirectly affected by the nature of state organization. A family that was spread across the new border did not cease to function as a family, for instance, merely because of the new state arrangements.

There is usually some tension between society and state. It is often thought that if "society" is too strong—that is, if pressure groups and special interests can easily force their views on the government—the state will be ineffective and will not be able to make clear policies. This is often cited as the reason the United States has difficulty setting clear economic policies and energy policies, for example. A reverse problem is that totalitarian states sometimes seek total control of society (this is why they are called "totalitarian"). Hitler's Germany abolished many private clubs and all labor unions, setting up instead its own organizations; it tried to undermine the family by drawing children away from their parents and into the Hitler Youth organizations.

In the relationship between state and society, an important subset of the overall society is what is called **civil society.** The civil society is the part of society that is organized and active, but neither controlled by the government nor focused on private concerns such as the family or economic activity. It consists, therefore, of organizations that deal with public questions, but that are not controlled by the government. It is often defined, in fact, as the set of all organizations that are not directly or indirectly part of the government, that are not families, and that are not set up for economic activity. Civil society is made up of religious organizations, hobby groups, political movements, professional societies, and so on.

What makes civil society important is that it is the natural counterweight to government in the affairs of the state. A rich and vigorous civil society is often thought to be important to the healthy functioning of democracy, for instance. And, civil society is often an important factor when spontaneous movements oppose governmental policies in either democratic or nondemocratic systems (see the discussion of such movements in Chapter 13).

This subtle distinction between state and society is a central concern in many theories of democratization and of economic policy making. We will see it again in Chapter 5, for instance, in our analysis of the economic progress of Ghana and South Korea. The distinction is hard to express other than through the theory of the autonomous state.

✦ Challenges to the State

The state may have evolved over the last few centuries to be the dominant form of political organization, but today it is under strong challenge from above and below.

Above the state, world leaders are groping for structures that would replace many functions of states and operate over a wider geographic range than the state. This has developed especially in economic matters. In Europe, a European Union established by twenty-seven states is in the process of taking over much of its member states' control of their own economies (the European Union is discussed in the example at the end of

German Soccer fans celebrate their team's victory over Costa Rica with waving flags. The sea of flags was controversial because many Germans are ambivalent about nationalism, given their state's history during the Hitler period.

Fabian Bimmer, Associated Press. *Star Tribune,* June 18, 2006, p. A10.

this chapter). The United States, Canada, and Mexico have established a free trade zone within which trade will not be taxed by the governments. Worldwide, states accepting loans from the International Monetary Fund (IMF) must shape their financial policies to conform with its requirements. In the area of environmental regulation, many cross-state bodies have been formed through which states give up their individual control of migratory species of wildlife, the production of pollutants, and so on. The challenge from above is not only in economic areas of policy. Across North Africa, the Middle East, and southern Asia, militant Islam—the most dynamic religion in the world—seeks to replace the secular states of the postwar period with religious political structures in which the state plays a relatively minor role, state boundaries would (ideally) fade, and the Islamic community would be ruled throughout by its religious leaders.

The state is also under attack from below. Far from fading away with the development of modern economies, as most scholars of all stripes thought they would do, ethnic and regional separatist movements have grown explosively. From the Walloons in Belgium to Tamil separatists in Sri Lanka, to French Canadians in Quebec, to the Croatians and Slovenians in former Yugoslavia, to the Eritreans in Ethiopia, to the Baltic republics in the former Soviet Union—the list could include dozens of other examples—regional or ethnic aspirations, which many years ago were quiet, built up over the 1980s and 1990s into serious political movements capable at the least of paralyzing their states.

What has been happening? Why the challenges to the state? One way to look at it is to note ways in which the state may have become less valuable in meeting societies' needs. This could help explain the challenge from "above" and the challenge from "below." From above, a series of environmental problems have appeared that are clearly going to become even more pressing in future years and are not readily dealt with by individual states. Swedish trees are dying because of pollution from industry in Britain, Germany, and other states; the chimney swift, which breeds in Canada and the United States but winters in eastern Peru, may cross the boundaries of eleven states in its annual migration; "greenhouse" gases warm every state in the world, regardless of whether they helped to produce them. These are problems that need broader, more overarching political structures.

Economically, the appropriate scale of industry increased in the twentieth century. Few small states were ever able to develop an automobile industry, for instance. There is no Norwegian auto company or Dutch auto company; auto companies developed mostly in such large states as the United States, Britain, France, Italy, and Japan. Such dynamic industries as nuclear technology, the aircraft industry, and space technology require an even larger scale to work economically. Is it any wonder that states are banding together?

From the other end, the experience of the latter half of the twentieth century was that centralized states were rather clumsy structures for fine-tuning responses to varying local needs in housing, education, health care, and so on. This helped to fuel pressures for local and regional autonomy. Perhaps, too, with a waning of the symbols of nationalism in a world in which most states cannot control their own destinies militarily, ancient local symbolic attachments or religious symbolic attachments have risen more to the fore and have come to satisfy people's yearning for symbolic identity. Thus, from "above"—problems too big for states to deal with—and from "below" at the local level, states find themselves challenged.

The previous paragraphs give rather a "choice"-oriented explanation of challenges to the state: Other structures can meet some of the people's needs better than the state, I have argued, and so they have begun to rival the state. One could also develop a "power"-based explanation: The state really evolved as a military structure; the one thing that defined a state—that still defines *sovereignty*—was that the state wielded a military force that could protect its people against invasion from outside its boundaries and could put down any internal challenge to the government's authority as well. Two developments in the latter half of the twentieth century, both born in the Second World War, have weakened this claim by the state to a monopoly of military power. First, nuclear weapons were invented. In the nuclear age, no government can protect its people against destruction from abroad; it may be able to reply in kind, but it cannot prevent its own destruction. Nuclear weapons are too devastating for that. From the other end, guerrilla warfare came into its own in the Second World War; techniques for local, sustained military effort against superior central forces were developed that are being used today by insurgent local forces in dozens of places around the world, most recently in Iraq. Militarily, the ability of states to control their destinies against other states and against internal insurgency has diminished.

Whether we can better understand this from a "choice" or a "power" perspective, it is clear that the state is seriously challenged.

✦ SOME POSSIBLE ALTERNATIVES

The world is still groping for alternatives to the state. However, the state still has a lot of life left in it; by no means is it clear that it will go away! Four possible alternatives of varying sorts are presented in the following sections:

1. Regional Integration

Many regions in the world have attempted to establish regional organizations that would have at least limited power to overrule and coordinate the actions of their member states. The Organization of American States in North and South America, the African Union, occasional attempts at economic union in Central America, and several abortive attempts to form a united Arab republic all attest to this wish, though none of these has succeeded very well. The European Union, which includes most of Europe, has had great success at integrating the politics of its member states, so much so that one can at least conceive of a time at which one might ask whether its members were still sovereign states. (The European Union is discussed in greater detail later in this chapter.)

At its best, **regional integration** would only represent a consolidation of the system of states into a smaller number of larger states. However, this might represent progress in its own right, and the process by which states were brought to yield up portions of their sovereignty voluntarily to a higher organization might teach us much about how the world system as a whole could begin to coordinate its members' activities.

2. The United Nations

There does exist an organization of almost all states of the world that is supposed to stand above them and lead them into peaceful coordination of their activities. The **United Nations** has little power to force states to cooperate, but it does have considerable persuasive power and has helped at least modestly to defuse several crises that could have led to war. With the decline of Soviet-American rivalry in the 1990s, it has seemed at least conceivable that the United Nations could emerge as a major structuring force in international relations. The United Nations is discussed in more detail in Chapter 18.

3. Communications and a "World Culture"

As electronic communication makes it possible to send messages easily from one end of the world to another, as people travel more widely and observe cultures that are new to them, the world is beginning to develop a more common set of attitudes. Different nations are becoming slightly less distinctive in their points of view. Blue jeans have become almost an international uniform of young people, and English has become an almost universal second language in which business is conducted among strangers. Children's symbols may originate from anywhere in the world: Big Bird and Elmo (the United States), smerfs (Denmark), Hello Kitty and anime (Japan). Much cultural richness may be lost in this homogenization, but it may become easier for populations of different states to understand each other's point of view. Too much faith should not be placed in this, however, because conflicts may as easily arise from understanding as from misunderstanding. Remember, most murders occur within families. Still, it may be a hopeful sign.

4. An Emerging International Law?

As we will see (pp. 401–403), in the late 1990s a body of law began to develop that might impose enforceable law on the leaders of states and thus on the states themselves. That is, an international community of law might supplant, or at least take its place along-side, the state as the maker of laws.

A key precedent was set when former Chilean President Augusto Pinochet, leader of a brutal military government, was arrested in Britain for Chile's violation under his presidency of the International Torture Convention; Pinochet was sent back to now-democratic Chile on Chile's promise to try him for the crime. This was the first time that any head of state, except the loser in a war, had been held responsible by the community of states for crimes committed in an official capacity. The Pinochet case was followed in 2001 by the trial in the Netherlands of former president Slobodan Milosevic of Serbia for the forcible deportation or murder of hundreds of thousands of ethnic Albanians in the Serbian province of Kosovo. These cases may be a straw in the wind. But, it is still a huge step to consider circumstances in which the sitting leader of a state (as opposed to disgraced former leaders like Pinochet or Milosevic) could be tried for the actions of the state in international tribunals.

 EXAMPLE

State-Building in Nigeria

No state's experience has been "typical," but it is useful to look at some examples to flesh out the concepts and analyses you have read so far in this chapter. In this section, we will take a brief look at how the Nigerian state was established; in the next section, we will consider the European Union and how it is drawing a number of European states into something new, which is beginning to look like a new, much broader "state."

Nigeria is a populous state on the west coast of Africa, with a population of 132 million. One out of five Africans lives in Nigeria, and its gross national product is second on the continent only to that of South Africa. The country is rich in oil, but it has so many people to feed that the average Nigerian is not especially well-off; the average annual income is $1,400 per person.

Until 1960, Nigeria was a British colony; like most colonies, it was not constructed for internal coherence but rather for the administrative convenience of the British. Over 250 different languages and dialects are spoken within its borders, and there is also an important religious split, as the north is primarily Muslim and the south is primarily Christian. After World War II, Britain experimented with various ways of handling this diversity. The plan eventually adopted was a decentralized system under which Nigeria was divided into three regions, each centered on one of the three main ethnic groups (see Figure 3.3): (1) the northern region, based on the Hausa-Fulani, (2) the western region, based on the Yorubas, and (3) the eastern region, based on the Ibos. These regions were administratively distinct, each having its own budget.

This arrangement continued in the initial democratic structure set up in 1960. The central government of the new state left many functions under the control of regional governments, in what is called a "federal" system. The situation was unstable, however, because tensions soon developed among the regions. The democratic procedures that were written into Nigeria's constitution favored the north, because it was the most populous region, and the north quickly established political control under the first prime minister, a northern Muslim named Abubakar Balewa.

However, the Ibos in the eastern region—a restless, economically active, and well-educated minority—felt stifled by the political domination of the north. Ibos all over Nigeria were disproportionately urban and held many technical and administrative positions. Three-quarters of Nigeria's diplomats were from the eastern region, as were about half the students who graduated from Nigerian universities in 1966.[20]

In 1966, a coup by Ibo officers toppled the democratic government and put an Ibo general at the head of the state. Six months later, Muslim soldiers struck back, and a new government under Yakubu Gowon, a northerner but a Christian, was installed. At this point the eastern region seceded from Nigeria and proclaimed itself the state of Biafra. The federal government refused to accept Biafra's right to secede, and there followed a bloody civil war lasting two and a half years in which over a million people died. Eventually, the Ibos were starved out and had to give up on secession. Gowon wisely followed a generous, conciliatory policy toward the defeated province and its leaders, one calculated to make it easy for them to rejoin the rest of the country.

Gowon had promised an eventual return to democracy, but he proved slow to deliver and was ousted in yet another military coup led by Murtala Muhammed. Muhammed was assassinated in 1976, and was replaced by General Olusegun Obasanjo, a Yoruba Christian who proceeded carefully to build the basis for a return to democracy. Elected local governments were established, and a new constitution was designed under which regional diversity would be respected in local affairs and no one region could dominate the central government. The state was divided into nineteen federal districts that, to some extent, broke down the old Hausa-Fulani, Yoruba, and Ibo regions. To be elected president, one had to receive not only at least one-third of the total popular vote but also at least one-fourth of the vote in two-thirds of the nineteen regions. Finally, power was divided between the president and a congress, so that regions that had not supported the president had a chance to defend themselves in the congress.

The first presidential election was held in 1979, and a northerner, Sheliu Shagari, was elected. He ruled for four years and was reelected in 1983, but his administration was marked by corruption and economic decay. Many Nigerians—most critically, the military—were dismayed by the greed of the new political class and their inability to overcome the regional/ tribal/religious divisions of the country. Shagari's government was overthrown shortly after his reelection in 1983.

From 1983 to 1999, the country was ruled almost continuously by the military. The military teased the public with promises of democracy while continually delaying its implementation. It took the death (of natural causes) in 1998 of the dictator at that time, General Sani Abacha, to allow a new opening in Nigerian politics. Elections were held in 1999, which resulted in the election of Olusegun Obasanjo, the general who had reestablished democracy after the 1975 coup, and who had not been implicated in the recent, corrupt regimes. Although Obasanjo was seen as clean politically, the election was dominated in all parties by the "big men" who had made money in the corrupt old regimes. After his election, Obasanjo moved cautiously to weed out a number of the most corrupt generals and officials. He has proved generally popular, and was reelected in 2003; he finished his second term in 2007 and stepped down, as he could not constitutionally run for a third term. This has been Nigeria's most lasting period of democracy since it became independent, but the democracy is still fragile.

The generals had left things in bad shape for the new democracy in 1999. They had proved adept at corruption and holding onto power but little else. They became wealthy during their

---

[20]Pauline H. Baker, "Nigeria: Lurching Toward Unity," *Wilson Quarterly* 4 (Winter 1980), p. 76.

years in power, but today the Nigerian economy is in deep distress. Oil revenues had declined under the generals because the government failed for years to invest in developing the oil and gas fields, and the country owes vast debts to foreign lenders. Even as the 1999 election was proceeding, the military had taken many last grabs out of the public pot.

Democratic government is hampered by the religious, ethnic, and regional divisions between the north and the south. Southerners believe that the Muslim north will never allow them to gain power. (The generals were all northerners; Chief Moshood K. O. Abiola, the winner of an annulled 1993 election who died in jail during the military regime, was from the south. Obasanjo is from the south, but was attacked as a turncoat supporter of the north during the 2003 election and got few votes in the south.) Northerners fear that since the south has the oil and most of the economic activity of the state, they will be left with nothing if they give up political power to the south. As of this writing, the 2007 election campaign had not produced any candidate to seize the public imagination.

 EXAMPLE

State-Building in the European Union

The **European Union (E.U.)** is an association of twenty-seven states in Europe that have agreed to coordinate much of their economic policy and some other policy areas; toward this end, they have set up a governmental structure that has limited but increasing power over the governments of the member states. The Union is of particular interest to political scientists because it represents the most serious experiment to date in getting states to give up some of their sovereignty voluntarily.

There had been mutterings about the need to unify Europe throughout the nineteenth and early twentieth centuries, but the first real push to do so came after World War II. Many people thought that France and Germany, which had twice in the century fought disastrously against one another, should be bound together in such a way that war between them would be inconceivable. Also, the advantages of operating as a large economic unit, with a single free market open to all, were obvious to those who were trying to rebuild Europe after the war.

With encouragement and some pressure from the American side, what would grow into the European Union was established in 1956. A French administrator, Jean Monnet, was a key figure in this. He had led several European states through earlier cooperative efforts in coordinating their policies on coal, steel, and nuclear power to a point at which they were willing to merge much of their economic policy making. Initially, only six states were members—West Germany, France, Italy, the Netherlands, Belgium, and Luxembourg. To Monnet's great disappointment, Great Britain refused at that time to join.

The main economic agreement among the initial members was that all trade would flow freely within their borders. That is, no member could place a tariff on imports of a product from another member to discourage local people from buying it. All the combined populations of the six member states were freely available as customers to any producer in any member state. Also, the member states soon coordinated their agricultural policy, giving up control of most agricultural policy within their borders to the governmental structure of the Union. It is the Union government that decides how high price supports will be for a given commodity, what will be charged for that commodity abroad, and so on. The Common Agricultural Policy was a breakthrough in regional integration, although it has proved in practice to be cumbersome and expensive, leading to large production surpluses and to high prices for consumers.

For about thirty years, the Union largely treaded water, gradually building somewhat greater institutional power but remaining held in check by strong nationalist sentiments on the part of some member states. During this relatively stagnant time, the entrance of Britain, Ireland, Denmark, Portugal, Greece and Spain was probably the biggest change to occur in the Union. Starting in 1985, however, the Union entered a period of intense reform and institution-building that continues today. Many internal barriers to trade were eliminated; the powers of the European Parliament were increased (see below); decision-making rules that had protected the special interests of member states were relaxed; and finally in 1999, the member states adopted a single common currency to replace the separate currencies of twelve of the then-fifteen member states. (Britain, Denmark, and Sweden decided to opt out.) These changes were significant, and difficult to achieve; the new treaties barely survived a referendum in France, and it took two tries to pass them in a referendum in Denmark. But pass they did, and the end result is that much of Europe now has something like a single economy; and politically, it is approaching something like a state.

Another huge change in the Union was its expansion in 2004, when ten mostly poor states from Eastern Europe and the Mediterranean joined the Union. These states increased the population of the E.U. by about 30 percent but only increased gross domestic product (GDP) by about 4 percent. They need a lot of help in developing to the economic level of older members, and their disparate political and economic interests are also likely to complicate decision making in the Union. These states were followed by Romania and Bulgaria in 2006, bringing the total membership of the European Union to twenty-seven.

Though it will need to be changed substantially with so many additional states, the current government structure of the Union has stood almost unchanged since the original six countries set up the Common Market in 1956. The two most important parts of the Union government are the Commission and the European Council, which make most of the rules and carry out executive functions. Two other parts are the Parliament and the Court of Justice. These have lesser powers but are still important.

The European Commission consists of twenty-seven appointed commissioners who head a bureaucracy of about 24,000 people. Commissioners are appointed by their home governments for a term of five years, but they must swear an oath to act on a European basis rather than in the interests of their home country. In practice, the commission has been the focal point of pan-European interests, as opposed to national interests. In this it has been cheered on by its thousands of bureaucrats, whose lives and careers are bound up in the Union. The commission has consistently pushed for a blending of states in the Union and has frequently been opposed in this by one or more member states fearful of giving up too much sovereignty.

The Commission has a great deal of power. It dominates the setting of most of the Union budget ($149 billion in 2007) and sets regulations for member states in a wide range of areas. As the only permanent part of the executive branch of the Union's government, it also takes the lead in initiating new proposals for policy.

The other part of the executive is the European Council, in which national interests are represented. It consists of the foreign ministers of the member states; these meet together several times a year to consider proposals from the Commission.[21] Any major policy proposal must be approved by the Council before it can go into effect. The Council votes on proposals, with large states getting extra votes. For many years, there was an unwritten rule that any state could veto a proposal if the proposal affected what the state considered to be a "vital national interest." This

---

[21]In addition, four times a year the Council consists of the prime ministers or presidents of the twenty-seven states. Important questions are saved for these "summit" meetings.

practice was limited, however, as part of the 1993 package of political reforms to achieve closer political union. Over the years, the European Council, with its emphasis on states' governments and their needs, has tended to retard the blending of the Union, but it has probably also made possible such blending as has occurred. Without this haven for the individual interests of member states, the Union might have fallen apart long ago.

The Union also has a parliament, which until the last decade or so had very little power. However, the expanded power of the Union vis-à-vis member states in the 1990s, brought about by the expansion of its powers in economic and monetary policy, has led to a concern for the "democratic deficit"—the fact that democratically elected national parliaments now have less control over their states' economies while the E.U. itself, which does increasingly control their economies, is run mainly by officials who never have to face voters. Since the members of the European Parliament are the one group directly elected by voters all over the Union, it has seemed natural to strengthen the role of the Parliament in order to introduce a minimal level of democratic accountability into Union decision making.

The Parliament has been scrapping for expanded power, with some success, but it is still the weakest of the big three institutions. In recent years the Parliament has gained the right to veto the budget, and it also approves new commissioners after they have been nominated by the government of their state. A number of laws now require the approval of the Parliament, but in many other areas, including such important topics as agriculture, economic policy, immigration, police cooperation, and transport, the Commission is only required to consult with the Parliament before it sets the law. And, a vast number of regulations are set directly by the Commission without ever requiring either a vote or consultation with the Parliament.

The fourth institution, the European Court of Justice, is a court of twelve justices serving six-year terms. It rules on disputes over the treaties the states signed on joining the Union. Most cases that come before the Court involve trade problems, but it also decides disputes among the governing institutions of the Union and about the individual rights of citizens in the member states. Over the years, the Court has pretty well established itself as dominant over the states' governments, although it has had to tread cautiously to avoid stepping on any government's toes. While the Court has been careful in approaching difficult cases, some of the cases it has decided have demonstrated an astonishing willingness on the part of member states to subordinate themselves to the Union's laws. Court decisions have included such questions as whether British teachers could legally whip their students, how soldiers could be disciplined in the Netherlands, and the conditions under which people could be put in prison to await trial in West Germany. (For a more detailed discussion of the European Court of Justice, see Chapter 17.)

Together, the members of the Union have great strength. As seen in Table 3.1, combined, the E.U. has a population greater than that of the United States; its members have more men and women under arms, and their combined gross domestic products are slightly larger than the gross domestic product of the United States. If they could pursue a unified foreign policy and develop a full-scale strategic nuclear force, they would be a superpower similar to the United States.

This is the governmental structure that evolved over a half-century from the original structure set up by the six founding states. In 2005, however, the future of this governmental structure was thrown into real question. There is general recognition that a governmental structure that was originally designed for just six countries can probably not work for a Union of twenty-seven, or at least not work very well. If nothing else, twenty-seven commissioners are surely too many. And should Malta (with its population of 398,534) have one commissioner, the same as Germany (with over 82 million people)? Does it still make sense to allow national vetoes in some policy areas? Also, many broad policies such as the large agricultural subsidies must change with the addition of large, poorer countries like Poland. How is this to be done?

To address such problems, the E.U. established a committee to write for the first time a formal constitution for the Union. The committee was charged to develop new structures of decision making that could work for the enlarged Union. It issued its recommended new constitution in

TABLE 3.1

European Union Compared with the United States

	Total Population	Total Armed Forces	Total Gross Domestic Product (billions of dollars)	Defense Expenditures (billions of dollars)
U.S.A.	298,444,215	1,506,000	$13,220	$495.3
E.U.	486,642,177	1,819,000	$13,620	$241.9

SOURCES: International Institute for Strategic Studies, *The Military Balance 2007* (London: Routledge, 2006); CIA, *CIA WorldFactbook online* (revised 8 February, 2007).

2004, but at this point the democratic deficit of the Union began to catch up with it. While the vast majority of political leaders favor the new constitution, it has not been broadly popular—not so much for the terms of the constitution itself, as for the "European project" it embodies. When the constitution faced referendums for approval in various countries, it first passed in Spain, but then was resoundingly defeated in both France and the Netherlands in May of 2005. Since it requires the approval of all twenty-seven states to become law, it seems as of this writing that it probably is a dead letter. This does not mean that the Union will dissolve, of course, but it does mean that its future decision-making structure remains in limbo, perhaps for a long time. It is possible that the long period of reform and integration that started in 1985 reached its end in 2005. At this point, the problem of integrating twelve new, poor members may have superseded—perhaps for a fairly long time — concerns about political design. If so, that would be a pity. The E.U. is a rather well-integrated economic entity, but it is still very creaky as a political structure.

How close is the European Union to being something like a state? The member states have given up a good deal of their sovereignty to the Union. The Union has independent taxing powers, collecting a sales tax of just over 1 percent to finance its operation. It sets its members' tariff and trade policies and their policies on agricultural price supports, and it regulates many other areas of daily life. For most of its members, the Union sets financial policy and maintains a unified currency. The European Court of Justice has successfully imposed surprisingly political judgments on member states. On the other hand, military control is the real core of statehood; in that area, the Union has not developed any control over its members, although it has taken some small steps in that direction. In 2003 the Union established its first common military force, a small mobile unit of 60,000 soldiers. And despite reservations expressed by the United States, the E.U. established a command center for its small force, independent of NATO. Just what the E.U. will become is still open to the tides and chance of time. Today it illustrates nicely the gray area in which it may become difficult to distinguish clearly just when a state is a state.

KEY TERMS

public good
nation
state
sovereignty
nationalism

nation-state
state-building
failed state
government
autonomous state

civil society
regional integration
United Nations
European Union

FURTHER READING

Anderson, Benedict. *Imagined Communities: Reflections on the Origin and Spread of Nationalism,* rev. ed. New York: Verso, 1991.

Cederman, Lars-Erik. *Emergent Actors in World Politics: How States and Nations Develop and Dissolve.* Princeton: Princeton University Press, 1997.

Dinan, Desmond. *Ever Closer Union: An Introduction to European Integration.* Boulder, CO.: Lynn Rienner Publishers, 1999.

Ertman, Thomas. *Birth of the Leviathan.* New York: Cambridge University Press, 1997.

European Union Encyclopedia and Directory 2006. London: Routledge, 2005.

Evans, P. B., Reuschmayer, D., and Skocpol, Theda, eds. *Bringing the State Back In.* New York: Cambridge University Press, 1990.

Hobsbawm, E. J. *Nations and Nationalism Since 1780: Programme, Myth, Reality.* New York: Cambridge University Press, 1990.

Mandel, Ernest. *Late Capitalism.* London: NLB, 1975, chap. 15.

Migdal, Joel. *Strong Societies and Weak States: State-Society Relations and State Capabilities in the Third World.* Princeton: Princeton University Press, 1988.

———. "Studying the State." In *Comparative Politics: Rationality, Culture, and Structure,* edited by Mark Lichbach and Alan Zuckerman. New York: Cambridge University Press, 1997.

Motyl, Alexander J., ed. *Encyclopedia of Nationalism.* San Diego, CA.: Academic Press, 2000.

Nettl, J. P. "The State as a Conceptual Variable." *World Politics* 20 (July 1968): 559–92.

Paul, T.V., Ikenberry, G. John, and Hall, John, eds. *The Nation-State in Question.* Princeton: Princeton University Press, 2003.

Rotberg, Robert I., ed. *When States Fail.* Princeton: Princeton University Press, 2004.

Skowronek, Stephen. *Building a New American State: The Expansion of National Administrative Capacities, 1877–1920.* New York: Cambridge University Press, 1982.

Spruyt, Hendrik. "The Origins, Development, and Possible Decline of the Modern State," *Annual Review of Politics* 5 (2002), pp. 127–49.

Tilly, Charles. *Coercion, Capital, and European States, A.D. 990–1992.* Cambridge, MA.: Blackwell, 1992.

Van Creveld, Martin. *The Rise and Decline of the State.* New York: Cambridge University Press, 1999.

WWW   WEB SITES OF INTEREST

A site of essays, news items, and so on about Nigerian politics:
http://nigeriaworld.com

A well-organized guide to the multifarious Web sites of different parts of the European Union governance structure:
http://www.europa.eu.int/

CHAPTER 4

POLICIES OF THE STATE

In Chapter 3, we saw that the modern state is a relatively recent invention. It developed gradually over the last several centuries and is still developing as people come to expect the state to take care of more aspects of their lives and as military operations—the special purview of the state—become more complex and expensive. In this chapter, we shall survey some of the most important policies of modern states to consider the variety of things the state does today.

Figure 4.1 charts the growth of overall state activity since the nineteenth century for Great Britain, Sweden, and the United States.

The most interesting thing about the figure is that these three countries have developed in much the same way, though they have had quite different types of governments and their experiences during the twentieth century varied a great deal. Britain had a socialist government from 1945 to 1951 and intermittently after that. Sweden was ruled uninterruptedly by a socialist party from 1932 to 1976 and intermittently thereafter, and is well known for its wide-ranging welfare state. The United States, on the other hand, has never had a socialist government, though the New Deal after 1932 was strongly oriented toward reform and the expansion of social programs. Britain and the United States participated in both world wars, while Sweden was neutral in both. Despite these political and historical differences, the three countries show a rather similar expansion of state activity. During the latter part of the nineteenth century and into the early twentieth, all three devoted a stable and relatively small percentage of their wealth to the government: approximately 8 to 10 percent of all economic activity. Beginning about the time of World War I, however, governmental spending began to take up more and more of the economy, until by the 1990s, it accounted for 40 percent (United States) to 61 percent (Sweden) of all economic activity.

The two world wars appear to have contributed to this growth. Britain showed great jumps in the government's role in the economy at both wars, while the United States surged at the Second World War. (The United States entered World War I only near the end of the war.) When the governments' roles subsided again after the wars, they

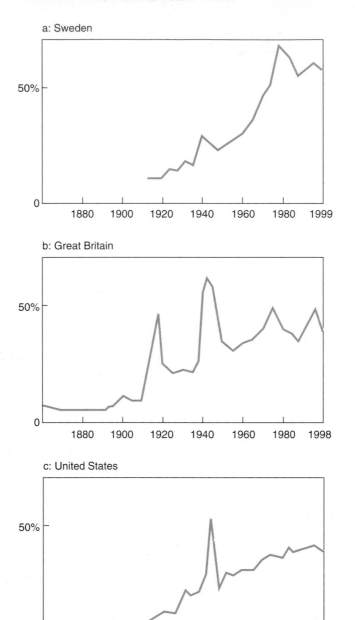

FIGURE 4.1   Government expenditures as a percentage of gross domestic product.

SOURCE: U.S. Department of Commerce, *Historical Statistics of the United States;* Peter Flora ed., *State, Economy, and Society in Western Europe, 1815–1975* (London: MacMillan, 1983); International Monetary Fund, *Government Finance Statistics Yearbook 2000.*

generally did not return to the same levels as before. This pattern is more pronounced in the British case, but it is evident in both. The lasting expansion of government as a result of these wars is probably due not only to the actual expenditures in the wars but also to the fact that in the "total warfare" of the twentieth century, governments became accustomed to controlling the lives of their people rather directly—rationing the goods they could buy, telling them what jobs they could work at, and so on. After the wars, the governments continued to intervene actively in people's lives and extended this intervention to a range of other policies as well.

Sweden was neutral during both wars, and so the conflicts did not have the same effect on Sweden as they had on Britain and the United States; but even neutral Sweden shows a modest spike in governmental activity around 1940. After the war, Sweden, too, left behind the stable, low level of expenditure that had characterized its public sector in the earlier part of the period and, with a socialist government, began in the 1930s a steady increase in the government's share of the economy. By the 1960s, this had brought Sweden up to the same levels as the other two countries, and during the 1970s, Sweden surpassed both.

A strong governmental role in society appeared to be typical of industrialized democracies late in the twentieth century. When we note that 40 percent of the U.S. gross national product consisted of governmental expenditures, this means that well over one-third of all purchasing of goods and services was done by the government. There seems to be a strong pressure in industrialized democracies to expand the role of the state. This was well illustrated by Sweden in the late 1970s. In 1976, a nonsocialist government replaced the Socialists, who had been in power almost continuously since 1932. This new government had pledged to avoid expanding the role of government, but as Sweden entered a period of economic difficulty and businesses looked as though they might fail, the government felt it had to take over some of them and keep them going to prevent unemployment. Thus, the *non*-socialist government ended up nationalizing a number of industries, including the country's largest ship-building firm.

As a result of such pressures, to which all industrialized democracies seem to be subject, the industrialized democracies do not vary a great deal with regard to the degree of governmental involvement in society and the economy. In all of them, the governmental role expanded greatly during the twentieth century and is now very large. We do see some reaction to the great expansion in a modest downward movement in the charts for Britain under Margaret Thatcher in the 1980s and for Sweden after 1978, a point at which governmental expenditures had risen to two-thirds of the gross domestic product (GDP). Obviously, the government's share of the economy cannot rise indefinitely, and resistance builds up. Still, the norm seems to be substantial governmental involvement; by 2003, the three countries for which we have information in Figure 4.1 ranged from 37 percent of GDP (United States) to 58 percent (Sweden). As noted, these figures actually represent a small pullback due to reductions in military spending in the aftermath of the Cold War's end and due also to the thrust of neoliberalism, with its attendant welfare reforms in the United States, and shrinkage of the welfare state in Sweden; in 1996, the similar figures had been 40 percent (United States) and 61 percent (Sweden).

In addition to this expansion of the government's role in the industrialized democracies, an even more marked expansion of this kind occurred with the establishment of communist governments in sixteen countries during the twentieth century. In the period after World War II, in the Communist states of Eastern Europe the government carried on almost all of the economic activity, as it owned most of the means of production. Most of these systems, however—at least, those in Europe—spent the 1990s in a massive move in the opposite direction, **privatizing** firms that had been owned and run by the state. This effort dwarfed the rather small privatization movement that also occurred in many Western democracies. Conservative British Prime Minister Margaret Thatcher, for instance, privatized two dozen firms over a twelve-year period; Poland privatized over three thousand in just a couple of years.

✦ THE ROLE OF GOVERNMENT IN THE THIRD WORLD

The governments discussed above are what we usually call "industrialized democracies"— prosperous states, typically with per capita annual income above $20,000 or so, which also usually are democracies.[1] North America, much of Europe, and certain other states such as Japan, Australia, and New Zealand make up this set of states. It is also simply called "the West," a term that is a holdover from the Cold War when the "West" was opposed to the Communist "East."

We have also noted that the set of formerly Communist states in Eastern Europe and Central Asia, because of their special shared history, has had a distinctive pattern of governmental development. Until about 1990 they had hyper-developed governments, but have been shrinking the reach of government since then; they are quite variable as to how far this has progressed, ranging from Estonia with a very liberal regime (in the sense we used the term in Chapter 2) to Belarus, which still has an essentially unreconstructed socialist state apparatus.

However, about two-thirds of the world's population is not found in either of these sets of states. Latin America, Africa, and Asia (except Japan) comprise a set of states that were mostly not involved in the Cold War and acquired the name "Third World" at that time (because they were neither "East" nor "West"). This term is still generally used today. Most of these states are poor, though a number of them have great mineral wealth (Saudi Arabia and other oil-producing states, for example), and some others, such as Mexico, Brazil, Singapore, Malaysia, Thailand, and South Korea, have industrialized and become fairly prosperous.

Politically, these states are a grab bag, ranging from still-Communist states like Cuba and China to traditional monarchies like Saudi Arabia. Many are democracies, but most of the nondemocracies of the world are also found in this region. The poverty of most of these countries constrains how much their governments can develop, as we will see especially in later parts of this chapter when we look at governmental policies. Generally government operates at a lower level of involvement than in the industrialized

---

[1]The figure of $20,0000 is based on the "purchasing power parity" measure of per capita income; this measure attempts to correct for currency exchange rates in order to compare what peoples in various countries can purchase, compared with residents of the United States.

TABLE 4.1

Central Government's Revenues as a Percentage of the Gross Domestic Product in Selected Third World States, 2004

Country	Government's Percent of Economic Activity	Location	Democratic/ Non since 1975
Argentina	11%	South America	mixed
Bangladesh	6	Asia	democratic
Caomeroon	10	Africa	nondemocratic
Côte d'Ivoire	8	Africa	mixed
India	11	Asia	democratic
Nigeria	21	Africa	mixed
Syria	13	Middle East	nondemocratic
Yemen	13	Middle East	nondemocratic

SOURCE: World Bank Group, *World Development Indicators Online*, 2007; "Democratic/non since 1975," adapted from Adam Przeworski et al., *Democracy and Development* (New York: Cambridge University Press, 2000), appendix 1.2.

democracies, but the size of government also ranges widely among these states, as we see in Table 4.1. The sources of these variations are not always very clear. It is perhaps no surprise that Syria, which has been governed by a one-person dictatorship for decades, does not have an especially active government; but then why does democratic India have a governmental profile that is not all that much higher than Syria's?

Whereas the politics of industrialized democracies involves a rather standard set of pressures from business, interest groups, and the international community—which result in a similar level of governmental activity from one such country to the next—politics in

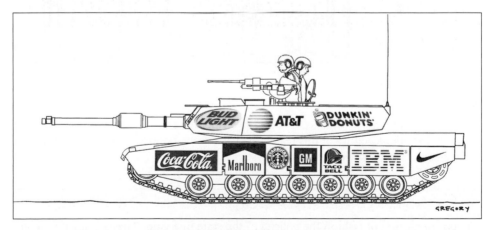

"How else are we going to pay for the war?"

Why Are The World's States Expanding?

Almost all states in the world have expanded in the degree to which they intervene in their people's lives. Why this is so is a challenging puzzle for political scientists. David Cameron ("The Expansion of the Public Economy: A Comparative Analysis," *American Political Science Review* 72 [December 1978]: 1243–61), reviewed five main explanations that have been advanced:

1. As people become more prosperous, they may want more done for them and are willing to pay for it. Therefore, as industrialization makes people more prosperous, the state naturally grows.
2. As governments have become more clever at using "hidden taxes" such as excise taxes and payroll withholding of income taxes, they can get away with taxing people more heavily, and the state grows.
3. Electoral democracy results in a "bidding up" of the state's operations as parties compete to see which can promise more services to the voters.
4. Once governmental bureaucracies are established, they develop internal pressures for expansion. Inevitably, they succeed in slowly ratcheting upward the scope of their operations.
5. As world trade grows and states' economies become more subject to disruption by events in the international economy, their governments are less able to control what is happening in the state. The governments must then grow to compensate for the greater difficulty they find in functioning.

   The jury is out, and will stay out for a long time, as to which among these explanations are valid. For examinations of evidence on the subject, see Cameron's article and also David Lowery and William D. Berry, "The Growth of Government in the United States," *American Journal of Political Science* 27 (November 1983): 665–94.

   Of the five proposed explanations, note that numbers 1 and 5 are based on the perspective of politics as choice, numbers 2 and 4 are based on the perspective of politics as power, and number 3 is ambiguous.

   Ironically, this expansion has coincided with growing challenges to the state (see pp. 64–66).

the Third World is more variable, less developed, and more fluid. Thus, it is more difficult to generalize about politics of this region than about the politics of either industrialized democracies or the formerly communist systems.

→ CONSTRAINTS AND CONDITIONS FOR POLICY

Governments do not fashion the policies of the state in a void. They work within constraints of what is possible, and that obviously helps to shape the policies they make. In addition to what is possible, power relationships within the state also help to determine the shape of policy, as those parts of society that hold power will usually shape policies at least in part to benefit themselves.

There are many constraints that limit the possible. Geographic location, natural resources, technology, and other things are all important. But probably the dominant constraint in what the state can do is how rich or poor it is. We measure this by **gross domestic product,** or GDP: the total amount of all economic transactions in the state. That is, the sum of all such things as the value of the food people have produced, the value of mechanics' work on automobiles, the value of educational activity, and so forth. The higher the GDP, the greater the total amount of economic activity in the state. To measure how economically well off the average person is, we divide GDP by the population, to get per capita GDP.

GDP is usually expressed in dollars, as I did when I noted in Table 3.1 that the combined GDPs of the members of the European Union totaled $13,620 billion. To give a truer comparison of individual well-being, however, economists prefer to use **PPP per capita GDP,** which is per capita GDP adjusted to take into account the fluctuations in value of other currencies relative to the dollar.[2] Instead of making the people of a state look poor or rich because of currency exchange rates, PPP per capita GDP expresses how much of comparable things people in different states can buy. So, when you see that the poor country of Niger has PPP per capita GDP of $800, that means that an average citizen of Niger can buy in a year, in Niger, approximately what an American could buy with $800 in the United States.

You already saw in Table 4.1 that the overall governmental activity of poorer countries is much lower than that of the well-off countries of Figure 4.1. In the sections that follow, you will see that the specific mix of policies pursued by poor countries is also very different than the policy mix in well-off countries.

Policy is shaped not only by constraints, but also by power relations in the state. For instance, in states that are ruled over long periods by the military, spending on defense equipment is almost always elevated relative to other policies. The most important distinction among states with regard to their policies, however, is whether or not they are democracies.[3] Democracies spread power at least to some limited extent across the full population of a state, rather than restricting power to some segment of the population such as the military, a priesthood, or an ethnic group. As a result, democracies often emphasize policy areas meeting broad needs in the population—education, housing, health. We will see this to some extent in the sections that follow. But more generally, Adam Przeworski and his collaborators demonstrate in a study using all states of the world that after we have taken into account how wealthy the states are, life expectancies tend to be higher in democracies than in dictatorships, and infant mortality is lower.[4] Population growth is higher in dictatorships, because contraception is less available. And school enrollments are higher in democracies than in dictatorships, for both boys and girls.

In the sections that follow, in most tables describing states' policies I have included the PPP per capita GDP of the state, and whether it has been consistently democratic or

---

[2]PPP stands for "purchasing power parity"; that is, this adjustment attempts to express per capita GDP in a way that compares purchasing power, i.e., how much people in varying countries can buy as a result of their economic activity.
[3]Democracies and autocracies are dealt with in detail in Chapter 7.
[4]Adam Przeworski, Mike Alvarez, José Antonio Cheibub, and Fernando Limongi, *Democracy and Development: Political Institutions and Material Well-Being in the World, 1950–1990* (New York: Cambridge University Press, 2000), Chapter 5.

nondemocratic since 1975. Be alert, as you read these sections, to see how much difference these two factors make on policy.

✦ DEFENSE POLICY

Defense is the one area of policy in which governments have almost without exception proceeded by developing and administering programs themselves and have insisted on holding a monopoly with regard to the policy. Private schools, private hospitals, and so on are sometimes tolerated by governments, but this is practically never true of private armies!

As Table 4.2 shows, states vary a great deal in the effort they expend on defense. The industrialized democracies spend a few percent of their GNP on defense. Canada,

TABLE 4.2

Defense Preparations for Selected States

	Democratic/ Non since 1975	Military Service	Percent of Population in Active Military	Percent of GDP Spent on Defense
Russia	mixed	18–24 months	0.7	3.7
Canada	democratic	voluntary	0.2	1.1
France	democratic	voluntary	0.4	2.5
Germany	democratic	9 months	0.3	1.4
Great Britain	democratic	voluntary	0.4	2.3
United States	democratic	voluntary	0.5	4.0
Israel	democratic	men: 3 years women: 24 months	2.7	8.0
Egypt	nondemocratic	12–36 months	0.6	4.1
Saudi Arabia	nondemocratic	voluntary	0.6	8.2
Algeria	nondemocratic	18 months (including civil duties)	0.4	3.2
Colombia	democratic	24 months	0.5	4.0
Paraguay	mixed	12 months	0.3	0.8
South Korea	mixed	26–30 months	1.4	2.6
North Korea*	nondemocratic	3–12 years	4.9	25.0
Tanzania	nondemocratic	voluntary	0.1	1.1
Madagascar	nondemocratic	18 months (including civil duties)	0.1	5.3
Myanmar*	nondemocratic	voluntary	1.0	5.0

*2002 figures.

SOURCE: International Institute for Strategic Studies, *The Military Balance 2006* (London: Routledge, 2006); World Bank Group, *World Development Indicators Online,* 2007; "Democratic/non since 1975," adapted from Adam Przeworski et al., *Democracy and Development* (New York: Cambridge University Press, 2000), appendix 1.2.

the United States, and Britain have volunteer armies, and none of the industrialized democracies in Table 4.2 spent more on defense than the United States (4.0 percent of the gross national product in 2006).

Poorer, Third World, countries vary tremendously in their military expenditures. Tanzania and Madagascar show up as fairly low in Table 4.2, but Israel, Saudi Arabia, North Korea, and Myanmar are quite high. Some Third World regions have been the scene of continuing tensions, with frequent threats of war, and countries in those regions may spend shocking sums on defense. North Korea, in particular, has ruined its economy by its massive military expenditures. In the late 1990s, the country experienced mass starvation while spending as much as a third of its total gross domestic product on defense! In international "hot spots" such as East Africa and the Middle East, many countries spend between 5 and 10 percent of their gross domestic product on defense. Even in calm parts of the world, military dictatorships such as that of Myanmar often support their military constituency with bloated defense spending. Large defense budgets in poor countries are tragic, because defense spending neither feeds people nor furthers economic development.

The actual use to which this investment in the military is put varies a great deal from one country to another. The two superpowers, the United States and Russia, invested substantially in nuclear weapons and missiles during the Cold War, although they have now cut back a great deal. Beyond this, Russia has always emphasized the development of a large land army, since it had long borders with potential enemies in China and Europe. The United States, with its peaceful borders, has emphasized more the development of its navy and air force, so that it can keep in touch with its allies around the world, head off trouble spots abroad, and address its global interests.

✦ EDUCATION

The most basic service that most governments are expected to offer their people is education. This is a prerequisite of economic development for the country as a whole, and it greatly expands the world of the individuals who are educated. Many nations of the Third World, whose populations were largely illiterate at the time independence was acquired, have had an uphill fight in bringing education to their peoples, but this story over the last fifty years is in the main one of success.

As Table 4.3 shows, most countries invest a substantial effort in this area of policy and most countries of the Third World have already accomplished a good deal along these lines. Many have had to overcome great difficulties.

One of these, Mozambique, exemplifies the problems faced by a poor state in attempting to educate its people. Mozambique's investment of 2.5 percent of its GDP is not all that much worse than other states, but even that does not provide a great deal; only 13 percent of boys between the ages of fourteen and seventeen, and 19 percent of girls, were enrolled in school. However, 47 percent of adults can read, a dramatic improvement over the nearly 100 percent illiteracy rate at the time the country attained independence.

TABLE 4.3

Educational Effort for Selected States

Country (per capita GDP in parentheses)**	Percent of GDP Spent on Education	Percent of Eligible Girls/Boys Enrolled in High School*	Adult Literacy Rate (percent)	Democratic/ Non since 1975
United States ($41,854)	5.8	87/87	—	democratic
Canada (32,886)	5.4	114/114	—	democratic
France (30,120)	6.0	113/110	—	democratic
Chile (12,635)	4.1	78/74	96	mixed
South Africa (12,347)	5.5	91/84	92	mixed
Botswana (10,790)	2.3	58/57	89	democratic
Turkey (8,430)	3.7	60/89	87	mixed
Indonesia (3,842)	4.2	47/50	88	mixed
Nicaragua (3,680)	3.2	56/43	77	mixed
Mozambique (1,364)	2.5	3/4	47	mixed

*May exceed 100 percent because it is the "gross" percent: total enrollment in a grade (of whatever ages) divided by the population of the age at which one would normally attend that grade. Percents greater than 100 generally mean that the state is attempting to catch up with older students (including adults) who missed out on education at their "proper" age.

**Purchasing power parity.

SOURCE: UNESCO, Web site, http://www.uis.unesco.org, December 2006; "Democratic/non since 1975," adapted from Adam Przeworski et al., *Democracy and Development* (New York: Cambridge University Press, 2000), appendix 1.2; GDP per capita from World Bank Group, *World Development Indicators Online*, 2007.

✦ RESEARCH AND DEVELOPMENT

If states of the Third World must concentrate on spreading basic education throughout their populations, the more highly developed economies of the industrialized democracies depend on continuing technological development to give them a competitive edge in making high-tech goods (computers, electrical machinery, aircraft, etc.) for export, and for increased efficiencies in their own economies. In most of these developed economies, labor costs are too high to allow basic industries such as the manufacture of clothing or of simple plastic goods to be competitive internationally. Third World states can produce such goods much more cheaply. The special province of the developed economies is in the production of high-tech goods and services, where their scientific and technological capacities allow them to outperform everyone else.

Table 4.4 shows how dependent the industrialized democracies, in particular, are on high-tech industry for their trade with other states. About a third of the United

TABLE 4.4

Involvement of Selected States in Research and Development

Country (per capita GDP in parentheses)*	Percent of Manufactured Exports High Technology	Scientists and Engineers per Million Population	Government Spending on Research and Development as a Percent of GDP	Net Gain (over expenditure) in License Fees (millions of $)	Democratic/Non democratic since 1975
United States ($41,854)	32	4,605	3	+33,083	democratic
Canada (32,886)	14	3,597	2	–2,852	democratic
Great Britain (32,005)	24	2,691	2	+3,944	democratic
Japan (30,821)	24	5,287	3	+3,002	democratic
France (30,120)	19	3,213	2	+2,742	democratic
Israel (25,670)	19	1,570	4	+58	democratic
South Korea (21,868)	33	3,187	3	–2,660	mixed
Brazil (8,730)	12	324	1	–1,303	mixed
Egypt (4,455)	1	NA	0	–8	nondemocratic
India (3,486)	5	120	1	–396	democratic
Madagascar (897)	1	15	0	–12	nondemocratic

*Purchasing power parity.

SOURCE: World Bank Group, *World Development Indicators Online*, 2007; "Democratic/non since 1945," adapted from Adam Przeworski et al., *Democracy and Development* (New York: Cambridge University Press, 2000), appendix 1.2.

The Peruvian government pursuing educational policy: children at school.
© Paul Conkin

States' manufactured exports were high-tech goods in 2003. And in addition, American firms netted over $33 billion through selling licenses for technical processes. This shows up in the fourth column of Table 4.4, "Net Gain (over expenditure) in License Fees." Brazil's companies, in contrast, paid out $1.3 billion more than they earned in license fees.

A fascinating example, however, of a Third World state that has successfully established an embryonic high-tech industry is Costa Rica, a relatively poor Central American democracy, with PPP per capita GDP of $9,985.[5] In the mid-1980s, the country cut its tariffs on computers from 133 percent to 10 percent in a successful effort to encourage computer use and literacy. The government assigns every Costa Rican an e-mail address that can be accessed at terminals in all post offices. And by law, expenditures on education must equal at least 6 percent of the gross domestic product (compare this with other states of the Third World in Table 4.3). As a result of these and other efforts, technological products have become the largest category of Costa Rica's exports, topping coffee and bananas. Partly this is the result of a large Intel Corporation chip-manufacturing plant that was established in 1997, but partly it is also a result of over 140 locally owned software-development companies.

---

[5]"Who Says the Chips Are Down?" *BusinessWeek,* 10 September 2001, p. 68E2.

Planning for Environmental Sustainability in Costa Rica*

Since the early 1980s Costa Rica has been working hard to transform its consumption patterns to rationalize human uses of natural resources and the environment.

In 1996 the country outlawed leaded petrol and has since cut its lead levels by two-thirds. All vehicles must now pass an annual emissions inspection, new imported cars must have catalytic converters, and industries are required to have systems to treat the contaminants that they produce. Last year the government, responding to citizens' protests, closed the Placer Dome Company's open-pit gold mine because of harm caused to the environment and local inhabitants.

Negative incentives are also used, such as higher import taxes on used imported vehicles without catalytic converters and fines for loggers who cut timber illegally. The hundred cleanest companies in Costa Rica are named annually, and a green seal of quality is given to gas stations with the best records in preventing air and water pollution and in treating waste water. A red stamp is for those with the worst records.

The government and civil society also apply moral suasion by using ad campaigns to convince people that a healthy environment is good in itself, contributes to human well-being, and is good for tourism. Civil society, responding to a governmental programme, has organized thirty-six natural resource vigilance committees nationwide. These groups provide more than 3,000 citizens to serve as voluntary inspectors of natural resource use and compliance with environmental statues.

In the late 1980s, in one year alone, Costa Rica felled 10 million cubic metres of forest, with an estimated timber value of $422 million. In 1988 the Netherlands purchased part of Costa Rica's external debt at a cost of $5 million and then wrote it off on the condition that Costa Rica spend an equivalent amount in local currency on forestry redevelopment. In 1989 Sweden purchased a further $5.5 million of Costa Rica's debt for a similar purpose. Such debt-for-nature swaps are helpful but need to be pursued on a much broader scale.

Home to about 5 percent of the world's species of flora and fauna, Costa Rica has been a global leader in environmental sustainability, setting aside about 25 percent of the country as conservation or protected areas and arranging debt-for-nature swaps.

*"Figure 5.11–Planning for Environmental Sustainability in Costa Rica," from *Human Development Report,* 2001 by United Nations Development Programme, copyright © 2001 by the United Nations Development Programme. Used by permission of Oxford University Press, Inc.

In all countries, the technology that makes this sort of industry possible is provided partly by government-sponsored research, partly by research carried on directly by the industries involved, and partly by basic research conducted in universities and other institutions of higher education. A good idea of the general level of such activity in a country may be gained by observing the number of scientists and engineers in the population. This figure is displayed for several states in the third column of Table 4.4, which gives the number of scientists and engineers engaged in research and development.

✦ HEALTH AND SOCIAL WELFARE

Most modern states have accepted some responsibility for maintaining their people in reasonable health, in adequate housing, with financial security in their old age, and with some security against disability or disaster. Developed economies devote considerable resources to these purposes, while states of the Third World do not do as much. For the people of many poor states, daily life is a series of catastrophes, and it is all they can do to deal with those, much less prepare for future ones. Third World governments must often use any surplus funds they have to develop systems of basic education or to build industrial plants for future economic growth. Finally, as we have already seen, some Third World states are burdened with large military budgets. All these circumstances put such strains on the economies of these states that social programs are usually put on a back burner.

This pattern is evident in the second column of Table 4.5, which lists the proportion of national budgets devoted to such items as health, recreation, unemployment insurance, pension systems, housing, and so on. The broad pattern is clear: The governments of developed economic systems make a considerable effort to ensure social welfare, whereas poorer governments do less. Another notable point in Table 4.5 is that the United States devotes a smaller portion of its public budget to social programs and health than Canada or the European states.

What sorts of things do governments do to promote social welfare? A vast number of programs have been used in one country or another for this purpose. To name a few: Governments may provide child care centers for working parents; psychiatric counseling for emotionally troubled people; medical care for their citizens—as the

TABLE 4.5

Social Welfare Activity by Selected Governments

Country (per capita GDP in parentheses)*	Percent of Governmental Expenditures Devoted to Social Programs and Health	Democratic/Non since 1975
United States ($41,854)	39.8	democratic
Canada (32,886)	49.0	democratic
Great Britain (32,005)	56.7	democratic
Germany (29,309)	59.9	democratic
Israel (25,670)	36.1	democratic
South Korea (21,868)	14.8	mixed
Tunisia (8,298)	27.4	nondemocratic
Philippines (4,920)	6.3	mixed
Syria (3,842)	7.7	nondemocratic
Myanmar (1,700)	7.4	nondemocratic
Madagascar (897)	9.9	nondemocratic

*Purchasing power parity.
SOURCE: International Monetary Fund, *Government Finance Statistics Yearbook, 2004* (includes all levels of government); "Democratic/non since 1975," adapted from Adam Przeworski et al., *Democracy and Development* (New York: Cambridge University Press, 2000), appendix 1.2; World Bank Group, *World Development Indicators Online,* 2007.

British government does and as the United States does for poor people and for all people over age sixty-five; governments may build residential housing and offer it at inexpensive rates; governments may give grants of money to all families with children to help them with the costs of child rearing (most European governments do this); governments may provide some sort of minimal national pension for people too old to work; and so on. There is quite an array of programs, and countries vary widely in the extent to which they give one or another type of aid.

A more detailed look at one area of social policy—the provision of health care—is presented in Table 4.6. The table displays the choice governments make of whether to provide a service directly or allow it to be dealt with privately. Outcomes of health care are also compared here, with life expectancy and infant mortality shown for each country.

In line with what we have seen in other policy areas, general expenditure on health is higher in the richer countries. And we see from the outcomes that this higher expenditure appears to work. Life expectancies are lower at the bottom of the table, and infant mortality rates are higher. The differences in life expectancies and rates of infant mortality between poor countries and rich countries are startling.

On the other hand, there are fairly large variations in expenditure among the rich countries, and among these countries, greater expenditure does *not* necessarily translate into better outcomes. The United States spends far more on health care than any of the other four rich, industrialized countries without achieving better health outcomes. In a ranking of overall performance put together by the World Health Organization (WHO), the United States ranks thirty-seventh, compared with Japan's rank of tenth, Britain's

TABLE 4.6

Health Expenditures and Outcomes for Selected States

Country (GDP per capita in parentheses)*	Government Spending on Health Care, % of GDP	Private Spending on Health Care, % of GDP	Total Spending on Health Care, % of GDP	Life Expectancy	Infant Mortality (per 1,000 live births)
United States ($41,854)	7	8	15	77	7
Canada (32,886)	7	3	10	80	5
Great Britain (32,005)	7	1	8	79	5
Sweden (31,062)	8	1	9	80	3
Japan (30,821)	6	2	8	82	3
South Korea (21,868)	8	3	11	77	5
Tunisia (8,298)	3	3	6	73	21
Philippines (4,920)	1	2	3	71	26
India (3,486)	1	4	5	63	62
Bolivia (2,856)	4	2	7	65	54
Nigeria (1,400)	1	4	5	44	101

*Purchasing power parity.

SOURCE: World Bank Group, *World Development Indicators Online,* 2007; GDP per capita from CIA, *World Factbook Online,* Field Listing, revised April 21, 2005.

rank of eighteenth, and Sweden's rank of twenty-third.[6] Of the five rich countries in the table, Japan, which spends the next to lowest percentage of its GDP on health, actually gets the best result: life expectancy of eighty-two, only three deaths in infancy for every thousand children born, and tenth place in the WHO rankings.

In fact, Japan spends only a bit more relative to its GDP than Bolivia does—but with dramatically different results. It is probably the case that the main determinants of the health outcomes are not private or governmental expenditures on health per se, but other things associated with overall poverty: nutrition, education, and public sanitation. This might also help to explain the poor showing in health of the United States, where inequality of incomes results in unexpectedly high levels of poverty for such a rich country.

✦ THE PLACE OF POWER IN POLICY ANALYSIS

It is easy to lapse into an almost pure "choice" perspective in this chapter, because we have been looking at policies, the product of the state. We are thus looking at a variety of choices that states have made, and it is easy to forget the interchanges of power that lie behind the states' decisions. The difference that democracy makes in policy, however, offers a good reminder that how power is organized in the state will have a lot to do with what kind of collective choice is made.

Good policy analysis will not only assess the objective merits of a policy but also take into account the power constraints under which the policy must work. For instance, any reasonable assessment of U.S. policy in banning the use of marijuana has to take into account the difficulty of enforcing that law, the connivance of local governments with marijuana farmers, and so on. Once again, we see that even when our subject matter pulls us rather strongly toward one of the poles of power and choice, good analysis requires that we retain both perspectives to some extent.

 EXAMPLE

The Demographic Challenge

 Industrialized countries face a major challenge over the next few decades because of dramatic changes in the age structure of their populations. Over the past half-century, medical advances have meant that people in prosperous countries live longer than they used to. And at the same time, a number of social and medical changes—the greater involvement of women outside their families, the availability of reliable contraceptive devices—have led to sharply decreased birth rates. As a result, from now through the year 2030 or so, the populations of prosperous countries are going to consist more and more of the aged.

This change has multiple implications for policy, including the question of where support for school expenditures will come from, the possibility that roads may be safer as the average driver

---

[6]World Health Organization. *World Health Report 2000.*

is more experienced and pumps less testosterone, and many others. But the most direct and most important challenge posed by the demographic shift is that national pension systems will become very hard to maintain under their present systems of finance.

At present, pension systems in all industrialized states are primarily "pay as you go" systems. That is, those who are engaged in the labor force pay taxes, which are then passed on to retired people as pensions. Those who are now working expect that when they retire the working population at that time will in turn support them in the same way. The demographic problem, though, means that as time passes there will be more of them, and fewer new workers to support them. The ratio of retired people to those who are working is going to go through the roof. In Europe today there are 35 people of an age to have retired for every 100 people of working age. By 2050, there are expected to be 75 people of an age to have retired for every 100 people of working age. This means that either pensions will have to be drastically reduced, or workers and their employers will have to pay about triple the taxes they now pay to fund the pensions. The situation is similar in the United States, though the United States is helped by the fact that it admits millions of immigrants each year, almost all of them young. So, the demographic shift in the ratio of pensioners to workers in the United States will be less extreme than that in other industrialized countries.

One solution to the problem could be to shift from "pay as you go" to a "prefunded" system in which workers gradually build retirement accounts through taxes they and their employers pay into a special fund that invests their money for them. Each worker, when she retires, would then have built up a large pot of money that would fund her pension. In other words, her pension would have been prefunded by her earlier taxes and those of her employers, rather than relying on current workers' and employers' taxes. This is happening in many companies' private pension systems, which have shifted from "defined benefit" (a worker gets a pension, funded out of current resources, at a level that has been stated and guaranteed in advance) to "defined contribution" (the worker and company make stated contributions each year the worker is employed, and when the worker retires, he gets whatever the resulting pot of cash yields). Chile has set up its national pension system as a "prefunded" system, and it seems to work well. President George Bush in 2005 proposed a partial change of this sort for the Social Security system in the United States, but his proposals were rejected.

A major problem with shifting from an established "pay as you go" system to a "prefunded" system is that there is a huge bulge that must be funded, because for thirty years or so the government will be paying off the pensions for which it is obligated under the old "pay as you go" system, but the taxes new workers are paying will be dedicated to prefunding their own future pensions, and cannot be used to support the older retirees. So, how do you pay for the bulge?

 # EXAMPLE

Economic Development Compared with "Human Development"

Economic growth is vital to people's well-being, but other things should also be taken into account—how equally the economic benefits are distributed, the state of the environment, the state of people's health, and so on. It is not enough to ask whether the people of a state are prospering; rather, we must ask, how well are they living?

This is hard to assess, because it involves so many diverse things, but a rough first stab has been taken in the "human development index" developed by the United Nations Development Programme (see Table 4.7).[7] The index combines indicators of gross domestic product per capita, life expectancy, school enrollment, and literacy into a single index; presumably, this measures

TABLE 4.7

The World's Most Prosperous States, Ranked on Gross Domestic Product per Capita and on the Human Development Index

State	PPP Gross Domestic Product per Capita, Worldwide Rank	Human Development Index, Worldwide Rank	Difference in Rankings
Luxembourg	1	12	−11
Equatorial Guinea	2	120	−118
United Arab Emirates	3	49	−46
Norway	4	1	+3
Ireland	5	4	+1
United States	6	8	−2
Iceland	7	2	+5
Denmark	8	15	−7
Hong Kong	9	22	−13
Austria	10	14	−4
Canada	11	6	+5
Switzerland	12	9	+3
Japan	13	7	+6
Australia	14	3	+11
Finland	15	11	+4
Belgium	16	13	+3
Netherlands	17	10	+7
Sweden	18	5	+13
Germany	19	21	−2
Great Britain	20	18	+2
Singapore	21	25	−4
France	22	16	+6
Italy	23	17	+6
Qatar	24	46	−22
Spain	25	19	+6
Israel	26	23	+3
New Zealand	27	20	+7
Brunei	28	34	−6
Bahrain	29	39	−10
South Korea	30	26	+4

SOURCE: United Nations Development Programme, *Human Development Report, 2006* (available at http://hdr.undp.org/).

[7]United Nations Development Programme, *Human Development Report, 2006* (available at http://hdr.undp.org/).

broad well-being better than gross domestic product alone, and it is interesting to examine how states compare with each other on the two measures.

Luxembourg, whose people have the world's highest incomes, ranks lower when life expectancy and education are added into the equation. The champion at providing a good life given their level of prosperity is Sweden, whose people are only the eighteenth richest but rank fifth on the human development index. A number of other industrialized Western states also do well, including Australia, New Zealand, and the Netherlands. States that have high income based on a restricted product, such as the Arab oil states, tend to do the worst in these comparisons. In particular, many Arab oil producers such as Qatar and the United Arab Emirates have accomplished little with great resources.

Equatorial Guinea stands out in this table. It ranks 120th on the human development index despite being the second highest state in the world in average income. But "average" here masks deep disparities in wealth. Equatorial Guinea is a nondemocratic one-party state with most businesses owned by government officials and members of their families. Recent discoveries of oil have made those who run the country rich, but most of the people rely on poor subsistence farming.

 EXAMPLE

Uganda, an African AIDS Success Story[8]

The southern two-thirds of Africa has been devastated since the 1980s by an epidemic of AIDS. It was estimated at the end of 2003 that 25 million children and adults in the region were ill with AIDS. In 2003, 2.2 million Africans died of the illness, and at that point 12 million children had been orphaned by it.[9]

Many African states have been slow to address the problem, which is devastating both to the families involved, and—because of the large numbers involved—to the economy as well. Partly the slow response has been due to the extreme poverty of many African states; AIDS is an expensive illness to treat once it has been contracted. While preventive measures are not especially expensive, even something as simple as a pack of condoms is not an insignificant purchase in a country like Niger, where the average income is $800 a year.

The problem has not been solely one of resources, however. Many African leaders have been hesitant to work on the AIDS problem either because its sexual character has meant that solutions clashed with their own religious values or because if they did take action, they immediately encountered resistance from powerful religious leaders. Additionally, in the 1980s there was some discussion in the scientific community as to whether the AIDS virus had originated in Africa; African leaders feared that this theory, combined with what appeared to them to be morally reprehensible sexual sources of the infection, would lead to further stereotyping of Africans of the sort that had been all too prevalent during the colonial period.

As a result of all these factors, many African countries have simply not taken effective action against AIDS. As late as 2000, for instance, President Thabo Mbeki of South Africa (where 21 percent of all adults and children suffer from AIDS) argued that AIDS is not caused by sexual

---

[8]I am much indebted in this section to James Putzel's case study, "The Politics of Action on AIDS: A Case Study of Uganda," *Public Administration and Development* 24 (2004), pp. 19–30.
[9]U.S. Census Board/Joint United Nations Programme on HIV/AIDS (UNAIDS), "Report on the Global HIV/AIDS Epidemic," July 2004.

behavior but by malnutrition and poor hygiene, and refused to provide the drug AZT to pregnant women to protect their fetuses.

Against this background, the success of Uganda, a poor country situated west of Kenya and east of the Democratic Republic of the Congo, stands out. UNAIDS estimates of infection rates in Uganda had reached about 15 percent by 1991, after a spread fueled by civil war (with the movement of troops from one part of the country to another) and by long-haul trucking routes with their associated brothels. But by 2005, after a concerted effort to arrest the illness, the rate of adult AIDS had dropped to 7 percent. How was this accomplished?

President Yoweri Museveni took power in Uganda in 1985 when his forces prevailed in the civil war; he established a one-party regime that continues in power today. He is a socially conservative figure, and initially joined in the skepticism of many African leaders about AIDS; for the first few years of his rule, for instance, he banned the distribution of condoms to combat the spread of the illness. By 1988, however, Museveni had become convinced that AIDS had to be combated. (A contributing factor in his conversion appears to have been that of sixty officers sent to Cuba for training in 1986, eighteen tested positive for AIDS.)

Once Musevini was committed, a number of things became possible. He was able to use both the army and his political party (the "Movement") to reach every village with educational materials and treatment. Also, his own socially conservative bent and his early opposition to condoms reassured religious leaders. Gradually, he was able to win them over to the program. His program, ABC ("Abstinence, Being Faithful, and Condoms"), in fact emphasized traditional values strongly.

The actual program, once the government was fully engaged in it, was rather straightforward. Musevini stressed education and preventive interventions. His army, for instance, conducted a national sampling of blood serum to map the incidence of AIDS in the country. He urged all officials to speak about AIDS at every single meeting they addressed. And he worked both with the churches and with international agencies to distribute condoms widely, even while casting their use in traditional terms as an enhancement of faithfulness.

The result is one of the best records in Africa of diminishing the AIDS epidemic.

KEY TERMS

privatization
gross domestic product
PPP per capita GDP

FURTHER READING

Alstott, Anne L. *No Exit: What Parents Owe Their Children and What Society Owes Parents.* New York: Oxford University Press, 2004.

Blank, Robert H., and Burau, Viola, eds. *Comparative Health Policy.* New York: Palgrave Macmillan, 2004.

Callahan, Daniel, and Wasunna, Angela A. *Medicine and the Market: Equity v. Choice.* Baltimore, MD: Johns Hopkins University Press, 2006.

Ellerman, A. Denny, Joskow, Paul L., Schmalensee, Richard, Montero, Juan-Pablo, and Bailey, Elizabeth M. *Markets for Clean Air: The U.S. Acid Rain Program.* New York: Cambridge University Press, 2000.

Esping-Anderson, Gosta. *The Three Worlds of Welfare Capitalism.* Princeton: Princeton University Press, 1990.

————. *Why We Need a New Welfare State.* New York: Oxford University Press, 2002.

Howell, William G., and Peterson, Paul E. *The Education Gap: Vouchers and Urban Schools.* Washington, DC: Brookings Institution, 2002.

Human Rights Watch World Report. serial. New York: Human Rights Watch, 2000.

Lomborg, Bjørn. *The Skeptical Environmentalist: Measuring the Real State of the World.* New York: Cambridge University Press, 2001.

Mead, Lawrence M. *Government Matters: Welfare Reform in Wisconsin.* Princeton: Princeton University Press, 2004.

Metz, Bert, Davidson, Ogunlade, Swart, Rob, and Pan, Jiahua. *Climate Change 2001: Mitigation.* New York: Cambridge University Press, 2001.

Moe, Terry M. *Schools, Vouchers, and the American Public.* Washington, DC: Brookings Institution, 2001.

Morone, James A., and Jacobs, Lawrence R. *Healthy, Wealthy, and Fair: Health Care and the Good Society.* New York: Oxford University Press, 2005.

Patterson, Amy S., ed. *The African State and the AIDS Crisis.* Burlington, VT: Ashgate, 2005.

Schick, Allen. *The Federal Budget: Politics, Policy, Process,* rev. ed. Washington, DC: Brookings Institution, 2000.

Scott, James C. *Seeing Like a State: How Certain Schemes to Improve the Human Condition Have Failed.* New Haven CT: Yale University Press, 1998.

Steinmo, Sven, and Watts, Jon. "It's the Institutions, Stupid! Why Comprehensive National Health Insurance Always Fails in America." *Journal of Health Politics Policy and Law* 20 (1995), pp. 329–72.

World Bank. *World Development Report.* serial. New York: Oxford University Press, 2001.

World Health Organization. *World Health Report.* serial.

WEB SITES OF INTEREST

Brookings Institution, a centrist policy research center:
http://www.brookings.org

American Enterprise Institute, a conservative research center:
http://www.aei.org

Economic Policy Institute, a research center with close ties to the labor movement:
http://www.epinet.org

Heritage Foundation, along with the American Enterprise Institute, one of the major conservative research centers in Washington, D.C.:
http://www.heritage.org

Moving Ideas Web page; links to over a hundred left-oriented policy sites:
http://www.movingideas.org

National Center For Public Policy Research, a conservative, free-market foundation:
http://www.nationalcenter.org

CHAPTER 5

❧

ECONOMIC
POLICY OF THE STATE[1]

In Chapter 4, we looked at the range of states' policies, but I left one especially important set of policies for separate treatment in this chapter. Economic policy is such a large part of a government's responsibilities and the questions involved in economic policy are sufficiently varied that it seemed to deserve treatment on its own. Also, the study of economic policy is intertwined with the broad subfield of *political economy* in political science. This is a part of political science with which you will want to become familiar, and it seemed easiest to present economic policy and political economy together in this chapter.

Certainly, the state of the economy bulks large in our evaluation of a government. Bill Clinton is famous for displaying a sign prominently in his campaign headquarters during his campaign for president in 1992 that said, "It's the economy, Stupid!" Governments fall into disfavor with their people when the economy is going badly—when prices are high and jobs are scarce. Conversely, when the economy is performing well, governments can count on support from their people. Bill Clinton's sexual and legal problems in his second term as president never seemed to evoke as strong a response from the electorate as they evoked from the media—at least partly, one might think, because unemployment and the rate of inflation reached their lowest points in decades at that time.

If nothing else, the centrality of economic policy in a government's responsibilities should be obvious to us from the fact that all of the policies we looked at in Chapter 4 require revenue. For everything else it wants to accomplish—developing military power, educating youth, providing good housing to its people—a government relies on a strong economy to give it the revenues it needs for the policies. Both in its own right

---

[1]Portions of this chapter are adapted from W. Phillips Shively, ed., *Comparative Governance* (New York: McGraw-Hill).

as well as instrumentally for the other policies it makes possible, a healthy economy is important to the state.

People's concerns about the economy generally boil down to two broad ones: (1) prosperity and economic growth, that is, the *performance* of the economy; and (2) the *distribution* of economic benefits (how evenly benefits are spread), and these are the main concerns of government policy. In the next three sections we will deal with the most important questions states deal with in making their economic policy, two having to do with performance, and one with distribution. After these sections we will look at some of the conditions that help or hinder them in dealing with these questions.

✦ ECONOMIC PERFORMANCE I: GROWTH

Probably the single thing by which governments are most judged is whether the economy of the state grows steadily and rapidly. States certainly vary in how well they provide prosperity and economic growth for their citizens. The map in Figure 5.1 shows the average per capita gross domestic product, or GDP, for the world's states in 2005. (For per capita GDP, see above, p. 81.)

 Baumol's Disease

Political science often uses simple economic analyses to answer tricky questions about politics. (This is part of the subfield "political economy," which is described below, pp. 120–122.) One part of an answer to the question I posed in the chapter on the state, "Why are the world's states growing bigger?" may be provided by an analysis of the economic dilemma of service activities such as the fine arts that William J. Baumol made in various publications across the 1960s.

His analysis started with the fact that as manufacturing industries become more productive (through more efficient operations, especially the use of new machines that allow a worker to produce more goods in a day), pay scales in manufacturing can increase at a rate greater than inflation.[2] This is great for manufacturing. However, some industries (the so-called "service" sector) produce services that one person does for another. Workers in the service sector cannot as easily increase their productivity, since there are typically no machines to help them produce more service in a day of work. A cellist cannot play more songs in a day. A barber cannot speed up the cutting of hair, or at least not by much. A teacher can only become more efficient by increasing the size of classes—but that usually reduces the quality of the teaching.

As manufacturing workers' pay increases, they would gradually pull away from service workers—if service workers' pay stood still. It does not, though. Over time, as other

Continued

---

[2]"Inflation" is defined on p. 105. Transportation, and distributional industries like retailing, also have a considerable capacity to increase productivity. So, this analysis is not based just on manufacturing alone, though it provides the clearest case.

Baumol's Disease   *Continued*

workers' pay increases, employers in the service sector have to increase their workers' pay similarly to keep them from all moving over into the manufacturing sector. Schools have to increase teachers' pay to keep them from quitting and taking jobs in software development, for instance.

As a result, pay in the service sector will increase at a rate greater than inflation, even though the workers in the sector are not producing any more than they have done before. And so, the services they provide will have to increase rapidly in price if they are not to deteriorate in quality (through larger class sizes, for instance). In a sense, there is nothing too awful about this. It just means that everyone in society benefits from the greater efficiency in manufacturing, rather than only those who happened to be lucky enough to work for someone who developed slick new machinery to help them. But it does lead to the disconcerting fact that, for instance, college tuition will generally rise at a rate greater than overall inflation, as will the costs of hospitalization, symphony concerts, and other labor-intensive services. This has come to be called "Baumol's disease."

How does this help to answer the question about why states expand? Most of what a state does is to provide labor-intensive services: education, health care, law enforcement, safety inspections, and the like. As the cost of these services increases, the cost of government will almost inevitably grow at a rate greater than inflation, just in order to keep providing the same set of services. Of course, there are plenty of other things that may be going on as well in the growth of states. Most states have increased the range of services they offer over the past century. But part of the story is that the cost of even constant services has inevitably risen. And, this is not a story of greedy bureaucrats. It is a story of the gains of productivity being shared with teachers, doctors, and hamburger inspectors.

There are tremendous variations here from one state to another. The average citizen of Luxembourg enjoys $74,573 per year compared with the average citizen of Burundi, with $653 per year. The states of North America and Western Europe are quite prosperous, along with a few East Asian states: Japan, Australia, New Zealand, and South Korea. With a few exceptions, the states of Africa and central and East Asia are poor. Latin American states, the states of the former Soviet Union, and the states of the Middle East fall in between.

Some of these differences are due to differences in natural resources (Saudi Arabians, who enjoy $14,729 per capita annually, are lucky enough to sit on a lake of oil) or to long and peaceful development as in the case of Canada or the United States. States and their governments, though, do make a difference. In 1972, Ghana and South Korea had roughly the same per capita GDP ($310 and $300, respectively), but by 2005, the per capita GDP of Ghana was only $2,402, while South Korea's had risen to $21,868.[3] Beyond the numbers, what this means is that Ghanaians are still mired in poverty, while South

---

[3]The 1972 figures are straight per capita GDP, because PPP-adjusted figures are not available; the 2005 figures are PPP per capita GDP.

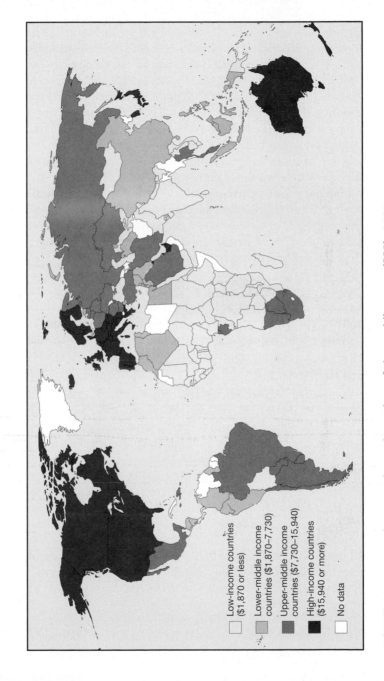

FIGURE 5.1 Per capita gross domestic product of the world's states (PPP), 2005.

SOURCE: © 2007 World Bank Group, *World Bank Atlas.* Used with permission.

Legend:

- Low-income countries ($1,870 or less)
- Lower-middle income countries ($1,870–7,730)
- Upper-middle income countries ($7,730–15,940)
- High-income countries ($15,940 or more)
- No data

Koreans have raised themselves to a level of reasonable comfort—in other words, these numbers really do mean something. However, South Korea is not especially well endowed with natural resources. What happened? The difference between the experiences of the two countries must lie in how they organized themselves and their economies.[4]

One obvious first crack at why countries vary in their growth is that some governments make big mistakes in guiding investment in the economy. Ghana, for instance, like most African states in their first few decades of independence, taxed farmers highly to subsidize food prices for the cities and to pay for ambitious, showy industrial projects. When the industrial projects flopped and at the same time farmers decided not to invest in improving operations on their farms because the government took most of their earnings, the economy was badly hurt.

A lesson that is often drawn from this type of experience is that governments should not try to make fine-tuned economic decisions. Economic decisions, it is said, require a nimbleness and capacity for handling detailed information that are simply beyond governments. Such decisions are better left to be made separately by individuals in thousands of specific investment decisions. An individual deciding whether to invest money in his or her farm, or perhaps in a nearby factory, can operate more efficiently and will more often choose rightly than the more cumbersome governmental operation. Of course, this leaves out of consideration some of the reasons why governments may have intervened in the first place—their concern that private market decisions would exacerbate inequalities, for instance, or that they would put investment into projects the government does not approve of. (The question of government's proper role in economic policy will be addressed in more detail, pro and con, in Chapter 6.)

Rents and Rent-Seeking

Another reason often advanced for governments to leave economic decisions to free markets is that governments are political arenas and those who are dominant within the government will use their control to extract what economists call **rents.** In this use, rent does not mean the fee one pays to live in an apartment. Rather, rents are transfers of money that do not relate to production. If a government uses tax money to build a road or educate children, that is a *productive* transfer of money because the investment (in transportation or in an educated work force) allows the society to produce more. However, if the government uses the general tax money to give its supporters a break on their own taxes, that transfer does not increase society's productivity. It is a *rent*. Other examples of rents would be farm price subsidies, pork-barrel projects, and the creation of unnecessary public jobs for patronage. Governments are in the business of maintaining public support, so if they engage actively in managing the economy, there is certainly a danger that they will gravitate to the economic tool that most easily allows them to buy support—rents.

In the case of Ghana, it was because the government's supporters were mostly from the cities that the government taxed the farmers to subsidize cheap food for city

---

[4]Another possibility would be that United States aid to South Korea after the Korean War helped that country to develop. But Ghana also attracted a good deal of aid, and South Korea was further handicapped by high military expenditures necessitated by its aggressive neighbor to the north. Probably all of these factors are roughly a wash.

dwellers. That is, the government used its power to provide its urban supporters with a rent.

The reason rent-seeking hurts economic growth is that it channels transfers of money into the pockets of the dominant coalition's supporters, rather than into what would be the most efficient economic use of the money. Some degree of rent-seeking occurs in every state. In the United States, for instance, the politically dominant middle class has seen to it that the government subsidizes the owners of houses by allowing them to deduct mortgage interest payments on their federal income tax. As a result, there is probably more money spent on housing in the United States (and, therefore, less invested in farms and factories) than makes economic sense. While some degree of rent-seeking occurs everywhere, the extent varies from one state to another. And like Ghana, most of the new states of Africa in the 1960s, 1970s, and 1980s were weak states, which could not easily force consideration of the interests of the unrepresented parts of society. The better organized parts of their societies—urban populations, the military, corrupt officials—made sure they were taken care of, as these states distributed rents with a vengeance. (You see now some of the reason for our consideration of the relative strengths of society and the state on page 63. When the state is weak relative to society, reliance on rents can flourish.)

Import-Substitution Industrialization

Another policy of the Ghanaian government that probably hurt the economy was the policy of **import-substitution industrialization.** This was a common practice for new, underdeveloped economies in the 1950s, 1960s, and 1970s. To transform their economies to advanced industrial economies, many governments in Latin America, Africa, and Asia tried to encourage the establishment of factories within their own states. They did this by setting high tariffs to discourage imports of manufactured goods from elsewhere. Without competition from producers in other countries, it was thought that these new factories would be able to prosper and thus transform the economy. Often, however, the owners of the factories (or their managers, if the factories were owned by the state) simply took advantage of the lack of competition to charge high prices for shoddy goods. This did not provide the hoped-for shot in the arm for the economy. Producing overpriced tractors that broke down frequently, for instance, did little to help boost agricultural production. The owners of the protected factories benefited from the policy, but the people as a whole did not get the expanding economy that was supposed to have resulted from this.

The South Korean Experience

The argument so far would seem to be for keeping governments out of economic decisions. Governments, one might argue, are not well suited to the rapid, finely detailed decisions that are required. When they involve themselves in the economy, the argument would go, they are prone to distribute rents unproductively to their supporters.

However, the South Korean side of the South Korea–Ghana comparison suggests another consideration. It is not because the government left it alone that the South Korean economy grew at a wonderful rate. The South Korean state has long intervened directly in business's investment decisions. For many years, for instance, the government controlled which corporations were allowed to borrow money and expand. In addition, in many areas of the economy that it wished to control, the government created large corporate monopolies, which then allowed themselves to be guided by the government in many respects. Finally, the government closed off much international competition by laying down prohibitive tariffs to protect domestic industries. However, instead of aiming at import-substitution industrialization, the government pushed the protected industries to become exporters to other countries. This meant that at least in their export markets, they were still exposed to the discipline of competition with other manufacturers.

If government intervention hurts economic growth, as so many economists say it does, how can it be that South Korea's economy grew rapidly under these conditions? Apparently, the difference between Ghana and South Korea is that South Korea's government was somehow able to intervene in ways that helped the economy rather than hurt it.

First, South Korea had an unusually autonomous state.[5] The population of South Korea is remarkably homogeneous, so there were relatively few societal divisions for the government to balance off. More important, perhaps, the country was faced throughout the period with a strong security threat from North Korea, which had invaded the South once in the 1950s and threatened to do so intermittently thereafter. This threat tended to unite South Koreans and so dominated politics that few other conflicts could emerge. All of this gave South Korea's military government a relatively free hand with policy, so much so that *the government did not have to deal much with rent-seeking.* Its supporters were mostly concerned with national security, and in the name of national security the government could pursue economically rational policies if it chose to do so, rather than diverting resources into subsidies to placate the farmers or pork-barrel projects to placate particular towns or regions. The government left many areas of the economy free to respond flexibly to market forces of supply and demand, even as it controlled certain other strategic parts of the economy tightly.

Some political scientists also credit South Korea's long-established Confucian political culture for the fact that the government did not abuse its power to enrich its followers. The Confucian culture was one that envisioned leaders and followers as being in a natural harmony of mutual obligations, and in this culture leaders were supposed to be modest in their personal demands and fair and farsighted in making policy. This pervades the culture. For example, in a recent study the average CEO compensation in South Korea was 5.6 times as great as the wages of the average manufacturing worker. By way of comparison, the average CEO compensation in the United States was 411 times as great as the average worker's pay.[6]

Finally, South Korea's authoritarian government organized itself in ways that apparently made it more nimble and flexible in economic decisions than is often the case. A good example is the government's response to the oil crisis of 1973, when Mideast oil

---

[5]See the discussion of the *autonomous state,* pp. 62–63.
[6]Sarah Anderson, John Cavanaugh, Chuck Collins, and Eric Benjamin, *Executive Excess 2006.* Published jointly by the Institute for Policy Studies, and United for a Fair Economy.

Southeast Asian stock markets, like this one in the Philippines, were swamped during the currency crisis of 1997.

© Enverga/Sipa Press

producers first founded the OPEC cartel of oil producers and oil prices shot up around the world. It took the South Korean government just five months to produce a sophisticated plan to deal with oil prices.[7] By contrast, U.S. President Jimmy Carter proposed a comprehensive energy policy to Congress at about the same time but could not get anything passed. The United States never has adopted a comprehensive energy policy.

This rosy picture of South Korean development could easily leave a misleading impression of perfection. The regime through this period was, after all, an authoritarian military regime. Also, while it is true that the government did a number of things right and while it is true that it did not have to apply large areas of policy to create rents, still a number of bad investment decisions were made, and individual government officers often were corrupt. In other words, this picture is not perfect, though it was good enough to bring substantial economic growth to the country. In an analysis based on surveys of businesspeople who were asked how often they had to bribe government officials to do business in various countries, the Transparency International organization ranked South Korea thirty-fifth out of 120 countries in its 2004 Corruption

---

[7]Dilip K. Das, *Korean Economic Dynamism* (New York: St. Martin's Press, 1992), p. 149.

Perception Index—ahead of most Third World countries, which tend to be plagued with governmental corruption, but behind almost all advanced industrial democracies. In addition to the drain of governmental corruption on the economy, the close relationships between governmental officials and the directors of state-sponsored monopolies sometimes led to unwise investments, in which a failing business would be propped up by loans engineered from friendly banks by government officials. These are warts on the system, albeit important warts. This remained a system that had lifted South Korea from deep poverty to become the eleventh largest economy in the world. A point was reached in 1997, however, at which the cumulative effects of such inefficiencies caught up with the Korean economy. Several banks either went into bankruptcy or proved to be on the verge of bankruptcy, and the South Korean state was forced, in what was a terrible blow to national pride, to seek financial help from the International Monetary Fund. This money came with strings attached and led to a large-scale reform of South Korea's banking systems. In 1999, South Korea emerged from the general Asian depression more quickly and more strongly than any of its neighbors. This time the state was again heavily involved, as South Korea reformed radically. Currently, South Korea's economy is growing strongly.

It is not clear what we should conclude from these two cases about governmental intervention and economic growth. There are a large number of states around the world—not just Ghana, but most African states, the former Soviet Union, and many others—in which governmental intervention has been associated with economic stagnation or even collapse. There are a smaller number where interventionist governments have been associated with strong growth—Japan and smaller Asian countries such as South Korea and Taiwan, but also a country such as France, which has long been noted for its state's strong intervention in the economy. There are several other states, among them Hong Kong and the United States, where noninterventionist governments have presided over prosperity. Finally, many other countries, especially in Latin America, have seen their economies improve markedly when their governments became less interventionist.

Let me offer a speculation, based on these cases: The South Korean case suggests that a crucial factor may be the autonomy of the state apparatus. It is possible that all noninterventionist governments, whether or not their state apparatus is autonomous, offer a good possibility for reliable growth, but that for interventionist governments, autonomy may be the thing that distinguishes success from failure.[8] According to this thesis, a relatively autonomous, interventionist government would be able to guide successful growth (witness the Korean and French governments). But less autonomous governments would be subject to so many rent-seeking claims that if they were interventionist the money they might wish to guide into constructive investment would be diverted instead to pay off supporters and cronies with wasteful projects or subsidies. In other words, it is possible that all noninterventionist states can grow reasonably well, but that of interventionist states, only those that are also fairly autonomous can grow well.

_____

[8]However, both the United States and Great Britain, with relatively noninterventionist governments, did go through years of stagnation in the 1970s.

I do not want to make too much of this argument—free-market systems like that of the United States often have their own sorts of waste—but state autonomy, interacting with interventionist or noninterventionist strategies, may be part of the explanation.

✦ ECONOMIC PERFORMANCE II: CONTROLLING INFLATION AND UNEMPLOYMENT

Another important question about the state and the economy is whether and how the state can control the twin problems of inflation and unemployment.

Inflation

Inflation is a general rise in prices, which means that the currency is worth less than it used to be. Prices of one or another thing will always go up or down, of course, but if prices of most things are rising, that is inflation; a dollar can then no longer buy as much as it could the year before. If everyone could simply adjust to such changes each year, inflation would be no problem. However, inflation hits different people differently. A person on a fixed income, such as an old person living on a pension, is badly hurt by inflation. Other people may make a great deal of money from it.

Inflation occurs when consumers and governments have a large amount of money to spend, relative to the supply of things they want to buy. This condition, called "excess demand," means that potential purchasers bid against each other for scarce goods; this then drives up the price of the goods. It is important to note that this is a relative relationship: a large amount of money, *relative* to the supply of things. As such, many different factors can shift this relative balance in the direction of inflation:

- A frequent cause is deficit spending by governments. If a government spends more than it takes in taxes, this puts extra money to work without taking a corresponding amount out of private consumption through taxes. In this way, the "money to spend" side of the inflationary balance is raised.

- Another possible cause is a shortage in important goods. Bad storms, resulting in a low harvest of grain, can cause inflation by reducing the "supply of things" side of the inflationary balance. A prolonged strike in a major industry such as steel or automobiles can have much the same effect. Similarly, in the 1970s, the major oil producers of the Mideast cut their production of oil in order to force prices up, and this kicked off serious inflation in all other countries of the world. Any of these things can reduce the "supply of things" side of the inflationary balance.

- Monopolies, which allow one company or a group of companies to raise prices without having to worry that their customers will shift to another provider, also contribute to inflation.

- Relatedly, trade restrictions between countries can give full or partial monopolies to local providers (since people cannot easily buy from producers in another country) and drive prices up.

Modern economies usually have some inflation, and societies are not badly disturbed by low, regular inflation of less than 5 percent or so a year. When inflation gets higher than that, it has two bad effects: (1) it churns the society up, accelerating the rise and fall of people's circumstances; social change accelerates, creating big winners and big losers in the process. And (2) it diverts a good deal of people's energy into figuring out how to circumvent the effects of inflation, rather than how to invest productively.

In many states, at various times inflation has run at high levels. In 1994, for instance, China's inflation rate was 21 percent, Venezuela's was 69 percent, Turkey's was 108 percent, Russia's was 150 percent, and Brazil's was 3,173 percent. That is, prices in Brazil were thirty-one times what they had been the year before! A popular joke in Brazil at the time was that it was cheaper to take a taxi than to ride a bus, because with a bus you paid when you got on, while with a taxi you paid at the end of the trip, when the money you gave the driver was worth less than at the beginning of the trip. Levels of inflation like this can cause terrible hardship; this type of inflation destroys everyone's savings as effectively as if every bank in the country had failed. If the money you had saved was worth one thirty-first at the end of the year what it was worth at the beginning of the year, you have effectively lost all of it. One of many stories of personal tragedy in the hyperinflation that struck Germany in the early 1920s (and that many historians think contributed to the rise of Adolph Hitler, because he offered hope from the misery) is of a retired conductor of the Berlin Philharmonic Orchestra who withdrew his life savings from the bank, bought a subway ticket with the money (all it would buy), rode once around his beloved city, went home, and put a bullet through his head.

A remarkable worldwide development in the late 1990s was that in most countries of the world, inflation dropped a great deal. There were a variety of causes for this. A number of countries reduced their government's budget deficits, which helped to cut inflation. Also, commodities such as oil remained reasonably cheap.[9] Probably the most important reason was that with the end of the Cold War and with various initiatives to make world trade more free and open, companies faced worldwide competition, making it difficult for them to raise prices. Disinflation almost took on a life of its own, sweeping all countries along. Whatever the cause, inflation in the United States was down to 2.4 percent in 2006, and in Canada to 2.0 percent—both relatively low levels compared with the 1990s. Of the countries previously mentioned, many had reduced inflation a good deal: China's inflation rate was down to 2.7 percent, Brazil's to 3.0 percent, Russia's to 7.8 percent, Turkey's to 10.2 percent, and Venezuela's to 20.4 percent.

✦ UNEMPLOYMENT

Unemployment is a situation in which not enough jobs are available for everyone who wants to work. There is always some amount of unemployment present in any economy as people move from one occupation to another and are temporarily without jobs. Often, however—in fact, most of the time—economies have more unemployment than this minimum base. If a factory closes in a town and unemployed workers do not move away immediately, 20 or 30 percent of available workers in that town may be unemployed. Or throughout a state, economic activity may lessen so that large numbers of people cannot find jobs even if they are prepared to move.

---

[9]Although, when they began rising again in the 2000s this did *not* kick off inflation.

Unemployment hurts society in two ways. First, those who are without work are devastated, because supporting oneself is a basic requirement for social respect in most societies. Being unable to find a productive use of one's time robs one of most claims to social standing, so a society with high unemployment is a society with many wasted souls. Second, unemployment is dreadfully inefficient. The economy would benefit if everyone who wanted to work productively could do so. There would be more manufactured goods, more food, more available medical care, more of everything.

To some extent, at least in the short run, controlling unemployment involves a trade-off with controlling inflation. As noted in the preceding section, inflation occurs when goods are in short supply and money is readily available, so that many buyers chase few goods and drive prices up by bidding against each other. Governments' main tool to counteract this is to raise the interest rates that people must pay for loans. (A form of government intervention that even economists like!) As interest rates go up, fewer people borrow money, and the amount of money in play declines. Therefore, governments can fairly readily lower inflation by reducing the amount of money available to chase goods.

The problem is that when interest rates go up like this, economic activity declines and, at least in the short term, unemployment rises. Stable, low rates of inflation will eventually allow interest rates to come back down and allow unemployment to drop again—in fact, it will usually drop to a lower level than it had been at before. In the short term, however, fighting inflation by raising interest rates usually cuts back on employment.

Unfortunately, we do not have as clear and simple tools to combat unemployment as we have for inflation. One might think that states could turn interest rates around and lower them to combat unemployment. But, just as the effect of higher interest rates on unemployment was short-term and temporary, so is the effect of lower interest rates. Lowering rates heats up the economy as people borrow more money and spend it, and initially this does produce jobs. Governments often try this, and that is one reason that inflation is no lower around the world than it is. However, this is a temporary effect. The inflation that results from deliberately holding interest rates down in this way causes enough economic dislocation after a short while that unemployment shoots back up anyway. Now you have managed to create inflation *and* unemployment.

Other state measures to combat unemployment have included creation of jobs through government projects. If governments could be quick at doing this, it would be a very effective tool. Surplus labor that would otherwise be wasted could be used for needed investment in roads and schools. The United States did this to a modest extent during the Great Depression under Franklin Roosevelt. However, it is the rare government that can discipline itself to turn job programs on and off quickly as needed. Once a set of jobs is established, a constituency has been created that will now use whatever political power it has in rent-seeking to preserve the jobs as a government subsidy even after the unemployment problem has passed. And, the reverse is true: Governments are not only slow to turn off job programs when they are no longer needed, they are also often unable to get a job program started before the emergency for which it was created is almost over.

One useful tool for governments is to reduce the "natural" unemployment, which is always present as workers move between jobs or look for new work after local factories have closed, by retraining displaced workers and encouraging them to relocate quickly. Sweden has been particularly successful at this, with large retraining programs and support for workers who relocate to find a job. However, while making the labor market operate better in ways like this is helpful, it cannot prevent all unemployment.

Evidence that governments find it difficult to reduce unemployment is offered by numerous Western European states whose governments are strong and skillful and have tried hard to reduce unemployment but continue to have unemployment levels of close to 10 percent. In early 2007, for instance, even though their economies were on the upswing, unemployment levels in some Western European countries were:

Germany	9.2 percent
France	8.6 percent
Italy	6.5 percent
Belgium	11.5 percent
Spain	8.6 percent

These numbers mean, for instance, that of all people in Belgium who were ready and willing to work, one out of every nine did not have a job.[10]

The key to governments' efforts to minimize both unemployment and inflation, as well as sustain economic growth, is to maintain a balance. Low inflation, low unemployment, and high rates of growth are all good things, but each of them is caused by numerous factors. And, tools that improve one of these three often make one or both of the others worse. (Raising interest rates to cool down inflation, for instance, will usually slow economic growth and raise unemployment.)

Some factors, however, improve all three simultaneously. Education, for instance, gives workers more flexible skills so that they are able to adapt more readily as jobs shift; it reduces inflation, by making work forces more efficient so that products can be priced more cheaply; and it feeds economic growth. Technological innovation also has a benign effect on all three. It lowers the cost of making things, which lowers inflation; and companies make strong profits because of their lowered costs, so they are able to expand their work forces. This means that unemployment stays low. Some think that the long period of strong growth in the United States starting in the 1990s, combined with low inflation and low unemployment, was the result of technological innovation in the computer industry and the World Wide Web. Technological innovation and good education are two of the best economic tools available to government.

→ MANAGING DISTRIBUTION TO ADDRESS INEQUALITY

At the outset of this chapter, I noted that not only was the overall performance of the economy important, but also the distribution of goods within the economy. We care not just about how much wealth is generated in the economy but how that wealth is shared among the people of the state.[11]

---

[10]By way of comparison, unemployment at the time in the United States was 4.5 percent and in Japan, 4.0 percent.
[11]In the present chapter, we will look primarily at economic policies and distribution; in Chapter 6 we will look at the normative questions lying behind the issue of how much the government *should* try to reduce inequalities and of which sorts.

Governments play a role not only in the overall level of economic activity but also in *distribution* within the economy. They have two options if they want to create greater equality: (1) special subsidies and aids for the poor and (2) systems of **progressive taxation.** A progressive tax is one that takes a greater percentage of income from a person who is relatively well off and a smaller percentage from one who is not doing so well. Graduated income taxes are designed to be progressive, though they are often filled with loopholes that benefit the better off (which makes the tax less progressive). For instance, if an income tax is set up so that a person earning $10,000 a year pays no tax, while a person earning $20,000 a year pays $2,000 (10 percent of that income) and a person earning $50,000 pays $10,000 (20 percent of that income), then the tax is progressive.

Not all taxes are progressive. Many are **regressive** in that they take a higher percentage of poor people's income than they do of the income of those who are better off. The Social Security tax in the United States is an example. In 2007, workers in the United States had to pay 6.2 percent of their income to Social Security, up to a maximum income of $97,500. Any income over this amount was untaxed; thus, a person earning

"I need some short-term economic stimulus."

TABLE 5.1

Income Inequality in Selected States, 2005

Country (GDP per capita in parentheses)*	Democratic/Non since 1975	Percent of Income Earned by Poorest 20% of Population	Percent of Income Earned by Richest 20% of Population	Difference
United States ($40,100)	democratic	5	46	41
Canada (31,500)	democratic	7	40	33
Great Britain (29,600)	democratic	6	44	38
Sweden (28,400)	democratic	9	37	28
Slovenia (19,600)	mixed	9	36	27
Portugal (17,900)	mixed	6	46	40
Brazil (8,100)	mixed	2	63	61
Belarus (6,800)	nondemocratic	8	39	31
Philippines (5,000)	mixed	5	52	47
India (3,100)	democratic	9	43	34
Côte d'Ivoire (1,500)	mixed	5	51	46

*Purchasing power parity.

SOURCE: World Bank Group, *World Development Indicators* online, 2007; "Democratic/non since 1945," adapted from Adam Przeworski et al., *Democracy and Development* (New York: Cambridge University Press, 2000), appendix 1.2; 2005 GDP per capita from CIA, *World Factbook Online,* Field Listing, revised April 21, 2005.

$30,000 a year paid 6.2 percent of that in Social Security, while a person earning $140,000 a year paid $6,045 (that is, 6.2 percent of $97,500) in tax, which was only 4.3 percent of the $140,000 income.

In the United States over recent years, taking all sorts of levies into account, the progressive and regressive taxes have just about canceled one another out, though with mild progressivity, so that people's relative incomes have been just about the same before and after taxes.[12] That is to say, tax policies overall have not changed the distribution of incomes very much.

Table 5.1 displays income inequalities in a number of countries. In the table, the percentage of all income that goes to the poorest 20 percent is compared with the percentage of all income that goes to the richest 20 percent of the population. The greater this difference is, the more unequally are incomes distributed.

---

[12]Thomas Piketty and Emmanuel Saez, "How Progressive Is the U.S. Federal Tax System? A Historical and International Perspective," National Bureau of Economic Research working paper #12404, July 2006. In 2004 the poorest group in the study, the second quintile of the population, had 6.1 percent of national income before taxes, and this rose to 7.2 percent of national income after federal taxes were taken into account; the richest group (the top one-hundredth of one percent) dipped from 3.0 percent of pre-tax national income to 2.5 percent of after-tax national income. Though the taxes were progressive, they operated very gently.

Several things are apparent in this table. First, poorer states are often burdened with considerably greater inequality of incomes than developed economies. It is paradoxical that in the midst of poverty, especially in Asian and Latin American states, there may be found a small group of people who are quite rich. Modern development—with its widespread education, mobility of populations, trade unions, and so on—alleviates inequality compared to countries with backward economies, where deep inequalities may be present. As seen from the first column (per capita GDP), the states are arrayed in the table from richest (top) to poorest (bottom). Although there are plenty of exceptions, in general as we move lower in the table, disparities between rich and poor become larger. The average difference between the poor and the rich (fifth column) is 34.5 for the six richest countries, 43.8 for the poorest five.

Second, we also see that democracy makes a difference, as was the case with regard to social welfare policies, as discussed in Chapter 4. Where government is accountable to the broad population, it is more likely to make an effort to ease the situation of the large numbers who are not well off. This shows up in Table 5.1, where it is likely to account for India's unusual performance.

The table also shows that when governments make a special effort to do so, they can redistribute incomes somewhat. Belarus, which was part of the Soviet Union, still has a rather unreconstructed communist-led government, and it continues the communist tradition of promoting equality. Among industrialized democracies, Sweden, with its string of socialist governments and a strongly communal culture, has made special efforts to redistribute income, through large and steeply progressive income taxes. India, one of the poorest states in Table 5.1, has made real efforts at redistribution. We can see in the table that these states' efforts have made a difference.

The clearest message of the table, however, is that incomes are unequal in *all* systems. On any absolute scale, variations among these governments have made rather little difference. The truth is, those who have high incomes usually also have a good deal of political clout and are able to defend their interests vigorously. Whether it is the landowners of Brazil or the privileged bureaucrats of Belarus, those who are well off in society generally make sure that governmental redistribution does not bite very deeply.

✦ INDEPENDENT CENTRAL BANKS

In the first four sections of this chapter, we have looked at three general areas in which governments take responsibility for the proper functioning of the economy: growth, inflation and unemployment, and inequality. In doing so, we have looked at a number of the things governments can do to accomplish these things, and we have looked at some of the things that stand in their way. We will conclude the chapter by looking at one major tool: independent central banks, discussed in this section; and at one major impediment: corruption, discussed in the next section.

One institutional tool that many think can help governments make effective economic policy is a relatively independent central bank. A **central bank** is a bank that is set up by a government to help handle its transactions; to coordinate the policies of private banks; and above all, to control interest rates either by lending its reserves freely (to lower interest charges by increasing the amount of money in circulation) or by increasing its reserves (to pull money out of circulation and thus raise interest rates). Every modern state has such a bank. In the United States, it is called the Federal Reserve Bank; in Britain, it is the Bank of England; in Germany, the Bundesbank.

Though each of these banks is set up by the state and is thus a public agency, central banks vary from one state to another in how autonomous they are of the state's political leaders. Some central banks operate independently, while some are controlled by political leaders. What constitutes "autonomy" may be fairly subtle since the political leaders do after all appoint the directors of the bank. Britain, for instance, extended greater autonomy to the Bank of England in 1994 by starting to publish the minutes of the monthly meeting of the governor of the bank and the chancellor of the Exchequer (similar to the Treasury secretary in the United States). Publishing the minutes made it more difficult for the chancellor to direct the bank to take actions that the bank's governor deemed unwise. This may not look like much, but in the stately world of high finance, it was seen as a major step toward bank independence.[13]

Why might it be important for the central bank to be independent of the government's political leaders? Using interest rates to control inflation requires unpopular decisions. In particular, raising interest rates to cut back on economic growth when jobs are expanding rapidly is not a good way to make friends! One chair of the Federal Reserve Bank once said that its job was "to take away the punch bowl when it looks as though people are beginning to enjoy the party." For this reason, political scientists and economists have long thought that a central bank that was closely controlled by political leaders would not work very hard to reduce inflation and that if a state wanted to keep inflation low, it should make its central bank fairly autonomous.

Indeed, as seen in Figure 5.2, states with relatively independent central banks tend to have stronger records on inflation than those whose central banks are more directly run by the government. Germany, with the most independent central bank, averaged about 4 percent inflation from 1972 to 1989, while Spain, Norway, and Belgium, with the least independent banks, averaged inflation of almost 9 percent. It is also the case, not shown on this figure, that when Britain extended more independence to the Bank of England in 1994, that change was indeed followed by an unusually bold increase in interest rates. Thus, there would seem to be something to this.

However, it often happens in political science that although two things coincide, it is not clear which causes which. It might appear obvious from the figure that independent central banks bring lower inflation, but it is at least possible that things are the other way around. It might be that in states where inflation is reasonably low, so that central banks do not have to do the unpopular thing too often, the state's leaders are willing to tolerate a good deal of autonomy in their central bank. If the bank has to make people angry fairly often, however, the leaders may act to take control of it and stop it from raising rates so frequently. In other words, it could be that low inflation creates the conditions for independent central banks, rather than the other way around. There is some evidence for this. Javier Ortiz Batalla shows that many Latin American

---

[13]In 1997, the newly elected Labour government went even further and gave the Bank of England full, formal independence from the cabinet.

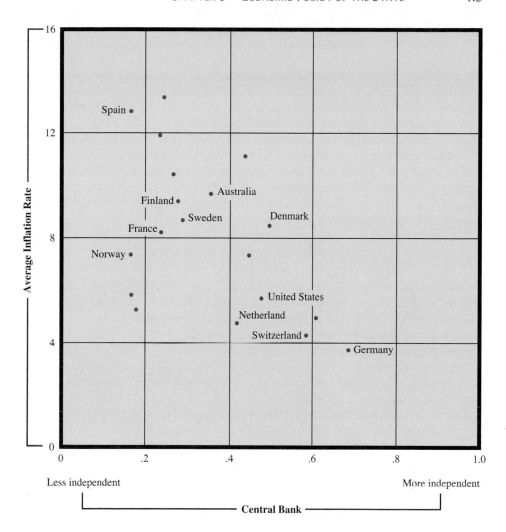

FIGURE 5.2   Inflation and central-bank independence. Annual average inflation rate (percent), 1972–1989.

SOURCES: World Bank, *World Development Indicators 2002;* Alex Cukierman, Steven B. Webb, and Bilin Neyapti, "Measuring the Independence of Central Banks and Its Effect on Policy Outcomes," 6 *World Bank Economic Review* (1992), pp. 353–398.

states had established rather autonomous central banks by the late 1920s but that under the pressures of the high inflation of the mid-1930s, most took away that autonomy.[14] In these cases, it looks as though high inflation may have produced central banks that were closely directed by their governments, rather than vice versa.

---

[14]Javier Ortiz Batalla, *Essays on the Early History of Latin American Central Banking,* Ph.D. dissertation in economics, University of California–Los Angeles, 1993.

Thus, there are two possible stories to tell about the picture in Figure 5.2 and some evidence for each. This is often the case in political science because we do not have the experimenter's luxury of controlling which things will vary and under what conditions. We have to take our coincidences where we find them and interpret them to the best of our ability. This does not mean we must throw up our hands, however. In this example, for instance, while both possibilities are plausible, the first is probably more compelling. There is strong reason to believe that political leaders, if they controlled banks, would allow higher inflation than independent bankers would otherwise have allowed, and thus most people would find it hard to reject that explanation.

On the other hand, the presence of a second potential explanation, with some attendant evidence, makes us keep our eyes open and seek further evidence to help us choose between the two. This is actually a fairly typical example of how political science develops its ideas in all areas.

✦ CORRUPTION

Another political-economic condition that affects the functioning of economies is the degree of **corruption** in the society: that is, the use of public resources for private gain. Our concern is with officials performing their public tasks improperly to receive personal benefits: elected officials selling their votes, police overlooking crimes in return for a bribe, a housing inspector ignoring an unsafe building in return for a favor, and so on.

Frankly, I have never been quite sure where to deal with corruption in this book. It is not a factor only in economic policy, which is the main focus of this chapter; certainly, corruption relates to politics and policy well beyond economics. If a voter accepts a payoff in exchange for voting a certain way, that is corruption, for instance, even though it is not part of economic policy. On the other hand, corruption usually does involve an exchange of cash or of something with cash value. In that sense, it represents a meeting ground of sorts for politics and the economy. And, as we will note in this section, the level of corruption in government influences powerfully how the economy functions. So, this chapter seems as reasonable a location as any for the discussion of corruption.

One might first ask, why bother about corruption? It has always been present in human exchange, and there does not seem to be much we can do about it. It may even be the case that corruption occasionally serves good purposes by greasing the skids for commerce. The answer to this is twofold. First, the effects of corruption are horrid, and it is not something society should tolerate. Second, while it does surely exist everywhere, it is worse in some places than in others, so there are clearly things we can do about it.

What does corruption do to the community? Its worst effect may be to produce cynicism, lack of faith, and disregard for the rule of law. This can also contribute to broader political instability; from the earlier description of Nigerian state building (p. 68), you will recall that the Nigerian military overthrew the democratic government over charges of corruption—and it was largely because of the corruption of the democratic government that the military takeover was widely accepted.

Corruption also has direct economic costs. Some of these are obvious and dramatic, such as the billions of dollars the dictator Saddam Hussein extracted from Iraq's economy for himself and his family. More generally, the cost of government services not properly provided and the inflated cost of government programs due to corruption reduce economic growth and the benefits we receive from governmental services. It is estimated that as of the early 1990s corruption had added as much as 15 percent, or $200 billion, to Italy's national debt.[15] The Turkish minister of energy and natural resources charged in 2003 that because of corruption honest citizens paid 36 percent more tax than they should pay.[16] A new Internet-based procurement system that Mexico introduced in the late 1990s reduced the Mexican government's purchasing costs by 15 percent, largely by eliminating the personal dealings that breed corruption.[17] Corruption does not always involve bribes. "Personal gain" may result from cozy relationships between vendors and government purchasing agents in the form of job prospects for the purchasing agents when they leave the government or from the connection between moneyed interests and candidates to whom they made large contributions, or in the form of large campaign contributions to candidates. These may be part of the background on the recurrent miniscandals in government purchasing in the United States, including no-bid contracts in the Iraq War that went to campaign contributors, and favorable treatment in Congressional bills for interest groups and corporations that have contributed to members' campaigns. Though illegal bribes for personal gain appear to be relatively rare in the United States, money clearly distorts policy through organizational behavior, in a system of "legal corruption."

Corruption becomes a culture that spills into all aspects of life. A vivid example of this is offered by parking tickets issued by New York City police to United Nations diplomats. Since they have diplomatic immunity, no states' diplomats to the United Nations may be prosecuted in New York; diplomats can, if they are so inclined, ignore "no parking" signs and throw away any tickets that are issued to them. It turns out that diplomats from states that do not have much corruption are law-abiding even when they do not have to be; it is a habit, a cultural predisposition. For instance, in a study of diplomats and parking tickets, there were no tickets issued to envoys from Sweden, Denmark, Japan, Israel, Norway, or Canada—all states with low levels of corruption. (See the box on page 116.) Members of the Kuwait mission averaged 246 unpaid tickets apiece, and diplomats from Chad, Sudan, Pakistan, and Ethiopia also had large numbers of tickets. All of these are states that score high on corruption in the box.[18]

What can be done about corruption? First, corruption is not equally pervasive everywhere, and that should give us some hope. If it varies, there must be reasons that cause it to be greater in one place than another. Unfortunately, a number of these reasons do not offer much leverage. Societies undergoing rapid change often appear susceptible to corruption, partly because norms of behavior are in flux so people do not have stable moral guides for behavior and partly because there are so many opportunities for corruption in a situation of rapid economic change. Two good examples of this today are China and Russia, where corruption has exploded in the shift away from planned economies. This doesn't help us much, though—should we tell societies not to undergo rapid change?

---

[15]"The Destructive Cost of Greasing Palms," *BusinessWeek,* 6 December 1993, p. 138.
[16]Transparency International daily corruption news, July 15, 2003, www.transparency.org.
[17]"Stopping the Rot in Public Life," *The Economist,* 16 September 2000, p. 41.
[18]David Brooks, "The Culture of Nations." *New York Times,* August 13, 2006, section 4, p. 11.

Corruption, on a Scale of 0 to 10

Transparency International, an international organization dedicated to documenting and tracing levels of governmental corruption, has ranked countries for 2004 by their level of corruption. The ranking was done by combining several polls of businesspeople rating agencies as to how much corruption there is in governments they've worked with. A score of 10 means politics is totally clean; 0 means that it is totally corrupt. Here are the scores of the 163 states and regions in the study.

Country	Score	Country	Score	Country	Score	Country	Score
Finland	9.6	South Korea	5.1	Madagascar	3.1	Russia	2.5
Iceland	9.6	Malaysia	5.0	Mauritania	3.1	Rwanda	2.5
New Zealand	9.6	Italy	4.9	Panama	3.1	Swaziland	2.5
Denmark	9.5	Czech Republic	4.8	Romania	3.1	Azerbaijan	2.4
Singapore	9.4	Kuwait	4.8	Sri Lanka	3.1	Burundi	2.4
Sweden	9.2	Lithuania	4.8	Gabon	3.0	Central African	
Switzerland	9.1	Latvia	4.7	Serbia	3.0	Republic	2.4
Norway	8.8	Slovakia	4.7	Suriname	3.0	Ethiopia	2.4
Australia	8.7	South Africa	4.6	Argentina	2.9	Indonesia	2.4
Netherlands	8.7	Tunisia	4.6	Armenia	2.9	Papua New	
Austria	8.6	Dominica	4.5	Bosnia/		Guinea	2.4
Luxembourg	8.6	Greece	4.4	Herzegovina	2.9	Togo	2.4
Great Britain	8.6	Costa Rica	4.1	Eritrea	2.9	Zimbabwe	2.4
Canada	8.5	Namibia	4.1	Syria	2.9	Cameroon	2.3
Hong Kong	8.3	Bulgaria	4.0	Tanzania	2.9	Ecuador	2.3
Germany	8.0	El Salvador	4.0	Dominican		Niger	2.3
Japan	7.6	Colombia	3.9	Republic	2.8	Venezuela	2.3
France	7.4	Turkey	3.8	Georgia	2.8	Angola	2.2
Ireland	7.4	Jamaica	3.7	Mali	2.8	Congo, Republic	2.2
Belgium	7.3	Poland	3.7	Mongolia	2.8	Kenya	2.2
Chile	7.3	Lebanon	3.6	Ukraine	2.8	Kyrgyzstan	2.2
United States	7.3	Seychelles	3.6	Bolivia	2.7	Nigeria	2.2
Spain	6.8	Thailand	3.6	Iran	2.7	Pakistan	2.2
Barbados	6.7	Belize	3.5	Libya	2.7	Sierra Leone	2.2
Estonia	6.7	Cuba	3.5	Macedonia	2.7	Tajikistan	2.2
Macao	6.6	Grenada	3.5	Malawi	2.7	Turkmenistan	2.2
Portugal	6.6	Croatia	3.4	Uganda	2.7	Belarus	2.1
Malta	6.4	Brazil	3.3	Albania	2.6	Cambodia	2.1
Slovenia	6.4	China	3.3	Guatemala	2.6	Côte d'Ivoire	2.1
Uruguay	6.4	Egypt	3.3	Kazakhstan	2.6	Equatorial	
United Arab		Ghana	3.3	Laos	2.6	Guinea	2.1
Emirates	6.2	India	3.3	Nicaragua	2.6	Uzbekistan	2.1
Bhutan	6.0	Mexico	3.3	Paraguay	2.6	Bangladesh	2.0
Qatar	6.0	Peru	3.3	Timor-Leste	2.6	Chad	2.0
Israel	5.9	Saudi Arabia	3.3	Vietnam	2.6	Congo, Democratic	
Taiwan	5.9	Senegal	3.3	Yemen	2.6	Republic	2.0
Bahrain	5.7	Burkina Faso	3.2	Zambia	2.6	Sudan	2.0
Botswana	5.6	Lesotho	3.2	Benin	2.5	Guinea	1.9
Cyprus	5.6	Moldova	3.2	Gambia	2.5	Iraq	1.9
Oman	5.4	Morocco	3.2	Guyana	2.5	Myanmar	1.9
Jordan	5.3	Trinidad and		Honduras	2.5	Haiti	1.8
Hungary	5.2	Tobago	3.2	Nepal	2.5		
Mauritius	5.1	Algeria	3.1	Philippines	2.5		

Continued

Corruption, on a Scale of 0 to 10   *Continued*

Prosperous, developed states of North America and Europe tend to have the cleanest records, though Singapore (9.4), Hong Kong (8.3), Chile (7.3), Barbados (6.7), Slovenia (6.4), and Uruguay (6.4) show that non-Western, poorer states are not necessarily corrupt; and Italy (4.9) shows that prosperous, industrialized states are not necessarily clean. The United States does not show up especially well with its score of 7.3. Canada looks good with its score of 8.5

The presence of foreign businesses has also been noted as a catalyst for corruption, because they may seem like easy marks and are often better situated financially than local officials, so that what may be a huge bribe to the official may look like a normal expense to the foreign business.

Other things that have been found to be associated with corruption are low average incomes, intense factional competition, non-Protestant religious traditions, and a history of colonial rule by some country other than Great Britain.[19]

These are interesting, but none of them are things we can do much about. However, Transparency International has developed a "National Integrity System" that does provide a framework for things a state can do to reduce corruption.[20] Essentially, the National Integrity System prescribes strong watchdog officials, especially in Congress or Parliament, and in an attorney-general and auditor-general; establishment of independent anticorruption agencies; clear and transparent procedures for public procurement; a free and open flow of information to the media; and encouragement of a highly developed civil society.

Many other specific measures can also help. The Foreign Corrupt Practices Act, which bans U.S. multinational corporations from including bribes as part of their operating budgets, has probably helped to reduce corruption in other countries. In an attempt to reduce bribery, Russia in 2001 reduced the number of business activities that require a license (an obvious opportunity for bribery) from 2,000 to just 100. Even a simple change like moving Mexico's border customs posts to the actual border, rather than miles away where it was difficult to oversee the inspectors, helped to reduce corruption.[21]

---

[19]Wayne Sandholtz and William Koetzle, "Accounting for Corruption: Economic Structure, Democracy, and Trade," *International Studies Quarterly* 44 (2000), pp. 31–50; Daniel Treisman, "The Causes of Corruption: A Cross-National Study," *Journal of Public Economics* 76 (2000), pp. 399–457; Marcia Walecki, "Political Corruption: Democracy's Hidden Disease," *Democracy at Large* 2 (Winter, 2006), pp. 16–19.
[20]The National Integrity System is assessed in a comparative case study of eighteen countries in Alan Doig and Stephanie McIvor, "The National Integrity System: Assessing Corruption and Reform," *Public Administration and Development* 23 (2003), pp. 317–32.
[21]Tina Rosenberg, "The Taint of the Greased Palm," *The New York Times Magazine*, August 10, 2003, pp. 28–33.

→ Other Measures Available to Government

A number of policies are available to governments to pursue their general goals of encouraging growth, controlling inflation and unemployment, and shaping the distribution of wealth. We have looked here in some detail at two such policies: maintenance of independent central banks and combating corruption. Others include:

- Measures to increase the rate at which people in the society save, which thus makes more money available for investment. The main tools for this are various tax breaks to benefit saving and investment.

- Measures to maintain competition among companies, which forces them to keep their prices down or risk losing their customers. The main tools for this are regulation to prevent a single company or a couple of companies establishing a monopoly in a particular product.

- Measures to increase education, which makes everyone in the society more productive.

- Measures to make it easier for workers to move from one job to another, which reduces unemployment. The main tools for this are retraining programs and unemployment compensation.

- Research and development to develop new technology that will build new businesses or make older ones more productive.

- Measures such as the graduated income tax or social welfare programs to redistribute the fruits of the economy.

In a sense, we have come full circle. I said at the beginning of Chapter 4 that we would set aside political economy and economic policy for separate treatment in this chapter. In looking back at the policies I have bulleted above, however, you should see that many of the policies a state can follow to direct its economy are policies we looked at in their own right in Chapter 4. The truth is that the economy is so bound together with society as a whole that all policies are economic policies and economic policy affects everything else in society as well. For all that, the economy is a particularly critical part of the society. We have only been able to scratch the surface of the concern for political economy in political science or of the variety of questions revolving around economic policy. These concerns will arise repeatedly in succeeding chapters.

→ Globalization: Are States Losing Their Ability to Make Economic Policy?

We have reviewed in this chapter the range of things states can do to manage their economies. However, the development of a freely moving global economy today calls into question how much room for maneuver governments will actually have in the future. States may see themselves diminished, not by a formal reallocation of their powers but by the growth of actors and processes they cannot control as worldwide economic and social functions begin to operate as a single unit in "globalization."[22] In this case, whole areas of economic policy in which the state might want to act may prove impossible for it to control. The state remains a state; it is just that the range of things the state has the capacity to control may have shrunk. In effect, the state is not challenged in its formal capacity but is hollowed out by a shrinkage in the range of things it can actually do. With the development of a large and fluid world economy, the world's investors and capital markets probably determine the state's economic development so strongly that the state—its government, its central bank—actually has only a rather narrow range of choice in economic policies.[23]

As late as 1970, trade (exports plus imports) was only 8 percent of the U.S. gross national product, but by 2006, it had grown to be 22 percent. For smaller countries, trade usually bulks even larger; for Denmark in the same year, the sum of exports and imports was 71 percent of the gross national product, and for Belgium, it was 182 percent. The international currency markets *each day* move more than a trillion dollars around the world—far more than any state's government or central bank can command. Most large corporations spread their operations over many states and, as a result, are not under strict control by any one state. In 1973, for instance, the U.S. government tried to order Exxon (an American company) to deliver oil to the United States despite an Arab oil embargo; Exxon replied that it could not do so, because it was subject to the laws not only of the United States but of the other states in which it operated.

Under these circumstances, states have begun to find that if their economic policies are too unlike those of their neighbors or look too suspicious to international investors, then capital flees their country and the economy turns down. As a result, all states have found themselves forced into the same relatively narrow range of economic policy alternatives.

The classic example of this is the socialist regime of Francois Mitterrand in France. In 1981, France elected Mitterrand to be its first socialist president since 1958. He immediately began a fairly radical expansionist and redistributive program. Family allowances (cash payments to families with children) were raised by 81 percent over two years. Housing allocations for the poor were raised 25 percent. All workers were given a fifth week of paid vacation. Pensions were increased. As a result of these efforts, unemployment dropped and the economy grew more rapidly than other European economies. Incomes became more equal.

However, the rapid expansion of people's purchasing power led to a surge of imports from other countries. France was soon importing far more than it exported, and the value of its currency dropped. Inflation climbed because this made all imported goods more expensive (each import had to be paid for with more francs). Inflation was also pushed up by the increase in domestic demand.

International investors (and French investors as well), fearful that the francs they were holding would lose value because of the inflation, exchanged their francs for dollars,

---

[22]See the discussion of globalization above, page 64.
[23]This theme is developed especially in Jeffrey A. Frieden, *Debt, Development and Democracy* (Princeton: Princeton University Press, 1991); Sven Steinmo, *Taxation and Democracy* (New Haven: Yale University Press, 1993); and Peter Hall, "The Political Economy of Europe in an Era of Interdependence," in *Continuity and Change in Contemporary Capitalism,* ed. Herbert Kitschelt et al. (New York: Cambridge University Press, 1999).

marks, and yen. No one wanted francs, so their value went even lower. Mitterrand's government was faced with a crisis, and within a year of having taken over as president, he abandoned his program to increase jobs and make incomes more equal. Never again in the twelve additional years that Mitterrand served as president would he move far from the middle of the road in economic policy.

A more recent example of international constraints on governmental policy was seen in 1998, when international investors suddenly became concerned about the financial reliability of several Southeast Asian states, such as Thailand, Indonesia, South Korea, and Malaysia, that had been growing rapidly. The investment community pulled out its money, and the economies of these countries went into abrupt recession. It was only after the governments of these states made changes in their financial regulation—especially of banks—that capital returned and economic recovery ensued.

A further constraint on many of the world's poorest states—which might otherwise be expected to be rather experimental and innovative with their economic policies, because their current circumstances are so bad—is that they are by now heavily in debt to richer countries and to international banks. The International Monetary Fund (IMF) monitors these states and sets conditions under which the holders of the debt will be willing to stretch out countries' repayments. The IMF's conditions usually involve cautious economic policies: restraining government spending (especially reducing transfers within the population through subsidies) and raising interest rates to fight inflation. Even though many of these policies will be unpopular, debtor states' governments often feel they must abide by them. The only alternative is to refuse to pay their debts at all, which means no one would lend them anything in the future. That is a dead end because they all need capital if they are to develop their economies.

The overall result of all this has been that the states of the world—from rich, industrial states such as France to poor states such as Côte d'Ivoire—are constrained to follow a more or less uniform set of economic policies, regardless of what their governments might otherwise have wished to do.

This is only the most dramatic instance of the general phenomenon of globalization. As world communications improve and as the world's states come to depend more on each other economically, if we are to understand what happens "within" a state's politics, we must look at least in part to the state's international environment. To paraphrase the British cleric, John Donne: No state is an island, entire of itself. (Even if it *is* an island; an island country such as Britain, with total trade equal to 44 percent of its gross national product, can no more ignore the world economy than could Mitterrand's France.)

✦ POLITICAL ECONOMY

The economy in its relationship to politics is so important that a whole subfield has opened up in the field of political science to study it. The subfield of **political economy** within political science focuses on how the state and the economy interact. A large part of this subfield involves analysis of economic policy, in which we look at how the state's government influences the economy. That is what we have looked at in this chapter.

But the economy also influences the state, and that is another important part of what is studied in political economy. As one example of this, an important set of questions addressed by political economy is, "Why do states exist?" You will recall that in Chapter 3, I raised the question of why states arose in Europe in the sixteenth, seventeenth, and eighteenth centuries. Though I did not label the discussion as such, this came right out of political economy; the question was whether the driving force was the new economic activity of the time that created a *need* for the state to be invented or whether it was the new technology of weapons and communication that *made it possible* for the state to be invented. In other words, we were looking at how economic developments influenced the development of states.[24]

Beyond asking how the state influences the economy and how the economy influences the state, another way in which political economy functions in political science is to bring the methods of economics to bear on political science questions. Economists have developed a distinctive style of analysis, which centers on a set of shared assumptions—especially the assumption of "rationality": the assumption that *individuals make their decisions in order to maximize specific goals.* Note that this is a specialized definition of *rational.* By *rational,* we do not mean "sensible" or "wise" but merely that actions are directed to achieving a goal or a set of goals and that they can be analyzed as strategies to meet those goals. Based on the assumption of rationality, plus (usually) other assumptions designed to address a particular theoretic question, economists then derive mathematically what the consequences of those assumptions should be. Such theories are called **rational choice** models. A good example is supply and demand analysis in economics. Based on an assumption that the seller and buyer are trying to maximize the amount of money they retain after a transaction (i.e., that they act "rationally"), plus some assumptions about the information they share, economists predict what price they will agree on under varying circumstances. Conclusions such as these can then be tested by observation, to see whether in the real world people act as one would assume they do based on the assumptions one has used. The box on pages 97–98, "Baumol's Disease," provided another example of this kind of economic reasoning.

This sort of analysis, which was brought into the field of political science by its political economy subfield, has now become so common throughout the field that it is often not labeled explicitly as "political economy." You will see numerous examples of it in the chapters to come. Two examples, which you will recognize when you hit them, are the question of whether it is rational for people to vote, given the small chance that their single vote will change the outcome of a national election (pages 244–245; and the question of under what circumstances rational actors will form an organization for common action (i.e., an "interest group"; box on p. 285). This latter is an application of the general problem of public goods, which was introduced in Chapter 3.

Let me hasten to add that while the "political economy" perspective is widely shared in political science, it does not have hegemony over the field. One of the good

---

[24]In a related argument, some political economists argue that for a market economy to operate, the one basic requirement is that property rights be defined and upheld. Since only the state can do this, they argue, that is the reason states exist. See Douglas North, *Institutions, Institutional Change and Economic Performance* (New York: Cambridge University Press, 1990).

things about political science is that a number of perspectives are able to compete in the field. Not all political scientists would take rationality as a good base assumption for analysis. For instance, another important subfield of political science, **political psychology,** looks at the roles of cognition, emotion, the framing of questions, and so forth in people's political decisions, none of which assume rationality.

Also, the questions we ask include normative questions that go behind the question of rationality to ask not "Are people making decisions in order to further specific goals" (our definition of rationality) but rather, "*Which* goals should people be furthering?" So, political economy is an important approach and probably comes closer than any other to providing the dominant approach in the field of political science—but no approach rules political science entirely.

EXAMPLE

Economic Policy in Germany

From the ruins of World War II, West Germany rose to be one of the world's major economies by the 1970s and 1980s. With its merger with formerly communist East Germany in 1990, united Germany clearly will be an economic giant, even though the East German economy will require a long time before it is a match for its western counterpart. Germany currently has the fifth-largest gross domestic product in the world, topped only by the United States, China, Japan, and India.

German political economy has been characterized by three special things: (1) labor relations and the training of workers that are set up to enhance cooperation and emphasize quality; (2) an economy that has been highly organized through a series of regulations and special government-corporation arrangements known as *Ordnungspolitik* (roughly "policy of structured arrangements" but difficult to translate); and (3) policy that has focused strongly on controlling inflation. We shall look here more specifically at each of these and then look also at a major new challenge: maintaining German productivity so that a high-wage, high-benefit labor system can continue in the face of growing international competition. It is fair to say that with the stresses of globalization, including competition from nearby neighbors like Poland, the German economic model is under intense pressure today.

Labor Policy

Relations between labor and management have been set up since the 1950s to emphasize coopera-tion and the peaceful resolution of conflicts. A German innovation after the war, and an institution that typifies German economic relationships, is the system of **codetermination.** For companies with over two thousand employees, by law half of the members of the board of directors must be representatives of the workers. Therefore, workers are involved, along with shareholders, in the management of each company. In practice, this has led to better pay and benefits, better worker training programs, and increased satisfaction among workers.[25] It may also have contributed to Germany's admirable strike record: In 2000, on any given day an American worker was twenty-nine times as likely to be out on strike as a German worker. Other things that have also probably contributed to this are Germany's pattern of industry-wide, rather than company-specific, nego-tiations between management and labor, and the pattern, seen throughout German politics, of a reliance on cooperation and negotiation more than on confrontation.

Germany also has an unusual system for worker training, which has helped the country build a highly skilled work force. About 30 percent of young Germans go on to the university after high school, but almost all of the remaining 70 percent enter an elaborate system of apprenticeships run by industry. Over 500,000 companies offer apprenticeship training programs in everything from hairdressing to computerized manufacture of optical equipment. High school graduates enroll in these programs for a period of three to three and a half years, receiving one or two days a week of formal academic training in school, with the other days spent at the plant. As of 1996, German firms spent more than $24 billion a year to train apprentices.

As German businesses have faced increasing international competition, however, the ap-prenticeship program, like other parts of the "German model," has come under pressure. Starting in 2000, when the economy hit a soft spot, business began to reduce the number of apprentice-ships they offer. As of 2004 the number had declined to 16 million, down from 18 million in 2000. In general, both businesses and labor have been adjusting to competitive pressures.

Ordnungspolitik

The German economy is highly regulated. The proper content for manufactured goods is stipu-lated in law and regulation, as are such things as the working condition of machinery or the hours stores may be open (no stores are allowed to be open on Sundays, for instance, and permissible hours on the other days are set by law). These regulations are often fine-tuned to a degree that seems strange to Americans. Under the original rules, for instance, an exception was allowed in the store-closing law, so travelers at train stations, airports, and gas stations could buy shaving sup-plies, magazines, and so forth. In 1992, a Hamburg court ruled that the gas station stores had to classify their goods as either essential or nonessential and sell only the essential ones on the week-ends. Thus, one could buy handkerchiefs at Hamburg gas stations on Sunday but not T-shirts![26]

As a result of the net of regulation of *Ordnungspolitik*, combined with a population of knowl-edgeable consumers who are not tolerant of defects, German industry has come to be known for consumer products that are finely engineered and of excellent quality but that are not inexpen-sive. Germany is not a throwaway society.

Anti-Inflation Policy

In fiscal policy (whether the government's budget operates in surplus or in deficit) and in mon-etary policy (regulation of the supply of money, which helps determine the value of the cur-rency), the German government has always emphasized as its chief goal controlling inflation. This

[25]Jutta Helm, "Codetermination in West Germany: What Difference Has It Made?" *West European Politics* 9 (1986): 637–58.
[26]Philip Glouchevitch, *Juggernaut: The German Way of Business* (New York: Simon & Schuster, 1992), p. 48.

may result partly from the historic experience of ruinous hyperinflation in the 1920s. It probably also results in part from so much decision making in Germany being by consensus, with a heavy involvement of the bureaucracy and a resultant lessening of the impact of elected officials. Elected officials have a weakness for inflation. If one spends money this year without raising the necessary funds to pay for what is purchased—that is, if one runs a deficit—the resulting inflation doesn't kick in until a year or two later. People can then feel artificially good for awhile, and if an election is coming up soon, elected officials have plenty of reason to make people feel artificially good. Therefore, democracies tend to run in deficit and to produce inflation. While the German system certainly is a democratic one, its officials have been hemmed in more than in most countries by a bureaucratic consensus that constrains them against indulging in this way.

Since February 28, 2002, monetary policy for all countries using the Euro (a common currency adopted by most members of the EU) has been taken over by a European Central Bank, based in Brussels. Therefore, the German central bank no longer controls interest rates in Germany, and the Germans no longer have that tool available to fight inflation. However, at the time the European Central Bank was being established the Germans insisted that its charter make it lean very strongly toward fighting inflation. Through its influence on the EU and the design of its central bank, in effect, Germany still pursued a strong anti-inflationary policy.

Ironically, the tough, anti-inflation central bank it helped to create is now exacerbating Germany's problems. As of this writing, Germany has skirted recession for some years, with high unemployment rates; it would benefit from some economic stimulus in the form of lower interest rates to help get businesses investing again, and consumers spending. The European Central Bank, however, has been steadfastly maintaining interest rates at levels that fight inflation, but do little to help the German economy recover.

The Challenge of Globalization

Labor peace, a passion for quality, and institutional structures that have provided low inflation—these helped for many years to give Germany enviable economic strength as a state and to give its people a high standard of living. Since the early 1990s, however, Germany has struggled to keep its economy competitive. Its problems have also been exacerbated by the hugely expensive reunification of East and West Germany at the end of the Cold War. Even just in direct costs of building infrastructure, the reunification cost the German government about $640 billion in the 1990s; and there were immense indirect costs as well.

Germany's economy is hugely dependent on selling goods to the rest of the world. The very traits that I described approvingly with the terms *labor peace* and *Ordnungspolitik*—the extensive regulatory structures that ensure broad security and benefits for workers and quality of products—may prove a drawback in the more competitive globalized world that is emerging, although they could also prove to work out well.

German labor input costs (the cost of wages and benefits per year) have long been higher than its competitors', as is seen in Table 5.2. This has meant that for German goods to be sold at competitive prices, each German worker had to produce about 15 percent more per hour than a worker in the United States—and had to produce about twenty times as much as a worker in nearby Poland. In other words, German productivity had to be much higher than its competitors'.

However, in a study in 1993 of nine industries in the United States, Germany, and Japan, Germany did not have the highest productivity in any of the industries. Japan led in five and the United States in four.[27] The trend in productivity was in the wrong direction as well.

---

[27]"Europe Has a Novel Idea: Cut Costs," *New York Times*, 17 July 1994, section 3, p. 1.

TABLE 5.2

Labor Cost per Worker in Manufacturing, 1998–2002

Germany	$33,226
Japan	31,687
USA	28,907
Britain	23,843
Hungary	3,755
Poland	1,714

SOURCE: World Bank, *World Development Indicators 2003.*

Throughout the late 1980s and early 1990s, while productivity in Germany improved at a rate of about half a percent a year, productivity increased more than twice that fast in Japan and the United States. Faced with such high costs and finding it difficult to reduce them in Germany's highly regulated economy, many large German firms moved part of their production abroad to lower-cost labor markets such as the United States (for skilled workers) or Eastern Europe (for less-skilled jobs). This was a major contributory factor to Germany's 10 percent plus unemployment. Note that the problem here was *not* high pay. If manufacturers can use highly educated workers with technological equipment to produce twenty times as much per hour as their competitors in Poland, then there is no problem paying them twenty times as much. The problem only occurs if they are producing ten times as much but are being paid twenty times as much.

In general throughout the postwar period, Germany and its workers prospered precisely because they were highly productive. And therefore German workers' high pay was a good thing and not a problem at all. To continue in this way, however, they will need to continually improve their productivity if they are not to fall behind rival industrial states. How can they do this? They will have to become flexible, with workers willing to move to new jobs and management innovating to reduce procedures and paperwork. This creates a tension, however, with the regulatory state that has served Germany well in the past. It may be that the real question is whether a highly regulated state can prosper under the competitive pressure of a globalized economy.

Germans have begun to talk about the challenge and how to handle it, and there are signs of progress. Germany's Social Democratic chancellor, Gerhard Schroeder, introduced changes in unemployment benefits in 2005 as part of an effort to make industry more competitive, a painful change that nearly split his party, and led to a sharp drop in its popularity. But by 2007 unemployment had dropped from 11.8 percent to 9.2 percent, and in 2006 productivity in Germany increased by a full two percent. From 2000 to 2006 Germany's relative labor costs declined dramatically compared to Spain and Italy.[28] So, it may be that Germany is adjusting successfully to meet its challenges.

---

[28]"Beggar Thy Neighbor," *The Economist*, January 27, 2007, p. 73.

EXAMPLE

Economic Policy in Indonesia

Indonesia is a vast state in Southeast Asia with 245 million people inhabiting several thousand islands. Since the state became free of the Netherlands at the end of World War II, it has been ruled by military governments, especially the government of General Suharto, which took power in 1967. Suharto was a clever and capable ruler who under most conditions was able to guarantee that his main real opposition was his own eventual mortality rather than any political force. He was brought down only by the regionwide economic crisis that swept over Southeast Asia in 1997.

The state Suharto took over in 1967 was poor and economically underdeveloped, but it had huge natural resources in oil, metal, and forests. Suharto pursued a policy of development hinging on education of the population, market-centered financial policies, and the use of revenue from the exploitation of natural resources to build economic infrastructure for the future. At the same time, he used the economy for his own political support and the support of his family and cronies, in ways that kept it from developing as well as it could have done.

By Third World standards, Indonesia by the mid-1990s had done reasonably well—per capita GDP was $1,100 in 1997. This was accomplished through economic growth that was usually in the range of 5 to 7 percent annually. By the 1990s, Indonesia had clearly turned the corner from a subsistence economy to one that was active and diversified. Early in that decade, for the first time, manufacturing accounted for a greater percentage of the gross national product than did agriculture. In 1997, however, Indonesia was caught up in the general economic tailspin of Southeast Asia as currencies crashed in value and foreign investors pulled their money out of the country. It is just now, still in a very tentative way, recovering from that shock.

Though it is certainly ironic at this point to talk about Indonesia's progress under Suharto in light of the economic collapse of 1997 and his removal from the presidency, it is still useful to look back at how Indonesia moved from a very primitive country to one on the verge of an industrial economy. The base for Indonesia's economic development under the Suharto regime was laid down, first, by educating the population. In 1973, just 60 percent of Indonesian children attended primary school, but attendance is almost universal today. The illiteracy rate has dropped from 43 percent of the adult population in the 1970s to 12 percent. In addition to emphasizing education, Suharto relied on a largely American-trained group of economists for his basic economic policies. These were led by Widjojo Nitisastro (Berkeley Ph.D.), who shaped the policies of the 1970s and 1980s.

Nitisastro lifted the tight controls that Indonesia had maintained on transfers of capital before 1967, and this made it possible for trade to operate much more freely and for foreign corporations to invest in Indonesia. Instead of trying vainly to hold the value of the currency at a fixed point, Indonesia allowed it to move several percent a year in its ratio to the dollar, so that pressures for revaluation did not build up. The government did not operate with too great a deficit, and therefore, its debt to foreigners did not get out of hand.

Along with these free-market-oriented financial policies, the government intervened on a huge scale in development of the country, with mixed results. "Mixed" in this case is not code for "terrible," however. The results were truly mixed. There were successes in a program for rice production and marketing and in the state's family planning program. Suharto also used such programs, however, to conduct a massive personal pork-barrel program of infrastructure projects in villages labeled "Presidential Instruction" programs. The resulting roads, wells, sewage disposal

Michel Camdessus, director of the I.M.F., watches President Suharto of Indonesia sign a 1998 agreement for fiscal austerity. Mr. Camdessus said later that he just did not know what to do with his arms, but outraged Indonesians thought the picture captured the arrogance of the I.M.F. and their country's subservience to it.

© AP/Wide World Photos

facilities, and so on undoubtedly helped cement Suharto's personal rule at the same time as they laid the basis for further economic development.

More questionable than these projects is what is reputed to have been a large "under the table" economy in which favors were done for businesses by the government and unreported personal donations were made by the businesses. Many of these business leaders were ethnic Chinese, a minority of about 4 percent of the population who have often been subject to racial violence in the past and find themselves in a vulnerable position vis-à-vis the government leaders who ask them for cash. You will recall that in the box on page 116, Indonesia ranked 130 (tied) out of 163 countries in the overall level of business leaders' perception of the depth of political corruption. All of this sets back normal economic operations. Rizal Ramli, an economist with Econit, a consultancy, was quoted by *The Economist* in 1997 as estimating that bribes and arbitrary fees made up 10 percent to 15 percent of the capital cost of setting up a new small business.[29] Much of this traffic in cash was reputed under Suharto to be formally organized in the government, especially through Pertamina (the state oil company) and the Logistics Affairs Agency (a state company that monopolized the importation of agricultural products and that controlled the domestic trade in rice).[30] Aside from economic inefficiencies like this, government and military officials' close collusion with businesses surely contributed to a sorry record of environmental spoilage in Indonesia. In the fall of 1997, for instance, all of Southeast Asia suffered under a huge cloud of smoke from the burning of Indonesia's rich hardwood forests.

---

[29]"Indonesia Survey," *The Economist,* 26 July 1997, p. 14.
[30]William Liddle, "Indonesia," in *Comparative Governance,* Primis database.

Large-scale business operations conducted by members of Suharto's family, especially his daughter Tutut and his son Tommy, also complicated the situation. One of Tommy's companies, for instance, was granted an exclusive import arrangement in 1996 to establish a national auto-mobile manufacturing industry. In addition to allowing him free imports (while other automo-bile importers had to pay a 125 percent tariff), the government forced a consortium of banks to lend him $690 million for the enterprise.

When the currency crisis hit Southeast Asia in 1997, at first most observers expected Indonesia to escape any pain. Its financial balances were in fairly good shape, and its currency should have weathered the storm. Indonesia did in the end get caught up in the crisis, however—partly because of the general panic in the region and partly because the government and the banks turned out to have colluded to make the country's debts seem artificially low (so that in fact, it was not in as good shape as people had thought—though it was still not in terrible shape).

Since 1997, Indonesia has gone through rapid changes. Suharto's government collapsed in the face of popular demonstrations in 1998; in the ensuing election after democracy had been established, an enigmatic politician, Abdurrahman Wahid, was elected president. Wahid was the leader of a major Islamic party and had a strong base of support in that movement. However, he frittered away his power in inconsistent decisions, glib jokes where serious statements were required, a revolving door in his cabinet, and general incapacity to lead. He was impeached in July 2001, nominally for corruption but in reality for incompetence, and was replaced by his vice president (from a rival party), Megawati Sukarnoputri. Sukarnoputri, in turn, lost her position in the election of 2004 to a former general, Susilo Mambang Yudhoyono. By now, Indonesia clearly has a lively democracy, with abundant competing media and some experience with the peaceful transfer of power through elections.

The economy actually recovered fairly well through this period, but economic progress was retarded by spectacular political and social crises that sapped the energy of the country. With re-gard to the economy, the government moved rapidly in 1998 to seize the failed banks' assets; even-tually, the government ended up owning industrial assets worth about one-quarter of Indonesia's GDP. Between 1998 and 2003, it gradually sold these off privately to achieve a new beginning for the economy. The effort to privatize the assets did not go smoothly, however, as old Suharto cronies were often able to buy back large parts of their old commercial empires at bargain prices. There have been some reforms. The Suharto family were ousted from their privileged positions in the economy, for instance, and the power of the National Logistics Board was trimmed. While growth in the economy was less than 1 percent in 1999, the growth rate averaged about 4 percent annually over the next three years, and hit 5.4 percent in 2006.

However, the political system over the last few years has done nothing to help the economy. Indonesia *should* be doing at least as well as its neighbors—if nothing else, it sits on a big lake of oil. Indonesia suffered both from the very long damming up of political conflict under Suharto, which burst out more sharply than in most countries with democratization in 1998, and from its deep ethnic divisions. In the aftermath of the economic collapse of 1997, vast anti-Chinese riots drove much of the entrepreneurial and middle-class Chinese population from the country—a loss Indonesia could not easily afford when rebuilding was needed. And immediately once democracy was established, the province of East Timor pushed for independence from the rest of the country; it won this, but only after military massacres and destruction that ruined its economy. Regional violence in another part of Indonesia, the Aceh province, caused Exxon in March 2001 to close its giant natural gas plant there, which alone produced about 3 percent of Indonesia's total GDP. The basic problems of Indonesia's economic collapse and recovery have all along been more political and social than economic.

With its educated work force, and abundant natural resources, Indonesia potentially has a lot going for it. After the 2004 election the new president pledged economic reforms, with a goal of 6 percent economic growth starting in 2005—a level that is necessary if the many young people now entering the labor market are to be able to find jobs; he came close, with growth of 5.4 percent. The two biggest problems Indonesia must now address are (1) the corruption and red tape that dog business activity, and (2) the infrastructure of roads, water, and so on that was neglected during the past several years of crisis. Bribery is rampant and expensive in Indonesia, and red tape slows down business formation. It takes an average of 151 days in Indonesia to complete all the paperwork required to start a company, compared with 30 days in Malaysia and 8 in Singapore. Spending on infrastructure dropped from almost $16 billion in 1996 to $3 billion in 2001; electric power is unreliable, roads are bad, and many Indonesians do not have access to clean water.[31]

President Yudhoyono has taken particular aim at corruption, appointing a tough attorney-general and an independent Corruption Eradication Commission. In 2005, for instance, both the president of the country's largest bank and the head of the national election commission were detained for questioning in corruption cases; and in 2006 the head of the state electricity company, PLN, was arrested. Work on the infrastructure problems is going more slowly.

---

[31]"Time to Deliver," *The Economist*, December 11, 2004, p. 5.

Key Terms

rent	progressive taxation	political economy
import-substitution	regressive taxation	rational choice models
industrialization	central bank	political psychology
inflation	corruption	codetermination

Further Reading

Alesina, Alberto. "Elections, Party Structure and the Economy." In *Modern Political Economy,* ed. Jeffrey Banks and Eric Hanushek. New York: Cambridge University Press, 1995.

Alt, James, and Alesina, Alberto. "Political Economy: An Overview." In *A New Handbook of Political Science,* ed. Robert Goodin and Hans-Dieter Klingemann. New York: Oxford University Press 1997, pp. 645–74.

APSA Task Force on Inequality and American Democracy. *Inequality and American Democracy.* New York: Russell Sage Foundation, 2004.

Bratton, Michael, Mattes, Robert, and Gyimah-Boadi, E. *Public Opinion, Democracy, and Market Reform in Africa.* New York: Cambridge University press, 2004.

Eichengreen, Barry. *The European Economy Since 1945: Coordinated Capitalism and Beyond.* Princeton, NJ: Princeton University Press, 2007.

Evans, Peter. *Embedded Autonomy: States and Industrial Transformation.* Princeton: Princeton University Press, 1995.

Frieden, Jeffry. *Debt, Development, and Democracy.* Princeton: Princeton University Press, 1991.

—. "Invested Interests: The Politics of National Economic Policies in a World of Global Finance." *International Organization* 45 (1991), pp. 425–51.

Frumkin, Norman. *Guide to Economic Indicators,* 4th ed. Armonk, NY: M.E. Sharpe, 2006.

Heidenheimer, Arnold, and Johnston, Michael, eds. *Political Corruption: A Handbook,* 3rd ed. New Brunswick, NJ: Transaction Press, 2002.

Iversen, Torben. *Contested Economic Institutions: The Politics of Macroeconomics and Wage Bargaining in Advanced Democracies.* New York: Cambridge University Press, 1999.

Johnson, Roberta Ann, ed. *The Struggle Against Corruption: A Comparative Study.* New York: Palgrave Macmillan, 2004.

Kohli, Atul. *State-Directed Development: Political Power and Industrialization in the Global Periphery.* New York: Cambridge University Press, 2004.

Landes, David S. *The Wealth and Poverty of Nations: Why Some Are So Rich and Some So Poor.* New York: W.W. Norton, 1999.

North, Douglas. *Institutions, Institutional Change and Economic Performance.* New York: Cambridge University Press, 1990.

Olson, Mancur. *The Rise and Decline of Nations.* New Haven: Yale University Press, 1982.

Rosenberg, Tina. "The Taint of the Greased Palm." *The New York Times Magazine,* August 10, 2003, pp. 28–33.

Sen, Amartya. *Development as Freedom.* New York: Knopf, 1999.

"Survey: The World Economy." *The Economist,* 30 September 2004.

Teague, Paul. "Lean Production and the German Model." *German Politics* 6 (1997), pp. 76–94.

Van de Walle, Nicolas. *African Economies and the Politics of Permanent Crisis, 1979–1999.* New York: Cambridge University Press, 2001.

Wilensky, Harold L. *Rich Democracies: Political Economy, Public Policy, and Performance.* Berkeley: University of California Press, 2002.

World Bank. *World Development Report 2007.* New York: Oxford University Press, 2006.

WEB SITES OF INTEREST

Organization for Economic Cooperation and Development (OECD):
http://www.oecd.org

International Monetary Fund:
http://www.imf.org

World Bank:
http://www.worldbank.org

CHAPTER 6

❧

WHAT LIES BEHIND POLICY: QUESTIONS OF JUSTICE AND EFFECTIVENESS[1]

In Chapters 4 and 5, we reviewed the varying things that governments do (or do not do) on behalf of their people. In this chapter, we will shift from the "is" to the "ought," as we review the ethical and moral basis of policy making. What are the considerations that lie behind these policies? What things must the leaders and their people think about in considering what the state should do? If you were the leader of a state, what sorts of policies would you opt for?

This is an unusual chapter in an introductory text, not because the questions are unimportant but because of how introductory courses are usually taught, and the inexorable pressure of only so many weeks in a term. In fact, I have sometimes been advised to eliminate this chapter and shift the material included here to other parts of the book. For instance, it has been suggested that I move the material on justice back to my later chapter on courts and legal systems. I considered doing this, but realized that *justice is not a consideration that comes up only in law.* Policies are just—or not just—at all stages where they are considered and implemented. At the end of the day, I believe that these questions of how we decide what policy *should* be need to be dealt with on their own, in a prominent way. This may not fit with every sort of course, but I hope that yours is able to include it.

There seem to be two broad characteristics that almost everyone wants to see in state policies: (1) policies should be "just"—that is, people in the state should be treated in the way they deserve; and (2) policies should be "effective," producing the greatest

---

[1]Any author of an introductory book owes debts to many people, but in this chapter, a special debt is owed to Charles Anderson, whose splendid book *Statecraft* (New York: Wiley, 1977) pursued similar themes in more detail and with greater elegance than I have done here.

131

good at the least cost. As you might expect, the problem with these criteria is that both are multifaceted and hard to pin down. In addition, even these two broad criteria sometimes come into conflict, because what is most "just" may not be most "effective," and vice versa. Sorting out the various factors that make one policy "good" and another "bad" is an art, and people of goodwill may frequently come up with differing conclusions regarding a policy. In this chapter, we shall look at some of the things that make a policy "just" or "effective" and also, perhaps, come to see how complex the final evaluation of a policy must be.

✦ THE PROBLEM OF JUSTICE[2]

What do we mean by **justice,** by the notion that people should be treated "as they deserve"? Does justice consist of treating everyone equally? Surely not, because we can think of many instances in which treating everyone equally would seem quite unjust. If you had worked especially hard on a paper but your instructor decided to give everyone in the class the same grade, this would seem unjust. You had worked hard while others sloughed off, yet all got the same reward. *Different members of the class had contributed different amounts, and justice would seem to require that they be rewarded accordingly.* A rather different consideration appears in the following example: Suppose six people were waiting on a corner on a cold, rainy day, and one of the six was suffering from asthma. Suppose further that a car came along that could take only one additional passenger. Equal treatment would require that the six draw lots to see who should get to go in the car. However, would not justice require that the other five defer to the asthma victim, who was suffering more from the rain than they were? In this case, justice would seem to require that the person whose *needs* were greatest should get special treatment.

Should justice, then, be based solely on the weight of contributions or solely on need? Neither of these can provide a sufficient basis for justice, though obviously both are part of the picture.

There are many problems with the "weight of contributions." People's contributions are frequently as much a matter of luck as of virtue, and we are often a bit queasy when rewards are based solely on such "lucky" contributions. To continue with the example of grades, what if you worked very hard on your paper but a friend, who was born very intelligent, dashed off a brilliant piece in one evening while drinking beer and got a better grade than you did? You would probably have mixed feelings about the justice of the grades. To follow the same line of thought, is it just that a ballplayer such as Sammy Sosa should be paid a very high salary because his shoulders and back are so constructed as to help him hit the long ball? Is it just that a worker living in West Virginia should have so few opportunities to find a job as compared with a worker living in Connecticut? Contribution alone, then, cannot provide a sufficient criterion for determining justice. Contribution may often involve elements of luck, so that we are

---

[2]Those who have used earlier editions of this book may notice that I have departed recently from my practice of treating justice as a component of a broader concept I called "fairness." That practice was always idiosyncratic, and I have concluded that the confusion it caused far outweighed any benefits. I want to thank A. P. Simonds for finally convincing me to change this section.

Officials in a small town in Pennsylvania notified a Mr. Selby that he would have to tear down a backyard tree house because he had not obtained a permit and the house exceeded the 40-foot height restriction. Mr. Selby ignored the notice, and the following month two police cars, a dump truck, and a powerline truck with a cherry picker returned to the tree house and demolished it. Justice? Of what sort?

uncertain how much it should be rewarded. Looking only at contributions would also cause us to ignore questions of need; even if four of the six people on the rainy corner had managed to stop a cab (thus contributing more than the other two), we might think it "just" if one of them were excluded to make a place for the asthma victim.

Similar problems arise if need alone is used as a criterion for justice. Like "contribution," "need" is a tricky thing, and we are not always sure that it should be rewarded. If some members of an office staff are having a hard time economically because of bad luck (or bad judgment) in the houses they bought and the debts they've run up, should they get bigger raises than members of the staff who are not in trouble economically? Should parents get better pay because they have children to support? Would this be unjust to single people who are doing the same work as the parents are doing? Again, if need alone were used as a criterion, this would mean that contribution would have to be ignored. To return finally to the example of grades, how would you feel if the papers were graded solely on the instructor's assessment of each student's need for a "positive self-image"?

Justice, then, is a complex issue. It involves a number of things that are often in conflict and need to be balanced—the contributions people have made, their varying needs, and even some further sense that people should not be treated *too* unequally. Not only do these things have to be balanced, but each of them is itself ambiguous and hard to pin down.

This does not mean that justice is an unworkable concept but simply that it is a difficult one. We all have a strong sense for the justice or injustice of certain things, and there is a good deal of agreement among us about these. If this were not so, I could not have expected the examples used previously to mean roughly the same thing to each reader. It is when we judge a question of justice differently, though, that we must tackle the problem of working out our disagreement. Different people will weigh contribution, need, and the necessity of equality differently; and they will also disagree on precisely what sort of need or what sort of contribution exists, or on what sorts of things need to be equal. Many would see no injustice in Sammy Sosa's salary. One could argue that the amount of pleasure he has given millions of people merited this pay, or one could see justice in a black being well paid, or one could note the limited period during which Sosa can play baseball, since he likely will need to retire in his thirties.

Justice is a complex question, but one on which we can talk productively. By bringing out and examining the differing ways people evaluate contribution, need, and the necessity for equality and by examining the differing weights people place on each, we may at least *clarify* disagreements about the justice of a policy.

✦ Other Aspects of Justice: Procedural Justice

The tack I have taken in the section on "The Problem of Justice" falls under the general rubric of **substantive justice**—any conception of justice that emphasizes people receiving what they need and deserve. This is in fact, to me, the central concept of justice. But the question of justice is sufficiently complex that it goes well beyond the already rich tension between need and contributions that I laid out in that section. Justice is a highly contested concept, a central philosophical problem in all of our consideration of life and humanity. Another conception of justice, less concerned with the fairness of distribution that I emphasized in the "Problem of Justice" section, emphasizes justice as embodied in the *procedures* by which decisions are reached about people. **Procedural justice** is a complex concept. I will raise in this section just some of the sorts of issues that are involved in procedural justice: (1) *whether governmental action is "arbitrary,"* (2) *whether special basic rights are violated, and* (3) *whether special overriding social needs are present.*

Arbitrary Policies and Due Process

Governmental action is **arbitrary** if decisions are made and communicated capriciously, that is, if the people affected by a decision do not know what to expect before the decision is made and do not learn on what grounds it was made. Decisions that single out particular individuals for punishment or reward are arbitrary. For instance, highway patrols sometimes appear to be especially strict in enforcing speed limits and other regulations on drivers of brightly colored sports cars just because of the cars' appearance. (And "racial profiling" is of course an especially abhorrent example of the same problem.)

This is arbitrary action. Librarians are acting arbitrarily when they allow people owing fines to escape without paying provided that they are "properly sorry about having been late." In some dictatorships such as Nazi Germany or Idi Amin's Uganda, a person could be killed because someone in the government bore a grudge against him or her. This was the worst sort of arbitrary terror.

The question of arbitrariness is not the same as a question of substantive justice. A policy we regard as substantively unjust might be reached by means we admit are not arbitrary. (A prohibitive tax on chocolate to reduce consumption might be regarded by many people as wrong; but if it were passed constitutionally and applied equally to everyone, it would not be arbitrary.) Arbitrary means could also produce results we considered substantively just.[3] Regardless of the substantive justice of the result, however, arbitrariness lessens the justice of a policy.

The notion of **due process** has evolved to help control arbitrary decision making. This is the idea that certain standard procedures must always be followed in making some policies and that if those procedures were not followed in making a given policy, then the policy should be void. This prevents policy makers from acting arbitrarily, since they want to see their policies stick. To keep from having their policies voided, they stay within the standard set of procedures in making policy.

This sort of standardization involves some costs in that it lessens governmental flexibility. It is not set up for all areas of policy making. Britain, the United States, and Canada especially emphasize due process in criminal trials, because historically those countries have been especially concerned with protecting their citizens from unfair prosecution by the government. In criminal trials in English-speaking countries, due process consists of the following:

1. People may not be accused of crimes unless they could have learned of the existence and meaning of the law before they committed their acts.
2. When people are accused of crimes, they are entitled to know what crimes are charged, they are entitled to know on what evidence the charges are based, and they are entitled to gather and present their own evidence to rebut the charges.
3. Judges must be disinterested, unbiased, and attentive.
4. Once a judgment has been made, some means for later reconsideration must be available.
5. If any of these conditions has been violated in an American, Canadian, or British court except under certain special circumstances, the trial is ruled invalid.[4]

In other areas of policy, such as the setting of regulations, assignment of people to schools, levying of taxes, and so on, the general spirit of due process is still supposed

---

[3]This often produces uneasiness about legal processes in the United States and other countries with protections against arbitrary criminal investigation. If the police had stopped a sports car and found a bloody ax in the back seat, justice would appear to require that the driver be investigated for murder. However, the initial search was arbitrary, and a court might dismiss the evidence on the grounds that it had been obtained unfairly. Citizens frequently find it difficult to appreciate these distinctions.

[4]This is of course an idealization of what happens. In fact, American courts, at least, are badly overworked and many shortcuts are tolerated to move the business through. For instance, in plea bargaining, a deal is struck between the accused, the prosecutor, and the judge by which the accused pleads guilty to a lesser charge, the prosecutor's original charge is withdrawn, and the trial ends. Therefore, many of the theoretical protections listed are avoided.

to be followed—that is, policy making is not to be arbitrary—but there are usually not such precise and strict rules to safeguard due process.

Special Basic Rights

Another added factor that enters into considerations of procedural justice is the existence of certain basic rights whose violation is thought to be unjust in and of itself. Such rights have a special status in that only extraordinary circumstances would make it appropriate for policy makers to violate them for anyone. Although almost everyone would think that some such rights exist, it is not always possible to get people to agree on exactly which rights have this status. Three rights that have frequently been held to have the special status are:

1. *The Right to Survive.* It can be argued that because death negates all other rights, the right not to be killed should be kept almost absolute. Opposition to capital punishment is often based on this idea, as is opposition to abortion.
2. *The Right of Free Speech.* It can be argued that because politics depends on the exchange of ideas, policy makers should be especially reluctant to regulate the expression of ideas. Decreasing the flow of ideas decreases politics itself.
3. *The Right to Privacy.* It can be argued that if one's very personality is to exist, there must be some space that can be called one's own, where no one else may peek in, and that governments must if at all possible respect those boundaries. It is for this reason that in British, Canadian, and American law, people may not be compelled to speak about themselves in court and wives or husbands may not be compelled to testify against their spouses.

Few people would hold any of these special rights to be *absolute*. Most people would agree that it would have been good if Hitler had been assassinated in 1942, even those who believe strongly in the right to survive. Almost everyone recognizes that the special right of free speech must have some restrictions, as well; the classic example is that no one should have the right to yell "Fire!" in a crowded theater. Similarly, there must also be some ultimate limits to the right to privacy.

Thus, "special rights" are not absolute. However, to the extent that the idea of special rights is accepted, a society sets aside those rights as having a top priority, so that it would take something unusual for us to compromise them. Under these circumstances, substantive justice, or even due process, might have to be tempered in the interests of one or another special right. As one example of this, many people have opposed the establishment of a central, computerized data file of information about Americans because they are concerned about the potential abuses of people's right to privacy that could result if all official information about a person—military record, tax returns, criminal record, health information, record in school, and so on—were brought together and made easily accessible. Those opposing the file grant that justice would be better served if such a file existed, because tax fraud and other crimes would be easier to detect, but they think that the right to privacy is more important than these other needs of justice.

Overriding Social Needs

Finally, justice in a broad sense may require that to be just to most of the people, the state must be less just to some people. That is, there may be overriding social needs that enter into considerations of justice. The best example is the military draft. In many countries, young men (and at least in Israel, women) are required to serve a fixed period of time in the military, whether they wish to do so or not. The reasoning behind this is that the people of the state need to have a strong army, but it is difficult to get people to serve in an army of their own free will. Therefore, some people must be compelled to do so for the greater general good. Similarly, affirmative action programs for employment in the United States often require that minorities and women should be given a slightly better than even break in hiring decisions (even though an even break would be the "just" decision) to help overcome historic patterns of unjust decisions going the opposite way. The argument is that society will benefit from an integrated work force and that at least modest levels of individual injustice during the transition period are not too great a price to pay.

Another example of this sort of consideration is seen during wars. When they are at war, most countries subordinate almost everything else to winning the war. Among the subordinated things is a concern for individual justice, due process, and special individual rights. Governments are often given extraordinary powers during wars, and they are not expected to be primarily concerned with justice to individuals. After 9/11, for instance, the United States government was able to take extraordinary steps in its war on terrorism, steps for which it probably never could have gained popular support under more normal circumstances. Sometimes governments do things during war that they later regret. The internment of hundreds of thousands of Japanese Americans in prison camps during World War II, because of their national origin, is a shameful piece of America's past that occurred under the excess and strain of war.

Revolutionary governments often justify suspensions of due process and justice because of the great good that will eventually result from the revolution. Thousands of British sympathizers were driven into Canada at the end of the American Revolution, aristocrats and many others were beheaded during the French Revolution, and millions of farmers were executed or deported to forced-labor camps in the Soviet Union in the 1930s.

Each of the examples given here—the draft, affirmative action, wartime civil liberties, the needs of a revolution—in fact, any claim to an overriding social need is based on an assumption that ends can justify means. This assumption should not be too easily accepted *or* too readily rejected. It would be wrong to read into the assumption an exaggerated claim that means can be ignored. Clearly, there are many means that cannot be justified by many ends. The internment of Japanese Americans by the U.S. government during World War II did nothing to help the American war effort; even if it had helped in small ways, the enormity of the injustice would not have been worth it. That internment was unjustified. Similarly, even if many Soviet citizens had benefited from the Russian Revolution, the immense human suffering during that revolution and the limitation of free speech throughout the existence of the Soviet Union were horribly unjustified.

However, if we should not accept too easily the notion that ends can justify means, neither should we reject it totally. Some social ends, such as secure national borders, may be worth modest degrees of individual injustice. *Some* ends can clearly justify *some* means—as anyone must agree who has ever told a "little white lie."

In the end, then, we see that justice may be a mix of several things: substantive justice (which is itself a mixture: of concerns for contribution, need, and equality); governmental action that is not arbitrary; consideration of special rights; and the possibility of overriding social needs. It is because so many things are involved that people can honestly disagree on whether a policy is just. At the same time, being aware of what goes into justice can help us to understand and resolve such disagreements.

✦ EFFECTIVENESS

We have seen that one question for the policy maker is whether a policy is *just,* both to individuals and to society more broadly. The other basic question is whether the policy is **effective.** An effective policy is *one that gives the state and the people of the state the greatest benefits at the least cost.* The trick in dealing with an effective policy is that often neither the benefits nor the costs of a policy are easy to calculate.

First, many of the effects of a policy are difficult to measure and compare. They bring up the old problem of "apples and oranges" in its severest form. How can we compare the amount of recreational value gained by building a dam and the value of the protection against flooding that is gained by building it against the cost of pain and inconvenience of those who have to leave their homes to make way for it, the economic loss of farm production on the flooded lands, and the government's cost in constructing it? There is no common unit by which to measure recreational value, protection against flooding, pain and inconvenience, and agricultural loss, and so it is difficult to say whether in this case the gains are greater than the costs.

A second reason the costs and benefits of a policy are not always clear is that policies always have a variety of effects, many of which one cannot anticipate when the policy is set up. These are often referred to as the *unanticipated consequences* of a policy.

As one example of such an unanticipated consequence, consider Germany's public-spirited effort to help slow global warming by relying more on solar energy. The government subsidizes solar energy heavily to encourage its use, but at least in the short run, this actually *reduces* the world's production of energy from the sun! By encouraging the use of solar power generators in Germany through subsidies, the government diverts the world's solar cell production to Germany (where frankly there is not that much sunshine) and away from sunnier, drier climates like Spain's, where the solar cells could be used more effectively.

As another example of unanticipated (and in this case, directly perverse) consequences of a policy, Douglas S. Massey and Kristin E. Espinosa have shown that a series of "get tough" policies against illegal immigration on the United States–Mexican border actually had an effect opposite of what was intended. The U.S. Immigration and Naturalization Service has added extra guards and imposed punishments on employers found to be employing illegal immigrants, and is now building a several-hundred mile wall along the border. Massey and Espinosa found that since the border crossing has been made tougher, illegal immigrants who originally would have come to the United States and stayed only for a few months of seasonal labor now stay year-round because they know that it will be hard to get back if they go home. The end result is that the number of illegal immigrants present at any given time is increased, not decreased, by the stepped-up enforcement.[5]

As a third example of the varied effects that a policy may have, consider the Social Security program of the United States. This is a fairly simple program. As of 2007, all employed workers except government employees paid a tax of 6.2 percent of their salary (up to a maximum salary of $97,500), and their employers paid a matching tax of the same amount.[6] From the proceeds of this tax, pensions are paid to people age sixty-five and older who have retired; also, support payments are paid to disabled workers and to children of workers who have died young. The direct purpose of the program is to provide a national system of pensions and catastrophe insurance. Among the many *side* effects of the program, some good and some bad, are the following:

1. People with low salaries are taxed relatively more heavily than people with high salaries (see Chapter 5). Therefore, the distribution of incomes in the state is made less equal.
2. Retired people have been made less dependent economically on their families. This has surely been a good thing for them, but it may also have helped to lessen the ties of the extended family, which are already weak in our highly mobile society.
3. The age of retirement has been made more or less standard nationally.
4. The overall production of goods and services has been reduced for the country and all the people are economically somewhat less well-off than they would otherwise be because people are encouraged to retire at age sixty-five rather than at a later age.
5. Conversely, the policy has allowed many who wish to stop working at age sixty-five to do so without being forced by economic need to work beyond that age.
6. The payroll tax on employers takes a higher percentage of the payroll for low-pay employees than for high-pay employees. For example, the employer pays a tax of 6.2 percent of the salary of an employee who earns $30,000 a year but only 4.3 percent of the salary of an employee who earns $140,000 a year (0.062 × $97,500 is $6,045, which is 4.3 percent of $140,000). Therefore, the policy encourages industries such as the electronics and computer industries, which have highly paid work forces, while it discriminates against industries such as steel and automobile manufacturing, which employ large numbers of workers at lower pay. This encourages the development of clean industries with a great deal of potential for export sales, but it also hurts economically weak areas of traditional industry.

As this example shows, even a fairly simple program like Social Security has many effects beyond those for which it was originally designed. Some of these were not anticipated by

---

[5]Douglas S. Massey and Kristin E. Espinosa, "What's Driving Mexico–U.S. Migration? A Theoretical, Empirical, and Policy Analysis," *American Journal of Sociology* 102 (January 1997), pp. 939–99.
[6]An additional 1.45 percent tax on *all* wages, also matched by employers, supports medical care for people over sixty-five years of age.

the designers, and some have probably not yet even been noticed by scholars. Certainly the previous list does not exhaust all the consequences of the Social Security plan.

As one last example of the unintended consequences of policy, some studies have suggested that stiffer penalties for those caught driving while intoxicated may have led to an increase in hit-and-run accidents, as drunk drivers flee the scene of accidents to avoid the tougher punishment for driving while intoxicated.

Any judgment of the *effectiveness* of a policy must take into account *all* its costs and benefits—so far as we can guess what these are—not just the *intended* costs and benefits. It is often hard to put a price tag on these, as we have seen in the example of Social Security; we are usually comparing apples, oranges, bananas, and grapefruit. Many of the consequences may be difficult to foresee. As a result, it is just as much an art to judge the effectiveness of a policy as to judge its justice. There is nothing terrible in recognizing that policy making is not an exact science; it is simply a good thing to realize that policy choices are neither simple nor direct.

✦ A BASIC QUESTION OF EFFECTIVENESS: AUTHORITY VERSUS THE MARKET

The most basic choice about effective policy is whether we want to rely more on *governmental authority* or on *market mechanisms* to carry it out, and which is better at accomplishing our goals effectively. "Governmental authority" is just what it sounds like. Under governmental authority, policy is made by the government telling people what they may or may not do, how much they may spend on X, how much the country is to invest in Y, and so on. Many policies with which you are familiar are matters of governmental authority. The public school system, in which the government fixes a minimum number of years of education that each child must receive and sets up free public schools to provide that education, is an instance of policy provided by governmental authority. The system of highways and streets, in which the government decides where streets should run and then uses public money to build and maintain them, is another example. So is the nationalized coal industry of China, in which the government owns all coal mines and decides how much coal is to be mined, what sort of equipment is to be built, how much the miners are to be paid, and how much the coal will cost.

Under a **market mechanism,** the government leaves the choice as to what people are to do, what goods they are to receive, and so on, up to the people to choose for themselves, through their exchanges of goods and services with each other. Through the operation of supply and demand, if large numbers of people want G.I. Joe dolls and are willing to pay high prices for them, producers will make more G.I. Joe dolls. If no one wants to pay people well to care for children during the day, there will not be many child care centers. Therefore, collective choices come to be made by millions of individual decisions about proper prices and what objects to purchase. The government depends on the *costs* of action, of goods and so on to restrain people in their choices so that they will end up choosing to do or buy only those things they most want (or can afford). In the coal industry of the United States, which is not nationalized, the choice as to how much coal is to be produced is a matter for a number of mine operators to decide on the basis of their operating costs; their decision is strongly affected by the choices of millions of customers as to how much coal they will buy at a given price. The policy decision—how much coal is to be produced—which in China is made directly by the government, is made in the United States by the interplay of a large number of individual decisions.

In a modification of the market mechanism, a government may leave a policy to be settled by the market but may intervene to structure the individual decisions that go to make up the market choice. Almost every country, for instance, taxes liquor and tobacco products heavily to raise their prices and make it less likely that people will choose to consume such unhealthy substances rather than, say, meat and vegetables. The choice as to what to consume is still the customer's, but the government has taken steps to help determine what that choice will be. By contrast, in banning the consumption of heroin, the U.S. government is relying on governmental authority rather than on a market mechanism to determine the level of consumption of a dangerous substance.

Whether authority or a market mechanism is a better way of making policy is a continual subject of debate. Is it better for the government to nationalize railroads, airlines, and such, and run them in the public interest? Or is it better to leave decisions on scheduling, allocation of investment, salaries, and so on, to be worked out by management, workers, and customers through their individual choices? In an energy shortage, should gasoline be rationed (with a set number of gallons allocated per family), or should the price be allowed to shoot up, so that those who do not need gasoline as much as others or who cannot afford it as readily will reduce their driving? Either policy would reduce consumption to meet the short supply, but they would have different side effects. *Both* types of policy—authority and the market—have considerable disadvantages, as well as advantages.

Problems with Authority-Based Policy

The two main problems with authority as a means of policy are that (1) authority is not good at getting things to the people who need them most or will value them most—that is, it does not *allocate optimally,* and (2) there is a lack of incentives to encourage authority-based policy to use resources as efficiently as they might be used.

Regarding the first of these problems, it stands to reason that if government officials make a choice on behalf of all the people, it is difficult for them to take into account the infinitely varying needs of those people. They might write a thousand exceptions and special conditions into their decision, but it would still be a clumsy instrument for deciding who is to get how much of what. Consider the example of gasoline rationing. If the government states that each family may receive forty-two gallons of gasoline a month, should they not allow rural families more than that because of the long distances they must drive? Then what about an urban resident who must drive to a job twenty miles away? Perhaps the government should allow less gas to those living near a bus line. How about people with weak hearts—should they receive extra gasoline? How about people with small children? People who own a vacation house forty miles out of town? This can go on forever, and even if the government writes terribly complicated rules, there will still be many people who do not receive gasoline in proportion to their

Reprinted by permission of ScienceCartoonsPlus.com.

desire and need for gasoline. As Lindblom has put it, authority systems have "strong thumbs, no fingers."[7]

The second main problem with policy made by authority is that it often does not lead to a very efficient use of resources.[8] When the government decides how much is to be invested in what ways in schools, highways, coal mining, or whatever, the government officials responsible do not *personally* gain much of anything from a wise decision or lose much of anything from an unwise one. Under a market arrangement, however, the people making such decisions save money directly from wise decisions and lose money directly from unwise ones. Even with the best intentions in the world, it is natural that, in systems of authority, decision makers may be more careless with resources than they would be under a market system. As an extreme example of the sort of inefficiency that can result, the Soviet Union at one time allowed its farmers to manage small plots themselves and to sell their produce in competitive markets, though most Soviet agricultural products

---

[7]Charles Lindblom, *Politics and Markets* (New York: Basic Books, 1977).
[8]This is not to say that private decision making does not involve any waste, however! Expensive wood-paneled executive conference rooms are just one of the possibilities. The point is that overall, the incentives of a market system push toward efficiency even if there are many lapses, while the incentives of an authority system do not.

came from large government-managed collective farms. On the private plots, on the average, it took four pounds of feed grain to produce a pound of meat; on the collective farms, it took up to *thirteen* pounds of feed grain to produce a pound of meat.[9]

Problems with the Market

Given these two serious problems, why would anyone ever use authority? Why don't governments leave the decisions to market mechanisms? The reason is that market mechanisms themselves suffer from several serious defects; we shall consider three of them here.[10]

First, as we saw in Chapter 5, wealth and income are distributed unequally in all societies, with some people poor and others better off. When decisions are left to the market, goods and opportunities flow to those who can afford them, and these will not necessarily be the people who need them most. In the section on "Problems with Authority-Based Policy," I wrote that authority systems could not easily sort out

Factories and their neighbors in South Boston, Massachusetts. A strong example of "externalities."
© Spencer Grant/Index Stock Imagery

varying levels of need in making allocations; market systems are terrific at doing this for two people who have the same amount of money. But when incomes vary, ability to pay enters along with need in determining what individuals choose, so the allocations will still probably not be the ideal ones. If medical care is allocated by letting the price rise, for instance, poor people who need surgery to avoid being crippled might have to do without, while richer people might be able to afford casual cosmetic surgery. Where a need is especially important, the government may step in to make certain that justice is done in a way that cannot be guaranteed by a market mechanism. This is part of the motivation behind systems of free public education, national health plans (such as the national medical care programs that serve people of all ages in Britain, Canada, and many European states, or Medicare, which serves those over age sixty-five in the United States), and the rationing of food during shortages.

A second problem with market mechanisms is that they are not very effective in producing *public goods*. As you recall from Chapter 3, a "public good" is something that benefits all members of the community and that no one can be prevented from using; every member of the community can enjoy the benefits of it whether that person has

---

[9]*The Economist,* 7 February 1981, p. 14.
[10]For a more thorough discussion, see Lindblom, *Politics and Markets,* chap. 6, n. 6.

helped pay for it or not. Some examples of public goods are national defense, medical research, weather forecasting, and public health programs to control the spread of disease. All members of the community benefit from such programs, whether or not they have helped pay for them. Left to the market, such public goods would be terribly difficult to finance. Each individual could quite sensibly think, "If I don't pay my share, the army will still be there, and I'll get all the benefits of it; why should I pay? I'll let someone else do it!" As a result, no one would pay to finance the army, there would be no army, and all would lose out. Rather than let such paradoxical failures occur, governments often decide not to rely on the voluntary choices of a market mechanism. Instead, they force the people to pay taxes, and they use those taxes to provide the public good that all (or most) desire.

A third problem with market mechanisms is that they do not take into account **externalities** of individual transactions. An "externality" exists when there are social costs or benefits beyond the individual costs and benefits between two individuals. For example, let us say that a couple contracts with a trash company to dump refuse on their land. For the landowners, the benefit is the money paid by the trash company; the cost is the odor, the sight of the trash, and the portion of their land that is occupied by the trash. Presumably, the landowners are satisfied with the deal (the benefit outweighs the costs), or there would have been no deal. And, the trash company presumably has greater benefits than costs from the deal. So, the trash company and the landowners are happy, and according to market practices, the deal will be struck. However, there is an externality. All the landowners' neighbors, including a nursing home and a day care center, must also suffer the sight and smell of the trash. They receive no benefits, and so there is a large *social cost* that should be taken into account but does not enter into market calculations. This is the problem of externalities, a problem in which governmental authority is often brought to bear to make certain that the broader social costs and benefits are taken into account in transactions, along with the narrower individual costs and benefits of those making the choices. The most obvious externalities are negative ones—pollution, the setting up of ugly structures, and so on. However, there can also be *positive externalities,* in which there are positive social benefits that would not be taken into account in individual transactions and that government may step in to guarantee. Two examples are the preservation of historic buildings and the requirement that every member of society acquire a basic education. (The notion in the latter case is that society as a whole benefits from literacy above and beyond the benefit any single individual gains from being literate.)

Governmental authority and market mechanisms, then, are two modes for the making of policy. There are problems with each, and so it is hard to argue an absolute case for one as opposed to the other; and personal preferences will play a role. Furthermore, it is clear that certain areas of policy lend themselves better to one mode than to the other. Defense is always provided by governmental authority, not by a market mechanism, probably because it is so difficult to provide collective goods through a market mechanism. Art and science seem to flourish best when left to a "marketplace of ideas" rather than being made to conform to decisions of governmental authority.

Many other policy areas—industrial production, health care, and others—seem suscep-tible to either mode of decision; and examples of both modes from numerous countries can be found.

→ POWER AND CHOICE

You will of course have realized that this whole chapter has been written from a "choice" perspective. "Why is defense always provided by governmental authority, but art and sciences usually provided by the 'marketplace of ideas'?" was answered, for in-stance, by stating that a collective good cannot be produced effectively by a market mechanism.

But I hope you realize by now that neither power nor choice, alone and in isola-tion, is likely to account fully for any political phenomenon. Our focus in this chap-ter has been on justice and effectiveness, which are very important in understanding what happens when policies are chosen, but we know that a lot of other things are going on as well. Power relationships will also have a lot to do with which policy is chosen. Political leaders may steer a lucrative contract to a friend, or may push for a policy benefiting an ethnic group that is part of their support base. These things happen a *lot*.

Once again, we recall that both the power perspective and the choice perspective are usually needed, to get a full picture of political outcomes.

→ THE NEED TO ACT, EVEN UNDER UNCERTAINTY

At this point, you might think the message of this chapter is that policy making is aw-fully complicated. This is understandable. We have seen that the question of justice is complex, and that reckoning efficiency is similarly tricky—that it is difficult to count accurately the costs and benefits of a policy to choose the one that gives the greatest benefits at the least cost.

Unfortunately, a description of the complexity of policy decisions could lead some people to give up in discouragement. If it is difficult to decide what policy is most just and most efficient, why bother to try? Carried too far, an appreciation of complexity can be paralyzing.

We must always carry on a difficult balancing act between recognizing that our decisions are fallible and therefore require continual reexamination, and being able to act decisively on our best judgment at any given time. The fact that analysis is complex does not mean that "anything goes" or that one opinion is always as good as another. These questions are important enough to justify hardheaded analysis. It is the duty of those who recognize the complexity of decisions to hold themselves always ready to act despite knowing that their choices might be wrong. Otherwise, the only people to act would be those who did not understand the complexity of policy choices, and the world would be ruled by simpletons.

 EXAMPLE

Political Choice

Here are four examples of policy questions that have concerned governmental decision makers. In each instance, the policy issue is stated; this is followed by some of the questions that those making a decision on the issue must consider:

1. ***The Problem of Need-Based Scholarships.*** Most systems for providing college scholarships are based on some definition of financial need, with scholarships generally being given only to those students who most need financial help to attend school.

   Is need, rather than academic ability, the best basis on which to choose those students who are to be encouraged to attend college?
   - Which way of choosing who gets aid is the more just?
   - Which is the more efficient? Is the overall educational level of society increased more by giving financial aid to bright students or to needy students? Presumably, the aid offers more leverage to needy students, because they all need the money to attend college, whereas many of the bright students would attend college in any case. However, is a smaller number of bright students the more important addition?

     Assuming we wish to use need as a basis, how do we determine "need"?
   - Is need a function of parents' income? What, then, do we do about children of wealthy parents who are living independently of them and get no aid from them? Should they be punished for their parents' wealth? If they are given aid, won't all students, to get aid, claim to be independent of their parents?
   - Is need solely a matter of family income, or shouldn't we take a family's financial obligations into account? Doesn't it make more sense to give aid to someone whose parents must put eight children through school than to someone from a family of four with the same income? In a possibly parallel situation, should a family that carries big mortgages on two large homes get preference because they don't have much money left to spend on college? (Many scholarship systems do count mortgage payments as contributing to need.) Does doing this merely reward imprudence? Is there a difference between the case of the eight children and the case of the large mortgages?
   - How should parents who are not married but are living together and supporting their children jointly be counted? Most systems allow just one of the parents to be counted as the "supporter," and if the one who earns less is so designated, the family will show up as more "needy" than most people would consider them to be. Is this fair to married couples? Does it discourage marriage? If it is not allowed, how can one address the problem of separated couples where one of the parents does not pay a fair share of support? In this case, the single responsible parent and children would appear as *less* needy than they really are. Whichever way you decide to define need in the case of unmarried parents, how can you police the system?

2. ***The Problem of Water Pollution.*** Most states have laws to limit the pollutants that can be dumped into the water.
   - How do we decide which pollutants to ban? Should we ban primarily those that are dangerous to human health? Those, such as phosphates or DDT, that have especially bad effects on fish, birds, and mammals? Those that discolor the water? Those that stink?
   - Who is to bear the cost of cleaning up the water?

- Is it better to use a flat ban on pollution or to charge people and corporations a stiff fee for polluting? (This is an example of the choice between government authority and market mechanisms.) The main argument against the latter is that it puts the government in the position of saying that pollution is acceptable (or at least legal) as long as one can pay the fee. The main argument in favor of this is that it adds flexibility to the law. Cleaning up pollution always carries costs and may lead to plant closings, higher prices for consumers, and other socially undesirable consequences. The fee system would allow some continued pollution where the cost of cleaning up would be prohibitive. Where the cost is not so high, people would choose to clean up rather than pay the fee. Therefore, the system would be made more efficient but at the expense of losing some of the moral and symbolic vigor of the law. Which is the better course?

3. ***Children as a Public Good.*** A society needs to raise children to replace its members who die, or the society would disappear over a couple of generations. One could, therefore, think of the production of children as a public good. Those who do not have children benefit from the child-raising labors of those who do; they enjoy a society of varied ages in which to live as they grow older, and a labor force of younger people is available to support them in their retirement. Should all then share in the economic costs of raising the children? In the United States, the cost of educating children is borne collectively through the system of public education, but most other costs of raising children are treated as private costs of the parents. In about half the world's states, however, the full society assumes some of the responsibility for all costs of child rearing by giving direct grants to families with children. These grants are often pegged to the median income of workers in the country: 10 percent of the country's median income might be given to any family raising two children, for example.
   - Should such aid go to all families with children or only to poor families? Public education goes to all families, but should this be treated the same?
   - How would it change society to define the raising of children as a collective effort, rather than a private effort of parents?
   - Would this be a good way to address such problems as malnutrition, child abuse, and poor education?
   - In a sense, this would mean the government was paying people to have children. Is this a wise policy in a period of massive worldwide population growth?

4. ***The Problem of Gender-Based Pension Payments.*** Almost all insurance companies have varying insurance rates for low- and high-risk categories of people. Many companies give lower insurance rates to students who maintain a B average, for instance, on the assumption that those students drive better (or less often) than others and therefore will have fewer accidents. Similarly, young drivers carry higher rates for auto insurance, nonsmokers have lower rates for life insurance with many companies, almost all companies give lower life insurance rates to women because women live longer than men, and so on. In the same spirit, many insurance-based pension plans pay women who retire at age seventy a lower monthly pension than men who retire at that age because, since women have a longer life expectancy, the companies can reasonably expect to make payments to the women for a greater length of time.
   - Is it just that a woman who has worked as hard as a man should not enjoy as comfortable a retirement as the man?
   - On the other hand, if payments are made equal, a man who has worked just as hard as a woman can expect to draw out a smaller total amount of retirement income before he dies. Is this just?
   - If the system is changed to give equal payments, will men reinvest their retirement savings in other ways that allow them to draw out their retirement income in whatever way

they wish? This could result in an insurance-based scheme with only female clients, thus defeating the purpose of the change.

- Why should gender be singled out as a basis for this distinction? People who live in Iowa live longer, on the average, than people from Rhode Island. If we're to be consistent, shouldn't Iowans draw a smaller pension than Rhode Islanders? How about people who exercise regularly, people who don't smoke, slender people, and so on?

KEY TERMS

justice	arbitrary action	market mechanism
substantive justice	due process	externality
procedural justice	effective policy	

FURTHER READING

Adler, Matthew D., and Posner, Eric A. *Cost-Benefit Analysis: Economic, Philosophical, and Legal Perspectives.* Chicago: University of Chicago Press, 2001.

Anderson, Charles. *Statecraft.* New York: Wiley, 1977, especially chaps. 1–6.

Fleischacker, Samuel. *A Short History of Distributive Justice.* Boston: Harvard University Press, 2005.

Hardin, Garret. "The Tragedy of the Commons." *Science* 162 (13 December 1968), pp. 1243–48 (the original statement on the problem of producing public goods through voluntary contributions).

Hochschild, Jennifer. *What's Fair? American Beliefs about Distributive Justice.* Cambridge: Harvard University Press, 1981.

Lane, Robert E. *The Loss of Happiness in Market Democracies.* New Haven: Yale University Press, 2001.

Lindblom, Charles. *The Market System: What It Is, How It Works, and What to Make of It.* New Haven: Yale University Press, 2001.

Olsaretti, Serena, ed. *Desert and Justice.* New York: Oxford University Press, 2003.

Ostrom, Elinor. *Governing the Commons: The Evolution of Institutions for Collective Action.* Cambridge: Cambridge University Press, 1991.

Scott, James C. *Seeing Like a State: How Certain Schemes to Improve the Human Condition Have Failed.* New Haven: Yale University Press, 1998.

Solomon, Robert C., and Murphy, Mark C., eds. *What Is Justice? Classic and Contemporary Readings.* Oxford: Oxford University Press, 1990.

Wildavsky, Aaron B. *Speaking Truth to Power.* New Brunswick, NJ: Transaction Books, 1987.

PART III

The Citizen and the Regime

CHAPTER 7

DEMOCRACY AND AUTOCRACY

In Part II, we looked at the state and at questions that go into the setting of state policies. Now we have reached a point in the text at which we should look inside the state. How does "the state"—which comprises many different people—choose a particular set of policies? What goes on within a state that determines the policies it will pursue? The state is not a simple decision-making mechanism, and its complex organizational structure strongly influences the processes of political choice. In the next two parts—Chapters 7 through 8 and 9 through 17—we will look at those internal structures.

In this chapter, we will examine two broad types of regime: democracy and autocracy. A **regime** is the general form of government of a state, including its constitution and rules of government. A regime generally continues beyond the terms of individual officeholders. The United States, for instance, has had a democratic regime for better than two centuries, across many presidents and lawmakers. A state, in turn, is in principle more enduring than a regime. For instance, a state may shift between different regimes, as Nigeria has moved back and forth between democracies and military governments. Thus a state is more lasting than a regime, which in turn is more lasting than individual officeholders.

✦ DEMOCRACY

A **democracy** is a regime in which all fully qualified citizens vote at regular intervals to choose, from among alternative candidates, the people who will be in charge of setting the state's policies. Democracy is "government of the people"; therefore, there is also a sense that the full population of citizens will be actively engaged between elections in debate over alternative policies and in the work of setting the policies. How fully engaged they are varies across democracies, and whether they are sufficiently engaged has long been a matter of debate. Examples of this debate include proposals for referendums, workplace democracy, and citizen caucuses, all of which are intended to give citizens more detailed involvement in policy-making than is possible just in voting for alternative leaders.

In fact, as we look at the states of the world that we characterize as "democracies," we must remember that although the full population of citizens have more access to the power of government in democracies than in autocracies, there is really no pure democracy, in the sense of a state in which every citizen has equal access to governmental power. The vote is important, but there are also other resources that give some citizens more access than others, as we will see in succeeding chapters—money, armed force (the military, in some states), education, and so forth. Democracies vary in just how equal the access to government is for ordinary citizens.

At the bottom range of democracies, we even find a broad gray area of **authoritarian democracies** where we are not sure whether there is enough democracy in the system to really merit the name. Examples include Russia, where the Constitution gives the President immense power and Vladimir Putin has built on this by cowing or seizing almost all of the press, and the African state of Zimbabwe, where President Robert Mugabe has won continued electoral victories in large part by campaigns of intimidation, assault, and beatings of opposition candidates.

So, "democracy" actually is a range of things rather than a single thing. But as we will see, there is a real difference between democracies (even if they constitute a range of things) and autocracy. Democracy does make a difference.

Most of you are familiar with democratic government from your own experience. Only a relatively small number of the world's states are stable democracies—though most of the world's states have been democracies at one time or another since the 1960s. Democracy requires an implicit agreement by the conflicting groups in a state to accept the possibility that they will lose out in the making of policy. In effect, it requires an agreement among labor unions, corporations, farm groups, environmentalists, vegetarians, motorcycle enthusiasts, and all other groups to take their chances on the outcome of a process of policy making in which the population as a whole gets the deciding voice. Each group accepts that it must abide by the end result and hopes that it will be able to get enough of what it wants out of the process. This is the "democratic bargain."

When we look at it in this way, it is easy to see why democracy might be fragile. All that is needed to make a democracy collapse is for one or more important groups to reject the results of the democratic bargain and to have access to enough power to overthrow the system. Many parts of the world are beset by problems of overpopulation, ethnic and religious conflict, poverty, and chancy positions in world trade—problems so fierce that it becomes difficult for powerful groups to face policy defeats philosophically; the stakes are too high. And military forces or popular movements usually lie close at hand, willing and able to overthrow the system.

As one might suspect, under these circumstances only a small number of the world's states are stable democracies. Of the 104 states that were independent as of 1960, only 29 have had an uninterrupted record of electoral democratic government over the time since then.[1] Most of these were prosperous industrialized states whose people can more easily afford to compromise on the "democratic bargain." However, poor states

---

[1]Adam Przeworski et al., *Democracy and Development* (New York: Cambridge University Press, 2000), appendix 1.2.

such as India, Jamaica, Malta, Botswana, and Costa Rica also had steady histories of democratic government.

✦ THE COMING AND GOING OF DEMOCRACY

The world's imagination was seized in 1989 when the Iron Curtain fell, and the Berlin Wall with it, and most of the communist states of Eastern Europe suddenly threw off their old systems and established democracies. The drama of the failed coup in the Soviet Union in 1991 and the victory of the pro-democratic forces there had people glued to their television sets. These dramatic changes were only part of a larger move toward democracy that covered two decades and ranged across many parts of the world.

Southern Europe saw three shifts from right-wing dictatorships to democracy in the late 1970s: in Greece, Portugal, and Spain. A bit later, a wave of democratization swept Latin America, as several states reestablished democracies after periods of military (mostly right-wing) dictatorship: Ecuador and Peru in 1978, Bolivia in 1982, Argentina in 1983, Uruguay in 1984, Brazil in 1985, and Chile in 1989.

Finally in 1989 and 1990, along with the wave of democratization in the formerly communist states of Eastern Europe (East Germany, which has since merged with former West Germany; Poland; Czechoslovakia; Hungary; Bulgaria; Romania; and Yugoslavia), several states scattered around the world moved to democracy: Algeria over the period 1989–1991 (and at the same time Egypt, Jordan, and Tunisia moved closer to being democracies); Haiti in 1990; South Korea in 1987; Nepal in 1990; Nicaragua in 1990; Pakistan in 1988; the Philippines in 1986; and South Africa in 1994.

However, this was not a story of uniformly forward progress. After establishing democracy in Algeria, the military was afraid that the fundamentalist Islam party would be victorious, and it abruptly banned elections in 1992. In Haiti, the military ousted newly elected President Jean-Bertrand Aristide in a 1991 coup; he was only reinstated in 1994 after strong pressure from the United States and the temporary occupation of Haiti by U.S. troops. The military overthrew the democratically elected government in Pakistan in 1999 and installed their commanding general in power. Democracy is tenuous in most parts of the former Soviet Union. And the new elections in Africa include only a few in which a government has actually been replaced; more often, the old dictators have managed to prevail under the new democratic rules, sometimes through ruthless violence. Overall, however, there has been a clear movement toward more democracy.

The shifts of the 1980s occurred in regional waves, but they were all part of a larger wave of democratization, often called simply the "Third Wave."[2] Movements to democracy have generally occurred in three worldwide waves. The first wave of democratization came in the wake of World War I, as Germany became a democracy in 1918 and new democracies were created in Eastern Europe; at about the same time, a number of Latin American states also established democratic regimes. Many of the democracies established at this time, however, failed either under the economic pressures of the Great Depression or in the violence of World War II. A second wave of democratization

---

[2]Samuel P. Huntington, *The Third Wave: Democratization in the Late Twentieth Century* (Norman: University of Oklahoma Press, 1991).

occurred after World War II, as democracy was reestablished in countries such as Germany and Italy and large numbers of former European colonies in the Third World achieved independence. Again, while many of those democracies survived, many also fell to military coups. The third wave is considered to have started in the late 1970s with the successful reintroduction of democracy to Spain and Portugal.

It is clear that movement to democracy is not a one-way street. We experienced a wave of democratization in the last few decades of the twentieth century, but at other periods during that century there were waves of dictatorship. The 1920s were such a period, as Germany, Italy, Spain, and various Eastern European states overthrew democracy; and in the 1950s and 1960s, a wave of dictatorship spread over South America and Africa. Democracy *is* fragile, even though it has many strengths, including especially the greater dignity it confers on all citizens, and its relatively strong protection against arbitrary treatment by governments. In the wake of the democratization of the former Soviet Union a number of commentators crowed prematurely about the triumph of democracy. There was even a very widely read essay with the rather silly title, "The End of History?" that argued that the question of democracy was now permanently answered and the ideological conflicts ushered in by the nineteenth century were dead.[3] But history does not stop. We are likely to see movements both to democracy and to autocracy over the coming decades.

→ POSSIBLE EXPLANATIONS

What brought about the push for democracy at this point in history? Four possible reasons are fatigue of some authoritarian regimes; international pressures; people's desire for security against arbitrary abuse; and people's desire for economic development.

In a few cases, authoritarian systems became "tired" and lost popular support. In Spain and Portugal, long-term dictators died, and their regimes lost steam long before their deaths. In Argentina, the military government lost a war with Britain. Most dramatically, the exhaustion of the Soviet Union at maintaining its control of Eastern Europe was a critical element in the wave of democratization in that region in 1989, and the corruption and senility of its Communist Party led to the victory of democracy in the Soviet Union. This was evident in the communists' botched countercoup in the Soviet Union in 1991; the old party could not muster enough imagination and organization to take advantage of a good opportunity to reestablish its rule.

Also, in many cases at this time there was international pressure on nondemocratic regimes to change, orchestrated by activist networks from around the world. Spain, Portugal, and Greece came under pressure from their neighbors to become democratic, and the carrot of membership in the European Union was offered to them implicitly if they established democratic systems.[4] South Africans were under international trade and investment sanctions for several years to force them to give democratic rights to their black majority, and those sanctions helped lead to democratic government in

---

[3]Francis Fukuyama, "The End of History?" *National Interest* 16 (Summer 1989), pp. 3–19.
[4]See Chapter 3, for a discussion of the European Union.

Reprinted by permission of ScienceCartoonsPlus.com

1994. Though pressure for democracy in China has been repulsed since the Tiananmen Square massacre in 1989, concern for international reactions has slightly softened the suppression of democratic movements there. Nicaragua's government held free elections under quasi-military pressure from the United States, which promoted a civil war in the country to force a change in regime.

Probably more important than either international pressures or the weakness of the old regimes, however, are the remaining two factors: a desire for human rights and security against abuse and, especially in the communist states of Eastern Europe, economic failure. A desire for security and dignity must have been high among the reasons for democratization in South America, where many of the military regimes had been brutally oppressive. In Argentina and Chile, thousands of people disappeared during the dictatorships and are presumed to have been tortured and killed. In the Philippines, the murder of Corazon Aquino's husband sparked the move for democracy. In East Germany, after the overthrow of the communist regime, it was learned that the secret police had maintained files on 6 million people, out of a total population of 16 million, and had employed hundreds of thousands of informants. In the formation of most democracies, a yearning for dignity and security has always played a large part. This was true in the establishment of the first democracies in Europe and North America in the nineteenth century, and it is true today.

The fourth factor in the surge to democracy was the economic stagnation of many authoritarian states, which contrasted with the dynamic prosperity of democracies such as Japan and (then West) Germany. This was particularly true of democratization in Eastern Europe, where establishing democracy was intermingled with the dismantling of inefficient socialist economies and the establishment of market economies. The connection between free markets, democracy, and prosperity is not all that clear, as we will see below; but in many democratizing states, part of the thrust for democracy came from a sense that the state had stagnated economically, that it was not "modern" (not up-to-date), and that democracy was part of being modern.

These are some of the factors that we think led to the widespread shift to democracy over the last forty years. Concentrating on the sources of democratization, as we have done here, does carry the risk that we can come to see the coming of democracy, and the continuation of democracy, as natural and normal. They are not. As we noted above, for example, a new democracy may often be established lacking a broad base of support that would allow it to survive. And, a shift to democracy may even bring with it some side effects that actually make democracy *more* difficult to sustain. Democracy's openness often unleashes regional nationalist pressures that had been held in check by more oppressive regimes. Unless the state is strong and lucky, it may be pulled apart. Or alternatively, the danger to the state may then prompt an antidemocratic reaction from the military, and we may end up back at dictatorship.

✦ WHAT DID WE LEARN FROM THE THIRD WAVE?

The challenge of explaining the Third Wave has helped to further a fairly substantial shift in the whole field of comparative politics. Explaining *distinct* and *specific events,* as compared with analyzing ongoing stable situations, leads us to emphasize individuals' choices and especially the choices of individual leaders and popular movements. Stable situations are often appropriately analyzed by looking at stable, broad background factors such as the constitution, the balance of groups' power, broad economic structures, and the historical background of the state. But a specific event that occurs at a given point in time is usually not determined in any precise way by such factors, so to analyze such an event, we must look more specifically at the particular actors involved—at their strategic situations and their decisions.[5] The great interest attracted by the wave(s) of democratization at the end of the twentieth century helped to shift the study of comparative politics somewhat in this direction. In the terms used in Chapter 1, it increased the "interpretive" aspect of comparative politics. (See above, p. 15.)

1.   ***The Importance of "Pacts."*** An early work that formed the basis for most further analysis of the Third Wave was a broad review by O'Donnell and Schmitter of what were then the most recent cases of democratization, primarily in Latin

---

[5]For an opposed view, see Nancy Bermeo, "Myths of Moderation: Confrontation and Conflict During Democratic Transitions," *Comparative Politics* 29 (April 1997), pp. 305–22.

A man holds a Romanian flag with the communist symbol torn from its center on a balcony overlooking
tanks, soldiers, and citizens filling Palace Square in Bucharest during the revolution of 1989.
© Peter Turnley/Corbis.

America and southern Europe.[6] This study did not so much develop a theory as
note and comment on similarities across cases.

One important conclusion the authors reached was that it may be important for
successful democratization that the democratizers form **pacts** with those whom they are
ousting to ensure a smooth transition and to lay a good base of support for the future
democracy. Such pacts might include, for instance, amnesty from prosecution for
crimes committed under the dictatorship; symbolic affirmation of the old regime, as
in the maintenance of a powerless or weak monarch; or guarantees of funding for the
army. "Pacts" figured importantly in the Spanish case, described in detail in an example
in this chapter.

As always in looking at democratization, however, there are few universal truths.
In the wave of democratization across Eastern Europe in 1989, which occurred after
the study by O'Donnell and his coauthors, pacts were not nearly so important. Unlike
southern Europe, this was not a case of ousting a military associated with powerful domestic forces, which had to be dealt with gingerly. Rather, the force being ousted was
primarily the Soviet army, and broad nationalist sentiment coincided with the democratic thrust. Therefore, the new democratic leaders in Eastern Europe did not need to
bargain very much with their discredited predecessors. Also, broad-based social movements were much more at the forefront of these moves to democracy than had been the

---

[6]Guillermo O'Donnell and Philippe C. Schmitter, *Transitions from Authoritarian Rule: Tentative Conclusions about Uncertain
Democracies* (Baltimore: Johns Hopkins University Press, 1986).

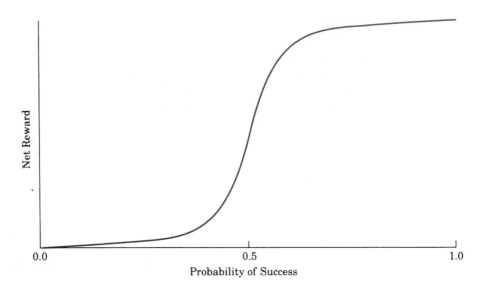

FIGURE 7.1   Probable reward for coming out in favor of democracy, as probability increases that democracy will in fact be established.

case in southern Europe. And the members of these movements had little tolerance for generous "pacts" with the old regime.

2.   ***Sudden Changes.*** Many of the recent shifts to democracy have taken observers by surprise. No one predicted in 1988, for instance, that by the end of 1989, many Eastern European states would be democracies. One scholar has provided a good explanation for why these shifts might be sudden and difficult to predict.[7]

Under an authoritarian regime, there are few rewards and many punishments for anyone coming out in favor of democracy. However, this is a function of how likely it is that democracy will be established; if democratization in the end succeeds, there will be many rewards and no punishments for those who had come out in favor of it. The key factor is that the net rewards of coming out may tip suddenly as the probability of success shifts over from less than even to greater than even. This is depicted graphically in Figure 7.1. As the probability of success rises from zero to 0.2, 0.3, or 0.4, the net rewards for favoring democracy do not increase much. In fact, regimes may crack down more on opponents as their situation becomes slightly less secure than it had been. Suddenly, however, at some point the danger in favoring democracy appears to decrease. People find that when they demonstrate in the street, there are thousands of other people there, too many for the government to take on. Almost overnight, favoring

---

[7]Adam Przeworski, "Some Problems in the Study of Transition to Democracy," in Guillermo O'Donnell, Philippe C. Schmitter, and Laurence Whitehead. eds., *Transitions from Authoritarian Rule: Comparative Perspectives* (Baltimore: Johns Hopkins University Press, 1986).

democracy may shift from being a dangerous activity, restricted to the hard core, to an easy activity that may carry future rewards.[8]

3. ***Economic Crisis or Not?*** Stephen Haggard and Robert Kaufman have pointed out that a transition to democracy occurs differently if it comes in response to an economic crisis in the state than if it occurs under good economic conditions.[9] Some examples of **crisis transitions** are the Eastern European transitions of 1989–1991 and most of the Latin American transitions. On the other hand, a number of East Asian transitions, such as those in Thailand and Korea, occurred in the presence of prosperity, as did transitions in Spain, Turkey, and Chile.

When a transition is spurred by economic crisis, the ruling authoritarian government often has little credibility and cannot influence the path of the transition much at all. Pacts are less important in such transitions, and the military are less likely to retain any influence in the new regime. In Turkey and Thailand, with their "noncrisis" transitions, the resulting democracies had to constantly look over their shoulders to see how the military viewed any decisions. When a pro-Islamic cabinet was formed in Turkey in 1997, for instance, the military forced it to dissolve after several months because they thought it would weaken the secular, Western-oriented doctrines they supported.[10]

Politics is also likely to be more open after crisis-driven transitions, with fewer restrictions on broad participation by a full range of parties and interest groups. As a result, the politics that follow are likely to be marked by greater representation of the political left, and to be more tumultuous, than the politics that follow a noncrisis transition.

➔ WHY ARE PROSPEROUS COUNTRIES LIKELY TO BE DEMOCRACIES?

One of the most regular and predictable things in the comparative study of politics is that prosperous countries are much more likely to be democracies than poor countries are. We noted noble exceptions above, such as India and Costa Rica, but there are really not all that many exceptions. The average per capita income of democracies in 2002 was $9,503, of non-democracies, $1,653.[11] There is nothing natural or inevitable about this. Poor people want dignity and security from abuse as much as rich people do. Why is it that they are less likely to enjoy democratic government?

One explanation, of course, could be that democracies are better at fostering economic growth than non-democracies, and so countries that are democracies become more prosperous over time than non-democracies. I do not think this is true, though. I will give my reasons in more detail at the end of this chapter, but for the moment it may be enough to note that democratic India did not grow more rapidly over the last

---

[8]I do not mean here that the process is automatic from this point on. China is an example of where this point had been reached in 1989; thousands were flocking to the democratic banner, but the government responded with the Tiananmen Square massacre, thus moving the probability of success back to a lower level.

[9]Stephen Haggard and Robert Kaufman. *The Political Economy of Democratic Transitions* (Princeton: Princeton University Press, 1995).

[10]Later, however, the military did acquiesce in 2003 in the formation of a moderately Islamic cabinet.

[11]Calculated from World Bank, World Development Indicators database, July 2003, www.worldbank.org.

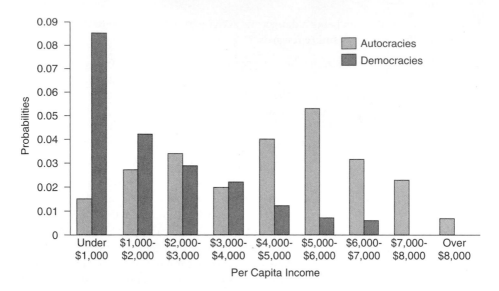

FIGURE 7.2   Probabilities of overthrow in democracies and autocracies.

SOURCE: Based on Adam Przeworski, "Political Regimes and Economic Development," in Richard Sisson and Edward Mansfield, eds., *The Evolution of Political Knowledge* (Columbus: The Ohio State University Press, 2004), table 1.

fifty years than Communist China did, though both started at about the same level of poverty.

At any rate, if you will allow me for now to stipulate that the economies of democracies do not grow more rapidly than the economies of non-democracies, then there must be something about prosperity that makes a state more likely to be a democracy. What could be the reason for this? Rather than look at ways prosperity might cause states to become democracies, it is probably more fruitful to realize that states become democracies for all sorts of reasons having little to do with economic prosperity—the collapse of Soviet military power in Eastern Europe in 1989, the breakup of colonial empires in Africa and Asia in the 1950s and 1960s, international pressure on South Africa in 1990, the United States' overthrow of Saddam Hussein in Iraq in 2003—and look instead at whether, once a state has for whatever reasons become a democracy, prosperity has anything to do with the chances that it will *remain* a democracy.[12]

Figure 7.2 shows a very clear relationship, in which the probability that democracies are overturned marches steadily lower with each increment of prosperity.[13] At per capita annual income under $1,000 (in purchasing power parity dollars), the probability that a democracy would have been overthrown in any given year from 1951 to 1999 was over .08; the probabilities decrease steadily, until they are approximately zero at per

---

[12]This idea is developed in Adam Przeworski and Fernando Limongi, "Modernization Theories and Facts," *World Politics* 49 (1997), pp. 155–83.

[13]W. Phillips Shively, "The Asymmetry of Democratization and Democratic Breakdown (Or Is It Authoritarianization and Authoritarian Breakdown?): Przeworski's 'Political Regimes and Economic Development,'" in Richard Sisson and Edward Mansfield, eds., *The Evolution of Political Knowledge* (Columbus: The Ohio State University Press, 2004).

capita annual income over $7,000. By contrast, the probability that an autocratic regime would have been overthrown and replaced with democracy is pretty much unrelated to the prosperity of the country; these probabilities wander throughout the figure.[14]

It appears that this holds the key to our question: why are prosperous countries more likely to be democracies? States may become democracies for all sorts of reasons, but once they have become a democracy, if they are prosperous they are much more likely to remain one than if they are poor. The same is not true of autocracies. Whether they are overthrown in any given year does not seem to have much to do with whether they are prosperous or poor.

What is it about democracy that might make its survival peculiarly dependent on prosperity? Remember that at the beginning of this chapter I wrote about the "democratic bargain," an agreement by which all groups in society agree to abide by the results of an election and await their chance at power in the future. In order for this to happen, the losers must feel reasonably secure for the present while they wait to take power at some point in the future, and this must surely be easier to do in a society with ample resources. If a drop of one-fourth in your income means that you must sell the cow, that will probably mean more to you and your children than a one-fourth drop in income means to an average West European. Since disaster is always closer to citizens of a poor country, it is likely that those citizens, more than the citizens of richer countries, would try to make their system provide predictable outcomes. That is, when under stress, poorer countries should be more apt to shed the unpredictable future of democratic power-sharing. However, it is not just the poorest people in those countries who will seek the certainties of autocracy. In fact, it will usually be a powerful group in the state, such as the military, a large ethnic group, or a business coalition, that seeks to tie things down rather than leave things open in the democratic bargain, often because they fear the poor. In an impoverished country, everyone is on edge.

✦ DEMOCRACY AND FREEDOM

Many people think of democracy and individual freedom as almost synonymous. Certainly, it is apparent that democracy and individual freedom must have some sort of connection. After all, democracy and a variety of individual freedoms derived originally from the same basic principles of liberalism.[15] And, for purely practical reasons, democracy requires at least minimal levels of freedom of speech and freedom of association if the public bargaining that is the essence of democracy is to proceed at all.

However, a variety of other freedoms—such as freedom of religion, free markets (see the next section, on "Democracy and Capitalism"), freedom to travel where you will, freedom to consume alcohol, and so on—are *not* necessarily companions of democracy, although we may find in practice that they usually go together.

A good example showing that freedom and democracy do not necessarily imply each other is Hong Kong, which as a British colony until 1997 never had democratic

---

[14]For a critique of some aspects of this interpretation, see Carles Boix and Susan Stokes, "Endogenous Democratization," *World Politics* 55 (2003), pp. 517–549.
[15]As we saw in Chapter 2.

government but which had an open society with many liberal freedoms—a free press, freedom of religion, freedom of speech and association, and so on. The United States also furnishes examples from its history in which, although we are a democracy, we have seen the level of freedoms rise and fall. The internment of Japanese-Americans during the Second World War, the system of legal racial segregation in many parts of the country through the first two-thirds of the twentieth century, the McCarthy period in which freedom of expression was limited—all help to demonstrate that there is not an automatic correspondence between democracy and freedom. Perhaps the most dramatic demonstration that freedom and democracy do not automatically coincide is that for the first half-century of its democratic history, the United States continued a brutal, institutionalized system of slavery.

Fareed Zakaria has presented an interesting argument along these lines, arguing first (as I have done above) that democracy and liberal freedoms do not always or necessarily imply one another, but then drawing the further argument that under some circumstances a less fully developed democracy may actually be more conducive to freedom than "all-out" democracy.[16] He points out that several countries in southeast Asia have gradually developed liberal freedoms *before* establishing electoral democracy (Singapore, for instance, which has very clean government, enjoys a much more open discussion of politics than in the past, but is still an essentially undemocratic government; Taiwan, which only instituted electoral democracy in the 1990s, but had a very open society well before that; and South Korea, which similarly instituted electoral democracy only in the 1990s). And, he notes that some states that opened up electoral democracy rapidly in a sudden transition from autocracy—Russia is one of his prime examples—only succeeded in creating a playground for shady characters and powerful economic interests.

The question of how and whether democracy and individual freedom are linked arises especially as autocracies move to democracy because in a number of countries authoritarian systems have gradually become more liberal and open, often with no shift to democracy for some years. Democracy has then come—or not come—only as a last step. Thus, it has been necessary, in analyzing the process of democratization, to separate the two processes. It appears that democratization may work best where it has been preceded by slow liberalization, which has provided time for opposition leadership to form, for organizations of representation to be established, and for working relationships to be established between the old regime and the forces for change. For example, in Brazil a process of *abertura*, or "opening," was begun by the military regime in 1974, under which discussion became more open, local governments became more independent, and political parties could form. It was not until 1985 that democracy was established.[17]

✦ Democracy and Capitalism

Another pairing that often seems natural to people is democracy and free-market capitalism. Partly this may be because the most prominent democracy in the world, the United States, is also the most prominent capitalist, free-market economy in the

---

[16]Fareed Zakaria, *The Future of Freedom: Illiberal Democracy at Home and Abroad* (New York: W.W. Norton, 2003).
[17]For a discussion of why military regimes might choose to yield up power in this way, see pages 166–167.

world. But to some extent the two also have a rough natural affinity, since both are based on the aggregation of individual choices as a way to make collective decisions and both reflect the basic liberal value of making individuals responsible for their choices.[18] And of course, both democracy and free-market capitalism were originally both backed by the same ideology, classical liberalism. So, these two have a lot in common, and it is no surprise that most democracies of the world have market-based economies.

However, there have been plenty of non-democratic states in the past that used market mechanisms for their economy.[19] Hong Kong, again, is a good example. It operates with an open market economy yet has never had fully democratic government, either under Britain or now as part of China. Many dictatorships and military governments in Africa rule states that essentially have market economies. Nazi Germany operated with a market economy; China, even as it has brutally been putting down the movement for democracy since 1989, has allowed a rapid evolution of its economy away from communist planning and toward market mechanisms.

Therefore, there is no automatic connection between democracy and capitalism, and the Eastern European states could in principle have made a shift away from communist economies without moving to democracy. Very likely, however, their rejection of the past and their desire for change and integration with the West were such that it seemed natural to become "Western" in politics as well as in economy. A radical change in the economy would have been very difficult without a thorough change of leaders; therefore, a basic governmental change of *some* sort was probably necessary, whether or not it was a move to democracy.

✦ AUTOCRACY

I noted at the beginning of this chapter that democracy is a fragile thing: of the 104 states that had been independent for at least forty-seven years in 2007, only 29 had had an uninterrupted record of electoral democratic government during that time. Autocratic government has its own fragilities, however. Of those same 104 states, only 13 had an uninterrupted autocratic regime across the same period of time. In the sections that follow, we will (1) look at some of the major forms of autocratic government and (2) explore the sources of their fragility and success.

What is **autocracy** like? The autocratic alternatives to democracy are by no means of one piece. Consider this sampling:

- **The Union of Soviet Socialist Republics (1917–1991)** From the Russian Revolution (1917) until a couple of years before the breakup of the union in 1991, power in the Soviet state was lodged clearly with the Communist Party. It was self-sustaining, recruiting new young members who could progress through it to build careers. Although Stalin's rise to power in the 1930s was bloody, after Stalin the party saw five peaceful, orderly transitions of leadership. As far as we know, decisions were

---

[18]See Charles Lindblom, *Politics and Markets* (New York: Basic Books, 1977), chap. 12.
[19]See Chapter 6 for a discussion of "market mechanisms."

made collectively within the party, with strong leadership by the party head and a great deal of influence from such groups as the army. Ordinary people did not have a great deal of personal freedom, but—compared with the bloody past—laws were at least predictable and dealings with the governmental apparatus were usually orderly.

• **Pakistan** Pakistan is a country of 150 million people in South Asia, adjoining India (on its east) and Iran (on its west). It achieved independence in 1947, along with India, and became the Moslem counterpart to Hindu India; the two have had tense relations ever since. Since attaining independence, Pakistan has alternated between democracy and military governments. The new country was a democracy until 1958, when a coup installed a military government. That government lasted until 1971, when democracy was restored. For the next six years, Pakistan once again had democratic government, with Z. A. Bhutto serving as its prime minister. In 1977, General Muhammad Zia ul-Haq took over the government. His military government executed Bhutto in 1979, and for several years Zia headed a repressive military regime that sought to establish Pakistan as an Islamic state. In 1983, a coalition of opposition leaders, many of them in exile, began a campaign called the Movement for the Restoration of Democracy. In 1985, General Zia yielded some power in a partial return to democracy: all military officers were removed from government posts except Zia himself, who remained as an extremely powerful president and head of the armed forces. In 1988, Zia was killed in a suspicious plane crash, and democracy was restored. Benazir Bhutto, Z. A. Bhutto's daughter, became the prime minister, but the democratic government had a rocky career. It was difficult to form a clear majority in a country deeply divided ethnically and economically, and the legacy of the constitution Zia had written in 1985 made it difficult for government to function. In the 1997 election, Bhutto's party lost badly, and Nawaz Sharif became prime minister in the first peaceful, democratic transfer of power in Pakistan's history. In 1999, however, after Pakistan suffered a defeat in a border skirmish with India, General Pervez Musharraf took over the government in yet another military coup. As has often been the case, the military takeover in 1999 was at least initially quite popular. The performance of the democratic government had not inspired respect.

Pakistan's sixty-year history of sporadic, brief democratic rule punctuated by military takeovers has not been good for the country. Over half of Pakistanis cannot read, and the economy is primitive.

• **Saudi Arabia** Saudi Arabia has been an absolute monarchy since early in the twentieth century, with power lodged in the Saud family. This is a large, extended family that provides not only the king but also most of the council of ministers and other high government officials. It appears that while the king figures importantly in the making of decisions, this is a genuinely collegial effort in which the council of ministers (including the king) discusses issues and decides on policies. The Saud family are conservative in religious matters and enforce strict Muslim standards of behavior, though they have been enthusiastic about economic modernization. Even the turmoil of the two Gulf Wars left this system essentially unchanged.

- **Democratic Republic of the Congo (formerly known as Zaire)** Zaire became independent from Belgium in 1960 and immediately plunged into a civil war fomented by Belgian mining interests. After a chaotic period of civil war, coups, assassinations, and attempts to establish democracy, power was seized in 1965 by Colonel Joseph-Désiré Mobutu, with strong support from the United States. Mobutu established a one-party state and remained in power from then until 1997, as president and, at various times, chair of the single party and head of the armed forces. His rule was characterized by charges of massive corruption and widespread abuses of human rights; but Mobutu proved adept at maintaining his rule despite unrest by giving ground at critical moments and retaking it when the opportunity arose. From about 1982, an organized opposition operated, based mainly abroad but sometimes openly, when circumstances permitted, in Zaire. In the 1990s, Mobutu fended off strong opposition pressure and student riots, while the country sank more deeply into social and economic disorganization. In 1997, a rebel group led by Laurent-Désiré Kabila, a long-time opponent of Mobutu from the eastern region of Zaire, finally defeated Mobutu's forces. Mobutu fled, and Kabila renamed the country and established himself as president. His regime was marked by the same sort of oppression as Mobutu's reign, but he was never able to establish full control of the country. He was assassinated in 2001 and succeeded by his son, Joseph Kabila. The country is a wreck; continuing civil wars, fomented by its neighbors, have almost broken it into a set of disparate regions.

These examples are roughly representative of autocratic systems. First, they are quite varied politically; they range from conservative Saudi Arabia to the bureaucratic Soviet Union to the personal dictatorship of Zaire. Second, many of the autocracies are not organized stably. Of these examples, Pakistan has alternated between democracy and military government. The Soviet Union disintegrated in 1991. Some of its parts have moved toward democracy, but often a shaky democracy; others are autocracies, masked by sham democracy. Mobutu did not ultimately retain power in Zaire, though his successor was as much an autocrat as he was. Saudi Arabia, on the other hand, appears to have a rather stable system.

✦ MILITARY GOVERNMENT

The most dramatic alternative to democratic government is **military government,** in which a group of officers use their troops to take over the governmental apparatus and run it themselves. This is called a **coup,** from the French *coup d'état* (strike at the state). Only a handful of the world's states are under military government.

"Only a handful"? We might have expected that military governments would be quite common. After all, the military in any state control more armed power than anyone else. If they choose, as a group, to oust the existing government—or even if only a part of the military choose to do so and the rest decide to sit it out—there is no one who can stop them. Civilian governments must depend for their safety on the military's satisfaction, on their disunity, or on their reluctance to take over the government. While each of these protective shields is evident in many military groups, it must not be so

Are Military Coups Contagious?

A number of observers have noticed that military coups cluster at certain times. Suddenly a rash of coups will break out in a region such as Latin America or southern Africa, and then coups will once again decrease. Statistical tests have shown that this is not coincidental. Coup makers apparently watch each other's success, and if they have seen a number of their neighbors succeed, they are likely to have fewer qualms about undertaking a coup themselves. Furthermore, if a number of coups have recently occurred in the neighborhood, this lessens the problems of legitimacy. If coups are a frequent thing in the region, initiating a coup will not seem as flagrantly illegitimate as if yours were the only army doing it.

Beyond considerations in any one state, then, coups appear to involve broad, wave-like regional processes. A good example of statistical analysis to measure these processes is Richard P. Y. Li and William R. Thompson, "The 'Coup Contagion' Hypothesis," *Journal of Conflict Resolution* 19 (March 1975), pp. 63–88.

Actually, it is likely that regime changes of *any* sort operate in this way, at least in part. As we saw earlier, democratization occurred in waves at different times, in different parts of the world. Most Eastern European states shifted to democracy between 1989 and 1991, for instance. There is evidence that movements for democracy in one area are often influenced by movements in another.*

*See, for instance, Douglas Anglin, "Southern African Responses to Eastern European Developments," *Journal of Modern African Studies* 28 (no. 3, 1990), pp. 431–56.

unusual that all three would from time to time fail and that the military would break out in a coup. This is particularly likely in a new state, where a tradition of civilian government has not had time to take hold. It is not surprising that military coups occur with some frequency around the world.

In a few states, coups have become so routine that they have almost been institutionalized as the normal method of governmental change. In such cases, other political forces have come to be involved informally, much as they would under other arrangements. Key groups such as labor unions may be sought out by one or another military faction as potential allies, and—even though they do not themselves bear arms—their weight is felt.[20]

In Bolivia, for instance, factions of the armed forces in the past regularly depended on other political groups when they were attempting a coup.[21] In 1978, a right-wing government was overthrown by the army, who were aided by left-wing allies in the unions and political parties. After an attempt at an election in 1979, a right-wing coup was tried, but it failed because its leaders were not able to get the support of Congress. In 1982, yet another military group was forced out of office by a general strike led by the

---

[20]Martin C. Needler, "Political Development and Military Intervention in Latin America," *American Political Science Review* 60 (September 1966), pp. 616–26.
[21]Bolivia experienced military coups regularly—almost annually—until 1985. Since 1985, Bolivia has had a democratic regime.

unions. In a bizarre way, coups under these circumstances become a system that draws a fairly wide range of people into the political process. Usually, however, they are more isolated events.

Military governments vary greatly in their political role. In Myanmar (formerly known as Burma), the military have ruled without interruption since they took power in 1962; theirs is a very repressive regime, with no dissent tolerated. In Nigeria, a series of military governments ruled from 1966 to 1978 and again from 1983 to 1999. During much of that time, except for the corrupt and vicious rule of General Sani Abacha from 1993 to 1998, there was considerable civilian support for the military regime. Greece was ruled by a right-wing group of officers from 1967 through 1973; this government maintained itself by harsh, repressive measures. It broke up in 1974, and democracy was reestablished. In Turkey, the military have taken over the government three times since World War II—in 1960, 1971, and 1980—each time when Turkey's democratic government was verging on chaos. The Turkish takeovers have been broadly supported and have been followed by a return to democracy after stability was restored.

Military governments also vary widely in the one thing in which we might have expected that they would be similar: their political direction. They are not all of the political right or of any other direction, even though the usual stereotype is of the right-wing officers' coup. Some coups are clearly of the right or the left, but many are not identifiable as either. Which sort results depends on which group of officers leads the coup; there are many officers of the left in most countries, as well as of the right,

"Good news. The 'Times' has upgraded us from a 'junta' to a military government."

especially if recruitment is not limited to the upper class. Studies that have compared fairly large numbers of military regimes with civilian regimes conclude, on the whole, that whether or not a state has a military regime has little effect on the state's rate of economic development. That is, as a group, military governments are neither especially good at guiding their states' economies nor especially poor at doing so.[22]

These two aspects of coups—that they sometimes become incorporated in the broader political process and that they have no clear political complexion, of the left or of the right—have made political scientists a bit cautious in assessing them. In a study of Venezuelans' views of democracy and military coups, David J. Myers and Robert E. O'Connor found that Venezuelans considered occasional coups part of the normal political process but distinguished sharply between coups and military dictatorships:

> … self-professed democratic Venezuelans perceive no incompatibility between
> endorsing democracy and supporting an occasional coup to rectify problem situations.
> Approving military intervention differs from favoring long-term military dictatorship.
> We find no evidence of the latter but widespread support of the former. Many
> respondents seemed to view coups as a device equivalent to a parliamentary vote of no
> confidence. It is indeed a serious action but is consistent with their understanding of
> democratic rules.[23]

And as Martin C. Needler noted some time ago:

> I would still affirm the general correctness of the position I took on this question ten
> years ago [that military coups are a repressive move backwards, thwarting necessary
> social change]. However, subsequent events have suggested that I underestimated the
> extent to which apparently democratic political processes could in fact be manipulated
> by elite economic interests to its advantage. This means that interruption of those
> processes by military seizures of power could, at least in some cases, be a force for
> promoting development instead of retarding it.[24]

✦ WHY AREN'T THERE MORE MILITARY GOVERNMENTS?

Good or bad, though, it is still surprising that more countries are not governed by the military. There are not as many coups as we might expect, and most military governments stay in power only a few years. This may be partly because most states take pains to imbue their military officers with inhibitions against political intervention. Adolf Hitler required officers to swear oaths of personal allegiance to him, for instance; and in the training of its officers, the U.S. government ensures in many ways that they will understand their proper role to be nonpolitical.

However, more important than such inhibitions are a series of significant problems faced by military governments—problems that make officers reluctant to take and

---

[22]See Robert Jackman, "Politicians in Uniform," *American Political Science Review* 70 (December 1976), pp. 1098–1109. See also the discussion below, pp. 170–172.
[23]David J. Myers and Robert E. O'Connor, "Support for Coups in Democratic Political Culture: A Venezuelan Exploration," *Comparative Politics* 30 (January 1998), p. 206.
[24]Martin C. Needler, "The Logic of Conspiracy: The Latin American Military Coup as a Problem in the Social Sciences," *Studies in Comparative International Development* 13 (Fall 1978), p. 31.

hold power. A uniquely serious one for them is that of legitimacy, which we will discuss in detail, as a general problem of all governments, in Chapter 8. Legitimacy is a widespread belief among the people of a state that a particular form of government is appropriate, and that its officials are therefore entitled to rule. We can see why this might pose special problems for a military government. A military government takes power through no regular process but simply seizes it, so how can it claim that no other group should similarly displace it? A democratic government is legitimized by the electoral process that produced it; a monarchy is legitimized by the rules of succession on which it is based; a communist government is legitimized by Lenin's theory that the Communist Party must lead the revolution. No process of selection legitimizes the military government, though. Those who live by the sword shall die by the sword, they say, and a military government must always be concerned to justify its existence. To this end, many military governments add civilians to their governing apparatus or set future dates for a return to democracy. Others try to rally the people through wars and appeals to nationalism.

Another problem of most military governments is that while their leaders *may* be skilled politically, there is little in the profession for which they have been trained that makes this especially likely. Military organization is usually marked by a fairly orderly passage of commands from higher officers to lower officers, without a great deal of argument in between. This orderliness should not be exaggerated, but many military officers are clearly frustrated by the jabber of daily political requests and arguments with which they must deal once they have taken over the power of the state.

Yet another problem for military governments is the problem of succession. How does the system provide for transfer of power from one leader to another, either on the first leader's death or because it appears to be time for a change? In democracies this is accomplished through regular elections. In a monarchy, it is accomplished by the designation of a child or other relative to be the monarch's successor. But in military governments there is no clear institutional basis for arranging the transfer of power.

Finally, many military governments are fairly shaky alliances, united primarily by their opposition to the regime they have displaced and likely to fall apart as new issues arise that may divide their members.

As a result of these problems, purely military governments are actually rather fragile. Unless they set up the institutions to transform themselves into one-party states (see the next section), there is a good chance that they will eventually yield to the establishment of democracy. If a military regime is internally divided or has problems generally in governing and if enough of the key figures concerned feel that the uncertainty of the outcome of democratic choice is preferable to the certainty of any other particular group being in control, the stage is set to introduce democracy—or reintroduce it, as the case may be.[25] In the last two decades of the past century, for example, twenty-two states switched at least for a time from purely military government to democracy.[26]

---

[25]For an expansion of this argument, see Adam Przeworski, "Some Problems in the Study of the Transition to Democracy," in Guillermo O'Donnell, Philippe C. Schmitter, and Laurence Whitehead, eds., *Transitions from Authoritarian Rule: Prospects for Democracy* (Baltimore: Johns Hopkins University Press, 1986), pp. 47–63.

[26]Argentina, Bangladesh, Bolivia, Brazil, Burkina Faso, Burundi, Chile, Ecuador, Fiji, Ghana, Honduras, Nigeria, Pakistan, Panama, Paraguay, Peru, the Philippines, Portugal, South Korea, Thailand, Turkey, and Uruguay.

✦ ONE-PARTY STATES

Most autocracies are not straight military governments but **one-party states.** The one-party state is distinguished by the fact that the government is based on and supports a political party, and that this is the only party allowed in the state. One-party arrangements have often had their origins in military coups. For example, in Libya, Colonel Muammar Khadaffi seized power in a coup in 1969 and established the Arab-Socialist Union as the sole political party; its general congress, chaired by Khadaffi, is in effect the chief governing body of the state. Other one-party arrangements originated in national independence movements, which were then institutionalized as the single party. In Tanzania, for example, Julius Nyerere led the movement for independence, and his independence movement, the Tanganyika Africa National Union, won seventy of the seventy-one seats in the first election to the National Assembly. Four years later, a constitution was written that established it as the state's sole party.[27] A number of one-party states originated in socialist revolutions, either indigenous, as in the cases of Cuba, China, or the U.S.S.R., or imposed by the U.S.S.R., as in the cases of (pre-1989) East Germany, Czechoslovakia, and other Eastern European states.

What distinguishes these states from other autocratic systems, especially from straightforward military governments, is the existence of a reasonably large national political party that bolsters the government and provides an institutional basis for it. Compared with military rule, the one-party state offers a more stable and responsive form of government. The military government is necessarily limited by the field of vision of the officers who hold power. There is little provision for dealing with broad factional conflict or for the intrusion of diverse opinions. The government itself came into being by irregular means; therefore, there exists no regular set of arrangements to provide for the replacement of old leaders by new. These are things that may be provided for by the single political party.

A national party is likely to embrace at least a reasonable range of the social groups in a state—labor leaders, industrialists, intellectuals, and military leaders. Not all of these may be equally happy with the party; however, they have little choice but to cooperate with it if asked. The party, on its side, needs to involve them if only to keep tabs on potential troublemakers. As a result, the single party as an organization is usually able to have a broad feel for opinion in the countryside. It provides institutional links between the government and the population.

Second, the party can provide an arena in which varied political positions can develop into factions. In this way, new conflicts may develop within an existing system rather than arising outside it and posing a threat to it.

Finally, the single party may provide a set of arrangements by which a transition of leadership can be accomplished. An example of this capacity was the fairly easy transition from Konstantin Chernenko to Mikhail Gorbachev in the Soviet Union after Chernenko's death in 1985. During Chernenko's illness, there had been some

---

[27]Although there is only one legal party, there are still many contests between individuals in elections. A majority of the seats in the National Assembly are filled by election, the rest being appointed. Defeats of individual incumbents in elections are common, though all candidates must come from the ruling party.

process at work by which the Communist party leadership decided who would take over from him.

The one-party state must be distinguished from a democracy with a dominant-party system.[28] A few democracies have party systems in which a single party has dominated government over a long period. Italy is a good example: From 1945 to 1994, without a break, the Christian Democratic Party received the largest vote of any party at each election, and except for a couple of years, it dominated all coalition cabinets during that period. (It finally fell from grace in 1993 due to its leaders' involvement in massive scandals.) What distinguished Italy from the one-party states during this period is that other parties were able to organize and did so; it was also universally recognized that those other parties would gain office if enough people voted for them—and in fact, this did happen in 1994.

To sum up our treatment of one-party systems: This is the most frequently seen form of autocratic government. It may originate in all sorts of ways—military coups, movements for national independence, socialist revolutions, and many others. Distinctively, the one-party state has one (and only one) political party that is fostered by the government. This party adds to the government's capacities and helps to make these regimes more stable than straight military governments.

✦ MONARCHIES AND THEOCRACIES

Two other significant forms of autocracy are found in the world:

- **Monarchies** are systems in which the power to rule is inherited through descent in a family. Most monarchies of the world are found in the Mideast or Asia, and are often relatively underdeveloped states not much touched by modernity. (Bhutan, on the northern border of India, is a good example.) Monarchies would not figure importantly in our study of politics today, except that several of them turned out to sit on huge reserves of oil. That is a good way to attract people's attention. Some examples of oil-rich monarchies in the Mideast are Saudi Arabia, Qatar, and Kuwait.

    Monarchies should not be confused with "constitutional monarchies" like Great Britain, Spain, or Sweden where a hereditary monarch exists as part of a democracy. Constitutional monarchs play a purely symbolic and ceremonial role. (These will be discussed further in Chapter 14.)

- A **theocracy** is a state ruled by a set of religious leaders, who derive their power from their positions in the religion. Its legitimacy comes from the shared faith of the citizens. Iran is the most prominent theocracy today. Vatican City, a tiny sovereign territory ruled by the Pope, is another example, if a minor one.

    There is no particular set of principles we can lay out for how a theocracy is ruled, because power in the state is simply a function of how power is acquired and exercised within the religion. Some religions, like the Catholic Church, are strictly hierarchical, with a single clear leader at the top. In contrast, Islam in all of its

---

[28]See below, pp. 266–269.

Muammar Khadaffi, leader of Libya: originally, leader
of a military coup; later, head of the single party.

© Reuters/Bettmann/Corbis

forms is very loosely organized, and power is a function of how widely respected a religious scholar is. At any given time there are usually many diverse leaders within an Islamic group.

Theocracies are few today, but popular movements in many Islamic states are pushing for the establishment of theocracies in their state.

✦ DEMOCRACY VERSUS AUTOCRACY: MATERIAL CONSIDERATIONS

It may seem odd to ask the question, which is better—democracy or autocracy? People all over the world have "voted" often for democracy through popular movements, revolutions, and "with their feet" through emigration. The basic appeal of democracy is surely the individual dignity it confers, at least implicitly, on each citizen, and the partial protection its rule of law offers against arbitrary actions by the government. But, there have often been arguments about other good things in life as well, and whether they were easier to achieve under democracy or under autocracy. It has often been argued, for instance, that economic growth is easier for a poor country to achieve if it is not burdened by the debates of democracy, but can instead focus its efforts under autocratic leadership.

TABLE 7.1

Life Expectancy under Autocracy and Democracy

Per Capita Income, $	Life Expectancy, Democracies	Life Expectancy, Autocracies	Difference
0–1,000	47.2	46.4	0.8
1,001–2,000	56.3	52.2	4.1
2,001–3,000	63.6	59.2	4.4
3,001–4,000	67.3	64.2	3.1
4,001–5,000	70.2	65.0	5.2
5,001–6,000	71.3	68.6	2.7
6,001–	73.2	67.6	5.6

SOURCE: From Adam Przeworski, Michael E. Alvarez, Jose Antonio Cheibub, and Fernando Limongi, *Democracy and Development: Political Institutions and Well-Being in the World, 1950–1990*. New York: Cambridge University Press, 2000. Reprinted with the permission of Cambridge University Press.

In this section, drawing on the research of Adam Przeworski, Michael E. Alvarez, José Cheibub, and Fernando Limongi, I will look both at the question of how democracies compare with autocracies in economic growth, and in the overall quality of life as measured by life expectancies.[29] In both of these comparisons, democracy looks good, so the more material aspects of life give the same answer as the basic values cited above—democracy trumps autocracy.

First, with regard to economic development, Przeworski and others show through careful measures both of democracy and of economic development that the average performance of democracies over four decades was about the same as that of autocracies. States with both sorts of regime grew at about a 4 percent annual rate. However, these averages conceal a major difference between autocracies and democracies. Though on the average both sorts of regime were equal, the range of possible outcomes for autocracies was wildly greater than for democracies. All of the states whose economies grew at an annual rate of 7 percent or more were autocracies, but so were almost all of the states whose economies grew at a rate of less than 1 percent annually. With democracies, given that economic policy will represent some sort of a negotiated bargain among the economic interests of society, you will get results that are all in the same, moderately positive ballpark. With autocracies, since the government is free to put all of its eggs in one basket, you can get results ranging from miracles to disasters.

With regard to general well being, consider Table 7.1, which shows the life expectancy of people in autocracies and democracies, for states at varying levels of prosperity.[30] The main thing determining life expectancy is how well-off the state is, but at each level

---

[29]Adam Przeworski, Michael E. Alvarez, José Antonio Cheibub, and Fernando Limongi, *Democracy and Development: Political Institutions and Well-Being in the World, 1950–1990* (New York: Cambridge University Press, 2000).
[30]Ibid, p. 230.

of per capita income those living in democracies can expect to live significantly longer than those in autocracies (as much as 5.6 years longer, for the most prosperous states).

I conclude this look at the material differences between democracy and autocracy with the triumphal note of Przeworski and his colleagues: "Thus, we did not find a shred of evidence that democracy need be sacrificed on the altar of development."[31]

✦ "POWER AND CHOICE" AGAIN

To return to the theme of our text, autocratic governments—especially the military governments—might appear to embody a rather pure strain of politics as power. After all, when political control depends on who has the guns, it is hard to deny that power is at work. On the other hand, it is a common mistake to think of autocratic governments simply as raw examples of power at work.

One-party governments often see themselves as pursuing communal objectives and develop organizational mechanisms for bringing a wide spectrum of opinion to bear on the government's decisions. Even military governments usually portray themselves as heeding the country's call, and there is often broad support among the people for a military coup. We shall deal with governments such as these more wisely if we remember that the picture is not black or white but that politics in these states—as in democracies—consists of power and choice.

EXAMPLE

Democratization in Spain

For a brief period in the 1930s, Spain had a democratic government; but the army, supported by Hitler and Mussolini, overthrew the government at the end of a long and bloody civil war in 1939 and established Francisco Franco as a fascist dictator. Franco ruled from 1939 until his death in 1975.

His dictatorship was ironfisted and authoritarian in the early years, but for the last decade or two of his rule, there was considerable liberalization in Spain. Labor unions, which were technically still illegal, were tolerated and bargained collectively for large numbers of workers. Public education, which had earlier been suppressed, blossomed: In 1957, there were only 120 high schools in Spain, one *fewer* than in the last year of the republic, but in the next decade, the number of students attending high school went up 1,000 percent. The Spanish economy, organized as a free market in contrast with the political structure, grew rapidly and diversified; the large landowners who formed the core of Franco's support became less and less central to the economy.

---

[31]Ibid, p. 271.

Thus, when Franco died in 1975, the stage was set for change. However, everyone was apprehensive. Against the promise of a more modern society in 1975 were set the bloody memories of the civil war of the 1930s, characterized by shocking brutality and atrocities.

There seems agreement that the transition was eased by unwritten agreements ("pacts") between the army and the democratic forces. The army apparently acquiesced in establishment of a democracy on three conditions:

1. The monarchy (which Franco had set up to succeed to power after his death) was to be retained.
2. The political right, rather than the army's old enemies on the left, were to lead the change.
3. The country's regions should be given no self-determination.

In 1976, King Juan Carlos and his conservative prime minister, Adolfo Suarez, put a democratic constitution before the people of Spain in a referendum. The referendum was important because it added the legitimacy of popular approval to the new democracy. The constitution, reflecting the king's wishes, established more of a democracy than the army had probably envisioned, one with a constitutional, mainly symbolic monarch.

Over the next few years, the new democracy was plagued by disorganized party conflict in the parliament, together with a rising campaign of terrorism by Basque nationalists. The terrorists' targets were primarily officers of the police and the army, which added to the tension because those institutions were potentially dangerous if they became disenchanted with the new system. In 1981, there was a serious attempt to overthrow the regime. A group of soldiers seized the parliament when it was in session, with the entire cabinet present, and announced that they were taking over the state in the name of the king. However, they failed to cut off communications into and out of the palace; Juan Carlos telephoned the commanders of the army, some of whom were already preparing to set out for Madrid in support of the coup, and told them they would have to depose him if they wished to overthrow the democracy. The coup failed, and the political leaders were freed.

Afterward, Juan Carlos reportedly met with the parliamentary party leaders and told them they would have to work out better techniques of decision making and compromise, because he doubted he could thwart another coup if one were attempted. In the next several years, Spanish democracy was solidified in several ways:

• In 1982, a moderate socialist, Felipe Gonzalez, became prime minister. His long, not very radical rule helped to calm fears of the "reds" and lay the civil war to rest.
• Considerable power of self-government was devolved onto the regions.
• Spain became a member of the European Community in 1986, integrating it into a democratic organization of democratic states.

Spain has by now successfully established a stable base for democracy, marked by a peaceful and straightforward replacement of Gonzalez's socialist government by a right-of-center cabinet following the 1996 election, and further movements back and forth since then. The transition to democracy in Spain involved less activity by popular movements than in most countries, perhaps partly because of everyone's concern, given the bloody history of the 1930s, not to ignite an open conflict over democratization. Because of this not only the forces for democracy, but also the army, moved carefully. Furthermore, most of the political elite recognized the need for democracy and acted publicly to bring it about, so there was not a strong antidemocratic side for popular movements to push against. Although it would be wrong to underestimate the hard work and courage of all those who brought democracy to Spain, it is true that in comparison with many other countries, democracy came in this case almost like a ripe fruit falling.

✳ EXAMPLE

Fragile Democracy in Peru

Peru is a poor country on the west coast of Latin America—a poor country, but one with a vibrant cultural life and a long history of intellectual contributions; three of its universities are over three hundred years old. The country has long been torn by ethnic, economic, and regional conflicts. Approximately half of its people are Amerindians, mostly living in the impoverished interior of the country. Economic disparities between the interior and the more prosperous coast are indicated by the fact that infant mortality in the coastal region is 46 per thousand births but 128 in the lower areas of the interior and 156 in the mountains.[32]

From the Second World War until 1978, except for a five-year interlude of democratic government from 1963 to 1968, Peru was ruled by various military groups, which replaced each other from time to time by seizing power in coups d'état. In 1977, General Francisco Morales Bermúdez announced a plan to restore civilian rule. A constitution-writing assembly was elected, the new constitution emerged in 1979, and a new president and congress were elected in 1980.

From 1980 to the present, there have been regular presidential and congressional elections every five years, so one might conclude that steady democracy had been established in the democratization of 1979. However, the experience of democracy since 1980 has not been that smooth, and while the outlook is positive, it remains uncertain. In this, Peru is probably fairly typical of newly established democracies.

Not long after the first election of the new democracy, a left-wing terrorist movement appeared in the interior that called itself *Sendero Luminoso,* the "Shining Path." It developed broad-based strength in the region and drew down on itself an unprincipled retaliation from the military that was almost as destructive of society as *Sendero Luminoso* itself. At the height of the movement's activities in 1989, the government reported that 3,198 people had been killed in terrorist violence. At the same time, it was estimated that since 1982 approximately three thousand people had been executed by the military, and another three thousand had "disappeared" in military jails and were assumed dead.[33] The government appointed peace commissions to investigate human rights abuses by the military, but both commissions eventually resigned, stating that they could get no cooperation from the military.

The economy also did badly during the initial years of the democracy. Real incomes in the area around the capital city of Lima declined by 1990 to about one-third what they had been in 1980.[34] By 1990, inflation was running at 7,650 percent a year. (If inflation were to run at that rate in the United States, a shirt that cost $10 at the beginning of a year would cost $765 by the end of the year!) Governmental economic policy had been crippled by

---

[32]James D. Rudolph, *Peru: The Evolution of a Crisis* (Westport, Conn.: Praeger, 1992), p. 8.
[33]Europa Publications Ltd., *Europa Yearbook 1995* (London: Unwin Brothers Ltd.), p. 2360.
[34]Susan C. Stokes, *Cultures in Conflict: Social Movements and the State in Peru* (Berkeley: University of California Press, 1995), p. 46.

opposition from businesses and labor unions. The latter had launched several general strikes at various times, in which all unions went out on strike simultaneously, for maximum political impact.

In the 1990 election, a little-known agronomist of Japanese descent, Alberto Fujimori, won on a pledge to fight inflation and corruption. He initiated an austerity plan for the economy—abolishing subsidies, breaking up monopolies, simplifying the tax system, and privatizing a number of publicly owned industries. In November 1991, Fujimori convinced the congress to give him 150 days of emergency dictatorial power to deal with economic problems; he used this power to deregulate most forms of transport and to open telecommunications, the postal services, the schools, and other services to private competition. He also gave the military added leeway in combating *Sendero Luminoso.*

His relations with congress deteriorated as a result of these actions, and on April 5, 1992, Fujimori carried out what has been called an *autogolpe* ("self-coup"). He announced suspension of the 1979 constitution, had troops seize the congress and all television and radio stations, and placed large numbers of labor leaders and leaders of congress under house arrest. Tanks patrolled the streets of Lima.

A week later, when censorship was lifted, opposition leaders called on the people to take up arms against the president, a right that had been guaranteed in the 1979 constitution. However, the *autogolpe* had been fairly popular, and there was no response to the opposition's call to arms. Fujimori presented his revised version of the 1979 constitution to the electorate in 1993, with new provisions allowing the president to run for reelection and setting a death sentence for terrorist activity. The revised constitution was approved with 52 percent of the vote.

Over the next couple of years, Fujimori maintained good relations with the military. He and his courts protected military officers from charges of human rights abuse, transferring even well-documented cases of murder from civil courts to the military courts, for instance, where the officers received relatively mild sentences. The government gradually won the twin battles against inflation and *Sendero Luminoso,* capturing *Sendero's* leader in 1994.

In the 1995 presidential election, Fujimori won in a landslide with 65 percent of the vote, and his party gained a majority in congress. Over the next few years, he cemented his relationship with the military further, issuing an amnesty in 1995 for all military officers and police convicted of human rights violations since 1980 in connection with the counterinsurgency campaign. He also claimed credit as a tough leader when a guerrilla group (not part of *Sendero Luminoso*) occupied the Japanese embassy in 1996, taking everyone in the building hostage. After four months of highly publicized deadlock in negotiations with the guerrillas, Fujimori ordered a military assault in which the hostages were successfully freed. The guerrillas were killed—some of them reportedly after they had surrendered.

During Fujimori's second term, even though he had successfully put down rebellion and gotten the economy into reasonable order, Peru still had intense lines of political animosity. The military remained highly political and was a lightning rod for angry passions on both sides, and Peru remained a poor country with huge disparities of income and education. Fujimori undermined any infant sense of constitutionalism that might have emerged in the country, operating fast and loose with the rule of law. The constitution he wrote in 1993 limited presidents to two terms, but Fujimori manipulated rules furiously during his second term to evade this provision and run for a third term in 2000. When three Constitutional Court justices ruled that he could not do so under the constitution, he removed them from the court. And when a television station aggressively investigated abuses by the Peruvian intelligence service, its Israeli-born owner was stripped of his Peruvian citizenship; thereupon, his shares in the station were impounded under a law stating that foreign citizens may not own Peruvian television stations.

The election in which Fujimori ran for his unconstitutional third term, in April 2000, was marked by massive irregularities, especially in the voting rolls. A popular alternative candidate who had arisen in the campaign, Alejandro Toledo, an economist of Amerindian heritage, rejected the first-round results of the election when they showed Fujimori had just under 50 percent of the vote. Toledo refused to participate in the runoff election in May (the constitution required that the two leading vote-getters face each other in a runoff if no one received 50 percent of the vote on the first round). Citing widespread rigging of the first round and the election commission's refusal to institute reforms for the second round, Toledo urged his supporters to vote spoiled ballots in protest, and he did not campaign for election. The outcome of the runoff was that Fujimori got 51 percent, Toledo (whose name was still on the ballot) garnered 17 percent, and written-in "No to fraud" got 32 percent.

Despite the controversy, and despite condemnation of the election by the Organization of American States (most of whose members did not send official representatives to his inauguration in August), Fujimori took office with a defiantly anti-reform cabinet. However, the street protests against his election, which had never stopped, took on a new ferocity when a few months later, a video was leaked to the media showing Fujimori's secret police head, Vladimiro Montesinos, bribing a member of congress. Montesinos was the "gray eminence" of Fujimori's regime, commanding an internal spy network of four hundred professional agents and sixteen thousand paid informants spread throughout the population. Under pressure of the pro-reform protests, the government's control of the country became ever more tenuous, and finally in November, Fujimori stepped down. A new election was called.

Three main candidates emerged in this election: Toledo again; Lourdes Flores, a woman representing the center-right; and Alan Garcia, a controversial populist former president (Fujimori's predecessor from 1985 to 1990) who had fled abroad in disgrace after a regime marked by hyperinflation and the rise of guerrilla violence. The campaign was remarkably dirty and personal, including charges of drug use and sexual scandals against Toledo. In the end, Flores—who had started out as a popular, fresh voice for reform—became too closely tied to Lima and the upper class, and finished third. In the runoff election, Toledo beat Garcia and was installed as president in June 2001. He symbolically held two inaugurations—one in Lima and another the next day at Cuzco, the ancient Inca capital in the Andes.

Toledo's presidency was dismal. He was fortunate in that the economy did well (5.2 percent growth in 2002), but he lacked the skill to pull various parts of society or of his own party together. By June 2003, when his entire cabinet resigned in protest amid a teachers' strike and widespread protests, his approval rating stood at just 11 percent.[35] And in 2003 the *Sendero Luminoso* reappeared on at least a small scale, with widespread graffiti, ambushes of army units that killed several soldiers, and a mass kidnapping of 71 workers on a gas pipeline. In the election of 2006, Toledo lost badly to Alan Garcia.

Peru's democracy has now operated almost continuously for over twenty years, and support for it is institutionalized in many ways, but it is not at all difficult to imagine circumstances in which it could still fail.

---

[35]"Running Out of Options," *The Economist,* June 28, 2003, p. 35.

 EXAMPLE

Theocracy in Iran[36]

 Iran has a government that is a blend of democracy and theocracy, but with the theocratic aspect clearly dominant. The present system emerged in 1979 from a revolution to overthrow the unpopular emperor of Iran, Shah Mahammed Reza. After a few years of indecisive internal conflict, the present system emerged.

The system is one in which there is a democratically elected parliament, the Majles, and a president. The elections are freely contested, but are managed indirectly by the clerics, who can veto any candidates they choose. Despite their managed character, the elections are lively events, and have in the past put into power reformers who wanted to gradually ease the Islamic character of Iranian life. Currently, because reformers boycotted the last election, conservative Islamic forces dominate the Majles. The president, Mahmoud Ahmadinejad, is a populist who gained office on promises to help the poor and conduct an aggressive foreign policy; as such, he does not pose a threat to Islamic control.

Existing alongside the democratic structure, but in fact much more powerful than the democratic structure, is a somewhat loosely organized theocratic governing body. The heart of this is the Supreme Leader, a figure who emerges by informal, consensual selection from among the learned elders of the faith in Iran. Once selected, the Supreme Leader rules for life. The first Supreme Leader was Ayatollah Khomeini, who had led the revolution against the Shah. At his death in 1989 he was succeeded by Ayatollah Ali Khameini, who rules today.[37]

The Supreme Leader has immense powers, and there are no checks on how he exercises them:

- He is commander-in-chief of the armed forces.
- He sets overall policy for Iran, and can annul acts of the president and Majles.
- He controls immensely rich foundations, which hold all of the wealth seized from the monarchy when it was overthrown.
- He appoints the Friday prayer leaders of the mosques, and controls the Shi'i seminaries.
- He appoints the heads of the radio and television networks.

The Supreme Leader is aided in his control of the democratic side of things by the Council of Guardians, who examine the compatibility of all laws on legislation with Islamic law and the Islamic Constitution of Iran. They can annul any law. They also review the credentials of all candidates for the Majles and the presidency, and can eliminate any candidates they choose. Half of the members of the Council of Guardians are appointed by the Supreme Leader; the other half are judges chosen by the Majles from a list prepared by the judicial branch of government.

In short, the Supreme Leader is indeed supreme. This does not mean, in practice, that he rules arbitrarily or by whim. He is chosen in the first place because he represents in his views something of a consensus of the clerical establishment. And, Shi'i Islam is a very open, free-wheeling

---

[36]I owe a debt in this section to Mohsen M. Milani, "Iran," in *Comparative Governance*, Primis database.
[37]"Ayatollah" signifies a religious leader with a significant following. Shi'i Islam, the dominant form of Islam in Iran, does not have a single leader; rather, various ayatollahs build sets of followers.

structure with lots of room for dissent. The Supreme Leader rules from within an establishment in which many viewpoints are continually being raised, and in a country where public opinion is a force to be reckoned with. If nothing else, the Islamic state always has to reckon with the possibilities of passive resistance by the public, and it has to be careful not to get totally out of step.

For instance, state censors prevent almost all Western films and music from entering the country—yet a large black market exists in which, at least in the cities, Iranians can get almost any sort of entertainment they want. This is tacitly tolerated by the theocratic state.

Like all autocratic states, we see that the Iranian theocracy is neither absolute nor unchallenged. The peculiar mix of democracy and theocracy in Iran, however, is probably unstable in the long run. If the Supreme Leader receives guidance from God, what does it matter whether 51 percent of the voters agree with him? Alternatively, if the people of Iran are to rule, what place is there for a Supreme Leader? Iran has suffered from a decades-long crisis of legitimacy. In the end, a basic question is, "What use [is] a Supreme Leader in a democracy, and what use [are] elections in a theocracy?"[38]

KEY TERMS

regime	crisis transitions	one-party state
democracy	autocracy	monarchy
authoritarian democracy	military government	theocracy
pacts	coup	

FURTHER READING

Almond, Gabriel A. "Capitalism and Democracy." *PS: Political Science & Politics* (September 1991), pp. 467–74.

Boix, Carles. *Democracy and Redistribution.* New York: Cambridge University Press, 2003.

Brooker, Paul. *Non-Democratic Regimes: Theory, Government, and Politics.* New York: St. Martin's Press, 2000.

Centeno, Miguel. *Democracy Within Reason: Technocratic Revolution in Mexico.* University Park: Penn State University Press, 1994.

Cheibub, José Antonio, Dahl, Robert, and Shapiro, Ian, eds. *Democracy Sourcebook.* Boston: MIT Press, 2003.

Diamond, Larry, Kirk-Greene, Anthony, and Oyediran, Oyeleye, eds. *Transition Without End: Nigerian Politics and Civil Society Under Babangida.* Boulder, CO.: Lynne Rienner Publishers, 1997.

———, and Morlino, Leonardo. *Assessing the Quality of Democracy.* Baltimore, MD: Johns Hopkins University Press, 2005.

---

[38]Laura Secor, "Whose Iran?" *New York Times Magazine,* January 28, 2007, p. 53.

————, Plattner, Marc F., Chu, Yun-han, and Tien, Hung-mao, eds. *Consolidating the Third Wave Democracies.* Baltimore: Johns Hopkins University Press, 1997.

Downing, Brian. *The Military Revolution and Political Change.* Princeton: Princeton University Press, 1992.

Drake, Paul, and McCubbins, Mathew, eds. *The Origins of Liberty: Political and Economic Liberalization in the Modern World.* Princeton: Princeton University Press, 1998.

Haggard, Stephan, and Kaufman, Robert R. *The Political Economy of Democratic Transitions.* Princeton: Princeton University Press, 1995.

Huntington, Samuel P. *The Third Wave: Democratization in the Late Twentieth Century.* Norman: Oklahoma University Press, 1991.

Maravall, José Maria. "The Myth of the Authoritarian Advantage." *Journal of Democracy* 5 (1994), pp. 17–31.

Needler, Martin C. "The Logic of Conspiracy: The Latin American Military Coup as a Problem in the Social Sciences." *Studies in Comparative International Development* 13 (Fall 1978), pp. 28–40.

Neumann, Franz. *Behemoth: The Structure and Practice of National Socialism, 1933–1944.* New York: Oxford University Press, 1944.

O'Donnell, Guillermo, and Schmitter, Philippe C. *Transitions from Authoritarian Rule.* Baltimore: Johns Hopkins University Press, 1986.

Opp, Karl Dieter, Voss, Peter, and Gern, Christiane. *Origins of a Spontaneous Revolution: East Germany 1989.* Ann Arbor: University of Michigan Press, 1995.

Osa, Maryjane. *Solidarity and Contention: The Networks of Polish Opposition, 1956–1981.* Minneapolis: University of Minnesota Press, 2003.

Przeworski, Adam. *Democracy and the Market.* Cambridge: Cambridge University Press, 1991.

————. *Sustainable Democracy.* Cambridge: Cambridge University Press, 1995.

————, Alvarez, Mike, Cheibub, José Antonio, and Limongi, Fernando. *Democracy and Development: Political Institutions and Material Well-Being in the World, 1950–1990.* New York: Cambridge University Press, 2000.

Reno, William. *Warlord Politics and African States.* Boulder, CO: Lynne Rienner Publishers, 1998.

Roeder, Philip G. *Red Sunset: The Failure of Soviet Politics.* Princeton: Princeton University Press, 1993.

Schmitter, Philippe, and Karl, Terry. "What Democracy Is . . . and Is Not." *Journal of Democracy* 2 (1991), pp. 75–88.

Sisk, Timothy. *Democratization in South Africa: The Elusive Social Contract.* Princeton: Princeton University Press, 1995.

Skidmore, Thomas E. *The Politics of Military Rule in Brazil, 1964–1984.* Oxford: Oxford University Press, 1988.

Wedeen, Lisa. *Ambiguities of Domination: Politics, Rhetoric and Symbols in Contemporary Syria.* Chicago: University of Chicago Press, 1999.

Zakaria, Fareed. *The Future of Freedom: Illiberal Democracy at Home and Abroad.* New York: W.W. Norton, 2003.

WEB SITES OF INTEREST

Political Database of the Americas, maintained by Georgetown University:
http://pdba.georgetown.edu

National Endowment for Democracy:
http://www.ned.org

International Institute for Democracy and Electoral Assistance (International IDEA), an intergovernmental organization supporting sustainable democracy:
http://www.idea.int/

Amnesty International, a global organization working to protect human rights, especially in autocratic systems:
http://www.amnesty.org/

Human Rights Web, with connections to a range of human rights sites:
http://www.hrw.org

United Nations Development Programme: Democratic Governance:
http://www.undp.org/governance

Network Institute for Global Democratization:
http://www.nigd.org/

Comparative Democratization Project, Stanford University:
http://democracy.stanford.edu

CHAPTER 8

How Individuals Relate to the State, and the State to the Individual

In this chapter, we shall consider the relationship between the state and its citizens. Every state has some sort of government, which sets its policies. A "government," when you think about it, is an unusual body within the state. It is the only group of people entitled to make decisions that everyone in the state has a duty to accept and obey.[1] There are many groups of people who have power over others, in that they can force others to do what they wish; for example, General Motors may induce a local government to give it a special tax break in return for locating a plant in the town, or a union may force an employer to increase wages.[2] The government, however, has a different kind of power, which we call **authority**.[3] (We used this term in Chapter 6 also, as an alternative to market mechanisms for making public choices.)

If General Motors tries to convince a family to sell their house and the family refuses, that is all there is to it. The family may have made a wise or an unwise decision; but whether they sold or not, the decision was theirs to make, and either decision is socially acceptable. If the school bully tells another child to eat dirt and the child runs away or fights the bully, no one faults the child for not doing what the bully commanded. General Motors does not have authority to make someone sell a house, and the bully does not have authority to make another child eat dirt.

Authority is power based on a general agreement (1) that a person or group has the right to issue certain sorts of commands and (2) that those commands should be obeyed. If a

---

[1]See Chapter 3, p. 62.
[2]See Chapter 1 for a fuller discussion of power.
[3]See also the discussion of authority above, p. 5.

person fails to obey authority, that failure is socially unacceptable, because the authority itself is based on a general acceptance of its exercise.

You will find in these sections that we deal with two somewhat similar terms—"authority" and "legitimacy"—which in turn might be thought to bear some relationship to a concept we worked with in Chapter 3, "sovereignty." I will introduce "legitimacy" in the next section, but at this point let me clarify the difference between "sovereignty" and "authority." "Sovereignty" is a trait of the state. No matter how power is organized within the state, or who holds that power, the state has sovereignty. *Within* the state, various individuals wield various kinds of power, and one kind of power is "authority," as defined here. Authority relationships within the state may change—even dramatically, as in a military coup—yet the sovereignty of the state continues unaffected.

Various individuals or groups in a society have limited sorts of authority that extend over specific ranges of behavior. A parent has authority to tell children of a certain age when they should go to bed, with whom they should play, and so on; but as children grow older, the range of activities over which a parent has authority dwindles until it disappears. A teacher in a classroom has the authority to tell students how they should prepare for classes, but the teacher does not have the authority to tell them whom they may date or what political candidate to support. A General Motors supervisor has the authority to tell an assembly-line worker which bolts to tighten, but he or she cannot tell the worker how to spend coffee breaks; and when the worker resigns, the supervisor has no authority at all.

A *government* is unique in society in that all of its power involves authority, and at least potentially, there is no limit to the range of activities over which it may exercise authority. Most governments themselves impose some limits on their authority; for instance, the U.S. government, in its Constitution, rules out the exercise of authority over what religion people are to follow, what people are to say to each other, and so on. However, these limitations are self-imposed and not necessarily "natural" to governments. Many governments around the world, at one time or another, have claimed authority to tell people what religion they should follow, what they should or should not say to one another, what sort of sexual activity they were permitted, what they might eat or drink, or what sorts of sports and recreation they could take part in. It is safe to say that there is no area of human activity over which some government or another has not at some time exercised authority. Government, then, is set apart from all other groups in society because all of its power is based on authority and, at least potentially, there is no limit to the range of activities over which it may exercise authority.

Authority is a particularly efficient kind of power. It may be backed up ultimately by the threat of coercion (the police will haul you off and punish you physically if you do not do what those in authority tell you to do), or it may be backed up ultimately by persuasion (if you keep your well clean, as the government tells you to do, you will be sick less often). However, if people do what the government tells them to do, without having to be coerced or persuaded, everything goes more smoothly and—at least from the government's point of view—more satisfactorily. In general, authority does not require the actual use of coercion or persuasion to any great extent. No one has to stand at street corners to *force* cars to stop at red lights, and no one has to stand there to *persuade* them to do so. One of the things that makes the modern state such an efficient form of political organization is the very fact that the state has *authority* and therefore can ensure that people will comply with its commands with a minimum of expensive and time-consuming coercion or persuasion.

People do obey the authority of the state. Actions against authority are by definition "outlaw" behavior and therefore extraordinary, so we can think of many vivid examples of refusals to obey authority—burglary, speeding on the highways, tax evasion, and so on. The startling thing, however, is that few people steal things even when it would be safe to do so, most people drive at or near speed limit even though only a sprinkling of police are available to monitor what they are doing, and most people pay the taxes they owe. It is authority that makes this system of commands and obedience work as smoothly as it does, and this makes the modern state appear to us to be the most natural form of political organization.

Authority is not a simple thing that is either present or absent. Rather, it is a matter of degree. Remember that authority exists because it is "generally agreed on"; that is, most people believe it exists. There will probably never be a state in which every person agrees on the existence and range of the state's authority. Often, when a state issues certain commands, a portion of the people do not accept its authority to do so. If enough people deny the authority of the state, the state has a problem. In the early twentieth century, the government of the United States attempted to command people not to drink alcohol. So many people denied the authority of the state in this area that enforcement proved impossible and the law was eventually abandoned. More seriously, in the 1860s, the whole southern region of the United States denied that the national government had any authority over it at all. The states in that region set up their own new government instead, and it took a long and bloody Civil War to reestablish the authority of the U.S. government over them.

✦ LEGITIMACY AND AUTHORITY

The crux of the state then, and of its ability to function effectively, is the government's wide-ranging authority to organize the lives of its people. Paradoxically, this authority exists only because the people believe it to exist and that it is appropriate. If authority were to fail, it might still be possible for a government to organize its people by coercion and persuasion but at such great cost that this approach could probably not be sustained over the long haul. A pure tyranny, existing without the benefit of at least some degree of authority, probably could not last long.

It is crucial to a government that large numbers of its people should believe not only that it has authority, but that it properly *should* have that authority. We call the existence of this sort of feeling, to the extent that it does exist, the **legitimacy** of the government. Legitimacy, like authority itself, is a matter of degree. Not everyone in a state will necessarily always agree that its government is legitimate or that a given type of governmental act is legitimate. Much of the violence of politics in Chechnya in the 1990s, for instance, resulted from a failure to agree on what sort of government could be legitimate.

➜ SOURCES OF LEGITIMACY

How does a government achieve a reasonable degree of legitimacy? There are many ways by which the people's allegiance may be bound to a government so that it is considered legitimate.

1. Legitimacy by Results. First and foremost, a government may gain and retain legitimacy from its people by providing for them the things they most want: security against physical assault, security of their country's borders against invasion, pride in their nation, and economic security. If the government can provide these things, its legitimacy will be greatly strengthened. If it cannot, its legitimacy is likely to be called into question.

A good example of "legitimacy by results" is the rule of Adolf Hitler in Germany in the 1930s. In 1933, Hitler took power through dubious maneuvers and with at most a bare majority of support. The most votes the Nazi party had received in a fully free election was 37 percent—enough to make it the largest party in the country but hardly a mandate for dictatorship. Once in power, Hitler could initially count on the free support of only about one-third of the Germans, and powerful forces were arrayed against him—the labor unions, the Catholic Church, much of the army's general staff. Hitler was a monster, but what solidified his hold on Germany and gave him a degree of legitimacy by the end of the 1930s were the *results* of his early policies. He reduced unemployment by large-scale

Legitimacy by results: Adolf Hitler dedicates his latest project, the Volkswagen; Fallersleben, Germany, 1938.

© Underwood & Underwood/Corbis

deficit spending; by some audacious bluffs, he outmaneuvered France and England and reestablished Germany as a great power; he built the autobahn system of superhighways; he even pioneered the Volkswagen "beetle" automobile. In spite of his suppression of free speech, his oppression of Jews, and his crude party comrades, these accomplishments brought him widespread support from the German people. By the late 1930s, it probably would have been impossible for anyone to seek to overthrow his rule. It was not until 1944, when he had obviously lost World War II, that a group of generals were able to muster sufficient strength to try to depose him; even then, the attempt failed.

2. Legitimacy by Habit. Once a government has been around for a while, people become accustomed to obeying its laws. People expect to operate under some government or other, and so whatever government is in place and has been obeyed in the past is likely to be regarded as legitimate—unless a particular crisis arises or some force (another state, perhaps) intervenes from outside. In other words, once a particular government has been in place for a while, so that the people have developed the habit of obeying it, it no longer has to perpetually justify its existence. Rather, the burden of proof lies with whoever would propose an alternative government. The existing government remains legitimate unless and until a compelling alternative comes along. We should not underestimate the importance of habit in maintaining governments in power.[4]

3. Legitimacy by Historical, Religious, or Ethnic Identity. Many governments enhance their legitimacy by the ties that exist between themselves and the people because of the government leaders' past accomplishments (their historic role) or because of the religious and/or ethnic similarity between the government leaders and the people.

This may be especially important in a new state, in which the government has not yet been in place long enough for the people to have developed the *habit* of treating it as legitimate and in which the many economic and social problems that plague most new states make it difficult for the government to achieve legitimacy by *results*.

Many governments of new states are able to buy time by virtue of the status they acquired in leading the state into independence in the first place. George Washington was revered as the "father of his country" after his success as commander of the Revolutionary Army. He and his associates enjoyed a couple of decades in which the people of the United States regarded them as their natural government, and this time allowed them to get the Constitution into place and to establish among the people the habit of obeying it. Similarly, the Labor Party in Israel, the Congress Party in India, the party of Julius Nyerere in Tanzania, and the National Liberation Front in Algeria had a breathing space in which their governments were accepted, because they had led the independence movements that had established their states in the first place. Religious or ethnic ties may also be used by a government to enhance its legitimacy. In Iran, the regime of the Ayatollah Khomeini and his successors used its ties to the dominant Shiite Muslim sect and has played on antagonisms between the Persian majority in the country and the

---

[4]Also, a government that is in place is usually able to foster a supportive mythology. For some examples, see Dan Nimmo and James Combs, *Subliminal Politics: Myths and Mythmakers in America* (Englewood Cliffs, N.J.: Prentice-Hall, 1980); and Barry Schwartz, *George Washington: The Making of an American Symbol* (New York: Free Press, 1982); and Lisa Wedeen, *Ambiguities of Domination: Politics, Rhetoric, and Symbols in Contemporary Syria* (Chicago: University of Chicago Press, 1999).

Arab populations in the rest of the Mideast to strengthen its legitimacy. Similarly, the former, white-dominated government of South Africa long used whites' fears of blacks to strengthen its legitimacy among the white population.

4. Legitimacy by Procedures. Finally, a state may strengthen the legitimacy of its government by following certain procedures in setting itself up—procedures in which many people have confidence, so that they will start off with a fund of trust for any government that has been established along these lines.

The best example of this is democracy—a state in which the citizens participate in selecting their leaders and perhaps also in determining the state's policies. Typically, democratic governments are chosen by competitive elections in which citizens vote to decide which of various alternative leadership teams are to govern. The resulting government has won broader support than any alternative; therefore, it gains a strong base of legitimacy. It is the government "of the people."

The *procedures* of democratic election are what give such a government a good part of its legitimacy. One may dislike particular leaders or think their policies unwise, but it is hard to argue with their right to govern as long as they have been selected by the proper procedures.

Democratic government is the preeminent example of legitimacy by procedures—so preeminent that democratic procedures are often imitated through staged elections in dictatorships. At other times, other procedures have served as the basis for legitimacy; all that is important is that the procedure be accepted as appropriate. Until a few centuries ago, for instance, and still in a few countries, it was accepted that political leadership was most properly passed on by inheritance. One king ruled; when he died, his heir became the new king. This procedure was so important as a basis of legitimacy that great care was taken to lay out precise rules of inheritance; if no clear heir was available, the result was sometimes civil war.

Authority, then, through the legitimacy on which it is based, depends on the relation between the state and its citizens. A particularly interesting problem in authority and legitimacy is posed by modern democracy. A democracy is a state in which fully qualified citizens vote at regular intervals to choose, among alternative candidates, the people who will be in charge of developing the state's policies. It is in one sense an odd sort of state, because the government has power over the citizens (it makes the laws), but the citizens also have power over the government (they can vote it out of office). What sort of relationship between state and citizens is best in a democracy?

✦ THE "DEMOCRATIC CITIZEN"

The one most special thing about the relationship between a democratic state and its citizens is that democracy requires citizens who will do more than obey and follow the government. In our previous discussion, it was more or less sufficient, for authority to exist, that the people regard the actions of the government as legitimate. This would ensure obedience to the laws.

Some nondemocratic states go a step further and try to generate *enthusiastic* support for the government. Hitler—through his pageantry, his rallies, and his network of youth organizations, sports clubs, and so on—tried to generate enthusiastic support for nazism that would help him to build a powerful German military force more rapidly. The Soviet Union and other communist countries always tried to build enthusiastic support through rallies, discussion groups, parades, and strenuous campaigning, even when their elections were restricted to a single party.

Democracy goes yet a step further than this. In a democracy, it is hoped not only that people will obey the laws and be enthusiastic citizens but that they will also and at the same time be *critical* citizens. Democratic citizens are expected to walk a difficult line along which they support enthusiastically the authority of their government leaders but, at the same time, are critical enough of those leaders that they might readily vote them out of office at the next election. This requires a complex and sophisticated view of politics. It is not easy to be a citizen of a democracy.

What characteristics would we look for in a "democratic citizen"?

1. *Tolerance.* If varied groups are to support their opinions, it is necessary that the people have a reasonable tolerance for diversity. If people could be prevented from setting forth unpopular ideas, then the democracy would not function well. Therefore, citizens must be at least minimally tolerant of different races, different social behaviors, different religions, and political beliefs that may depart sharply from their own. At the very least, most citizens in a democracy must be willing to allow these various groups to present their cases freely. If they are not, then there is a danger that the voters will not be allowed a full range of options from which to choose.

2. *Active Participation.* Democracy requires that citizens do more than just obey the laws the government lays down. Authority in a democracy is a two-way street; therefore, the citizens must take concrete political actions to exercise their authority over the government. At the very least, they should vote in elections. Better yet, they should maintain frequent contact with the government by writing to their representatives, serving on citizen committees, and so on. If the citizens do not do this, a state simply cannot be a democracy. Its government will have authority over its citizens, *but not vice versa.*

3. *High Level of Interest and Information.* It is not enough that citizens participate actively. If they do not know what is going on, they can be as active as they wish but they will have little effect on what the government does. Action based on no interest or understanding would be aimless, and one person's act would tend to cancel the other's out. If the citizens' active participation is to be constructive, democracy requires also that those citizens be well informed.

4. *Varying Support for the State, the Regime, and the Government.* Finally, while the three characteristics noted are required in order for the people to maintain authority over the government, democracy requires also that the government maintain authority over the people. This is difficult, since the people are required to remain skeptical about the holders of government positions and must stand ready to vote them out of office if that is necessary. What is necessary, if this balancing trick is to work, is that citizens (1) identify with and support the state (without this there is real danger of things falling apart); (2) retain an abstract

support for the regime, the ongoing set of rules and procedures that place certain individuals into positions in the government (see discussion of "regime" on p. 149); but (3) remain skeptical about the particular individuals currently holding those positions.

⇥ HOW WELL ARE THESE REQUIREMENTS MET?

As you see, it takes work to be a citizen in a democracy. How well do the citizens of modern democracies measure up? In particular, how do citizens of the United States measure up?

1. Tolerance. The citizens of most democracies will readily agree with abstract statements guaranteeing minorities the right to express their opinions freely. However, concrete applications of this principle may be another matter. For instance, people often think that even conventional political participation should be banned for those who they think are wrong or dangerous. In a 1987 study in the United States, people were asked to name the political group they liked the least. (For instance, one might ask them to choose among skinheads, militant gays, born-again Christians, secular humanists, the American Civil Liberties Union, the Ku Klux Klan, etc.) They were then asked several questions about what rights that group should have to participate in politics. Only 27 percent thought that members of the group they disliked should be allowed to serve as president if elected, only 18 percent thought that members of that group should be allowed to teach in the public schools, and only 32 percent thought that the group should not be outlawed. A related study in Israel showed Israelis to be even less tolerant in these

"Is it OK to discriminate against bigots?"

TABLE 8.1

Percentage of Americans Engaging in Seven Different Acts of Political Participation

Type of Political Participation	Percent
Voted in the most recent presidential election	70
Worked in a campaign for the most recent election	8
Made a campaign contribution for the most recent election	24
Contacted a government official within the past year	34
Attended a protest, march, or demonstration within the past two years	6
Worked informally with others in the community to deal with some community issue or problem within the past year	17
Served in a voluntary capacity on a local governing board or attended meetings of such a board on a regular basis within the past two years	3

SOURCE: From *Voice and Equality* by Sidney Verba, Kay Lehman Schlozman, Henry E. Brady, p. 72. Cambridge, MA: Harvard University Press (1995). Copyright © 1995 by the President and Fellows of Harvard College.

ways than Americans.[5] A study of Moscow citizens in newly democratic Russia, while it yields the same disturbing levels of tolerance as the American and Israeli studies, is probably encouraging for the prognosis for democracy in Russia, in that the tolerance levels are not much lower than those in the well-established democracies of the other two countries. Only 24 percent of Moscow citizens thought that a member of their least-liked group should be allowed to run for public office, and only 28 percent thought the group should not be outlawed.[6]

2. **Active Participation.** At the very least, citizens in a democracy should vote regularly in elections. As we shall see in Chapter 10, even this cannot be taken for granted. However, it is also necessary, if the democracy is to function well, that good numbers of citizens go beyond voting to involve themselves in more demanding tasks such as writing or phoning officials, organizing neighborhood groups, working in political campaigns, and so on.

Table 8.1 presents the results of a survey of the American public in which people were asked whether they participated in a variety of ways. In looking at this table, you must bear in mind that people usually tell pollsters that they are more active than they truly are; actual turnout in that presidential election was 50.2 percent, for instance, although 70 percent of the people polled said that they had voted. Still, the figures give a rough idea of the relative frequency with which people participated in these various ways.

---

[5]John L. Sullivan, Pat Walsh, Michal Shamir, David G. Barnum, and James L. Gibson, "Why Politicians Are More Tolerant: Selective Recruitment and Socialization Among Political Elites in Britain, Israel, New Zealand and the United States," *British Journal of Political Science* 23 (January 1993), p. 60.
[6]James L. Gibson and Raymond M. Duch, "Emerging Democratic Values in Soviet Political Culture," in A. H. Miller, W. M. Reisinger, and V. L. Hesli, eds., *Public Opinion and Regime Change* (Boulder, CO: Westview Press, 1993), p. 76.

TABLE 8.2

Percentage That Have Ever Engaged in a Variety of Actions More Demanding Than Voting, for Selected Countries

Country (per capita GDP in parentheses)*	USA ($41,854)	Canada ($32,886)	Germany ($29,309)	Brazil ($8,730)	India ($3,486)	Nigeria ($1,183)
Signed a petition	81.1	73.3	50.6	47.1	28.9	6.7
Joined a boycott	25.6	20.5	10.2	6.4	13.3	7.6
Attended a lawful demonstration	21.4	19.5	27.0	24.8	22.9	19.5
Occupied a building or factory	4.1	3.0	.7	6.5	4.5	9.1

*Purchasing power parity.

SOURCE: Ronald Inglehart, Miguel Basáñez, Jaime Díez-Medrano, Loek Halman, and Ruud Luijkx, *Human Beliefs and Values: A Cross-Cultural Sourcebook Based on the 1999–2000 Surveys,* supplemental CD, tables E025, E026, E027, and E029.

Do the people depicted here participate a lot or a little? Political science is often the science of the half-filled glass. (Is it half full, or is it half empty?) Against a standard of what a democracy *should* be, these citizens fall short. Only 17 percent of them (or fewer, if some were exaggerating) had worked with others to solve a local problem. On the other hand, against a standard of what we might feel we could realistically expect, these figures show considerable activity. To turn the earlier sentence around, fully 17 percent of the people polled had worked with others to solve a local problem in that year.

Table 8.2 presents similar information comparatively across several democracies. The states in the table range from developed democracies like the United States, Germany, and Canada, through poorer democracies like Brazil, India, and Nigeria. In the case of Nigeria the democratic system was just a few years old in 2000, when the survey was taken. Interestingly, the less demanding, more individualistic acts of signing a petition or joining a boycott are much more common in the developed democracies. The somewhat more demanding, collective act of demonstrating does not vary much across the countries. And the most demanding, aggressive, collective act of occupying buildings—while uncommon in all of the states—is more common in the poorer states.

These differing trends across the states probably reflect, first, the fact that overall political participation is lower in the poorer states. (Two-thirds of all Nigerians, for instance, said they would never sign a petition under any circumstances.) But, second, the tensions and conflicts surrounding politics in poorer states may be such that when participation does come, it escalates more easily and more often to demanding and potentially violent actions like occupying buildings.

3. High Level of Interest and Information. Of course, people who regularly turn out and vote in elections might know little or nothing about the candidates among whom they were choosing; in that case, they would contribute little to the working of democracy. How interested are citizens of democracies in what goes on politically, and how accurately informed are they? Voters in the United States are rather interested in

TABLE 8.3

Percentage Accurately Stating Candidate's Position

	Correct Answer (yes)	Incorrect Answer (no)	Don't Know
Gore: favor free prescription drugs for the elderly?	58%	8%	36%
Bush: favor large cut in income taxes?	52%	11%	37%

SOURCE: Thomas E. Patterson, *The Vanishing Voter* (New York: Alfred P. Knopf, 2003).

politics, according to most studies. For instance, a poll of Americans in 2004 showed that 26 percent said they followed what was going on in government and public affairs most of the time, 41 percent said they followed it some of the time, 24 percent now and then, and 10 percent hardly at all.[7]

However, most people will exaggerate to a stranger how much they do something as virtuous as following public affairs. In actuality, how well informed are these virtuous-sounding people? Not very. Only 29 percent of a national survey of American adults can name their representative in Congress, and only 30 percent can name both of the senators from their state.[8]

In a study of the 2000 presidential election, Thomas E. Patterson asked citizens to identify where George W. Bush or Al Gore stood on each of twelve issue questions, each of which had figured prominently in the campaign (see Table 8.3). On what were probably the key issues for each candidate, a narrow majority of citizens were able to identify correctly the candidate's position.

So, on their signature issues, the candidates had only gotten through correctly to about half of the electorate. On the average, across all twelve issue areas, only 38 percent correctly identified a candidate's position, while 16 percent identified it wrongly, and 46 percent said they did not know the candidate's position.

4. Support for the State. You will recall that what is needed here is a general abstract support for the state and for the regime (the state's constitution and rules of government), which can coexist with skepticism about the qualities of individual officeholders. Many democracies seem to be fairly successful at commanding this type of respect from their people.

In a survey in 1959, Americans were asked, "Generally speaking, what are the things about this country that you are most proud of?" They could mention anything they wished to, including religious values, the wealth of the country, landscape, culture, and so on. Over 60 percent of the things mentioned were aspects of government and politics.[9] At about the same time, in a survey in 1958, 73 percent of those polled said that they trusted the government in Washington to do what was right either "most of the

---

[7]University of Michigan, Center for Political Studies, 2004 National Election Study.
[8]Michael X. Delli Carpini and Scott Keeter, *What Americans Know About Politics and Why It Matters* (New Haven: Yale University Press, 1995).
[9]Gabriel Almond and Sidney Verba, *The Civic Culture* (Boston: Little, Brown, 1965), p. 102.

time" or "just about always."[10] As we shall see later in this chapter, there has been an erosion since then of this sort of generalized confidence and support of their government by the American people. The point is, such support was maintained at a time when, in the same study, Americans felt considerable skepticism about the *people* running the government. In 1958, 24 percent thought that "quite a lot" of the people running the government were crooked, 37 percent said that the people running the government did not usually know what they were doing, and 85 percent said that the people in government wasted "some" or "a lot" of the money they paid in taxes. At about this time also, the American electorate repudiated their Republican president Dwight Eisenhower by giving the Democrats a landslide victory in the congressional election of 1958.

This balance between support for state institutions and skepticism about officials is hard to maintain, and many shaky democracies are rarely able to achieve it. As we shall see in examples later, one democracy, West Germany, had to build it up over a twenty-year period, while another, the United States, may have to some extent lost it.

✦ SOCIAL CAPITAL

Robert Putnam and his coauthors, in a study of what makes democratic government effective in Italy, concluded that the necessary ingredient is what they called **social capital:** intricate webs of voluntary involvement in organizations that bind people together and give them the political resources and mutual trust that are needed to make any cooperative form of government work. Democracy is the quintessentially cooperative government form. Examples of the interwoven organizations they addressed would be people's involvement in trade unions, community choirs, PTAs, bird-watching clubs, professional organizations, social service organizations to help the needy, the American Legion, churches, book clubs, and so on. In parts of Italy where people were involved in rich networks of such participation, democratic government worked well; in parts where people were not so involved, democratic government did not work well.

"Social capital" might seem slightly out of place in this chapter, because it is not an attitude or a set of attitudes. Rather, it is a pattern of community interaction that *produces* desirable attitudes of efficacy and trust, and that gives people practical experience in persuasion and collective action that helps them to function well in a democracy. It appears vital to an understanding of democratic citizenship, however, and that is why I have included it here.

The United States has long been considered a society with high voluntary participation in community organizations, although there is a debate whether that high level of participation is diminishing.[11] Putnam argues that Americans are turning inward and individualistic. He points out, for instance, that while bowling alley use is up in the United States, bowling league membership is down; more Americans are "bowling

---

[10]University of Michigan, Center for Political Studies, 1958 National Election Study. Data made available by the Inter-University Consortium for Political and Social Research.

[11]For a pessimistic view, see Robert Putnam, "Bowling Alone: America's Declining Social Capital," *Journal of Democracy* (January 1995); "The Strange Disappearance of Civic America," *American Prospect* (Winter 1996): 34–48; and *Bowling Alone* (New York: Simon & Schuster, 2000). For an opposed view, see the June/July 1996 issue of *Public Perspective:* Everett C. Ladd, "The Data Just Don't Show Erosion of America's 'Social Capital,' " *Public Perspective* (7 June/July 1996), p. 1; and associated reports, pp. 7–47.

alone." Whether or not voluntarism and participation in civic organizations have declined in the United States, though, they still appear to be relatively high compared with other countries. A set of surveys in the early 1990s found that 49 percent of Americans had done volunteer work in the preceding twelve months compared with 13 percent of Germans and 19 percent of French respondents.[12]

✦ POLITICAL CULTURE

Political scientists have given the name **political culture** to the types of basic attitudes addressed in this chapter. The political culture of a society consists of all attitudes and beliefs held communally by a people, which form the basis for their political behavior. We have borrowed the term from anthropology, in which the term *culture* (a people's whole interrelated set of beliefs and ways of thinking) forms a central organizing concept.

It is clear that political culture varies a good deal from one state to another and that it is responsible for major differences in how politics is conducted. We can often detect differences in culture by looking at popular behaviors and sayings. For instance, we sense that the Japanese put a greater emphasis on consensus than do Americans and value conflict less than Americans, when we compare two popular sayings:

The nail that sticks out will get pounded down. (Japan)

and

The squeaking wheel gets the grease. (United States)

Basic differences such as those reflected in these sayings must surely have something to do with the fact that compared with the United States, political decisions in Japan are more likely to be made on the basis of unanimous consent rather than by a vote (with one side losing). Individualistic assertion and challenges are less highly valued in Japan than in the United States.

Political culture is important, but it is a difficult thing to evaluate concretely. It almost seems that such a big concept resists precision and invites fuzzy generalization. There is always a temptation to lapse into stereotyping of peoples: lockstep, obedient, efficient Germans; unflappable British; breezy, pragmatic Americans; hot-blooded Latins. However, even with these difficulties, political culture is too important to ignore. A work that demonstrates the potential importance of cultural analysis is *Culture Shift in Advanced Industrial Society* by Ronald Inglehart (see p. 36).[13] Inglehart argues that prosperous, industrial societies are undergoing a shift in culture in which concerns for security are being replaced by concerns for self-expression, and he uses this shift to account for broad generational changes occurring across Europe.

One striking characteristic of political cultures is that they usually change slowly. A good example of this is provided by Alexis de Tocqueville in *Democracy in America*.[14] De Tocqueville visited the United States in the early nineteenth century to examine the

---

[12]Helmut K. Anheier, Lester M. Salamon, and Edith Archambault, "Participating Citizens: U.S.–Europe Comparisons in Volunteer Action," *Public Perspective* 5 (March–April 1994), p. 17.
[13]Inglehart, Ronald. *Culture Shift in Advanced Industrial Society* (Princeton, NJ: Princeton University Press, 1990).
[14]Alexis de Tocqueville, *Democracy in America* (New York: Knopf, 1980).

workings of U.S. democracy, but his description of the American approach to politics is still recognizable—the emphasis on individuality and freedom, reliance on local politics and voluntary organizations, the restlessness and desire for progress. This despite the fact that the America he saw was an almost totally agricultural society, without modern means of communication and without the quasi-imperial world role the United States has adopted since the Second World War, and despite the fact that since his study, American society has absorbed many waves of immigrants who initially came to America with very different cultures. Our state and society have changed immensely since he wrote his book, but the underlying culture has remained recognizably the same.

The role of political culture in political science theory is somewhat like the role of history. Essentially, political science theory is a search for levers that might at least potentially help us to change society. This is why almost all political science theory is causal (see the methodological appendix, pp. 429–431.) If we understand causal relationships, they allow us to predict that a change in A (something under our control) will cause a change in B (the thing we wish to change); in this way, they offer us at least a potential lever for change. Thus, we are interested in the sources of political parties' influence because that knowledge can at least potentially help us to make parties more influential or less influential. Similarly, we look at the roles of political institutions, the effects of regulating campaign finance, the impacts of different systems of organizing health care, because understanding these things can offer us tools that might help us to effect change.

History and political culture play a slightly different role in our theories; they do not themselves offer levers, because we cannot easily change them. History is beyond our manipulation, and a culture is very difficult to change. It is in this sense that Hernando de Soto, a community activist, once said:

Culture is interesting to read about, but what does one do with it?[15]

History and culture are important, however, as the *context* within which any levers will succeed or fail. They may not be things we can control, but the effects of all the things we *can* control will vary depending on the history and culture of the society within which we try to use them. Political parties, for instance, can be expected to operate differently and to have different effects in Japan than they do in the United States.

We must understand the effects of the historical and cultural context if we are to understand properly how any of our levers will work. A common mistake is to export an institution from Western democracies to a new democracy and assume it will work there as we expect it to. The tragedy of the Balkans in the 1990s was due in part to NATO leaders' failure to understand the political culture of that region and the burden of history there.

→ AN APPLICATION OF POLITICAL CULTURE: ROBERT KAGAN'S *OF PARADISE AND POWER*

A good example of how political culture can be used to help us understand important questions is Robert Kagan's *Of Paradise and Power*.[16] Kagan is concerned to explain why the United States and its traditional European allies have diverged so sharply in their foreign

---

[15]Matthew Miller, "The Poor Man's Capitalist," *New York Times Magazine,* 1 July 2001, p. 47.
[16]Robert Kagan, *Of Paradise and Power* (New York: Knopf, 2003).

policies in the early twenty-first century, especially over the issue of whether or not Iraq should have been invaded. He finds the explanation in a change in their political cultures, especially the culture of Europe, with regard to how they regard power in politics:

> ... on major strategic and international questions today, Americans are from Mars and Europeans are from Venus: They agree on little and understand one another less and less. And this state of affairs is not transitory—the product of one American election or one catastrophic event. The reasons for the transatlantic divide are deep, long in development, and likely to endure. When it comes to setting national priorities, determining threats, defining challenges, and fashioning and implementing foreign and defense policies, the United States and Europe have parted ways.[17]

Kagan explains that Europeans, based on their experience in subordinating national differences to unify the continent in the European Union, have come to be suspicious of the unilateral use of power in international affairs, and believe the world should be ordered by cooperative arrangements under multilateral auspices such as those of the United Nations. In their own experience, they have been able to end centuries of interstate warfare in Europe by establishing systems of multilateral cooperation. The United States, on the other hand, feels heavily the responsibility of its own hegemonic power, wants to use it for what it regards as good purposes, and does not want to be hemmed in by a "rule by committee." In many ways, the two sides have reversed from a century ago, when the states of Europe rushed into World War I each for their own purposes, and the United States held forth Woodrow Wilson's vision of a "League of Nations" that would henceforth resolve issues multilaterally rather than through individual states' resort to military force. In Kagan's view, these different perspectives have jelled into lasting cultural differences in the way power is viewed—differences that, because they have entered strong ideological and cultural systems of belief, will be "deep . . . and likely to endure."

Interestingly, Kagan does not use culture here to tap deep-rooted aspects of national character. Even though culture is long-lasting and resists change, it of course can also change given a sufficiently hard push. Like Inglehart, Kagan examines here a critical change in culture, based in a momentous historic change, to explain important changes in the nature of politics—in this case, a basic divide over foreign policies.

✦ RELIGION AND POLITICAL CULTURE

A religion is an encompassing set of ideas about our creation, our relationship to a creator, and ethical and moral imperatives that flow from that relationship. Religion may have very little to do with politics—the ethical and moral imperatives of a religion may all have to do with personal faith and one's private life. Or, religion may have a great deal to do with politics. To the extent that a religion is political, it becomes a facet of the political culture. And when that is the case, the emotional strength of religious beliefs is such that they become a very important part of the political culture.

Religion in the early twenty-first century appears to be increasingly important in politics. In the United States religious issues such as abortion, homosexuals' rights, and teaching the theory of evolution in schools occupy much of the public debate. And around

---

[17]Ibid., pp. 3–4.

TABLE 8.4

Change in the Percent Believing in God, 1947–2001

	1947	2001
Canada	95%	88%
Australia	95	75
United States	94	94
Sweden	80	46
France	66	56

SOURCE: Adapted from Pippa Norris and Ronald Inglehart, *Sacred and Secular: Religion and Politics Worldwide.* New York: Cambridge University Press, 2004. Used by permission of Cambridge University Press.

TABLE 8.5

Frequency of Attending Religious Services, USA 1972–2002

	1972	2002
Attend weekly or more	35	24%
Never attend service	9%	19%

SOURCE: Adapted from Pippa Norris and Ronald Inglehart, *Sacred and Secular: Religion and Politics Worldwide.* New York: Cambridge University Press, 2004. Used by permission of Cambridge University Press.

the world religious or at least partially religious conflicts such as al Quaeda's attacks on the United States and its allies have increased in number and intensity.

Ironically, this increase in religious political activity comes at a time when at least in North America and Europe, religious belief and participation in religious services has been declining or standing still, as we see in Tables 8.4 and 8.5.

If religion and its practice are in some decline, at least in North America and Europe, how is it that it seems to play an increasingly prominent role in politics? A number of things, coming together, may have brought this about. First, the decline in organized conflict about class issues as socialist parties have splintered and lost support may have simply created a vacuum that religion could fill. And, new forms of communication such as television and the Internet may have made it easier for those outside the usual political elite to organize effectively and bring their issues into the body politic. After all, religious issues in politics are not all that new (witness the prohibition movement in the United States in the early twentieth century); the new thing is that religious leaders can easily reach a million people at a time. Finally, the increasingly broad and graphic portrayal of sexual matters in a secular world is simply abhorrent to many believers. Religious politics may be a push-back.

Outside the United States, the most dramatic manifestation of religion's increased role in politics is the rise of political Islam. Most versions of Islam are rather nonpolitical, playing down the role of the state; people should be governed not so much by governments as by God. However, various groups within Islam have developed political agendas in the last few decades and, like the politically religious in the United States, have been able to use modern technology and communications skillfully to pursue their goals. Their appeal has been heightened not only by Muslims' discomfort with the sex culture of a secular society, but by Arab feelings of disrespect and exploitation by the West. The Islamic state in Iran, Islamists in other countries like Pakistan, extreme groups like al Quaeda, all attest to the growing importance of political Islam. Samuel Huntington's *The Clash of Civilizations and the Remaking of World Order* in fact argues that with the decline of class politics in the twenty-first century world politics will be driven by clashes between different "civilizations" with differing sets of values—especially a clash between Islam and Christianity.[18] Interestingly, however, despite all of the flash-points of the unresolved Israeli-Palestinian conflict, the American occupation of Iraq, and tensions between (Islamic) producers of oil and (mainly Christian) consumers, differences in values between Islamic populations and, say, those in the United States are not all that great.

Table 8.6 compares the values of people in the United States and people in Jordan, a Muslim country. As you see in the table, on issues such as support for democracy and

TABLE 8.6

Values of Americans and Jordanians

	USA	Jordan
I. Democracy and Religion:		
Agree: Democracy may have problems, but it is better than any other form of government	88%	89%
Agree: Politicians who don't believe in God are unfit for public office	36%	17%
Agree: Religious leaders should not influence how people vote	64%	75%
II. Social Values:		
Agree: Homosexuality is never justified	32%	98%
Agree: Abortion is never justified	30%	85%
Agree: Divorce is never justified	8%	42%

SOURCE: Adapted from "Values of Americans and Jordanians." From World Values Studies 2000, reported in Inglehart, Basáñez, Díez-Medrano, Halman, and Luijkx, editors, *Human Beliefs and Values* (Coyoacar, Mexico: Siglo XXI Editores: 2004).

---

[18]Samuel P. Huntington, *The Clash of Civilizations and the Remaking of World Order* (New York: Simon & Schuster, 1996).

the role religion should play in public life, the two peoples are not very different.[19] On social issues such as homosexuality, abortion, and divorce there are distinct differences, but these hardly seem the stuff of a "clash of civilizations."

✦ POLITICAL SOCIALIZATION

The values and assumptions people hold about politics are acquired in a process called **political socialization,** which simply means the learning of political values and factual assumptions about politics.[20] In principle, this can occur at any age and under any circumstances, but it tends to be concentrated at certain points of our lives.

The importance of political socialization is evident, if nothing else, in the fact that without it, any political culture would disappear after one generation. All of the cultural underpinnings of politics, and many other more transient values, are learned by children and other new citizens through political socialization. It is political socialization that allowed the United States to absorb millions of Irish, Italians, Russians, Poles, Chinese, Vietnamese, and so many other peoples and yet maintain political continuity.

Like most learning, political socialization apparently comes most easily and fully in childhood, and diminishes as we grow older. However, explicit and detailed information about politics tends not to be picked up much before the teen years. Children learn in their families many basic social attitudes, such as trust in people and attitudes toward authority, that will be important in shaping their later response to politics. But most children acquire only rather primitive ideas about what government is and how politics works. These things are primarily learned in adolescence and early adulthood and continue to be learned throughout adult life. For example, Table 8.7 shows the percentage of Swedish youths of varying ages who were undecided as to which political party was the best. Among eleven- to twelve-year-olds, 73 percent did not have a preference among the parties. This indecision declined to 35 percent by early adulthood. (I realize that these findings come from quite an old study, but I have not found a more recent study that gets at this; enumerating attitudes of young people as they age has rather gone out of style. I believe most political scientists would expect that similar relationships are not much different today.)

One of the concerns of political scientists studying socialization is to assess the varying roles of different **agents of socialization.** We must learn about politics *from* someone, and the various sources of learning are what we call the agents of socialization. Different agents operate in different ways and affect different areas of our values and assumptions about politics. We learn about politics from many different agents, but a few particularly important ones are our families, schools, and peer groups.

---

[19]Even in Iraq as it was moving toward a sectarian civil war, a survey conducted in December 2004 found that six times as many Iraqis thought democracy was good for Iraq as thought it was bad. Mark Tessler, Mansoor Moaddel, and Ronald Inglehart, "What Do Iraqis Want?" *Journal of Democracy* 17 (January 2006), p. 41.

[20]A good general review of political socialization is Richard G. Niemi and Mary A. Hepburn, "The Rebirth of Political Socialization," *Perspectives on Political Science* 24 (Winter, 1995), pp. 7–16. Other useful sources are Pamela Johnston Conover, "Political Socialization: Where's the Politics?" in William Crotty, ed., *Political Science: Looking to the Future,* vol. 3 (Evanston, Ill.: Northwestern University Press, 1991), pp. 125–52; Stanley W. Moore et al., *The Child's Political World* (New York: Praeger, 1985); Orit Ichilov, *Political Socialization, Citizenship Education, and Democracy* (New York: Teachers College Press, 1990); and Roberta S. Sigel, *Political Learning in Adulthood* (Chicago: University of Chicago Press, 1989).

TABLE 8.7

Development of Political Orientations among Swedish Youth

Age	Percent Undecided as to Best Party
11–12	73
13–15	66
16–18	55
19–21	47
22–24	32
25–27	35

SOURCE: Adapted with the permission of The Free Press, a Division of Simon & Schuster Adult Publishing Group, from *Political Socialization: A Study in the Psychology of Political Behavior* by Herbert H. Hyman. Copyright © 1959 by The Free Press. Copyright renewed © 1987 by Helen Hyman. All rights reserved.

From our parents we acquire a number of social values that will apply to politics as they do to other aspects of our lives. It is also thought that we may gain expectations about how politics should occur in the state by extension from the way politics (the making of family decisions by the use of power) is conducted in the family; an authoritarian family may prepare one for an authoritarian state and a democratic family for a democratic state.[21] More specific political values and assumptions do not develop as much through the family as we might suppose, since they tend to be acquired during adolescence—a period when most children are trying to establish an independent identity.

Schools are of particular interest to students of political socialization because they are agents of socialization that the state controls and through which the leaders of the state can attempt to mold the citizenry. In all states, there is some degree of guided socialization through the schools. Schools in the United States try to develop informed, patriotic citizens directly through civics classes and salutes to the flag and indirectly through class materials in history, literature, and other courses. Some states such as Cuba, China, and Nazi Germany have used the schools vigorously and directly to attempt to remake their citizens. In general, however, governments have had relatively little success in doing this. The Nazis failed notably, for example, in their attempts to produce the "new German man."

One group of schools that do seem to have been successful at socializing young people and shaping their political beliefs are the *madrassas,* Koranic schools supported

---

[21]This is a controversial position; many scholars think it oversimplifies a complex process of the development of values. A good presentation of the position is Harry Eckstein and Ted Robert Gurr, *Patterns of Authority* (New York: Wiley, 1975).

across the Mideast by Saudi Arabia. The success of the *madrassas* may stem from the fact that unlike most government-sponsored socialization efforts in schools, which have attempted to move children away from the belief systems of their parents, the *madrassas* seek to exaggerate parents' Islamic beliefs rather than to oppose them, and then add political direction to those beliefs.

Peer groups are extremely influential in developing adolescents' tastes and their view of the world, but they vary considerably in their political impact. In most friendship groups of adolescents, politics does not figure importantly in the attention of the group. Normally, the group will influence its members' choices in clothes or social behavior strongly but will not affect their political identity very much. However, youths who are already somewhat involved in politics may gravitate together as a friendship group, and when this happens, the group may have a profound impact on the political development of all its members.

From our discussion of schools as socializing agents, one would probably conclude that governments do not have much of an impact on political culture, even if they try. One instance, however, in which governments were able to affect political culture rather strongly is offered by the cultures of East and West Germany at the time they were united in 1991. After the Second World War, Germany was divided into two states, the Federal Republic of Germany (West) and the German Democratic Republic (East). The two states were aligned with opposite sides in the Cold War, and though they had shared a common history and culture leading up to the defeat in 1945, for the next forty-five years, they were separated by international events. Indeed, from 1960 on, any travel between the two was made impossible by the infamous Berlin Wall.

When scholars began to study the culture of newly united Germany after 1991, they found many sharp contrasts between the cultures of West Germans and of East Germans. For instance, 31 percent of West Germans but only 11 percent of those from the East prided themselves on the democratic institutions of Germany.[22] And 81 percent of easterners but only 44 percent of westerners agreed with the statement "Socialism is basically a good idea that was only badly carried out."[23]

Why was Germany an exception? One factor is probably just the long time that the two governments had at their disposal; they had from 1945 to 1991 to work on the cultures of their states. Also, at least after 1960, the two populations were forcibly isolated from each other; anthropologists have even found that villages a few miles apart but separated by the Wall developed over that period of time recognizably different accents and dialects of German. And finally, as described in the example on Germany in this chapter, the culture of defeated Germany was in many ways a shattered remnant and was probably easier than most cultures to reshape. Whatever the explanation, Germany provides an example demonstrating that major cultural shaping is not impossible—though it may take an unusual constellation of advantageous circumstances for it to occur.

---

[22]David P. Conradt, "Political Culture in Unified Germany: Will the Bonn Republic Survive and Thrive in Berlin?" *German Studies Review* 21 (1998), p. 92.
[23]David P. Conradt, *The German Polity*, 7th ed. (New York: Longman, 2001), p. 85.

EXAMPLE

Building Authority and Legitimacy in West Germany after World War II[24]

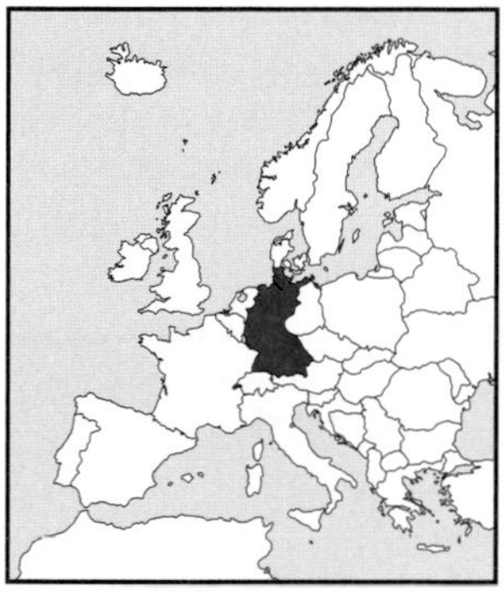

After the defeat of Germany in 1945, the Germans as a people were demoralized politically. They had bought a dream of greatness from Adolf Hitler, but he had brought them defeat and international disgrace. They were hated throughout Europe, their country had been cut up on the map, and their industries and farms were in ruins. Germans who were fifty years old in 1945 could not be blamed if, having been dazzled by politics, they now withdrew from it. They had grown up under the kaiser's monarchy and had seen it overthrown in disgrace at the end of World War I, when they were in their early twenties. They had then lived through fifteen years of a chaotic attempt at democracy, which never really established its authority and legitimacy with the people and ended in Hitler's dictatorship. They were thirty-eight years old when Hitler came to power; in the next twelve years, they saw Germany approach world conquest and then come close to total destruction. They could be pardoned if they were shy of politics after all of this.

In many ways, West Germany after 1945 gave political scientists much the same opportunity to observe an evolutionary development as a new volcanic island rising from the sea offers to biologists. When a new island is formed, biologists get a rare chance to observe which animals are the first to appear on it and see how long it takes a diverse flora and fauna to be established. Similarly, political scientists get few chances to see attitudes toward politics establish themselves among a people who initially have essentially no attitudes. West Germany after the war did provide such a case.

For many years, political observers asked themselves whether democratic behavior and attitudes could possibly develop among Germans. Some said that the people who had put Hitler into office could not develop into democrats. Others thought that if Germany was lucky enough to have a period of peace and economic stability, democracy would be able to establish itself. No one could hazard a guess as to how long the process would take.

As we can see in Tables 8.8, 8.9, and 8.10, the optimists were correct; in fact, the development of democratic support occurred steadily and fairly rapidly. As we see in Table 8.8, during the first twenty years, the democratic regime established itself as the best arrangement Germany had known—better than Hitler's dictatorship or the kaiser's monarchy.

It was not simply that the country was economically well off. The political institutions of democracy became more popular during this period. In 1959, in a survey similar to that mentioned earlier for the United States, Germans were asked what they were proud of about their country. Only 7 percent pointed to Germany's political institutions. In 1978, the question was repeated in a survey. By that time, 31 percent of the things mentioned were aspects of government and politics. By 1988, the figure had grown to 51 percent.[25]

---

[24]West Germany and East Germany were reunified as Germany in 1991.

[25]David Conradt, *The German Polity,* 5th ed. (New York: Longmann, 1993), p. 55.

TABLE 8.8

Attitudes toward the "Past," 1951–1970

Q.: When in this century do you think Germany has been best off?

	Year of Survey			
	1951 (Percent)	1959 (Percent)	1963 (Percent)	1970 (Percent)
Federal Republic (present)	2	42	62	81
Under Hitler before the war (1933–1939)	42	18	10	5
Under the kaiser, before World War I	45	28	16	5

Source: Adapted from David Conradt, "Changing German Political Culture," *The Civic Culture Revisited,* edited by Gabriel Almond and Sidney Verba, p. 226. Copyright © 1980 by Sage Publications Inc. Reprinted by permission of Sage Publications, Inc.

TABLE 8.9

Trust and Hostility among Germans, 1948–1976

a. Percent "trusting most people"

1948	1959	1967	1973	1976
9%	19%	26%	32%	39%

b. Percent thinking more people are evil minded than good minded

1949	1951	1953	1971	1976
46%	43%	34%	17%	16%

Source: Adapted from David Conradt, "Changing German Political Culture," *The Civic Culture Revisited,* edited by Gabriel Almond and Sidney Verba, p. 226. Copyright © 1980 Sage Publications Inc. Reprinted by permission of Sage Publications, Inc.

TABLE 8.10

Frequency of Political Discussion, 1953–1972

	1953 (Percent)	1959 (Percent)	1961 (Percent)	1965 (Percent)	1969 (Percent)	1972 (Percent)
Daily	9	11	10	10	37	50
Occasionally	29	50	51	66	40	34
Never	63	39	39	25	23	16

Source: Reprinted by permission of the publisher from *Germany Transformed: Political Culture and the New Politics* by Kendall L. Baker, R. J. Dalton, and K. Hildebrandt, Cambridge, Mass.: Harvard University Press. Copyright © 1981 by the President and Fellows of Harvard College.

Support for democracy in the abstract also grew across the first two decades. In 1953, only a bit over 55 percent of the Germans stated in the abstract that democracy was the best form of government.[26] By 1976, 90 percent answered yes to the same question.[27]

The sort of social relations among people that are required if a loose system of authority (such as democracy) is to work was also developing. In a society where people are hostile and suspicious of each other, democracy cannot work well. As we see in Table 8.9, trust grew steadily and social hostility decreased during this time.

Finally, it is necessary that the people begin to be active and interested citizens. As we see in Table 8.10, this also developed steadily.

West Germany did not necessarily become an ideal democracy, but it is interesting to see that there were established, over a couple of decades, patterns of behavior and support similar to those of such democracies as the United States or Great Britain. No one would have predicted this with any confidence in 1950, and it was an eye-opener for political scientists.

 ## EXAMPLE

Declining Democratic Legitimacy in the United States

 The story of the last few decades in the United States has been in some respects the opposite of what we have seen in Germany. Since about the mid-1960s, there has been a puzzling decline in people's confidence in officials and in the political system. It might not seem so strange that the political turmoil of the 1960s and the Watergate scandal of 1973 shook people's faith, but there appeared to be further erosion during the calmer period of the late 1970s and the 1980s.

Table 8.11 shows a drop from the 1950s and 1960s in the percentage of Americans thinking that one can trust the government to do what is right most of the time or always and an increase in the percentage thinking that the government is run for the benefit of a few big interests and that quite a lot of people running the government are crooked. The steadiness of the trend across various events and various presidents makes it look as though it were not a response to particular disappointments, but political scientists are frankly at a loss to say just what *did* cause the decline.[28] Interestingly, although levels of trust have gone up and down fairly unsystematically since about 1980, they do seem to have jogged up in 2004.

Interestingly, while this drop in trust and legitimacy was occurring, Americans remained an attentive and reasonably active citizenry. As you can see in Figure 8.1, while turnout in elections dropped somewhat in the 1970s and 1980s, it is unchanged over the past half-century, with 59 percent of the electorate voting in the 1956 presidential election and 61 percent in 2004.

---

[26]Kendall Baker, Russell Dalton, and Kai Hildebrandt, *Germany Transformed* (Cambridge: Harvard University Press, 1981), p. 24.

[27]David Conradt, "Changing German Political Culture," in Gabriel Almond and Sidney Verba, eds., *The Civic Culture Revisited* (Boston: Little, Brown, 1980), p. 234.

[28]Arthur Miller and Jack Citrin present an interesting interchange concerning the possible causes of the decline in "Political Issues and Trust in Government 1964–70," *American Political Science Review* 68 (September 1974), pp. 951–1001; see also Arthur H. Miller and Stephen A. Borrelli, "Confidence in Government During the 1980s," *American Politics Quarterly* 19 (April 1991), pp. 147–73; and Burns Roper, "Democracy in America: How Are We Doing?" *Public Perspective* 5 (March–April 1994), pp. 3–5.

TABLE 8.11

Decline of Confidence, 1958–2004

	1958	1964	1968	1972	1976	1980	1984	1988	1992	1996	2000	2004
Percent who trust the government to do what is right "most of the time" or "always"	73	76	61	53	33	25	44	40	29	33	44	50
Percent thinking the government is run for a few big interests	—	29	40	53	66	70	55	64	75	70	61	56
Percent thinking "quite a lot" of government people are crooked	24	29	25	36	42	47	32	40*	46*	44*	36*	35*

*Slightly different question wording after 1988: "quite a few" crooked.

Source: University of Michigan, Center for Political Studies, National Elections Studies. Data made available by the Inter-University Consortium for Political and Social Research.

The number of people performing the more substantial act of writing to members of Congress has risen steadily, from 6 percent in 1958 to 36 percent in 1992.[29]

Finally, the percentage who state that they follow what is going on in government and public affairs some or most of the time has remained essentially unchanged: 63 percent said that they did so in 1960 and 67 percent in 2004.[30]

One implication for democracy when citizens' trust in government declines is at least hinted at in the widely differing experiences of the three large blackouts in the northeastern United States in 1965, 1977, and 2003. In 1965, New York lost all of its power for a day, and people responded constructively and helpfully to each other; there was little anger or resentment at what was obviously a mechanism gone wrong. In 1977, when the same thing happened, there was a crisis of public order, with widespread violence and looting. But when it happened again in 2003, the

---

[29]*Public Perspective* (June–July 1996), p. 12.
[30]University of Michigan, Center for Political Studies, National Election Studies. Data made available by the Inter-University Consortium for Political and Social Research.

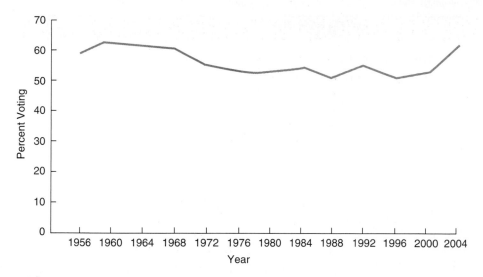

FIGURE 8.1   Percentage of voting-age population voting, United States.

SOURCE: U.S. Bureau of the Census, *Statistical Abstract of the United States.*

response was reminiscent of 1965. Citizens stepped into intersections and took over directing traffic when the traffic lights went out, trucks stopped and carried strangers who needed a ride, and there was no looting or arson. What can account for the difference? Note that in 1964 (our nearest year to 1965 in Table 8.11) 76 percent of Americans trusted the government to do what was right, by 1976 this had dropped to 33 percent; by 2000 it had risen back a bit to 44 percent. It may be that when citizens have sufficient confidence in government to respond well, they can accept adversity, but not when they are distrustful of government.[31] (And of course, in 2003, New Yorkers had also had the events of September 11, 2001, as a lesson in civic cooperation.)

The decline in Americans' trust in government has many varied effects, but surely a combination of a still attentive citizenry who have lost some of their faith in government must be alarming. It does not bode well for a continuation of stable, constructive democracy, and it is important that we find out the causes of the change. The person who does so will have made an important contribution to our understanding of democracy.[32]

---

[31]William Schneider made this suggestion on CNN News, August 15, 2003.
[32]Part of the explanation may lie in the fact that something similar appears to have been happening in most of the world's mature democracies over the same period. See Susan J. Pharr and Robert Putnam, eds., *Disaffected Democracies: What's Troubling the Trilateral Countries?* (Princeton: Princeton University Press, 2000).

KEY TERMS

authority	political socialization	political culture
social capital	legitimacy	agents of socialization

FURTHER READING

Almond, Gabriel, and Verba, Sidney. *The Civic Culture.* Boston: Little Brown, 1965.

"Authority." In *International Encyclopedia of the Social Sciences.*

Cohen, Mitchell. *Why the French Don't Like Headscarves: Islam, the State, and Public Space.* Princeton NJ: Princeton University Press, 2006.

Conover, Pamela Johnston. "Political Socialization: Where's the Politics?" In *Political Science: Looking to the Future,* vol. 3, edited by William Crotty. Evanston, IL.: Northwestern University Press, 1991, pp. 125–152.

Dalton, Russell J. "Communists and Democrats: Democratic Attitudes in the Two Germanies." *British Journal of Political Science* 24 (1994), pp. 469–93.

Delli Carpini, Michael X., and Keeter, Scott. *What Americans Know About Politics and Why It Matters.* New Haven: Yale University Press, 1996.

Gibson, James L., and Gouws, Amand. *Overcoming Intolerance in South Africa: Experiments in Democratic Persuasion.* New York: Cambridge University Press, 2002.

Harris-Lacewell, Melissa Victoria. *Barbershops, Bibles, and BET: Everyday Talk and Black Political Thought.* Princeton: Princeton University Press, 2004.

Hibbing, John R., and Theiss-Morse, Elizabeth, eds. *What Is It About Government That Americans Dislike?* New York: Cambridge University Press, 2001.

Hooghe, Marc, and Stolle, Dietlind, eds. *Generating Social Capital: Civil Society and Institutions in Comparative Perspective.* New York: Palgrave Macmillan, 2003.

Huntington, Samuel P. *The Clash of Civilizations and the Remaking of World Order.* New York: Simon & Schuster, 1996.

Inglehart, Ronald. *Culture Shift in Advanced Industrial Society.* Princeton: Princeton University Press, 1990.

Laitin, David. *Hegemony and Culture.* Chicago: University of Chicago Press, 1986.

Lane, Robert E. *Political Ideology: Why the American Common Man Believes What He Does.* New York: Free Press, 1962.

"Legitimacy." In *International Encyclopedia of the Social Sciences.*

Marcus, George E., Sullivan, John L., Theiss-Morse, Elizabeth, and Wood, Sandra L. *With Malice Towards Some: How People Make Civil Liberties Judgments.* New York: Cambridge University Press, 1995.

Norris, Pippa, and Inglehart, Ronald. *Sacred and Secular: Religion and Politics Worldwide.* New York: Cambridge University Press, 2004.

Nye, Joseph S., Jr., Zelikow, Philip D., and King, David C. *Why People Don't Trust Government.* Cambridge: Harvard University Press, 1997.

Patterson, Thomas E. *Out of Order: How the Decline of Political Parties and the Growing Power of the News Media Undermine the American Way of Electing Presidents.* New York: Knopf, 1994.

Pharr, Susan J., and Putnam, Robert D. *Disaffected Democracies: What's Troubling the Trilateral Countries?* Princeton: Princeton University Press, 2000.

Putnam, Robert D. "Bowling Alone: America's Declining Social Capital." *Journal of Democracy* 6 (January 1995), pp. 65–78.

———. *Making Democracy Work: Civic Traditions in Modern Italy.* Princeton: Princeton University Press, 1994.

Rokeach, Milton. *The Open and Closed Mind: Investigations into the Nature of Belief Systems and Personality Systems.* New York: Basic Books, 1960.

Sapiro, Virginia. "Political Socialization During Adulthood: Clarifying the Political Time of Our Lives." In *New Directions in Political Psychology,* edited by Robert Y. Shapiro, Michael X. Delli Carpini, and Leonie Huddy. London: JAI Press, 1994.

Sears, David O., Huddy, Leonie, and Jervis, Robert, eds. *Oxford Handbook of Political Psychology.* New York: Oxford University Press, 2003.

Sniderman, Paul. *Personality and Democratic Politics.* Berkeley: University of California Press, 1975.

Stern, Jessica. *Terror in the Name of God: Why Religious Militants Kill.* New York: Ecco, 2003.

Sullivan, John L., Shamir, Michal, Walsh, Patrick, and Roberts, Nigel S. *Political Tolerance in Context: Support for Civil Liberties in the United States, Israel, and New Zealand.* Boulder, CO: Westview Press, 1985.

Verba, Sidney, Schlozman, Kay Lehman, and Brady, Henry E. *Voice and Equality: Civic Voluntarism in American Politics.* Cambridge: Harvard University Press, 1995.

Wilson, Richard W. "The Many Voices of Political Culture: Assessing Different Approaches," *World Politics* (January 2000), pp. 246–273.

Zaller, John R. *The Nature and Origins of Mass Opinion.* New York: Cambridge University Press, 1992.

WEB SITES OF INTEREST

National Election Studies Guide to Public Opinion and Electoral Behavior:

http://electionstudies.org/nesguide/nesguide.htm

The Gallup Polls:

http://www.gallup.com/

Tolerance Web site of the Southern Poverty Law Center:

http://www.tolerance.org

Saguaro Seminar Web page to promote social capital:

http://www.bettertogether.org

Partnership for Trust in Government:

http://www.trustingov.org

PART IV

The Apparatus of Governance

CHAPTER 9

CONSTITUTIONS AND THE DESIGN OF GOVERNMENT

Every state—in fact, every political organization, club, or other group—has a **constitution,** or set of rules by which power is distributed among the members. No group of people engaged in politics could exist without rules of this kind.

We speak of such an encompassing set of rules as a "constitution with a small *c,*" meaning the understood rules, both formal and informal, by which power is distributed in any political group—rules that have come to be accepted over time. These rules may be either formally laid down in statutes and other documents or informally understood.

Most organizations and states have as a part of their constitution a formal set of central rules that outline the basic ways in which they conduct their affairs. The Constitution of the United States (note the *capital C*) is such a document, as are Canada's Constitution Act of 1982, the Basic Law of Germany, and the Constitution of the Netherlands. Typically, such a document tells who is to carry out the major functions of politics (proposing, deciding on, and implementing laws); how the people holding those positions are to be chosen; who is to be in charge during an emergency; and by what procedures the constitution itself may be changed. Often there is also a section, such as the Bill of Rights in the U.S. Constitution, that sets out certain basic rights of the citizen or basic aims of the state. Thus, a constitution may state that citizens are guaranteed the right of freedom of speech (U.S.A.) or that the state guarantees full employment (France) or that the state is socialist (China).

Before the United States was ever founded as a state, the American Indian Iroquois Confederation had an elaborate constitution, maintained in an oral tradition. It takes several days for elders to recite the constitution, which specifies a veto right for each member nation but dominance for the Mohawk nation in making new initiatives; the establishment of a ruling council and procedures for selecting confederation leaders;

special elevation for those excelling at war; and provisions for relations with other nations not in the confederation.[1]

No state can put *all* the rules governing the distribution of power into its formal constitution: Much must always be left to informal arrangements or to other documents. In the United States, the Constitution lays out a basic structure for politics. However, the "constitution with a small *c*" includes a great deal more than just the Constitution. It includes the understanding that the U.S. Supreme Court may overturn an act of Congress—a rule not written into the Constitution but only developed later under the strong Chief Justice John Marshall. Furthermore, it includes the tradition that presidents take a leading role in the making of foreign policy, and it includes much else besides. All these things are rules governing the distribution of power, which are not part of the Constitution but *are* part of our constitution.

There is often some disparity between the formal rules of the Constitution and actual political power. In the United States, a reading of the Constitution would lead one to think that the members of the electoral college have great power, because they are elected to meet and select a president; in fact, however, the practice and expectation have developed that the members of the electoral college ratify the vote of the citizens of their states, so that in practice, they have essentially no political power. As another example of the frequent disparity between formal political power and actual power, consider that no constitutions in Europe or North America mention the great political power of newspapers and television networks other than in passing.

✦ VARIATIONS IN FORMALITY

Constitutions vary as to how much is set out formally in a central document and how much has gradually developed outside of it. Older constitutions put less into a central document; newer ones, more. Two of the oldest political bodies in the world, Great Britain and the Catholic Church, have no central written constitution. Rather, the rules of politics for each are embodied in a variety of documents, traditions, and accepted practices. Each has a constitution (with a small *c*); people are aware of it and cite it frequently in British or church politics, but they are not referring to a single document when they do.

The United States is a relatively old state, and the original U.S. Constitution was approximately forty-three hundred words long; approximately twenty-nine hundred words have been added in amendments. Germany is a new state, and its Basic Law, written in 1949, is approximately 19,700 words long; this includes numerous amendments. France's most recent constitution, published in 1958 and amended only slightly since, is about ninety-one hundred words long. Perhaps constitutions that have been written in more recent years are longer because their writers are aware of the greater size and importance of the state and have taken greater pains to protect the state's power from difficulties that might arise. A large part of Germany's Basic Law is devoted to who is to

---

[1]Donald S. Lutz, "The Iroquois Confederation Constitution: An Analysis," *Publius* 28 (1998): pp. 99–127; the Constitution of the Iroquois Nations is available at www.constitution.org/cons/iroquois.htm.

govern during emergencies, though this is unusual. The one thing that is true of recent constitutions is that they are *specific* and complicated.

✦ THE VIRTUE OF VAGUENESS

Such specificity is by no means always an advantage. Napoleon once said that a constitution should be short and obscure. If rules are stated specifically, it becomes difficult to adapt a constitution to unforeseen or changing circumstances. Just as French generals in the period from 1919 to 1933 devised a marvelous fortification (the Maginot line) that would have served well for the trench warfare of World War I but was useless against the changed strategies of World War II, writers of constitutions often include in their design solutions to the problems with which *they* have become familiar. If these solutions are precise and inflexible, they are likely to produce new problems. Republican lawmakers in the United States were upset that Franklin Delano Roosevelt (a Democrat) had served more than the customary two terms as president. After his death, they wrote a stern amendment into the Constitution, limiting presidents to two terms of service. A few years later, they were faced with Dwight Eisenhower, a popular Republican candidate whom they would have loved to nominate for a third term but who was constitutionally barred from running again.

Similarly, the writers of the Basic Law of Germany were preoccupied, after the war, with the fact that Hitler had been able to take over the democratic government of Germany peacefully and more or less legally in 1933 and transform it into a dictatorship. In dozens of ways, they tried to make their new constitution "Hitlerproof." One of the many devices they added was a restriction on the ability of the parliament to unseat the chancellor and his cabinet. This power of parliament was hemmed about by numerous conditions, which led to an unpleasant comic opera when in 1972, the socialist-led government of Willy Brandt had lost so much support in the parliament that it could not even pass the national budget. Brandt and his cabinet wished to step down and call for a new election, since, under the circumstances, they could not govern effectively. But for six months, no one could think of a way by which this could be arranged under Germany's complicated constitutional provisions, without the embarrassment of the socialists formally voting themselves out of office (which they were not willing to do). The authors' precise and detailed constitutional tinkering with the Basic Law, designed to "win the last war," led to unforeseen difficulties in governing Germany.

Another example of misplaced specificity in writing constitutions comes from a regional political science association in the United States. This group publishes a scholarly journal, the editor of which is changed every three years. At one time, it was suggested that the term of the editor might be lengthened to four years, since it cost the association a few thousand dollars each time the editor was changed and the journal's operations had to be moved from one campus to another. This was not a big issue, but everyone agreed that the change would be a good idea because it would save some money and inconvenience. On looking at the association's constitution, however, it was found that the change could not be made easily. This document, instead of sensibly stating that the editor should serve a term "to be determined by the association's council," plainly said that "the editor shall serve a term of three years. . . ." An amendment to the constitution, tedious and difficult to arrange, would have been required to change the editor's term; therefore, the idea was dropped. One would think that the political scientists who wrote this document would have known better!

→ OTHER PRINCIPLES OF CONSTITUTIONAL DESIGN

Let us assume that you are in a position to help design or amend a state's constitution. Are there any additional principles that might help guide you? Beyond the general principle that you should not try to be too specific, a few additional rules of thumb you might consider are as follows: (1) The constitution should preferably not break drastically with long-standing traditions of government, (2) the constitution should be relatively easy to change, and (3) "incentive compatibility" should be built in as much as possible, so that the holders of power will find it personally advantageous to do what society as a whole needs from them. Let us consider each of these in some detail.

The Importance of Long-Standing Traditions

If a set of rules is to work, it must not be too far out of line with what most people in the state wish to do. One famous instance of a rule that did not work because it deviated too far from the people's wishes was the prohibition of liquor in the United States in the 1920s. In 1919, a constitutional amendment forbidding the possession or consumption of alcoholic beverages in the United States was passed. While many people supported this amendment (else it would not have been passed), many opposed it. The law was openly disobeyed, and criminals such as Al Capone flourished from the illegal traffic in liquor. Eventually, the state gave up, and in 1933, the Constitution was amended to make alcoholic beverages legal again.

It is not enough, either, to set up rules that the people are willing to obey only reluctantly; something more is needed than bare acquiescence. As we saw in Chapter 8, it is important that a state have a reservoir of goodwill and positive support from its people to carry it over the occasional rough times. A good constitution will be not only one that people are *willing* to obey but also one that comes close enough to their preconceptions that they will be able to identify enthusiastically with the system. Many historians think it is unfortunate that when Germany lost World War I, the monarchy to which its people were accustomed was destroyed. The democratic constitution of 1919 did not provide for the sort of personal, emotional attachment that the monarch always had. Instead, the first president of the new system was a quiet man, the son of a lowly saddle maker, with no dash or glamour. Hitler was later able to exploit the people's hunger for an exciting focus of patriotic devotion. How much better if the constitution of 1919 could have made a less dramatic break with the past by including a powerless but handsomely dressed monarch. This of itself would not have solved all of Germany's problems, but it might have helped.

This is not to say that a constitution can never depart from what the people expect. Many revolutionary states—such as China, in 1949, for example—have imposed new systems of government and society that transformed their people's expectations. There has always been a great deal of tension associated with this, however, and such states have had to keep tight control of things, causing much human suffering, to ensure the state's stability. There is inevitably a price to be paid in instituting rules for which the people are not prepared; but in some instances, this price might be considered worth paying.

The Importance of Amendability

If a new constitution must come reasonably close to reflecting the people's expectations, it must also be open to revision or amendment in response to changing needs. It is always a temptation, when writing a formal document, to "protect" it by making it difficult to change.

The U.S. Constitution, for example, was designed to be difficult to change. As a result, in the more than two hundred years that it has been in force, only seventeen amendments beyond the original Bill of Rights have been added. Such inflexibility could have been dangerous, because the conditions of U.S. politics obviously have changed immensely over two or more centuries. Fortunately, a new device for adaptation appeared when the Supreme Court took onto itself the power to interpret the Constitution with a certain amount of discretion. The Constitution was sufficiently "obscure," in Napoleon's sense, that the Court could adapt it with reasonable ease to changed circumstances. In 1954, for instance, the Court ruled that, in light of modern sociological theory, "separate but equal" schools for blacks and whites could not be taken to provide the equal protection under the laws that the Constitution guarantees. The Court ruled in this way despite that in earlier decisions, without the benefit of such theory, it had ruled that segregated school systems were constitutional.[2] Allowing nine judges who are appointed for life the discretion to adapt the Constitution may not be the best or the most democratic way to proceed, but it has at least provided a flexibility that the authors of the Constitution were not wise enough to build in.

In many states, provisions for adapting the constitution are much simpler. Often, a simple majority in the parliament is sufficient.

The Importance of Incentive Compatibility

In any political system, it is important that people in positions of power have personal incentives to do what society as a whole needs from them. That is, holders of power should find that they are personally rewarded when they do what society needs done and personally punished when they do not; there should be **incentive compatibility.**

We may safely assume that when people find that what is good for them personally conflicts with what is good for the state, they will usually choose what is good for themselves. This is not necessarily because they are especially selfish. It is easy for the individual to conclude that the damage to the state will be tiny compared with the benefit to him or her because the state and the individual are so different in size. As a result, people can usually make the "selfish" choice without feeling that they are doing much damage to the state. If a little cheating on my income tax can save me $300, what does that matter to a national budget of billions upon billions of dollars?

---

[2]Brown v. Board of Education, 347 U.S. 483 (1954).

The problem, of course, is that if large numbers of people find themselves in a similar position, the result can be serious. Precisely this problem occurs in constitutions. The constitution—the set of rules determining who has what kinds of political power—places individuals in positions in which they will make certain choices that society needs to have made. Presidents and members of a congress or parliament are expected to make laws for the state, public health officials are expected to watch out for epidemics, judges are expected to settle legal disputes fairly, police officers are expected to keep order, members of town councils are expected to set rules within their towns, and so on.

It is not enough to *say* what a person is to do in one of these positions, however. If costs and benefits are not set up to encourage officials to act in the intended manner, there is a good chance that they will act in ways that suit their personal interests rather than those of society.

For instance, the U.S. Congress was set up to make rules for the country as a whole. However, members of Congress are rewarded or punished not by the country as a whole but by the voters of their districts. It is a well-known problem of American democracy

"THE HECK WITH THE CONSTITUTION—
I'M GOING TO SHOUT 'FIRE'."

(In 1919 Supreme Court Justice Oliver Wendell Holmes wrote in a famous decision that illustrates the flexibility necessary to constitutional interpretation: ". . . protection of free speech would not protect a man falsely shouting 'Fire' in a theater and causing a panic.")

Reprinted by permission of ScienceCartoonsPlus.com.

that if the two conflict, members of Congress will frequently pursue the needs of their districts rather than those of the country as a whole. If the United States had stronger political parties, which could develop national programs and punish members of the Congress who did not support their party's program, then the personal incentives to members of the Congress would be different, and we might expect to see them support national interests even when these conflicted with their own districts' interests. As we will see in Chapter 11, many of the world's states do have political parties of this sort, and there we find that members of the parliament are less prone to place local needs over national ones. In the United States, however, which has relatively weak parties, this source of incentive incompatibility poses a serious problem.

As another example, consider the role of civil servants. Society needs to have civil servants develop programs creatively and administer them to the public efficiently, that is, at as low a cost as possible. However, in almost all countries, civil servants are personally rewarded most highly if they are cautious about innovation (in this way they will avoid ever making a dramatic mistake) and always spend all the money that had been allocated to them (if they show that they can do the job for less money, they're likely to be given less money the next year). These rewards have the effect of pushing civil servants toward uncreative, inefficient administration of programs.

Other examples could be drawn to show the importance of designing incentive structures to reward people for doing what the constitution intends them to do rather than for something else. It should be stressed that this is necessary *not* because holders of public office are especially greedy or cynical or selfish. Rather, like the income tax cheater, they are faced with differences in scale such that important things for them personally (security in their jobs, advancement) are balanced against almost trivial losses to the state. (What does it really matter if I vote for an inefficient project for my district? It is tiny compared with the overall budget. Is it really that important to the United States that my office—the transcribing division of the Southwest Regional Advisory Branch of the Weedgit Marketing and Regulatory Board—function at top form?) As with the problem of tax evasion, the problem here is that from the point of view of the single official, little damage is done to the state; but because there are thousands of officials like this, their combined impact may be grave. We can expect most of these individuals to do what they are actually rewarded for doing, not necessarily what they are meant to do. Therefore, we must try to design our constitution so that rewards follow for what officials are meant to do.

✧ CONSTITUTION-WRITING

The preceding few pages sound very detached and academic. In effect, they are the view of constitutions from 30,000 feet. The actual writing of a constitution for a new or transformed state is a messy business, in which the competing claims of different groups in the population have to be balanced with sufficient care that all of them (or almost all) will buy into the new procedures for allocating power. If some groups fear other groups and think that power going to those groups will mean oppression or obliteration for themselves, then striking the balance may take political skills of a very high order.

A famous example of this is the creation of the U.S. Senate in 1789, to give small states a platform to defend themselves against larger states. Another example is the partial independence of provinces from the central government written into Canada's two Constitution Acts, in order to protect various geographic minorities. It has been suggested that where deeply divided ethnic groups fear each other, formal division of power between the groups should be written into constitutions.[3] For instance, in Lebanon, the president must always be a Maronite Christian, the prime minister a Sunni Moslem, and the speaker of the assembly a Shiite Moslem.

A good current example of the difficulty of writing constitutions is the new constitution for the state of Iraq. Iraq comprises of three large ethnic/religious groups which have historically been very suspicious of each other: Kurds in the North, Sunni Arabs in the central part of the country, and Shiite Arabs in the South. All are Moslems, but the Kurds are ethnically different from the Arabs, and the Sunni and Shiite Arabs represent the two main forms of Islam. Of the three groups the Shiites are the largest in Iraq, making up a majority of the population.

The Sunnis, who make up only 20 percent of the population, had historically dominated Iraq (including under Saddam Hussein, who was a Sunni). Even after the American overthrow of Hussein, they were not reconciled to their loss of control, and wanted to keep Iraq tightly unified, looking ahead to what they hoped would be a restoration of their dominant position. The Kurds, on the other hand, wanted to have the right to secede. Finally, the Shiites wanted the country more-or-less held together so that with their majority they would have the possibility of controlling it, but they also wanted some autonomy for themselves in the South in case that failed. Add to all this the fact that a civil war between the Sunnis and Shiites was developing over the period when the constitution was being written and implemented, and you can see the difficulties!

A constitution was finally drafted in the fall of 2005, and barely passed in a referendum. In order to reassure the Sunni and Kurd minorities, the rule had been set that if three of the country's eighteen provinces rejected the draft constitution in the referendum by votes of more than two-thirds, it would not go into effect. Two heavily Sunni provinces rejected the draft by votes of over 90 percent, but a third, in which there was a sizable Kurdish minority, rejected it by only 55 percent. All fifteen Kurdish and Shiite provinces supported the constitution strongly in their votes, so it went into effect, on October 15, 2005.

The major provisions of the constitution are:

- The state is a "federal" system (i.e., decentralized; see below for an explanation of federalism), with provinces having a great deal of autonomy. Provinces are also allowed to unite among themselves into "super-regions," which would have similar autonomy. This includes the right of super-regions to maintain a regional guard, their own armed militia.

- The question of how to divide oil revenues is a contentious issue because the Sunni region has no oil and wants to share the revenue. This question was ducked in the writing of the constitution, and was passed on to the parliament to take care of as a regular law. (It was not until February 2007 that the various factions were able to work out a compromise law governing oil revenues.)

---

[3]Arend Lijphart, *Democracy in Plural Societies: A Comparative Exploration* (New Haven: Yale University Press, 1977); see also his *Power-Sharing in South Africa* (Berkeley: Institute of International Studies, University of California, 1985).

- The state was given a muted religious character. The constitution states, "Islam is a basic source of law," and the Supreme Court (which can overturn acts of the government) is a mix of legal specialists and religious scholars.
- There is an extensive set of provisions for individual rights.
- A democratically elected parliament vests the executive powers of government in a prime minister and cabinet. The office of president is a largely ceremonial figure. (This is a "parliamentary" system; parliamentary systems are discussed in detail in Chapter 14.)
- At least one-fourth of the members of the parliament must be women.

Of course, with a civil war under way between the Sunnis and Shiites, as of this writing it would be foolish to bet on the future of Iraq. But, this is the structure that has been laid down for a democratic Iraq, if it survives.

✦ THE GEOGRAPHIC CONCENTRATION OF POWER

In later chapters, we will look at a variety of questions on one aspect or another of constitutional design: how officials should be chosen, how laws should be passed, what is the best way of administering policies, and so on. However, one general question of constitutional design deserves treatment in this chapter.

That is the question of how much political power should be concentrated in the central government and how much should be distributed among the governments of cities, of "states" (as in the United "States"), or of regions. Some constitutions place almost all political power in the central government, with little independent decision making left to localities or regions. Others create a relatively weak central government, with many political decisions being made at lower levels. A variety of arrangements that fall between the two are possible.

What makes this a particularly important question is that all over the world, hot conflicts frequently rage between central governments and local groups. This is the single greatest cause of political conflict—a more incendiary one, for instance, than the perennial conflict between haves and have-nots or any of the newer conflicts such as those associated with feminism or protection of the environment. In Spain, separatists have for years waged an intermittent campaign of terror on behalf of their claims for a separate Basque state or at least for a greater degree of local independence in making political decisions. Since 1982, Canada has been involved in a divisive constitutional crisis over the relationship between Quebec and the rest of the country. In Britain, a Scottish nationalist party has regularly gotten a significant vote in British parliamentary elections with its claim for greater independence for Scotland and has been rewarded by the establishment of a separate Scottish Parliament. India is divided into many districts speaking different languages; these districts operate fairly independently of the central government, and disputes over language policies and job preferences for those speaking different languages are always hot political items. Until 1991, the Soviet Union consisted of fifteen governmental units called "republics" (one of which was Russia); many of these had their own languages, and there were frequent conflicts among them. In the end, the union had to be dismantled, with each of the republics declaring independence.

In another part of the world, many parts of Africa have had intense center-region conflicts; civil wars have been fought in Nigeria, Ethiopia, the Sudan, and Zaire between the central government and one or more regions that wished to break away. In the Mideast, Kurdish regions of Turkey, Syria, Iraq, and Iran have been a source of political tension for those countries for many years. As one last example, remember that the one time that politics in the United States has heated up to the level of civil war was 1861, in a dispute between the central government and a region of the country.

✦ "Federal" and "Unitary" States

The question of central versus local control is thus a hot item of politics; how is it dealt with constitutionally? There is a formal distinction between states that are **unitary** and those that are **federal.** We shall look first at the formal distinction (a characteristic of constitutions with a capital *C*) and then consider less formally (and more realistically) the division of power between central governments and their local or regional units.

A *unitary state* is one in which no other governmental body but the central government has any areas of policy that are exclusively under its control. In a unitary state, local and regional political bodies may potentially be overruled by the central government in any political decision they make. In a *federal state,* by contrast, local governmental authorities of some sort are set up by the Constitution (usually for regions of the state, as in the "states" of the United States or the "republics" of the Soviet Union), and these authorities are given certain political decisions over which they have a legal monopoly of control.[4] In a *federation,* then—a federal state—two governments control the same group of people but with regard to different political questions.

Germany is an example of a federation. The regional governments, called *Länder,* have total control of education, television, and radio; the central government has total control of defense, diplomacy, the postal service, railroads and air transport, and copyrights; the central government and *Länder* share responsibility for all other areas of policy.[5]

A federal system has often been the result of a compromise by which reluctant members were induced to join in a state; this is how the United States was originally formed, for instance. Federal systems usually exist where there was some difficulty in uniting the state or where the state is so large or so culturally diverse that it is thought there might be problems holding it together. Small states are less likely to be federal systems than large ones because problems like these are more likely to have cropped up in large states with diverse populations.

As of 2007, a total of twenty-one states were federal systems while 172 were unitary. From this it might appear that the question of federalism is unimportant, because so few states are federal systems. However, the federal states tend to be the larger ones. Though these twenty-one states represent only 11 percent of the world's states, they contain 38 percent of the world's people and cover 49 percent of the world's land area. The twenty-one states are indicated in Figure 9.1.

---

[4]William Riker, *Federalism: Origin, Operation, Significance* (Boston: Little, Brown, 1964), chap. 1.

[5]In what is coming to be called "layered sovereignty," the central government of Germany in turn yields total control of certain policies—especially currency, monetary policy, and agricultural policy—to the European Union, of which it is itself just one geographic unit. Thus German sovereignty is exercised in three layers, though it ultimately resides in the German state.

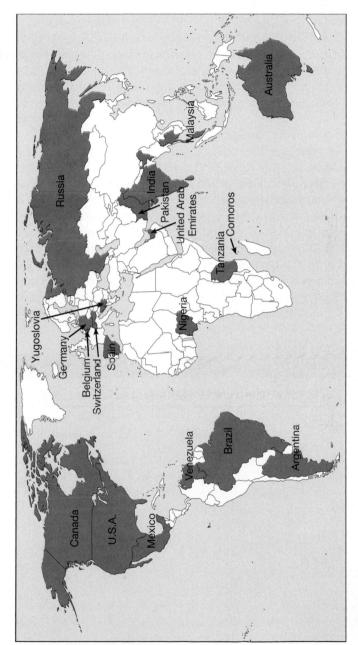

FIGURE 9.1 Federal systems (shaded areas) of the world.

✦ THE DISTINCTION BETWEEN "UNITARY" AND "CENTRALIZED" STATES

A formal definition like that given in the " 'Federal' and 'Unitary' States" section usually needs to be supplemented by an understanding of informal arrangements. I stated that in a federal system, separate governmental units coexist on the same territory, each with its own constitutionally set areas of policy. In a unitary system, by contrast, the central government is given the authority to make all policies, although it may deputize other governmental structures to act on its behalf. From this, we can see that in at least a formal sense, political power is more *centralized* (concentrated more on a central authority) in unitary systems than in federal ones.

However, politics is filled with surprises, and there are many informal arrangements that modify the centralizing tendency of the unitary state and the opposite tendency of the federal state. First, actual control of money counts at least as much in politics as the formal authority to make decisions. "Who pays the piper, calls the tune," as they say. Table 9.1 shows the percentage of governmental revenues collected and controlled by central, regional, or local governments in a variety of federal and unitary systems. While the central government usually controls more of the money in unitary systems than in federal systems, there is considerable variation within each category and some overlap across the two. Sweden's central government, with a unitary system, draws only 65 percent of governmental revenues, well under the 91 percent drawn by Malaysia's central government, the most centralized of the federal systems displayed

TABLE 9.1

Percentage of Revenue Collected by Different Levels of Government

	Central Government	"State," Regional, and/or Local Governments
Federal Systems		
Malaysia	91	9
Germany	67	33
Brazil	58	42
United States	54	46
Switzerland	51	49
Canada	48	52
Unitary Systems		
Israel	93	7
Chile	92	8
Great Britain	91	9
France	76	24
Sweden	65	35

SOURCE: International Monetary Fund, *Government Finance Statistics Yearbook 2006.*

here. Clearly, if we look at the control of cash, there is considerable variation in degrees of government centralization that goes beyond the constitutional distinction between "federal" and "unitary."

In other ways, less easily measured than revenues, states vary in their degree of centralization. France and Britain, for example, look fairly similar on Table 9.1. Both are unitary states, and the central government of France draws 76 percent of revenues while the central government of Great Britain draws 91 percent. However, *how* authority and revenues are used is as important as *whether* they are used. In Britain, the central government has traditionally kept only a loose control over local governments' actions and expenditures. For instance, in the last few years Great Britain has given its regions of Scotland and Wales extensive control over spending within their borders, even though all the revenue is technically revenue of the central government.

In France, on the other hand, power was for centuries lodged firmly in Paris. A minister of education in the late nineteenth century is said to have demonstrated this to a visitor, when, checking his watch, he looked up and said, "My friend, at this moment every third-grade pupil in France is reciting 'The Blue Bird.' " Power in France was quite centralized for many years; there was a time when for almost any major decision—whether to build a new town hall or school, for instance—cities had to gain the approval of the government in Paris. In 1981 President François Mitterrand instituted a number of decentralizing reforms, devolving many functions on new regional and departmental councils. But the system remains, on balance, centralized.[6]

To sum up, the degree of centralization in politics is greatly influenced by the formal constitutional choice between federalism and a unitary arrangement, but it is also strongly affected by all sorts of less formal arrangements.

✤ HOW MUCH CENTRALIZATION IS GOOD?

Any country has to strike some balance between centralized and decentralized politics. With totally decentralized politics, the state would cease to exist; it would be broken up into many small independent states. Even short of this, strong decentralization might lead to uncoordinated policies and confusion. Strong centralization, on the other hand, especially in a state that is large or geographically varied, could make for inflexible and insensitive government.

How much centralization is good will vary from state to state and with the circumstances the state faces. Large and diverse states find it necessary to be less centralized than other states in order to meet varying local needs flexibly. If a given state is faced with an emergency, as in time of war, it may feel that all power must be pulled together centrally so that it will be able to concentrate its resources on the single goal of meeting the emergency. (Most decentralized systems do give their central governments extraordinary temporary power during war.) There is no single level of centralization of politics that one should necessarily prescribe for all states at all times.

---

[6]See Vivien A. Schmidt, *Democratizing France: The Political and Administrative History of Decentralization* (Cambridge, England: Cambridge University Press, 1991).

The industrialized states of the world have shown signs of converging toward a fairly similar degree of centralization. Apparently, the circumstances in which these states find themselves are sufficiently similar that a common level of centralization has seemed appropriate to the leaders of each.

For instance, super-centralized France moved over the latter half of the twentieth century to decrease the centralization of power. The Mitterrand reforms of 1981 sharply decreased the powers of the "prefects," civil servants who had used to be responsible for keeping Paris in control of what local governments were doing. On the other side of the coin, in the decentralized United States, the last fifty years—despite recurrent attempts to reverse the trend—have been marked by an extension of power by the central government over the states and localities. This has often been accomplished by aid grants from the central government to the state or local government that carry with them some control over how the money is to be spent. As one example of this, the central government now has the power to order school districts to supply certain services to handicapped students. This would have been unthinkable fifty years ago.

We cannot give a simple answer to the question of how much centralization of government is good. However, around the world, complex industrialized states are indicating by their own choices that they are most comfortable with a considerable but limited degree of centralization. The main exceptions are states such as Belgium and Canada, where deep ethnic conflicts have boiled up to threaten the state, and a radical decentralization may be the best solution.

✦ CONSTITUTIONS AND GUARANTEES OF RIGHTS

As noted above, constitutions may include things beyond the distribution of power among institutions. One thing that almost all constitutions include is some enumeration of basic individual rights. In fact, these can be just as important as a clear set of rules assigning and governing power. They can establish the role of citizens in the state, just as other provisions establish the role of government; and, they can provide protection for individuals against abuse.

For instance, the Bill of Rights (the first ten amendments to the U.S. Constitution) guarantees United States citizens freedom of speech, freedom of religion, freedom of association, and other basic rights. As another example, the Danish Basic Law guarantees to all citizens that they "shall not in any manner whatever be deprived of their liberty because of their political or religious convictions or because of their descent." And more specifically, it protects them against unreasonable searches, against being held in jail without being charged with a crime, and against having their property expropriated. It also guarantees them free and equal access to trade; the right to a job or, if unemployed, to public assistance; the right to free education through elementary school; the right to free speech; and the right of free association.

Most constitutions include some set of guarantees like this, but not all do. For instance, the Canadian Constitution does not. Instead, it leaves the protection of individuals' rights up to the judiciary, through the body of precedents they develop. The Canadian example demonstrates that although it is often good and useful to guarantee rights in a constitution, there can be other ways to achieve protection for individuals as well.

In contrast, there is *no* other way to lay out the rules by which power is assigned among institutions and exercised by them. Only a constitution can do this.

✦ "CONSTITUTIONALISM" AND THE RULE OF LAW

Constitutions are a tool to build the **rule of law,** that is, an assurance that actions of the government are based on general principles that are applied equally to all people. Under the rule of law, governmental actions are not arbitrary, and are not based on personal connections or pay-offs.[7]

Constitutions, by laying out rules about power and its exercise, provide the platform for a rule of law. We have seen in the preceding section that guarantees of individual rights may contribute to this, but it is also true of the structural elements of the constitution, which assign power to various parts of government.

However, another factor—beyond the rules of the constitution—is also critical to the rule of law. **Constitutionalism** consists of faithful adherence to the letter and spirit of the constitution: Given that each state has a constitution, how faithful is a state to its constitution? That is, how fully do the leaders of the state honor the rules of politics in the state? "Constitutionalism" is the doctrine that states should be faithful to their constitutions because the rules so provided are all that can protect the citizens from arbitrary decisions by powerful people. There is also a notion in "constitutionalism" that constitutions should be designed fairly, rather than to give undue advantage to one particular group.

Constitutionalism is strong in Britain, the United States, Canada, Australia, and New Zealand. In the United States, for example, the Supreme Court, rather insulated from political pressure, has the power to overturn any act of government if it finds that the act is unconstitutional. The Court has been particularly active in guarding the Bill of Rights. Britain, Australia, Canada, and New Zealand do not have a supreme court to enforce the formal constitution, but in all of them, there is a long tradition of impartial obedience to the rules of politics and to the protection of individuals from arbitrary official action. Even in these five countries, however, constitutionalism is only *relatively* strong. It is not, and probably can never be, an absolute. Especially in times of national emergency, the governments of these countries have sometimes felt that it was necessary to temporarily suspend rights that they would ordinarily honor. Great Britain, for instance, held no elections for the duration of World War II, even though an election had been due in 1940; Churchill and the other party leaders thought that an election would be an unnecessary distraction during wartime, and they were critical of the United States for going ahead and holding its presidential election in 1944. Similarly, President Roosevelt ordered the internment of most Japanese-Americans during the war on the grounds that they were security risks. The president would never have had the power to do this in peacetime.

A country in which traditions of constitutionalism are slightly weaker is France. While individual rights are secure there, leaders' faithfulness to the rules of politics is a

---

[7]For "arbitrary" actions see above, pp. 134–135.

more fragile thing than in the United States, Canada, or Britain. Over the last century, France has had four constitutions, and it has had a total of nine systems for holding elections. Election laws, in particular, have often been manipulated to benefit the party in power. Also, the party in power has often manipulated news reports on public television and radio to enhance its election chances, and French embassies abroad have in the past tried to manipulate absentee voting to help the party in power. Finally, aside from these cynical manipulations of the rules of electoral politics, three times in the twentieth century French military leaders gave up on democratic rules altogether and tried to seize power; twice they were successful.

If France is a bit weak in its constitutionalism, though, many states are far weaker. Many of the world's people live in systems that give them only small protections against arbitrary power. In China from 1966 to 1976, over a million people were killed in the Cultural Revolution, which the state's leader, Mao Tse-tung, initiated to restore the Communist Party to its original revolutionary zeal. A similar disregard for individuals was shown in the 1989 suppression of the student movement at Tiananmen Square. In the late 1970s under a right-wing military regime, several thousand Argentinians "disappeared" when they were seized by the state police; they were never tried and were not seen again. Currently, the government of Sudan has unleashed rape and murder on its citizens in Darfur province.

EXAMPLE

Constitutional Government in Great Britain

Great Britain is an unusual example of constitutional government in that it has no written constitution—no single document that claims to set out the central principles of the organization of power.

What does the British constitution consist of? Some of it is made up of statute, or acts that Parliament has passed; the Parliament has the power, by a simple majority vote, to change any aspect of the British constitution. Much of the rest of the constitution consists of court precedent, decisions that have been made by judges in cases of constitutional significance. And some important parts consist of practice—behavior that has arisen in the day-to-day conduct of government and is not written down anywhere. In all of this, Parliament is ultimately supreme, because a new statute passed by it would override decisions by any court and would, of course, override any practices that had grown up. In the absence of contrary action by the Parliament, however, court decisions or practices stand. Much of the British constitution consists exactly of this: practices and court precedent that the Parliament has not chosen to change by statute.

The Magna Carta is one of the earliest parts of the British constitution. In 1215, an unpopular king (John) was forced by rebellious barons to sign this document limiting the king's authority over them in a number of ways. This document was later read into statute in 1295. Other important statutes have settled the system for determining who succeeds to the crown when a king or

Queen Elizabeth II, the ceremonial head of state of the United Kingdom.
© Tim Graham/Corbis

queen dies (Act of Settlement of 1701) and have laid out the powers of the two houses of Parliament (Parliament Acts of 1911 and 1949). Many smaller matters are also dealt with in statutes.

Court precedents have also contributed importantly to the constitution. For instance, the
powers of the queen are largely determined by a long series of precedents from court cases over
the centuries. The definitions of individual rights—which in the United States are written into the
Constitution as the Bill of Rights—evolved over centuries of court decisions in Britain.

Finally, and this is perhaps the most puzzling thing to non-British readers, important parts of
the constitution are not written in any document whatever but exist in practice. They are "what one
does." For instance, the prime minister and cabinet are probably the most powerful single part of
the process of government in Britain. All but a few of the bills considered by Parliament each year
are initiated by the cabinet, and the cabinet controls closely what happens in the Parliament. (You
will see more about this in Chapter 14.) But nowhere in any statute or in the decision of any court
is the cabinet set up or its powers defined. The only law that mentions the cabinet even indirectly is

one setting the salaries of cabinet ministers.[8] The rules governing the cabinet's behavior and defining its powers have arisen in practice and remain as unwritten understandings.

One might ask how a constitution like this gets enforced. How do we make sure that people play by the rules if not all of the rules are even written down? For instance, the prime minister is dominant within the cabinet and can ask members to resign or to exchange posts. This is a matter of practice. What would happen if a prime minister fired a cabinet minister, but the cabinet minister did not leave? As another example, an important aspect of the British constitution is that a British monarch will always sign into law a bill passed by the Parliament. Without the signature, the bill does not become a law, and in principle, the monarch has a right to veto acts of Parliament. In practice, however, this is not done. (What would happen if a monarch were to try to exercise the right? The answer, probably, is a constitutional crisis in which the monarchy would be eliminated.)

"Ancient and unwritten," by the way, does not mean unchanging. At present, there is a great deal of constitutional ferment in Britain. The state's entry into the European Union was itself a major constitutional change, and it in turn stimulated a movement to develop an official British code of individual legal rights (like the United States' Bill of Rights) to allow British law to function more easily with the European Court. On another front, when Tony Blair became prime minister in 1997, he undertook several major constitutional revisions. In its first couple of years, his cabinet moved through the Parliament seventeen constitutional bills, including bills to establish quasi-federal autonomy for Scotland and Wales, a bill to incorporate the European Convention on Human Rights into English law, and a bill to remove most hereditary peers from the House of Lords.

The British themselves puzzle over how an uncodified system like this can work. The authors of a British textbook write:

> Why have countries found it necessary to draw up [formal constitutions]? Three reasons can be advanced. First, they are needed when nations make a fresh start with their institutions, as when India, Pakistan, Ceylon, etc. gained their independence after World War II. Secondly, the country may contain groups of people distinct from each other through race, religion or language. In order to incorporate all people within the nation, each group must be given some guarantee that its identity will be maintained. Thirdly, in large countries, people in different parts may have particular interests and needs which they feel cannot be adequately provided for by a government in a remote capital. Here some form of federalism is likely, the division of powers between federal and state authorities being laid down in a written constitution. None of these considerations applies to Britain.[9]

This does not ring true, however. Certainly, Britain has been subject to major stresses, especially the breaking away of Ireland in the early twentieth century and the continuing troubles in Northern Ireland. It is not plausible that the British have been so peaceful that they have not needed a set of rules to govern them. In the end, one must conclude that the system depends on the goodwill of those who are involved in it. They must *want* to have the system work and see this as in their interest; otherwise, it would not work. It may be that the existence of an unwritten constitution pushes people to behave cooperatively. Where there is a formal set of rules, clever people often feel challenged to find loopholes. Where there is only a set of practices based on certain commonsense principles, clever people will find it necessary always to cite those central commonsense principles and to tailor their arguments and their behavior to them.

---

[8]Ministers of the Crown Act 1937; from S. B. Chrines, *English Constitutional History* (London: Oxford University Press, 1947), p. 21.
[9]J. Harvey and L. Bather, *The British Constitution*, 3d ed. (London: Macmillan, 1974), p. 510.

For good or bad, however, an "unwritten" constitution is not something a state can decide to start at any time. It must be received from the past, and so it is unlikely that a state could deliberately imitate Britain and set up an unwritten constitution! However, we may draw the lesson from Britain that it is well to leave some aspects of our constitution to custom, if that is practical, rather than trying to write everything down.

 EXAMPLE

Constitutional Government in Russia

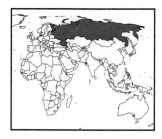

One of the many challenges facing the new Russian government after the breakup of the Soviet Union in 1991 and the subsequent collapse of the communist regime was establishing a new constitutional order for the state. Russia did not bring from the Soviet period much of a tradition of constitutionalism. Constitutions had never been seen in the Soviet Union as a solid foundation for government, which should regulate the government's actions. Rather, they were seen as ratifications of whatever power relationships were currently in place. From the Soviet revolution of 1917 until the breakup of the union in 1991, the Soviet Union had four different constitutions. These were seen more as descriptions of how the government operated than as guides to how government should operate; when power relations shifted, a new constitution was written to reflect the new situation.

Not only were constitutions seen as readily exchangeable, they also were seen as only minimally binding even while they were in place. Great disparities between the constitutional description and actual political reality were tolerated. For instance, the Soviet Constitution of 1977 gave each of the fifteen republics of the Soviet Union (units such as Russia; Ukraine; the three Baltic republics of Latvia, Lithuania, and Estonia) the right to secede from the union; in fact, the republics were kept under tight control through the army and party structures. Similarly, the Constitution assigned to the Soviet parliament the supreme power to pass laws. However, the parliament met only twice a year for a few days, during which time it heard long reports from the Central Committee of the Communist Party and ratified the reports unanimously with a show of hands. Constitutionalism was almost nil in the Soviet Union.

In truth, the Soviet constitution (with a small *c—not* the formal Constitution) could have been summarized very simply just by noting that the Communist Party was supreme in running the country. Regardless of the formal governmental structure, the party maintained its control in a practical sense by carefully placing party members in key positions in the armed forces, universities, bureaucracies, and the government.

With the collapse of communist rule, therefore, Russia's leaders needed to start from the beginning. President Boris Yeltsin presented a draft constitution in November 1993, and the Constitution was ratified in a referendum a month later. This was a document clearly designed to benefit Yeltsin (it gives the president massive power), and it was never certain how long it would last beyond his presidency. The uncertainty was not helped by the fact that in the turbulent period of 1991 to 1993, when Yeltsin was locked in a conflict with the old parliament, *everyone* played fast and loose with the still-valid Soviet Constitution. This period of extraconstitutional jockeying culminated in Yeltsin sending tanks to destroy the Parliament Building. If the old Constitution could be violated so casually, what did that say about the new one?

With the election in 2000 of President Vladimir Putin, however, and with his re-election in 2004, the new heavily presidential Constitution seems to be settling in. Whether this is a good thing or a bad thing is not entirely clear, as there are some real danger signs of the development of authoritarian government in Russia. It is an electoral democracy, but one in which the democratic function of elections is fragile. Under the new Constitution, citizens elect a president and a Federal Assembly that consists of two chambers. The president has direct and immediate control of all parts of the government that use weapons—the armed forces, the police, and what is left of the old secret police and intelligence networks. This is particularly important, given the extent of armed confrontation in politics in the past. Other operations of the state, such as economic policy, health policy, education, and so on, are administered under a prime minister who is appointed by the president but who must also work closely with the Federal Assembly and who can be voted out of office by the Federal Assembly.

The Federal Assembly has the sole power to pass laws for Russia. In December 2003, Putin's party swept to a two-thirds majority in the lower house of the Federal Assembly, and he has clear control of the Assembly. Combined with the immense power residing in the office of president, this has given him almost unchallenged control of Russia.

Most ominously, outside of the formal governmental structure Putin has moved systematically to remove any opposition. He has suppressed all independent television and most newspapers that opposed him. In 2004, he trumped up charges against the Yukos oil company, Russia's largest oil company, and drove it into bankruptcy because its chief executive, Mikhail Khodorkovsky, had tried to finance an opposition to him.

Russia, like the Soviet Union of which it used to be a part, is a federal system, with eighty-nine separate federal units.[10] But the federal arrangements still leave a great deal of power to the central government. All legislation passed by the parliaments of the federal units, for instance, must be approved by a head of administration appointed by the president. The president may suspend any administrative act of a federal unit. And in 2004, Putin further tightened central control by changing the Constitution to have the governors of provinces appointed (by him), rather than elected.

Despite such ominous signs the Russian Constitution is still the constitution of a democracy—just. The president and the lower house of the Federal Assembly are both directly elected, and although the electoral process has been badly distorted by corruption and a (mostly) controlled press, the pieces of democracy are still there. The moment of truth may occur in 2008, when President Putin's second term will end. The president is allowed to serve two terms under the Constitution. If Putin does not change the Constitution to allow himself further terms, the democratic possibility in Russia's future will remain at least minimally alive.

KEY TERMS

constitution	unitary state	rule of law
incentive compatibility	federal state	constitutionalism

---

[10]The basis for "federal units" varies a good deal. The cities of Moscow and St. Petersburg are federal units, for instance; other federal units are ethnically distinct regions such as the Tatar territory; and others are more general geographic divisions of Russia.

FURTHER READING

Bakvis, Herman, and Chandler, William M. *Federalism and the Role of the State*. Toronto: University of Toronto Press, 1987.

"Constitutions and Constitutionalism." In *International Encyclopedia of the Social Sciences*.

Erk, Jan. "Does Federalism Really Matter?" *Comparative Politics* 39 (2006), pp. 103–120.

Ferejohn, John, Rakove, Jack N., and Riley, Jonathan. *Constitutional Culture and Democratic Rule*. New York: Cambridge University Press, 2001.

Filippov, Mikhail, Ordeshook, Peter C., and Shvetsova, Olga. *Designing Federalism: A Theory of Self-Sustainable Federal Institutions*. New York: Cambridge University Press, 2003.

Friedrich, Carl. *Limited Government: A Comparison*. Englewood Cliffs, NJ: Prentice-Hall, 1974.

Gerston, Larry N. *American Federalism*. Armonk, N.Y.: M. E. Sharpe, 2007.

Goldwin, Robert A., Kaufman, Art, and Schambra, William A., eds. *Forging Unity Out of Diversity: The Approaches of Eight Nations*. Washington, DC: American Enterprise Institute, 1989.

Griffiths, Ann L., and Nernberg, Karl, eds. *Handbook of Federal Countries, 2002*. Montreal: McGill-Queen's University Press, 2002.

Horowitz, Donald G. *A Democratic South Africa? Constitutional Engineering in a Divided Society*. Berkeley: University of California Press, 1991.

Maravall, José Mariá, and Przeworski, Adam. *Democracy and the Rule of Law*. New York: Cambridge University Press, 2003.

McHugh, James T., ed. *Comparative Constitutional Traditions*. New York: Peter Lang, 2002.

Reynolds, Andrew. *The Architecture of Democracy: Constitutional Design, Conflict Management, and Democracy*. New York: Oxford University Press, 2002.

Riker, William. *Federalism: Origin, Operation, Significance*. Boston: Little, Brown, 1964.

Schlesinger, Joseph. *Ambition and Politics: Political Careers in the United States*. Chicago: Rand McNally, 1966 (especially with regard to incentive compatibility).

Sunstein, Cass R. *Designing Democracy: What Constitutions Do*. New York: Oxford University Press, 2001.

Weiler, J. H. H. *The Constitution of Europe*. New York: Cambridge University Press, 1999.

Ziblatt, Daniel. "Rethinking the Origins of Federalism: Puzzle, Theory, and Evidence from Nineteenth-Century Europe." *World Politics* 57 (2004), pp. 70–98.

WEB SITES OF INTEREST

Constitution of the United States—Analysis and Interpretation, maintained by the Congressional Research Service:

www.gpoaccess.gov/constitution/browse.html

International Constitutional Law Project, a site with the constitutions, amendments, and recent constitutional commentaries for most states of the world:

http://www.servat.unibe.ch/law/icl

University of Michigan site with links to many Web sites regarding constitutions of the world:

http://www.lib.umich.edu/govdocs/forcons.html

Web site of the Constitution Society, a libertarian group:

http://www.constitution.org

CHAPTER 10

ELECTIONS

In the long swing of history, elections with broad mass participation are rather new. Such elections originated with democratic government, which means that they came along at the end of the eighteenth century and the beginning of the nineteenth. Today elections are widespread around the world, even though a number of the world's states are not democracies. Even many nondemocratic states, such as Syria, have held them regularly. Why are elections so in vogue?

Part of the answer, of course, is that *democracy* is a word that purrs with respectability. Even states that are not democratic wish to appear democratic, and holding elections is one of the easiest ways to follow some of the forms of democracy even if the state is not democratic.

A second reason is that elections can serve more purposes for the state than just the democratic one of allowing the mass of people to help in the selection of leaders and policies. Elections were invented to make democracy possible; but once invented, they turned out to have further uses. This is an interesting aspect of political institutions that we shall encounter frequently in later chapters. Institutions may be devised to serve a particular purpose, but once they are in existence, they may be adaptable to a variety of purposes.

In this case, the thing that recommends elections to the leaders of autocratic states is that they can serve *two* main purposes: *not only* (1) the purely democratic purpose of allowing the mass of people to have some direct say in the *choice of leaders and policies,* but also (2) the more or less universal purpose of *allowing the state to mobilize its people and to build up their support for the state by acting out support and participating in the process of government.*

✦ ELECTIONS AS A MEANS OF BUILDING SUPPORT

Let us consider the second of these first. Many autocracies around the world hold elections, and often invest quite a lot of effort and money to ensure a large turnout. In modern times, such states as Guatemala, Egypt, Syria, Romania, Algeria, North and South Korea, Paraguay, Belarus, Cuba, Côte d'Ivoire, Singapore, and many others have

Rene Preval, a presidential candidate in Haiti, greets supporters.

© Tim Perching/AFP/Getty Images

staged elaborate elections of which the outcome was never in doubt.[1] And, they have accomplished electoral turnout in these non-contests that are equal to or better than the turnout in United States presidential elections: Syria, 63 percent in the 2003 election; Belarus, 93 percent in 2006; Singapore, 92 percent in 2006.

In the Soviet Union (before it dissolved in 1991) intense efforts by the Communist Party ensured a 99 percent turnout:

> The network of agitators is fully activated during the ten days preceding the election. Agitators must visit each voter in the precinct, explaining the virtues and qualifications of the sole candidate. The mass media publicize the biography of each candidate to the larger soviets and urge a resounding vote of confidence for the regime. The candidate spends no money campaigning but holds meetings with voters. . . . Refusal to vote is regarded as an unpatriotic act. Even the sick are expected to vote and ballot boxes are brought to the bedsides of hospital patients. Voting occurs on ships that are at sea on election day if there are at least twenty-five voters aboard; the votes are added to those cast in the ship's home port. Passengers on long-distance trains vote in special precincts while in transit.[2]

---

[1]Some of these countries are now electoral democracies, but were autocracies within the last few decades, and staged elaborate elections.

[2]John S. Reshetar, Jr., *The Soviet Polity,* 2d ed. (New York: Harper & Row, 1978), p. 196.

TABLE 10.1

Percentage Agreeing That Ordinary People Have Little Say in Government

	Voters	1968 Nonvoters	Total
Before the election	71	83	74
After the election	37	58	42
Change	−34	−25	−32
	Voters	1972 Nonvoters	Total
Before the election	34	58	40
After the election	29	54	36
Change	−5	−4	−4

SOURCE: Recalculated from Benjamin Ginsberg, *The Consequences of Consent: Elections, Citizen Control, and Popular Acquiescence* (Reading, MA: Addison-Wesley, 1982), pp. 167 and 170.

The elections took up a great deal of time and cost a lot of money. Over 2 million candidates were elected each time—better than one out of every hundred adults—and they invested a great deal of time and energy in the campaign. Millions more were engaged in agitation, in serving on electoral commissions, and so on. It was an expensive business. And yet, the single candidate of the Communist Party was going to win each seat. Why did they go to all of this effort?

The most reasonable guess is that the main purpose of elections in the Soviet Union was to renew the people's enthusiasm and support for the regime. Elections provided a recurring opportunity for the newspapers to pour out praise for the leaders of the state and for citizens, through their actions, to feel that they were a part of it. As behavioral therapists know, a good way to ingrain a particular point of view in a person's consciousness is to have the person act it out. This would be reason enough for the Soviet Union to have put its population "through their paces" at regular intervals.

While we do not normally think of elections in democracies as functioning to build support for the system, it can be shown that elections serve this purpose in democracies as well as in autocracies. A study of presidential elections in America highlighted this quite well.[3] At the 1968 and 1972 presidential elections, a sample of American adults were asked before and after the election whether they agreed or disagreed with the statement "People like me don't have any say about what the government does." Before the 1968 election most people, whether or not they ended up voting in the election, agreed with the statement, as can be seen in Table 10.1. The electorate in 1968 was quite disillusioned and had lost a great deal of its faith in the nation's leaders. Conflict over civil rights and American

---

[3]Benjamin Ginsberg, *The Consequences of Consent: Elections, Citizen Control, and Popular Acquiescence* (Reading, MA: Addison-Wesley, 1982), pp. 166–170.

involvement in the Vietnam War had soured people on politics, and the American public had seen the Democratic nominating convention in Chicago torn apart by demonstrations and by the reaction of the police to the demonstrations. Of those who voted in that election, 71 percent initially agreed that ordinary people do not have any say in government, as did 83 percent of those who ended up not voting. Over the campaign and the election, this outlook changed considerably. After the election, only 37 percent of those who had voted agreed with the cynical view of government, for a drop of 34 percentage points. Among those who did not vote but who experienced the period of campaigning and election, the figure also dropped, but by somewhat less–25 percentage points.

The circumstances in 1972 were different, but there again the election apparently served to reassure the public about the political system. The pre-election public in 1972, in contrast to that of 1968, was not turned off to politics. The incumbent Nixon administration was popular (Nixon would get 61 percent of the vote), and the Vietnam trauma had passed. Only 34 percent of those who would eventually vote and 58 percent of those who would not initially agreed with the cynical view of government. The campaign was not one to inspire confidence in the system. It was marked by the forced withdrawal of Thomas Eagleton as the Democrats' vice-presidential nominee because it became known that he had a history of mental illness; by a great deal of personal vituperation between the candidates; and by rumors of corruption and "dirty tricks" that would later produce the painful Watergate scandal.

In spite of this, the campaign period and election of 1972 produced small moves toward greater support of the system, even among an electorate who were already rather supportive before the election. After the election, 5 percent fewer voters and 4 percent fewer nonvoters agreed with the cynical view.

The figures in Table 10.1 were based on the National Election Studies (hereafter NES) surveys for 1968 and 1972.[4] The only other United States election for which a similar analysis is possible from NES data is 1996. For that election, Wendy M. Rahn, John Brehm, and Neil Carlson found exactly the same process as was shown for the earlier elections in Table 10.1.[5]

Still further evidence for the effect comes from a study of Canadian elections in the 1980s. For all Canadians (not distinguishing between those who voted and those who did not vote), regard for Parliament, on a scale of 0 to 100, rose from an average of 53 before the 1988 election to 59 after the election. And a dozen similar comparisons worked in the same way.[6]

From all of this, it appears that such renewal of support for the system is a widespread attribute of elections. In Chapter 8, we examined the state's need to maintain sufficient support among its citizens so that its authority would continue undiminished.

---

[4]National Election Studies, Center for Political Studies, University of Michigan.

[5]Wendy M. Rahn, John Brehm, and Neil Carlson, "National Elections as Institutions for Generating Social Capital," in Theda Skocpol and Morris P. Fiorina, eds., *Civic Engagement in American Democracy* (Washington, DC: Brookings Institution, 1999), pp. 111–62. Simply looking at the overall result for voters and nonvoters combined, they found that from before the election to after the election, Americans reduced their agreement with the cynical position by 8.4 percentage points. And, in a careful multivariate analysis of the sources of this change, they found that whether or not a person had voted in the election added significantly to the effect.

[6]Allan Kornberg and Harold C. Clarke, *Citizens and Community* (New York: Cambridge University Press, 1992), pp. 187–191.

Difficulties of Elections in a New Democracy

All new democracies find the actual conduct of elections difficult at first, especially if they are poor and lack a good infrastructure for communication. Papua New Guinea's election in 2002 offers a particularly horrific example, complicated by poor internal communications in an impoverished country, ethnic warfare in its highland region, and continued tensions coming from its war of independence from Australia. The story, however, is as much one of great hope at the efforts made by local democrats and their international partners to establish democracy in a country that faces great problems.

Voting in the 2002 election started on June 15, 2002, and polls were supposed to close on June 29. (The two-week duration was required by the difficulty of people reaching the polling places on a single day.) In fact, the polling was so marred by gangs intimidating officials and voters, by tampering with ballots, and by arson at polling places that the voting was extended for another month, to July 29. Even then, election results could only be declared for 80 of the 109 seats; the rest, all in the southern highlands, were decided in a supplemental election in June 2003.

Transparency International (an international anti-corruption organization; see p. 116) has worked with the government to change the electoral system to limited preferential voting, in which not only voters' first choices count, but also their second and third choices. The intent is to make vote-buying and bribery difficult; since all votes count in the end, there are too many people to bribe easily. The new system was introduced for the 2007 election.

The press releases of the Papua New Guinea Electoral Commission in its early years of 2002 and 2003 provided a fascinating and moving picture of good people dealing with politics in the raw. The commission complained of attacks by thugs, of police inaction, of bribery, and of obstruction by local officials. The language was blunt and vivid. Yet what remains at least for me is a strong sense of the faith and dedication of these officials, working under the worst of circumstances, to establish democracy and the rule of law.

For democracies and autocracies alike, elections apparently furnish a potent tool to help ensure this popular base of support. At regular intervals, people's acceptance of the system is reinforced as citizens act out their identification with the state and its leaders.

❖ ELECTIONS AS A MEANS OF SELECTING LEADERS AND POLICIES

In many countries, however, elections are meant to do more than bolster support for the regime. They are the means by which leaders and (sometimes) actual policies are chosen by the people. For this to be the case, an election must involve a choice between candidates or a choice whether a particular policy is to be followed. In democratic states, elections are set up in this way. And in some states that are not democratic at the level of national government, elections are allowed to function in this way at least at the local level.

In democracies, the choice of political leaders at all levels is made by competitive elections. In addition, some democracies provide for the **referendum,** a device by which the voters choose directly through their ballots whether a particular proposal will become law. Controlled referendums are also sometimes used in autocracies to exhibit and stimulate support in the same way as other elections. The referendum is discussed in the "Referendums" section of this chapter.

✦ ELECTORAL SYSTEMS

If elections are to be used to choose political leaders, there must be some rule for translating people's votes into a particular selection of leaders. This is not as simple a matter as one might think. For instance, one might state simply that the candidate who gets the most votes will win the election and take office. What of the people who voted for a losing candidate: Should their votes count for nothing? What if there were a dozen candidates and the one who got the greatest number of votes had only about 20 percent of the vote: Would we want that person to take office? There is no single obvious way to translate the votes cast by the electorate into the people who will take office. States need to design rules determining which people win office as a result of any particular result in the voting; these rules are called the **electoral system** of the state.

Rulers of states can, if they wish, write many detailed differences into their electoral systems. At one or another time and place, for instance, a party has been required to win at least 5 percent of the vote to get a seat in the legislature, owners of businesses have been given double votes to increase their weight in the electoral choice, some seats in a legislature have been reserved for members of one or another race, and votes have been counted separately and weighed differently for rich people and poor people. The possibilities are limited only by the imagination of those in charge of the state.

However, two broad types of electoral system are used in almost all democracies: **single-member-district plurality systems** and **proportional representation systems.** For convenience, they will be referred to from this point on by their initials, SMDP and PR.

SMDP and PR Systems

In the SMDP system, the state is divided into a set of districts, usually having roughly equal populations. One representative is elected from each district to be a member of the legislative body of the state, and whoever gets a plurality of the votes wins the seat. (A *plurality* is the largest number of votes cast for any candidate; if there are many candidates running, the plurality may be less than a majority of votes cast.) Hence the name: A *single member* is elected from each *district* by a *plurality* of votes.

This arrangement is familiar to U.S. and Canadian students, because both countries use versions of the SMDP system. In Canada, the members of Parliament are elected by the SMDP system. In the United States, members of the House of Representatives are elected by an SMDP system and members of the Senate by a variant of SMDP. (There are two senators from each state of the United States, but they are elected in separate years by a plurality so that, in effect, the senatorial electoral system is SMDP.)

Britain is an SMDP system, and indeed these systems tend to be limited, worldwide, to Britain and its former colonies such as the United States, Canada, and India.

Most electoral democracies of the world use versions of proportional representation (PR). PR is simple. Though various formulas and methods are used to calculate the proportional result, the basic principle of PR is that political parties' representation in the legislative body is set roughly proportional to their strength in the electorate. That is, if the Fundamentalist Neopejorative Party got 18 percent of the votes cast in the election, it would get roughly 18 percent of the seats in the legislative body; if it got 30 percent of the votes, it would get roughly 30 percent of the seats.

The most common form of PR is "list PR." In list PR the state is divided into a relatively small number of large districts, each of which sends a large-ish number of members to the parliament. There may even be only one "district," the entire state itself. (The Netherlands and Israel do this, for instance.) But, most states set up a number of districts in order to ensure that all regions get their fair share of representation. Sweden, for instance, is divided into 29 districts that elect 310 representatives, for an average of about 11 representatives per district.

Before the election each party prepares a ranked list of candidates for each district (hence the name, "list PR") and registers that list with the election commission. After the election the commission determines the number of seats each party should have, based on its proportion of the vote, and counts down the ranked list from the top, awarding places to that number of candidates. If the Socialist Party gets 40 percent of the vote in a district with fifteen members, for instance, the commission will award six seats (40 percent of the 15) to the Socialists; the first six names on their list will then become members of the parliament.

The proportional outcome may not seem an unreasonable result, but PR was invented precisely because SMDP does *not* give a proportional result. Instead, SMDP generally favors large parties and hurts small ones. This is because a small party, if its voters are spread evenly geographically, will have only a small number of voters in each district and may not have enough in any one district to achieve a plurality and win there. This is illustrated in Figure 10.1. The hypothetical country of Aksala is divided into twenty districts,

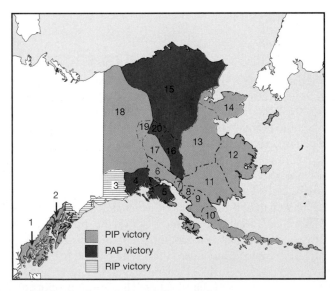

FIGURE 10.1   Aksala: A hypothetical SMDP result.

TABLE 10.2

Percent of the Vote for the RIP, by District

District	Vote	Percent
1	12,500	25%
2	13,500	27
3	21,000	42
4	14,000	28
5	13,000	26
6	11,000	22
7	5,000	10
8	6,500	13
9	8,500	17
10	10,500	21
11	12,000	24
12	9,500	19
13	9,500	19
14	3,100	6
15	1,500	3
16	2,300	5
17	14,600	29
18	2,000	4
19	14,300	29
20	15,700	31

each having 50,000 voters. In its most recent election, the Prudential Improvidence Party (PIP) polled 450,000 votes, or 45 percent of the total; the Protection of Artifacts Party (PAP) polled 350,000 votes, or 35 percent of the total; and the Revolutionary Inaction Party (RIP) came in third with a still substantial poll of 200,000, or 20 percent of the votes. As you can see from the map, the PIP won fourteen seats with its 450,000 votes, the PAP won five seats with its 350,000 votes, and the poor RIP got only one seat for its 200,000 votes. That is, 45 percent of the vote got 70 percent of the seats, 35 percent of the vote got just 25 percent of the seats, and 20 percent of the vote got only 5 percent of the seats.

How is it that RIP did so badly, getting just one out of the twenty seats for its one-fifth of the votes? As we see in Table 10.2, RIP's votes were spread around so that it got 25 percent in one district, 13 percent in another, 29 percent in another, 3 percent in another, and so on. Only in district number 3 did RIP's 42 percent share of the vote top the shares of both PIP and PAP, so that it won.

This is a fairly typical result of SMDP. Although the example is made up, it was not deliberately constructed to produce this result beyond stating the initial condition that the three parties were of those sizes and had a fairly even distribution of their voters across the country. Most "real life" examples of SMDP fit the same pattern. In the British election of 2005, for instance, the Liberal Democrats polled 22 percent of the votes but won only 10 percent of the seats in the House of Commons.

In their early elections, most European states used electoral systems similar to SMDP. It was at the urging of small or new parties that felt unfairly discriminated against that most states changed to PR systems in the early part of the twentieth century. Why, you may ask, do any states retain SMDP as an electoral system when it is so unfair? The reason is that there is a practical benefit to the distortion in favor of large parties, which many observers think may compensate for the unfairness to smaller parties. Small parties are disadvantaged by SMDP; therefore, there is a tendency for them to disappear or to merge over time. As a result, SMDP electoral systems tend to encourage the emergence of two large parties rather than a variety of smaller parties.[7] With only one major exception—Canada—SMDP systems have only two major parties, which may make it easier to govern the state. And with only occasional exceptions, all PR systems have more than two major parties. This may make it difficult to govern the state, but only if parties have difficulty cooperating; while in some notable cases multiparty government has been associated with instability, most PR/multiparty governments function smoothly. (We will discuss the relative merits of having two parties in Chapter 11—there are arguments on both sides!)

The trade-off between the two systems is one of fairness to minorities and small parties, on the one hand, versus simplifying the party system by weeding out small parties, on the other. Two other issues that may enter into a choice between the two electoral systems are:

- Electoral participation is likely to be higher under PR than under SMDP. Under SMDP, voters who are in the minority in their district (a Republican in Boston, a Conservative in Quebec City, a Democrat in suburban San Diego) may feel that there is no sense in voting, because their candidates cannot win. And more important, since PR usually produces a system of more than just two parties, the voter is likely to have a wider range of choices under PR and find a party that is a close fit to her values.

- SMDP provides legislators with a tie to a particular locality, with a particular set of constituents, while most PR systems do not make this kind of connection.[8]

---

[7]The standard statement on the effects of electoral systems is Maurice Duverger, *Political Parties* (New York: Wiley, 1954). See also Douglas Rae, *The Political Consequences of Electoral Laws,* rev. ed. (New Haven: Yale University Press, 1971); Rein Taagepera and Matthew S. Shugart, *Seats and Votes: The Effects and Determinants of Electoral Systems* (New Haven: Yale University Press, 1989); Gary Cox, *Making Votes Count: Strategic Coordination in the World's Electoral Systems* (New York: Cambridge University Press, 1997).

[8]A variant of PR, which was first invented by Germany in the early 1950s, elects half of the representatives from *single*-member districts, but then tops off those members (who, as one would expect, overrepresent the larger parties) with an additional and equal number of seats distributed among the parties in such a way that the overall membership of the parliament is made proportional. This provides each district in the country with an identifiable member who is "their" member in the parliament, while arranging that the overall distribution of seats is proportional, so that small parties are not disadvantaged. This blend of the two systems has proved very popular in new democracies since the 1990s.

Two Conditions for the SMDP Bias

The bias of SMDP in favor of large parties is a function of two conditions: *First, if a small party has most of its strength concentrated in just a few districts, it may not be hurt by the SMDP system,* because it may have enough strength in those few districts to win there. Consider if a Southwestern Autonomy Party had appeared in Aksala and had polled 60,000 votes spread across the four southwestern districts. Depending on how its votes were spread among the four districts, it might well have won in one or two of them. (It would have averaged 30 percent of the vote across the four districts, and the rest of the vote would have been spread among three parties.)

Again, there are plenty of "real life" examples of this exception to the rule of SMDP bias. One is the Plaid Cymru, a Welsh nationalist party, which in the British election of May 2005 polled only one-half of 1 percent of the vote nationally but, by concentrating that vote in Wales, won three of the 645 seats in the House of Commons. (Remember that in that same election the Liberal Democrats, with their strength spread more evenly across the country, got 22.1 percent of the vote, but only 62 of the 645 seats.)

Another good example is Canada, which, as noted, is the major exception to the rule that SMDP electoral systems tend to limit a country to two major parties. Four major parties are active in Canadian politics, but each of them has a distinct regional identity, so that there is little selective pressure on them from the SMDP system.

Second, the smaller the number of districts, the more likely it is that small parties will be hurt by SMDP. If the state is divided into a small number of large districts, there is less chance that a small party will happen to have enough votes to win in a particular district.

This is illustrated in Figure 10.2, in which the districts of Aksala from Figure 10.1 have been grouped by fours, so that there are five larger districts. Under this arrangement,

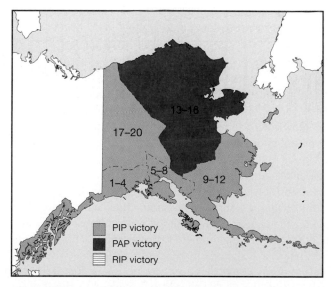

FIGURE 10.2 A hypothetical election by SMDP, with Aksala divided into only five districts.

the largest party (PIP) expands its share of the seats from 70 to 80 percent, the PAP drops from 25 to 20 percent, and the "small" RIP (with 20 percent of the vote) disappears.

To carry this to an extreme, if there were only one seat in the legislative body, the whole country would be one single-member district, with a plurality winning. In this case, the ultimate distortion would occur, with the candidate of the PIP winning 100 percent of the "seats" (i.e., the one seat), even though PIP had gained only 45 percent of the total vote.

This last extreme possibility sounds silly, but I mention it because it actually does happen in the real world, and is important. If a state has a president who is popularly elected by all the voters, the election functions, in effect, as a legislative election with one seat under SMDP. (Most democracies do not have an elected president, but some do— the United States, France, Mexico, and others. Presidential government is discussed at length in Chapter 15.) Where there is a presidency, small parties are driven out of contention, and there is strong pressure for the system to evolve into one with two large parties. An example of this is France, which in 1962 shifted to a popularly elected presidency. Since that time, small parties have been gradually declining, until today there are four parties arranged by pairs in loose alliance into a bloc of the Left and a bloc of the Right, plus a fifth party off on its own dimension of opposition to immigrants. The conclusion is unavoidable that the institution of the presidency has forced France's quarrelsome parties to coalesce into something like two large parties.

To summarize the point of this section dealing with electoral systems: *The SMDP system tends to drive out small parties and ultimately to produce an arrangement consisting of two large parties. This effect is less strong if the parties have geographic concentration of voters and may disappear altogether, as in the case of Canada, if all parties' strengths are concentrated by region. The effect is heightened by reducing the number of districts and is especially strong when the state is a single district, as in presidential elections.*

✦ Referendums

Many democracies restrict their citizens' involvement in the affairs of state to a vote that expresses their choice among potential political leaders. The state's policies are then set by the elected leaders, without any direct input from the voters. Some democracies, however, allow voters under some circumstances to choose directly, in an election, whether a given policy should be followed. Such an electoral choice is called a referendum. The United States does not have any provision for national referendums, but many localities and states do provide for them. California is particularly noted for their use, as in the Proposition 71 referendum in 2004, in which the state's voters established a large trust fund to sponsor stem-cell research. Outside the United States, a few democracies provide for the regular use of national referendums. France and Switzerland are two examples, the latter relying on them rather heavily.

Beyond these few instances, many democracies that would not accept the regular use of referendums *do* use them on rare occasions for decisions of great gravity, where it is felt that all the people should be involved in the decision. Spain, for instance, when it initiated its new democratic Constitution in 1978, held a referendum so that the Constitution could be ratified by the people. Similarly, when the powers of the

European Union were to be expanded in a new constitution in 2005, Spain, France and the Netherlands held referendums to allow their people to decide whether it should be approved. (Spain voted yes, but defeats in France and the Netherlands killed the draft constitution.)

Why are democracies so reluctant to give "power to the people" by using the referendum to make laws? The main objection is that a proposed law cannot get the sort of careful consideration and detailed examination in an election campaign that it would get in a legislature or parliament. Voters typically do not have the time or resources to inform themselves about the intricacies of a bill. In a sense, that is "what they hire politicians for." Especially when many bills are voted on in a single campaign—as in California, where twenty or more may appear on a single ballot— only one or two will have been widely discussed among the voters. The other bills will be decided by chance factors such as how enticingly they are worded or where they appear on the ballot, or by the small number of people who may stand to gain from them in special ways and therefore take a special interest in them.

✦ ELECTORAL PARTICIPATION

Let us shift from elections and electoral systems to examine how voters act in elections. We shall confine our attention to voters in democratic elections.

It is evident that not all of those who are entitled to vote do vote. In the 2004 American presidential election, for instance, only 61 percent of those who were eligible to vote did so; in most elections for local office, the turnout is even less than this.

There is great variation from one place to another, and among different sorts of people in any one place, as to how active people are in elections. At roughly the same time that 61 percent of eligible Americans voted in the 2004 presidential election, the following percentages of the eligible electorate voted in a variety of European elections: Great Britain, 58 percent; Czech Republic, 58 percent; Germany, 79 percent; Sweden, 80 percent. European democracies usually exhibit higher levels of electoral participation than the United States, but in the very high-interest election of 2004 (with turnout up from 50 percent in 2000 to 61 percent in 2004), the United States got as high as some of Europe's laggards. Within the United States, electoral turnout varies a good deal as well. Hawaii had the lowest turnout among the fifty states in 2004, with only 49 percent; Minnesota had the highest, 77 percent.

Beyond geographic variation, certain types of people seem especially likely to vote. Table 10.3 lists various types of people who seem especially likely or especially unlikely to vote.

What is it that leads some people to vote more regularly than others? Partly it seems to be a matter of cultural traditions. The high electoral turnout in Minnesota, for instance, seems likely to be a result of the tradition of constructive citizenship that was strong among the Scandinavian immigrants who made up a large part of Minnesota's early population.

Partly it is a function of practical, almost mundane questions—whether polling day is on a working day (as in the United States), which is less convenient than a Sunday, or whether registration to vote is a cumbersome procedure or an easy one. (In

TABLE 10.3

Who Is Likely or Unlikely to Vote?

Groups Unusually High in Participation	Groups Unusually Low in Participation
Suburban residents	Young people
Well-educated people	Poor people
Well-off people	Women (except in Europe and North America)
Farmers (U.S.A.)	Ethnic minorities (U.S.A.)
Old people	

some countries, registration is automatically done by the local authorities and requires no specific action by the person being registered.)

Partly it is a function of the difficulty of making political decisions. This may help explain why well-educated people are more likely to vote than people with less education; those with less education presumably find politics more puzzling and confusing than those who are better educated. This problem surely helps to explain why voting turnout is low in referendums, which demand more from a voter than choosing a party or a candidate.

Finally, it is partly a function of the political circumstances under which the election is held. A close election stimulates greater turnout than one that promises to be a walkaway for one side. National elections, because of the great stakes of war and peace that are involved, get a higher turnout than they probably deserve as compared with local elections. As noted, elections conducted under a PR electoral system get higher participation than those under SMDP, because under PR no one need worry about "wasting" a vote on a candidate who has no chance to win. Blue-collar workers in Europe participate more faithfully than those in the United States partly because unions in Europe are more active than American unions in mobilizing their voters. In most European states—unlike the United States—there are explicitly working-class socialist parties that draw blue-collar workers into political activity.

The fact that some social groups are more likely to vote than others makes a real difference in what views are brought to bear on the election—and therefore on what views elected officials will pay attention to. In the United States, young, poor, ethnic citizens are less likely to vote than older, better-off, white citizens, and the impact on the views officials must consider is dramatic. In September 1998, the *New York Times* ran a poll in which it distinguished those citizens most likely to vote in the next election.[9] (Such citizens said they definitely expected to vote in the 1998 election, they were paying a lot of attention to the campaign, and they had voted in both 1994 and 1996.) How did registered voters as a whole compare with those who were really likely to vote?

---

[9]"Likeliest Voters Favor Republicans," *New York Times,* 25 September 1998, p. A18.

What Is the Best Level of Participation?

A major argument among political scientists in the 1960s and 1970s turned on this question: Is more participation always better, or is there some optimal level of participation that is lower than 100 percent? Among others suggesting that more was not always better, Gabriel Almond and Sidney Verba expressed the opinion, in *The Civic Culture* (Boston: Little, Brown, 1965), that the ideal citizen participated up to a point but then sat back and trusted government officials to take things from there. This guaranteed an attentive citizenry, but one that would also give its government trust and support. Seymour M. Lipset also fueled the distrust of excessive participation by his finding, in *Political Man* (Garden City, NY: Doubleday, 1960), that the high turnout in the German elections of 1932 and 1933 had had a great deal to do with Adolf Hitler's victories.

Of the several responses, that of E. E. Schattschneider—*The Semisovereign People* (New York: Holt, Rinehart and Winston, 1960)—suggested that nonparticipants were like a time bomb waiting to disrupt the system. They were not building patterns of support for the existing system by participating; therefore, they could cause dangerous results, if they suddenly flooded in as the German voters for Hitler did. Schattschneider concluded that we should try to get everyone to participate as much as possible. Carole Pateman, in *Participation and Democratic Theory* (Cambridge: Cambridge University Press, 1970), drew an argument straight from classical liberal theory. A main purpose of participation was to help people improve themselves by exercising their judgment and by informing themselves of what was going on. Whether or not instability results, more participation is in and of itself a good thing; the more there is, the better.

The argument seems to have been resolved for now in favor of the defenders of participation. Today, one does not often hear arguments against full and extensive participation. But this argument has been going on sporadically since the time of the ancient Greeks. We may anticipate that it will come up again.

Of registered voters as a whole:

- 44 percent favored the Democrats, 39 percent the Republicans.
- 66 percent approved of President Bill Clinton's performance in office.
- Only 29 percent thought that Clinton should be impeached.

Of registered voters who appeared most likely to actually vote:

- 41 percent favored the Democrats, 53 percent the Republicans.
- 48 percent approved of President Bill Clinton's performance in office.
- 50 percent thought Clinton should be impeached.

Since elected officials only need to worry about what *voters* want, and can ignore those who do not vote, it was the latter group that called the shots.

❧ EFFECTS OF CHOICE AND INFORMATION ON TURNOUT

Sometimes factors that determine political behavior work in unexpected ways. And, this can be especially notable when combinations of factors interact with each other.

I noted earlier (p. 242) that we think citizens should be more likely to vote in PR systems than in SMDP systems, because the multiple parties that typically result from PR offer a wider range of choices to pick from. This is, roughly, true. But it interacts in an odd and perverse way with how well informed voters are about politics. Once we see this, it is not so clear which electoral system produces "better" participation.

Figure 10.3 presents the results of a statistical analysis, conducted across 25 countries, of how frequently well-informed and less-informed citizens vote, in the presence of party systems that give them varying ranges of choice.

As you see in the figure, the analysis shows that as the number of parties increases, participation increases for well-informed voters (the dashed line), just as we would expect. But look at the less-informed voters! The solid line representing their participation decreases as the line moves across the graph to larger numbers of parties. Apparently, for the less-informed the greater difficulty of choosing among larger numbers of parties affects them more greatly than the fact that they now have more options available, and so they quit in discouragement.

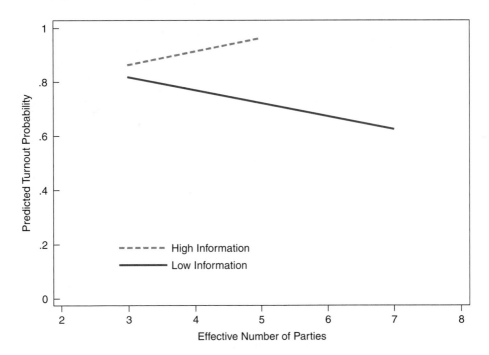

FIGURE 10.3   Turnout by number of parties, for well-informed and less-informed voters.

Adapted from Karen Long Jusko and W. Phillips Shively, "Applying a Two-Step Strategy to the Analysis of Cross-National Public Opinion Data" 13 *Political Analysis* (2005), pp. 327–344, Figure 3.

The perverse effect of this is that PR, the electoral system that is supposedly designed to get better participation, produces an electorate that is less and less representative of the full public. As the well-informed flock to vote and the less-informed quit in discouragement, the end result is an electorate more and more skewed to the well-informed. Now, you might think that is great: what's wrong with a country dominated by the well-informed? But, the well-informed tend to be those parts of society that have been able to benefit from education. The poor, ethnic minorities, older generations (depending on the country) are likely to cluster among the less-informed.

As you see, it is at least an open question whether the broader choice likely to be found associated with PR systems really improves participation.

✦ THE PARADOX OF VOTING

We might also flip the question of participation around, and instead of asking "Why doesn't everyone vote?" ask, "Why are all these people voting?" Looked at in one way, it appears irrational to take the trouble to vote. Seeing how unlikely it would be for a single vote to decide a U.S. presidential election, one might consider it hardly worthwhile to spend a half hour and 8 cents worth of gasoline to get to the polling place. (The odds must be less than one in a trillion that the other 80 million voters would split exactly evenly, so that one vote could decide the outcome.) As a character in Skinner's *Walden Two* remarks to his friend,

> "How is the people's will ascertained? In an election. But what a travesty! In a small committee meeting, or even a town hall, I can see some point in voting, especially on a yes-or-no question. But fifty million voters choosing a president—that's quite another thing."
>
> "I can't see that the number of voters changes the principle," said Castle.
>
> "The chance that one man's vote will decide the issue in a national election is less than the chance that he will be killed on his way to the polls. We pay no attention to chances of that magnitude in our daily affairs. We should call a man a fool who bought a sweepstakes ticket with similar odds against him."[10]

This is what we call the **paradox of voting**.[11] It is paradoxical because, if things are considered from this perspective, *no one who is sensible should vote*. If the result of the election is nearly certain to be the same whether you vote or not, why should you take the time and go to the expense? To put it in the concrete terms alluded to in the quotation from Skinner, over the years more people are hit by trucks and killed on the way to the polls than change the results of national elections by their single votes. On the average and over the long run, voting looks like a dangerous and unproductive act.

Paradoxes have solutions, and we can try two possible solutions for this one. First, the paradox obviously holds only for voters taken one at a time. If a large group of voters chose to sit out an election, it is quite possible that their absence could change the outcome, as we saw above in our example from the *New York Times* poll. In fact, most

---

[10]B. F. Skinner, *Walden Two* (New York: Macmillan, 1948), pp. 220–221.
[11]William H. Riker and Peter C. Ordeshook, *An Introduction to Positive Political Theory* (Englewood Cliffs, NJ: Prentice-Hall, 1973), pp. 45–68, esp. pp. 57–58.

politicians spend more time and effort in their campaigns in trying to make sure that the right people get to the polls than in trying to change the minds of people who are planning to vote for their opponents.[12] Politicians certainly recognize the importance of turnout rates in determining elections. Therefore, the paradox of participation is a paradox only for voters taken individually. This might resolve the problem for us—except that a voter's decision whether to vote is taken individually. That is, groups do not decide whether to vote, *voters* decide whether to vote. So the paradox remains.

A second way of addressing the paradox is to note that it looks at voting solely as an act to provide benefits to the individual voting. The paradox arises only if we think that voters vote solely because of their wish to exercise their own power in making the government's policies. While it is true that this is the democratic justification for hold-ing elections, we must realize that it casts voting as essentially a *selfish* act in which voters participate only to increase their own political power. However, we saw at the beginning of this chapter that in many countries, high electoral turnout occurs even though the voters have no choice of candidates. Clearly, voters in those countries are voting for some reason other than to exercise their individual political power, because *their* votes represent no individual political power whatever. They are voting out of a desire to do their duty, out of a love of country, and often because of a good deal of social pressure from those around them. In other words, voting for them may be more of a communal act than an individual one.

There is no reason to think that these communal aspects of voting are absent in a democracy. This would certainly help to explain what is otherwise unexplainable—that millions of people vote in elections even though it can easily be demonstrated that vot-ing is of no benefit to them as individuals. This seems an attractive resolution to the paradox partly because it elevates our discussion of voting above selfish calculations of individual costs and benefits. Love of community and country is a noble sentiment, and if electoral participation is based partly on it, all the better for elections.

✢ THE BASES OF INDIVIDUALS' ELECTORAL CHOICES

For whatever reason, great numbers of people vote in elections. How do they choose which party or candidate to vote for? Any number of things may serve as the basis for voting choice in one country or another.

We can distinguish usefully between short-term factors and long-term factors in voting choice. Short-term factors are things about a particular election that may lead a person to vote one way or another. The state of the economy usually operates in this way, for instance. If times are bad, a number of people will vote against whoever is in office as a way of showing their unhappiness, and in good times they will reward the party in office. Michael S. Lewis-Beck and Tom W. Rice have estimated that for a drop of 2 percent in national income the president's party would lose four seats in the U.S.

---

[12]However, see W. Phillips Shively, "From Differential Abstention to Conversion: A Change in Electoral Change, 1864–1988," *American Journal of Political Science* 36 (May 1992), pp. 309–30.

House of Representatives in a mid-year election or twenty seats in a presidential election year.[13] François Gélineau and Éric Bélanger, reviewing Canadian elections from 1953 to 2000, estimated that an increase in the unemployment rate of 1 percent led to a drop of 1.3 percent in the vote for candidates of the governing party, while an increase of 1 percent in the rate of inflation led to a drop of 0.4 percent in the vote. Candidates in provincial elections were also punished and rewarded for the performance of the national economy when their party was in power nationally, even though they themselves had nothing to do with national economic policy.[14]

Other short-term factors may include the particular appeal (or lack of same) of a candidate. This appears to be particularly the case in the United States and Canada, where the personalities of possible presidents and prime ministers sway a large number of voters. In most European countries, on the other hand, the voters have often seemed to weigh primarily the various political parties as whole organizations, with less emphasis on the personal characteristics of a party's leading candidate. In 1979, for instance, polls in Britain showed that Margaret Thatcher, the Conservative candidate for prime minister, was less admired and respected personally than James Callaghan, the candidate of the Labour Party. However, the British electorate did not hesitate to defeat Labour soundly and put the Conservatives—and Thatcher—in power. As will be seen in Chapter 11, political parties in the United States and Canada are weak organizations compared with those in most countries; as a result, individual candidates in American or Canadian elections carry more personal weight. In countries with strong parties, the focus of the electorate is more on the parties, and individual candidates do not count for as much.[15]

A particular candidacy, the state of the economy, an international crisis— such short-term factors can be potent in deciding an election. However, most elections most of the time are determined largely by things that do not change much or that change only gradually.

One such long-term factor is the identification of some people with a particular political party. We all know some older person who says he or she has been a Democrat (or a Republican or a Conservative or a Liberal or a Labour voter or whatever) "since I was a young child." To such a voter, a particular candidacy or the state of the economy makes less difference than to other voters. Most of the time this person is going to vote by party no matter what is going on. Political scientists call this sort of continuing tie **party identification.**[16] It adds a good deal of stability and predictability over time to election results. We will discuss party identification in more detail in Chapter 11.

---

[13]Michael S. Lewis-Beck and Tom W. Rice, *Forecasting Elections* (Washington, DC, Congressional Quarterly Press, 1992).
[14]François Gélineau and Éric Bélanger, "Electoral Accountability in a Federal System," paper presented at the annual meeting of the Canadian Political Science Association, Winnipeg, June 3–5, 2004.
[15]Over recent decades this difference has been diminishing, however, as electorates everywhere shift more to an emphasis on candidates. For instance, in the 2002 election in Germany, an initial 10 percent advantage in the polls for the Christian Democratic Party dwindled over the course of the campaign to a virtual tie in the election, due almost solely to the bland personality of its candidate, Angela Merkel. Despite these shifts, however, the United States and Canada still stand out in this regard.
[16]Angus Campbell, Philip Converse, Warren E. Miller, and Donald Stokes, *The American Voter* (New York: Wiley, 1960), chaps. 6 and 7.

"HOW BINDING ARE CAMPAIGN PROMISES MADE ONLY IN PRIMARIES?"

Reprinted from *Minneapolis Star Tribune,* 11/7/06.

Another long-term factor that adds stability over time is the commitment of various social groups to one or another party. As we see in Table 10.4, the basic commitment of the working class and the less religious to the Social Democratic Party of West Germany was fairly stable from 1953 to 1972; the flip side of this is that the middle class and the religious were rather consistent in *not* supporting the Social Democratic Party.

These two bases of support also have held fairly stably into recent elections, even with the large change in the German electorate after merging former East Germany into the country. In the 1998 election class continued to be a strong factor in SPD support, with 61 percent of workers voting for the party, and 48 percent of "new middle class" (salaried white collar workers and government workers), but only 24 percent of "old middle class" (farmers, shopkeepers, professionals, etc.). Religion also continued to matter: 52 percent of those who never attended church voted for the party, as did 48 percent of those who occasionally attended church, but only 26 percent of those who attended church weekly.[17]

---

[17]Russell J. Dalton, *Citizen Politics* (New York: Chatham House Publishers, 2002), pp. 149 and 159.

TABLE 10.4

**Social Bases of Support for the Social Democratic Party
of West Germany, 1953–1972**

	1953	1957	1965	1969	1972
Percent voting socialist of:					
Working class	58	60	57	58	70
Middle class	28	23	31	46	53
Those who never attend church	63	64	64	77	74
Those who occasionally attend church	48	39	48	45	61
Those who frequently attend church	17	19	17	32	28

SOURCE: Calculated from *Germany Transformed: Political Culture and the New Politics,* by Kendall Baker, Russell Dalton, and Kai Hildebrandt, Cambridge: Harvard University Press, Copyright © 1981, by the President and Fellows of Harvard College.

In other countries and at other times, the following social differences have functioned importantly as bases for voting distinctions:

- Region (The "solid Democratic South" of the United States from the 1870s to the 1960s is an example, or the regional basis of all Canadian parties.)
- Language (The Swedish People's Party of Finland is an example.)
- Farming (Many countries have had Agrarian parties; Norway and Sweden are two examples.)
- Country of origin (Irish and Italian voters in the United States tend to be Democrats; German and Anglo-Saxon voters tend to be Republicans.)
- Race (Blacks tend strongly to vote Democratic in the United States; the politics of Guyana has been almost totally determined by conflicts between blacks and East Indians.)
- Gender (Women in many countries favor conservative parties, although this may be an indirect effect of religion rather than a direct effect of differences between men and women; by contrast, a "gender gap" has opened in the United States and several European countries, with *men* voting more conservatively than women.)
- Age (In 1999, for instance, only 28 percent of Germans aged fifteen to twenty-five expressed a preference for the Christian-Democratic Party, while 51 percent of those over fifty did so.)[18]

---

[18]World Values Survey (www.worldvaluessurvey.org).

✳ EXAMPLE

Proportional Representation Elections in Israel

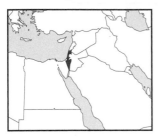

The Knesset (Israel's parliament, with 120 seats) is elected every four years by an unusually simple and direct form of proportional representation. Parties submit lists of candidates (in ranked order) to the electoral commission. Any party that receives 2.0 percent or more of the vote nationally gets at least one seat in the Knesset, and each party's number of seats is proportional to how large a proportion of the vote it received. Compared with most countries, this is a simple and straightforward PR system. The accounting is done across the state as a whole, rather than separately for different regions of the state. The threshold of 2.0 percent is low enough to be quite generous to small parties; in Germany, for instance, a party receives no representation unless it has received at least 5 percent of the vote.

To put a list on the ballot, the party must submit a petition containing a few thousand signatures and pay a fairly small deposit (usually a couple of thousand dollars). Usually twenty or more lists are on the ballot.

Voters then cast their vote for a list. Candidates on the list enter the Knesset according to their rank in the list; for instance, the Shas Party qualified for twelve seats in the Knesset in 2006, so the first twelve names on the list became Knesset members. If a seat is vacated before the next election, the next person on the list steps in.

Where candidates rank on their party's list is obviously important. Parties put their key leaders at the top of their lists, to make sure that they are elected, but beyond that, groups and factions compete to get their people placed high. Who does the placing varies by party. Of the two traditionally largest parties, Labour uses a primary election to determine the internal placement of its candidates on its list; in the Likud Party, the "center" (a gathering of one thousand to three thousand leaders of the party, broadly representative of its constituent parts) does the ordering.

Larger parties do get a slight advantage in the distribution of seats under Israel's system, because of the formulae for the distribution of "surplus" votes. "Surplus" votes occur when a party gets less than 2.0 percent of the vote so that its votes do not count toward any party's share, or when rounding off in assigning Knesset seats to parties leaves some votes unused. And as in almost all other proportional representation systems in the world, in Israel the formulae used to allocate the surplus votes among the various parties favor the larger parties slightly. In 2006, these leftover votes gave Kadima (with 22.0 percent of the vote) 29 of the 120 seats in the Knesset, or 24.2 percent of the seats; Labour, with 15.1 percent of the vote, got 15.8 percent of the seats. This is only a minor advantage, however. The bottom line is that the Israeli system of PR is unusually straightforward and faithful to proportionality.

As a result, a lot of parties usually get into the Knesset. In 2006, the results were:

	Votes (%)	Seats
Kadima (centrist party, new in 2006)	22.0	29
Labour	15.1	19
Shas (ultra-orthodox)	9.5	12

Likud (nationalist)	9.0	12
Israel Beytenu	9.0	11
National Union/National Religious	7.1	9
Gil	5.9	7
United Torah Judaism	4.7	6
Meretz (left-oriented)	3.8	5
National Arab Party/National Democratic	3.0	4
Hadash	2.7	3
United Arab List	2.3	3
Green Party	1.5	0
Ale Yarok	1.3	0
Other parties	3.0	0

Such a diverse party system—twelve different parties in the Knesset!—could produce unstable government, as it might prove difficult to combine enough different parties to make up a working majority in the parliament (especially when, as in Israel, they are deeply divided on policies). This has not proved the case in Israel, possibly because the country's constant exposure to external danger has forced the parties to cooperate in spite of their inclinations. However, one major result of the dispersion of the parties is evident. It is almost impossible to form a governing majority without including at least one of the religious parties; this has given them a good deal of leverage, by which they have commanded patronage and policy concessions way out of proportion to their electoral strength.

 # EXAMPLE

Elections in Nigeria

Nigeria has had elected democratic government for only sixteen of its more than forty years of independence—from 1960 to 1966, from 1979 to 1983, and again starting in 1999. Obviously, Nigeria's democracy is fragile; elections there illustrate well the difficulties of conducting an election in a large, new state whose diverse ethnic elements are still only weakly united.

Even aside from the military's propensity to throw out the results, electoral politics is difficult for any country like Nigeria. First, it tends to bring out sectarian conflicts between ethnic groups and regions of different religions, which always threaten to tear the state apart. Nigeria fought a bloody regional civil war from 1966 to 1969, and thousands of people have died in Christian-Moslem riots. Violence between ethnic groups is also common.

Second, Nigeria is a large, spread-out country. The difficult logistics of an election, together with the passions of hostility that an election awakens, leave the process open to violence and fraud. When democracy replaced the military regime in 1999, for instance, a system for elections had to be established. Because of the huge logistical challenge, the elections were spread out over several weeks. Local elections were held in December 1998, state elections in January, and elections for Parliament and president held two weeks apart in February. Hundreds of millions of dollars were spent on the campaigns. One particular problem arose when about 20 million of the 60 million registration cards were bought up by politicians. To prevent the use of these cards in fraudulent multiple voting, the polling stations required all voters in the district to register on the day of the election. Voters then were required to wait in the registration station until everyone had registered, at which point all voted together, so that no one could come back and vote more than once. Devices such as this were apparently successful; international observers declared the elections to be generally free and fair.

The parliamentary election had only about a 20 percent turnout, since the eviscerated Parliament of the period of military rule had inspired no respect. But the presidential election generated great excitement and a respectable turnout. The two final candidates, Olusegun Obasanjo and Olu Falae, were both members of the Yoruba ethnic group from the southwestern part of the country. This reflected the fact that issues other than ethnicity have begun to broaden politics in Nigeria; the Yoruba are probably the only ethnic group today whose members vote unitedly on a "one-issue" basis for their group. Obasanjo was in the end distrusted by his own group, partly because he had generated a good deal of support in the rest of the country. He won handily, with majorities in twenty-seven of the country's thirty-six states; but he lost heavily in the six home states of his Yoruba group. In the state of Lagos, the financial center of Nigeria, he got only 12 percent of the vote.

Parliamentary and presidential elections in 2003 showed that Nigeria has matured as a democracy, though it is certainly still fragile. These elections marked the first time in the country's history that it moved peacefully from one democratically elected civilian government to another. In the parliamentary election, turnout was about 30 percent, much better than the previous election's 20 percent. Violence was more isolated than in previous elections, and even though in some places voting was clearly not secret—and in some places had to be canceled entirely because of violence—election monitors from South Africa's Institute for Democracy judged the election overall a success. In the presidential election, which was held the next week with 70 percent turnout, President Obasanjo was reelected in a closely fought race.

As of this writing Nigeria was in the midst of the campaign for its 2007 election. Because President Obasanjo was constitutionally barred from running for a third term, this would be a key event in Nigeria's democracy—the first time that one civilian president would replace another through elections. There was some worry, however, that the election might not come off successfully. Atiku Abubakar, the vice president, had been barred from running because the National Electoral Commission had included him on a list of officials too corrupt to be allowed to run, but he charged that the decision was rigged politically, and challenged it in court. The election was also threatened by armed insurrection in the oil-producing Niger delta region. Finally, Umaru Yaradua, the candidate nominated by Obasanjo's party, was a little-known figure in poor health. He was the governor of a small northwestern state and a Moslem, thus balancing Obasanjo's Christianity; but many people suspected that he was chosen so that Obasanjo could continue to dominate politics even while out of office. All friends of Nigerian democracy were keeping their fingers crossed.

KEY TERMS

referendum

electoral system

single-member-district
  electoral system

proportional
  representation electoral
  system

paradox of voting

party identification

FURTHER READING

Abramson, Paul R., Aldrich, John H., and Rohde, David W. *Change and Continuity in the 2004 and 2006 Elections.* Washington, DC: CQ Press, 2007.

Bowler, Shaun, Donovan, Todd, and Tolbert, Caroline J., eds. *Citizens as Legislators: Direct Democracy in the United States.* Columbus: Ohio State University Press, 1998.

Burns, Nancy, Schlozman, Kay Lehman, and Verba, Sidney. *The Private Roots of Public Action: Gender, Equality, and Political Participation.* Cambridge: Harvard University Press, 2001.

Cox, Gary W. *Making Votes Count: Strategic Coordination in the World's Electoral Systems.* New York: Cambridge University Press, 1997.

_____, and Katz, Jonathan N. *Elbridge Gerry's Salamander: The Electoral Consequences of the Reapportionment Revolution.* New York: Cambridge University Press, 2002.

Dalton, Russell J. *Citizen Politics in Western Democracies,* 4th ed. Washington, DC: CQ Press, 2006.

Diamond, Larry, and Plattner, Marc, eds. *Electoral Systems and Democracy.* Baltimore: Johns Hopkins University Press, 2006.

Duverger, Maurice. *Political Parties.* New York: Wiley, 1954.

Edwards, George C., III. *Why the Electoral College Is Bad for America.* New Haven: Yale University Press, 2004.

Flanigan, William H., and Zingale, Nancy H. *Political Behavior of the American Electorate.* 11th ed. Washington, DC: Congressional Quarterly Press, 2005.

Geer, John G. *In Defense of Negativity: Attack Ads in Presidential Campaigns.* Chicago: University of Chicago Press, 2006.

Jamieson, Kathleen Hall, and Waldman, Paul. *The Press Effect: Politicians, Journalists, and the Stories That Shape the Political World.* New York: Oxford University Press, 2003.

Johnston, Richard, Hagen, Michael G., and Jamieson, Kathleen Hall. *The 2000 Presidential Election and the Foundations of Party Politics.* New York: Cambridge University Press, 2004.

Lindberg, Staffan I. *Democracy and Elections in Africa.* Baltimore: Johns Hopkins University Press, 2006.

Patterson, Thomas E. *Out of Order: How the Decline of Political Parties and the Growing Power of the News Media Undermine the American Way of Electing Presidents.* New York: Knopf, 1994.

_____. *The Vanishing Voter.* New York: Alfred A. Knopf, 2003.

Popkin, Samuel L. *The Reasoning Voter.* Chicago: University of Chicago Press, 1991.

Romer, Daniel, Kenski, Kate, Waldman, Paul, Adasiewicz, Christopher, Jamieson, Kathleen Hall. *Capturing Campaign Dynamics: The National Annenberg Election Survey.* New York: Oxford University Press, 2003.

Rosenstone, Steven J., and Hansen, John Mark. *Mobilization, Participation and Democracy in America.* New York: Macmillan, 1993.

Shugart, Matthew Soberg, and Wattenberg, Martin P. *Mixed-Member Electoral Systems: The Best of Both Worlds?* New York: Oxford University Press, 2001.

Stokes, Susan C. *Mandates and Democracy: Neoliberalism by Surprise in Latin America.* New York: Cambridge University Press, 2001.

Thompson, Dennis F. *Just Elections: Creating a Fair Electoral Process in the United States.* Chicago: University of Chicago Press, 2002.

Wattenberg, Martin P. *Where Have All the Voters Gone?* Cambridge: Harvard University Press, 2002.

WEB SITES OF INTEREST

Elections Around the World, a good source for the background and results of recent elections:

http://www.electionworld.org

Elections Canada Web site:

http:www.nodice.ca/elections/canada

International Institute for Democracy and Electoral Assistance; worldwide data on turnout in elections:

http://www.idea.int/

Federal Election Commission. A source on campaign contributions and expenditures in U.S. elections:

http://www.fec.gov

Project Vote Smart. Information on voting records of members of U.S. Congress:

http://www.vote-smart.org

CHAPTER 11

PARTIES: A LINKING AND LEADING MECHANISM IN POLITICS

In preceding chapters, I have talked a good deal about political parties. The **political party** crops up in all aspects of politics. It is an invention that first developed in the nineteenth century in response to the appearance of elections involving large numbers of voters. Politicians developed the political party at that time as a device to help themselves and like-minded friends get elected, but the party proved to have many other uses as well and went on to become a ubiquitous feature of modern politics.

I shall explore this theme in later sections, but first, questions of definition.

✦ THE POLITICAL PARTY

A political party is a group of officials or would-be officials who are linked with a sizable group of citizens into an organization; a chief object of this organization is to ensure that its officials attain power or are maintained in power.

The latter part of this definition distinguishes the political party from the "interest group," which will be discussed in Chapter 12. In most countries, there are many interest groups—such as the American Medical Association, the American Dairy Farmers' Organization, the Natural Gas Supply Association, Friends of the Earth, and so on—groups of people with a common interest who band together to try by way of lobbying, campaign contributions, and other tactics to make sure that the government's policies will be in tune with their wishes. Interest groups are distinguished from political parties in that they try to influence which policies are chosen without actually taking power or setting policies; parties, on the other hand, have as their central purpose the acquisition of power and the direction of policy.

There is nothing about the definition that says political parties are restricted to democracies and to electoral activity. Revolutionary parties may be organized not to win elections but to seize control of the government by force. And parties like the Nazi

Party of Germany, the Communist Party in the Soviet Union, or the Ba'ath Party in Syria today (and in Iraq until Saddam Hussein's overthrow in 2003) may oversee the machinery of a nondemocratic state.

Finally, a party joins people together in a formally organized structure. U.S. political parties surely fall at an extreme in the looseness of their organization, but in most countries, the parties are clearly delineated, with formal membership that sets those who are in the party apart from the rest. For instance, the Conservative Party of Britain has about 300,000 dues-paying members. The Communist Party of China has about 58 million members, who must pass a probationary and training period, generally taking more than a year and a half, before they are accepted for full membership.

The party's nature as a structure, tying together a large group of officials and citizens, provides an avenue by which one part may control or communicate with another. It is this that has made it such a versatile tool of modern politics. This will be explored in more detail.

✦ ORIGINS OF THE MODERN PARTY

Although the party has turned out to be useful for a variety of tasks that require control or communication, it was first invented for more limited and self-serving purposes. Long before the coming of electoral democracy, the state had had a varied structure of public officials—mayors, members of parliament, ministers for defense, and so on. Before democracy arrived, people attained these offices in a variety of ways: by being born into them, by buying the office (much as we might today purchase a fried-chicken franchise), by bribery, by appointment.

Once democracy was introduced, however, many of these positions were filled by election. This was different from the old ways of choosing officials in one important respect: In the old ways, the person who wished to have the office dealt with a single king or perhaps with a few people who could be bribed; under democracy, the would-be official had to seek the votes of a thousand or more people—too many to bribe.

It did not take long for politicians in the new democracies to see that some sort of club or organization that bound them together with large numbers of voters would help them to mobilize voters, in order to attain and hold office. Furthermore, large national clubs binding together a whole set of officials with voters throughout the country could function more effectively than a local club built around a single official. With a nationwide organization, voters were not lost to the club as they moved from one place to another; a popular official could go from place to place, helping to convince the voters to choose other candidates of the organization; and there would be enough money to hire professional staff who could help with the job of organizing thousands of voters. Thus, the political party was born.

The first modern electoral democracy was the United States of America, and it was here that the first parties developed. By the 1820s, there were well-organized parties, and the Democratic Party, which can trace its roots back to that time, is the oldest political party in the world.

In Britain, 1867 was the first year in which there was a reasonably widespread extension of the vote. As of that year, 10 percent of the population was entitled to vote, and the establishment of organized political parties followed over the next couple of decades. Indeed, the possibility that an expanded suffrage would lead to the development of political parties was one of the arguments raised by some members of Parliament against expanding the suffrage in 1867:

> . . . with a widely enlarged suffrage the candidate would find himself less and less able to come face to face with his constituency, and would be compelled in consequence . . . to rely more and more on the aid of the election agent, and, as in America, of that of committees and canvassers whose mouthpiece and delegate he would have to make himself.[1]

Similarly, all over Europe, whenever a reasonably large and varied electorate was established with the coming of democracy, the political party appeared.

Like elections themselves, political parties have been widely copied and are found in many countries that are not electoral democracies. Egypt, for instance, is governed by the National Democratic Party, China by the Communist Party, Zimbabwe by the Zimbabwe African National Union–Patriotic Front, and Syria by the Ba'ath Party, which also governed Iraq until the fall of Saddam Hussein. Many more examples could be noted, for many regimes that do not require parties to win elections have found that the modern political party—with the links it creates between masses of people and a set of political leaders—is useful to them. One of the wonders of modern politics is that this invention, originally devised in order that some officeholders could keep their jobs, has proved

A powerful image of mobilization: from the stage in the foreground, George A. Papandreou addresses a rally of Greece's Pasok party.

© Louisa Gouliamaki/AFP/Getty Images

---

[1]M. Ostrogorski, *Democracy and the Organization of Political Parties*, vol. 1 (Garden City, N.Y.: Doubleday, 1964), p. 78.

adaptable to all sorts of other purposes. The political party has become a "miracle glue" of sorts for politics. Whenever one group of people is to be controlled by another group or even just kept in contact with them, the party has turned out to be a useful tool.

Let us look at some of the ways in which the political party has been used to do these things. Parties provide the following: a basis for the mobilization of masses of citizens; a means of recruiting and socializing political leaders; structured political identity at the mass and elite levels; and a method of control within a government structure. We shall look at each of these in turn.

✦ POLITICAL PARTIES AND THE MOBILIZATION OF THE MASSES

I argued in Chapter 10 that one of the main effects of holding elections was to involve the masses of ordinary citizens in acting out their support for the state and, by so doing, strengthen that support. For this to happen, millions of voters must be stimulated to go out and take the trouble to vote. Governments cannot easily get people out to the polls, so how to reap this particular advantage of elections poses a bit of a problem. The problem is particularly great where only one slate of candidates is allowed, so that there is no suspense whatever about the outcome of the election. How can the voters be mobilized to get out and vote under these circumstances? A political party is a handy instrument with which to stir up the electorate and get them to the polls. It is controlled by its leaders, who are at the same time the rulers of the state; and it may have a membership that extends down into every village, so it is strategically placed to turn out large numbers of people.

In the United States, political parties make great efforts to get out the vote. They do this not to bolster support for the regime, although that is a side effect, but to help themselves win elections. In Singapore the People's Action Party (which holds 82 of the 84 seats in Parliament) has no such motive for stirring up the electorate, but its leaders are anxious to generate a good show of support, and so the party does much the same things as American parties do at election time.

Aside from elections, political parties may serve to **mobilize** the people for special purposes or to meet crises. When President Anwar Sadat of Egypt was assassinated in 1981 and was succeeded by Vice President Hosni Mubarak, over a million people joined a demonstration in Cairo to show their support for Mubarak. The demonstration was partly organized by the government apparatus itself but also, in large part, by the ruling National Democratic Party. When the regime of Charles de Gaulle was threatened in France by a general strike in 1969, the turning point at which his opponents were defeated came when his Union of Democrats for the Republic Party organized a massive demonstration in Paris for which over 100,000 supporters were bused in from the countryside. When Syria came under intense international pressure in 2005 to withdraw its troops from the neighboring state of Lebanon, its allies in the Lebanese Hizbullah Party mobilized a demonstration of 500,000 supporters (Lebanon has only 3.7 million people!) to support Syria's role there.

A party may also mobilize masses of people *against* a regime. Many of today's political parties in Third World states—the Congress Party in India, for example, or the National Front for Liberation in Algeria—were initially organized to carry out a campaign to overthrow a colonial ruler such as Britain or France. When German armies occupied much of Europe during World War II, it was the churches and the political parties that provided the basis for a resistance movement because these were the only structures binding together large and widespread groups of people in ways that made coordinated resistance possible. Today, the most important focus of opposition to many regimes lies with political parties.

✦ POLITICAL PARTIES AND THE RECRUITMENT AND SOCIALIZATION OF LEADERS

Another use to which parties have lent themselves, beyond what they were originally designed for, is the recruitment and socialization of leaders. Somebody has to do this in any society, and where there are political parties, they are an obvious choice for the task. What other organization could better seek out promising young people, give them experience at relatively small jobs, and gradually move those who do well to more important jobs, while imbuing them with the values that the political leadership wishes to encourage?

In Britain, for instance, an ambitious young woman who was interested in entering politics might work for a while at lesser tasks for one of the major parties, such as the Conservative Party. Before too long, if she were interested in standing for Parliament, she might be nominated from a district. To get the nomination, she would have to convince the local selection committee of the Conservative Party in that district that she was their best nominee. As a beginner, she would probably be selected in a hopeless district, where no Conservative had much of a chance; but once she had proved that she could campaign well in one or two lost causes, she might get the nomination from a decent district, win, and enter the House. In the House, she would continue to be molded and guided by the party. If she were the sort that party leaders like—witty in debate, hard working, and above all a faithful party voter—she might advance into positions of real responsibility, such as party spokesperson on defense or on health. Eventually, she might aim so high as to be prime minister. To be selected for this position, she would have to win an internal election at which all the Conservative members of the House of Commons vote to narrow the choice of nominees to two of their members; the 300,000 enrolled members of the party then vote by mail ballot to choose which of the two will be party leader. Throughout this career, her advancement would have been primarily due to her support from her party organization, and she would have risen to the top only because she was the sort of person her party wanted and because, in each position she held, she would have learned from the rest of the party how to behave in the ways they preferred. This is essentially the only way to make a political career in Great Britain.

In the United States, too, parties are important as devices for the recruitment and socialization of leaders. However, parties in the United States are weaker organizationally than those in Britain, and so they do not hold the same monopoly in this regard that British parties do. Most political leaders have worked their way into place through the apparatus of either the Democratic or Republican Party, starting at fairly lowly positions. However, primary elections at which a candidate can appeal directly to the voters for nomination, rather than relying on party leaders, can also allow a popular celebrity such as the actor Arnold Schwarzenegger to enter directly into politics at a high level. (The existence of primary elections, which take the selection of candidates out of the hands of party leaders, is often considered the single most important cause of American parties' organizational weakness.) Furthermore, people who have distinguished themselves at some other career are often appointed to a president's cabinet directly without any prior political career and thus without any screening by a party. When John Kennedy appointed his brother Robert as attorney general, when George W. Bush appointed Stanford professor Condoleeza Rice to be national security adviser, or when Bill Clinton appointed career civil servant Madeleine Albright to be secretary of state, no party experience was involved.

In a one-party state such as Yugoslavia was before 1990, the single party may serve as the major avenue to any sort of political or economic advancement. The Yugoslav Communist Party actually restricted its membership to keep out opportunists who would join to advance themselves. By strict entrance requirements and by purges, the party was limited to a membership comprising about 5 percent of Yugoslavia's population. Party leaders had good cause to be concerned about the problem of opportunism. There was ample reason for ambitious young people to seek membership no matter what their political beliefs because all factory directors, all important public officials, and most leaders of institutions such as universities were required to be Communists.

✦ POLITICAL PARTIES AS A SOURCE OF POLITICAL IDENTITY

Another unforeseen effect of political parties was the extent to which parties, once one was associated with them, became an important part of one's identity. Party is probably not the first thing a person would mention when asked "What are you?" A more likely reply would be "I am a Presbyterian," "I am a woman," "I am a student," "I am a Canadian," and so on. Along the way, if you keep prompting, you may well be given the name of the political party with which that person feels associated. As we saw in Chapter 10, this source of identity is called **party identification.**[2] For those who become quite active, the political party may become a vital and central personal concern. What would Bill Clinton have been without the Democratic Party? What would Angela Merkel of Germany have been without the Christian Democratic Party, or Hu Jintao of China without the Communist Party?

One important thing about party as a source of identity is that it can provide continuity in a political world that is otherwise quite fluid. Candidates come and go, wars start and end, political issues arise and fade and are replaced by others, but parties may go on and on. The two major parties of the United States are over a century old; the Communist

---

[2]The concept of "party identification" was first developed fully in Angus Campbell et al., *The American Voter* (New York: Wiley, 1960), chaps. 6 and 7. For a review, see W. Phillips Shively, "The Nature of Party Identification: A Review of Recent Developments," in John C. Pierce and John L. Sullivan, eds., *The Electorate Reconsidered* (Beverly Hills, CA: Sage, 1980).

"WHAT I DON'T UNDERSTAND IS HOW, IN A FEW YEARS, WE'LL BECOME CONSERVATIVE REPUBLICANS."

Reprinted by permission of ScienceCartoonsPlus.com.

Party of the Soviet Union was over seventy years old at the time of its collapse; Britain's Conservative Party is over a century old, and its Labour Party is almost ninety years old.

By furnishing individuals and politically active people with a lasting political identity, the party can give them a source of political community throughout their lives. Parties may provide an even longer-range continuity in politics than that of a single lifetime if party connections are passed on from parents to children or if local party organizations continue their activity across generations. An ironic instance of the way in which parties can create this sort of continuity is provided by the state of Indiana.[3] Since the Civil War, there has been a political split between the southern part of the state and the northern part. There was a good deal of sympathy for the Confederacy in the 1860s in southern Indiana; this translated into support for the Democratic Party, which was more sympathetic to the Confederacy at that time. In northern Indiana, abolitionist and Union sentiment ran strong, and this led northern voters to support the Republican Party. One hundred forty years later, this pattern still holds! As may be seen in Figure 11.1, most of the counties in which Democratic presidential candidate Al Gore

[3]This case was first presented by V. O. Key, Jr., and Frank Munger in Eugene Burdick and Arthur J. Brodbeck, eds., *American Voting Behavior* (Glencoe, IL: Free Press, 1959), chap. 15. Their analysis has been updated here.

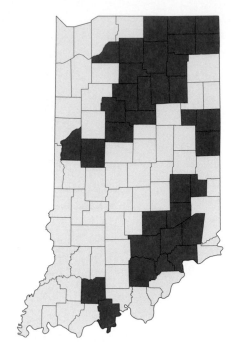

FIGURE 11.1   Indiana counties that voted 40 percent or more Democratic, 2000.

FIGURE 11.2   Indiana counties with over 30 percent of the labor force employed in manufacturing, 2000.

received 40 percent or more of the vote in 2000 fell in the southern part of the state. In northern Indiana, Gore got as much as 40 percent of the vote in only a handful of counties, which is to say that Republican George W. Bush got over 60 percent of the vote almost everywhere in northern Indiana.

This distribution of support bears little relation to what we think of as the basis for Democratic and Republican voting. Figure 11.2 shows the counties in Indiana in which over 30 percent of the labor force consists of workers in manufacturing industries. Such workers are commonly thought to be the mainstay of the Democratic Party, yet a comparison of the two maps show that whether a county is heavily industrial has little to do with whether it is strongly Democratic. Indeed, there is a negative relationship between the two: While 43 percent of the counties that are "nonindustrial" in Figure 11.2 are unusually Democratic in Figure 11.1, only 21 percent of the "industrial" counties are unusually Democratic.

The basic north-south split in the state has been a political fact of life continually since the 1860s. The chief determinant of the geographic distribution of party support is not the economy and not the distribution of industry but events that occurred and were pretty well disposed of 140 years ago. The ability of parties—through their organizational structure and through their grip on people's consciousness—to establish stable lines of conflict is impressive. In this case, the results border on the ludicrous, because it must make little sense that Indiana elections in 2000 were determined by who took what position on slavery and secession in 1860.

✦ POLITICAL PARTIES AS A CHANNEL OF CONTROL

A final unforeseen effect of political parties was to provide some political leaders with a new channel through which to exert control over other leaders. This has been an important factor in modern politics.

Remember that a party is an organization that binds a sizable group of political leaders together with a sizable number of ordinary citizens. It is the only sort of organization that regularly does this. It spreads so widely within the set of political leaders and out into the mass of people that it offers an excellent channel for power through which political leaders can control the actions either of other political leaders or of the citizens.

As a channel for controlling other political leaders, the party is important in all sorts of states. The leaders of a party have many punishments and rewards at their disposal—nomination for various offices, support in passing favored legislation, and so on. Perhaps the greatest carrot or stick most of the time is the chance to advance to more powerful positions within the party. Leaders use these inducements deliberately to force obedience on lesser party figures in legislative votes, campaign activity, and so on. Sam Rayburn, who was for many years the leader of the Democratic Party in the U.S. House of Representatives, used to caution new members, "To get ahead, get along." That is, to advance within the House hierarchy, obey orders. In the British House of Commons, the party organizations expect such pure obedience in voting that the life of ordinary members is in some ways rather dull, because they are following orders in how they vote.

As we shall see in Chapter 14, this channel of control is crucial in making the parliamentary governments of Western Europe and other parts of the world work. However, party functions as a channel for power in all sorts of other systems as well. In one-party states, the party may provide a means by which the apparatus of the state, especially in touchy areas such as the armed forces, is kept under the control of the party leaders. As much as possible, only party members were allowed to serve as high-ranking officers in the armies of the communist countries, for instance, and their advancement was strongly affected by their standing in the party.

Parties may also be used as a channel for power by which the leaders of the state control the mass of citizens. This is more common in authoritarian states than in democracies, where direct control of citizens is supposed to be the exception rather than the rule. For example, one particular problem for authoritarian systems is the control of intellectual activity, which might pose a threat to the leaders of the state if it proceeded freely. By placing party members in leadership positions in writers' organizations, universities, professional associations, and the media, the leaders of the state can help to ensure their control over what the citizenry thinks and says. This has particularly been the practice in communist systems, although military dictatorships, the fascist regimes of the 1930s, and other authoritarian regimes have attempted it as well.

✦ PARTY ORGANIZATION

Political parties in the United States are unusual in their organizational structure because they are loose and informal. Any other organization in the country—a savings bank, a birders' club, a church—has some sort of formal membership, for which one applies and in return receives a membership card of some sort. Political parties in the United States do not require this of their "members"; in fact, it is often difficult for people to be sure whether or not they are members of a party. Political scientists have some difficulty specifying just what group of people they are describing when they speak of the "Republican Party." Do they mean only the elected Republican officials in Congress and elsewhere? Do they mean the people who run the party's offices? Do they mean just the people who work for Republicans in election campaigns? Do they mean those who are "registered" as Republicans (even if they regularly vote Democratic)? Do they mean those who sympathize with the Republicans? There is no formal organization defining those who "belong" and those who do not, so anyone is free to define the set as desired.[4]

In other states, however, parties are set up in a more normal way as formal organizations; if one wishes to be a member of the party, one applies for membership, pays some sort of dues, and is formally enrolled with a membership card. As explicit, well-defined organizations, these parties have *organizational structure*, which may greatly affect their political role.

The Conservative Party of Great Britain offers a fairly typical example of organizational structure. As we see in Figure 11.3, the party consists of several parts. The key position is occupied by the leader of the party, who is a Conservative member of the House of Commons, elected by the other Conservative members of the House. If the Conservative Party is in power, the leader serves as prime minister for Britain.[5]

One-way arrows (indicating power) go out from the leader to all other units with which the leader interacts except the members of the House. With regard to the latter, power is a two-way street—the members may unseat the leader, and this occurred several times in the twentieth century; but the leader directs the business of the Conservative Party in the House.

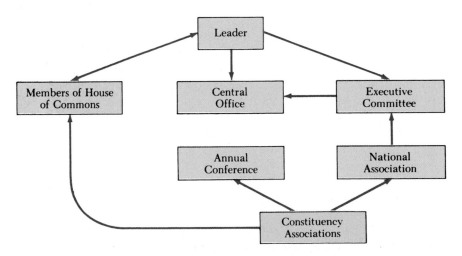

FIGURE 11.3   Organizational structure of Great Britain's Conservative Party.

---

[4]For a more detailed analysis of this problem, see Marjorie Randon Hershey and Paul Allen Beck, *Party Politics in America,* 11th ed. (Lexington, MA: Longman, 2005), chap. 1.
[5]This arrangement is discussed in more detail in Chapter 14.

Other parts of the party serve as a supporting structure for the leader and the party's members in the House. There are about 300,000 dues-paying party members organized into constituency associations. These determine local party policy—including the important question of who will be the party's candidate from that district—but they have little say otherwise in national party policies. Their only influence in this regard is to send delegates to the party's annual conference, from which, as seen in Figure 11.3, *no* arrows of power go anywhere. Issues are discussed at the conference and resolutions passed; these are not binding on anyone, although the party's leaders may treat them as important symptoms of discontent that must be taken seriously. Members also participate in the choice of a leader, but only after candidates have been narrowed to two by the Conservative members of the House of Commons. Party members vote to choose which of these two should be leader.

The National Association is not elected but consists of members of Parliament, prospective candidates, party officials, representatives of the constituency associations, and others: about three thousand in all. It meets annually and elects an executive committee of 150, which meets several times a year. These bodies consider the direction of the party, organizational questions, and so on, but the fact that they meet so infrequently indicates that what they do is not terribly important.

The Central Office is a large and well-financed party bureaucracy that hires regional and local party agents, conducts research on policy, and publishes propaganda. The Central Office is closely controlled by the leader, who directly appoints most of its top officials.

Thus, the Conservative Party has a complex structure, dominated by the members of the House of Commons through their leader. Other parts of the structure are important to the members of the House as a support group, but except for the important power over nominations held by local constituency associations, they have little power over the party's policies. This is not to say that the outside structure is unimportant; if nothing else, the dues paid by its members are the major source of party finance.

Most parties outside the United States have organizational structures more or less similar to this. They may vary in the degree of power given to the outside structure. (The Labour Party of Britain, for instance, gives more real power to its annual conference than does the Conservative Party.) Or, they may vary in how tightly control is exercised. In communist parties, "lower" units in power generally have to toe the line much more precisely than in noncommunist parties; this allows the leader to direct party policies more completely and more efficiently than leaders of other parties can.

✦ PARTY FINANCE

Parties get the money with which to finance their activities from a variety of sources. In the United States, parties do not have a monopoly on political finance, since much of it is raised directly by candidates from individual contributors and organized interest groups. Since a reform in 2003, independent groups, loosely aligned with candidates but not under their control, have also played a major role in campaigns. Parties still are able to generate enough resources from individual contributors, often solicited over the Internet, to function actively; but they do not dominate campaign finance.

Outside of the United States, parties generally raise the money and determine its use themselves.[6] The money may come from many kinds of sources:

- *Public finance:* Most states pay a portion of their parties' campaign expenses from public funds. It is always difficult to decide how much money to give to which parties. And established parties benefit disproportionately, since a new party, with no prior electoral success as a claim to funds, is on its own.

- *Individual memberships:* These may provide a good deal of income to a party, especially one with a large membership.

- *Bribes and kickbacks:* Especially where a single party is associated with a dictatorship, the closeness of the party to government allows it to organize corruption on its own behalf. In 1993, the Liberal Democratic Party of Japan, which had ruled without interruption for so long that it closely approximated one-party government, became embroiled in a huge scandal involving kickbacks of millions of dollars from construction contractors.

- *Interest-group donations:* Business and labor groups, and a few others, may subsidize favored parties heavily.

- *Profits from business enterprise:* Many parties own their own newspapers, banks, and other service firms, which they operate for the benefit of their members. Usually these cost money rather than make it, but some may be profitable.

- *Subsidies from foreign countries:* The United States, Venezuela, Libya, China, Israel, France, Japan, and other states have, at times, subsidized parties in other countries to further their own policies.

→ POLITICAL PARTY SYSTEMS

So far I have addressed the questions of what a political party does, how it is structured, and so on. All these questions have involved a single political party, looked at by itself. Another important set of questions revolves around the *pattern* formed by the political parties in a state. We speak of a **party system** as the set of all parties. Political scientists distinguish such systems primarily by the number and relative size of the parties.[7]

A **one-party system** is one in which only a single political party is allowed to be active. The former communist states of Eastern Europe; Egypt, Tanzania, Syria, and many other new states of the Third World; and the right-wing dictatorships of Nazi Germany or Franco's Spain are examples of the one-party system. In such systems, the government and the party are closely identified, because the government enforces the rule that other parties are not allowed to be active. The party may closely control the

---

[6]Two general reviews of party finance in various countries are Herbert Alexander and Rei Shiratori, *Comparative Political Finance Among the Democracies* (Boulder, CO: Westview Press, 1994); and Robert Williams, ed., *Party Finance and Political Corruption* (New York: Palgrave Macmillan, 2000). A fine reference is Reginald Austin and Maja Tjernström, eds., *Handbook on the Funding of Political Parties and Election Campaigns* (Stockholm, Sweden: International IDEA, 2003). It is accessible, along with an associated, current database, at **http://www.idea.int/parties/finance/**.

[7]For good discussions of each of the party systems examined here, see Maurice Duverger, *Political Parties* (New York: Wiley, 1954); and Giovanni Sartori, *Parties and Party Systems* (Cambridge, England: Cambridge University Press, 1964).

governmental apparatus, as was the case in communist states, or the party may simply have been created by those in charge of government. The party in a one-party system concentrates heavily on the tasks of mobilization, communication, and control. It cannot serve well as an alternative source of political ideas because it is so closely tied to those who are already running the state.

A **dominant-party system** is similar to the one-party system in that a single party holds power all the time, but it differs from the one-party system in that other political parties are allowed to function openly and with reasonable effectiveness.[8]

A good example of a dominant-party system is that of Mexico. This system broke down in 1997 and looks unlikely to reestablish itself, but it provides a good illustration of the system. For seventy years, a single party, the Party of the Institutionalized Revolution (PRI), won every presidential election, usually with 60 to 70 percent of the vote. It was well understood in Mexico that serious politics occured only within the PRI. Because of this party's long dominance of politics, the whole governmental structure from the civil service on up had intimate ties to it, and the party had an identification with the system (which it dominated) of the sort that we observe also in one-party states. Thus, the PRI was concerned about raising electoral turnout not because it thought it would be more likely to win a high-turnout election—it would win in any case—but because the system that it dominated needed high electoral participation to build citizen support for the regime. In many ways, then, a dominant-party system is like a one-party system.

However, the tolerance of other parties in the system does lead to important differences. For one thing, the existence of alternative parties provides a base for criticism of the government and guarantees that there will be more open debate about politics than in a one-party system. Alternative points of view must inevitably be openly present in a dominant-party system. The largest opposition party in Mexico, for instance, was for many years the National Action Party, a party of the middle class that had been opposed to the PRI's emphasis on labor and the poor. In 1982, for the first time, a group of socialist parties to the left of the PRI also figured significantly in a presidential election, gaining about 10 percent of the vote. In the 1988 election, the candidate of the Left almost beat the PRI candidate—would have beaten him, most observers believe, but for fraudulent counting of the votes. The 1994 election was more genuinely competitive— and the PRI did not win automatically. In the 1997 election, the PRI lost control of the lower house of Congress and lost the powerful mayoralty of Mexico City. And finally, in 2000, Vicente Fox of the National Action Party won the presidency, the first non-PRI figure to hold the post since the constitution was written. It appears that Mexico's party system will be an open one from now on.

This pattern of long-term dominance eventually giving way to true competition is typical of dominant party systems.

A frequent pattern associated with dominant-party systems in Third World states is for the independence movement and its leaders to form a political party once independence has been achieved. They will have been united in the movement for independence,

---

[8]See Alan Arian and Samuel Barnes, "The Dominant Party System: A Neglected Model of Democratic Stability," *Journal of Politics* 36 (August 1974), pp. 592–614. Also Ariel Levite and Sidney Tarrow, "Legitimation of Excluded Parties in Dominant Party Systems: A Comparison of Israel and Italy," *Comparative Politics* 15 (April 1983), pp. 295–327.

Michels' "Iron Law of Oligarchy"

In *Political Parties* (first published in 1915), Robert Michels argues that a political party can never be faithful to the program and constituency for which it was originally founded. For the party to vie successfully for power, he wrote, it is necessary that it be organized through a specialized division of labor in which certain people become full-time leaders. Once this has happened, however, the leadership group inevitably develops a set of values and perspectives that is different from the original aims of the party. The leaders deal daily with the enemy, sitting with them in parliament, bargaining with them; the party may develop its own stake in the status quo (many European parties, for instance, own banks, newspapers, and other business enterprises) that makes its leaders cautious about rocking the boat; and finally, it is in the leaders' interests for the party to grow as large as possible, and the easiest way to effect this is to moderate the party's positions so as to bring in new groups that had previously not been willing to support it. In short, a political party is caught in a dilemma: It may refuse to develop central leadership, in which case it will probably not attain power; or it may develop central leadership, but at the cost of losing its soul.

Political Parties was perhaps the most influential social scientific work of the twentieth century. Michels's theme has been picked up time and again to explain why parties disappoint their followers. It was popular among Eastern European critics of their communist regimes. It provided the theme of George Orwell's novel *Animal Farm.* The Green parties of several Western European states (radical environmental protection parties) have taken it to heart, with the West German Greens at times rotating their leadership at short intervals so that they will not develop a "leadership class."

Whether one regrets Michels's conclusion depends to some extent on whether one likes radical parties. However you feel about the question, though, two factors put it in a slightly different light:

1. All the factors that Michels sees at work (contact with the enemy, development of a stake in society, etc.) are things that occur over time. If a movement is successful quickly, we might expect to see Michels not apply. The Bolshevik seizure of power in Russia in 1917 and the Nazi seizure of power in Germany from 1930 to 1933 are two such cases, and both parties followed their original programs fairly closely. On the other hand, large communist parties attempted unsuccessfully across the second half of the twentieth century to gain power in France and Italy, and both moderated their positions considerably; in fact, the Italian party dropped the title "communist" in 1991. This suggests that for the opponents of a radical movement, "buying time" is not a trivial strategy but can systematically help to change the movement.

2. Even if Michels is right, all is not lost from the radical standpoint. It may be true that every radical party gradually becomes more moderate, yet we might also see party systems in which, over long periods of time, there were always radical parties present, because new parties would replace older parties. This apparent paradox depends on whether we look at things from the viewpoint of the individual party or of the party system. A similar paradox exists with regard to our own lives. Everyone is constantly growing older and, à la Michels, "youth is impossible to maintain." This is true for each individual, but it is not true for society because new young persons are continually being born to replace their elders. Similarly, if a party system is very open to new parties, young radical parties may always be ready at hand.

and so it is easy for them to come together in a single party. Furthermore, the problems facing a new state are so awesome that its leaders often agree that it would be better if the state were spared internal disagreement for some time. However, once the dominant party that results from this has ruled for a few decades, it may begin to lose its dominance. Corruption may set in with a group of entrenched officials; the state, now better established, can more easily afford internal disagreements; and the issues of independence fade while new issues that may divide the old ruling group arise. Indeed, this is part of what happened in Mexico; governmental corruption was one of the most important issues in the 1997 and 2000 elections.

In addition to Mexico, two other examples of this pattern are provided by India and Israel. For three decades after attaining independence in 1947, India was dominated by the Congress Party, which represented Mohandas K. Gandhi's independence movement. Elections during this period were sure to provide a Congress majority in Parliament, and important political maneuvers occurred solely within the Congress Party. In 1977, however, Congress slipped below 50 percent of the vote and a coalition of many small, opposed parties came into power. Since then, Congress has held power most of the time, but its dominance has not been ensured in the way it was in the decades after independence.

Israel provides another example. After the state of Israel was established in 1948, the Labour Party (formed by the mainly European leaders of the Zionist movement) held nearly unchallenged power until 1977. It was a great surprise to everyone when, in that year, a coalition of opposition parties called Likud, led by Menachem Begin, defeated Labour at the polls. In this case, the usual problems of a party that had been in power too long were magnified by demographic change. In the 1950s and 1960s, there had been massive immigration into Israel of Jews from other parts of the Mideast, and by 1977, the country was split about evenly between voters of European origin and those of non-European origin. The almost exclusively European-led Labour Party had drifted badly out of touch with about half of the electorate.

A new example of a dominant party system may now be developing in South Africa. In 1990 South Africa ended *apartheid*, the period of undemocratic, exclusive white domination, after a long struggle led by the African National Congress Party. In the first three elections of the new democracy, the African National Congress received 63 percent of the vote in 1994, 66 percent of the vote in 1999, and 70 percent in 2004. Meanwhile, parties opposed to the African National Congress were quite fragmented; the party that ran second in 2004 got only 12.3 percent of the vote, to the ANC's 70 percent.

The point of these examples is that, while a dominant-party system is similar in important ways to a one-party system, the availability of other active parties does guarantee that there will be fairly open discussion and debate, and it also provides for possible long-term flexibility and adjustment in the system.

A third variant is the **two-party system.** This is typified by the fact that no one party can count on always holding power but only two parties can normally expect to have a chance at doing so. In a two-party system, the two major parties will typically receive over 90 percent of the votes cast, but neither party will very often receive more than 55 or 60 percent of the vote. A prime example is the U.S. party system, in which only the Republican and Democratic parties are normally serious contenders for power. A two-party system does not necessarily *have* only two parties; a dozen or so parties run regularly in a U.S. presidential election, including the Libertarians and the Socialist Workers' Party. But only the two major parties usually have any expectation of winning. Other examples of two-party or nearly two-party systems are those of Great Britain and Austria.

In contrast to a dominant-party system, a two-party system offers somewhat more regular variety and choices in policies and candidates. At the same time, a single party usually wins an election cleanly and is able to govern by itself without forming a coalition with other parties. Thus, two-party systems are typified by a certain amount of choice combined with fairly stable and straightforward governance.

The final type of party system dealt with here is the **multiparty system.** This system consists of more than two major parties. A good example is Norway, whose Parliament, after the election of 2005, consisted of representatives from the following parties:

Labour Party	61 seats
Progress Party (anti-tax)	38 seats
Conservative Party	23 seats
Left Socialists	15 seats
Christian People's Party	11 seats
Centre Party (environmentalist, agrarian)	11 seats
Liberal Party	10 seats

There are 169 seats; therefore, eighty-five are required to control a majority vote in the Parliament, and no one party had enough seats to rule by itself. The Labour Party, the Left Socialists, and the Centre Party, with 87 seats, formed a coalition to govern. The leader of the Labour party, Jens Stoltenberg, was named prime minister, since Labour was the largest member of the coalition.

Most democratic systems are multiparty systems. The one factor that seems strongly to determine whether a given state will have a two-party or a multiparty system is its electoral system. If a state uses a form of single-member district plurality electoral system, it will almost surely have a two-party system. If it uses a proportional representation system, it will almost surely have a multiparty system. The reason for this should be clear from the discussion in Chapter 10. Under a plurality system, large parties have such an advantage that small parties are driven out, until only two major parties are left.

Compared with a two-party system, a multiparty system offers the voter a wider range of choice. Not only are there *more* choices, but the parties are able to be more distinctive than they could be in a two-party system. In a two-party system, because a party must command half or more of all votes cast in the election to succeed, there is great pressure on both parties to appeal simultaneously to many different groups. A party may not stake out a clear appeal to farmers, for instance, because it might alienate its supporters in the cities; it cannot appeal clearly to the East because it might lose votes in the West, and so on. Such parties are apt to present a pretty fuzzy picture to the electorate. Parties in a multiparty system do not have this problem. The formation of a coalition is likely in any case; therefore, a party does not *have* to be huge to get some share of the power. In the Norwegian example, the Labour Party represents the special interests of the labor unions, fishing crews, and various other groups; it is a bit bland. The Conservative Party represents especially the urban middle class, who want taxes kept down and do not want moralistic constraints imposed by the state. The Christian People's Party represents devout Lutheranism and favors prohibition of liquor, religious instruction in the schools, and a ban on abortion. The Centre Party has a special concern for farmers but as these have declined in numbers it has also taken up special concerns of white-collar workers and the environment. The Left Socialists have a variety of programs but have been most noted for their opposition to Norwegian membership in NATO and protection of the environment. The Progress Party is a right-wing party sharply opposed to the welfare state and to immigration. What a "smorgasbord," compared with any existing two-party system! The voter simply has a greater range of choice in multiparty systems than in two-party systems.

However, there is a balancing advantage to the two-party system. Most of the time, multiparty systems require a coalition government to operate smoothly; therefore, a government cannot be set up unless two or more parties agree to cooperate by forming a coalition. Now this may be fine. Sweden, Norway, Finland, Germany, and other countries have been ruled by stable coalitions of one sort or another through most of their postwar history. If the need for a coalition coincides with a great deal of animosity among the political parties, however, there may be trouble. Under this combination of circumstances, it may be difficult to put together a coalition of parties; or if one is formed, it may be torn apart by mutual mistrust before it has lasted very long. A prime example of this problem is Italy, governed by sixty-one different coalitions since 1945.[9]

✦ POWER AND CHOICE

The disjunction between politics as choice and politics as power has led to some distortion in our view of political parties in a democracy. We have viewed the party much as what Michels wishes it could be—an instrument that expresses politically the unified choice of its members. We have viewed parties as unitary actors and have thought of them, from the standpoint of their members, predominantly in terms of choice. We have not thought of a party as consisting of various groups that may be at odds with each other and that exercise power over one another.

More often than not, a chief function of a party is to serve as a conduit by which one part may exercise power over another. It is this that has made the party almost as important to nondemocracies as to democracies, and we have seen that it is also an important function of democratic parties.

Our emphasis on the party as a vehicle for expressing choice has often helped make us insensitive to its importance as a channel for the use of power. Once again, power and choice are necessary to a full understanding of politics.

---

[9]To address this problem, Italy changed its electoral system at the end of the century from proportional representation to a mostly single-member-district electoral system, and the 2001 election produced, for the first time, a cabinet with a stable majority of support in the parliament.

✳ EXAMPLE

The Communist Party of China

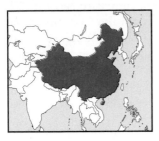

For thousands of years, China was a powerful empire, the premier force in eastern Asia. But throughout the nineteenth century and the first half of the twentieth century, it was weak and corrupt, dominated by European powers that carved it up into spheres of influence.

During World War II the country was occupied brutally by Japan, but in the aftermath of the war, and following a further civil war, China became unified again, this time under the Communist Party, led by Mao Tse-tung. The Party established a one-party socialist state, which Mao led until his death in 1976.

Under Mao the Party saw itself as the leader of a socialist revolution and therefore would not tolerate any other political organizations, which it worried would get in the way of the revolution. It established a society in which there was very little private property. People's lives revolved around their factory or their collective farm, which provided them with housing, health care, old-age care, and care for their children.

After Mao's death a new leader, Deng Xiaoping, turned the economic direction of China on its head, shifting the country instead to a largely capitalist economy, with individually owned farms, private property, and considerable scope for entrepreneurs. Just as the Party had guided the socialist revolution, it guided this shift away from socialism as well, arguing that China needed to rapidly develop economically in order to take its rightful place in the world. It continued to ban all other political organizations, presumably because clear and unified leadership was needed to accomplish the changes that would bring rapid economic growth.

In effect, the party first led a socialist revolution, and would allow no opposition because clear leadership was needed. And then, it led a nationalist revolution with an emphasis on capitalism, but would still not allow opposition.

This is not to say there is no dissent or conflict under the Communist Party's rule. China has always been a big, sprawling, rather loosely organized country, and the Party has simply not been able to control people's lives tightly. The Party has tolerated vocal individual dissent, as long as it does not crystallize into a broader organization opposed to the Party. For the last couple of decades, for instance, there has been a lively tradition of "wall posters" on which individuals could write scathing criticism of governmental policies. And more recently, a large and lively community of bloggers has developed in China. But when the Party thinks that a group has organized formally in a way that might pose a potential threat, it comes down hard. Obviously, no other political parties are allowed, but even cultural and religious organizations like the Falun Gong cult are repressed strenuously.

Though no other organizations are allowed to maintain themselves, there are many spontaneous, unorganized demonstrations around the country that the Party worries about, but cannot really control. ("Social movements" of this sort will be discussed in Chapter 13.) In 2006, there were an estimated 23,000 riots or protests in rural areas, mostly over land seizures, increases in fees, or local government corruption. One of these was a protest of 20,000 people in Hunan province against a doubling of bus fares, which was put down brutally by 1,500 police. Scores of people were injured, and one student was beaten to death.[10]

The Party rules as the sole political organization, but it rules over a rather loosely organized state. How does it maintain its central control? The Communist Party of China is a huge organization,

---

[10]"Rural Unrest in China," *Economic Intelligence Reports*, March 15, 2007, **www.economist.com.**

with 63 million members. It actually has to take pains to keep itself relatively small, and has a goal of never exceeding 5 percent of the population. In order to become a member one must pass a one-year probationary period. Members are expected to implement the directives of Party leaders.

With such a large number of picked members, the Party can insert itself into all of the points of power of the state. Most judges are Party members, for instance, and subject to its discipline. Most high-ranking military officers are Party members. And as we can see below, the party organizes itself in committees parallel to all of the organs of the state, to keep control of them.

The Party is organized hierarchically. The top national leadership of the Party is lodged with the Politburo, a group of twenty-four officials, who in turn actually are led by their Standing Committee, a subgroup of nine members who constitute the real leaders of the state as well as the Party. (Two members of the Politburo Standing Committee, for instance, are the president and vice president of China.) Parallel to the Politburo is the Party's Central Military Commission, which coordinates military affairs. And below the Politburo, in descending order of scope, are provincial Party committees, prefecture Party committees, county Party committees, township Party committees, and village Party committees—all set up to coordinate with and control their respective governmental units.

The Party's control of the state apparatus is thus fairly close. But this does not result in a lockstep, totalitarian society, partly because the Party is itself not monolithic. The same looseness that characterizes China itself also shows up in the Party. Factional conflict guarantees fairly lively political debate within the Party.

For instance, a new law to define and protect private property was introduced in 2006 in the normally docile National People's Congress, but there was so much uproar about it from the left wing of the Party, who have not given up on the spirit of Mao's revolution, that it had to be pulled. It was passed the next year, in 2007, but only after the Party had taken the unusual step of banning all press coverage and pressuring universities to keep some prominent critics quiet.

The Party faces an uncertain future. Many in China look at the chaos of post-Communist Russia and are thankful that their state chose economic reform rather than political reform. And, a noncompetitive political structure that does, however, allow at least limited debate and dissent may be able to continue for a long time. On the other hand, the freewheeling flows of information that characterize capitalism must inevitably create at least some tension with a political monopoly. This is not to predict the fall of the Party at any time soon, but rather to note that there will inevitably be some tension with the economy it has unleashed, and that this might eventually lead to a new political system.

EXAMPLE

Canada's Political Parties

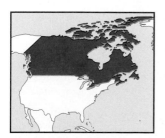

Canada's party system is unusual in that it has several major parties, despite having a single-member-district plurality (SMDP) electoral system.[11] Currently there are five significant parties in Canada, with shares of the vote in the 2006 election varying from 4.5 percent to 36.3 percent.[12] These five parties are:

- The *Liberal Party,* for most of the postwar period the largest party in Canada; but in the 2006 election it dropped from its dominant position to get just

---

[11]See the discussion of SMDP systems above, pp. 235–239.
[12]As of this writing another election looked likely sometime in 2007, so the relative strengths of the parties noted here may well be out of date when you read this.

30 percent of the vote, and 102 seats in the House of Commons. It had been in power for a number of years when it became embroiled in a scandal before the election over the use of national funds to put some of its supporters on the payroll of firms hired by the government. It is a broad party without a particularly clear set of programs or principles, but has generally favored holding the Canadian state together as a loose federation (i.e., not having Quebec secede to become an independent state), and has been opposed to religiously based social policies such as banning same-sex marriages. Regionally, its core strength has always been in the huge central province of Ontario (which elects about one-third of all seats in the House of Commons), plus significant strength in the other very large province, Quebec. Additionally, it has often done well in the small maritime provinces of Nova Scotia, New Brunswick, Prince Edward Island, and Newfoundland/Labrador. One reason why its current strength of 135 seats is relatively low is the rise since 1993 of the Bloc Québécois Party, which has largely displaced it in Quebec (see below).

• The *Conservative Party of Canada.* This was traditionally the second-largest party of Canada, but was almost destroyed when it lost badly in the 1993 election and limped badly thereafter. However, one of the agents of its destruction at that time, a new "Reform Party" which arose as a fairly conservative antiparty party in 1993, merged with the remnants of the old Conservative Party just before the 2004 election, and their newly re-created Conservative Party of Canada received 30 percent of the vote and 99 seats in that election. When the Liberal leader had to call an election in early 2006 in the midst of his scandal problems, the Conservatives came out best with 36 percent of the vote and 124 seats. Their leader Stephen Harper, who had engineered the reunification of conservative parties in 2004, took over as prime minister. Like the Liberal Party, the Conservative Party does not have a very clear set of programs, except that most of its members support religiously based social positions such as banning same-sex marriage and abolishing abortion. The Conservative Party is strongest in western Canada, where its largest share of the vote generally comes from the prairie provinces; in 2006 it received 57 percent of the vote across Manitoba, Saskatchewan, and Alberta.

• *Bloc Québécois,* the third party in the House, with 51 seats. It is a regional party, operating only in Quebec, and its program is primarily just one of autonomy or independence for Quebec. In 2006 it received 42 percent of the vote in Quebec, taking 51 of Quebec's 75 seats, but that vote was down from 49 percent in 2004, because the Conservatives made inroads in the province. The Bloc's main strength lies in its control of the provincial government in Quebec. In 1995 a provincial government led by the party held a referendum vote on whether Quebec should become an independent state; the referendum failed narrowly, 50.6 percent to 49.4 percent.

• The *New Democratic Party* is a socialist party with origins in prairie populism, but also with considerable support from organized labor. It is the fourth party in the House, with 29 seats, though it drew 18 percent of the vote nationally in 2006. Aside from its weakness in Quebec it is more generally spread nationally in its support than the other parties, and this hurts it in the SMDP electoral system.

• The *Green Party* is fairly new to Canada. It drew just 4.5 percent of the vote in 2006, but polls in 2007 were suggesting it would draw 8 percent in the next election. Its strength is distributed across most regions, and so it did not win any seats with its 4.5 percent vote in 2006. It espouses a "green" environmentalist program.

The explanation for one of the mysteries about Canadian parties—how a multiparty system survives the SMDP electoral system—may be evident from the descriptions above. Of the four parties, three have distinctive regional bases of support, and as we saw in Chapter 10 (see especially page 239), small parties with regionally concentrated support do not suffer diminution from SMDP in the same way that those with geographically broad support do.

One puzzle left unexplained, however, is why the (rather) broadly based New Democratic Party does not disappear under this electoral system. The answer may be that it is the one party with a truly distinctive set of positions on economic and foreign policy questions. The Bloc Québécois focuses primarily just on the Quebec question, and the other two parties are large, inclusive "umbrella" parties that until recently did not have programs that were very distinct from each other, and now differ only on rather narrow "social" issues.

This explanation leads us on to the second important puzzle about Canadian parties—just why is it that the two main parties have remained so indistinct on issues of policy? R. Kenneth Carty argues that the reason is that parties in Canada are condemned to link a very mobile, regionally diverse society to a governmental system (parliamentary government, which we will examine in detail in Chapter 14) that requires tightly disciplined, centralized decision making.[13] The only way the parties can remain loose, yet disciplined, he says, is for them to be disciplined holding companies at the national level, but open and loosely defined at the local level. They accept whoever will support them at the local level, even if the end result is a very diverse set of views across the whole national party; but they require disciplined voting by members of Parliament at the national level, and provide the incentives needed to enforce this discipline by maintaining strong programs of pork-barrel legislation and jobs patronage. The result is parties that do not have a very clear programmatic basis but that are effective patronage and pork-barrel machines.

This interpretation of the parties may also help to explain a final, third puzzle about Canadian parties. Canadian voters are considerably more volatile than those in most other North American or European democracies.[14] Parties have fairly often come and gone over the past few decades—a "Social Credit" party based in western Canada regularly garnered from 5 to 10 percent of the vote in the 1960s and 1970s, but then petered out; both the Reform Party (now gone by merger) and the Bloc Québécois popped up in 1993. And, turnover in Canada's House of Commons is considerably greater than in U.S. House of Representatives elections or British House of Commons elections. Since 1935 turnover in the Canadian House has averaged about 30 percent, reaching 75 percent in the unusual election of 1993.[15]

It may be that the nonprogrammatic, patronage/pork basis of Canadian parties helps the electorate to behave in such a volatile way. Party identification in Canada is about as high as in most industrialized countries, but Canadians seem to view their parties as tools rather than homes. This also shows up in quite varying patterns of votes for the same party in provincial as compared to national elections. A voter may identify with one party for national purposes, another one for provincial purposes.

Whatever the cause of the volatility, it is probably quite salutary for the quality of democracy in Canada. Most democracies—and certainly the United States, where most members of Congress sit in almost unassailable seats—could benefit from active accountability of the Canadian sort.

---

[13]R. Kenneth Carty, "Canada's Nineteenth-Century Cadre Parties at the Millennium," in Paul Webb, David Farrell, and Ian Holliday, eds., *Political Parties in Advanced Industrial Democracies* (New York: Oxford University Press, 2002), p. 347.
[14]Bakvis, Herman, "Canada," in *Comparative Governance*, Primis database.
[15]Ibid., footnote 9.

KEY TERMS

political party	party system	two-party system
mobilization	one-party system	multiparty system
party identification	dominant-party system	

FURTHER READING

Aldrich, John. *Why Parties? The Origin and Transformation of Party Politics in America.* Chicago: University of Chicago Press, 1995.

Burnham, Walter Dean. *Critical Elections and the Mainsprings of American Politics.* New York: Norton, 1970.

Dalton, Russell J., and Wattenberg, Martin P., eds. *Parties Without Partisans: Political Change in Advanced Industrial Democracies.* New York: Oxford University Press, 2000.

Downs, Anthony. *An Economic Theory of Democracy.* New York: Harper & Row, 1957.

Duverger, Maurice. *Political Parties.* London: Methuen, 1954.

Hale, Henry E. *Why Not Parties in Russia?* New York: Cambridge University Press, 2005.

Hershey, Marjorie Randon. *Party Politics in America.* 11th ed. Lexington, MA: Longman, 2005.

Katz, Richard S., and Mair, Peter. *How Parties Organize: Change and Adaptation in Party Organizations in Western Democracies.* Thousand Oaks, CA: Sage, 1995.

———, eds. *Party Organizations: A Data Handbook.* Thousand Oaks, CA: Sage, 1992.

Lipset, Seymour Martin, and Rokkan, Stein. *Party Systems and Voter Alignments.* New York: Free Press, 1967.

Mainwaring, Scott. "Party Systems in the Third Wave." *Journal of Democracy* 9 (1998): pp. 67–71.

———, and Scully, Timothy, eds. *Building Democratic Institutions: Party Systems in Latin America.* Stanford, CA: Stanford University Press, 1995.

Maisel, L. Sandy, ed. *The Parties Respond: Changes in the American Party System.* 4th ed. Boulder, CO: Westview, 2002.

Malbin, Michael J. *Life After Reform: When the Bipartisan Campaign Reform Act Meets Politics.* Lanham, MD: Rowman & Littlefield, 2003.

McCormick, Richard L., ed. *Political Parties and the Modern State.* New Brunswick, NJ: Rutgers University Press, 1984.

Panebianco, Angelo. *Political Parties: Organization and Power.* New York: Cambridge University Press, 1988.

Party Politics is a specialized journal of political science research about parties.

Przeworski, Adam, and Sprague, John. *Paper Stones: A History of Electoral Socialism.* Chicago: University of Chicago Press, 1986.

Scheiner, Ethan. *Democracy Without Competition in Japan: Opposition Failure in a One-Party Dominant State.* New York: Cambridge University Press, 2005.

Stokes, Susan C. "Political Parties and Democracy." *Annual Review of Political Science* 2 (1999): pp. 243–67.

Strøm, Kaare, and Svåsand, Lars, eds. *Challenges to Political Parties: The Case of Norway.* Ann Arbor: University of Michigan Press, 1996.

Webb, Paul, Farrell, David, and Holliday, Ian, eds. *Political Parties in Advanced Industrial Democracies.* New York: Oxford University Press, 2002.

WEB SITES OF INTEREST

Political Parties site with links and resources:

http://www.psr.keele.ac.uk/parties.htm

Canadian political parties site:

http://home.ican.net/~alexng/can.html

Democratic Party:

http://www.democrats.org

Republican Party:

http://www.rnc.org/

Labour Party:

http://www.labour.org.uk/

Conservative Party:

http://www.conservatives.com/

Liberal Democratic Party:

http://www.libdems.org.uk/

Scottish National Party:

http://www.snp.org.uk/

Reform Party of the United States:

http://www.reformparty.org/

College Republicans of America (check out activities on your campus):

http://www.crnc.org

College Democrats of America (check out activities on your campus):

http://www.collegedems.com

Green Party of the United States:

http://www.gp.org/

Campaign Finance Institute:

http://www.cfinst.org

CHAPTER 12

STRUCTURED CONFLICT: INTEREST GROUPS AND POLITICS

In Chapter 11, we distinguished the political party from the **interest group.** A party is concerned with the process of leadership selection and the organization of government, while an interest group is concerned primarily with trying to affect what those in power do. *The interest group is an organized group of citizens one of whose goals is to ensure that the state follows certain policies.*

All sorts of organized groups may function as interest groups. Some are organized solely to lobby governmental officials on behalf of one or another cause. The Sierra Club, a U.S. organization that lobbies for the preservation of wilderness areas, is an example of such an organization. Other groups may be organized primarily for other purposes but take on lobbying and other ways of influencing policy as an important task. Examples of such groups are labor unions, primarily organized to bargain with an employer but also usually active politically. Still others focus on other goals but give some attention to politics. An example would be a university, whose first concern is to educate students and conduct research but is likely to maintain one or two people to lobby the government on bills that concern it. And, a number of interest "groups" are individual corporations that lobby the government for a contract or a regulatory decision.

There are many interest groups in a modern state, so many that it is hard to form a precise idea of their numbers. There is available a reasonably good census of interest groups in Germany in the mid-1990s; it is presented in Table 12.1. Note how many of these are economic interest groups (industrial organizations, trade unions, and professional organizations); this is fairly typical of industrialized countries. However, non-economic groups have been growing relative to economic groups, which is also fairly typical, at least for Western European and North American countries. In a comparable census of interest groups in Germany twenty years earlier in 1974, 79 percent of all groups were economic groups; we can see from Table 12.1 that by 1994, this figure had

TABLE 12.1

German Interest Groups, 1994, by Type

Category	Number of Organizations	
Economic	65%	
Corporate groups		41%
Unions		5%
Professions		15%
Other		3%
General	35%	
Ideological		3%
Social help		16%
Cultural		11%
Recreation, sports		2%
Environmental		3%

SOURCE: Martin Sebaldt, *Organisierter Pluralismus* (Opladen, Germany: Westdeutscher Verlag GmbH, 1997), pp. 79–82.

dropped to 65 percent. The major gainers over the twenty years were cultural, recreational, and environmental groups.

No one knows exactly how many different interest groups a large and diverse country such as the United States has, but there must be many thousands.[1] In 1997, it was estimated that thirty-five hundred to four thousand interest groups lobbied the German government in Bonn.[2] The 1996 directory of pressure groups lobbying the European Union offices counted over seventeen hundred groups, about 80 percent of which were corporate or trade associations; the other 20 percent consisted of unions and humanitarian and religious groups.[3]

Interest groups are not confined to democracies or open societies. All states have interest groups. Some do not permit a wide diversity of formally organized, politically active groups to exist, since this would seem threatening to their governments. However, even in such states, organizations set up for other purposes—the army, universities, natural history clubs, scientific associations, sports clubs, factories—exert political influence to help mold government policies.

---

[1]A recent estimate is that there were approximately 24,000 national interest groups active in the United States in 1995. And beyond this, there were many local interest groups that were not active in Washington. Martin Sebaldt, *Transformation der Verbändedemokratie: Die Modernisierung des Systems Organisierter Interresen in den USA* (Wiesbaden, Germany: Westdeutscher Verlag, 2001), p. 48.
[2]Thomas Saalfeld, "Germany: From Dictatorship to Parliamentary Democracy," *Parliamentary Affairs* 50 (July 1997), p. 386.
[3]Alan Butt Philip and Oliver Gray, eds., *Directory of Pressure Groups in the EU* (London: Cartermill, 1996).

The cartoonist appears to think that the liquor and restaurant lobbies have been feeding Congress's habit.

Copyright 1998 by Herblock in *The Washington Post*.

❖ Interest Groups and Representation

Interest groups are probably the main vehicle in most states for representing public opinion and bringing it to bear in an organized (and therefore effective) way on the governmental authorities. Political parties cannot do this very well, because they are involved in trying to acquire governmental power for themselves. This quest for power forces parties to incorporate many compromises in their programs to appeal to the broadest spectrum of support. If the state is a democracy, this may take the form of an attempt to appeal to a wide range of voters; if the state is not a democracy, it may mean trying to have such a broad appeal that neither the army, the air force, the navy, urban workers, the church, nor any other major group will try to overthrow them. Whatever the case, a political party, by virtue of its most basic goal, cannot serve to articulate and represent people's wishes. It has a different task: to blend various wishes into a larger coalition. The party seeks to make differences fuzzy, but each interest group is free to present its group's wishes clearly and precisely. The task of representing the people's desires, then, falls primarily on the interest group. How well do interest groups do this?

TABLE 12.2

Percentage of Eligible Employees in the United States Who Are Enrolled in Labor Organizations, by Industry, 2004

Type of Industry	
Agriculture	3
Mining	8
Construction	13
Manufacturing	13
Transportation and public utilities	24
Leisure and hospitality	3
Finance, insurance, real estate	2
Government	37

SOURCE: U.S. Bureau of Labor Statistics, *Union Membership* (online, January 26, 2007, modification), Table 3.

Interest groups usually accomplish this fairly well; otherwise, they would not be the workhorses of political advocacy that they are. However, there are three important barriers that keep interest groups from functioning as well in this area as we might wish:

1. *Not all interests are equally well organized.* Groups whose members have enough leisure to be active in politics are likely to enlist more of their potential clientele than other groups. Similarly, we will see high enrollment among interests whose members are concentrated in particular localities, rather than spread out; have a basic economic stake in the outcome of politics; are well educated; and so on. Table 12.2, for example, lists enrollment percentages for labor organizations in several different occupational groups.

Perhaps the most universal and significant break between groups that are readily organized and those that are difficult to organize is represented by "producer" interests and "consumer" interests. A producer interest is any group of people involved in producing something. For any product, there may be a few producer interests: a corporation, a trade union, one or more professional organizations. Examples of producer interests are Microsoft Corporation, the AFL-CIO, the American Medical Association, and the National Farmers' Union—any economic entity made up of those who produce something. A consumer interest is a group of people consuming a product. Examples would include the National Association of Homebuyers and the American Automobile Association; it is harder to come up with examples of consumer groups, however, because most groups of people who share in consuming a product are not formally organized.

Producer interests are always easier to organize than consumer interests, because their interest is more concentrated. Consider the price of milk, for instance. For the hundreds of millions of milk consumers in the United States, an increase of 10 cents a gallon for milk would be a nuisance, but it is not something they would give up evenings and weekends to organize against. However, 10 cents a gallon produces a large total sum of

Migrant farm workers, Imperial Valley, California. Moving frequently, working long hours, lacking education and political skills, such workers find it difficult to organize themselves for political action. Note in Table 12.2 that only 3 percent of agricultural workers are in labor organizations.

© Peter Menzel/Stock Boston

money when it is accumulated over many million gallons sold; since that large sum of money is concentrated on perhaps a couple of thousand dairies and their workers nationwide, the small price increase might mean a difference of 10 or 20 percent in the profits of the companies and the earnings of their workers. This is something people *will* give up evenings and weekends for. You can bet that Washington would be saturated with letters, campaign contributions, and lobbying visits from the affected companies and their unions—but would hear very little from the people who are to pay the extra dime.

In every country of the world, producers are more fully organized than consumers, and the result is a general skewing of government policies in favor of producers. In Germany, for instance, as shown in Table 12.1, 61 percent of all German interest groups were corporate groups, unions, or professional associations. Only 3 percent were "other" economic groups (mostly consumer groups).

As a result of these and other disparities, some interest groups can speak strongly and confidently as representatives of their interest, and they are listened to with respect. Other interest groups, which formally represent only a small percentage of their potential clientele, must speak with a more muted voice. The overall system of interest groups, as a result, does not represent all interests equally well. Those that are easy to organize bulk larger in the system, and their voices are heard more loudly than they should deserve on the basis of their numbers.

2. *Also, some groups command a disproportionate voice in the interest-group system because they have special advantages.* Consider the following examples:
    * In almost all Western countries, business groups have influence beyond what one would expect based on the size of their memberships. They gain added influence for several reasons: they have a great deal of money to spend on politics; they have a good deal of expertise in advertising and organization, which can be used to political benefit; and the well-being of the country is so closely tied to their own well-being that they must be listened to with respect.
    * In many states whose governments are shaky, large landowners as a group gain exaggerated political influence because of their ties to the army, which may be expected to intervene politically on their behalf.
    * In Israel over past decades, rather small groups of fundamentalist Jewish sects have wielded influence out of proportion to their numbers because the Labour and Likud parties have been so evenly matched in elections that the small religious parties have held the balance of power.
    * In almost all countries with much coastline, the fishing industry has had disproportionate influence because its members are concentrated in what are often key locations politically and because they are willing to go to great lengths to protect their livelihood and their traditional way of life. (It is for this reason, for instance, that it has been so difficult for other countries to get Japan to stop the hunting of whales, even though only a few thousand members of Japan's huge labor force are involved in the whaling industry.)

    Such examples are numerous. Partly because not all interests are equally well organized and because some have special advantages such as these, the sum total of interest-group representation may give quite a distorted picture of the interests in a country.

3. *Finally, most interest groups lack structures to ensure that leaders will be closely responsive to the members' wishes.* The leaders of an interest group are usually able to build a base of support within the administrative structure of the group and among its members, which makes it difficult to unseat them. Even where the members of the group elect the leader periodically—as is true of most labor unions, for instance—an "inside" group usually dominates the election, so that the same person is elected year after year.[4] Many interest groups—such as universities, armies, and factories—are not even set up to allow periodic elections.

The internal structure of interest groups is not very democratic; therefore, there is a real danger that their leaders may gradually drift away from the ordinary members and follow their own political line. Democratic accountability to the membership could prevent this, but in its absence, there is little to keep it from happening.

We might expect that the free market would provide a control over this. That is, if the leaders drifted too far from the ordinary members, the latter would be able to "vote with their feet" and join a competing group. For example, there are many different

---

[4]Seymour Martin Lipset, Martin A. Trow, and James S. Coleman explored an exception to this rule in *Union Democracy* (Garden City, N.Y.: Doubleday, 1962). Another, more recent example was the running battle during the 1990s between the reform and the traditional factions in the Teamsters union.

TABLE 12.3

Percentage of Members Who Would Stay in the Association If It Did Not Lobby at All

Minnesota Farm Bureau	77
Minnesota Farmers' Union	63
Minnesota Retail Federation	57
Minnesota-Dakotas Hardware Association	70
Printing Industries of the Twin Cities	94

SOURCE: From *The Organization of Interests* by Terry M. Moe, The University of Chicago Press, 1980. Copyright © 1980 The University of Chicago Press. Reprinted with permission.

conservation societies, and so we might expect that if some members of, say, Friends of the Earth did not like their leaders' positions, they would drop their membership and join some other group, such as the National Wildlife Association.

The trouble with this solution is that the situation with regard to conservation groups is rather atypical. Often, a group's political positions are *not* major factors determining an individual's continued membership in the group; this is especially true of economic interest groups. For most union members, the important thing is how skillful their union is in negotiating a good contract with their employer. Another important consideration is the package of extra benefits the union can provide—low-cost group insurance, educational and entertainment programs, low-cost package vacations, and so on. For many members, the union's political activity is a weak runner-up among the things that matter to them.[5]

A survey of several business and agricultural associations asked members whether they would stay in their association if it stopped its political activity altogether but continued to offer them the other benefits they enjoyed. As seen in Table 12.3, a majority of each group said that the association's other benefits were important enough to them that they would continue their membership even if the group did nothing in politics.

These side benefits, which the leaders of groups may manipulate to maintain membership in the group, are called **selective incentives.** (They give members an *incentive* for being in the group; they are *selective* in that they may be targeted selectively to members of the group.) If the selective incentives available through an organization are sufficiently attractive, they can provide the leaders of the organization with a great deal of leeway in their choice of political positions. Leaders of labor unions have been able to take political positions varying from rather conservative Republican (the Teamsters union in the United States, at various times) to communist (many French and Italian unions), and their members have not objected strongly as long as their wage settlements and other benefits were good.[6]

---

[5]Mancur Olson, *The Logic of Collective Action* (Cambridge: Harvard University Press, 1965).
[6]An added factor that may hold members in groups and that certainly operates in the case of many labor unions is *coercion.* "Union shop" contracts often require that a worker must be a member of the union to hold a job.

The Logic of Collective Action

One of the more interesting works of abstract theory in the social sciences is Mancur Olson's *The Logic of Collective Action* (Cambridge: Harvard University Press, 1965). This was one of the earliest works to develop the general problem of public goods (you will recall from Chapter 3 that a public good is one that no member of the group can be prevented from enjoying). However, it was developed particularly to account for when interest groups organize or do not organize. Olson notes that organized groups will be plagued by the problem of public goods. Even if a business owner does not join the local chamber of commerce, for example, he or she will still benefit from its lobbying activities with the state government.

To Olson, this means that the potential members of the group will be inclined to save their dues money and not join the group, because they can enjoy the benefits of the group's activity whether or not they join. What is rational for the individual may be tragic for the group, however, because if every potential member did what was rational, there would be no interest group at all and no benefits for anyone.

Olson notes four possibilities that help to explain how one might be able to organize groups in spite of the problem of collective goods:

1. If a group is *sufficiently small*, it may be easier to organize. Each member's contribution is then not trivially small, and so all potential members can see that there will be less of the collective good available if they withhold their contribution to the group.
2. The group may offer *selective incentives*, such as life insurance programs or travel packages, that can be withheld from those who do not enter the group.
3. The group may be able to *coerce* members to join whether they wish to or not. The closed shop is an example of this in labor relations. In "neocorporatist" systems (see pages 294–296), the government may require that the group be formed so that it can help to carry out the government's policies.
4. If one member of the group bulks large relative to the others, then that member may see that the collective good would be impossible to attain without its participation. Therefore, that member may join and carry things forward even though smaller members who do not join get a free ride. The largest department store in town, for instance, can hardly avoid joining the chamber of commerce. For a slightly different "group," this helps to explain why the United States figures so importantly in the NATO alliance and provides its smaller allies with a partially free ride.

Note that of the four possibilities, the first, second, and fourth are concerned only with politics as choice. The third, which I had to pull from a later chapter of Olson's book because it actually does not come up in his core chapter, takes into account the fact that decisions in politics are made through the use of power. This emphasis on choice rather than on power in politics is typical of models based on economic theory (like Olson's).

Interest groups, then, are not on the whole democratically organized, and their leaders may depart considerably from the members' views. Add to this our two earlier points (that the groups themselves may be rather unrepresentative of the population as a whole, because some kinds of people participate more in groups than others; and that some groups, because of strategic advantage, are able to have more impact than they would deserve on the basis of their numbers), and we can see that the overall result of lobbying and other political activity on the part of interest-group leaders may be quite unrepresentative of the overall wishes of the population.

As a few examples of how the interest-group system may distort public opinion, consider the following:

- In Israel, in deference to small orthodox groups, the national airline El Al does not fly on the Sabbath even though it is expensive to have the planes sit idle and most Israelis would prefer to have Sabbath flights.[7]

- In the United States, a majority of those sampled in public opinion polls favor tighter regulation of handguns, but the National Rifle Association has effectively blocked such laws in most localities.

- In countries with state-run television networks, programming is almost always more "educational" (and dull) than the people would prefer. Leaders of cultural associations are in part responsible for this.

✦ TYPES OF INTEREST GROUPS

Three major types of interest groups are **sectoral** interest groups, **institutional** interest groups, and **promotional** interest groups:

1. Sectoral Groups. Sectoral groups are those that represent a sector of the economy—a corporation, a union, an association of members of a profession, or, less frequently, a consumer group. Examples would include the National Manufacturers' Association, Ford Motor Company, the National Farmers' Union, the AFL-CIO, and the American Automobile Association. Since these are groups associated with the economy, they often combine great financial resources with fairly narrow concerns. An industrial organization might find, for instance, that the issue making the greatest difference to its members' earnings is an obscure and highly technical rule about depreciation rates, a rule that falls below most other groups' radar. And with its resources, the organization can vigorously pursue changing that rule. Needless to say, sectoral groups are usually effective. They also dominate most interest-group systems. We saw in Table 12.1 that 65 percent of Germany's interest groups are "economic" (sectoral).

2. Institutional Groups. Institutional groups are set up primarily for purposes other than political activity and would certainly exist even if they did not deal with politics; they become politically active only to defend their own interests in the state's policy decisions.

---

[7]In 2004, the Israeli government transferred El Al to private owners—in part to get it out of politics and to allow it to stop losing money because of shutting down for one day each week. In 2006 the airline did begin to schedule Sabbath flights, but after a boycott by ultra-orthodox Israelis, the airline backed down and promised not to fly on the Sabbath.

Jeff MacNelly. Tribune Media Services. Reprinted with permission.

Examples of this sort of group would include an army, set up to defend the state, that may become active—even dominant—in the politics of the state to help the defense budget and further the common interests of its members; a public university, set up to educate students and conduct research, that may hire lobbyists to procure a larger annual budget from the government; the Red Cross, set up to help people in emergencies, that may become actively engaged in lobbying for national emergency help grants; and so on.

3. Promotional Groups. Promotional groups organize around an idea or a point of view—to support an ethnic group (the National Association for the Advancement of Colored People), a foreign policy position (Women Against Military Madness), religious values (the Christian Coalition), a position on the environment (National Audubon Society), a recreational activity (National Rifle Association), or whatever. These are the groups we commonly think of first when we hear the words "interest group."

　　Around the world, promotional interest groups have increased in recent decades. We noted in connection with Table 12.1 that the fastest-growing categories of interest groups in Germany from 1974 to 1994 were the cultural, recreational, and environmental groups. In Britain, the Royal Society for the Protection of Birds has more members than the three major political parties combined and increased in size by 1,300 percent between 1971 and 1998.[8] Amnesty International, an organization that campaigns against political oppression, has 195,000 members.[9] Fathers4Justice, a deliberately disruptive "guerrilla" interest group promoting fathers' rights (in 2004 they pelted the prime minister with purple flour bombs), has 6,500 members.

---

[8]"A Nation of Groupies," *The Economist,* 13 August 1994, pp. 49–51.
[9]195,000 members in Britain; worldwide, Amnesty International has approximately 1.8 million members.

Promotional interest groups appear to be especially important in the politics of the United States, compared with most other states of the world. This is probably because (1) United States parties are weaker and less unified on policy than most other states' parties and thus are not well equipped to lead in a debate over ideas; and (2) the two-party system does not provide room for small, specialized parties such as Israel's religious parties, able to directly seek a portion of the governmental power through participation in coalitions. Instead, those seeking to pursue an ideological goal in the United States must usually operate indirectly through an interest group to *influence* those who have attained power.

In contrast to the promotional groups, sectoral groups probably vary less in their role from one state to another. The economy is such a central part of any modern society that sectoral interest groups have a natural entrée to government everywhere. Therefore, their presence and their activities are probably less variable than is true of promotional interest groups. Some states such as the United States and Sweden have active feminist groups, for instance—although in Sweden, this interest is channeled somewhat more through political parties—while in others such as Japan, there is almost no feminist presence. Nearly every state, however, has a politically active manufacturers' association.

✦ TACTICS OF INTEREST GROUPS

The tactics an interest group will use are determined by the sources of its power and by the opportunities that the political system offers for the use of power. An interest group with many members but little money will concentrate on tactics that take advantage of numbers rather than money, while a group with few members but plenty of money will follow different tactics. Groups that have similar sources of power but find themselves faced with different sorts of political structures may also be expected to follow different tactics. In their political activity, U.S. labor unions, for instance, emphasize electoral activity and campaign contributions to public officials. For Solidarity, the labor union that transformed the politics of Poland in the 1970s and 1980s in spite of suppression by the communist government, these focuses of political activity were not available, and so it concentrated instead on sit-ins and mass demonstrations.

Let us look specifically at several tactics available to interest groups in a democracy. What leads a group to choose one or more of these?

1. **Control of Information and Expertise.** Sometimes the members of an interest group control specialized information that is important to the government—information that may even be required if the group is to be controlled by the government. Doctors, for example, are the only people with the necessary expertise to judge the quality of medical treatment. Scientists are the only ones sufficiently skilled technically to judge a variety of scientific questions. Oil corporations know more about the oil business than anyone else. In all these cases, a government that wishes to make policy relating to an interest group must depend on the members of the group for the necessary information and expertise. This gives the group a great deal of power, because the resulting interpretation of things is likely to be slanted a good deal toward the group's prejudices. It does not require that anyone operate dishonestly. Everyone always has a certain slant on

things, and if the members of an interest group are the only ones giving the government analysis and interpretation, their slant is inevitably going to enter in.

This tactic requires that relevant information and technical skills be scarce. Labor unions, religious groups, or hobby organizations cannot make good use of the tactic, because the skills and information they have are widely available. A dramatic example of power based on the control of information appeared in lawsuits and investigations in 2006, where it was revealed that the United States Department of the Interior had no independent source of information on how much oil companies were drilling on public lands. It had to rely on the companies to tell the government how much drilling was going on.

2. Electoral Activity. Electoral activity is especially suitable for groups with a large number of members who are at least moderately committed. Such a group may raise money from among its members to contribute to candidates, provide campaign workers to candidates, and deliver its own members' votes for candidates—all in an effort to ensure that people favorably disposed to the group end up in office. If the members of the group are not sufficiently committed to it to choose their vote on the basis of its recommendations, this tactic is of little use; an automobile club, for instance, would not be able to deliver its members' votes. Groups that have used this tactic successfully include labor unions, large religious organizations, and ethnic groups. Some other special organizations such as the National Rifle Association in the United States or the wine growers of France have also been successful in this way.

3. Use of Economic Power. An interest group of economic importance to the state may influence the state by threatening to disrupt its economic contribution. Strategically placed unions, such as those of railroad or postal workers, have often been able to enlist the government's help by threatening a strike that would be catastrophically disruptive to the state. At some times, as in France in 1968 or Germany in the 1920s, a *general strike* in which all unions stop working at the same time has been used to try to force an unpopular government out of office. Businesses often threaten communities by telling them that if they don't give them tax advantages or other considerations, they will move their operations elsewhere. Professional sports franchises have been particularly skillful at this kind of threat, forcing communities to provide them with subsidies and build stadiums to house them. The civil rights movement of the 1960s in the United States gained great impetus when an unknown preacher named Martin Luther King, Jr. organized a boycott of the city bus system of Montgomery, Alabama, to force the city to allow blacks to sit anywhere they wished on the buses. Similarly, economic boycotts of white businesses were an effective tool for blacks in South Africa in the late 1980s.

This tactic requires that a large economic stake be maneuverable. That is, the group must be able to turn on or turn off a large enough part of the economy to threaten dire results. This can be accomplished either by a single large corporation, for which it is usually fairly easy, or by a large number of people who, though they are not individually that important to the economy, are willing to coordinate economic disruption (a strike or boycott) so that their combined impact is important. Mass action like this is usually difficult to accomplish, because it requires a large number of people to make an economic sacrifice by stopping work, finding an alternative to riding buses, or whatever. It requires a large and unusually devoted membership.

4. Campaign Contributions. Another, considerably cheaper, way in which economic power can be used is in contributions to political candidates. Here the group's economic strength is not used to produce the threat of disruption but rather to buy access to political leaders, and it is sometimes astonishing how cheaply influence can be bought in this way. Contributions in the hundred thousands of dollars may net a corporation or trade group a special provision in a bill that is worth many millions of dollars to it. Ballooning expenditures on political campaigns in the United States have made political leaders more dependent on interests that can provide money. Around the world, states vary considerably with regard to the importance of interest groups' money for campaigns, depending on election laws and on custom. In most European states, campaign expenditures are regulated and do not bulk as large as they do in the United States. Japan, on the other hand, is another state where the appetite of parties for campaign finance is insatiable.

5. Public Information Campaigns. A group that does not necessarily have a large mass base but does have substantial access to the media may try to change policy by the most indirect of means—by changing the minds of the entire population in the hope that this will influence government policy. Institutional interest groups frequently use this tactic, because many other tactics are barred to them. The U.S. Air Force helps to encourage movies that put the Air Force in a good light. Government agencies in all states use "public service advertisements"—giving health advice, moral admonition, and so on—to keep themselves in the public eye while they also accomplish indirectly a secondary goal of the advertisements: to build public support for the agency.

This tactic is also useful for an interest with enough money to buy advertising time, especially if other tactics do not look promising. In the 1970s, American corporations were faced with a new environmental movement that was difficult to combat. How could a group argue effectively for dirty air? An expensive and skillfully executed ad campaign on the theme "businesses don't cause pollution, people cause pollution" helped them to shift the terms of national debate.

In the United States in the 1990s, this technique was further refined as interest groups learned to target public opinion in the districts of members of Congress who were seen as swing votes on important bills. In 1997, for instance, labor unions targeted about thirty congressional districts with television ads against expanding free trade when Congress was considering legislation to give the president special negotiating powers to arrange lower trade barriers between the United States and other countries. In the same year, a consortium of businesses opposed to an international pact to limit the emission of greenhouse gases conducted a widespread television ad campaign against the proposed Global Warming Treaty.

6. Violence and Disruption. An interest group may also try to dramatize its case by violent or disruptive activity, or it may try by violence and disruption to convince the leaders of the state that they will pay a high price in turmoil by not yielding to the group's demands. Disruptive but nonviolent protest may be an effective way for an interest group to bring attention to its cause, especially if it has few resources other than a dedicated mass following.

Violent terrorism has grave drawbacks as a technique, since it is likely to cost the terrorist group what public sympathy it has and to call forth strenuous efforts at control by the authorities. However, it may work well when one region is united in its opposition to the rest of a state and wishes to separate from it or at least to change its legal relationship to the government. A separatist group under these conditions can launch violent attacks on the rest of the state without losing the sympathy of the only "public" that counts for them, the people in their part of the state. The violence is likely to bring down harsher regulation and police activity in their region, which will serve to further strengthen local support for the separatist cause. Many separatist movements—the Irish Republican Army in Britain, the Basque separatists in Spain, Moslem separatists in the Philippines—have used this tactic with success. By the same logic, international terrorist groups like al Quaeda, who attack people of other nationalities or religion on behalf of their own group, may find a sympathetic home among their own people, whom they do *not* attack. (For more on terrorism, see below, pp. 415–417.)

7. **Litigation.** In litigation an interest group attempts to affect policy by working within the court system. The historic reversal of segregated schooling in the United States was begun in this way when, in 1954, the National Association for the Advancement of Colored People (NAACP) sponsored a constitutional test of segregation in the courts. A black student, with the help of the NAACP, sued her school board to force it to admit her to the white school, and she won.

Through court cases, an interest group may hope to change the interpretation of a law or, in some countries, even get it thrown out as unconstitutional. Also, court procedures can be so slow and expensive that the mere threat of tying a governmental agency up in court may get the agency to compromise.

However, litigation is a strategy based on weakness. For a group to be successful at litigation, it must depend on the way the law was initially written—something over which it has little control if litigation is its main tactic. It must depend on finding a sympathetic court, which is also rather chancy. The great appeal of litigation is that it does not require large numbers (all one has to have is a lawyer) or enormous economic power. Therefore, it appeals particularly to small weak groups. Groups that have depended fairly heavily on litigation in the United States include environmentalists, the handicapped, and groups favoring abortion rights. These are relatively weak groups that have usually been on the defensive.[10]

The history of the civil rights movement in the United States provides varied examples of how circumstances determine strategy. In the 1940s and 1950s, the movement for civil rights for blacks was relatively weak. The majority of blacks were still barred from voting in the South; blacks were poor and did not have a great deal of money to contribute; and the movement did not have many white allies, either in public office or outside it. The chief civil rights organization at this time was the NAACP, and its chief tactic was litigation. It achieved several important successes in court, among other things overturning segregated schooling in the South and outlawing the exclusion of black voters from primary elections.

---

[10]See, for example, Susan M. Olson, *Clients and Lawyers: Securing the Rights of Disabled Persons* (Westport, CT: Greenwood Press, 1984). In 1989, the abortion rights movement strengthened a good deal in a popular reaction to an unfavorable court decision, and with its increased strength, it began to shift its attention from litigation to electoral activity.

With the increase in support for civil rights in the 1960s and partly as a result of these successes, more money and resources became available to the movement. Blacks had become bolder politically; many more were willing to march in demonstrations to help draw attention to their cause, and they began to acquire significant white allies. At this time, new, rival organizations using different tactics appeared. The Congress on Racial Equality (CORE) and Martin Luther King, Jr.'s Southern Christian Leadership Conference (SCLC) were two new organizations that emphasized, as ways of attracting sympathy and forcing segregationists to yield, the use of economic power and the provocation of segregationists into violence. (Note the clever twist on the use of violence as a tactic—here white officials were goaded into violence so that they would lose public sympathy.) Massive demonstrations were held, requiring large numbers of dedicated black and white participants. Violence of their own was never a part of these leaders' strategy; but the provocation of white violence was useful, and the black urban riots of 1965–68, which occurred spontaneously, were used by civil rights leaders as evidence for their claims that blacks had to be treated more fairly.

At this time, electoral activity was not especially emphasized because, first, during the 1960s many southern blacks could not vote or were just acquiring the vote and, second, demonstrations and disruption were proving to be such powerful tools. By the 1970s and 1980s, however, demonstrations began to be less effective. The public was more used to them and therefore less impressed by them, and police and public officials had learned not to respond in the picturesquely violent ways that demonstrators had once counted on. At the same time, the electoral importance of blacks had grown. The black percentage of the electorate in many northern cities had reached a point at which blacks could often determine the outcome of mayoral and other elections. In the South, thanks to the gains of the 1960s, most blacks were free to vote and could determine many elections. In the 1970s and 1980s, accordingly, the activity of black civil rights groups shifted to emphasize more their importance in elections.

We can see in this evolution of the tactics of the civil rights movement a good illustration of our general principle that interest groups will pick those tactics that best fit the group's resources and the political opportunities offered by those resources.

✦ PATTERNS OF ORGANIZED INTEREST-GROUP ACTIVITY

In all of our discussions of interest groups, we have talked about them primarily from the point of view of the individual group. However, we must also look at the pattern of all group activity in a state. In looking at political parties, we found that the overall pattern formed by the system of parties was important to the state's politics; similarly, we will see that the overall pattern of interest-group activity is also important. Interest-group systems vary in (at least) two important ways.

1. Degree of Organization. In some countries, people are heavily organized by groups; in others, they are not heavily organized at all. Most states of the Third World are only weakly organized. Institutional interest groups such as the church and the army bulk much larger in the politics of these states than they would otherwise, because interest groups of other sorts are weak.

Among industrialized states, there is also a good deal of variation. In authoritarian states such as China, the formation of groups is suppressed, and here again institutional interest groups gain in importance by default. Even among open societies, there is a good deal of variation. The Scandinavian countries are probably more thoroughly organized than any others in the world. For example, 88 percent of Danish workers are members of trade unions, compared with 29 percent for Great Britain and 13 percent for the United States.[11] The percentage of people belonging to political organizations is about twice as high in Norway as in the United States.[12]

2. Degree of Direct, Formal Involvement of Interest Groups in Government and Administration. We saw earlier in this chapter that government officials must often depend on interest groups for information and expertise. The way in which governments may tap into this varies from casual arrangements, in which officials occasionally call up interest-group representatives or look up a figure in the group's publication, to quite formal arrangements in which interest-group representatives may sit by right on administrative committees of the government. Under the latter arrangement, which is fairly common in northern Europe, it may be hard to draw the line between interest groups and government.

Two important types of interest-group systems can be identified by variations on these two dimensions. These are *pluralism* and *neocorporatism*. They are important concepts for understanding how interest groups operate in democratic systems.[13]

➔ PLURALISM

Pluralism is an idealized system in which all interests organize and compete freely and no one group is able to dominate. The government is open to pressure from the interest groups, and politics consists largely of the competition among these interest groups to see that the policies they favor are adopted by the government.[14] In terms of our two dimensions listed in the section on "Patterns of Organized Interest-Group Activity," the ideal of pluralism is high on the scale of "organization" and low on "direct involvement of interest groups in government"; that is, interest groups are well organized but are quite distinct from the government. There is, however, no state that is truly "pluralist"; the term is an abstraction. The United States approaches the type more closely than most and is often used as a chief example of pluralism at work, but even the United States falls far short of the full organization of all groups that is envisioned in pluralism.

Those who favor a pluralist system of politics point out that with numerous groups operating, there is a good deal of spontaneity. It is relatively easy for new ideas

---

[11]European Foundation for the Improvement of Living and Working Conditions. *Industrial Relations in the EU, Japan, and USA, 2003–2004,* **www.eurofound.eu.int/publications.publications.htm,** 2004, Figure 1.

[12]Robert B. Kvavik, *Interest Groups in Norwegian Politics* (Oslo: Universitetsforlaget, 1976), p. 46; a dated source, but the difference is probably about the same today.

[13]Here, as in our discussion of interest-group tactics in this chapter, we will focus attention on democracies.

[14]The chief source is David Truman, *The Governmental Process* (New York: Knopf, 1951). See also "Pluralism" in *The International Encyclopedia of the Social Sciences.*

to appear from the grass roots, and there is a good deal of flexibility. Furthermore, because the government is simultaneously influenced by many competing groups, negotiation and compromise should be the order of the day. Politics should typically be pragmatic and nonradical.

Pluralist writers see pluralism as an ideal way to reach the common ground of society. The various interests in society pull in their varying directions, and the government responds to their pressure by ending up at a kind of equilibrium point where the pressures balance. With a minimum of distortion, the most desired mix of policy is reached.

However, in any real state—as distinct from the idealized abstraction—the set of interest groups cannot represent the people of the state very well, because not all interests are equally able to "organize and compete freely." This was discussed at the beginning of this chapter in the section "Interest Groups and Representation." Therefore a pluralist system might have the advantages cited by those who favor it, yet it would still have serious drawbacks because policies based on "pluralist" deliberations could be expected to slant systematically in favor of those groups that can operate effectively and against those that cannot.

✦ NEOCORPORATISM

Neocorporatism is another abstraction. It takes its name from a system popular in the early twentieth century called *corporatism,* in which instead of individuals being represented by right of being citizens, as in liberal democracy, *functions* of society were to be represented in governmental decisions. The basis of corporatism was the idea that the various functional parts of society (business, labor, agriculture, universities, etc.) were all vital and must be taken into account, much like the parts of the body (hence the word's root in *corpus,* Latin for *body*). And like the parts of the body, the various functional units should not be in conflict with each other (how can the heart fight the liver, for instance?). This notion of representation came up in various settings at that time, including the left wing of the Labour Party in Britain, but was most noteworthy in its adoption by Mussolini's fascist dictatorship in Italy. The latter, of course, left it with a strong and unpleasant odor. Neocorporatism consists of corporatist-like practices that have appeared in a number of countries since the fall of Mussolini: they have often arisen more or less spontaneously in well-established democracies like Sweden, but in their non-democratic form, they have also sometimes been imposed from above, as in Brazil's military dictatorship in the 1970s.

It is a system in which all interests are organized and the government deals directly with all affected interests at all stages in the making and administration of policy. Unlike pluralism, under neocorporatism the government does not merely respond to the interest groups' pressure but actively involves the groups in the job of governing.[15] In terms of our two dimensions listed in the "Patterns of Organized Interest-Group Activity" section, neocorporatism is high on the scales of "organization" and "direct involvement of interest groups." And it is higher than pluralism on the "organization"

---

[15]A good presentation of the model is Martin O. Heisler and Robert B. Kvavik, "Patterns of European Politics: The 'European Polity' Model," in Martin O. Heisler, ed., *Politics in Europe* (New York: David McKay, 1974), pp. 27–90.

scale; the practice of involving interest groups in government generally stimulates an especially high degree of participation in interest groups, just because the stakes of interest group activity become higher.

Not only does the government draw interest groups into the governmental process in neocorporatism, but parts of the government may also act rather like interest groups. This is not so much a matter of "institutional interest groups" lobbying for their own perquisites and budgets as it is active engagement in political debate on behalf of certain policies: Parts of the bureaucratic apparatus may take on a greater role of representing popular constituencies and initiating policy demands than is common under pluralism. They are in effect "self-starters" who try to mobilize popular support for their positions. An example is the founding of the European Common Market in 1956; the campaign for unification was spearheaded not by party leaders but by civil servants. From both sides, then, the boundary between government and interest groups becomes fuzzier in a neocorporatist system.

Unlike what we saw in the case of pluralism, some states do follow the neocorporatist model fairly closely. This is especially true of the Scandinavian countries. For instance, in Denmark:

- The government is constitutionally required to send copies of any bill it is drafting to affected interest groups and to solicit their responses at all stages of the legislative process.

- The drafting of most bills is shaped by discussions in a special commission set up to consider the bill. Civil servants and representatives of all affected interest groups sit on such a commission.

- Once the bill is passed, its administration will often be turned over to the affected group. For instance, the government's unemployment compensation program is administered not by a governmental agency, but by the trade unions.

- Policies are set in a spirit of cooperation and compromise. There is a reluctance to push any affected group to the wall.

Those who admire neocorporatism point to the cooperative attitude brought forth by such a system. For such a system to work, there *must* be a cooperative spirit, and putting the system in place may therefore help to call forth the required cooperation.

Also, neocorporatism eases the problem of unequal organization of groups, which flaws pluralism. Groups must be well organized to take part in governing; therefore, it becomes more important that they organize their members, and they tend to do so. Indeed, the government sometimes writes a law in such a way that its administration requires the creation of a group that does not yet exist; when this situation has arisen, the government has organized the group![16]

On the other hand, the neocorporatist system is a fragile one, because it depends so much on cooperation and on everyone's willingness to avoid rocking the boat.

---

[16]This illustrates what is probably the most basic difference between the pluralist and neocorporatist models. Under pluralism, it is assumed that the state apparatus responds to the system of interest groups. Under neocorporatism, the state is taken to have a good deal of autonomy; to some extent, it creates the system of interest groups and determines how it operates.

Neocorporatism sets up an officially sanctioned set of actors in the system, each with rights to a piece of the pie; therefore, no group can go for the jugular of another without endangering the whole system.

This suggests a second important problem in neocorporatism. It defines a set of groups with claims on the state and routinizes the process by which the state consults with them. As a result, the neocorporatist system tends to petrify the existing line of conflict as of the time it was established. In effect, the government "licenses" an existing set of interest groups. We can expect that lines of conflict will change over time, as old conflicts fade and new ones arise. It is difficult for the neocorporatist system, with its intricate organizational structure of established and "entitled" interest groups, to adjust to such change. As an example of this problem, one of the more difficult challenges faced by Danish politics in the 2000s has been to find a way of providing political expression to the new concern over immigration and a multicultural society.

In this section, we have considered what one might call "cooperative" neocorporatism of the sort typified by politics in the Scandinavian states. Neocorporatism of this sort arises from the desires of the government and the interests to develop consensus and minimize conflict in policy making. Another form of neocorporatism, usually called "state neocorporatism," was found especially in Latin America (Brazil in the 1970s and Perón's Argentina in the 1950s). This system is imposed on the interests by the state to keep them under its control. Though both types of government are "corporatist" in that the government deals directly with groups, the nature of politics is very different in the two types.

→ PLURALISM AND NEOCORPORATISM: POWER AND CHOICE

Of "power and choice," pluralist writers certainly emphasize a "choice" perspective. The public choice—policy—is seen as a balanced outcome of the different pressures of organized interests, almost like a physical equilibrium, and the government is treated rather as an unexamined "black box." Power relations within the government, and especially the difference in power of various interest groups, tend to be played down in this abstraction.

One might expect that the main alternative abstraction, neocorporatism, would take an opposed side of this great divide, but oddly it, too, embodies more of a "choice" than a "power" perspective—at least in the "cooperative" form we have looked at here. (Where corporatism is analyzed as a tool by which authoritarian governments construct their control of society, the emphasis is more on a "power" perspective.) In its "cooperative" form, neocorporatism is seen as a system in which, as in pluralism, the interests of society in a rather natural way come together to produce their most-preferred mix of policies. The main difference between the two abstractions is in the role accorded government in the process: Under pluralism, the government is a passive receiver of pressures from interests; under neocorporatism, it is seen as a stimulator and shaper of those pressures, and the government blends with the system of interest groups. In both abstractions, the production of policy is portrayed as the natural outcome of a process designed to produce public choices. An interesting exercise would be to design an alternative abstraction of interest-group activities in democracies that is based more on a "power" perspective.

✵ EXAMPLE

Interest Groups in France

France has a system that probably falls somewhere between the pluralist and neocorporatist models of politics. It also shows interesting peculiarities of its own, especially in a certain looseness and unpredictability of structure. French interest groups are rather fragmented, and compared with groups in other states, they are relatively more likely to engage in provocative violence.

These characteristics are often attributed to two aspects of French political culture: (1) the French tradition of a strong state, relating directly to the population, which leads to disdain and disapproval of intermediary organizations such as interest groups; and (2) a second French tradition that romanticizes direct political action, "taking politics to the streets."[17]

French interest groups have fairly low enrollments from their potential members. Labor unions enroll only 8 percent of their potential membership, and other sorts of groups have similarly low enrollments.

Furthermore, the organized groups are deeply divided. Frequently, several different organizations compete for the same membership, which in other countries would be united behind a single organization. Workers, for instance, are organized in five major, separate unions: the CGT (a communist union with 38 percent of the total union strength), the CFDT (an independent-minded, socialist union with 28 percent), Force Ouvrier (a reformist union independent of parties with 16 percent), the CGC (a union of managers, engineers, and technicians with 7 percent), and the Catholic Confederation (with 7 percent); independent unions account for the rest.[18]

Promotional interest groups, such as environmental groups, veterans' groups, and feminist groups, are mostly local in their organization rather than national, which means that there are thousands of them, but that they have little clout in national politics.

French politics at all levels is punctuated by sporadic, intense activity against a background of cynical disengagement, and this holds as true of interest groups as it does of other aspects of politics. In fact, the line between interest groups and social movements is even harder to draw in France than in other countries (see "social movements," Chapter 13.) The weakly organized interest groups of France flare up from time to time into what really should be thought of as social movements. This is most notable in the periodic national crises that engulf France. One of these occurred in May 1968, when a dispute between the students and administration of a provincial university flared up into a national confrontation between students on the one hand and administrators and police on the other. More normally, large street demonstrations (and occasionally more dramatic barricades, etc.) are a not uncommon tactic of many groups, including unions, farmers' organizations, and public employees.

In their relations with the government, French interest groups are in some instances bound to the government by formal ties of intimacy of the sort we associate with neocorporatism. More often, interest groups and government maintain the sort of distance we expect under pluralism. The agricultural sector comes closest to the neocorporatist model. Not all agricultural interest

---

[17]Andrew Appleton, "France: Party-Group Relations in the Shadow of the State," in Clive S. Thomas, ed., *Political Parties & Interest Groups* (Boulder, CO: Lynne Reinner, 2001), p. 48.
[18]Ministry of the Economy, INSEE, *Annuaire Statistique de la France,* 2005, p. 115.

groups are tied intimately to the government, but one group, the Federation Nationale des Syndicats d'Exploitants Agricoles (FNSEA), has become something like the "official" agricultural group for the government. The FNSEA dominates French agricultural politics, and performs a number of administrative duties, including most of the educational and training tasks carried out in other countries by agricultural extension agents. In most areas, the government recognizes the FNSEA as the coordinating representative of farming interests.[19] The presence of strong representation for agriculture in an otherwise often fragmented interest-group system is reflected in a history of very strong programs of price supports and subsidies for farmers.

Like everything else in French politics, the activities of interest groups have been hugely reshaped by the growing importance of the policies of the European Union. Interest groups have responded to this in two ways: by establishing lobbying activities directly at the EU Commission in Brussels, and by lobbying the French government to protect their interests in EU decisions. Sectoral groups have actually been rather slow to respond to the growth of EU policy making and have reacted to it for the most part defensively. Promotional interest groups, however, have found that the EU offers them new and better opportunities than they have formerly found at home. After being routinely brushed aside in Paris, groups such as antihunting organizations have found that they can combine with similarly minded groups from other EU member states to accomplish much of what they want through Union policies.[20]

✳ EXAMPLE

Interest Groups in Japan: Attenuated Neocorporatism

The Japanese system of interest groups is a strongly neocorporatist system. However, it is one that is sharply attenuated, by European standards; labor does not play the important role in the system that we usually see in neocorporatism, and many noneconomic groups that we often see in Europe and North America are missing.

The bureaucracy is the key to the Japanese system. The higher civil service in Japan is an elite that is almost autonomous in making policy. It is a well-respected elite, drawing the best university graduates and trading on the general public scorn for politicians to maintain its independence. Until the early 1990s, the Japanese system was a three-way arrangement among the bureaucracy, big business interest groups, and the Liberal Democratic Party (LDP). Agricultural groups, critical to maintaining the LDP in power, played a supporting role in return for subsidies and agricultural trade protection. Business interests gave the LDP the huge amounts of money on which Japanese electoral politics was based ($2.6 billion in 1989), and the LDP cooperated as the bureaucracy and the business interests set up most public policies.[21]

---

[19]Adam D. Sheingate, *The Rise of the Agricultural Welfare State: Institutions and Interest Group Power in the United States, France, and Japan* (Princeton: Princeton University Press, 2001), pp. 192–93. For a dissenting view, see Pepper D. Culpepper, "Organizational Competition and the Neo-Corporatist Fallacy in French Agriculture," *West European Politics* 16 (July 1993), pp. 295–315.

[20]Emiliano Grossman and Sabine Saurugger, "Challenging French Interest Groups: The State, Europe and the International Political System," *French Politics* 2 (2004), p. 205.

[21]Ronald J. Hrebenar, "Japan: Strong State, Spectator Democracy, and Modified Corporatism," in Clive S. Thomas, *Political Parties & Interest Groups* (Boulder, CO: Lynne Rienner, 2001), p. 169.

The LDP was the dominant party in a "dominant party system" (see pages 267–270), and it remains clearly the leading party of Japan. Since 1993, however, its dominant position has been challenged. Public disgust with the system of corruption and "big-money politics" has led to the rise of reform movements, and voters have proved willing to consider alternatives to the LDP, so the party corner of the LDP-business-bureaucracy triangle is undergoing change. The role of the bureaucracy appears unchanged, however, and may be strengthened because no clear party leadership has yet emerged to take the place of the weakened LDP hegemony. Interest groups and the bureaucracy mingle closely. As is so often the case in neocorporatist systems, government advisory committees heavily weighted to the bureaucracy and interest groups are important in policy making. Bureaucrats often take high-level positions in the interest groups when they retire from the civil service.

One reason for the dominance of economic interest groups in Japan (at least business groups and agriculture) is that paradoxically, although Japanese society is oriented to social groups—one's family or factory or association demands intense loyalty and support—the Japanese are rather apathetic about politics and groups formed around political issues. There are few environmental or consumer-oriented groups in Japan, and there is essentially no feminist movement. There are rather important ideological groups on the right, which are anti-labor, honor the emperor, and refuse to apologize for Japan's role in World War II. As of late 1988, it was estimated that these groups had over 125,000 members.[22] The Left is not as well organized; it is represented primarily by the National Teacher's Union, which is aggressively of the Left.

So economic groups fill most of the political space: business groups, agricultural groups, and labor. Of these, only the first two figure importantly; labor is almost excluded from the political process.

There are a large number of business groups in Japan, but one group, the Japanese Federation of Economic Organizations, is accepted as speaking on behalf of "business." It represents primarily large businesses; its members make up only 1 percent of Japanese firms but account for 40 percent of sales.[23] In addition, there are many trade organizations, often for quite specific activities, such as an association for manufacturers of tea services or an association of manufacturers of pens. Beyond these organizations, much business policy is made by a business leader directly approaching a bureaucrat.

Agriculture's peak organizations are based on the agricultural cooperatives. These are organizations of farmers that have the right to be the sole marketers of rice; they also distribute some services on behalf of the government. As a result, farmers have little choice but to be members of their cooperative; Japanese society is so group-oriented, however, that this does not appear to be viewed as an imposition. The cooperatives have about 8 million members, but their political power is greater even than this would suggest, due to their close ties to the LDP. The farmers have also proved to be politically flexible. In 1989, for instance, they shifted many of their members' votes to the Socialist Party to punish the LDP for being too open to free trade; this was a major reason for the LDP's loss of the upper house of parliament in that year, and it demonstrated to everyone that the agricultural cooperatives could not be taken for granted. As a result of their power, Japanese farmers are among the most highly subsidized in the world. In 1997 "producer subsidy equivalents," or PSEs (a measure used to sum up all government support for agriculture) equaled nearly 70 percent of Japanese agricultural production; by way of comparison, PSEs in the European Union equaled between 40 and 50 percent of production in that year, in Canada they equaled 20 percent, and in the United States they equaled 16 percent.[24]

---

[22]Ibid., p. 161.
[23]Ibid., p. 159.
[24]Adam D. Sheingate, *The Rise of the Agricultural Welfare State: Institutions and Interest Group Power in the United States, France, and Japan* (Princeton: Princeton University Press, 2001), p. 236.

The power of the agricultural groups is also one of the main reasons for Japanese-American tensions over trade; political leaders are reluctant to open up the Japanese market to American agriculture products.

T. J. Pempel has dubbed the Japanese system "corporatism without labor."[25] Most Japanese workers are organized in company unions, not industrywide unions, and these organizations tend to be less politically active and more compliant and to look to their companies' interests. The main exceptions are the public employees' unions, such as the National Teachers' Union. These unions have been marginalized in Japan's generally conservative society because they are quite far to the left on almost all issues. Labor is also split into two main organizations, one based on company unions and the other based on the public employees' unions. As a result, political leadership in Japan has been able to safely ignore labor on most issues.

Change is in the wind in Japan, however. Scandals have publicized the reliance of parties, especially the LDP, on large illegal contributions of cash. (One scandal involved a bribe so large that the firm's secretary had to use a supermarket cart to carry the cash across a parking lot.) The electoral system was changed in 1996, and public financing of campaigns was instituted; reformers claim that the changes are altering the system of campaign finance. The two labor organizations have made fitful attempts to combine in a cooperative political movement. And finally, the Finance Ministry—the most powerful of the powerful bureaucracies—lost a great deal of its prestige during the long-lasting economic crisis of the 1990s. So this is probably a system in transition. On the other hand, the Japanese culture still reveres scholarly "nonpolitical" authority such as that of the bureaucrats. And Japan still sees much of its postwar prosperity as having been accomplished by an alliance between government and business.

In the clearest indication that Japan might indeed be entering a period of reform after several years of economic and national disappointment, Junichiro Koizumi, a maverick politician, won the leadership of the LDP in 2001, which automatically also made him the prime minister. He was not really the old politicos' choice, but they were desperate. Shortly thereafter, the electorate gave him a mandate for change by giving the LDP a majority in the upper house, something that would never have happened without him.

Koizumi used this power to push through a number of reforms. He took out of governmental control the state-owned bank and life insurance company, for instance, privatizing $3 trillion in assets, and broke up the post office's $13 trillion "pork barrel fund." To force this last reform through, he had a number of LDP members of the Diet thrown out of the party.

Koizumi's flamboyant style and tough leadership sat well with Japanese voters, who supported him consistently while he was in office. However, he has been succeeded by an old-school LDP politician, Shinzo Abe. Abe has signaled that he will carry on Koizumi's foreign policy (aggressive support for the United States, and push-back for China), but not his domestic agenda of reform. Among other things, Abe has readmitted eleven of the LDP Diet members whom Koizumi had kicked out of the party.

What remains to be seen is whether Koizumi was a one-shot phenomenon, or whether the changes in the electoral system, together with Koizumi's demonstration that the electorate will welcome tough reform, have put Japan on a new and different trajectory, no matter what Abe might want to do. Most analysts are betting on the new and different trajectory.

---

[25]T. J. Pempel and Keiichi Tsunekawa, "Corporatism Without Labor? The Japanese Anomaly," in Philippe Schmitter and Gerhard Lehmbruch, eds., *Trends Toward Corporatist Intermediation* (Beverly Hills, CA: Sage, 1979).

KEY TERMS

interest group

selective incentive

sectoral interest group

institutional interest group

promotional interest group

pluralism

neocorporatism

FURTHER READING

Baumgartner, Frank, and Leech, Beth. *Basic Interests: The Importance of Groups in Politics and Political Science.* Princeton: Princeton University Press, 1998.

Berry, Jeffrey M., and Wilcox, Clyde. *The Interest Group Society.* 4th ed. New York: Longman, 2007.

Christiansen, Peter Mark, and Rommetvedt, Hilmar. "From Corporatism to Lobbyism? Parliaments, Executives, and Organized Interests in Denmark and Norway." *Scandinavian Political Studies* 22 (1999), pp. 195–220.

Gerber, Elisabeth R. *The Populist Paradox: Interest Group Influence and the Promise of Direct Legislation.* Princeton: Princeton University Press, 1999.

Greenwood, Justin. *Interest Representation in the European Union.* New York: Palgrave Macmillan, 2003.

Horowitz, Donald L. *Ethnic Groups in Conflict.* Berkeley: University of California Press, 1985.

Lehmbruch, Gerhard, and Schmitter, Philippe C., eds. *Patterns of Corporatist Policy-Making.* Beverly Hills, CA: Sage, 1982.

Loomis, Burdett A., and Cigler, Allan J., eds. *Interest Group Politics.* 7th ed. Washington, DC: Congressional Quarterly, 2006.

Moe, Terry. *The Organization of Interests.* Chicago: University of Chicago Press, 1980.

Norton, Philip, ed. *Parliaments and Pressure Groups in Western Europe.* London: Frank Cass, 1999.

Olson, Mancur. *The Logic of Collective Action.* Cambridge: Harvard University Press, 1965.

Ramseyer, J. Mark, and Rosenbluth, Frances. *Japan's Political Marketplace.* Cambridge: Harvard University Press, 1993.

Sheingate, Adam. *The Rise of the Agricultural Welfare State: Institutions and Interest Group Power in the United States, France, and Japan.* Princeton: Princeton University Press, 2001.

Siaroff, Alan. "Corporatism in 24 Industrial Democracies: Meaning and Measurement." *European Journal of Political Research* 36 (1999), pp. 175–205.

Skocpol, Theda, Lizos, Ariane, and Ganz, Marshall. *What a Mighty Power We Can Be: African American Fraternal Groups and the Struggle for Racial Equality.* Princeton, NJ: Princeton University Press, 2006.

Thomas, Clive S., ed. *Political Parties and Interest Groups.* Boulder, CO: Lynn Rienner, 2001.

Wilson, James Q. *Political Organizations.* New York: Basic Books, 1973.

WEB SITES OF INTEREST

Emily's List (organization endorsing women candidates, mostly Democrats, for office):

http://www.emilyslist.org

National Right to Life:

http://www.nrlc.org

Planned Parenthood:

http://www.plannedparenthood.org

National Rifle Association:

http://www.nra.org

Environmental Defense Fund:

http://www.environmentaldefense.org

U.S. Chamber of Commerce, interest group for industry:

http://www.uschamber.com/

AFL-CIO, interest group for labor:

http://www.aflcio.org/

Children's Defense Fund, an interest group for children's issue advocacy:

http://www.childrensdefense.org/

Christian Coalition:

http://www.cc.org/

European Foundation for the Improvement of Living and Working Conditions, with information on European trade unions and labor relations:

http://www.eurofound.europa.eu/

CHAPTER 13

❧

SOCIAL MOVEMENTS AND CONTENTIOUS POLITICS

The last two chapters dealt with formally organized, institutionalized ways that citizens and interests enter into the political process: political parties and interest groups. But, there has always been a more flexible, less formal way that broad groups of citizens have engaged in politics. "Grass roots," often ephemeral organization of people has taken many forms, from sudden riots, to petition drives, to well developed but still fairly informal organizations that have persisted for as long as a few decades. Such efforts have often had major political impacts. In England in the eighteenth century an underground pro-democracy movement gathered millions of signatures in just a few months on a petition urging the king to establish a democratic constitution; the effort failed at the time, but as is often the case, its goal was realized a century later. When the Jewish foreign minister of Germany, Walter Rathenau, was assassinated in 1922, over a million Berliners took to the streets within hours in a demonstration supporting the new democratic government. India achieved independence of Britain in 1947 through the efforts of Mahatma Gandhi's massive civil disobedience movement, in which millions of Indians passively disobeyed the British administration. The civil rights movement of the 1960s in the United States was pursued partly by established interest groups like the NAACP, but much more by informal organizations like Martin Luther King's boycott of the Montgomery, Alabama bus system. Much of the Islamic fundamentalist presence in countries of the Mideast, Africa, and Asia is based on loosely organized movements following various religious leaders. In 2003, massive protests against a proposed natural gas pipeline (and implicitly, against globalization) forced the president of Bolivia to resign. And probably the most momentous accomplishment of social movements in the last century was the Third Wave of democratization, especially in the formerly Communist states of Eastern Europe.[1]

---

[1]See Chapter 7; in Czechoslovakia, for instance, in November of 1989 hundreds of thousands of protesters gathered each Sunday in Wenceslas Square in Prague, ringing bells to call for democratic government. The demonstrations increased in size each week, culminating in a mass demonstration of 750,000 people in Letna Park on November 25 and a general strike, called on November 27. On November 29 the Communist government capitulated to the pro-democracy forces.

Demonstrators against a new pipeline for natural gas crowd the streets of La Paz, Bolivia. After weeks of such demonstrations, with eighty deaths, the president of Bolivia had to step down.

© Aizar Raldes/AFP/Getty Images

But not all such efforts have been on as large a scale as these. Often a local issue will ignite a sudden, fairly specific protest. In Minneapolis, Minnesota, for instance, an energetic movement tried in 1998 to stop the extension of Route 55 through a grove of bur oaks held to be sacred by Native Americans. In the end the movement failed, but only after it had tied up local politics (and the highway construction) for months. Its bumper stickers, "Go Oaks! Stop 55!" were everywhere.

Such informal movements are called **social movements.** They are spawned by "contentious politics"—confrontations between ordinary people and governing or economic elites. A social movement is *an informal collective movement of people, loosely coordinated in their actions and using flexible tactics, with some sort of leadership group to give its actions coherence.* A truly leaderless group, such as spontaneous looters after a storm, is not a social movement. A social movement, even though it is very informally organized, has purpose and direction; and so some sort of leadership is necessary to focus the efforts of the group.

Social movements often draw their energy from civil society, and in general, where there is a vibrant civil society, social movements are very active. You will recall from page 63 that civil society consists of all organizations that are not directly or indirectly part of the government, are not families, and are not set up for economic activity. Since social movements require a leadership catalyst and some sort of network for communication, we can readily see why abundant religious organizations, hobby groups, professional associations, and so on, could help social movements to form and operate. For instance, African-American churches were key sources of leadership and support for the civil rights movement in the United States in the 1960s.

The one major exception to this rule is that in some states where alternative organization is actively repressed, so that there is only "one game in town"—the government game—the repressed desire for an outlet for opposition to government policies can emerge in very *ad hoc* social protests, even without the help of a strong civil society. China, where the Communist Party maintains a monopoly on organized political expression, is a prime example of this; you will recall the discussion of the Chinese Communist Party and *ad hoc* rural unrest (page 272, above).

Social movements have driven more and more of politics in recent years. In the Introduction of *Power in Movement,* Sidney Tarrow takes up a single issue of the *International Herald Tribune* (March 17, 1997) and notes that the lead story covers a riot in Albania that brought down the government. He goes on:

> The same issue of the *Trib* features seven other stories relating to social movements, protests, and rebellions from around the world. Also on page 1 are a report on the armed rebellion in eastern Zaire and another on the peaceful march of Belgian, French, and Spanish workers to protest the recent closure of an auto plant in Belgium. Page 4 covers both a peaceful protest march of twenty thousand poor people in Thailand against a government development project and a violent clash between rival ethnic groups in Indonesia. Page 8 features brief reports of a gunfight between Algerian troops and the Islamic militants who have been locked in a savage civil war with the regime for the past five years, and on the Salvadoran elections, which promise to bring the Farabundo Marti National Front—a former guerrilla movement—into the government. Even the business pages cannot avoid contention: a story on page 15 describes the previous week's protest of German coal miners threatened with layoffs. One ordinary day's newspaper coverage: ten stories coming from places as different as Belgium and Borneo, indicating the continuing power of contentious politics and social movements.[2]

✦ WHY NOW?

Why have social movements blossomed in the twentieth and twenty-first centuries? They have always been around (the mobs of Rome were an important political force). But as indicated by the examination of one issue of the newspaper above, they are far more widespread and influential today than at earlier times. At least one reason for their explosive development in the last several decades may be that social movements depend heavily on rapid and easy communication—how else can one mobilize the unmobilized? Technical advances in communication have always gone hand in hand with social movement politics. The French Revolution could probably not have occurred without the invention of printing. And more recently, communist governments in the 1970s and 1980s drastically limited access to new tools of communication in a vain attempt to keep the lid on social change. In 1989, for instance, Romania's nuclear power plant had still not been allowed by the government to buy a photocopier! The twentieth century saw the greatest advances in communications in human history. At the beginning of the

---

[2]Sidney Tarrow, *Power in Movement: Social Movements and Contentious Politics,* 2d ed. (New York: Cambridge University Press, 1998), p. 1.

century people communicated by letter, by telegraph, and by newspapers; at its end, they were communicating by cell phones, faxes, email, television, and the Internet. It may be this, together with the democratic doctrine that ordinary people should share in the making of governmental policies, that has led to the explosive growth of social movements in the last decades.

Two additional possibilities are: (1) Social movements may have burgeoned because of the rise of "post-material" political issues such as the environment, women's rights, and ethnic relations that are not so easily handled by the political parties and interest-group systems that developed out of the older class and ideological conflicts associated with industrialization. Or, (2) it may also be that a general decline in the centrality of political parties to politics, as evidenced by declining memberships in parties over the last few decades and increasing volatility of party-voting by the electorate, has opened up opportunities for new, more flexible organizations.

The explanations above attempt to account for the increased presence of social movements as a whole. However, political scientists studying social movements have also developed a wide variety of more specific explanations for the rise of particular social movements. Doug McAdam, John D. McCarthy, and Mayer N. Zald group these into three types: opportunity, mobilizing structures, and framing processes.[3]

- **"Opportunity structures'"** refers to aspects of the broader political system that offer a social movement advantages, such as the presence of potential allies in the government or opposition, international organizations that are sympathetic to them, a breakdown in confidence in an incumbent leader, and so on.

- **"Mobilizing structures"** refers to the nature of the movement itself; one reason that the indigenous people's movement of Chiapas Province in Mexico has been more successful than most indigenous movements, for example, appears to be that it has some members who have been especially adept at communication in the Internet age. (The Chiapas movement—"Zapatistas"—is discussed in more detail in the next section.)

- **"Framing"** notes that in order to form a social movement a group must both feel a grievance and have some hope that by collective action they can redress the grievance. What changed between the 1950s in the United States, for example, when there was essentially no feminist movement, and the 1970s? The major change appears to have been a growing sense among many women that they shared common interests and that there was something they could do to further those interests by collective action; certainly, the opportunities in the system had not changed much, nor had the political skills and other organizational attributes of American women.

Having categorized the types of explanation, McAdam and his coauthors conclude that all three types of explanation normally are needed to account for any given social movement and how well it succeeds; the types of explanation are complementary, not competing.

---

[3]Doug McAdam, John D. McCarthy, and Mayer N. Zald, *Comparative Perspectives on Social Movements* (New York: Cambridge University Press, 1996), especially pp. 3–20.

Whatever the causes, loose and informal political movements are more and more active as we enter the twenty-first century, and have become adept at marshalling ephemeral international coalitions that are very difficult for states to deal with. From the anti-globalization movement to al Quaeda, from transnational environmental movements to local groups protesting noise from an airport, social movements are engaged in every part of international and domestic politics.

✦ SOCIAL MOVEMENTS AS A PUBLIC GOODS PROBLEM

Social movements provide an interesting example of our old friend, the problem of public goods. (See above, pp. 52–53.) Dennis Chong, in his excellent book on the United States civil rights movement, develops the concept of "public-spirited collective action": large-scale political action driven by broad public goals such as civil rights, protection of the environment, or women's rights.[4] These are all public goods, in that if they are achieved they cannot be parceled out just to some people and denied to others. Thus the dread problem of free riders appears: since all citizens will reap the fruits of the effort, whether or not they have contributed to it, why should I stick my neck out and participate?

As Chong points out, social movements enjoy some advantages in overcoming free ridership, in that the movement itself can be an enjoyable social group, with value in and of itself to the individual. Also, social movements usually involve goals that evoke strong emotions; potential supporters may well feel so strongly about the goal that they do not require much of a personal incentive to participate.

However, Chong does identify one particular factor that is critical to maintaining participation—the ultimate probability of the movement's success. If participants do not feel that they have a reasonable chance to succeed, it is hard for them to keep participating. In this case, social movements rapidly dwindle to a small, irrelevant group of demonstrators huddled on a street corner under a couple of signs.

Accordingly, Chong says, an important dynamic of social movements is that the movement's leaders will actively talk up their chances of success; and conversely, the government (or corporation, or whatever the movement is opposing) will try to convince everyone that it will hold out forever. This is a very recognizable aspect of unions' strikes against companies, and Chong shows that it was also the usual story in civil rights demonstrations against Southern governments in the 1960s.

✦ ADVANTAGES (AND DISADVANTAGES) OF INFORMAL ORGANIZATION

It is the loose organization of social movements that sets them apart from both parties and interest groups. You will recall that parties were distinguished from interest groups because parties seek to control the government, but interest groups seek to influence one

---

[4]Dennis Chong, *Collective Action and the Civil Rights Movement* (Chicago: University of Chicago Press, 1991).

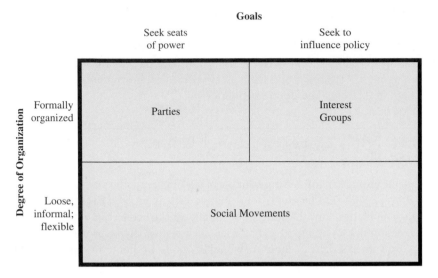

FIGURE 13.1   Parties, interest groups, and social movements.

or more policies of the government. Social movements may seek either of these goals. A social movement may seek to oust a leader of a country and replace him or her with someone else, as in the case of the "Orange Revolution" movement that forced President Viktor Yanukovich out of power in Ukraine in 2004, or the general strike organized in Venezuela in 2003 in an attempt to oust President Hugo Chavez of Venezuela. Or, a social movement may seek to change a specific policy of the government, as in the Montgomery bus boycott that achieved the right of African-Americans to sit anywhere they wish in buses in Montgomery, or the attempt to stop the extension of Highway 55 in Minneapolis. The thing that always typifies social movements is not their goal, but the way they are organized (loosely) and conducted (flexibly). This is illustrated in the charting of parties, interest groups, and social movements in Figure 13.1.

Social movements vary in how loosely they are organized. At their more organized end they may be difficult to distinguish from traditional interest groups. A Canadian group, the Castle-Crown Wilderness Coalition, while it was the subject of a study titled "New Social Movements and the Environmental Policy Process," actually operates more like a very grass-roots, volunteer-based interest group—it negotiates with government agencies, it does not engage in "direct action," and it is not particularly flamboyant in its media relations.[5] At the other end of the spectrum of loose organization, a series of demonstrations in 2005 by retired Russians protesting proposed cuts in their subsidies appears to have been almost entirely spontaneous, with no organizational structure and no apparent leadership. Thousands of desperate elderly people simply appeared at street

---

[5]Lorna Stefanick, "New Social Movements and the Environmental Policy Process: The Case of Alberta's Castle Wilderness Area," in Joanna Everitt and Brenda O'Neill, *Citizen Politics: Research and Theory in Canadian Political Behaviour* (New York: Oxford University Press, 2002), pp. 426–38; the activities of the Castle-Crown Wilderness Coalition can be reviewed on their Web site, **http://www.castlewilderness.ca.**

corners and started spontaneous actions to protest the cuts; they were very effective in changing the Putin government's policies.

Informal, loose organization carries with it two huge disadvantages. First, because by definition the movement does not have a well-organized and established staff and structure, it is difficult for it to amass many of the sorts of resources political leaders respond to. Social movements typically do not have much money. They also do not typically have specialized expertise that governments will want to tap into. And, they do not have ongoing staffs capable of doing long-term, tedious organizational jobs like amassing databases of voters and getting them to the polls.

Second, because social movements usually are ephemeral, counting their organizational lives not in decades, but in months or years, policy makers often know that they can outlast them. A corporation, trade union, or church will be around for a politician's entire career, but social movements come together and disband fairly easily. A politician may feel able to wait them out.

However, social movements' informality also gives them some distinct advantages: First, because they do not have an entrenched staff and old, established members who must be deferred to, they can be very nimble in defining and framing their issues. They can shift quickly if tactical necessity arises. In the case of the rubber gatherers of Acre province in Brazil, for instance, as described in the example at the end of this chapter, the rubber gatherers were able to frame their movement variously as a movement for indigenous people's rights, as an environmental movement, or as a labor movement, depending on whom they were dealing with. All of these framings were true, but the point is that since the rubber gatherers had only the most informal of organizations they were not bound by an organization's self-definition and the set of people an organization gathers around it. They could bob and weave a bit, and this gave them real advantages.

In another example of flexible framing, the question of female circumcision did not really take off until a campaign initiated by a group of women's and human rights organizations reformulated the issue as one of "female genital mutilation," which sounded (a) more horrible, and (b) less voluntary than "circumcision."[6]

Al Quaeda is not exactly what we usually think of as a social movement, because it is a secretive group of terrorists rather than an open, broad movement. Other than its use of terror as a strategy, however, it is actually fairly typical of social movements. Osama Bin Laden is adept at using the media, and the group uses its loose organization masterfully as a way of evading interventions by governments. And like other social movements, al Quaeda has also proved to be flexible in framing its goals: at its start it was formed to get American troops out of Saudi Arabia, and explicitly did not involve itself in the Israeli-Palestinian conflict; but after the Iraq war, it saw opportunities in linking its goals to the generalized anti-Americanism of the Arab "street" and moved to accomplish this by taking up the cause of Palestinians.

Now, social movements are not the only political groups that can re-frame issues creatively. Americans for Tax Reform, a well-established and thoroughly organized interest group—i.e., no social movement—brilliantly recast the estate tax in the 1990s

---

[6]Margaret E. Keck and Kathryn Sikkink, *Activists Beyond Borders: Advocacy Networks in International Politics* (Ithaca, New York: Cornell University Press, 1998), p. 20

as the "death tax," and succeeded in getting it repealed in 2002. The point, though, is that social movements are much more nimble than well-organized groups in making these shifts. They make a virtue out of their weakness by relying on the flexibility they gain from *not* having resources and organization.

Second, the lack of resources and organization also allows social movements to change tactics quickly and be very opportunistic. Indigenous peoples, who started out appealing to labor groups and human rights groups for help, quickly realized that they should shift more to environmentalists and anti-globalization groups. Social movements can also capitalize quickly on opportunities when they arise. Underground pro-democracy movements in the Soviet Union responded quickly when disagreements among the Communist leadership made Mikhail Gorbachev available to them as an ally.

Third, social movements have the ability to form networks beyond the boundaries of their state. More formal organizations tend to be inward looking, and do not often form effective partnerships with similar organizations in other states. The Chamber of Commerce of the United States, for instance, does not get together in concerted action with the Chamber of Commerce of Canada, and pro-life organizations in the United States do not form partnerships with Christian-Democratic parties in Europe that also oppose abortion. But social movements often draw on similar movements in other states for support. Margaret Keck and Kathryn Sikkink describe what they call the "boomerang pattern," in which a social movement that is blocked by its own government from accomplishing its goals asks a similar movement in another country to get *its* government to pressure the first government to yield to the social movement within its borders.[7] For instance, a human rights group trying to get a political prisoner released in Zimbabwe might enlist human rights groups in Britain to get the British government to pressure the government of Zimbabwe to release the prisoner.

Because they are nimble, and also because communication and the flow of information are so important in their own mobilization, social movements are often adept at communication and at using information effectively. A good example is the Zapatista movement of indigenous communities in the Chiapas province of Mexico. The movement has been engaged in sporadic armed conflict with the Mexican government, but has been able to transcend its role as a disaffected region by creative use of the Internet and other venues of communication. They developed a romantic, dramatic figure as leader, Subcomandante Marcos, who appears frequently in Mexico City and elsewhere, giving speeches and reading poems about the movement. Their Internet presence can easily be accessed from **http://studentorgs.utexas.edu/nave/zaps.html,** a server in the United States, indicating once again the frequent reliance of social movements on international ties. They have been able to draw widespread support from around the world.

Most of the examples of social movements above are of the left, but the right also has its social movements. In the United States, skinheads, militias, white power groups, and various kinds of tax protest groups flourish in exactly the same kind of nimble informal organization as social movements of the left. Like movements of the left, they are heavily represented on the Internet, and also have developed effective networks of private discussion groups. And like other social groups, they also utilize international ties.[8]

---

[7]Ibid., p. 13.

[8]The Fall 2001 issue of the Southern Poverty Law Center's *Intelligence Report* has several articles describing U.S. right-wing social movements' strategic partnerships with groups outside the United States.

Subcomandante Marcos, the charismatic leader of the Zapatista movement, addresses reporters at the outset of a 1,900 mile protest drive and march from Chiapas to Mexico City.

© Arturo Fuentes/AFP/Getty Images

 EXAMPLE

The Rubber Tappers of Acre[9]

The rubber tappers of Acre were initially brought to the western Amazon from the northeast by rubber barons anxious to profit from the rubber boom at the end of the nineteenth century. They have a long history of fighting for survival, first against pervasive debt peonage, and later to eke out a living after the collapse of the rubber economy. Over time, they developed a diversified strategy for economic survival that mixed subsistence farming and sale of rubber and Brazil nuts. In the 1970s, a land boom fueled by government incentives and road building attracted investors from the south, desirous of obtaining large stretches of land for either cattle ranching or speculation. A process of concentration of landholdings ensued, with conflicts over dubious and often overlapping land titles. The rights of rubber tappers and other small farmers to the land they occupied came from long-standing possession rather than formal property titles; for the ranchers, these groups stood in the way of forest clearing and the consolidation of holdings. Around 1973 ranchers in Acre began to resort to violence to clear them off the land.

[9]Excerpted from Margaret E. Keck, "Social Equity and Environmental Politics in Brazil: Lessons from the Rubber Tappers of Acre," *Comparative Politics* 27 (July 1995), pp. 409–24. Article first appeared in *Comparative Politics.* Reprinted with permission.

In 1974, rubber tappers began to organize to defend their livelihoods and their tenure on the land. Helped to organize by the Catholic church and by the arrival in 1975 of a delegate from the National Confederation of Agricultural Workers, CONTAG, the rubber tappers started in 1976 to use their signature tactic, the *empate,* or standoff,[10] in which they collectively expelled the work teams sent by the ranchers to clear forested areas. Although these expulsions did not involve violence against persons, they were considerable shows of force. Large groups of rubber tapper families surrounded teams of workers using chain saws to cut forested areas either where they were cutting or in their headquarters; they set fire to the headquarters and persuaded the work teams to leave the area.

The domestic political context in which rubber tappers organized contained favorable and unfavorable elements. The military government in power since 1964 began to liberalize the regime in 1974. The political opportunity structure was significantly more open than it had been just a few years earlier, and the rubber tappers could develop alliances with other social movement organizations springing up in Brazilian civil society during the 1970s. Over the same period, however, ranchers and other large rural landowners also became more organized. Fearing (correctly) that the transition to democracy would create greater pressure for agrarian reform, landowners in the 1980s increasingly resorted to violence to eliminate rural organizers they saw as threats to their interests.

The political liberalization that began in Brazil in 1974 sparked myriad forms of grass-roots organizing, many under the umbrella of the Catholic Church. Catholic base communities multiplied during the second half of the 1970s. In 1975 the National Conference of Brazilian Bishops, CNBB, created the Pastoral Land Commission, CPT, whose first coordinator was the Acrean bishop Dom Moacir Grechi. A proponent of liberation theology, Dom Moacir supported early attempts to organize rubber tappers and small farmers in the state. The CPT played a major role in making land conflicts more viable, at considerable risk to members. According to Dom Moacir:

> Until 1975 the land problem was not discussed in newspapers, on television, or in the media in general. After that we showed people in and out of the Church and also in government that we existed. So [the government] did all it could to demoralize us, even imprisoning priests who were linked to the CPT. . . . They saw that where unions didn't exist, the CPT got them started. Where serious injustices occurred, it denounced them to the newspapers. I mean, they considered it dangerous because it raised awareness among workers, leading to the formation of unions and workers' organization, while simultaneously exposing a whole world of crime, exploitation, land theft, where often high level authorities were involved.[11]

At the same time, the National Confederation of Agricultural Workers, CONTAG, grew rapidly, as a progressive leadership elected in 1968 used a new government policy to have rural welfare benefits (FUNRURAL) administered through unions to expand the base of rural organizing.[12] João Maia, a CONTAG organizer, arrived in Acre in 1975 and began to give the institutional support of the national rural labor movement to the struggles begun by rubber tappers and small farmers. CONTAG trained union organizers and brought a series of legal suits demanding just

---

[10]It is interesting that the first translation offered for *empate* in the *Novo Michaelis* is "act or effect of being or becoming equal, equality." Others, besides stalemate, are "unprofitable investment of capital" and "obstacle, hindrance." I use "stand-off" rather than the more habitually used "stalemate," as it seems to capture the confrontational nature of the action.

[11]Author's interview with Dom Moacir Grechi, Rio Branco, Acre, December 19, 1982.

[12]See Alan Biorn Henning Maybury-Lewis, "The Politics of the Possible: The Growth and Political Development of the Brazilian Rural Workers' Trade Union Movement, 1964–1985" (Ph.D. diss., Columbia University, 1991).

recompense for those being expelled from their land, many of which it won. The new landowners were not prepared to take this lying down. In João Maia's words:

> The ranchers who came to Acre had already opened ranches in São Paulo, Mato Grosso, Goiás and Rondônia, moving north, and they had never met with difficulties. Then they got to the end of the line and they came up against an organized union. So that's where the ranchers really began to react. Politically, they went to Brasília, to the National Security Council. We went too, via CONTAG. We explained the situation on the land and in the forest, and made an argument about rights of possession. This is a military area, and it was important to go about this carefully. We're an institutional organ, so we have to use institutional channels. Eventually, the ranchers began to feel they were up against a brick wall with the union, and realized that our lawyer could beat them in court. The workers were also getting organized and the practice of embargoing [physically preventing] deforestation was spreading, and we were starting to convince public opinion that intensive deforestation is a problem here in the Amazon and is going to be a serious problem for the future. So apparently they decided that the trick was to do something about the leadership, and in 1980 they killed the president of the Brasiléia union, the most combative one. It was to be a kind of warning so that people would be afraid and would stop the embargoes.[13]

The assassination of Wilson Pinheiros, president of the rural workers' union of Brasiléia, took place in the context of intensive political organization at the national level. The 1979 party reform eliminated the existing political parties; it both called for and made it possible to create new ones. The Workers' Party, PT, was organized in Acre based on precisely the same grass-roots initiatives that had helped to reinforce the rubber tappers' struggles at the end of the 1970s, drawing its base from church and union movements.[14] João Maia and many rubber tapper leaders were early proponents of the PT in Acre. At a rally to protest the assassination of Pinheiros, PT leaders Luís Inácio da Silva (known as Lula) and Jacó Bittar shared a platform with CONTAG president José Francisco da Silva, João Maia, and Chico Mendes, helping to give the incident national visibility. The day after the rally, a group of workers met the ranch foreman who was generally believed to have commissioned the assassination and killed him. Subsequently, the government used this act as a pretext to indict the speakers at the rally under the National Security Law for having incited the workers to violence. According to João Maia:

> The government wanted an excuse to curtail CONTAG's and the PT's activities nationally and in Acre, and to find a way to get at the Church people. This murder after a public rally provided a way of getting at all of them in one fell swoop. CONTAG and the Church in the rural area, and the PT too since our union supported the PT. It was really just a pretext, because this was the fourth time a foreman had been killed here in Acre. . . . But because it was a politicized moment and the government really had an interest in repressing the PT that was growing fast and also repressing CONTAG, they took advantage of it. Indictment under the National Security Law is a political charge, so they took advantage of a pretext.[15]

---

[13]Author's interview with João Maia, Rio Branco, Acre, December 18, 1982.
[14]See Margaret Keck, *The Workers' Party and Democratization in Brazil* (New Haven: Yale University Press, 1992), ch. 5.
[15]Author's interview with João Maia, Rio Branco, Acre, December 18, 1982. The National Security Law could be used widely in Acre because virtually the whole state was designated a national security area, either by a decree dating from the time of Juscelino Kubitschek so designating areas within 150 km from the national border or by a 1970 decree establishing national security areas for 100 km on each side of a national road in the Amazon region.

These charges were finally dropped in 1983. Although the PT performed disappointingly in Acre in the 1982 elections, it established an important foothold in Acre from the beginning and helped bring the struggles of the Acre rubber tappers to national attention. The party's national research and cultural institute is named after Wilson Pinheiros.

Thus, the rubber tappers' struggle was heating up at precisely the moment when the climate for linkage with other forms of grass-roots organization was especially propitious. Many Brazilians saw this kind of organization as part of a wider struggle for democracy. Democratization was an uneven process. The military eased the strictures on political and social organization in fits and starts, and political opening was accompanied by frequent repressive measures intended to keep it within bounds. In particular, the military did not want political liberalization to bring social upheaval.

Even so, groups like the rubber tappers had a better chance of finding domestic allies than they would have had the Acre land boom begun ten years earlier. But although these allies were sufficient to reinforce the rubber tappers' struggle, they were insufficient to win it. CONTAG could help to negotiate between tappers and ranchers and could win for them in the courts recompense for livelihoods lost, but it could guarantee neither long-term tenure on the land nor a livelihood should tenure be won. The PT could help provide the tappers with a political voice, but it was still too weak electorally to give them access to the corridors of power. While the church could shelter organizing initiatives, its capacity to denounce injustice was far stronger than its ability to correct it. As Brazil's democratization progressed, violence against rural organizers increased, especially in the north and northeast, and civilian authorities proved unable or unwilling to control it.

In the early 1980s, the rubber tappers' movement began to seek alternatives that could insure their long-term survival. Soon after the 1982 elections, Chico Mendes said that he thought it was time to change course.

> Now I have to change the way I work. Before, I fought to defend land, even in the face of threats from hired gunmen. Now it's clear that wasn't enough, because we didn't take the time to establish priorities for what came next. That's what I'm thinking about now. The only solution I can see is to try a new kind of struggle within the union, for a popular education campaign in the countryside, and for medical care. We also need to open trails [estradas] for those who won the land through that union struggle, and to fight alongside these people for a way to transport their product. We need to try to organize an autonomous cooperative. These are the things I think we need to fight for. It's the only way to recover the space we've lost.[16]

The process had already begun. In 1980–81 Mendes with Paraná anthropologist Mary Allegretti and others designed *Projeto Seringueiro* (Rubber Tappers' Project) to include a cooperative, a literacy project organized on Paulo Freire's principles around the rubber tappers' experience, and training for health monitors. It was to be run by the Xapuri rural workers' union, to whose presidency Chico was elected in 1981. The project received funding from Oxfam, whose regional representative Tony Gross, like Allegretti, had initially come to Acre to work on a dissertation on the rubber tappers. It also won support from the Brazilian organizations CEDI (Ecumenical Center for Documentation and Information) and CEDOP (Center for Documentation and Research of Amazonia).

---

[16]Author's interview with Chico Mendes and Nilson Morão, Rio Branco, Acre, December 18, 1982.

✳ EXAMPLE

The "Orange Revolution" in Ukraine

Ukraine is a large state southwest of Russia, part of the Soviet Union until 1991. It established electoral democracy in 1991, but the democracy was manipulated by corrupt governments dominated by former Communist officials. While a growing reform movement began to challenge the old leaders for control during the late 1990s, at the time of the presidential election on November 21, 2004, the old guard was still firmly in control.

The election campaign was very dirty. The establishment candidate was Viktor Yanukovich, an unsavory official who had once been convicted of robbery and assault and who had close ties to corrupt businessmen. During the campaign, the reform leader, another Viktor (Viktor Yushchenko) was poisoned and nearly died. He had to cease campaigning for a month to recover, and his face is still horribly scarred. The reform opposition was harassed in many ways, and barred from almost all television channels.

> Students living in university housing were told by university officials that if their districts voted for the challenger, they would be evicted from their dorms in the middle of winter. When election day came, at polling sites in several areas where support for Yushchenko was high, monitors discovered that pens had been filled with disappearing ink so that ballots would appear blank after they were cast.[17]

The election was clearly going to be close. Though the reform movement was strong in western and central Ukraine where most of the population are ethnic Ukrainians, the old guard was popular in eastern Ukraine, where in many provinces a majority of the population are ethnic Russians. The Russians favored the old Communist leaders because they felt they would keep closer ties between Ukraine and Russia than the reformers would. On election night, nonpartisan exit polls showed the reformer Yushchenko having won by 52 percent over Yanukovich's 43 percent. But after a mysterious delay of several hours in which a number of eastern districts revised their original reports of turnout upward to incredible figures, the official result was reported to be Yanukovich 49 percent, Yushchenko 47 percent.

Yushchenko's supporters, in a fairly spontaneous movement, descended on the capital, Kiev, and set up a huge camp in Independence Square, with tens of thousands of demonstrators all wearing Yushchenko's trademark orange colors. There was some organization to the movement; a side effect of the old government barring Yushchenko from the television had meant that he was forced to go from town to town speaking directly to voters, and this had allowed him to build up a large, loose network of supporters. But it was hardly what we would call an organized party.

For seventeen days the demonstration grew in Independence Square, and the campers vowed to stay until a new election was called. The capital was shut down. During this time two important sets of forces were also engaged in the standoff, and played key roles in the outcome.

First of all, the demonstration and the crisis of the regime attracted intervention from outside Ukraine. President Putin of Russia intervened strongly for dismissal of the demonstrators and the establishment of Yanukovich as president. But at the same time the European Union, and

---

[17]Adrian Karatnycky, "Ukraine's Orange Revolution," *Foreign Affairs* 84 (March–April 2005), pp. 35–52.

especially Poland and Lithuania, intervened on behalf of Yushchenko. And the Soros Foundation and other international organizations sent money and advisors to help the demonstration.

Second, and most surprisingly, a major faction of the Ukrainian secret police were concerned enough at the prospect of bloodshed and chaos that they intervened vigorously behind the scenes to protect the demonstrators. On November 28, the government ordered ten thousand troops to attack the demonstration in Kiev, but officials of the secret police hurried to Independence Square to warn the demonstrators, while others warned the government that if their forces attacked the demonstrators, forces from the army and the secret police would attack the attackers. The crisis was defused.[18]

After two and a half weeks the government gave in and a new election was held, at which Yushchenko was decisively elected president.

The importance of outside factors in the Orange Revolution is quite a common pattern in social movements, which usually succeed only when they can also find some outside sources of power and energy to complement their own. The revolution would probably have failed but for the support of the secret police and some of the army. And, it might have failed if the EU, Poland, Lithuania, and international organizations had not intervened. But none of this is to minimize or trivialize the accomplishment of the courageous demonstrators of Independence Square. They probably could not have succeeded without the help of the secret police, the EU, and others. But if they had not first put their bodies on the line, nothing at all would have happened.

Afterword: This was the "Orange Revolution," and it was in fact glorious. But sadly, not all revolutions turn out well. After the election, Yushchenko took up the office of president and Yulia Tymoshenko, who had helped lead the revolution, became prime minister and leader of Yushchenko's supporters in the Parliament. It did not take long, however, before Yushchenko and Tymoshenko fell out over a mix of largely personal squabbles. The resulting paralysis of policy-making discredited the new regime, and in the parliamentary election of August 2006, Yushchenko's old rival Yanukovich took over control of the parliament. The result has been gridlock between the president and Parliament, and a steady decline in Yushchenko's popularity and authority.

---

[18]C. J. Chivers, "How Ukraine's Top Spies Changed the Nation's Path," *New York Times*, January 17, 2005, p. A1.

KEY TERMS

social movement   opportunity structures

FURTHER READING

Alexander, Amanda, and Mbali, Mandisa, eds. "Problematizing Resistance," special issue of *Journal of Asian and African Studies* 41 (Nos. 1, 2; April 2006).

Armstrong, Elizabeth. *Forging Gay Identities.* Chicago: University of Chicago Press, 2002.

Barker, Colin, Johnson, Alan, and Lavalette, Michael, eds. *Leadership and Social Movements.* Manchester, UK: Manchester University Press, 2001.

Chong, Dennis. *Collective Action and the Civil Rights Movement.* Chicago: University of Chicago Press, 1991.

Della Porta, Donnatella, and Diani, Mario. *Social Movements: An Introduction,* 2nd ed. Oxford, UK: Blackwell, 2006.

Della Porta, Donna, and Tarrow, Sidney, eds. *Transnational Protest & Global Activism.* Lanham, MD: Rowman & Littlefield, 2005.

Goodwin, Jeff, and Jasper, James M., eds. *Rethinking Social Movements: Structure, Meaning, and Emotion.* Lanham, MD: Rowman & Littlefield, 2004.

Haber, Paul Lawrence. "Identity and Political Process: Recent Trends in the Study of Latin American Social Movements." *Latin American Research Review* 31 (1996), pp. 171–88.

Keck, Margaret E., and Sikkink, Kathryn. *Activists Beyond Borders: Advocacy Networks in International Politics.* Ithaca, New York: Cornell University Press, 1998.

Levi, Margaret, and Murphy, Gillian H. "Coalitions of Contention: The Case of the WTO Protests in Seattle," *Political Studies* 54 (2006), pp. 651–670.

McAdam, Doug. *Political Process and the Black Insurgency,* rev. ed. Chicago: University of Chicago Press, 2000.

_____, McCarthy, John, and Zald, Mayer, eds. *Comparative Perspectives on Social Movements: Political Opportunities, Mobilizing Structures, and Cultural Framings.* New York, Cambridge University Press, 1996.

Mcyer, David S., and Tarrow, Sidney, eds. *The Social Movement Society: Contentious Politics for a New Century.* Lanham, MD: Rowman & Littlefield, 1998.

Morris, Aldon. *The Origins of the Civil Rights Movement: Black Communities Organizing for Change.* New York: Free Press, 1984.

O'Brien, Kevin J., and Li, Lianjiang. *Rightful Resistance in Rural China.* New York: Cambridge University Press, 2006.

Rootes, Christopher, ed. *Environmental Protest in Western Europe.* New York: Oxford University Press, 2004.

Scott, James C. *Weapons of the Weak: Everyday Forms of Peasant Resistance.* New Haven: Yale University Press, 1985.

Tarrow, Sidney. *Power in Movement.* 2nd ed. Cambridge: Cambridge University Press, 1998.

_____, McAdam, Doug, and Tilly, Charles. *Dynamics of Contention.* Cambridge, 2001.

WWW   WEB SITES OF INTEREST

Political Advocacy Groups: A Directory of United States Lobbyists:

http://www.csuchico.edu/ kcfount/

American Sociological Association's section on collective behavior and social movements:

http://www.asanet.org (click on "sections"; then click on "collective behavior and social movements")

Social Movements and Culture, a resource site:

http://www.wsu.edu/ amerstu/smc/smcframe.html

Fourth World Documentation Project: Indigenous peoples information for the online community:

http://www.cwis.org/fwdp/fwdp.html

Social Movements in South Asia: Selected Internet Resources:

http://www.lib.berkeley.edu/SSEAL/SouthAsia/movements.html

CHAPTER 14

❧

NATIONAL DECISION-MAKING INSTITUTIONS: PARLIAMENTARY GOVERNMENT

In this and Chapter 15, we will examine formal arrangements for governing democracies. This chapter will deal with **parliamentary government,** while Chapter 15 will deal with "presidential" government. Parliamentary government is conceptually the simpler of the two and is the form found in most democracies. As you can see from the map in Figure 14.1, most European states are parliamentary systems, as are a large number of African and Asian states. Parliamentary government will seem unusual to many American readers, however, since the United States is one of the democracies that operates with a presidential system.

In presidential systems, the executive and legislature are selected in separate elections. (Even if the elections are held at the same time; in the United States, for instance, the President and members of the Congress are elected on the same day, but voters choose them separately, on separate parts of the ballot.) In a parliamentary system the only vote a citizen casts is for members of the parliament. The executive is then set up by the parliament.

The basic principles of a pure parliamentary system are as follows:

1. A parliament of representatives is elected by the citizens of the state. It normally consists of from two hundred to several hundred representatives. The parliament is the only elected body in the state. Bills passed by the parliament are the law, and no one can overrule them.

2. The executive power of the state (managing the bureaucracy, conducting relations with other states, etc.) is lodged with a **cabinet** of women and men who are selected by the parliament to conduct the affairs of the state. Most or all members

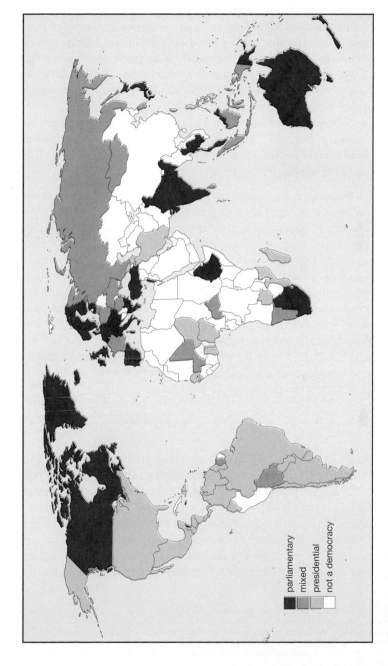

FIGURE 14.1 Parliamentary and presidential systems.

SOURCE: John Gerring, Strom C. Thacker, and Carola Moreno, "Are Parliamentary Systems Better?" (unpublished paper, October 6, 2005) table 1.

parliamentary
mixed
presidential
not a democracy

319

of the cabinet are usually members of the parliament who take on executive responsibilities in addition to their legislative chores.

3. The cabinet retains executive power only as long as it has the "confidence" of the parliament; that is, only as long as it can command a majority of the votes. At any time, a majority vote in the parliament may unseat a cabinet and cause a new set of people to be selected as a cabinet.[1] This is referred to as the "government falling." If no vote is actually taken to unseat the cabinet but the cabinet finds that it is unable to put together majorities to pass its important bills, it is expected that the cabinet will resign.

4. Just as the parliament holds the cabinet in jeopardy, the leader of the cabinet (called variously "premier," "prime minister," "chancellor," etc.) usually has the right to have the parliament disbanded, forcing a new election that will lead to a new distribution of power.

This, in a nutshell, is parliamentary government. We will examine some finer points and some variations, but these four principles are basic. It is a simpler form than presidential government because, at least in its pure form, it does not allow for any separation of powers. The parliament and the cabinet (that operates only by the support of the parliament) hold all the state's governmental political power. The cabinet runs the operations of government, and takes the lead in developing proposals to be put into law by the parliament; rather than being opposed forces like those in a presidential system such as the United States, the two are joined at the hip. The bottom line is that in a parliamentary system, with this simple concentration of power, political decisions should in principle be made clearly and directly with a minimum of delay. The cabinet and the parliament should at least most of the time be in agreement on important issues—if they were not, presumably the cabinet would fall. And in most systems their will cannot be blocked by a court or any other body.

✦ HEAD OF STATE

How, exactly, does all of this work? First of all, every parliamentary system has a separate, almost purely symbolic figure, called the **head of state.** In some countries (for instance, Great Britain, Denmark, the Netherlands), the head of state is a **constitutional monarch**—that is, a monarch who carries out ceremonial functions but has little or no real political power.[2] In other states (Germany and Italy, for example), an official called "president" fills this role. Such states are not presidential systems, in which a president directs the politics of the state; we will deal with presidential systems in Chapter 15. Rather, such presidents conduct only the ceremonial functions of the state.

---

[1] In May 2005, for example, the Conservative Party introduced a motion of no confidence in the Canadian House of Commons, seeking to take advantage of a scandal plaguing the Liberal-led cabinet. They wanted to force an early election, which they expected they could win. The motion failed by just a single vote, after the Liberal prime minister lured a Conservative member to vote against the motion by giving her a cabinet position.

[2] This is why we did not include countries like Spain or Great Britain under "monarchies" among autocratic systems in Chapter 7. Their monarchs are not the rulers of their states.

The head of state is the ceremonial and symbolic leader of the state. It is the head of state who dedicates hospitals, welcomes dignitaries, and so on. In most parliamentary systems there is a further sense that in a time of great emergency and breakdown of the state, the head of state (who otherwise has little power) would assume great emergency power to pull the state through. For instance, when Germany suddenly occupied Norway during the Second World War it was the king, not the cabinet, who rallied the Norwegians to resist, and set up a government in exile.

In normal times, however, the main political function of a head of state in a parliamentary system is to ask one of the parties' leaders in the parliament to form a cabinet. Even in this, the head of state normally has little choice in the matter of whom to ask; most parliamentary systems have rules the head of state must follow, such as the rule that the leader of the largest party is the one who must be asked to form a cabinet.

✧ THE CABINET

Once a party leader has been asked to form a cabinet, if one party has a majority of seats in the parliament the process is pretty simple. The leader becomes the head of the cabinet (variously called "prime minister," "premier," or "chancellor"), and appoints other members from the party to oversee different parts of policy: foreign minister, minister of defense, health minister, agriculture minister, and so forth.

If no one party holds a majority of the seats, then two or more parties, which among them total a majority of seats in the parliament, must form a **coalition** to lead the parliament. In forming a coalition, they will divide up the positions of the cabinet among themselves (party A gets to name the premier, the minister of economics, the foreign minister, and the minister for agriculture; party B gets to name the minister for defense and the minister for industry; etc.). In the parliament, they agree that their combined parties' votes will always be cast on behalf of legislation proposed by the cabinet.

A cabinet always has to be constituted after an election, of course. But if for any number of reasons a cabinet has to be replaced at a time when elections are not due, that can happen readily without a new election as well. If the members of a coalition cease to agree about governing together, for instance, the cabinet may "fall" in the sense that it no longer commands a majority of votes in the parliament, and a new coalition must be put together. In that case, the head of state will ask a leader of another party to negotiate a new coalition.

Less dramatically, after the Labour Party of Great Britain won a majority of seats in the House of Commons in the 2005 election, Prime Minister Tony Blair promised that he would not stay in office the full time till the next election, but would step down by 2007. He had served a long time, and his personal popularity was compromised by his support for the Iraq War. When he stepped down, the process was simple. A new election was not needed; rather, the Labour Party selected a new leader—Gordon Brown—to be the prime minister.

✦ CABINET CONTROL

If parliamentary government is to function smoothly, the cabinet must be able to control what goes on in the parliament. If a cabinet could be voted out casually because the mood of the parliament had changed, no one would find that a satisfactory situation; government would be far too unstable. Particularly if the cabinet is based on a coalition of parties, the basis for bargaining on the makeup of the cabinet is the number of votes each party can deliver. If the cabinet was not able to count regularly on the votes of one or another of the parties, the rest of the coalition would feel cheated and the coalition would not last long. As it happens, this was a large part of the problem for many years in Italy; the Christian Democratic Party was an important part of almost every coalition from 1945 to 1994, but it was a fragmented party and was never able to guarantee its parliamentary support very well.

On the basis of this reasoning, we might expect to see, in the many smoothly functioning parliamentary systems, that the cabinets dominate their parliaments. And this is indeed the case. The usual situation is that legislation is proposed by the cabinet and is *debated* in the parliament; after all, it is only there that the opposition parties have their innings. Aside from the addition of minor amendments, however, there is rarely any question but that the legislation will be passed by the parliament. In effect, the parliament is a rubber stamp for the cabinet.

It is ironic that a body that is elected by the parliament and can be brought down at any time by it—a body that is, in effect, created by the parliament—can turn around and control what the parliament does. It is readily understandable that this should be the case, however, if we recall that the members of the cabinet are top leaders of their parties. They are skillful politicians, and they have every reason to find ways to control what happens in the parliament to protect the power they enjoy as cabinet members.

In Chapter 11, we saw that a side effect of political parties was that, as organizations, they bind a number of people together and provide a channel by which some of those people can control others. It is by this channel that cabinets control their parliaments. The members of a cabinet participate in parliamentary debates; they vote in parliament; but most important, they are leaders or powerful members of their party organizations in the parliament. For the other members, the party provides the avenue for advancement in the parliament. Debate time, committee assignments, the chance of a cabinet post someday—these are controlled for members of parliament by their party. Those who do not cooperate with their party's leaders do not advance. It is by this source of discipline, in their capacity as the leaders of their party, that the cabinet members are able to impose their will on the parliament.

✦ WHAT DOES A PARLIAMENT DO?

The governmental role of a parliament, because it is so controlled by the cabinet, is difficult for students from the United States to appreciate. With regard to the passage of legislation, most parliaments are rubber stamps. From 1945 to 1978, for instance, of bills that the British cabinet submitted to the House of Commons for consideration, 97 percent were approved by the House. Amendments to bills are also tightly controlled by the cabinet in Britain. From 1967 to 1971, the cabinet proposed 1,772 amendments to various bills; of these, 1,770 were approved. By contrast, other members of the House proposed 4,198 amendments during the same period, but only 210 of these passed.[3]

It is apparent that whatever things parliaments do, deciding what legislation is to become law is not chief among them. In the unified governmental arrangement of a parliamentary system, it is expected that the executive and legislative parts of government will work together to make legislation; and because over the years cabinets have learned to protect themselves by controlling their parliaments, it is generally accepted that cabinets call the tune in designing laws.

Is parliament then a useless appendage? No, because it still serves a number of purposes that are similar to those of the U.S. Congress, and one further purpose that is peculiar to parliamentary systems:

Public debate. First, a parliament furnishes a forum for the public debate of bills. The opposition parties have a chance, before a bill is passed into law, to present their position on it and to stimulate public discussion. Often, bills do evolve under pressure of public opinion stimulated by parliamentary debate.

Scrutiny. Second, a parliament is a place where a bill that the cabinet wants to enact into law is submitted to detailed scrutiny both by the friends of the cabinet and by its enemies. It may be that a number of small problems may be uncovered in a complicated bill, problems that the cabinet is happy enough to have brought to its attention. In the British example, almost all of the 1,772 amendments introduced by the cabinet were amendments to its *own bills*, because almost no legislation is considered by the House of Commons except legislation submitted by the cabinet. Most of those amendments were cabinet responses to problems that were discovered in the course of parliamentary consideration of their bills.

Oversight of policy. Third, a parliament is one of the few parts of the governmental apparatus that has an interest in keeping a critical eye on how the cabinet is administering public policy. The opposition parties are especially eager participants in this, for obvious reasons, but there is also a tradition that the cabinet must report regularly to the parliament how it is managing the affairs of the state. This sort of accounting takes many forms. In most parliamentary systems, there is some sort of annual speech made to the parliament describing in broad outlines the state of things and the cabinet's plans for the coming year, and this speech leads to a significant debate on the overall program of the cabinet. In addition, many parliaments use a device called **question time,** in which various cabinet members appear regularly to answer questions from other members of the parliament about the way their ministry is being run. The answers they give may spark lively debates.

This third function of parliaments—watching what the executive part of the government does—is not met as well in parliamentary as in presidential systems. The

[3]Richard Rose, "Still the Era of Party Government," *Parliamentary Affairs* 36 (Summer 1983), pp. 284–85.

"Delegate" and "Trustee" Models of Representation

An enduring debate in political science centers on what role representatives should assume vis-à-vis their constituents. In the "delegate" model, they should regard themselves as speaking for the constituents and should cast each vote as they think the constituents would wish it to be cast. In the "trustee" model, it is assumed that representatives learn more about an issue than any of their constituents could possibly know and have been chosen on the basis of their superior judgment; we would then expect that on at least a few occasions they would vote differently than their constituents would wish them to vote.

Edmund Burke put the case for the trustee model beautifully in a speech to the electors of Bristol on November 3, 1774, after they had chosen him to represent them:

> Certainly, gentlemen, it ought to be the happiness and glory of a representative, to live in the strictest union, the closest correspondence, and the most unreserved communication with his constituents. Their wishes ought to have great weight with him; their opinion high respect; their business unremitted attention. It is his duty to sacrifice his repose, his pleasures, his satisfactions, to theirs; and, above all, ever, and in all cases, to prefer their interest to his own. But, his unbiased opinion, his mature judgment, his enlightened conscience, he ought not to sacrifice to you, to any man, or to any set of men living. These he does not derive from your pleasure; no, nor from the law and the constitution. They are a trust from Providence, for the abuse of which he is deeply answerable. Your representative owes you, not his industry only, but his judgment; and he betrays, instead of serving you, if he sacrifices it to your opinion.
>
> My worthy colleague says, his will ought to be subservient to yours. If that be all, the thing is innocent. If government were a matter of will upon any side, yours, without question, ought to be superior. But government and legislation are matters of reason and judgment, and not of inclination; and, what sort of reason is that, in which the determination precedes the discussion; in which one set of men deliberate, and another decide; and where those who form the conclusion are perhaps three hundred miles distant from those who hear the arguments?
>
> To deliver an opinion, is the right of all men; that of constituents is a weighty and respectable opinion, which a representative ought always to rejoice to hear; and which he ought always most seriously to consider. But *authoritative* instructions; *mandates* issued, which the member is bound blindly and implicitly to obey, to vote and to argue for, though contrary to the clearest conviction of his judgment and conscience; these are things utterly unknown to the laws of this land, and which arise from a fundamental mistake of the whole order and tenor of our constitution.

Source: Works of Edmund Burke (Boston, 1839: Charles C. Little and James Brown), vol. 2, p. 12.

reason is that committees are not strong in parliaments, as will be seen. Committees in a legislature have the potential to provide a powerful site for overseeing the executive. They are groups of legislators who specialize in a particular area of policy and who may become expert in it over the years. If they have a good professional staff, they may be able to match the offices of the executive in expertise and in the ability to handle evidence. If the committee can hold hearings and subpoena witnesses, it can provide a strong investigative force. But committees in parliamentary systems are usually weak, and so the oversight function devolves primarily on individual members of the parliament, who are not much of a match for the experts of the executive office. In presidential systems like that of the United States, in contrast, congressional committees can at their best operate as tough and knowledgeable watchdogs. (At their worst, of course, they can be tough, cranky, and perverse watchdogs—to some extent, this depends on one's point of view.)

From the discussion up to this point, it might seem that a parliament is a poor fish. It has little control over legislation except inasmuch as the cabinet can be persuaded to amend its own bills, and it is not as powerful in oversight of the executive as legislatures elsewhere. The one thing we have noted that it does well is to conduct public debate of bills. All this looks meager as compared, say, with the Congress of the United States.

Source of the executive. However, there is another function of parliaments that is peculiar to parliamentary systems. The fourth function of a parliament in a parliamentary system is to provide a pool of trained people for service in the executive and a setting in which they operate while serving in the executive; a legislature like the U.S. Congress does not do this. In most parliamentary systems, nearly all members of the cabinet and other political appointments in the executive are members of parliament. In Britain in 2007, for instance, 91 members of the House of Commons were serving in such positions as prime minister, minister for defense, first lord of the admiralty, other cabinet positions, or lesser executive positions such as parliamentary undersecretary to the minister for defense. These were members from the Labour Party, the party that had a majority in the House, and so at the same time, something like another hundred members of the opposition parties were hoping for electoral success that would give *their* parties control of parliament and put them into executive positions. At any given time, therefore, about one-third of the members of the House of Commons either hold executive positions or are waiting for them; and of course, most of the rest are hoping to eventually be in this position.

The members of the political executive in a parliamentary system are men and women who have been selected by the other members of their party for executive tasks, and that selection is based largely on how well they have performed in debate and other tasks in the House. They are selected after some years of service in the House, which, like any organization, imposes norms of behavior on its members and in many subtle ways changes their behavior and the manner in which they react to things. Once they are in executive positions, these people are still sitting members of the House and take part in its daily business of debate, voting on bills, and so on. Even while they hold executive office, they rub shoulders daily with their colleagues in the House.

Thus, an important task of parliament in a parliamentary system is to produce those who will hold executive office, train them in the ways of politics, select them, and then serve as the site from which they conduct the executive functions. In a presidential system, the legislative part of government exercises its strength in opposing the executive; but in a parliamentary system, it exercises its strength through the executive.

✦ PARLIAMENTARY COMMITTEES

Committees of the U.S. House of Representatives and Senate are well known as independent, bristly bodies that presidents, bureaucrats, and even other members of the Congress defy only at their own risk. The State Department quivered in the 1950s when the House UnAmerican Affairs Committee investigated some of its younger personnel. Most bills that are introduced in the U.S. Congress are killed by a committee that refuses to vote them out with a recommendation, or else they die through delay in committees. This may even be true of bills originating in the presidential office.[4]

Such independent bodies within a parliament would greatly weaken the central unity of parliament with the executive, because as independent sources of power, the committees would make it more difficult for the executive leaders to control what happened in the parliament. For a parliamentary system to work well, power must as much as possible be lodged with the leaders of the parties and no one else.

Debate in the Canadian House of Commons.
© CP Images

---

[4]A good example is the refusal in 1997 of Jesse Helms, chair of the Senate Committee on Foreign Relations, to hold hearings on President Bill Clinton's nomination of William Weld for the position of ambassador to Mexico. Eventually, the president had to withdraw his nomination because he could not get the Senate to act on it as long as Helms' committee kept it bottled up.

For this reason, **committees** of a parliament are generally a good deal weaker and less assertive than those in the U.S. Congress. All parliaments must have committees, of course. If hundreds of bills are to be submitted to a parliament in a year, the work of scrutinizing those bills carefully must be divided up among the membership in some way or other; there is simply not time for each member of the parliament to do a careful job on all bills that come down in a year. But care is taken that the committees do not operate too independently in doing their work.

As an extreme example of this, consider committees in the British House of Commons. Where the U.S. Congress uses "standing committees"—such as the Committee on Foreign Affairs, with a set group of members who serve for years and may become expert in the areas of policy that they cover—the British set up an ad hoc committee for each bill as it comes in. The members of this committee are not people who regularly work together; they have been put together to consider this bill. They have not had years of specialized experience in a particular area of policy. They cannot subpoena witnesses and do not hold open hearings on their bill. They have no permanent staff. As one might imagine, their ability to transform legislation and put their own stamp on it is quite limited. The cabinet need not fear that its bill will be stopped or mangled by a committee in the House of Commons.

Other parliamentary systems are not so extreme. It is more convenient to use standing committees, so that a new group does not have to be constituted for each bill. Even the British have set up limited standing committees for the House of Commons (to oversee the executive and bureaucracy, not to review proposed bills). In smoothly working systems, however, even standing committees still do not operate with the independence of the committees in the U.S. Congress.

✦ ADVANTAGES AND DISADVANTAGES OF PARLIAMENTARY GOVERNMENT

Parliamentary government has two special advantages and disadvantages:

Advantages

1. The government can respond fairly directly to changed circumstances because power is unified. For example, parliamentary systems were more successful than fragmented systems such as the United States at developing national energy policies in response to the shortages of oil in the 1970s. In a parliamentary system, all it takes to make a law is a majority of the votes in the parliament, and so it is straightforward for the party or parties in power to develop a policy and write it into law. In more fragmented systems such as that of the United States, many barriers are raised that can slow down or halt the passage of a law. The president may veto the law, the Supreme Court may rule it unconstitutional, states may have proper jurisdiction over it, and so on.
2. A second advantage to a parliamentary system is that the lines of responsibility for policy making are clear. Elections should mean more, because voters can

know exactly whom to blame for their current situation: the party or parties in power. Parties can be held pretty well to their election promises once they are in office, because there is nothing to prevent them from accomplishing in office what they had said they would do. In a more fragmented system such as that of the United States, this is not so. There are so many independent centers of power that an unhappy policy cannot be blamed on any one of them. The president can say that Congress did it, Congress can point to the Supreme Court, and so on. President Harry Truman was famous for his desk-top slogan, "The buck stops here"; but in 1948, he campaigned across the country on the theme that the "do-nothing" Congress, controlled by the Republican Party, was to blame for his not having accomplished his goals as president. Elections can mean more with regard to public policy in a parliamentary system than in a more fragmented system because once election results are in, the party or parties that have won control of the parliament have no excuse for not enacting the policies they had promised.

Disadvantages

1. In a parliamentary system, there are few protections for a minority that feels it is being wronged. In a presidential system, a minority may hope that even if it has lost its fight in the legislature, it may retrieve things with the president, or vice versa. As a result, the support of a bare majority is usually not enough to get a law enacted.

    This may be seen as either an advantage or a disadvantage. It is the flip side of the advantage noted previously, that in a parliamentary system policy making is straightforward. Though this is in general a good thing, it is clear that there must be some times when we would wish that the government had been slowed down and had been prevented from taking hasty action or action that did not have fairly broad support. A parliamentary system, because of its efficiency, does not necessarily do this.

2. A second disadvantage to the parliamentary system is that it *may* produce unstable government. If no single party holds a majority of seats, as I have noted above, a coalition of parties must form a cabinet. This is fine if the partners of the coalition are in general agreement on most issues. But the coalition is strictly a marriage of convenience. If the parties in it disagree on enough things, it may be hard to keep them together and cooperating for very long. A socialist party may pull out because the coalition has not been able to agree on a program to stimulate employment, a Hindu party may pull out over a question of religious policy. At that point, the government "falls," and a new coalition must be negotiated.

    If this happens only occasionally, it is no problem. Political change must come from time to time. But in a parliamentary system, it sometimes happens that the numerical strength of the parties and their relationships with each other are such that it is always difficult to find a coalition that will keep together. This may lead to a paralyzing succession of governmental breakups, in which governmental control is so unstable that people lose confidence in the whole process. Germany suffered from this problem from 1918 to 1933, when Hitler overthrew the weakened democracy. France suffered from it until 1958, when the military intervened and imposed a presidential system. Italy has suffered from it chronically since 1945; in sixty-two years (as of 2007), Italians have had sixty different governments.[5] On the other hand, most parliamentary systems have not had this problem. The Scandinavian countries, the Low Countries, Germany, and others have had long histories of stable government by coalitions.

✦ LET'S MAKE SURE I HAVEN'T MADE THIS SOUND TOO SIMPLE

I have described above a "pure case" of parliamentarism, which is probably not met with exactly in any country of the world, although Great Britain comes close. You may have noticed that in describing parliamentary government, I hedged many of my statements with qualifiers like "usually" and "generally." I am a little concerned that you may have drawn the impression that lawmaking in a parliamentary system is easy for the cabinet, that it can just shoehorn bills through. Compared with most presidential systems (which we will look at in the next chapter), lawmaking in parliamentary systems is indeed more straightforward. But it is not automatic, and it does not come without conflict or debate.

Actually, many parliamentary systems have incorporated various rules or institutions that soften the cabinet's or parliament's monopoly on power. For instance, Germany, Canada, India, and some other parliamentary systems are federal states; this means that important areas of policy are taken out of the hands of the cabinet and parliament. Also, Germany and some other parliamentary systems tolerate fairly strong and independent committees in parliament, which obviously lessens the cabinet's domination of the parliament. Finally, a few parliamentary systems—Austria and Germany are two examples—have courts that can overrule an act of parliament.

In these and other ways, most parliamentary systems incorporate a few exceptions to the basic principles listed at the opening of this chapter. Overall however, even with these exceptions, the principles I have laid out hold, and those systems still have relatively more straightforward lawmaking than presidential systems.

✦ "CONSENSUS" PARLIAMENTARISM

The most notable exception to "pure case" parliamentarism is a variant called **consensus parliamentarism** that is found in a number of northern European states. Germany, Austria, the Scandinavian states, the Netherlands, and Belgium—roughly those states

---

[5]To address this problem, Italy changed its electoral system from proportional representation to a mostly single-member-district electoral system in 1999, and the 2001 election produced, for the first time, a cabinet with a stable majority of support in the Chamber of Deputies. (Not content with a good thing though, Premier Berlusconi forced through a return to PR in 2006 because he thought his party would do better under PR. Despite the maneuver his party and its allies lost their majority.)

that have "neocorporatist" interest representation (see above, pp. 294–296)—have parliamentary systems in which the distinction between government and opposition is more muted than in the "pure" sort of parliamentary system I have sketched above. These states comprise a very important exception, obviously covering a lot of real estate and making up a major part of the world economy.

Consistent with the thrust toward consensus in neocorporatist interest representation, the emphasis in these states is on forming a consensus among all parties in parliament, whether they are in the cabinet or in the opposition. Therefore, the cabinet does not run things so single-handedly, but negotiates and compromises at many points.

How does such cooperation work? First of all, as we saw when we looked at neocorporatism in Chapter 12, significant parts of the political process are removed from parliament (where the cabinet could control things) and are given to royal commissions or similar consultative committees, in which all interested parties are brought together. And then, once the process enters the parliament, the cabinet does not exert ruthless control over outcomes. Typically, for instance, parliaments in these states have fairly strong committees—and most importantly, the cabinet does not maintain control over the direction of the committees. Committee chairmanships are allocated to all of the parties in the parliament, whether they are in the cabinet or not, proportionally to how many members they have in the house. As a result, important policies tend to be developed over a longish period of negotiation, involving all parties.

Since in such a system it does not matter so hugely whether a party is in the cabinet or not, it is not uncommon to see a **minority cabinet,** one based on a coalition holding less than 50 percent of the votes in the parliament. Often, a party will decide that it would just as soon not be in the cabinet at that point in time, possibly for tactical reasons; and so it will promise not to vote for motions of no confidence, thus letting a set of parties, which could not otherwise survive as a cabinet, serve at its pleasure.

There are clearly some advantages to consensus parliamentarism. One important advantage is that policy remains more consistent over changes in the party makeup of cabinets. When a Labour-led coalition replaced a Conservative-led coalition in Norway in 2005, for instance, there was some change in emphasis, but no really dramatic changes in policy—for the simple reason that Labour had been in on the making of these policies all along.

The main disadvantage of consensus parliamentarism is that it loses the clean accountability that I earlier noted as one of the advantages of pure parliamentarism. In "pure" parliamentarism of the British sort we always know which party is responsible for government policy. Elections can function effectively to enforce accountability, as voters look over the government's record and decide whether to "throw the rascals out." Under consensus parliamentarism it is harder to do this. In a sense, all of the parties are equally "rascals" (or not), since they have all been involved in the making of the policies.

How did consensus parliamentarism come about? These are all states with proportional representation electoral systems, which means that they have multiparty systems, which in turn means that they must have coalition governments. It has been argued by some that it is this need for coalition that has led habits of cooperation to develop, and that it is therefore the proportional representation electoral system that lies at the heart of consensus parliamentarism.[6] However, many multiparty-based parliaments elsewhere—Canada, India, Italy, Spain, Greece, and others—have not developed the same sort of consensus and cooperation between government and opposition. It appears more likely that the political culture of northern Europe provides hospitable ground for such cooperation, which shows up both in neocorporatism and in consensus parliamentarism.

The contrast between consensus parliamentarism and "pure" parliamentarism may offer another instance of the distinction between power and choice. Certainly, the exercise of power is direct and uncompromising in "pure" parliamentarism, while in consensus parliamentarism one has a sense of governing parties yielding some of the power advantages they might otherwise enjoy, in order to help reach more stable solutions to collective choices.

✦ PARLIAMENTS IN AUTOCRATIC SYSTEMS

Many states that are not parliamentary systems as described still have a parliamentary body. We saw in Chapter 10 that many nondemocratic systems have found it useful to hold elections for a variety of reasons; similarly, many of them find it useful to have a parliament. All a parliament is, after all, is a set of people who are designated to represent other groups of people, usually with some sort of geographic focus to the represented groups. It is not necessary that the parliament be able to operate independently or that it have discretion over laws. It can still do a number of useful things.

China's National People's Congress, for instance, is expected to—and does—ratify all laws that are submitted to it by the cabinet. It is not an elected body. Rather, its members are selected by municipal and provincial congresses, whose members are also not elected. Selection at all levels is controlled by the single legal party, the Communist Party, and the Party makes sure that mavericks do not get into the Congress.

The Congress is not intended as a body to control the making of laws, or in any other way to control the politics of China. It is obvious just from its size of about three thousand members, and from the fact that it meets only once annually for ten days, that it is not meant to do demanding work. About 70 percent of its members are government officials, and are not about to kick up dust. The meetings of the Congress consist of listening to speeches, voting to approve bills submitted by the government (which always pass), and appointing officials (who are always approved).[7]

---

[6]Arend Lijphart, *Patterns of Democracy: Government Forms and Performance in Thirty-Six Countries* (New Haven: Yale University Press, 1999); G. Bingham Powell, Jr., *Elections as Instruments of Democracy: Majoritarian and Proportional Visions* (New Haven: Yale University Press, 2000).

[7]In a rare show of independence, the national People's Congress did refuse in 2006 to ratify a new law explicitly protecting private property, which left-wing factions of the Party were very uncomfortable with. It was pushed through in 2007, however. See above, page 272.

"TODAY THE PRIME MINISTER SIGNED TWO TREATIES, HELPED INCREASE OUR STEEL PRODUCTION, NARROWLY AVERTED WAR, AND SUGGESTED YOU BOTH SIGN UP AT SUNNYVALE RETIREMENT VILLAGE."

Reprinted by permission of ScienceCartoonsplus.com.

Is this institution purely a decoration, then? The National People's Congress does not make law, but it does serve other useful purposes. Many of the members, especially those who are not government officials, submit bills of their own; these are not expected to pass, but they provide an occasion for debate, which helps the cabinet and the rest of the Party establishment get a sense of what people outside Beijing are concerned about. Each year, over a thousand such proposals are submitted.[8]

Another thing the Congress does is to serve as a symbol of a unified nation. Three thousand delegates drawn broadly from across the country serve as a fine platform from which to lay down both symbolic and real statements about national purpose. And of course, the formality of enacting a law or appointing an official adds legal finality to a process that primarily has occurred within the Party.

The Congress, like the Party, serves as a useful conduit for popular feeling in a governmental system that permits neither a fully free press nor the formation of organizations that might serve as rival foci of power.

---

[8]"In China's Congress, A New Sense of Responsiveness," *New York Times,* March 8, 2005, p. A8.

❋ EXAMPLE

Parliamentary Government in India

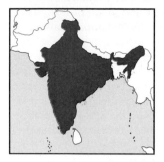

The general constitutional arrangement chosen for the new state of India in 1947 was largely drawn from the British parliamentary model, but a few devices were also borrowed from the United States. As is the case with any new state, including the United States in the early nineteenth century, India provides an interesting example of the evolution of governmental structure through custom and practice. It took the first four decades of politics in India to straighten out the relative power of the various parts of the government.

In the general outline of its constitution, India has a parliament consisting of two houses: The lower house is the Lok Sabha, or Council of the People, and the upper house is the Council of the States. A powerful prime minister and cabinet are responsible to the Lok Sabha, and a rather weak president oversees the whole structure. Thus far, India is a fairly standard parliamentary system, but it departs from common practice in two ways: (1) It is a federal system, with state governments that have a good deal of programmatic discretion, and (2) it has a powerful Supreme Court that can overturn actions of the rest of the government.

India faced grave problems on independence. Its people are relatively poor, with an average annual income per person of $3,700. This places the country among the bottom one-third of the world's states. At the same time, India's population of 1 billion people makes it the second largest state in the world and an important power on the international stage. India is deeply divided internally along ethnic and religious lines, with three major religions (Hindu, Sikh, and Moslem) and over fifteen major languages.

Until 1947, India was a colony of Great Britain. The pacifist leader Mohandas K. Gandhi and his Congress Party led a prolonged movement for independence, which succeeded in 1947. The Congress Party dominated early elections in the young democracy, and it was only in 1977 that an opposition coalition was able to break Congress's hold on power. Until 1989, a somewhat changed Congress Party ruled under Prime Minister Rajiv Gandhi, but throughout the 1990s, the situation was fluid, with Congress sometimes controlling the government, sometimes not. The 2004 elections resulted in a victory for Congress, defeating the previous government, which had been led by the Hindu BJP and fifteen smaller allies. The situation today is clearly one of competition, rather than a dominant-party system.

Against this background, let us look at the development of India's governmental institutions and particularly the Lok Sabha. One important issue that had to be worked out in practice over the early decades of independence was the power of the president, who is elected by an electoral college consisting of the members of both houses of Parliament plus the members of the state legislatures. Thus, it is conceivable that a president could be of a different party than the party that controlled the Lok Sabha and cabinet. The written constitution initially gave the president broad powers—among others, the power to rule by decree when Parliament was not in session, to declare a state of emergency and rule directly, and to dissolve Parliament or any state government and declare new elections. It might have happened that a strong, independent presidency would have evolved in India.

The dominance of the Congress Party in the early years ensured that this did not happen, however. Congress controlled both houses of Parliament and most state governments; and so a series of electoral colleges selected a series of presidents from the Congress Party. The prime ministers, who led Congress, made certain that weak and unaggressive people who would be willing to do what the prime minister told them to do were put into the presidency. Thus, the presidency developed into an office much like that of the queen in Great Britain. In a formal sense, all of the powers enumerated are the president's, but the president will exercise them only on the advice of the prime minister. This was formalized in an amendment to the Constitution in 1976, stating that the president "shall" act in accordance with the advice of the cabinet and prime minister. The practice was fixed even more firmly during a constitutional crisis the next year. In 1977, the Janata coalition won a majority of seats in the Lok Sabha, ousting the Congress Party after twenty years of dominance, and puts its own cabinet into place. This cabinet asked the president—B. D. Jatti, of the Congress Party—to dissolve the legislatures of the nine states that had Congress majorities and force new elections in those states. President Jatti hesitated for a day in doing what the cabinet requested, amid demonstrations and uproar, but finally gave in. Thus, the cabinet's supremacy over the president was established by something more dependable than words in a constitution; it was established by practice and precedent.

A second important question that had to be settled during this period was the relative power of Parliament and its cabinet vis-à-vis the Supreme Court. This question came to a point of crisis in 1967, when the Supreme Court ruled that an earlier amendment under which government land reforms were being administered was unconstitutional because it violated the fundamental rights guaranteed elsewhere in the Constitution.[9] (Among other things, the fundamental rights include a right against the expropriation of property.) Therefore, the government could not constitutionally carry out land reform programs of the sort it wanted, and there was no way in which the Constitution could be amended that would allow it to do so. In effect, the court ruled that the fundamental rights constituted a special part of the Constitution that was above all parliamentary action.

As one might expect, this ruling caused considerable uproar. Over the next few years, the court held to its position that the fundamental rights occupied a special place in the Constitution and struck down various acts of Parliament in their name. A crisis was finally reached in 1971, when Prime Minister Indira Gandhi, frustrated at her inability to pass her reform programs, asked the president to dissolve the Lok Sabha and call for new elections. The single theme of this election was the question of parliamentary supremacy over the court. When her Congress Party swept to victory with 352 of the 518 seats in the Lok Sabha, the prime minister had a popular mandate to establish Parliament as supreme. Parliament amended the Constitution with this simple addition:

> Notwithstanding anything in this constitution, Parliament may, in exercise of its
> constituent power, amend by way of addition, variation or repeal, any provision of this
> Constitution in accordance with the procedure laid down in this Article.

The next year this amendment was challenged in the Supreme Court. After the longest series of arguments ever heard there, the court gave in and sustained Parliament's right to amend any part of the Constitution.

Between these two developments—the establishment of the supremacy of Parliament and its cabinet first over the president and then over the Supreme Court—a basically parliamentary framework similar to that of Britain's was ensured. A third crisis was required, however, to establish firmly the principle of democratic government itself. In 1975, Prime Minister Gandhi was found guilty in a state court of minor campaign irregularities. The opposition parties in Parliament, and some members of her own party, pressed her to resign as prime minister.

---

[9]Under the Indian Constitution, Parliament is responsible for initiating amendments to the Constitution. Many sorts of amendment can be passed by a simple majority in both houses, while certain sensitive areas require a two-thirds majority in both houses. Ratification by half the states is then necessary for the amendment to become law.

To forestall such efforts, Gandhi struck first. She persuaded the president to declare a state of emergency so that she could rule dictatorially through him. She then had most of the leaders of the opposition arrested, banned a number of opposition organizations, and introduced a considerable degree of censorship for the press. In all, perhaps fifty thousand people were arrested for political reasons.[10]

This crisis for democracy was resolved in 1977, when Gandhi called for a new election to the Lok Sabha. Presumably, she thought that her party would win this election, but in a massive rejection of her seizure of power, the voters reduced the Congress Party to 153 out of the 543 seats in the Lok Sabha. Congress was out of power for the first time since 1945. Though Congress and Indira Gandhi returned to power in 1980 after the opposition parties proved incapable of governing effectively, the point had been made.[11] The 1977 election was a strong reaffirmation by the Indian people of their desire for democratic government.

To focus more specifically on the Parliament of India and how it operates, let us first note that the upper house, the Council of States, has less power than the lower house. This is typical of parliamentary systems; another good example is the British House of Lords, whose members have the power only to delay, not block, bills passed by the House of Commons. The members of the Council of States are not directly elected by voters, which would give them more prestige and legitimacy, but rather are chosen by the state legislatures and are sent to the Council of States to represent their states. Most bills require the Council of States' assent to become law, but there is an important limitation on this power. No money bills, including the annual budget and all tax laws, require the assent of the Council of States. The Council discusses each money bill and may make suggestions to the Lok Sabha, but the Lok Sabha has sole authority to pass the bill. Finally, the most important of all limitations on the power of the Council of States is that the prime minister and cabinet are responsible only to the lower house. This is almost universally true of parliamentary systems. It means that the prime minister and cabinet require the support of a majority of the Lok Sabha to exercise their power (they can be ousted at any time by a majority vote on a motion of "no confidence"), but they cannot be ousted by the Council of States.

The Lok Sabha plays a role much like that of the House of Commons in Britain. It has full powers to pass or deny legislation, and the cabinet depends on it for its power. However, because of party discipline, the Lok Sabha is controlled by the cabinet and its members do not feel individually all that powerful. From 1998 to 1999, for instance, of 71 bills introduced by the cabinet, 60 were passed; of 122 bills introduced by individual members, not one was passed.[12]

Aside from the usual informal cabinet domination of Parliament via party discipline, the Indian Constitution also gives the cabinet some formal powers that allow it further to dominate the parliament. The most important of these is the power to rule by decree when Parliament is not sitting. This was originally intended to allow for small matters that might need immediate attention when Parliament was not in session, but cabinets have come to use it as a device for taking measures they are not sure they could get through Parliament. Such actions as wage freezes, excise taxes, and rules to control smuggling have become law in this way, sometimes just days before or after Parliament was in session.

Still, the Lok Sabha functions importantly as a place for debate and one where the opposition can regularly scrutinize what the cabinet is doing. "Question time" has been borrowed from the British and has taken on a vigorous life in India. During the first hour of each parliamentary day, members of the cabinet are questioned by members of the house and their answers debated.

---

[10]D. C. Gupta, *Indian Government and Politics,* 4th ed. (New Delhi: Vikas, 1978), p. 657.

[11]Indira Gandhi was assassinated in 1984 by her Sikh bodyguards, as a result of tensions with militant Sikhs. Her son Rajiv took her place as prime minister and leader of the Congress Party, but he was in turn assassinated in 1991 by Tamil separatists.

[12]Lok Sabha Secretariat, *The Twelfth Lok Sabha, 1998–1999: A Study* (New Delhi: Lok Sabha Secretariat, 2000), pp. 135–36.

During the Twelfth Lok Sabha (March 23, 1998, to April 26, 1999), 197 questions were debated in this way, out of 1,362 that had been submitted.[13] All in all, though the Lok Sabha has had the usual rocky road of an institution with a new constitution that is being "broken in," the parliamentary system of which it is a part seems to have established itself reasonably well in India.

✼ EXAMPLE

Parliamentary Government in Germany

Germany has a parliamentary system of the "consensus" sort, but with an emphasis on dividing power at numerous points so that negotiation is unavoidable. (This contrasts with a system like that of Sweden or Norway, which does not have so many possible places that a policy can be vetoed, but emphasize more engendering cooperation by pulling policy out of parliament altogether, through the use of royal commissions.) The system was first set up in West Germany and has been extended, since German unification in 1990, to the eastern portion of the state as well. When the system was first set up in 1949, the disaster of Hitler's rule was still vivid in everyone's mind. The occupying forces from France, Britain, and the United States were anxious to prevent the rise of another dictator, as were the Germans who wrote the new Constitution with them. Accordingly, power was deliberately fragmented, so that it would be hard for any one person to seize it all. The resulting system of "checks and balances" may seem natural to American readers, but it is unusual in parliamentary government, even of the consensus sort.

Parliament is not wholly supreme in Germany, as it would be in a "pure" parliamentary system and as it nearly is in India. First, Germany, like India, is a federal system, so there are many areas of governmental activity that are not controlled by the national government. And compared with India, the national government has not devised as many ways to control what the state governments do. Furthermore, there is an active system of judicial review in Germany, with perhaps the most accessible Supreme Court in the world.[14] Among other things, the court has, for example, barred national administrations from outlawing the Communist Party and from establishing a national television network, and has determined the shape of Germany's laws on abortion. Federalism and the system of judicial review were new constitutional devices for Germany in 1949, inserted into the Constitution to diffuse and limit the exercise of power.

Another limitation on the power of the lower house, the Bundestag, and its cabinet is that Germany's parliament has a powerful upper house that may bar the lower house from many actions. We have seen that the House of Lords in Britain and the Council of States in India have little power to block a bill. However, the upper house of the German parliament, the Bundesrat, does have the power to block bills of many kinds.

The Bundesrat was strengthened in the Constitution to protect the powers of the newly established states. Its members are not directly elected but are appointed by the governments of

---

[13]Ibid., p. 112.
[14]Any German citizen may bring a case directly to the Supreme Court by simple petition; this does not even require a lawyer.

the states. Under the Constitution, its consent is required for constitutional amendments and for any law that affects the administrative, tax, or territorial interests of the states. Such bills require the support of a majority in the Bundesrat to become law. An amendment to the constitution in 2006 reduced the number of bills deemed to fit this requirement to a bit over one-third of all bills. On all other bills, the lower house may override a Bundesrat veto.

As a result of these provisions, the lower house and its cabinet often do not have the free play to make policy that should theoretically be theirs in a parliamentary system. Whole areas of policy, such as education, are under the control of the states. Also, the cabinet and lower house may find that what they wish to do is ruled unconstitutional by the Supreme Court. Finally, if the Bundesrat is controlled by a different party than the lower house, the cabinet may find that it continually has to compromise with the opposition to get its bills through. From 1991 to 2005, there was only one year in which a governing coalition in the Bundestag also had a majority in the Bundesrat. (Since 2005, with the two largest parties united in a coalition of convenience, one or the other of the two coalition partners has controlled every state, and so the Bundesrat has been controlled by the cabinet parties.)

The system generally produces compromise, but it can sometimes produce gridlock. A good example was the government's failure in July 1997 to pass a major tax reform. The Christian Democratic–controlled cabinet passed in the Bundestag a program to reduce high-end income taxes. This was defeated in the Social Democratic–controlled Bundesrat. The Social Democrats then passed in the Bundesrat their own counterproposal, to reduce labor costs in return for increased taxes and social benefits; this plan in turn was defeated in the Bundestag. End result— no change.

The lower house is set up along the familiar lines of parliamentary government. The cabinet is responsible only to the lower house, as is standard parliamentary practice, and so the lower house controls who sits in the executive. In its turn, the cabinet uses its control of party organization to ensure strict party voting in support of its bills. From 1961 to 1980, there were only fifteen instances in which a member of a party broke ranks and voted against the party position in the Bundestag.[15]

Even within the lower house, however, there are more checks and balances than we find in a pure parliamentary system. While party leaders expect total support for their parties' positions, ordinary members have more influence over what those positions will be than is the case in Britain.

First, the parties meet regularly as caucuses to determine their positions on bills. Members actually spend more of their time in meetings of the party caucus than in full meetings of the house. Policies are debated extensively within the party caucus, and the parties have full committee structures within the caucus, parallel to the committees of the Bundestag itself, to give careful and skilled scrutiny to each proposed bill. Thus, the party position on bills is not dictated to ordinary members by the party leaders so strongly as it is in Britain.

Second, unlike the British House of Commons, there are about two dozen specialized standing committees with professional staffs, which scrutinize bills before they go to the full house. Parties are given strength on the committees proportional to their strength in the house, and each committee selects its own chair. Each bill must be considered twice by one of these committees before it comes before the full house for a vote, and it may be heavily amended by the committee.

The general tone of the Bundestag is businesslike and rather dull, with a strong overtone of interest-group neocorporatism. The members are highly skilled (about one-third hold doctorates)

---

[15]Tony Burkett, "Developments in the West German Bundestag in the 1970s," *Parliamentary Affairs* 34 (Summer 1981), p. 302.

but tend not to be politically combative. In a survey in the late 1970s, 47 percent of the members were civil servants who had gone on leave to serve in the Bundestag, while a further 13 percent were officials of interest groups.[16] In a survey in the early 1990s, 10.3 percent of members of the Bundestag were senior officials of interest groups.[17] Full sessions of the house do not provide ringing rhetoric. For example, the Bundestag, like many parliaments, has a "question hour," but answers are often provided in writing by the minister rather than in person and are read to the Bundestag by an assistant.

The end result of all this is that German parliamentarism does not provide simple lines of responsibility. Even a defeat of the cabinet on a major bill in the lower house does not necessarily lead to the fall of the cabinet, because the Constitution provides for the ouster of a cabinet only under carefully specified conditions.[18]

The ruling parties cannot necessarily be held responsible by the electorate for the state of public policy, because the policy may actually not have been their choice. It may have been forced on them by the Bundesrat or the Supreme Court, or it might be policy of the "states" rather than of the central government. German parliamentarism, while it retains the general form and most of the flexibility of parliamentarism, lacks the usual advantage of a clean line of responsibility.

---

[16]Ibid., p. 305. Interest-group officials generally take a special interest in their group's concerns, seeking positions on useful committees and in general binding the parliament and the interest-group system tightly together. This helps to produce a "neocorporatist" blending of interest groups and government.

[17]Thomas Saalfeld, "Germany: Bundestag and Interest Groups in a 'Party Democracy,' " in Philip Norton, ed., *Parliaments and Pressure Groups in Western Europe* (London: Frank Cass, 1999), p. 48.

[18]The only way a cabinet can be brought down is for the opposition to propose a motion of no confidence, including a statement of who the new chancellor would be; the motion requires a majority to pass. The cabinet is not required to resign if one of its major bills fails to pass.

KEY TERMS

parliamentary government	constitutional monarch	consensus parliamentarism
cabinet	coalition	minority cabinet
head of state	question time	
	legislative committees	

FURTHER READING

Bowler, Shaun, Farrell, David M., and Katz, Richard S., eds. *Party Discipline and Parliamentary Government.* Columbus: Ohio State University Press, 1999.

Cain, Bruce, Ferejohn, John, and Fiorina, Morris. *The Personal Vote.* Cambridge: Harvard University Press, 1987.

Cox, Gary W. *The Efficient Secret.* New York: Cambridge University Press, 1987.

———, and McCubbins, Mathew D. *Legislative Leviathan: Party Government in the House.* Los Angeles: University of California Press, 1993.

Fenno, Richard F., Jr. *Learning to Legislate: The Senate Education of Arlen Specter.* Washington, DC: Congressional Quarterly Press, 1991.

Jennings, Ivor. *Cabinet Government.* 3d ed. New York: Cambridge University Press, 1969.

Kurian, George Thomas. *World Encyclopedia of Parliaments and Legislatures.* Washington, DC: Congressional Quarterly Books, 1997.

Laver, Michael, and Schofield, Norman. *Multiparty Government: The Politics of Coalition in Europe.* Oxford: Oxford University Press, 1990.

Lijphart, Arend. *Patterns of Democracy: Government Forms and Performance in Thirty-Six Countries.* New Haven: Yale University Press, 1999.

Loewenberg, Gerhard, Squire, Peverill, and Kiewit, D. Roderick, eds. *Legislatures: Comparative Perspectives on Representative Assemblies.* Ann Arbor: University of Michigan Press, 2002.

Miller, Warren E., Pierce, Roy, Thomassen, Jacques, Herrera, Richard, Holmberg, Sören, Esaiasson, Peter, and Wessels, Bernhard. *Policy Representation in Western Democracies.* New York: Oxford University Press, 1999.

Pitkin, Hanna Fenichel. *The Concept of Representation.* Berkeley: University of California Press, 1967.

Poguntke, Thomas, and Webb, Paul. *The Presidentialization of Politics: A Comparative Study of Modern Democracies.* New York: Oxford University Press, 2004.

Przeworski, Adam, Stokes, Susan C., and Manin, Bernard, eds. *Democracy, Accountability, and Representation.* New York: Cambridge University Press, 1999.

Rose, Richard. *The Problem of Party Government.* New York: Free Press, 1974.

Sawer, Marian, Tremblay, Manon, and Trimble, Linda. *Representing Women in Parliament: A Comparative Study.* Oxford, UK: Routledge, 2006.

Searing, Donald D. *Westminster's World: Understanding Political Roles.* Cambridge: Harvard University Press, 1994.

Strøm, Kaare. *Minority Government and Majority Rule.* New York: Cambridge University Press, 1990.

————. "The Presthus Debacle: Intraparty Politics and Bargaining Failure in Norway." *American Political Science Review* 88 (March 1994), pp. 112–27.

————, Müller, Wolfgang C., and Bergman, Torbjørn. *Delegation and Accountability in Parliamentary Democracies.* New York: Oxford University Press, 2004.

Parliamentary Affairs and *Legislative Studies Quarterly* are useful specialized journals relevant to this chapter.

WEB SITES OF INTEREST

Inter-Parliamentary Union, with links to the parliaments of many countries:

http://www.ipu.org

U.S. Senate:

http://www.senate.gov

U.S. House of Representatives:

http://www.house.gov

Roll Call, a daily newspaper covering the U.S. Congress:

http://www.rollcall.com

Project Vote Smart, a site with information about campaign finance and voting records of members of Congress:

http://www.vote-smart.org

British Parliament:

http://www.parliament.uk

Canadian government, with wide range of features on the Canadian Parliament, prime minister, and cabinet:

http://canada.gc.ca/main_e.html

Hansard Society, non-partisan British group promoting effective parliamentary democracy:

http://www.hansard-society.org.uk/

CHAPTER 15

NATIONAL DECISION-MAKING INSTITUTIONS: PRESIDENTIAL GOVERNMENT

Presidential government is a democratic system in which the legislature and the executive exist independently and are elected independently of each other. Both parts of the governmental apparatus are responsible for the making and carrying out of law; but they are independent, so it often happens that they compete and find themselves in conflict. The executive and the legislature are not forced into the kind of cooperation that tends to be ensured in a parliamentary system, where the two depend closely on one another.

As you note from the map in Figure 14.1, there are a large number of presidential systems in the world. The United States is probably the best known, but most Latin American states are also presidential systems, including large and important states like Mexico and Brazil. Most of the democracies found in Africa are presidential systems, as are some Asian democracies. A number of East European states—including the hugely important country of Russia—are presidential systems. Let us see how these systems work, and how they compare with parliamentary systems. I will emphasize the United States in these comparisons, because of its greater familiarity to students.

Just as the political party provides a glue that allows the parliament and its cabinet to function in intimate cooperation, so, in a presidential system, the political party may operate to soften the natural competition between independent executives and legislatures. In the United States, for example, the president, as head of one of the two great parties, is always guaranteed a large number of friends in the Congress. The system does not force the sort of unity on the president and his party's members of Congress that we would see in a parliamentary system, but still the bond of party allows for a good deal of coordination and cooperation.

However, note two things about presidential-legislative cooperation via party ties:

1. Parties are often more loosely unified in presidential systems than in parliamentary systems. In parliamentary systems, the premier and cabinet hold over the heads of ordinary members of parliament the threat that they may not advance into executive office if they do not cooperate with the leadership. In a presidential system, the president has little control over the careers and advancement of members of the legislature and cannot force unity on them. Even when the president's party has a majority of the seats in the legislature, the president will usually not be able to control what happens in the legislature as closely as most cabinets can control their parliaments in parliamentary systems.

2. There is no guarantee that the party that holds the presidency will also control the legislature. The two parts of the governmental apparatus are elected independently, so it may well happen that one party will have prevailed in the presidential election and another in elections for the legislature. For instance, throughout the 1980s, the Republican Party held the U.S. presidency and at times controlled the Senate, but the Democratic Party controlled the House of Representatives. And the same situation held in reverse for much of the 1990s. After the 2006 election the Democratic Party controlled both houses of Congress but George W. Bush, a Republican, was President. When there is divided control such as this, cooperation between the two branches of government is even more fragile.

In some multiparty, presidential systems (Brazil is an example), presidents negotiate formal coalitions of parties to support their program, awarding cabinet posts to their leaders. This may help to lessen the possibility of gridlock. However, the continued existence of the cabinet does not depend on its ability to get its program passed, as it would in a parliamentary system. The president is independently elected and will continue in office no matter what happens to his bills. Not being "joined at the hip" as in a parliamentary system, presidents and their supporters, even those in a legislative coalition, have a much looser relationship than a cabinet and its supporters in a parliamentary system.

In some other presidential systems, unified parties provide for more coordination than is found in the United States. Russia, for instance, has a presidential system that has come to be dominated by Vladimir Putin, president from 2000 to 2008. After the 2003 parliamentary elections his party, United Russia, held 309 of the 450 seats. In the run-up to the 2007 parliamentary elections a second party, Just Russia, was formed, which pledged to support Putin just as much as United Russia. All other parties have been marginalized through legalities, control of the media, and intimidation, so it appears that the 2007 election will be mainly "contested" by two parties equally pledged to the support of President Putin.

With the exception of questionable, controlled democracies like Russia, presidential systems do generally exhibit a good deal less coordination between the executive and the legislature than we see in parliamentary systems.

The legislature is a coequal body to the executive in a presidential system, so how is the legislature organized and how does it function? In a parliamentary system, the cabinet organizes the business of the legislature, but in a presidential system, the legislature must organize itself. How is this done? The U.S. Congress provides a good example.

A president has to straddle a range of supporters in Congress.
Copyright Gene Basset. Reprinted with permission.

The U.S. Congress consists of two equal houses, the House of Representatives and the Senate. Each house is governed by leaders elected by the party that has a majority in the house and by strong, independent committees whose chairs are appointed from among members of the majority party. Seniority—the length of time one has served in the house—is an important factor in deciding who will chair committees. For instance, in 2007, the Democratic Party had a majority in both the House of Representatives and the Senate. The majority leader of the Senate was Harry Reid of Nevada, and the speaker of the House was Nancy Pelosi of California. These two leaders exercised considerable influence over the business of their two houses, partly through their ability to persuade and partly through formal powers, such as the power to influence appointments to committees, to assign bills to committees, and to preside over debate.

However, the leaders cannot dominate their houses. Any bill must first be considered by a committee, and these committees operate independently and put their own considerable mark on bills that they bring to the full house. Power in each of the houses is so diffused—among leaders, committees, the minority party, and so on—that no one can be said to control what happens in either one.

The absence of control is heightened by the fact that voting in Congress is much less a party affair than it would be in a parliament. As we have seen, in a parliamentary system, regular failure by members to support their party's position would lead to collapse of the cabinet; for this reason, among others, members usually vote tightly along party lines. In the Congress, this incentive for discipline is lacking, and so members of Congress choose their votes more individually. Though congressional parties are more united than they used to be, it is still the case that fewer than half of all bills passed by the House of Representatives are "party votes" even in the modest sense that over half the Democrats voted on one side and over half the Republicans on the other.

✦ PRESIDENTIAL AND PARLIAMENTARY SYSTEMS COMPARED

What difference does it make whether a state is a parliamentary or a presidential system? Some differences include the following (I will expand on each of these in the next several sections):

- Policy leadership is often more clearly lodged with a president than with a parliamentary cabinet.
- Responsibility for policy is more difficult to identify in a presidential system.
- Comprehensive policy is more difficult to accomplish in a presidential system than in a parliamentary system.
- Recruitment of executive leaders differs in the two systems.
- There are special problems for review and control of the executive in a presidential system.
- The political process is less flexible in presidential systems than in parliamentary systems, because of presidents' fixed terms.
- The symbolic and political aspects of the executive are unified in a presidential system but split in a parliamentary system.
- Constitutional review of some sort seems to be more necessary in a presidential system, as is true in general of divided systems of power.

Let us first consider the question of policy leadership. Presidents have a personal mandate from the voters; therefore, they are able to take more direct personal charge of policy than the cabinet can in a parliamentary system. A parliamentary cabinet owes its position to its parties' members in the parliament, and it must operate with them as a team. The president, on the other hand, is personally elected by the voters of the nation, and this is true of no other public official. This personal mandate focuses attention on the president, who is accordingly thrust into a position of policy leadership.

Unlike the cabinet in a parliamentary system, the presidential cabinet does not consist of party notables whose appointments are obligatory. Rather, presidents appoint a group of cabinet officials who will be beholden to them personally. Often, these officials come from positions in which they have had little political exposure: Over the last several decades, presidential cabinets in the United States have included college professors, lawyers, auto company executives, military officers, school superintendents, a president's brother, and other relatively nonpolitical figures. In general, prominent political figures are *not* included, and this helps to focus attention directly on the president and the president's staff.

In most presidential systems, the president is constitutionally designated as the commander in chief of the state's armed forces and is personally charged with the responsibility to direct the affairs of the state, dictatorially if necessary, in the event of war or emergency. The president is also given personal responsibility for the direction of foreign policy.

Finally, in the making of laws, the legislative branch in a presidential system habitually puts itself in a passive stance, waiting to respond to proposals that the president is expected to put forward.

A presidential system, then, provides for a coherent and unified policy leadership that may be lacking in a parliamentary cabinet, especially if that cabinet is formed of a coalition of parties and most especially if the state suffers from cabinet instability.

✦ RESPONSIBILITY FOR POLICY

Though a presidential system provides a clear focus for *leadership,* ironically, it blurs the final *responsibility* for policies. In a presidential system, no one part of the governmental apparatus can be held responsible for any particular policy or any particular lack of policy. If the president proposes a new energy tax and the tax is defeated in Congress, who is responsible for the lack of tax reform? Is the Congress obstinate? Should the president have proposed a tax that would have been more apt to pass? Should the president have lobbied harder for the bill? It might also happen that the bill would pass, but with amendments that changed it substantially. Is it now the president's bill? Congress's? No one's?

Presidential systems do not present a clear picture of the responsibility for policies, and this leads to two important weaknesses. First, when voters cannot pin the responsibility for policies on any particular official, their electoral choices become less significant. Should a voter upset at inflation in the United States in 1948 have voted Republican? That would have been a vote against the party of President Harry Truman, who should perhaps have been held responsible for the inflation. What if the "do-nothing" Republican-controlled Congress was at fault, as Truman claimed? Faced with a choice like this, the poor bewildered voter must vote on less policy-related criteria, such as a candidate's personality or personal favors that an incumbent candidate has been able to do while in office. Eventually, elections come to function less as vehicles by which voters can affect the making of policy.[1]

A second weakness of presidential government caused by its blurring of responsibility is that when public officials do not have clear responsibility for a policy, they may literally begin to behave irresponsibly. If Congress is not directly held responsible for producing a balanced budget, it is easy for members of Congress to vote simultaneously to cut taxes (which will look good to their constituents) and to build highways (which will also look good). "Through the fault of no one in particular," the government may spend more than it takes in.

Campaign platforms of U.S. parties provide another example of the chronic irresponsibility of presidential systems. Because a party's president cannot be blamed for failing to enact into law the party's promises—after all, Congress might not cooperate—it becomes easy for the parties to promise in their campaign platforms whatever they think the voters would like to hear. With power as fragmented as it is in a presidential system, the parties will never lack for an alibi if the voters should take them to task for not delivering on their promises.

---

[1] A large body of literature has long urged that the United States should try to accomplish "responsible party government" similar to that of Britain. The argument has been that U.S. parties should become more tightly disciplined, not that the constitutional division of power should be changed. A good example is E. E. Schattschneider, *Party Government* (New York: Holt, Rinehart and Winston, 1942).

✦ PRESIDENTIAL SYSTEMS AND COMPREHENSIVE POLICY

It is more difficult to make comprehensive policies in a presidential system than in a parliamentary one. Policies are more likely to be patched together of varied compromises or perhaps not put together at all. The United States is one of the few democracies that lacks a national energy policy, though this has not been for want of trying. Presidents have proposed energy policies to Congress but have never been able to get agreement on anything recognizable as a policy.

It is not enough that a mere majority of the people want something done, because a bill can be blocked at the many points in a fragmented system; considerably more than a majority is required if all the defensive positions provided by a fragmented system are to be overrun. Handgun control, prayer in the schools, and the equal rights amendment are examples of policies that a majority of the U.S. population probably want but that have been impossible to enact into law.

If you are suspicious of majorities, as many of the authors of the U.S. Constitution were, this may be seen as a good effect of the fragmentation of power. But there is no denying that it makes the government slow to respond to change.

✦ RECRUITMENT OF EXECUTIVE LEADERS

There is a significant difference between the sorts of leaders who emerge in parliamentary and presidential systems. In a parliamentary system, all or almost all the leaders in the executive have emerged from careers in parliament; indeed, they continue to serve in the parliament while they hold executive office. This means that they will have had fairly similar lives before they entered the executive. For a decade or two, their jobs will have consisted of crafting the wording of bills and serving the voters in their constituency. They will have had a long period of exposure to the wide range of issues facing the state in diplomacy, tax policy, education, defense, and so on.

The similarity of these executive officers is made greater by the fact that they are mostly selected from among the members of the parliament on the basis of a common set of criteria. Members who move up to executive office are those who do a good job of being a member of parliament: They debate well, they keep their noses to the grindstone, they vote with the party.

Recruitment in a parliamentary system has the virtue that officials are chosen by those who know them and their work (their fellow members of parliament) during a career that has made them familiar with most of the issues they will have to face. It has the disadvantage that there is not much variety among the types of people chosen, they have had little experience in managing things (legislators spend most of their time responding to initiatives of others), and there are few "mavericks" or adventurers included.

In a presidential system, recruitment into executive office is fairly independent of the legislative parts of government. While a president may have started off with a legislative career, this is by no means necessary. Consider the last ten presidents of the United States:

President	Background
Dwight D. Eisenhower	Army general
John F. Kennedy	Senator
Lyndon B. Johnson	Senator
Richard M. Nixon	Senator; vice president
Gerald Ford	Member of Congress
Jimmy Carter	Farmer; governor of Georgia
Ronald Reagan	Film actor; governor of California
George H.W. Bush	Appointee to various foreign policy positions; vice president
William Clinton	Governor of Arkansas
George W. Bush	Governor of Texas

More than half of these men had established themselves with the public by something other than service in one of the houses of Congress.

Furthermore, the recruitment of other officials to staff the executive does not draw heavily on Congress in the United States, or in most other presidential systems. Only a minority of the membership of recent U.S. presidents' cabinets have been drawn from careers in the Senate or House. Many of the most distinctive and interesting cabinet members have been drawn from careers that were far from Congress, careers that gave them interesting points of view of their own. Four examples are Henry Kissinger, secretary of state under Nixon and Ford, a university professor; Donna Shalala, secretary of health and human services under Clinton, chancellor of the University of Wisconsin; Colin Powell, secretary of state under George W. Bush, Army general; and Henry Paulson, secretary of the treasury under George W. Bush, CEO of Goldman Sachs.

This sort of selection has the advantage that it brings varied talents and backgrounds to the task of executive so that through the introduction of new blood, problems may be seen in a new light. New points of view and the zeal of amateurs may be brought into policy making at a high level, as in Jimmy Carter's campaigns on behalf of human rights.

On the other hand, selection is often haphazard, because it is not done by those who have worked directly with the candidates; candidates may have had little previous experience in important areas (Carter, Reagan, Clinton, and George W. Bush, for instance, had had no experience with foreign policy before they became president); and inappropriate choices are more likely than in a parliamentary system.[2]

In short, in a parliamentary system you know much more what you are getting than in a presidential system. For better or for worse, executive officials will not surprise you in a parliamentary system—but they will not disappoint you, either.

✦ REVIEW AND CONTROL OF THE EXECUTIVE

Most organizations have some sort of plural board to which the executive leader is responsible and reports regularly. The president of a business corporation must report regularly to a board of directors, the president of a university reports to the board of trustees of the university, a superintendent of schools reports to a school board, and so on.

[2]An argument for the desirability of recruitment in the parliamentary mode is made in Harold W. Chase, Robert Holt, and John Turner, *American Government in Comparative Perspective* (New York: Franklin Watts, 1980), chap. 2.

Cartoon by Dana Summers in *The Orlando Sentinel.* Reprinted by permission.

In a parliamentary system, the parliament serves this purpose. The prime minister and cabinet regularly report to the parliament on the conduct of their business, questions are asked, and so on. There is regular and frequent contact between the cabinet and the parliament regarding the conduct of government.[3]

In a presidential system, however, the members of the executive operate in relative isolation. The media looks over their shoulders constantly, of course, and there is occasionally contact between them and the legislature regarding a particular bill or investigation. However, there is no broader body to which the president or other members of the executive regularly report.

This isolation of the presidency often leads to an inward-looking presidential office, with "inside" staff persons accused by those on the outside of arrogance and insensitivity. More seriously the lack of some regular device for review and control of the president made the Watergate crisis a good deal more traumatic for the United States than it might otherwise have been. When President Nixon was implicated in petty crimes at the Watergate office complex and it became apparent that some airing of the question was needed, there was no regular stage available for this, and extraordinary procedures for impeachment were required. Had he been a prime minister, he would have been called to task in the parliament as a matter of ordinary business.

---

[3]For further comparison along these lines, see William S. Livingston, "Britain and America: The Institutionalization of Accountability," *Journal of Politics* 38 (November 1976), pp. 870–94.

→ FLEXIBILITY OF THE POLITICAL PROCESS

Parliamentary systems are able to adjust readily to changing circumstances. If a parliamentary leader loses support after a couple of years, or if new political issues arise that rearrange the political landscape, it is not very complicated for the system to adjust. The existing cabinet can be ousted if some of the parties that originally supported it withdraw their support, or if the current leader is discredited, and then a new cabinet can be negotiated—with a new leader, or arranged along different political lines, or whatever is needed to accommodate the changed circumstances. A presidential system, however, exists unchanged for a fixed term of years, until the next presidential election. The president cannot easily be ousted if circumstances change. A particularly difficult problem is posed if the president becomes very ill, in which case there is always a good deal of uncertainty about who has the power to declare the president incompetent to govern and replace him or her with someone else. And if the president dies, in many presidential systems this means that a vice president will succeed to supreme power—someone typically who would never otherwise have attained the leadership of the state, and who may be quite inappropriate for the job.[4]

→ THE SPLIT EXECUTIVE OF PARLIAMENTARY SYSTEMS

Oddly enough, given that parliamentary systems are based on the principle of unifying power, the executive is split in parliamentary systems into the prime minister and cabinet who are responsible for political and administrative leadership, and a head of state who is responsible for the symbolic leadership of the state (see above, pp. 320–321). In a presidential system, these functions are united in a single person—the president.

In Britain, the prime minister and cabinet are responsible for political and administrative leadership, but it is the queen who carries on the ceremonies and personifies the state. It is she who opens new hospitals and bridges; it is her health and that of her family that the media subjects to ghoulish scrutiny; it is she at whose death the nation will go into deep mourning. Like the president of the United States, she is greeted by a special song when she enters a room, and crowds press in on her wherever she goes. The prime minister remains a more mundane figure, one who goes about the daily business of governing but does not personally represent the state.

It is clear why the two kinds of executive function are united in one person in a presidential system. The executive is weakened in a presidential system by the fact that its legislature is not under its control; for strong leadership to be available to the state, almost everything that *can* be done to strengthen the president's hand *must* be done. One such thing, an important one, is to give presidents an aura of majesty that they can use to bolster their political power. More than one member of Congress has gone into

---

[4]Juan Linz, "The Perils of Presidentialism," in Arend Lijphart, ed., *Parliamentary Versus Presidential Government* (New York: Oxford University Press, 1992).

the White House and walked out shaken, muttering, "When the president of the United States asks you to vote in the country's interest, what can you do?"

In a parliamentary system, there is no need to add to the power of the cabinet in this way, because the cabinet is capable of providing effective leadership without it. If it is not necessary to combine the two faces of the executive in a single office, as is done in presidential systems, there are some obvious advantages to separating them.[5]

First, the symbolic representation of the state in a person appears to fill a deep need of a modern people. The devotion people feel for those who personify their state is real. Consider the following examples. At John F. Kennedy's assassination in 1963, many Americans felt what they later reported as an almost religious experience; in fact, some people felt his wounds as *stigmata,* just as some devout Christians feel Christ's wounds on the cross. In Britain, the most disturbing political event of the twentieth century, with the sole exception of the two world wars, occurred when Prince Edward VIII left the throne to marry a divorced American. Norwegians credit King Haakon VII with having almost singlehandedly kept the government from surrendering to Germany in 1941, taking his family into exile and making it possible for Norwegians to fight on in the Resistance. Finally, consider the heart-wrenching difficulty with which Americans faced what would have been a fairly simple task if they had not revered the presidency so much—the ouster of Richard M. Nixon in 1974 when he had been implicated in petty crimes.

If modern people need a person on whom to focus their reverence for the state, it is better if this is someone who has little involvement in day-to-day politics. The queen of Britain, the king of Sweden, the emperor of Japan, the president of Germany (not a president as the term is used in this chapter, but an almost purely ceremonial head of state)—these people have almost no political power and are not involved in routine decision making. This allows them to serve as unblemished objects of national affection. Presidents of the United States, in contrast, must excite mixed feelings among the many people who find themselves in political disagreement with them. On the one hand, these people want to revere the president, but on the other hand, they find themselves faced with a political leader whose policies they may despise. Conservative Republicans were in many ways deprived of an object for national reverence during the presidency of Bill Clinton. George W. Bush has been a very polarizing president.

Thus, one problem of blending the political executive and the symbolic executive in a single office is that the symbolic function cannot be performed as well when it is located in an office that is inevitably involved in controversy.

The flip side of this problem is that political leadership does not operate as cleanly when reverence for the state gets mixed up with it. A president of the United States gains unfair political advantage from serving as the symbol of the state. Franklin Roosevelt, Lyndon Johnson, Richard Nixon, and Ronald Reagan were adept at taking positions that had questionable public support, appearing on radio or television with the sober attention

---

[5]Note that my interpretation above is based on *choice* rather than power. I have been trying to explain why the two kinds of executive function are united in presidential systems but not in parliamentary systems, and my explanation has rested on the claim that the needs of society will have led systems to sort out in this way. In other words, since the collective choice of unified executive power is better for presidential systems, that is what will be made; since unified executive power is not needed in parliamentary systems, it will not occur there. A *power* interpretation might have been given instead, based perhaps on the greater opportunities a president has to aggrandize all executive power to herself.

that a president can command, and selling that endangered program to the public. After all, this man is the president of the United States! Whom can we trust more than him?

We may welcome this as a way to cut through the confusion of the divided powers of a presidential system, but it is still unfortunate that, on any public issue at a given time, only one side is able to take advantage of this reverential response. In a parliamentary system, the cabinet and the opposition operate on more even terms in seeking public support for their political positions.[6]

⤳ WHY AREN'T ALL DEMOCRACIES PARLIAMENTARY SYSTEMS?

Let us review for a moment what we have looked at in this chapter. I first described how presidential government operates, and I noted the main difference between a parliamentary system and a presidential system: that the one unifies power and the other divides it. I then examined several aspects of presidential government that result from this difference:

- Concentration of policy leadership with the president
- Difficulty of locating responsibility for policies
- Difficulty of making comprehensive policy
- A different pattern of recruitment for executive leaders
- Special problems for review and control
- A merger of the symbolic and political aspects of the executive in a single person

While not every one of these differences showed the presidential system to disadvantage, most did. You have probably been left with the impression that parliamentary systems are better than presidential ones. The parliamentary system is a simpler, more direct, and usually more efficient way of making public choices. Why aren't all democracies parliamentary systems?

The main reason lies in the very faithfulness with which a parliamentary system transposes political divisions into the policy-making machinery. Policy is set and administered in a parliamentary system by a party or a cooperative coalition of parties that controls a majority of the votes in the parliament. This makes for straightforward policy making if a stable majority is possible in the parliament. If the country is divided into numerous parties that are intensely hostile to each other, however, it may be impossible to find a large enough number of members of parliament who can work together cooperatively as a governing coalition. It may be that no working majority is available.

Under these circumstances, a parliamentary system may limp along with an unstable government, as Italy did from 1945 until very recently, or the country may prefer to use some system that divides power but is more stable than what parliamentarism could provide.

---

[6]Related arguments may be found in Edward Shils and Michael Young, "The Meaning of the Coronation," *Sociological Review* 1 (December 1953), pp. 63–81; and in Lewis Lipsitz, "If, as Verba Says, the State Functions as a Religion, What Are We to Do Then to Save Our Souls?" *American Political Science Review* 52 (June 1968), pp. 527–35; see also William E. Scheuerman, "American Kingship? Monarchical Origins of Modern Presidentialism," *Polity* 37 (2005), pp. 24–53.

Presidential Leadership

The presidency offers us a particularly good chance to study a vital aspect of politics that is much neglected in political science—leadership. Certainly, few things are more important to politics than the qualities that produce effective political leadership, but leadership is a difficult thing to pin down for analysis. Most political figures—members of Congress, prime ministers, cabinet officials—operate within such constraints of power that their main accomplishments come through bargaining and deal-making or through coalitions where their role is blended with that of others. It is often hard to pull out of a particular political outcome the contribution of any one person's leadership.

The American presidency, however, offers us an office whose leadership is available for examination every day in almost all political questions that face the country. Further, it is exceedingly well documented, with huge libraries of the papers of all postwar presidents. Various scholars have taken this opportunity to study leadership by studying the presidency—notably Richard E. Neustadt, who analyzed presidents' political strategies in *Presidential Power and the Modern Presidents* (New York: Free Press, 1991), and James David Barber, who analyzed presidents' emotional security and its effect on how productively they could provide leadership in *The Presidential Character* (Englewood Cliffs, NJ: Prentice-Hall, 1977). A superbly broad view of presidential leadership, based on decades of observation and reflection, is Fred I. Greenstein's *The Presidential Difference: Leadership Style from FDR to George W. Bush* (Princeton: Princeton University Press, 2004).

Greenstein views leadership as a function of six qualities, which could probably never all be perfected in any one person; for him, each of our modern presidents has represented a mix of strengths and weaknesses on these six qualities:

- *proficiency as a public communicator*
- *organizational capacity*—the ability to choose good advisors and to use them in such a way that they did not just parrot back his desired opinion but helped him to work through policy choices in a thoughtful way
- *political skill*—the ability to get other people to do what he wanted
- *vision*—having an overarching goal and the ability to see how specific policies would help bring about that goal
- *cognitive style*—the ability to process the torrent of advice and information the president receives on every issue. In other words, the ability to understand the policies he was pushing for.
- *emotional intelligence*—"the ability to manage his emotions and turn them to constructive purposes, rather than being dominated by them and allowing them to diminish his leadership."[7]

Greenstein does not rank these six characteristics (and resists in his book playing the cheap and easy game of ranking the presidents), but it appears that for him, the most critical

---

[7]Fred I. Greenstein, *The Presidential Difference: Leadership Style from FDR to George W. Bush* (Princeton: Princeton University Press, 2004), p. 6. Both Greenstein and I, by the way, use the exclusively male pronoun here to describe an office that until now has always been held by men. This almost certainly will not be the case for much longer.

qualities are proficiency as a public communicator and emotional intelligence. Cognitive style appears to rank surprisingly low among the criteria for success. As Greenstein points out, two presidents whom he regards as weak in cognitive capacity—Truman, because he relied too much on oversimplified analogies drawn from his readings of popular history, and Reagan because he just didn't care about details—were two presidents who had a major impact on the country.

France after World War II was plagued by parliamentary instability similar to that of Italy. The Communists could not cooperate with any of the other parties, Catholic parties had trouble cooperating with Socialists, and so on. In 1958, the regime collapsed through a revolt by French settlers in Algeria. The military terminated the fourth Republic and asked Charles de Gaulle to design a new system; his new constitution replaced parliamentary government with what is known as a **hybrid presidential system,** a mixture of parliamentary and presidential government, leaning heavily toward the latter. (See the French example presented in detail, pp. 357–359.)

In much of the Third World, too, democracies, whether or not they started out as parliamentary systems, have often found that they must provide a more stable base for executive leadership than is possible under parliamentarism, even at the cost of fragmenting and complicating public decision-making processes. Many Latin American democracies, under the influence of the United States, used presidential systems from the start; Mexico and Costa Rica are good examples. Many African and Asian democracies—faced with the political stresses of poverty, modernization, and ethnic diversity—have had to modify what started out as parliamentary systems. Nigeria, for example, abandoned parliamentarism when democratic government was reestablished in 1975 and set up a system with an independent presidency rather like that of the United States.[8] Russia has a strong presidency.

Perhaps the message of this chapter, in the end, is that a parliamentary system is the best form of democracy *if* a country is sufficiently unified to cooperate in parliamentary politics.

✦ CONSTITUTIONAL REVIEW AND THE FRAGMENTATION OF POWER

Wherever power is fragmented, there is a need for some institution that can operate as a referee to adjudicate disputes among the various holders of power. If a president has part of the power and a legislature has another part, how do we resolve the kind of dispute that must inevitably occur when the legislature says to the president, "You've just done something that's supposed to be left up to us"—or vice versa? The solution is to have some third institution that is empowered to serve as a referee. In the United States, this is the Supreme Court.

---

[8]This, in turn, succumbed to a military coup in 1983, but an elected presidency was reestablished in 1999.

TABLE 15.1

**Constitutional Review and Presidential Government:
Western Europe and North America**

	Constitutional Review?	
Presidential or Hybrid Systems		
France	Yes	
Mexico	Yes	
U.S.A.	Yes	
Parliamentary Systems		
Austria	Yes	
Belgium		No
Canada	Yes	
Denmark		No
Germany	Yes	
Great Britain		No
Iceland		No
Ireland	Yes	
Italy	Yes	
Luxembourg		No
Netherlands		No
Norway		No
Portugal	Yes	
Spain	Yes	
Sweden		No
Switzerland		No

Over the last two centuries, the U.S. Supreme Court has established that it has the right to annul acts of presidents and laws passed by Congress whenever it deems either body to have exceeded its proper powers. Although there is occasional grumbling about the Court and its power, it is striking how readily this essentially undemocratic arrangement is tolerated. Think of it! Nine people who are appointed by the president and the Senate and thereafter serve for the rest of their lives without ever being subject to popular election—these nine people wield huge power in our otherwise democratic system. The only explanation for Americans' ready toleration of this is their recognition that the fragmentation of power requires something like this to make their system work.

Constitutional review is found in almost all systems that fragment power and is rare in those that do not. In Table 15.1, the states of Western Europe and North America are divided according to whether the governmental system is parliamentary or presidential/ hybrid; we then note for each state whether it has a system of constitutional review. Note that all three presidential or hybrid systems have some form of constitutional review. Of the parliamentary systems, only seven of the sixteen countries have constitutional review.

A president does many things—President George
W. Bush shakes hands with Milwaukee Brewers'
manager Davey Lopes, left, after throwing out
the ceremonial first pitch before the start of the
Brewers' home opener.

© AP/Wide World Photos

And of these, four (Austria, Canada, Germany, and Spain) might have been expected to
have constitutional review in any case, because they are federal systems (see Chapter 9).
Federal systems, with their division of power between a central government and regional
governments, need constitutional review to function as a referee, just as presidential systems, with their division between executive and legislature, do.

The main exception to this rule (that fragmented power is the reason for constitutional review) is that constitutional review has also had some popularity since World
War II as a means of protecting individuals from the arbitrary use of state power. That
is, constitutional review has come to be seen as a tool of "constitutionalism," in which a
relatively nonpolitical court can help to place limits on the authority of the government.[9]
This helps to explain the popularity of constitutional review in Germany after the Nazi
dictatorship, although the federal system there probably would have required it in any
case. More to the point, it also helps to explain the institution of constitutional review in
Ireland and Italy, which have neither federal systems nor presidential governments.

---

[9]See the discussion of constitutionalism in Chapter 9.

✦ A NOTE ON CONSTITUTIONS AND POWER

Having looked at formal governmental arrangements in this chapter and in Chapter 14, I should note an important principle of constitutions that is well illustrated by the development of some of the governmental institutions we have examined.

We saw in Chapter 9 that written constitutions are not static but change and develop as they are put to use. One predictable way in which constitutions change is this: *If power is given constitutionally to a body that lacks the resources to exercise it, informal mechanisms usually develop that lead to the de facto loss of that power even though the formality of power remains.*

One excellent example of this principle at work is the domination of parliaments by their cabinets. Parliaments are vested with supreme authority in the constitutions of parliamentary systems, but a parliament is too large and diverse a group to actually take charge of governmental policy by itself. Over the years, cabinets have developed ways to bully parliaments through the informal mechanism of the disciplined political party. This has shifted actual power from the parliament to its cabinet, which allows policy to be made coherently; but the parliaments remain formally supreme. Political parties are rarely even mentioned in the constitutions of democracies, but they are an important part of living constitutions.

A second example is provided by the Bundesrat, the upper house of the German parliament, described in Chapter 14. The Bundesrat, you will recall, was established in the Constitution to protect the independence of the new "states" from the central government. If Germany was to be a federal system, it was reasoned, the states needed a lever in the central government to allow them a veto over actions that would take away their rights. Therefore, the Bundesrat was established. It consists of representatives from the state governments and must give its consent to any action affecting their tax, administrative, or territorial interests.

Ironically, setting up the Bundesrat and giving it these powers has made it, and the states that appoint its members, sufficiently important to national political leaders that they try to control what goes on in state politics and have undermined the independence of state leaders in important ways. Elections for state governments often turn on a national issue rather than on those of the state. Figures from the central government campaign hard in the state, not for local figures or for the local party but on national political questions. And once a state election is over, national leaders often put pressure on local leaders to form a particular sort of coalition in the state parliament solely because of the effect the nature of the local coalition will have on the state's votes in the Bundesrat. The existence of the Bundesrat has arguably had an effect just the opposite of what was intended by the framers of Germany's Constitution. The states' prerogatives would have probably been protected adequately by the Supreme Court if the Bundesrat had never been set up, and local political leaders would have been free to operate more independently of national leaders.

In these examples, actual power relationships—the living constitution—have fit themselves to the power of groups in ways quite different from what was intended by those who designed the formal document. Such mismatches between reality and formal rules usually result from a failure to appreciate fully the "power" in "power and choice."

If one thinks of politics primarily as a question of working out proper choices for the state, it will seem that an appropriate set of procedures should do that, and good politics will follow from good written procedures. This ignores the necessities and possibilities of power and can lead to surprises for those who write rules.

✷ EXAMPLE

Presidential Hybrid in France

After World War II, France set up a fairly standard parliamentary system. It was immobilized, however, by the hostility of various parties to each other and by weak discipline within many of them, which made it difficult for coalitions to form and hold together. The average life of a cabinet was about six months, and because ministers did not stay in place long enough to get full control of their offices, France was governed by its bureaucracy rather than by its elected leadership.[10] There was a sense of drift, and when in 1958 tensions associated with Algeria's war for independence were added to the mix, things fell apart. The military took over, and Charles de Gaulle, the hero of World War II, was brought in to set up a new system.

De Gaulle and his advisers designed a new type of democracy with elements of presidential and parliamentary government in which, however, the presidential elements have gradually come to dominate. As first designed, the system consisted of a cabinet responsible to the National Assembly (the lower house of parliament) and of a rather powerful but nonpolitical president. The president, indirectly elected by an assembly of parliament and of mayors, was, in turn, to designate the premier and to preside over the affairs of government, especially foreign affairs and defense policy. The president could bring issues before the French electorate in the form of a referendum and could, if necessary, declare a state of emergency and take over power for up to six months at a time. The president could not veto acts of parliament.

Although this was a powerful position, it did not provide much more than what is implicit in the powers of the queen of England or what was implicit in the powers of the French president from 1945 to 1958. The key question was whether the French president would act as a primarily symbolic figure, performing these functions only on the advice of the cabinet, or would realize the full potential of the office's powers. De Gaulle served as the first president under the new system from 1958 to 1969. He exercised his potential power strongly and added to that power in three important ways:

- In 1962, he had the Constitution changed so that the president was directly elected. The president has since then carried great prestige as the only official elected by all the people of France.
- He set up an executive office with a structure that paralleled the ministries of the cabinet. Any bill that a ministry wished to submit to parliament had to be cleared by its counterpart

---

[10]Ironically, the bureaucracy governed France rather well. During this period, France pioneered in establishing the European Economic Community, and its per capita income grew at a rate of 3.5 percent annually in real terms throughout the 1950s.

bureau in the executive office. Eventually, many important policies began to be set in the executive office even without the knowledge of the minister involved.

- He established the principle that a president could dismiss a premier at will. The Constitution states that the president "designates" the premier but says nothing about dismissal. In 1962, de Gaulle asked his first premier, Michel Debre, to resign, and Debre did so. From that point on, another important element of presidential power had been established.

Today, as long as the same party simultaneously holds the presidency and controls the parliament, the premier and cabinet function as agents of the president, conducting much of the day-to-day business of the state and representing the president in relations with the parliament.

The new Constitution included a large number of constraints on the independence of the parliament, intended to prevent the immobility that had characterized French government before 1958. An absolute majority of members is required to overthrow a cabinet, so that abstentions or absent members count as votes in favor of the cabinet on a motion of confidence. When the cabinet submits a bill to the parliament, the cabinet has the right to list the priority within which the bill will be debated and the rules of debate; therefore, the cabinet is given considerable power in scheduling the work of the parliament. (Among other rules, the cabinet can require that a bill be voted on as a whole, rather than having a separate vote on any amendment; this frequently used device makes it difficult to amend a bill.) Members of the parliament are constitutionally barred from offering amendments to a bill that would have the effect of either adding to state expenditures or decreasing state revenues; an amendment requiring new expenditure, for instance, must include either a compensating cut in some other expenditure or an increase in taxes. Finally, the independence and power of parliamentary committees were decreased by the simple device of limiting their number to six. This ensured that they would be large bodies (the average size of committees is over a hundred members) covering broad areas of policy and that they would never again be able to develop into tight-knit groups of specialists.

By laying down these rules, the new French Constitution brought about executive supremacy of the sort that in most parliamentary systems is achieved informally through the political party. Constitutional design was used to ensure executive supremacy because parties had failed to establish the necessary discipline. One could argue that the informal device is better because it is more flexible, but the constitutional devices appear to have worked well in France.

These rules established executive domination over the parliament, and—as things have developed in France—"executive" usually means the president. However, an oddity of the French hybrid of parliamentary and presidential systems is that, because the president governs through a cabinet that can be turned out of office at will by the National Assembly, it is crucial whether the same party controls the presidency and the National Assembly. If the president's party has a majority (or close to it) in the National Assembly, things work smoothly in the way I have described previously; the president names a cabinet, and the party's majority in the National Assembly supports it. This has been the situation for all but ten of the almost fifty years since the establishment of the Fifth Republic.

However, if the president's party does not control the National Assembly, there is a possibility of deadlock. It is at least theoretically possible that the president could name cabinet upon cabinet that would be voted down by the National Assembly as quickly as they were named. The president could not rule under these circumstances.

Split control of the presidency and National Assembly has occurred three times. In 1985, conservatives won a majority in the National Assembly, and President François Mitterrand, a socialist, had to appoint Jacques Chirac, a Gaullist, to the premiership. No one knew how this would work; but it turned out that when the premier and the president are of different parties, more of the executive power rests with the premier than with the president, although both are then powerful. Mitterrand chose the ministers for defense and foreign affairs, while Chirac chose the rest; legislative initiatives lay wholly with Chirac and his cabinet, although Mitterrand limited Chirac's ability to promulgate decrees; and at international conferences both Mitterrand and Chirac represented France, dividing allotted speaking time between them (!).

This period of split control, dubbed "cohabitation" by the French, lasted only three years. In 1988, a newly reelected President Mitterrand took advantage of the enthusiasm over his victory and dissolved the National Assembly, calling for a new election of its members. The Socialists regained control, and the old constitutional system of presidential dominance was reestablished. Cohabitation emerged for a second time, however, when in 1993 the Socialists once again lost control of the National Assembly. This time it proceeded with less friction as the prickly Chirac decided not to serve under Mitterrand, and the new premier, Edouard Balladur, got along well with Mitterrand while still establishing clear dominance in the executive. In 1995, the system returned to "normal" when Chirac was elected president with a conservative majority in the National Assembly, but it reverted to "cohabitation" again when the Socialists won control of the National Assembly in the elections of 1997. From 1997 to 2002, Lionel Jospin headed a Socialist-led cabinet and Chirac receded into the role of president-as-head-of-state. Things went smoothly, and Jospin proved a popular premier. In 2002, a new election returned a large majority for the right-of-center coalition, ending cohabitation again and returning Chirac to his role as dominant president. By now, the French have worked out good precedents and traditions to handle cohabitation and indeed appear to like having the president and the cabinet be of different parties.

Nonetheless, this is still a constitutional oddity. In all sorts of ways, the constitution of France (constitution with a small *c*) changes abruptly when different parties come to control the National Assembly and the presidency. It is almost as if France has two constitutions, which switch on and off like lights.

 EXAMPLE

Presidential Government in Mexico

The presidency of Mexico offers a fascinating example of a political institution in transition. The Mexican presidential system arose out of a decade and a half of chaos, from 1910 to 1925. In a swirling tumult of banditry, revolutionary battles, and civil war, approximately a million Mexicans starved or were killed. The period of violence ended in the establishment of the dominant Party of the Institutionalized Revolution (PRI), which we examined in Chapter 11.[11] By the 1930s, the rule of the party had come to be centered on a strong presidency, and that regime has continued.

Under the system as it arose at that time and as it lasted until well into the 1990s, the president dominated Mexican politics. Although the Constitution provided for an independent Congress and Supreme Court much like those of the United States, neither of these bodies operated

---

[11]Actually, initially there was formed the Mexican Revolutionary Party; it restructured itself and changed its name to the PRI in 1946.

independently of the president. Until 1988, all but a handful of members of Congress were from the PRI, and even after 1988, the PRI always had clear majorities in both houses until 1997. The opposition was divided in the Congress, so that in the rare instances in which the president needed help (passing a constitutional amendment, for example, which requires a two-thirds majority), he was easily able to gain support from one of the other parties.

The Supreme Court had always been somewhat more insulated from the power of the president and not infrequently ruled in favor of citizens who were suing the presidential office on minor technical matters. However, the court always avoided confrontation with the president on important questions of policy.

A president in office had great power. What saved the system from an unbearable concentration of power was the firm tradition that presidents must step down after a single six-year term. For six years, a single person ruled, but then the party (influenced strongly by the incumbent president) chose another person to serve the next six years.[12] It was at this point that the system showed some flexibility over the years. The outgoing president based his decision on a combination of negotiations among party leaders, consultations with the PRI's three "sectors," interest-group pressures, and consideration of the popular mood, or "temper of the times."[13] Therefore, when the mood was to the left, a president emerged from the left; corrupt presidents were often succeeded by reformers; and so on. Not only the holder of the presidential office changed, but so did most other executive officers, as the new president found jobs for the members of his faction. The holder of a job under one president in the past had only a 30 percent chance of holding a job under the next president.[14]

Such concentration of power, even if it was temporary, encouraged corruption and personal gain, which has been a chronic problem of Mexican politics. Mexico under the PRI appeared to go through alternate waves of corruption and reform. The administration of President Miguel Alemán from 1946 to 1952 was marked by large-scale corruption, as was that of López Portillo from 1976 to 1982. Various officials of the López Portillo administration are widely thought to have taken $3 billion or more from public funds; his successor, Miguel de la Madrid Hurtado, came to office pledged to a clean government and prosecuted some of the offenders of the previous regime. Although presidential corruption was obviously costly and broad, some speculated cynically that it had the hidden virtue of making possible the regular six-year transition in power. If it were not for the illicit wealth on which they could retire, so this reasoning went, some officials would have devised a way of subverting the six-year rule so that they could stay in office!

During the period of reform from 1982 to 2000, however, a series of three reform PRI presidents oversaw the gradual opening of the political and economic system that culminated in the PRI's final loss of power in the 2000 election. The last of the PRI presidents, Lopez Zedillo, was especially active in reform and in opening up the political system. In the congressional elections of 1997, the PRI lost control of the lower house of Congress, although it kept control of the Senate. This had enormous implications for the all-powerful Mexican presidency, since without control of the Congress, President Zedillo was unable to continue the one-man show that had always been the Mexican presidency. Fortunately, he was already oriented toward reform of the system. He had been trying to open up the party and take control away from the "dinosaurs"; for instance, he had encouraged his attorney general to fire all twenty-three hundred officers in the corrupt

---

[12]Again, with increasing competition from opposition parties, the party's nomination will probably never again confer the office as automatically as it did through and including the 1988 election. In all elections since then, the outcome was open and competitive; the PRI candidate lost in the 2000 election.
[13]Rubio F. Luis, "The Presidential Nomination Process," in George W. Grayson, ed., *Prospects for Democracy in Mexico* (New Brunswick, NJ: Transaction Publishers, 1990), p. 76.
[14]Peter H. Smith, "Does Mexico Have a Power Elite?" in Jose L. Reyna and Richard S. Weinert, eds., *Authoritarianism in Mexico* (Philadelphia: Institute for the Study of Human Issues, 1977), p. 139.

narcotics investigation agency, rehiring only six hundred who were judged reliable. With the PRI's loss of dominance in the Congress, Zedillo appeared almost to welcome his party's losses as a chance to establish more reasonable working relations with the Congress. He was patient with the inevitable growing pains of a new opposition who had never before held real power, and while he lost on several significant issues—elimination of his huge secret "President's discretionary fund"; establishment of a new fund that he opposed, which sent several hundred million dollars of federal money back to towns and cities with no strings attached; and a cut in the value-added tax—he was able to get his budget through the opposition-controlled Congress in essentially the form he had requested.

In 2000, the transformation was completed by the ousting of PRI from the presidency with Vicente Fox's election. Fox's experience in the presidency, however, showed that with openness and competition, it is also possible to have gridlock. While his PAN party started off as the largest party in the Congress, it did not have a majority. And Fox himself was also a good deal more centrist than most of his fairly conservative party. He found that he had to maneuver and bargain to get what he wanted, and even though he started off with great personal popularity, he had many setbacks. He successfully used his control of the administrative apparatus to fight corruption, continuing the efforts that were started under Zedillo. But PRI majorities in Congress, and PRI appointees on the Supreme Court, exercised the checks and balances that were already implicit in the Constitution—stymieing Fox in almost his entire legislative agenda. This was probably healthy for Mexican democracy, but certainly not helpful for Fox. In a frustrating judgment of his administration, Mexico's voters cut his PAN party's representation in Congress from 207 to 155 in elections in July 2003. However, in 2006 they elected as Fox's successor yet another PAN president, Felipe Calderón.

The immense changes in the working of Mexican government over just twenty years illustrate how closely the formal governmental structures of politics interact with informal structures such as parties, interest groups, and the media. The written Constitution of Mexico did not change from the 1980s to 2003, but Mexico's governmental institutions changed immeasurably. They changed because the way in which parties structured political conflict changed. Just as we saw in Chapter 14 that parliamentary cabinet government depends crucially on parties that are internally disciplined, we see in the Mexican example that presidential government also depends crucially on the informal structures of politics to define how it works.

KEY TERMS

presidential government	hybrid presidential government	constitutional review

FURTHER READINGS

Abraham, Henry J. *The Judicial Process.* New York: Oxford University Press, 1998. Chapters on judicial review.

Edwards, George C., III, and Wayne, Stephen. *Presidential Leadership.* 7th ed. New York: Bedford St. Martins, 2005.

Fiorina, Morris P. *Congress: Keystone of the Washington Establishment.* 2d ed. New Haven: Yale University Press, 1989.

Greenstein, Fred I. *The Presidential Difference: Leadership Style from FDR to George W. Bush.* Princeton: Princeton University Press, 2004.

Howell, William G. *Power Without Persuasion: The Politics of Direct Presidential Action.* Princeton: Princeton University Press, 2003.

Jacobs, Lawrence R., and Shapiro, Robert Y. *Politicians Don't Pander.* Chicago: University of Chicago Press, 2000.

Levy, Daniel C., and Bruhn, Kathleen. *Mexico: The Struggle for Democratic Development.* Berkeley: University of California Press, 2001.

Lijphart, Arend. *Patterns of Democracy: Government Forms and Performance in Thirty-Six Countries.* New Haven: Yale University Press, 1999.

———, ed. *Parliamentary Versus Presidential Government.* New York: Oxford University Press, 1992.

Linz, Juan J., and Valenzuela, Arturo, eds. *The Failure of Presidential Democracy.* Baltimore: Johns Hopkins University Press, 1994.

Mainwaring, Scott. "Presidentialism, Multipartism, and Democracy: The Difficult Combination." *Comparative Political Studies* 26 (1993), pp. 198–228.

———, and Shugart, Matthew Soberg, eds. *Presidentialism and Democracy in Latin America.* New York: Cambridge University Press, 1997.

Neustadt, Richard E. *Presidential Power and the Modern Presidents.* New York: Free Press, 1991.

Pfiffner, James P. *The Modern Presidency.* 4th ed. Beverly, MA: Wadsworth, 2005.

"Presidential and Parliamentary Democracies: Which Works Best?" Special Conference Issue, *Political Science Quarterly* 109 (no. 3, 1994).

Rudalevige, Andrew. *Managing the President's Program: Presidential Leadership and Legislative Policy Formulation.* Princeton: Princeton University Press, 2002.

Shugart, Matthew Soberg, and Carey, John M. *Presidents and Assemblies: Constitutional Design and Electoral Dynamics.* New York: Cambridge University Press, 1992.

Skowronek, Stephen. *The Politics Presidents Make: Leadership from John Adams to George Bush.* Cambridge: Harvard University Press, 1993.

Wills, Gary. *Cincinnatus: George Washington and the Enlightenment.* Garden City, NY: Doubleday, 1984.

 # WEB SITES OF INTEREST

White House:
http://www.whitehouse.gov

CHAPTER 16

BUREAUCRACY AND
THE PUBLIC SECTOR

In the last few chapters, we reviewed the structure of governments. However, a great deal goes into policy making beyond what government leaders do. The government may establish by law that the speed limit on highways is fifty-five miles per hour, but what this means in detail is determined by thousands of traffic patrol officers across the country. It is they who decide whether this means that you are ticketed if you drive fifty-six miles per hour or whether there is a "zone of grace" so that you are ticketed only for speeds of sixty miles per hour or above. It is they who decide whether a woman with a bleeding wound in her arm is in bad enough shape that she is justified in speeding to the hospital at seventy-five miles per hour. It is they who decide whether to treat a well-dressed man in a dark blue sedan differently from a young person in blue jeans who is driving a red sports car, warning the one and ticketing the other.

The local police officer, the public health inspector, the president of the state university, the teacher in a public school—these are as much a part of the policy-making machinery as the legislator, judge, or U.S. president. For most citizens, it is *these* people—and not the legislator, judge, or president—who embody the state and its policies. People receive the policies of the state from police officers, immigration officials, IRS agents, schoolteachers, agricultural extension agents, and members of fire departments, not from the nation's president or members of Congress.

Any state, if its operations are at all complex, must have a large number of people like this—people who are not directly involved in politics in the sense that they share in making major decisions but who are involved in the construction and implementation of the policies that carry out those decisions. These are collectively called the **public administration** of the state. A modern state has a large number of people in its public administration. Figure 16.1 charts the growth of the public administration of the United States since 1950.

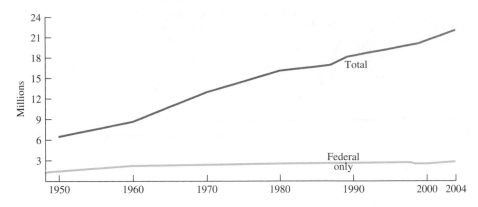

FIGURE 16.1   Total number of civilian public employees (combined local, state, and federal) in the United States, 1950–2004.

SOURCE: U.S. Bureau of the Census, *Statistical Abstract of the United States.*

The number of public employees in the United States climbed from 6.4 million in 1950 to over 21 million in 2004, almost wholly from increases at the state and local levels. (Federal civilian employment increased over this period by about 1.2 million.) Public employment climbed not only in absolute numbers but also as a proportion of the total civilian labor force. In 1950, 11 percent of employed civilians were public employees; by 2004, this had risen to 16 percent. In other words, by 2004, better than one out of six employed persons was a member of the U.S. public administration.

This actually understates the growth of government *operations* by a good deal. Federal operations grew by much more than the growth in federal employment shown in the chart. What happened is that the federal government has tended over the years to expand its operations by contracting out jobs to private research firms and service providers not directly in the government.

✢ PUBLIC ADMINISTRATION
AS A POLITICAL PROBLEM

That some part of policy making is done by such a large number of people poses something of a problem for the state. Public administrators as a group have significant governmental power, yet they are too numerous and individually too unimportant to be controlled effectively. Therefore, *a significant part of the governmental power of any state is of necessity not under close political control.*

Examples of the governmental discretion of administrators are numerous. American police officers have a good deal of discretion, for instance, in whom they stop to search for weapons or illegal substances; investigations of the New Jersey state police in 1999 revealed policies of "racial profiling"—identifying possible suspects based on certain physical characteristics—for stop-and-search actions that are probably widespread around the country. As another example, consider the agents of the IRS in the United

The state meets a citizen, Woodstock, New York.
© Mark Antman/Stock Boston

States who audit taxpayers' returns. Inevitably, given the complexity of our tax laws, interpretation of the laws will vary from one agent to the next. As a result, the outcome of a tax audit depends at least to some extent on which agent handles it. Finally, consider that the teachers of America determine, by their individual actions, the grading system that has such important ultimate effects on students' careers.

These and other examples show that even rather minor administrators make a good deal of governmental policy. The politically responsive part of government (elected officials, party leaders, military juntas, courts, or whatever) must be concerned to make certain that, at least in broad outline, they control the policies implemented by administrators. This control is not easy to design, however. An early study in this area illustrates the problem. In 1948, the U.S. Supreme Court ruled that it was unconstitutional for school districts to schedule certain hours during the day in which religious groups would come to school and provide classes in religion for those students who desired it. (Students who did not wish to have religious instruction were sent to study hall.) The Court ruled that this practice violated the constitutional separation of church and state. Nearly ten years later, in a survey of Pennsylvania school superintendents, one-tenth of those responding stated that their school districts continued this practice, even though it was unconstitutional. The survey also ascertained that the superintendents understood the Court decision fully; they were acting not out of ignorance but deliberately.[1]

---

[1]Frank J. Sorauf, "Zorach v. Clausen: The Impact of a Supreme Court Decision," *American Political Review* 53 (September 1959), pp. 777–91.

Reprinted by permission of ScienceCartoonsplus.com.

✦ CHARACTERISTICS OF GOOD PUBLIC ADMINISTRATION

The way in which we organize our public administration should aim to help us maximize some desirable traits. Among these are the following:

1. *Honest, accurate translation of political leaders' decisions into more specifically designed policies:* This addresses the problem of making sure that political leaders control at least the broad outlines of policy.

2. *Flexibility in dealing with special cases at the point of delivery:* While administrators should be obedient to directions from above, they should not be slavishly obedient. If a police officer pulls a driver over for speeding and discovers that the driver is trying to get a child with a gaping wound to the hospital, we do not want the officer to write a ticket.

3. *But this flexibility should not be used arbitrarily:* "Arbitrary" action is action taken capriciously, without regard to the important circumstances of a case. Stopping and searching blacks because of their race is an arbitrary act, for example. Another example would be to allow some students to take a makeup

examination but to deny the makeup opportunity to others who had had the same excuse.

4. *Feedback of expert advice; active imagination and assertive inquiry on the part of administrators:* We hope that administrators, since they know more about their areas of work than anyone else, will not hang back from sharing their expertise with the public and their political leaders.

5. *Efficiency:* We hope that all this can be done without costing too much.

All of these are desirable traits. However, since some of them are to a certain extent mutually contradictory, not all of them can be fully met simultaneously. For instance, there is some tension between item 1 (honest, accurate translation) and item 2 (expecting administrators to follow their own judgment). Item 3 is difficult because one person's capriciousness is another person's courageous judgment. Item 4 (feedback of expert advice) assumes an independent-minded set of administrators who may fit oddly item (1): honest, accurate translation.

It follows that there is no one best way to organize public administration; various modes of organization will emphasize one or another of these good things. Therefore, under varying circumstances, varying modes may be preferred.

✦ "BUREAUCRACY": A REFORM OF THE NINETEENTH CENTURY

Bureaucracy is one way to organize the public administration, one that has become fairly standard, at least as an ideal, throughout the world. The word *bureaucracy* is often used in common language to mean the public administration, usually with a connotation of distaste. However, social scientists have a precise meaning for it: a particular mode of administrative organization that was developed as a reform in the nineteenth century and spread widely to be the most generally used mode today.

Let us first set the stage of the eighteenth and early nineteenth centuries to show how bureaucracy developed as a reform of the systems then in place. At that time, in Europe and North America, positions in the public administration were treated as pieces of property, to be exchanged among people. In the United States, this took the form of the infamous "spoils system," in which administrative jobs were treated as commodities with which victorious candidates rewarded their party's workers. When the presidency changed hands, for instance, all post office managers in the country were fired and new people from the victorious party were put in their place. The same thing happened with state highway and surveyor jobs when one party replaced another in a state capital; so also with fire and police jobs when city hall changed hands.

In Europe, positions in the public administration were individually bought and sold more or less as investments. A wealthy family wishing to establish a son in a comfortable life would buy him a position in the customs service, an officer's commission in the army, or some similar position.

Such loose arrangements produced inefficient service, and there was little control over the quality of officials. In the United States, for example, some post office managers could not read. For most officials, getting the job in the first place was the only trick (what they did once they were there did not bear consequences for them), so controlling officials' actions was difficult.

In the nineteenth century, there arose a new reform method of organizing public administration, one that social scientists call "bureaucracy."[2] Under a system of bureaucracy:

1. Members of the public administration are appointed and promoted on the basis of their qualifications for the job they are to do.
2. Special requirements of training or experience are set for the position.
3. Administrative procedures are standardized, so that relatively little is left to individual officials' biases or passions.
4. Clear lines of command are established, in which an order from a high official goes to a lower official, who then passes the order on to the next level, and so on until it reaches the point of operation. This arrangement is called a **hierarchical command structure.**
5. Finally, public administrators are shielded from day-to-day political pressure, usually with a system of tenure.

This new, cleaner, and more efficient way of organizing the public administration was first used in appointments for procurement officers with the French and Prussian armies in the eighteenth and early nineteenth centuries. It demonstrated its usefulness in this area and spread rapidly. In the United States, the coming of the bureaucratic mode was embodied in the move for civil service reform at the beginning of the twentieth century, which eventually took most administrative positions out of party control and based them on competitive civil service exams. By World War II, some form or another of bureaucracy was the usual method of organizing public administration throughout Europe and North America. As new states attained their independence, they also adopted some form of bureaucracy. It is today the usual mode of administrative organization throughout the world, although there are many variations on its themes.

✦ BUREAUCRACY VERSUS FLEXIBILITY

As noted previously, there is no ideal way to organize administration. Of the various things that may be desirable in public administration, bureaucracy is particularly strong on the accurate translation of leaders' decisions and on preventing arbitrary behavior. Believe it or not, it is also rather efficient. (Bureaucracy has to some extent been identified in the public mind as wasteful because the public has high expectations for how cheaply one might expect administration to be done. The administrative costs of public agencies are not that different from those of private businesses.)

However, the standardization and clarity of command that accomplish these good things mean that bureaucracy cannot easily provide for local flexibility. Also, although the requirements for training and for decisions based on merit produce well-qualified

---

[2]For the definitive statement, see Max Weber, "Bureaucracy," in H. H. Gerth and C. Wright Mills, *From Max Weber* (New York: Oxford University Press, 1958), pp. 196–244.

officials, the system of standardization does not encourage independent-mindedness on their part, and so bureaucracy does not especially tend to produce helpful expert advice to political leaders. Administrators under most versions of bureaucracy tend to hold their advice until it is asked for.

This means that the bureaucratic form of organization will fit some administrative needs better than others. Where standardization and obedience are especially important, bureaucratic organization fits well. Where independence and flexible judgment are especially important, it does not. Military service is one area in which standardization and obedience are important, because if a general is conducting a wheeling motion on a battlefield, everything could be lost if one battalion wheeled in the wrong direction. The bureaucratic model fits military operations well, and indeed the military—with its clean lines of command and its tendency to "do things by the book"—exemplifies the bureaucratic model. On the other hand, public enterprises in which obedience is less important than individuality are not as well served by bureaucratic organization. A university or college is such a place: The object is to put a gifted individual in the lab or in front of a class and let that person do creative things.

It follows that bureaucracy is a better form of organization for some areas of the public administration than for others, depending on the relative needs for smooth obedience and individualistic judgment. To a considerable extent, these differences are reflected in the organization of various agencies; almost universally the armed forces are the most bureaucratically organized agencies in any state's public administration, and universities tend to be rather decentralized.

However, there is often a tilt *toward* bureaucracy, with most operations being organized more bureaucratically than would really be necessary. Most public administrators appear to incline toward standardization and away from individual initiative, a natural result of the human desire for safety and security. An official working within standardized procedures, unlike one who is supposed to make independent choices, cannot be blamed for the results. Procedures shelter bureaucracies, so bureaucracies foster procedures. Impressionistic evidence for this, at least, is that there are apparently no armed forces in the world set up in anything but a straightforward bureaucratic mode; whereas universities, which would not require bureaucratic organization and would almost surely benefit by its absence, are nonetheless often hemmed in by tight rules.[3]

→ THE PROBLEM OF PROTECTED INCOMPETENCE

Another common problem of bureaucratic organization stems from a combination of two factors: (1) the difficulty in *public* administration, as compared with private business, of evaluating how well a person has performed a job, and (2) the requirement in a bureaucracy that administrators be shielded from direct political pressure, usually by a system of tenure.

---

[3]For example, in some European universities, there are official limits on the number of pages that students may be required to read. In Norway in 1983, the limit for a political science course was six hundred pages, total, across a fifteen-week semester.

In private business, a standard yardstick is available to evaluate how well a person has done in a job. If profits have gone up in that person's sector, if sales have been high, or whatever—if the person has made money for the company—then the job has been done well. You and your boss know whether or not you have sold a million dollars of insurance this year. But how do we evaluate the performance of public administrators? There is no notion of "profit" in the operations of a public school, the army, or a state's highway department. A professor is supposed to teach well, but there is no dollar figure that can tell us *how* well the professor has taught. A highway superintendent is supposed to maintain the roads well, but there is no dollar figure that can tell us how well they have been maintained.

Combine this with the fact that political intervention against members of the bureaucracy is difficult and unlikely, and you have a situation in which incompetent administrators will rarely be removed from their positions. Few unambiguous standards of their performance are available, and—in the absence of clear-cut evidence—superiors will be reluctant to take action for fear that they will be accused of favoritism or political interference.

As a result, although bureaucracies do not particularly attract incompetent people—and although, by their entrance requirements, they have some success at selecting unusually competent people—those incompetents who do get in are less likely to be removed than they would be in private businesses.

✦ ADJUSTMENTS TO BUREAUCRACY

Although bureaucracy is only one way to organize the public administration, it is the dominant mode of organization across the world, as we have seen. Indeed, it is so dominant that the word *bureaucracy* has become almost a synonym for public administration, in much the way that *Kleenex* has come to be synonymous with facial tissues or *Xerox* with photocopies.

As a term loosely signifying public administration, *bureaucracy* has a number of unpleasant connotations. Bureaucrats are thought to be lazy, arrogant, inflexible, shortsighted—and too numerous. Partly this derives from the fact that it is impossible to construct an ultimate, best form of organization for the public administration; as we have seen, the various characteristics we would wish to see in a good public administration are to some extent mutually contradictory. Partly it derives from real weaknesses of bureaucracy.

In various parts of the world, adjustments have evolved or have been invented that can soften bureaucracy when it is excessively "bureaucratic." Among these are the office of *ombudsman,* provisions for opening government files for inspection, informal interference in the bureaucracy by political leaders, and pressure from public opinion.

1. ***The office of ombudsman*** is a Swedish invention. An **ombudsman** is a government official whose primary duty is to seek out citizens' complaints of abuse by public administrators and to negotiate changes in the offending practices. The ombudsman idea has been copied in many other countries. In the United States, it has not been used at the national level; but Hawaii, Florida, and other states have established ombudsman offices. Many nongovernmental institutions have

also found it an attractive idea. Universities have established ombudsman offices for their students or faculty, newspapers have set up a readers' ombudsman, and so on.

2. *Freedom of information laws* have been passed in many countries, and the United States has been a pioneer in this direction. Under such laws, individuals are guaranteed the right to examine most kinds of "internal" governmental documents, including dossiers that may have been gathered on them personally. The intent of the laws is to allow citizens to find out what procedures administrators are following in processes that are of interest to them; more specifically, it allows citizens to check and correct any information the government has gathered about them.

3. *"Interference" in administration by political leaders* may act as a safety valve to help correct abuses. You will recall that in the bureaucratic mode of organization, administrators are shielded from much direct intervention by political leaders. This was intended to avoid the excesses of a spoils system.

   However, it does not compromise the bureaucratic model greatly if political leaders take advantage of their potential power over administrative budgets to seize bureaucrats' attention and get them to deal with a constituent's problem. In the United States, in particular, this has become a major part of the job of a member of Congress and has developed into an important corrective for bureaucratic inflexibility. It is well understood that if you are having trouble getting a passport or your Social Security check has been held up, you should call your member of Congress for help. In 2004, for instance, the office of Representative Betty McCollum (Fourth Congressional District, Minnesota) assisted over four hundred constituents with a wide variety of concerns. The most common problems involved the Social Security Administration, the Bureau for Citizenship and Immigration Services, and the Veterans Administration.[4]

4. *Pressure from public opinion* can help to correct bureaucratic sluggishness and abuse. Administrators are ultimately dependent on political processes for their offices' budgets, and so they must be attentive to public opinion. Also, because they are human, they want to be liked and admired for what they do. Public criticism hurts them and will usually lead to improvements where there have been problems. Agricultural agencies, welfare services, research agencies, the postal service—all are worried by stories in the media about shortcomings in their operations and keep in reasonably close touch with their "clients," the groups most affected by their policies.

→ SOCIAL REPRESENTATIVENESS OF PUBLIC ADMINISTRATION

Members of the public administration are not under direct political control, and adjustments such as those I have described can go only so far. Therefore, there has been recurrent concern over how socially representative top bureaucratic decision makers are; that

---

[4]Personal communication.

Immigration Services as an Example

Perhaps the best evidence that public opinion serves as an important corrective to bureaucracy may be found by looking at an agency that is *not* under much direct pressure from public opinion. In democracies all over the world, immigration services are relatively free from pressures of public opinion because their "client group"—those who wish to enter the country as immigrants—cannot vote in elections and usually lack powerful friends. It is almost universally true that these offices are less responsive to their clients and more inclined to make arbitrary judgments than other government agencies:

- *Item:* The U.S. Bureau for Citizenship and Immigration Services (BCIS) some years ago tried to save about $20 million by setting a rule that no visas could be renewed under any circumstances. It would have saved the money by eliminating the positions of clerks who at that time handled applications for renewal. This decision ignored several important things: the hundreds of millions of dollars that would not have been spent in the United States by visitors who were unable to prolong their stay; the human hardship and ill will that would have resulted; and the fact that there would still have had to be some provision for emergency cases, such as heart attacks and appendectomies on the day of departure. The BCIS was eventually talked out of this silly idea.
- *Item:* A German visiting the United States on a valid visa was turned back at the Minneapolis airport and forced to return home because he had a pornographic homosexual magazine in his suitcase.
- *Item:* When the Norwegian government in 1980 decided to reduce the number of work permits it would grant to foreigners by 50 percent, the Norwegian Immigration Service also reduced the staff to deal with those requests by 50 percent. It forgot that although it was going to say yes only half as often, just as many people would be *asking*. It was not long before the office had such a backlog that applicants were required to wait nine months to a year for an answer.
- *Item:* In 1997, the U.S. Congress empowered BCIS border agents, after a brief examination and with no procedure for appeal, to turn back foreign citizens at the border and bar them from crossing the border for five years. In the first seven months of the new rule, twenty-three thousand people were barred, and in several incidents, it was clear that these were foreign citizens trying to visit family members in the United States, Canadians working for United States–based firms, and so on.[5]
- *Item:* In 2001, the BCIS, which was at that time taking more than two months to process applications for temporary work visas, offered a special expedited service that would take only fifteen days—for a fee of one thousand dollars!
- *Item:* In the late 1970s, until it was dissuaded by embarrassing publicity, the British Immigration Service required a virginity test of women who were applying for permission to immigrate to Britain.

[5]*New York Times*, 14 November 1997, p. 1.

TABLE 16.1

Backgrounds of European and American Senior Civil Servants

	Britain	France	Germany	Italy	Netherlands	U.S.A.
Social class origin (percent)						
Management/professional	68%	96%	67%	82%	60%	69%
Middle	21%	3%	21%	16%	37%	18%
Working	13%	1%	12%	3%	4%	14%

SOURCE: Calculated from Joel D. Aberbach, Robert D. Putnam, and Bert A. Rockman, *Bureaucrats and Politicians in Western Democracies* (Cambridge: Harvard University Press, 1981), table 3.3.

is, there has been a concern that they should not be too different from the population as a whole in such things as class background, race, or gender. There has been some controversy over this. On the one hand, advocates of **representative bureaucracy** urge that if administrators are not politically responsible, we should at least do all we can to ensure that they will look at things in the same ways that the common people would. On the other hand, skeptics have responded that we should not want "common people" in positions of uncommon importance and that we should not expect top public administrators to be any more socially representative than the leaders of corporations, universities, or other large institutions.[6]

Whatever our feelings on this, certainly many governments have made efforts to ensure that top public administrators will be reasonably representative. After World War II, many European countries (France, for example) attempted to increase the proportion of their officials who were from the working class. They did this by changing their entrance procedures and providing for internal promotions from less important administrative posts. As Table 16.1 shows, as of the 1970s, the class backgrounds of senior administrative officials were rather similar across a fairly varied set of countries, although France and Italy did stand out. Newer information on France, however, shows that by 1997, France had changed a good deal. Only 46 percent of senior civil servants were now from the upper class, 35 percent from the middle class, and 17 percent from the working class.[7]

In recent years, a similar concern in most countries has been to increase the representation of women and minorities in the bureaucracy. The United States has long tried by affirmative action programs to increase numbers of minority and women officials. By the mid-1990s women comprised 45 percent of senior civil servants in the Netherlands and 23 percent of senior civil servants in Sweden.[8]

---

[6]See discussions in Samuel Krislov, *Representative Bureaucracy* (Englewood Cliffs, NJ: Prentice-Hall, 1974); Kenneth John Meier, "Representative Bureaucracy: An Empirical Analysis," *American Political Science Review* 69 (June 1975), pp. 526–42; Sally Coleman Selden, *The Promise of Representative Bureaucracy* (London: M. E. Sharpe, 1997); and Kenneth J. Meier, Robert D. Winkle, and J. L. Polinard, "Representative Bureaucracy and Distributional Equity: Addressing the Hard Question," *Journal of Politics* 61 (November 1999), pp. 1025–39.
[7]Luc Roban, "The Civil Service in France," in Edward C. Page and Vincent Wright, *Bureaucratic Elites in Western European States* (New York: Oxford University Press, 1999), calculated from figures 4.1 and 4.4.
[8]Ibid., essays by Marleen Brans and Annie Hondeghem ("The Senior Civil Service in Belgium," p. 138) and Jon Pierre and Peter Ehn ("Senior Civil Servants in Sweden," p. 258).

✤ EXAMPLE

The French Bureaucracy

The "ordinary" bureaucracies of industrialized states do not vary greatly from one country to another. Mail carriers, teachers, agricultural extension agents, and so on, are organized and do their jobs in fairly similar ways around the industrialized world. Where there is considerable variation is in how the **higher civil service**—the managers, diplomats, specialists, and so on—are organized and work. In this realm, the French are quite distinctive; theirs is arguably the best civil service in the world.

In this section, we shall address almost solely the higher civil service. First, however, I should note one thing that *is* unusual about the "ordinary" French civil service: It is relatively large, perhaps due in part to the French state's high level of regulatory activity. There are approximately 6 million full-time local and national civil servants in France, including the military. They make up about 25 percent of the labor force, compared with 13 percent in Germany and Britain.[9]

The higher civil service of France consists of about four to six thousand highly trained persons. Most of these work within one of the ministries (defense, health, etc.), but at any given time, over a thousand of them are working in more independent ways, either as staff advisers to the premier or ministers or in relatively autonomous administrative bodies, which I shall describe. Furthermore, a certain number of them are at any time on loan to businesses, universities, or local government.

One of the things that distinguishes the French higher civil service is the training and ability of its members, which leads also to a high degree of self-confidence and pride. There are two main routes of entry into the higher civil service. If one wishes to be a specialist, such as a scientist or statistician, one usually receives a university education from one of the "great" technical schools, such as the Polytechnic or the School of Agronomy, followed by more specialized training at an institution such as the School of Mines or School of Statistics and Economic Administration. If one wishes to be a generalist, after university one enters the famous National School of Administration (the ENA). One of the most difficult schools in the world to enter, the ENA gives its graduates a general training in administration and in the social sciences. Whether from one of the "great schools" or the ENA, higher civil servants in France are noted for their verbal skill and for a tendency to abstraction and mathematical reasoning. They are pragmatic rather than ideological and usually emphasize economics over politics. Many French presidents and premiers have been alumni of the ENA.

The second thing that sets French higher civil servants apart is the tradition of "detached service," whereby they may leave the national civil service for periods of time either on personal leave or on loan by the national government to work in business, local government, or the universities or to hold elective office. In the 1970s, for example, about one-fourth of the members of the parliament were civil servants on leave from their administrative posts, and in 1984, there were twenty-five national civil servants on loan to the city of Paris.

---

[9]"France's Public Sector—They Love It," *The Economist*, 26 May 2001, p. 50.

Under these circumstances, the French have developed a more politicized civil service than that of most countries, one that lives on the frontier between "politics" and administration.[10] For instance, one set of high national officials in France are the **prefects,** who oversee the operations of local and regional government. Prefects coordinate the operations of all state agencies, including the police, for a city or region. They also oversee the operations of the elected city or regional governments, holding them to account if they question the legality of their operations. Inevitably, these are sensitive political positions. Such politicization appears to have added vigor to the higher civil service and has allowed French civil servants to lead aggressively in the development of such new political thrusts as the campaign for a tunnel under the English Channel, the adoption of the value-added tax, and the formation of the Common Market.

It was stated previously that the French higher civil service is "arguably" the best in the world. The other side of the "argument" is raised by those who see the civil service as too insulated from the rest of the population, too haughty, and overly given to technical fixes:

> Instead of a homogenous administration equally open to everyone, one sees established an aristocracy of a few thousand young men produced through privileged channels; the isolation of their education easily persuades them that they are destined to retain among themselves (and for themselves) the administration of the state, and above all its best jobs. Less and less are they touched by doubts; the assurance of their elders and their own success convinces them that it is enough to advance confidently under cover of their technique to make obstacles disappear. The sharing of a certain exoticism of language or of modern administrative techniques or of economics; the sense of making up a kind of network between the bosses and dauphins of the great public and private businesses; the exhilaration, still hardly acknowledged, of feeling in their hands such means of action, and such docile underlings; all these make up the psychology of a senior civil servant, young and ardent, certainly devoted to what he considers the public good, but more inclined to define it himself, or to let it be defined by the boss, than to listen on this subject to the aspiration of the country.[11]

EXAMPLE

Bureaucratic Cultures in Europe and Africa

The bureaucratic model of public administration may work out very differently, depending on the culture of the civil servants—their collective attitudes on the best ways to make decisions, the importance of remaining flexible, and so on. Many states in Africa, Asia, and Latin America are thought to have especially "bureaucratic" civil servants, who are not very flexible, emphasize the hierarchical nature of authority, and follow written rules whether or not they fit a situation well. John C. Munene, Shalom H. Schwartz, and Peter B. Smith have

---

[10]This also fits the more general culture of the French and other continental Europeans. English is the only European language that distinguishes between *politics* and *policy*; in French, both are called *politique.*
[11]"Le Regime des 'Jeunes Messieurs,'" *Courrier de la Republique,* November 1965, quoted in Anthony Sampson, *The New Europeans* (London: Hodder and Stoughton, 1968), p. 345.

compared ways in which European and African civil service managers make decisions, and the results are rather dramatic.[12]

In a larger study of forty-four countries, they had asked managers what sources they would turn to for guidance in making a variety of common decisions, such as whether or not to order a new piece of equipment or how to introduce new work rules into a department. They asked, among some other options, how often managers would rely on their own experience, would rely on unwritten rules, or would consult the people working under them (all of which would be "unbureaucratic") or would rely on formal rules or consult their boss ("bureaucratic"). Table 16.2 compares European and African managers.

In the table, the managers for each country are compared with all forty-four countries in the study, and their rank is given. Therefore, a low score means that they rank high among the forty-four countries—that is, a low score means that they are unusually likely to seek guidance in that way. The highest score is 1 (ranked first among the forty-four countries), and the lowest is forty-four (ranked last among the forty-four). Under "rely on own experience," for example, Finland's score of 3 means that Finnish managers were the third most likely among all forty-four countries to rely on their own experience.

TABLE 16.2

Managers Ranked by Country (Out of 44) in How Frequently They Would Rely on a Given Source

	Unbureaucratic			Bureaucratic	
Nations	**Rely on Own Experience**	**Follow Unwritten Rules**	**Consult Subordinates**	**Consult Boss**	**Follow Formal Rules**
Europe:					
Finland	3	11	3	34	44
France	17	5	8	18	38
Germany	7	37	4	23	41
Netherlands	5	19	2	43	40
Sweden	16	33	7	41	18
Africa:					
Kenya	34	38	34	8	4
Nigeria	44	32	20	42	8
S. Africa	31	29	42	11	10
Tanzania	NA	42	16	26	13
Uganda	38	34	40	2	3
Zimbabwe	29	31	37	5	2

Source: Adapted from John C. Munene, Shalom H. Schwartz, and Peter B. Smith, "Development in Sub-Saharan Africa: Cultural Influences and Managers' Decision Behaviour," *Public Administration and Development* 20 (2000), p. 347.

---

[12]John C. Munene, Shalom H. Schwartz, and Peter B. Smith, "Development in Sub-Saharan Africa: Cultural Influences and Managers' Decision Behaviour," *Public Administration and Development* 20 (2000), pp. 339–51.

As we see here, the African managers are distinctly more "bureaucratic" than the Europeans. All five European countries, for instance, rank among the top ten countries in the extent to which they would consult the people working under them when they made a decision—a distinctly "unbureaucratic" thing to do. The six African countries all rank high in following formal rules, that is, "going by the book."

One could bemoan this bureaucratic culture as one that will make progress difficult in these mostly very poor countries, but that is probably not very fruitful; as we have noted elsewhere, culture is usually difficult to change. So, if we hope for progress in these countries, bemoaning the bureaucratic culture is not going to get us very far. Munene and his coauthors note that one implication of their findings is that those seeking change in African countries must learn to know the culture they are working with among officials, and find ways to work with that culture. Though it is not like the European culture, it is certainly not a bad one—the emphasis on hierarchical organization and the tendency to avoid individual responsibility probably fit with a general African culture that emphasizes embeddedness in groups and family, in contrast to individualistic Western culture.

Often, however, international organizations or foreign aid donors approach African government agencies assuming that the agencies must operate just like Western agencies, and then spend much time and energy being frustrated. Studies like this one can help donors understand better how to work within the cultural expectations of local officials.

KEY TERMS

public administration	ombudsman	higher civil service
bureaucracy	representative	prefect
hierarchical command structure	bureaucracy	

FURTHER READING

Aberbach, Joel D., and Rockman, Bert A. *In the Web of Politics: Three Decades of the U.S. Federal Executive.* Washington, DC: Brookings Institution, 2000.

"Bureaucracy" in the *International Encyclopedia of the Social Sciences.*

Crozier, Michel. *The Bureaucratic Phenomenon.* Chicago: University of Chicago Press, 1987.

Glazer, Amihai, and Rothenberg, Lawrence S. *Why Government Succeeds and Why It Fails.* Cambridge: Harvard University Press, 2001.

Kettl, Donald F., Ingraham, Patricia W., Sanders, Ronald P., and Horner, Constance. *Civil Service Reform: Building a Government That Works.* Washington, DC: Brookings Institution, 1996.

Naff, Katherine C. *To Look Like America.* Boulder, CO: Westview Press, 2001.

Page, Edward C., and Wright, Vincent. *Bureaucratic Elites in Western European States.* New York: Oxford University Press, 1999.

Peters, B. Guy. *Politics of Bureaucracy: An Introduction to Comparative Public Administration,* 6th ed. Oxford, UK: Routledge, 2006.

Peters, B. Guy, and Pierre, Jon. *The Politicization of the Civil Service in Comparative Perspective.* New York: Routledge, 2004.

Selden, Sally Coleman. *The Promise of Representative Bureaucracy.* London: M. E. Sharpe, 1997.

Wilson, James Q. *Bureaucracy: What Government Agencies Do and Why They Do It.* New York: Basic Books, 1989.

WEB SITES OF INTEREST

U.S. Federal Government Agencies Directory, with links to all agencies that have Web sites:

http://www.lib.Lsu.edu/gov/fedgov.html

Institute of Public Administration of Canada, an organization "dedicated to excellence in public sector management and governance":

http://www.ipaciapc.ca

CHAPTER 17

LAW AND THE COURTS

The **law** is a collection of rules laid down by the government, binding all members of the state, including members of the government itself. The law does two things: (1) It sets society's norms and rules for behavior; for instance, it may state that one may not steal others' property, that one may not expose oneself indecently, or that religious practice other than the state religion is illegal. (2) It sets the rules by which individuals in the state must relate to each other—rules governing divorce procedures, rules for the honoring of contracts, and so on.

The rules making up the "law" may reside in the state's constitution, may be statutes passed by the state's legislature, or may be decrees announced by the state's executive officers such as the president, military junta, dictator, or whatever. They may also, in some states, develop out of decisions of courts.

Courts are an odd part of the government in that they have the responsibility for interpreting all parts of the law and adjudicating—when various parts of the law are in conflict—which part takes precedence. Their oddity lies in that they are part of the government but must judge fairly among citizens of the state, including those in the government. Thus, while courts are part of the government, they must be to some extent independent of it. This independence has developed so far in some states that the courts are able to share independently in creating the law.

The tension implicit in being part of the government but at the same time independent of the government, and how this tension is resolved, are important aspects of the world's major legal systems, which we shall examine. **Legal systems** are general, organized sets of legal principles that form the basis of law and adjudication in states. They organize legal practice for states in a way somewhat parallel to the role ideologies play in organizing the thought processes of individuals.

→ ANGLO-SAXON CASE LAW

The legal system that is most familiar to Americans and Canadians is Anglo-Saxon **case law.** This is the system that developed in England during the late Middle Ages and early modern period and spread to such former British colonies as the United States, Canada, India, and Nigeria. It is also often called "common law," though that term is more often applied to the specific body of English law that developed over centuries of case experience.

In the system of case law, courts are seen as largely independent of the state's government, so independent that in the cases they decide they share to some extent in the making of the law, because those cases serve as precedents for future decisions. This is why the system is called "case law."

The heart of the system is a belief that the law is something that exists partially independent of the government. From this there follow several important aspects of case law:

- The task of judges is to find proper law, and the law evolves over time with a certain degree of flexibility. Thus, the U.S. Supreme Court in its landmark *Brown v. Board of Education* decision took note of changing sociological evidence to decide that segregated schools (which had once been considered legal) were against the law.[1]

- Training of judges and lawyers proceeds in special schools, separate from the rest of the university; their training—largely by other lawyers—emphasizes clarity of thought and expression, and skills at searching out and applying precedents.

- The role of the judge is to be a neutral arbiter, ruling on behalf of the law after listening fairly passively to opposed arguments by the lawyers.

- Especially where the government brings charges against an individual (a criminal case), the law protects the individual against the disproportionate power of the government. The burden of proof lies with the government (the defendant is "considered innocent until proven guilty"), and a whole series of protections hold: An individual may not be held more than twenty-four hours without being charged (right of **habeas corpus**), spouses may not be forced to testify against each other, and so on.

I do not mean to suggest that in case law systems, the law is manufactured by judges. The courts base their decision not only on precedents but also on statutes passed by the government, including (in the case of the United States) the Constitution. If the government changes the law by statute, the courts follow its directions, and so the government is the *final* authority on the law. If the United States government were to amend the Constitution to make racially segregated schools constitutional, for instance, *Brown v. Board of Education* would be annulled. However, in the absence of government action, and by filling in the details of government statutes, the courts work with the government to make the law. For instance, when a tax code revision is passed in the United States, commentators will note that we need to wait for two or three years of

---

[1]Brown v. Board of Education, 347 U.S. 484 (1954).

court cases to know exactly what the new law means. In a case law system, then, courts operate largely independently of the rest of the government, although statutes and the constitution have the final word.

✦ CONTINENTAL EUROPEAN CODE LAW

Case law developed in England out of local customs and was popular especially with the same emerging commercial elites who would help to develop the ideology of liberalism.[2] With its emphasis on the law as something existing at some remove from the government and on the law's capacity to restrain illegal governmental action, case law has a clear affinity with liberalism's desire for limited government.

On the continent of Europe, forces for the limitation of governmental power were never as strong as in England, probably because the establishment and maintenance of the continental states were usually more difficult than the establishment of a secure state in England, protected as it was by the English Channel. Where the state was difficult to establish and fragile to maintain, governments may have felt more that they needed to keep everything under direct control. The legal tradition on the continent has been to rely on variants of the Roman system of law, which involves a detailed code of law produced and interpreted by the government. The law, in this tradition, is an expression of governmental policy. Napoleon, when he was building his French Empire in the early nineteenth century, gave this tradition added life by encoding existing French law in the Code Napoleon; he later imposed similar codes in many of the European states he conquered. In one way or another, **code law** eventually dominated across the continent.

From the basic principle that the law is an instrument of the government rather than something that exists semi-independently of the government, there follow several notable characteristics of code law:

- It is not based nearly as much as case law on the accumulation of precedents. While code law judges of course try to keep in step with each other, lest the law degenerate into chaos, they rely more on the statute or code as an authority—not on previous judges' decisions. They do not "make the law" as case law judges do.

- The training of code law lawyers and judges, accordingly, is more general and not as specialized as what one finds in case law systems. Legal officials are seen primarily as just another kind of civil servant, so they are trained in the general university rather than in a separate school by special professors of law.

- The distinction between law as a tool of the state (code law) and law as something above the state (case law) is most marked in criminal cases, where the state itself (in the person of the prosecutor) is a party to the case. Under most code law systems, in a criminal case the judge is not a neutral arbiter of the arguments between the prosecution and defense; rather, as a servant of the state, the judge enters directly into argument, questioning witnesses and even, in some systems, directing the police investigation of the crime. The judge's role is not to pass judgment on the

---

[2]See Chapter 2.

Emile Durkheim's Theory of Law

Law is the set of rules that bind a society together, and so theorists of society have often looked to law as the critical point for analyzing society. Emile Durkheim, a great French sociologist of the nineteenth century, analyzed law in his work *The Division of Labor in Society* to address the question, "How do societies hold themselves together?" He saw law as functioning in varying ways at different stages of societal development to provide the mechanism for maintaining the society intact. In analyzing the role of law, he had a lot to say about why law develops as it does.

He first asked the question, "Why would people be moved to stay together as a society?" As an answer, he pointed to two bases for staying together: "mechanical solidarity," or the similarity among people of the same society that makes them feel akin to each other and comfortable with each other, and different from people not in that society; and "organic solidarity," the benefits of economic cooperation by which, for instance, a group of people with varying specialized skills are able by cooperating to build an automobile—something no one of them could possibly have done alone.

These two reasons for staying together as a society, however, operate under a natural tension. To build the kind of division of labor that yields large returns of organic solidarity, it is necessary for people to be *different* from each other. One person must be a designer, another a capable machinist, and so on. This must diminish the similarity that builds mechanical solidarity. Therefore, as society comes to rely more on organic solidarity, it must rely less on mechanical solidarity.

What does this imply for law? Durkheim points out that the two kinds of solidarity require different things of the law. Mechanical solidarity, based on people feeling similar to each other, requires law that makes people behave like each other and—when this similarity is broken—law that gives dramatic, public punishment. This reemphasizes the rules and reassures the public that the break has been compensated for. Laws will prescribe sexual practice, dietary practice, religion, dress, and so on; and punishment will be revengeful and memorable—stoning to death, hanging, confinement in the stocks, electrocution, and so on.

Organic solidarity, based on cooperation, needs law that ensures and regulates that cooperation—law enforcing the fulfillment of contracts, law regulating ownership of property, and so on. Where a law has been broken, what is needed is monetary compensation or enforcement of a contract, rather than societal retribution.

The development of law in modern societies—as improved technology makes the payoffs of cooperation ever greater, and we appear to rely more and more on "organic" rather than "mechanical" solidarity—does seem to bear Durkheim out. Punishments for crimes have become less dramatic and emphasize rehabilitation more than revenge. Public hangings were common in criminal cases in the United States in the nineteenth century, for instance, but are not used today. The vast body of contract law is a relatively "recent" addition of the last few centuries.

Durkheim is squarely on the "choice" side of "power and choice." He emphasizes legal structures arising to suit the needs of individuals making up society, not because someone imposes them. The question Durkheim poses at the beginning is based on the idea that people choose to be in a society, that the existence of society is based not on the use of power but on an accumulation of individual choices.

state's case but rather, as a servant of the state, to try actively on behalf of the state to learn the truth in the case. There is no presumption of innocence, as in case law; there is no presumption at all. The state, through the court, simply tries to find out what happened. Finally, in most code law systems, there do not exist the elaborate structures of protection for the accused that we see under case law—right of habeas corpus, right against self-incrimination, right against spouse's testimony, and so on. The task of the court is not to "prove guilt beyond any reasonable doubt"; rather, it is to decide what is most probably true in the case.

To an American raised on "innocent until proven guilty," this may seem strange.

The original code law systems were European. As new states were established in other parts of the world, unless they were former British colonies, they adopted some form of code law. When a revolutionary government or a new state based on an independence movement has needed to make an abrupt break with the past, it has seemed more straightforward to design a code of law directly, rather than build one gradually through an accretion of judicial decisions.

✦ THE BLENDING OF CASE LAW AND CODE LAW

I have probably exaggerated how sharp the distinction is between case law and code law. The differences between them are mostly differences of degree. For instance, case law is not "made by judges"; statute is also an important part of the law, and the state can always change "judge-made" law by passing a new law or amending the constitution. In code law, similarly, judges do not totally ignore precedent. They cannot decide a case by looking at the code and ignoring what other judges are doing, or things would become quite chaotic; nobody would know what the law was, because different judges might decide similar cases quite differently.

Therefore, the distinction between these two types is a matter of degree. Still, matters of degree can matter a great deal, as we have seen in comparing how criminal cases are handled in the two systems.

In recent years, we find that even these distinctions between the systems have been becoming less clear, as code law systems adopt some aspects of case law, and vice versa. For instance, in the general spirit of "constitutionalism," protections of individuals against abuse by the state have become popular even in many code law systems.[3] In 1959, France established for the first time the right of habeas corpus. In the mid-1990s, Italy changed its practice of putting judges in charge of the police investigation of a crime. And, in 1999, the French parliament passed a bill to establish the presumption that an accused person is innocent until proven guilty.

Furthermore, most industrialized states with complex governmental structures have found it necessary to set up some sort of avenue for individuals to sue the state; if the state was supposed to pay you a pension through the social security system but did not, for example, you need some way to force it to honor its obligation. In standard

---

[3]For a discussion of "constitutionalism," see Chapter 9.

code law systems, this was difficult because the law was a tool of the state and could not stand judge over it. Furthermore, faced with the complex governmental regulations of the twentieth century, government agencies often find themselves operating in quasi-judicial roles. An antitrust office, for instance, must rule on whether a proposed merger of companies will restrict trade unduly. Such decisions require "judicial" procedures within an administrative agency.

To handle questions like these, a wholly separate system of *administrative courts* has developed in many states, and these make law by precedent. In France, the administrative court system has a caseload larger than that of the regular courts, and its law is developed on a case basis.

Therefore, many code law systems are evolving to look more like case law systems. The opposite process has not been as marked, but some case law systems are becoming more like code law in certain ways. Legislatures and parliaments in some case law systems have begun to write codes in various areas to which judges are bound. For instance, many states in the United States have set up codes of uniform sentencing guidelines that set narrow ranges within which a judge may set the sentence of a person convicted of any particular crime. Also, in Great Britain—where case law started—after long debate, the European Convention on Human Rights was incorporated into English law in 2000, in effect inserting a code of human rights into the English legal system.

The historic differences in how legal systems originated in Europe may be receding far enough that the differences they produced are being overridden by the great *similarity* of conditions across modern industrialized states. These states need the strong coherence that code law can provide, but at the same time, their governmental operations are so large and complex that individuals feel a need for some protection against abuse by government. It may be that under these circumstances, a blend of code and case law is most appropriate.

Notice, by the way, that my account of the convergence of case law and code systems in the above paragraph is based on a choice perspective, rather than a power perspective. The evolution of the legal systems is accounted for by the needs of contemporary states.

✦ RELIGIOUS LAW: THE SHARIA

All states of the world have some version of case law or code law, often referred to as "Western law," introduced by the European powers or borrowed from them. A number of other legal systems survive partially, however. The most enduring are various forms of religious law; and of these, the most important is the **Sharia**—Islamic law—which makes up part of the legal system of such Islamic states as Morocco, Tunisia, Indonesia, Egypt, Syria, Iraq, Mauritania, Yemen, Iran, Afghanistan, and Pakistan.

No state is governed exclusively by the Sharia, and this is true of other traditional legal systems in use; rather, where it is used, it supplements and blends with Western law. For instance, the code systems of Egypt and Syria instruct judges to fill any gaps in the code according to principles of Islamic law. Many states, like Indonesia and Pakistan, have essentially Western law but use Sharia for some aspects of marriage and family law. Militant Islamic movements in many parts of the world are currently pushing

Defendant facing the judges of a Sharia Islamic court, Nigeria.
© AFP/Corbis

for the expansion of Sharia law, however. This has led to clashes between militant Islam and more secular parts of Islamic society, and to conflict as well in states like Nigeria where a variety of religions live together.

The two states that use the Sharia most extensively are Iran and Saudi Arabia, and it comes close to being the dominant form of law in these two countries. In both countries, between 2000 and 2007 there were scores of amputations for thievery, and several individuals were stoned to death, mostly for sexual transgressions. In other states the role of Sharia is more minor. In Jordan, for instance, the only role of Sharia is to provide separate courts for divorce proceedings for Christians and Muslims (in the Islamic courts the testimony of two women is held to be equivalent to the testimony of one man; in Christian courts the two are equal).[4] Even in countries like Iran or Saudi Arabia, harsh punishments like amputation and stoning are now unusual and controversial; but the one pervasive area in which the Sharia continues to clash most with modern sensibilities is in the role it prescribes for women.

The two broad divisions of Islam differ in how they define the body of Islamic law. Shia Islam, which is dominant in Iran and eastern Iraq, and is present in patches of Moslem populations elsewhere, holds that the true Sharia consists only of the Qu'ran and the traditions and sayings of Prophet Mohammed. Sunni Islam, which is dominant in the rest of the Moslem world, sees the Sharia as broader and somewhat more flexible. In addition to the Qu'ran and the traditions and sayings of Prophet Mohammed, it includes in the law both *ijma,* the discussions of Mohammed's friends, and also *Qiyas,* arguments by analogy from these sources. Analogies, especially, offer some room for flexibility.

---

[4]"A World of Ways to Say 'Islamic Law,'" *New York Times,* March 13, 2005, sec. 4, p. 4.

Beyond this basic division, Sharia in many regions incorporates local customs as well as the basic, shared principles. So, Sharia is not one single set of Islamic laws, but has to be considered as it exists in any particular region.

Although the parts of Sharia that deal with sexual morality and that prescribe harsh punishments like amputation are jarring, the underlying principles of Sharia are rather attractive. Sharia centers on obligations—to God and to other people—rather than on rights or entitlements. It is based on central Islamic principles of justice, good deeds, equality, and human brotherhood, as these were applied in the first few centuries after Muhammad to specific questions of behavior. The law was set by the tenth century A.D.; many elements that seem odd in modern society made sense for the medieval society in which they developed, but they have not changed since. What seem to us unbearably harsh punishments, such as cutting off a hand for thievery, were common and perhaps enlightened in the tenth century; certainly, they did not differ from European practice of that time.

Unfortunately, because Islamic law is based on divine inspiration, it is not easily adapted by judges. It is not totally inflexible, however. New circumstances can be adjudicated by analogy to older cases, and complex evasions can be worked out that honor the letter, if not the spirit, of the old laws. For instance, the Sharia bars charging interest on loans, because loans should be given out of a generous heart; but various evasions are used to get around this, such as giving a valuable gift in return for the "gift" of a loan, or treating the borrower and lender as partners in an enterprise, who share its profits.[5] At its heart, however, a God-given law cannot be as flexible as human law.

It is perhaps the flexibility of Western systems that has led them to be so widely used. Modern commercial transactions, especially, require rules of a kind that most traditional legal systems never envisioned: enforcement of contracts, for instance. Where traditional law is used, it is always combined with many elements of Western law.

✦ Courts

Courts are organized in sometimes rather complicated ways to take care of the variety of questions that come before them. The one common element to all courts is that, to the extent that a state has a tradition of constitutionalism, the courts are organized to be at some remove from other sources of political power. This is necessary if the courts are to be *independent* and able to give fair decisions no matter who is involved in a case.

Judges and other court officials in most of Europe are professional civil servants and are protected by the traditions of the bureaucratic model from political pressure.[6] In the United States, federal judges are appointed by the president with approval of the Senate, but the appointments are lifetime appointments so that no judge can be threatened with expulsion for having made an unpopular decision. Judges for state and

---

[5]In recent years, with the growing wealth and growing financial sophistication of a number of Islamic countries, special Sharia-compliant financial products have begun to be significant in international finance. In particular, *sukuk* (a bond-like instrument) issues of $1 billion or more have become common. This is still a small part of international finance, but it is growing.
[6]For the "bureaucratic model," see Chapter 16.

"I WAS IN JAPAN FOR A WHILE. VERY BORING.
NOBODY SUES ANYBODY THERE."

Reprinted by permission of ScienceCartoonsPlus.com.

local courts are elected in many states, but those elections are usually set for long terms in office and are often formally nonpartisan, to insulate the judges from the ordinary give-and-take of politics.

Where constitutionalism is less well established, however, the judiciary may have little independence. In Paraguay under Stroessner's military government, for example, the courts were subordinate to the military, and the president's office directed judicial decisions in all cases involving political prisoners.[7]

Courts are often organized separately to handle different kinds of law, especially:

- **Criminal law** involves a charge that a person has disobeyed a law prescribing proper conduct. In such cases, the state (through a prosecutor, district attorney, etc.) is the party that brings the case, and the person charged is the "defendant." The outcome of a criminal case is either acquittal of the defendant or punishment such as imprisonment or a fine.

  Civil law regulates relations between people. Civil cases may include disputes about the meaning of a contract, suits for damages in cases of injury, questions of mutual responsibility in marriage or divorce, and so on. The outcome of a civil case is some decision by the court as to mutual responsibilities—how much money is to be paid in child support, how a contract is to be met, or whatever. Civil cases usually involve private disputes rather than the breaking of a law that affects the broad public, so civil cases are usually conducted between individuals, without the state being involved as a party to the case.

  It is possible in civil law not only to get compensation for something that has happened in the past but to prevent a person from doing something in the future

---

[7]George Thomas Kurian, *Encyclopedia of the Third World* (New York: Facts on File, 1987), p. 1572.

that will harm you or force them to do something that you wish. To do this, the court declares an *injunction* that the person should (or should not) do the thing required. An example would be an injunction against a neighbor draining a marsh that you share; the injunction might be necessary if the marsh, once drained, could never be the same again biologically, so that undoing the damage after the fact would not be possible.

- **Constitutional law** involves disputes about the nature of the political process and about whether laws are consistent with the constitution.

Aside from being organized by *substance,* courts may also be organized by *jurisdiction:*

- *Lower courts* handle disputes directly.
- *Appeals courts* handle disputes about whether lower courts have decided cases properly.
- *Juvenile courts* handle criminal cases involving defendants who are not yet adults. Using separate courts here allows for more flexible, private proceedings for defendants who are considered not yet fully responsible for their actions.
- *"State" courts* (federal systems only) handle cases under the separate "state" laws in a federal system.
- *Religious courts* are used in a state such as Iran, where religious law coexists with Western law.
- Many others.

 # EXAMPLE

The Law in China

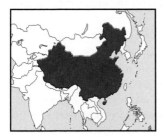

Chinese law is shaped by China's Confucian tradition and by the needs of the state's leaders. For thousands of years, until the end of the nineteenth century, China was dominated by Confucian thought. In the Confucian view of the world, society was meant to be in harmony. This harmony was thought to be maintained by leaders' continual demonstration of virtue, which instilled a sense of virtue into the rest of the people; and it was maintained also by complex networks of rites and mutual obligations based on the family and clan.

Problems were supposed to be worked out among disputants, perhaps with the help of a local person of superior rank, in a way that was conciliatory and that left everyone in agreement. No one was to lose; no one was to lose face. There were lawyers and law in China then, but they were to be appealed to as a last resort. The truth is, Confucian China *did not like law* and disapproved of it. Legal proceedings were made so unpleasant that most Chinese would go to any lengths to avoid them; and avoiding them was easier because the alternative of mediation and conciliation was urged on the disputants by their families and communities with a good deal of social pressure. Proceedings were deliberately made difficult and dangerous by Confucian rulers to discourage use of the law. The seventh-century emperor K'ang Hsi is quoted as saying:

> Lawsuits would tend to increase to a frightful amount, if people were not afraid of the tribunals, and if they felt confident of always finding in them ready and perfect justice. As man is apt to delude himself concerning his own interests, contests would then be interminable, and the half of the Empire would not suffice to settle the lawsuits of the other half. I desire, therefore, that those who have recourse to the tribunals should be treated without any pity, and in such a manner that they shall be disgusted with law, and tremble to appear before a magistrate.[8]

When the communists gained power in China after World War II, they continued the tradition of minimizing use of the law and legal procedures. While continuing that general tradition, however, they transformed it from the Confucian system to their own brand of informal rule. The old aristocratic leadership and old networks of obligation and ancestral rites were replaced by factory committees, neighborhood committees, and party officials. However, the basic principle remained: disputes were resolved by conciliation and mediation processes with a great deal of social pressure on the disputants to reach a mutually acceptable solution.

From 1949 until 1976, the government passed little legislation, preferring to govern less formally through enunciation of doctrines by party leaders. Courts and the legal process were rarely used. In 1981, on the eve of Deng Xiaoping's opening of the system, there were only five thousand lawyers for a Chinese population of approximately 1 billion, compared with half a million lawyers for a U.S. population a quarter the size of China's.[9]

With the death of Mao Tse-tung in 1976, a power struggle developed between Mao's supporters, who had pushed society in a radical left direction during the Cultural Revolution of 1966–76, and more centrist leaders such as Deng Xiaoping, who had been victims of the Cultural Revolution. Deng and his supporters prevailed, and among the changes they introduced was a much greater reliance on law and legal proceedings than what had gone before. The body of statutes was expanded dramatically, with codes of law for many areas previously not ruled by law, including industrial safety, environmental protection, and patents. Criminal law, marriage law, and many areas of civil law were expanded. The legal profession grew dramatically as well, with a tenfold increase by 1990. Especially in criminal law, changes were dramatic, with procedures set up rather along the lines of European code law.

These changes were probably made for two reasons:

1. *To establish a "rule of law":* The informal procedures of Confucian China, once the Confucian structure of society had been destroyed, left the way open for purely arbitrary power. Deng and his friends had suffered grievously from informal, arbitrary proceedings during the Cultural Revolution—Deng, for instance, was sentenced to hard labor, and his son was permanently crippled when his back was broken during interrogation—and they wanted to set up somewhat greater protections for the individual.

---

[8]Cited in René David and John E. C. Brierly, *Major Legal Systems in the World Today,* 3d ed. (London: Steven, 1985), p. 520n.
[9]Xinhua General Overseas News Service, Item 1009065, 9 October 1990.

2. *To handle the problem of economic disputes:* Deng wished to liberalize the Chinese economy, introducing large elements of market choice. Before 1976, there was little civil law in China. There was practically no individual property under communism, so there were few private disputes except for matters such as marriage that could be handled reasonably in conciliation by local bodies. With the development of a partial market economy, however, there would be long-distance disputes between suppliers and customers, partners, and so on, and these could not be handled locally. Also, economic exchanges required precise, dependable rules—not informal social processes for resolution. With the use of market mechanisms, civil law was necessary, and this could not easily be provided without building a more formal legal structure.

Economic development proved Deng right; by 2004, 4,300,000 civil cases were heard in Chinese courts annually, mostly involving disputes between businesses.[10]

Individuals have also begun to sue government agencies in increasing numbers. In 1990, there were thirteen thousand such suits, but in just five years, the number grew to 51,370. The outcomes are chancy. In one well-known case, three women who were forced to retire at age fifty-four by the China National Fisheries Group, even though Personnel Ministry regulations set the retirement age at sixty, sued and won in two different courts. But the courts have no power of enforcement, and the fisheries group simply ignored the judgments. On the other hand, in 1996, a restaurateur who had been jailed for fifteen days on charges that he had put opium in his hot pots successfully sued the police for false arrest. Overall, Professor Minxin Pei estimates that by the late 1990s, 39 percent of such suits were bringing at least partial victory for the person bringing the suit.[11]

The legal system cannot change overnight, though. Even with rapid increases in the number of lawyers over the 1980s and 1990s, there were only 110,000 lawyers in China in 2002. Furthermore, many of these were part-time and not fully trained, especially in such areas as finance and securities. These are clearly insufficient to operate a full-scale legal system in a country of a billion people. And, old Confucian attitudes of disdain for the legal process die hard, especially if an argument can be made that enforcing the law would set back economic growth. In January 2000, the *New York Times* quoted the official *China Youth Daily* saying that the use of confessions extracted by torture is still common: "It is commonplace for citizens to be arbitrarily summoned, forcibly seized, detained and even detained beyond legal time limits, and for citizens whose freedom has been restricted to be treated inhumanely."[12]

Just how Chinese law will develop also depends on how the Communist Party's monopoly of political power is maintained. The Party is caught in a dilemma with regard to the rule of law. On the one hand, the Party's leaders recognize that they need an effective legal system in order for China to realize its potential economically. But on the other hand, they do not want an independent source of political power to develop in the state. Judges are required to clear their decisions with trial committees appointed and controlled by the Party. And lawyers who refuse to be warned off by the Party from taking on controversial cases (such as defense of Christian churches or the Falun Gong sect, or of poor people protesting governmental expropriation of their property) may lose their license to practice law. But, since the Party also needs to modernize economic relations, it actually allows many challenges to go through. The situation remains in flux.

---

[10]Joseph Kahn, "Legal Gadfly Bites Hard, and the Party Slaps Him," *New York Times* 13, December 2005, p. A1.
[11]Elisabeth Rosenthal, "A Day in Court, and Sometimes Justices, for Chinese," *New York Times,* 27 April 1998, p. A1.
[12]Elisabeth Rosenthal, "In China's Legal Evolution, the Lawyers Are Handcuffed," *New York Times,* 6 January 2000, p. A1.

✳ EXAMPLE

The European Court of Justice

A s you saw in the example at the end of Chapter 3, the European Union is an organization of twenty-seven European states attempting to merge their markets and economies. The Union has an elaborate governing structure, although the members remain independent, sovereign states.

One of the governing structures is a court, the European Court of Justice; observing this court provides us with a fascinating case of how a court may develop a body of law in "new ground"—twenty-seven independent states that are bound together to form a common market. The court consists of twenty-seven justices, one from each member state, who are appointed by the unanimous consent of the member states. A justice serves a term of six years and is sworn to act on behalf of the Union.

The original basis of the European Union is the 1957 Treaty of Rome, which comes as close as anything to serving as the Union's constitution—at least until and if the European Union manages to adopt a formal constitution. The treaty was rather vague about the status and duties of the court. It stated that the court must ensure that "the law is observed" in applying the treaty (Article 164), and at various other points, it suggested that the court should apply general principles of law; but it did not spell out clearly the court's jurisdiction or powers.

Much like John Marshall's Supreme Court in the early days of the United States, the Court of Justice has made its place in the order of things through a series of decisions, in effect defining its powers by what it has been able to get away with. It has moved cautiously, but steadily, to make its law supreme within the European Union.

In an important early decision, the court ruled that the Rome Treaty set up a new order for the members, which was not governed by international law; in effect, the court established that the European Union would have an internal system of law. The key question was whether a member state could retaliate in kind if it was injured by another member violating the Rome Treaty. Under international law, this would be permitted; and so if the Rome Treaty were simply a treaty among sovereign states, a member could do this. The court ruled, however, that one member could not retaliate against another but must instead seek relief through the Union's institutions. It thereby transformed the Treaty of Rome from a treaty into a constitution.

In a later decision, the Court of Justice expanded the right to bring cases from member states to include also individuals and corporations in those states. Therefore, citizens of states in the Union could bring cases against their own governments. Most cases in the court have involved trade regulations because the Union is, after all, primarily an organization to enforce free trade within its borders. Perhaps the most dramatic development of law by the Court of Justice, however, has been in the area of individual rights.

The Treaty of Rome did not specify many rights for individuals. It was a document intended to set up a free market, and most of the few rights that are mentioned in it are economic: the right to free movement of capital, the right to bargain collectively, the right of women to earn pay equal to that of men, and so on. The court, however, has gradually developed across several dozen cases a set of rights based on "the constitutional traditions common to the Member States" and on other treaties that member states may have signed, such as the European Convention on Human Rights—even though the court is nowhere directly empowered to enforce those treaties. Some of these cases have gone deeply into what would be considered the independent responsibilities of member states: British schools have been directed to stop using corporal punishment, the Dutch army has had to change its disciplinary procedures, German courts have had to provide access to lawyers before a suspect is charged with a crime. Among rights that the court has written into European Union law are freedom to practice religion; a right against *any* kind of discrimination based on gender, not only discrimination in pay; the right to education; and freedom from arbitrary governmental decision.

Because so little was written into the Treaty of Rome along these lines, the Court of Justice has proceeded by building a body of case law. As is usually true where case law develops, the court has been tolerated in this because it has been seen as a constructive force in the development of the Union and because the alternative—states retaliating against each other for trade violations, for instance—could bring chaos.

As is often the case with courts when expanding their powers, the European Court of Justice, in making the moves described above, appears to have followed a strategy of choosing relatively inconsequential cases in which neither side could easily protest the outcome. Since no serious ox is gored in such a case, it is less likely that anyone will cry foul, so an expansion of court powers can slip through in the absence of a more general protest against the actual outcome. A good example is *Costa v. ENEL* (1964), in which Flaminio Costa, a shareholder in an Italian utility company, sued when the Italian government nationalized the company. He argued that the nationalization violated E.E.C. rules (the European Union was at that time called the European Economic Community), but his claim was rejected by the Italian courts. The basic substance of the case was simple: E.E.C. rules clearly did not prohibit the nationalization, and the European Court of Justice ruled so. But the court took advantage of this case to insert into its decision another point that probably was not really required for its ruling: it first asked, Is E.E.C. law superior to national law, and does it confer a right on individuals to sue their national governments under the body of E.E.C. law? In this way the court ruled that E.E.C. law was superior, thus expanding its jurisdiction. Neither side had a good basis from which to challenge the decision. A decision in which the court had upheld the actions of the Italian government gave the government no reason to protest the ruling—even though it was a decision that had the effect of taking power from the government. Costa might protest the outcome, but the critical jurisdictional part of the court's decision was a part in which the court had actually ruled in his favor, saying that he did, indeed, have the right to sue the government in the European Court of Justice. He could hardly protest that part of the court's decision.[13]

Like courts everywhere, a basic problem for the Court of Justice is enforcing its decisions. Its authority could never have developed as it has if member states did not heed it when it ruled on a case. It has no power to force compliance and must rely on member states' governments to enforce its rulings, which could have posed grave problems except that there has been a remarkable record of compliance. There have been exceptions, though. An order to France to desist from restricting imports of mutton was defied for a couple of years. In general, states have followed the court's directions, and the more often this happens, the more solidly the court's power becomes rooted in habit and expectations.

---

[13]I am grateful to Gordon Silverstein for bringing this case to my attention.

KEY TERMS

law	habeas corpus	civil law
courts	code law	constitutional law
legal systems	Sharia	
case law	criminal law	

FURTHER READING

Abraham, Henry J. *The Judicial Process: An Introductory Analysis of the Courts of the United States, England, and France.* New York: Oxford University Press, 1998.

Alter, Karen J. "The European Court's Political Power." *West European Politics* 19 (July 1996), pp. 458–87.

Bartlett, Katherine T., and Kennedy, Rosanne, eds. *Feminist Legal Theory.* Boulder, CO: Westview, 1991.

Baum, Lawrence. *The Puzzle of Judicial Behavior.* Ann Arbor: University of Michigan Press, 1997.

David, René, and Brierley, John E. C. *Major Legal Systems in the World Today.* 3d ed. London: Steven, 1985.

Elster, Jon. *Closing the Books: Transitional Justice in Historical Perspective.* New York: Cambridge University Press, 2004.

Epstein, Lee, ed. *Contemplating Courts.* Washington, DC: Congressional Quarterly Press, 1995.

Farber, Daniel A., and Sherry, Suzanna. *Desperately Seeking Certainty: The Misguided Quest for Constitutional Foundations.* Chicago: University of Chicago Press, 2002.

Gibson, James L., and Caldeira, Gregory A. "The Legal Cultures of Europe." *Law and Society Review* 30 (1996), pp. 55–85.

Gilman, Howard. *The Votes That Counted: How the Court Decided the 2000 Presidential Election.* Chicago: University of Chicago Press, 2001.

Ginsburg, Tom. *Judicial Review in New Democracies.* New York: Cambridge University Press, 2003.

Judicature 81 (May–June 1998), special issue, "Courts and Justice Abroad."

Kagan, Robert. *Adversarial Legalism: The American Way of Law.* Cambridge, MA: Harvard University Press, 2005.

Koopmans, Tim. *Courts and Political Institutions: A Comparative View.* New York: Cambridge University Press, 2003.

Widner, Jennifer. *Building the Rule of Law: Francis Najalai and the Road to Judicial Independence in Africa.* New York: W. W. Norton, 2001.

WWW. WEB SITES OF INTEREST

United States federal judiciary:
http://www.uscourts.gov/courtlinks/

Canadian Courts, with links to federal, provincial and territorial courts:
http://www.canadianlawsite.com/courts.htm

Oyez,oyez,oyez: a database of major U.S. Supreme Court cases, including multimedia capacity to listen to the oral arguments of counsel:

http://www.oyez.org/

Foreign and International Law Sources on the Internet: Annotated; maintained by the Cornell Law Library:

http://library.lawschool.cornell.edu/guides/foreign2/

PART V

International Politics

CHAPTER 18
⌘

GLOBAL POLITICS: POLITICS AMONG STATES (AND OTHERS)

In the preceding chapters, we looked at the manner in which politics—the use of power to make collective choices for a group of people—is carried on within a state. However, states also carry on politics *among* themselves. For instance, they sign trade agreements setting up special arrangements for the exchange of goods between firms in two or more countries. Or a number of states may agree to coordinate their military activities, as in the NATO alliance. Regular exchanges of scientific information are set up among states. Agreements are drawn up in which groups of states commit themselves to such things as a promise not to test nuclear weapons in the open air. Treaties are drawn up to protect wildlife that migrates across state borders. Wars are fought and settled. Each of these events makes a collective choice for a group of two or more states, and so these are examples of politics—the use of power to make collective choices—*among* states, for a group of states, rather than within one state.[1] This is commonly called **international politics** or **global politics.** The two terms mean approximately the same thing, except that "global politics" emphasizes by connotation that more than just states are involved in the politics. The states are central participants, but international social movements, multinational corporations, and other nongovernmental actors are involved as well.

✦ THE EVOLUTION OF THE INTERNATIONAL SYSTEM SINCE WORLD WAR II

Before analyzing international politics abstractly, it will be useful to review the development of the international system since World War II.

---

[1]Recall the definition of politics in Chapter 1: making of common decisions for a group through the use of power. Here the "group" is a group of states.

From the seventeenth century until the twentieth, most of the world's wealth and military power were concentrated in Europe, and various European states used that power to subjugate large populations around the world and form them into colonial empires. By the early twentieth century, European dominance was weakening, especially because of the increasing power of the United States and Japan. The Europeans then hastened their slide from power by squandering their wealth and slaughtering their youth in World Wars I and II. Although other powers such as the United States and Japan were eventually involved in these wars and they have been called "world wars," almost all of the fighting and destruction centered in Europe. The European states emerged from World War II in 1945 exhausted, with only enough strength left to reconstruct themselves internally.

Two major changes in international politics resulted from this exhaustion of Europe: (1) Two new superpowers—the Soviet Union and the United States—arose to fill the power vacuum, and (2) the European states' empires threw off European rule, because the Europeans no longer had the power to hold them in subjugation.

The rise of the Soviet Union and the United States to dominate world politics created quite a different kind of system than what had gone before. When Europe dominated world politics, a number of substantial powers were involved in the system because Europe was so fragmented. Britain, France, Germany, Italy, and to some extent the Soviet Union, Japan, and the United States could figure in alliances. Many varying combinations of states in alliance were possible, and patterns of alliance shifted as states jockeyed for position. In the world after 1945, however, and especially from 1945 to about 1960, the system of politics consisted of a bipolar rivalry between the United States and the Soviet Union.

The two superpowers had been allies in the war against Hitler and initially set out into their domination of the world with pledges to cooperate in building a new, peaceful political order. However, they differed deeply in political philosophy, and they had conflicting political and economic goals. The Soviet Union used its dominating military force in the region to bring most of Eastern Europe under its control for economic advantage and to insulate itself militarily and politically from Western European states such as Germany and France (which had frequently attacked it earlier in the century). By 1946, Winston Churchill had coined the phrase "Iron Curtain" in his famous speech at Westminster College, Missouri:

> From Stettin in the Baltic to Trieste in the Adriatic, an iron curtain has descended across the continent. Behind that line lie all the capitals of the ancient states of Central and Eastern Europe. Warsaw, Berlin, Prague, Vienna, Budapest, Belgrade, Bucharest and Sofia, all these famous cities and populations around them lie in what I must call the Soviet sphere, and all are subject in one form or another not only to Soviet influence but to a very high and, in many cases, increasing measure of control from Moscow.[2]

---

[2]Randolph S. Churchill, ed., *The Sinews of* **Peace: Post-War Speeches by Winston S. Churchill** (London: Cassell, 1948), p. 100.

In 1947, President Harry S. Truman announced that the United States was sending economic aid to the embattled anticommunist government of Greece, and the Cold War was joined.

The period of rivalry between the Soviet Union and the United States from 1945 on into the 1960s (and periodically until 1989) is called the "Cold War" because while at times it involved intense animosity, it never developed into full-scale "hot" warfare. Various skirmishes were fought—the Soviet blockade of West Berlin in 1948, war between the United States and the Soviet client state of North Korea in 1950—but there was never direct fighting between the two superpowers. There is a clear reason for this. Not only was the international system turned into a bipolar system after 1945, but the two superpowers of that system were armed with a new kind of weapon that made a war between them essentially unwinnable. Nuclear weapons are so destructive that in an all-out nuclear war, either combatant would be able to ruin the other.[3] As a result, the bipolar system that followed World War II was marked by a frustrated rivalry in which the two superpowers chewed on their animosity toward each other but were not able to do much about it.

The other main result of Europe's exhaustion after World War II was the breakup of the old colonial empires. One hundred of today's 193 states were colonies of European states at the outbreak of World War II. In other words, there are more than twice as many states in the world now as there were in 1941. These new states receive sympathy and support from some of the older states—such as China, Egypt, and the states of Latin America—which, although they were independent before World War II, find that they share a common set of problems with the newer states. Together, these new and older states make up the Third World.

The growth in numbers and importance of the Third World states has changed the international system markedly. The Third World commands many of the world's natural resources and comprises about three-fourths of its population. However, it does not command anything close to a proportional share of wealth or military power. Most of the states of the Third World are individually weak, although some such as India and Brazil have developed into moderately important powers, and China has become a major power. As a group, they account for so much of the world that they cannot and should not be ignored. Many Third World states, as they grow in wealth and military strength, have a great potential as future powers; China, in particular, is likely to rival the United States in size and importance within a few decades, and India also has that potential.

---

[3]A revisionist literature has questioned whether nuclear weapons prevent war. This literature points out that in the 1920s, many people thought that the existence of poison gas, in combination with the development of modern air forces, had made all-out war unwinnable. Any power, even if it were going down in defeat, could launch such deathly attacks with gas canisters that the winner of the war would be destroyed. Therefore, it was agreed, no one would dare wage war against a power that had poison gas weapons. As it turned out, full-scale war was waged in World War II, but without gas. The participating powers had chemical weapons, but none used them for fear of retaliation in kind. The revisionist literature argues that all-out conventional warfare could similarly occur today without the use of nuclear weapons. See, for example, John Ellis van Courtland Moon, "Chemical Weapons and Deterrence: The World War II Experience," *International Security* 8 (Spring 1984), pp. 3–35.

✦ THE WORLD SINCE THE COLD WAR

As of the mid-1970s, then, the world could have been described as a fairly stable system of states dominated by two main conflicts—a military standoff in the Cold War animosity between the Soviet bloc and the bloc led by the United States, and an economic and political "north-south" tension between the Third World and the industrialized states of both blocs. Over the next three decades, however, five major developments changed this system into the more fluid, more complicated, but less tense one we face today:

1. **Steadily the set of actors involved in international politics expanded and became more varied.** At the beginning of this period, international politics were conducted pretty much by the states of the world, plus the United Nations and its agencies. Starting in the early 1970s, however, the number of **nongovernmental international organizations (NGOs)** began to grow explosively—growth that continues, as we see in Figure 18.1.

Not all of these organizations are actively engaged in international politics. The International Political Science Association, for instance, exists mainly to promote communication among scholars, although it will occasionally act to promote or defend academic freedom in various parts of the world. Many others, however—Amnesty International, the Pugwash Conferences on Science and World Affairs, the Union of National Radio and Television Organizations of Africa, the International Federation of Journalists, GreenPeace, to name only a few—are politically active in all sorts of ways.

Perhaps the most important group of nongovernmental actors in international politics consists of **intergovernmental organizations,** or **IGOs.** These are organizations founded by treaties among governments, but which operate with an independent

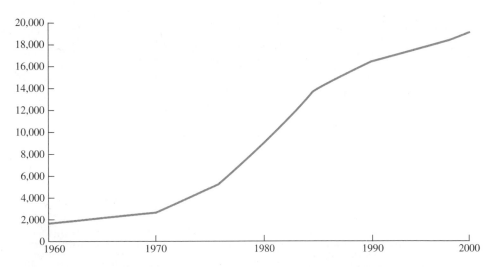

FIGURE 18.1 Growth of nongovernmental international organizations.

SOURCE: Yearbook of International Organizations, various years.

governing structure and staff so that they are not under the direct control of any particular government. They include the United Nations, various arms of the UN such as UNICEF (the United Nations International Childrens Fund), international financial structures such as the Bank for International Settlements, other specialized international coordinating organizations such as the International Whaling Commission and the World Trade Organization, and regional groups such as the Asian & Pacific Coconut Community. These organizations play a different role than NGOs. Usually they administer and implement international agreements among states—but as we saw in Chapter 16, those who implement a decision often put their own stamp on it. And compared with NGOs, these organizations usually operate with legal authority under treaties to make decisions. Where NGOs play more the role of gadflies or watchdogs in international politics, IGOs operate with authority of their own, removing a number of international decisions from the individual states.

In addition to formal organizations, other kinds of new actors have joined the scene. We noted in Chapter 3 that many corporations are so large and their operations spread across so many states' boundaries that they bargain directly with the states almost as equals. Terrorist groups, too, have become significant actors in international politics. The terrorist attack on the United States on September 11, 2001, reshaped the whole role of the United States in the world. Nonstate actors have become major factors in international politics. Another example of how important nonstate actors have become in international politics is provided in the box, "Banning Land Mines."

2. *The interdependence of the world's states grew enormously.* One way this has shown up is in the dependence of states' economies on their trade with each other. For the United States, for instance, trade as a proportion of economic activity was fairly stable through the 1950s and 1960s, but it became an increasingly significant part of the United States economy in the 1970s and 1980s. As seen in Figure 18.2, it doubled as a proportion of the United States' gross national product between 1970 and 1980. Not only did international trade play a larger role in states' economies, but because many of a state's largest corporations were spread across numerous countries, states' economies depended more on what was going on in other states than was the case in the first half of the twentieth century.

Environmental policy is another area in which interdependence has increased explosively. As the world becomes more industrialized, the environmental impact of what we do is less a matter of concern only for the polluting state. The depletion of the ozone layer and the increase in carbon dioxide in the atmosphere that causes global warming affect all states' populations. These and other problems are the ultimate "externality"; as we saw earlier (p. 144), any externality forces a search for collective decisions. The Kyoto Accords to reduce global warming, signed by 178 states in 2001 (but not by the United States), are a good example of the environmental collective choice that externalities from the industrial economy increasingly require.

Finally, partly through the expansion of worldwide communications such as Cable News Network and Al Jazeera network, and partly because the people of the world are more literate and better educated than in the past, we seem more aware of what happens in other states than we used to be. What once would have been claimed to be "internal

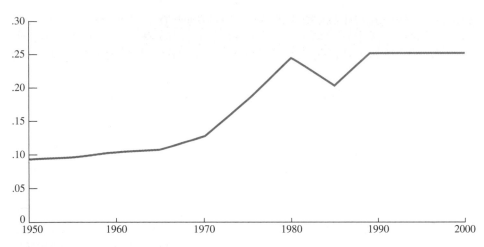

FIGURE 18.2   Trade in goods and services (exports plus imports) as a proportion of U.S. gross national product.

SOURCE: U.S. Bureau of the Census, *Statistical Abstract of the United States,* various years.

affairs" of sovereign states—apartheid in South Africa, human rights abuses in many other states—are now part of international politics.

It is a cliché, but still a good one, that the world is becoming a smaller place.

3. *The bipolar system of rivalry between the Soviet Union and the United States disappeared.* This had already been happening, fairly slowly, for about twenty years as the U.S.S.R. and the U.S.A. gradually lost their monopolies of economic and military power to such upstarts (communist and noncommunist) as Japan, China, Germany, and France. The system of rivalry finally ended rather suddenly with the economic exhaustion of the Soviet Union about 1989 and its internal collapse in 1991.

The results of this shift were momentous. The very way we defined the system of states—West, East, "Third World"—had been based on the old rivalry. Defense establishments suddenly found themselves searching for a new raison d'etre. Client states, such as Cuba or the Suharto regime of Indonesia, found themselves abandoned by their superpower partners.

4. *Starting roughly in the mid-1980s, a large number of states around the world shifted their economies more in the direction of open markets; as a result of this, the states of the world became somewhat more alike.* Partly this shift resulted from the collapse of formerly communist systems. Partly it resulted from the formation of new trade alliances and the necessity of meshing the economies of once heavily regulated states with the more open economies of their new partners; Mexico's economy moved to a more open condition after formation of the NAFTA partnership with the United States, for instance. Finally, a number of economies in Africa (early 1990s) and East Asia (after 1997) were forced by the International Monetary Fund to become more open following financial collapses.

Banning Land Mines

In September 1997, nearly one hundred states signed an international treaty in which they agreed not to use land mines, and to destroy any they had already laid down. Land mines are a weapon that is especially dangerous for civilians. After a war is over, they usually remain hidden in the ground for years, so most of the victims they claim are farmers plowing fields or children at play.

The ban was not engineered by the states that signed it. Rather, it is a prime example of the growing influence of nonstate actors in international politics. In 1990, a coalition of the Vietnam Veterans of America (United States), Human Rights Watch (United States), Physicians for Human Rights (United States), Medico International (Germany), Handicap International (France), and the Mines Advisory Group (Britain) began to work for an international ban. They waged a vivid public relations campaign featuring the late Princess Diana of Britain comforting land mine victims in Bosnia and Angola, and importantly they gained a key ally among the world's states in Canada, whose foreign minister took on the ban as a personal cause. In 1995, the International Red Cross joined in with a large ad campaign—the first time that this prestigious organization had ever joined a controversial cause. Canada called a special conference of states in 1996 to discuss a general ban, and from there, the process moved swiftly.

The states of the world therefore grew more similar to one another. There were fewer autocratic regimes at the end of the 1990s than there were twenty years before. Governments have become more interested in open trade relations than they were when their economics were treated as fortresses. The technocrats who run most states' economic policies "speak the same language" and often were educated at the same American universities; therefore, negotiations for cooperative economic policy have become somewhat easier.[4]

5. *In the late 1990s, a body of international law began to develop that has the potential to impose enforceable law on the leaders of states and thus on the states themselves.* A number of treaties had been in effect since the Second World War that brought the actions of states under international jurisdiction, but no one had tried seriously to enforce them. For instance, most of the states of the world had signed a convention against genocide in 1948. In the late 1990s, however, human rights organizations and their supporters in governmental posts successfully began to use these treaties to bring former heads of state to judgment for their actions. The first instance of this was the arrest of former President Augusto Pinochet of Chile, who had presided over a military dictatorship marked by the use of torture and kidnappings. After the return of democracy to Chile, Pinochet had lived in peaceful retirement as a result of the pacts by which

---

[4]In the early years of the new century a key partner in this process pulled away from it, however, as the United States became less interested in multilateral international cooperation. In particular, by raising farm subsidies and (for a time) tariffs on steel, the United States made it more difficult for states of the Third World to sell their products to it and build their mutual trading relations. In fact, open free trade came to be questioned more worldwide than it had been in the 1990s.

The internationally maintained peace in Bosnia's civil war felt a lot like war. A cartoonist's view . . .

democracy had been restored; but when he traveled to Britain in 1998, a Spanish judge asked for his extradition to Spain so that he could be tried for crimes against international law. Although heads of state traditionally had not been held personally liable for their actions as leaders of their state, the British Law Lords (the highest court in Britain) ruled in an important precedent that Pinochet was indeed liable as president for violations of the International Torture Convention, which Chile had signed. It is important to note that the International Torture Conventions treaty, under which Pinochet was tried, is one of the few international treaties that includes international jurisdiction—that is, it allows any country to punish violators of the treaty.

In a second important case, Serbia in 2001 surrendered its former president, Slobodan Milosevic, to NATO to be tried by the United Nations War Crimes Tribunal in the Netherlands for crimes associated with the deportation of hundreds of thousands of ethnic Albanians from the Serbian province of Kosovo. Unlike the trial of Pinochet, which was decided on very narrow grounds (the Law Lords ruled that Pinochet could be tried only for violations of the International Torture Conventions and then only for tortures committed after 1988, when Chile had signed the convention), the UN court worked with a broad case law based on the Nuremberg trials of Nazi war criminals and the general development of international law since those trials, including the Torture Convention and the International Convention on Genocide.

Finally, the **International Criminal Court** was established in 2003, based in the Netherlands—able to try any individuals, including heads of state and other government officials, for a broad range of crimes, including genocide, "crimes against humanity," war crimes, and the crime of aggression. As of 2007 the treaty establishing the Court has been signed by 104 countries, and even the United States has begun to support it and see its value, though it is not a member and had earlier been worried that its officials might be charged with international crimes and have to deal with the court. The Court tried its first case in 2007—Thomas Lubanga, a Congolese warlord who had forced children to serve as soldiers.

We are still only beginning to work out the implications of these changes in the international system. There are many dangers inherent in some of the changes. There are likely to be more "small wars," for instance, as the superpowers no longer feel a need to keep a lid on boundary disputes around the world; and while these may be "small" wars, we have seen in Bosnia, Somalia, Kosovo, Rwanda, and Darfur that they can be dirty and cruel. However, the new, fluid system also offers rich opportunities. Before those opportunities can be realized, however, we will have to see what norms and rules emerge to govern states' intervention in other states in this new world that is emerging.

Some of the pieces that will add up to what the new international system looks like are:

- The rapid rise of China and India, especially the former, to the status of major powers, both economically and militarily. The rise of new powers is always stressful for a region, as it shakes old connections and patterned relationships.
- Increasing Islamic militancy, exacerbated both by the unpopularity of existing, undemocratic governments in many Islamic states, and by American foreign policy over the last several years with regard to the Palestinian question and to Iraq.
- The negative reaction to globalization, which may turn many states inward rather than outward in their policy focus.
- The growing crisis of resource sustainability and global warming, which puts added strain on all states.

Each of these things probably embodies as many promises and opportunities as it does hazards and danger. But at the least, finding the opportunities and avoiding the dangers is going to call for skilled leadership, and some luck.

As someone once said, "The future lies before us."

✦ INTERNATIONAL POLITICS

The world has a full agenda of problems to address: the problem of environmental degradation; help for the poorest states of the world (mostly in Africa), which are becoming poorer rather than better off; the population explosion, which again is occurring most rapidly in the poorest countries; the control of diseases like SARS and AIDS, which spread more rapidly now that the world is smaller; the maintenance of international trade in the face of protectionist competition; the control of nuclear arms; and many more.

How are these to be addressed? The changes of the last two decades may—*may*—provide new opportunities to find solutions to common problems. However, international politics has some special characteristics, as compared with other types of politics, that make it unusually difficult to find common solutions. These enduring weaknesses may or may not stymie any hopes of progress in the post–Cold War world.

Let us look a bit more abstractly at international politics. We will first consider a few ways in which politics *among* states differs from politics *within* a state, the sort of politics with which we have been concerned so far in this book. It will be necessary, in doing this, to add one new concept, the "fiduciary political role." After we have looked at this question, we will conclude by examining the nature of power in international politics and the mechanisms of war and diplomacy by which international politics is carried on.

How is international politics like that which we have been looking at so far in this book, and how is it different? In its main outlines, politics among states is a good deal like politics within states. The same sorts of policy questions are addressed in both—regulation of potentially harmful behavior, aid programs for the weak, guarantees of standard weights and measures, and so on. Like politics within states, politics among states is marked by the use of force and by appeals to the common good, that is, by power and choice. Political decisions—decisions on behalf of groups—are reached in both types of politics. However, in important ways international politics differs from politics within a state. *The most important difference is that there is no single central authority to provide ultimate settlement of a dispute among states. Also, political figures are more likely to follow overtly selfish* ("selfish," that is, on behalf of their states' interests) *strategies in politics among states. Finally, political interchange does not proceed as easily in politics among states as it does in politics within a state.* Let us look at each of these points.

→ THE ABSENCE OF CENTRAL AUTHORITY

In politics as it is carried on within a state, the various antagonists are subject to a central authority that has the authority to settle a question firmly. If environmentalists square off in conflict with a mining company, both sides know that ultimately their dispute will be resolved by some higher authority that has the power to make them accept that decision, even if they do not agree with it. In the United States, that authority would be Congress, the president, or perhaps the Supreme Court; in Britain, it would be the Parliament; in Saudi Arabia, it would be the king. Within any state, there is some central authority, more powerful than any single political force, that can enforce decisions on any question. The only exception to this would be a state involved in a civil war, which is precisely a situation in which there is no clearly established central authority.

In politics conducted *among* states, however, there is no central position of authority. Therefore, states that become involved in disputes must ultimately settle the disputes themselves, whether by negotiations or through war. Other states may give helpful advice and exert pressure on the disputants, but there is no central body of any sort that can impose a settlement.

The **United Nations** would be a potential body of authority. It is an organization of 192 states, almost all of the states of the world, that accepts responsibility for many of the things a government would do within a state. That is, it is concerned to preserve law and order by preventing violent solutions to disputes (i.e., wars); it promotes health programs, education, and research; it tries to see that poorer states are helped.

While the United Nations tries to do the *things* a government does, it cannot do them *the way a government would do them.* It has no army or police force of its own to enforce its decisions. Rather, it must depend on voluntary help from its member states. Few states are going to send their soldiers voluntarily into a place where they are not wanted—and risk war with the people on whom they are enforcing the United Nations' decision; therefore, this has effectively meant that the UN can almost never send in a police force unless the disputants agree voluntarily to accept it. (The Gulf War of 1991, in which a United Nations force drawn from a number of countries and led by the United States ousted Iraq from Kuwait, was the first exception to this rule in decades.)

Despite these limitations, the UN has frequently been able to play a helpful role when the nations involved in a dispute want to bring in a neutral group to police their negotiated settlement. For instance, United Nations forces successfully enforced the peace agreement that ended civil war in Mozambique in 1992. This is a far cry from the real policing power that would give the United Nations the authority to force a decision on the parties in dispute, but it has helped on a number of occasions to reduce international violence. (The United Nations is discussed in more detail in an example at the end of this chapter.)

Another potentially ultimate authority in the system of states is the **International Court of Justice,** headquartered in the Netherlands. The court is a branch of the United Nations, but the body of "international law" over which it decides goes back far beyond the United Nations, which was founded only in 1945. Since that time (as of 2007), 79 cases have been tried in the court, but again, any solution laid down by the court sticks only if the parties of the dispute voluntarily abide by the court's ruling. In 1984, for instance, Nicaragua brought suit against the United States for mining its harbors. When the United States refused to admit that the court had jurisdiction, the court could do little. Most cases that come to the court are not of this sort but are cases in which those involved have agreed in advance to accept the court's decision, whatever it may be. In these circumstances, the court can serve as a useful tool for resolving disputes. Overall, however, it cannot play the role a government would play.

We noted above (pp. 401–403) that developments in the late 1990s may produce new strands of international law in which heads of state (or at least former heads of state) may be punished for crimes committed by their states. The enforcing agents in these cases would be other states, bolstered by broad consensus among the people of the world, rather than a formal international authority. Even if this process continues, however, we will still be a long way from holding sitting rulers of powerful states—in contrast to disgraced former rulers of weak states—accountable for their states' actions.

With no ultimate governmental authority in the world, politics among states is in many ways what we might expect politics within a state to be if that state had no government. States that are large and strong are able to bully smaller states, and they usually get what they want. Small states must attach themselves to stronger states, through alliances, for protection. In effect, gangs of states join together for mutual protection just as, in a governmentless state, people would form gangs.

✦ FIDUCIARY POLITICAL ROLES AND INTERNATIONAL MORALITY

Before we consider the second special aspect of international politics, we must define a new concept—the **fiduciary role** in politics.[5] Someone acts in a fiduciary role if that person operates as an agent on behalf of another person's interest. A real estate agent acts in a fiduciary role on behalf of a person who wishes to sell a house, or a lawyer acts in a fiduciary role for a client.

The important thing about fiduciary roles for our purposes is that a person acting in a fiduciary role stands in a peculiar moral position. Let us assume that the fiduciary agent is personally upright and moral and that among the agent's "upright" traits is a strong sense of duty toward the person whose interests are being represented. Now let us suppose that the agent is caught in circumstances in which doing the thing that is personally moral will hurt the interests of the person who is represented. Consider the lawyer, for instance, who may need to browbeat a timid witness to defend a client. What is the right thing to do? We hope such a lawyer would never browbeat a timid person on her own behalf, but is it right for her to impose her personal scruples on the client's case and thereby injure the client's interests?

This sort of situation arises frequently in modern life because we have given more and more of our activities over to agents. A corporation president might be generous personally and wish to pay the company's workers more than the going rate, but it is the stockholders who will pay if the company does this, not the president. Is it right for the president to be generous with their money? A real estate agent might not remain silent about that tiny leak in the north gable in trying to sell his own house, but is he right to impose his openness on his client? We recognize that a different moral situation exists when people do something on behalf of others than when they do it to help themselves. We feel differently about a woman who shoplifts caviar than we do about a mother, in dire straits, who steals food for her children.

How does all this relate to international politics? It is important to international politics because here, more than in the politics within a state, almost all decisions are made by those who see themselves as acting in fiduciary roles, on behalf of the people in the state they represent. In politics as it occurs *within* a state, political figures act to some extent as fiduciary agents (members of Congress, for instance, represent their

---

[5]William H. Riker presents the concept of fiduciary role in much the way it is used here in *A Theory of Political Coalitions* (New Haven: Yale University Press, 1962), pp. 24–27.

constituents); but they are largely personal decision makers who represent no clear single interest. Leaders of states (and the diplomats and others who help them to construct the state's position in international politics), however, work on behalf of a single clear "client," the people of that state. It is well understood that a state's leader owes first duty in international politics to the state and its interests, and that anything or anyone else in the world for whom the leader feels affection must run a distant second. We expect George W. Bush to serve the interests of the United States, Jacques Chirac to serve the interests of France, and Hosni Mubarak to serve the interests of Egypt.

This gives a different and colder moral tone to international politics than we find in politics within states. We expect leaders of states to be more cold-blooded in international politics than they would be domestically. What is regarded as personal virtue in domestic affairs may be seen as perverse and harmful in international politics.

Leaders of states have often been forgiven for official acts that, if done for personal gain, would have blackened their names forever. Harry Truman, for instance, killed thousands of Japanese civilians when he ordered atomic bombs dropped on Hiroshima and Nagasaki, and Winston Churchill launched devastating firebomb attacks on German cities. However, they were judged at least partly in light of their official positions. Nationalism further reinforces the view of leaders as filling fiduciary roles, as it can lead us to see other peoples as less human, less deserving of justice and mercy, than our own. This makes the leaders and populations of states more comfortable than they might otherwise be with their states' amoral behavior.

This case should not be overstated, however, because the political actions of states are not *solely* based on calculations of cold rationality. Emotions play a role, and some of these may be generous. For instance, U.S. support for Great Britain in World War II was based on more than rational considerations, although there were elements of rationality involved. U.S. support of Israel over the last few decades has certainly involved something beyond rationality. In its broad outlines, however, international politics is distinguished from politics within states by its relatively greater tone of calculation.

✦ IMPEDIMENTS TO INTERNATIONAL COMMUNICATION

A third major difference between international politics and politics within states is that communication between leaders is more cumbersome and more vulnerable to misunderstanding than communication within any one state. Within a state, the various political leaders speak the same language. More important, they "speak the same language" in that they know each other fairly well, have a common fund of experiences and stories, and share the same culture.

In international politics, the people involved must often use interpreters to converse, which makes the proceedings more formal and slow, and leaves a good deal of room for misunderstanding. The problem of interpretation can lead to amusing moments, as when President Jimmy Carter's statement that he was happy to be in Poland was translated as "I lust for Poland."

More serious yet are deep cultural and religious differences, and the frequent lack of shared assumptions and motivations, which may lead to a failure of communication between states. After World War I, U.S. diplomacy was deeply flawed by President Woodrow Wilson's inability to understand the motives of the United States' allies, Britain, France, and Italy. The leaders of Britain and France in the 1930s responded to Hitler in what was probably an inappropriately gentle way because they did not understand what he wanted to do. Most recently, the United States and North Korea have had continual trouble dealing with one another appropriately because they have approached their mutual interchanges with very different historical and political assumptions.

✦ POWER AND INTERNATIONAL POLITICS

Under these circumstances—with most decisions made by reciprocal bargaining or through conflict, with a relatively naked rationality operating and with severe difficulties of communication—international politics is a rough game. More simply and directly than in politics within a state, the raw power of the participants determines the outcomes.

On what is this power based? First and foremost, a state's *military power* determines its overall power in international politics. Military power is hard to assess. Different states emphasize different types of arms. Israel does not have much of a navy, but it has an excellent small army and air force. How do we compare it with Great Britain, which has an excellent small navy? How does nuclear capacity figure in our calculations? Beyond this problem of comparing apples and oranges, there are imponderable questions such as toughness, morale, and battle readiness that must be considered. Israel's armed forces are stronger than their small size would suggest, because of their spirit and their level of training and because they have had frequent combat experience; they are "tried and true."

Finally, any armed force will fight better when defending its home soil. A smaller and weaker army may be able to defend itself successfully against a stronger army under some circumstances. A good example of this is the tough resistance that Argentina was able to maintain in 1982 against the more imposing and experienced British armed forces in the Falkland Islands war, although Argentina eventually lost. An even better example is the defeat dealt to the large and powerful U.S. forces by North Vietnam in the early 1970s. Table 18.1 displays a few aspects of the military strength of the twelve states that are certainly among the strongest military powers in the world.

The United States found in the first years of the twenty-first century, however, that the Bush administration's reliance simply on military power was not very effective. As the United States became more and more isolated in the world, it became clear that multinational cooperation, appeals to shared ideas, personal links between elites, willingness to consult with others—a whole set of things often referred to as "soft power"— were at least as important.[6] Military might alone will carry you only so far.

---

[6]Joseph S. Nye, *Soft Power: The Means to Success in World Politics* (New York: Public Affairs Press, 2005).

TABLE 18.1

Twelve Major Military Powers

	Defense Expenditure (billions of dollars, 2006)	Persons in Uniform	Of These, Air Force and Missiles	Nuclear Weapons?
United States	535	1,546,372	347,400	Yes
Great Britain	50	216,890	50,370	Yes
France	42	254,895	63,600	Yes
Japan	41	260,250	45,600	No
China	35	2,255,000	400,000	Yes
Germany	29	284,500	67,500	No
India	24	1,325,000	170,000	Yes
Russia	24	1,027,000	240,000	Yes
South Korea	24	687,700	64,000	No
Italy	15	191,152	45,152	No
Israel	5	168,300	35,000	Yes
North Korea	2	1,106,000	110,000	Yes

SOURCE: International Institute for Strategic Studies, *The Military Balance, 2006* (Oxford, UK: Routledge, 2006).

Population

A state with a large number of people—such as India, Indonesia, or Nigeria—gains power from the mass of its population. Nigeria is a leading state of sub-Saharan Africa primarily because it has the largest population of the region. This large population gives it sufficient "critical mass" so that it is the natural center for cultural and economic activity in the region; it therefore becomes a hub of communication.

Another reason population per se serves as a basis of power is that in wartime, even if a state does not have a particularly good army, it may be difficult to defeat if it has a large population. Hitler discovered this when he invaded the Soviet Union in 1941. The Soviet army was initially no match for the Germans and retreated rapidly. However, the Germans kept going and going, and were still only part of the way into Russia. Their lines of communication stretched over a thousand miles, they were sitting in the midst of a hostile population, winter came on, and still there was a large population left in regions they had not yet occupied. From the remnant of Russia, Stalin was able to build a powerful army that eventually defeated the Germans.

Population alone will not make a state strong. In the nineteenth century, China, the largest state in the world, was dominated easily by the smaller European powers. Today, the two largest states in the world, India and China, are still only intermediate powers, though both are now on the verge of becoming major powers.

Economic Power

Even if it is not militarily powerful, a state may figure importantly in international politics if it controls something of economic importance. Saudi Arabia has only a small military force, for instance, but it has often been able to get other states to do what it wishes because they depend on it for their oil imports. Germany's army is reasonably effective, but it is constitutionally limited to defense or to multilateral action, and so cannot realistically be used as a threat to make other states do what it wishes. Greater leverage for Germany comes from the fact that until its economic problems caused by reunification in 1990, it had the strongest, most stable economy in Europe. Its central bank so dominated the European economies that Germany, in effect, set economic policy for many of them until the establishment in 1998 of the European Central Bank—designed to Germany's specifications—for most members of the European Union.

Economic position may also *fail* to provide a political tool, however, as is illustrated by the various attempts of the United States in the 1970s to use threats of economic punishment to get the Soviet Union to do what it wanted. The United States could not credibly threaten the Soviet Union militarily (a war between the two superpowers would be so destructive that no one would dare to start it); therefore, the United States at various times tried to use its economic muscle to influence the Soviets. When the Soviet Union invaded Afghanistan, the United States canceled its exports of grain to the Soviets, promising to start them up again if the Soviets changed their policy. Similarly, in the 1970s, the United States tried through economic sanctions to get Soviet and Polish leaders to liberalize the regime in Poland. These efforts did not work because the United States was not important enough economically to the Soviet bloc countries, whose economies were rather self-contained, to force them to back down on policies that were important to them. Economic sanctions as a tool of international politics are discussed in more detail in the "The Process of International Politics" section.

Geography

Many states are protected by natural formations that render them more secure militarily than their armed power alone would suggest they should be. Great Britain has always benefited from the fact that it is an island, separated from the rest of Europe by the English Channel. It was this that prevented Hitler from invading England during World War II. Similarly, Switzerland has always been rather secure in its rough mountains. Until the coming of air transportation, the United States was sufficiently isolated from Europe that it could get by with a small army. Germany has suffered over the centuries because it sits in the middle of a wide plain stretching from northern France into Russia, a plain along which armies can move easily.

Leadership

Finally, skilled leadership may make a difference in the weight a state carries in international politics. Charles de Gaulle, by skillful diplomacy and a flair for public relations, was able to make France the leading state of Western Europe in the late 1960s and 1970s. Woodrow Wilson's leadership probably diminished the influence of the United States at the end of World War I. Hitler and Mussolini led their states into disastrous, overreaching wars of conquest.

✦ THE PROCESS OF INTERNATIONAL POLITICS

If power is the basic tool of international politics, how exactly does it work? What do the leaders of states, of international organizations, and of nongovernmental organizations do as they make collective choices in international politics?

Diplomacy and Other Nonmilitary Measures

Though ultimately the military power of states remains in the background of most major international decisions, the vast majority of things that happen in international politics do not directly invoke military power. Thousands of small decisions are made every day—small-scale trade decisions, issuing of amnesty to refugees, visits of scholarly delegations—and these do not involve the full power of a state. Also, many large and important actions take place without any military involvement: the formation and expansion of the European Union, for instance, or the international agreement to ban the use of land mines (see box, p. 401).

The process of reaching international decisions in such ways is called **diplomacy.** States maintain a formal diplomatic apparatus for conducting politics with other states. The United States, for instance, employs over two thousand foreign service officers to conduct its diplomacy; in addition, a number of ambassadors and high-ranking officials in the State Department are directly appointed by the president from outside the professional ranks of foreign service officers.

Small-scale transactions, such as handling visitors' problems or promoting local business deals, are dealt with through a system of **consulates.** These are local offices to represent a state in major cities of another state. Germany, for instance, operates ten consulates in major cities in the United States. Consuls, who are in charge of the consulates, do not represent their governments in major international negotiations; their job is to maintain a ceremonial presence locally for the state (U.S. consuls host a Thanksgiving dinner each year for local notables in their city, for instance) and to take care of the myriad of small problems and decisions that come up from day to day.

Ambassadors are the officials charged by their state to conduct high-level politics with the state to which they are posted. A state appoints only a single ambassador to another state, and that person will be based in the capital city. Ambassadors, or even higher officials from the foreign ministry, will represent the state in negotiations over major agreements.

Another major function of ambassadors and the rest of the diplomatic corps is to gather information about the state to which they are posted—commercial information, political information, and military information. They do this openly, by reading the press and talking to the state's leaders and citizens. But these efforts are often supplemented by spying operations (the United States' Central Intelligence Agency, for instance) that mix open and clandestine information gathering.

It is in diplomacy, rather than military action, that most activity by IGOs and NGOs takes place. The box on p. 401 describes one such set of activities by nongovernmental actors; another example would be the active lobbying of the European Community governing structures by international interest groups such as the Cereal Producers' Association. Another example would be the initiatives of Amnesty International to obtain better treatment of political prisoners in numerous states by publicizing the cases and bringing international public opinion to bear on those states. The one exception to the "non-military" nature of nongovernmental actors is international terrorism, in which non-state groups seek to meet their international goals by independent violent action such as bombings or kidnappings. (See the discussion of terrorism below, pp. 415–417.)

That diplomacy does not directly involve military action does not mean that it is purely cooperative. The use of power in diplomacy, like the use of power in any other sort of politics, may run the full range from persuasion to coercion. In persuasion, diplomats will try to convince another state that it is in that state's interest to do what the first state wants. A good example might be trade negotiations, in which one state might try to convince another that open trade in a certain commodity would benefit both. Relations between states such as Canada and the United States consist primarily of persuasion.

Further along the coercion continuum, diplomats of a state might argue with leaders of another state that if the state does not open its markets, the first state might choose to shift its trade elsewhere.

Furthest along the continuum, short of military action, would be a threat by diplomats of the possibility of military action. United States diplomats have often cautioned various Mideast states that if they did not do what the United States was asking, the United States might attack them. This is still diplomacy, not military activity; but it certainly is not warm and fuzzy. Or as Will Rogers is supposed to have said, "Diplomacy [can be] the art of saying 'nice doggy' while looking around for a rock to smash it with."

Economic Sanctions

A form of nonmilitary coercion that is often used by the United States, even in dealing with friends, is the imposition of **economic sanctions.** Imposition of an economic sanction consists of a state or group of states deliberately withholding normal economic relations to punish another state. For instance, the United Nations asked its members to withhold most trade from Iraq from 1990 to 2003 to force it to destroy its weapons of mass destruction.

An economic sanction is certainly direct coercion, though it involves no military activity. It is the analogue, in international relations, of a strike or consumer boycott in domestic politics. In a few important instances, economic sanctions have been successful. For instance, the United Nations' boycott of trade with Iraq in the 1990s kept Iraq involved for several years in a grudging process of disarmament and inspections. The most successful use of economic sanctions was an international boycott of investment in South Africa that led to the fall of that country's undemocratic, white-dominated government.

The key to success in economic sanctions is that one must be able to close the spigot completely. In the Iraq and South Africa cases, nearly all states of the world cooperated in the boycotts, so Iraq and South Africa had no alternative sources of supply.

The United States has often been tempted to pursue unilateral economic boycotts of other states because all by itself it is such a large economic force in the world. These have almost never been successful, yet we keep trying. At various times, we have withheld trade from Cuba, Iran, the Soviet Union, Vietnam, China, and numerous other countries. At the same time, "states" and cities of the United States, pursuing their own miniforeign policies, have enforced economic sanctions on such states as Pakistan, Switzerland, and Indonesia. Inevitably, the target country has bought from Germany, France, or some other supplier the things we were unwilling to sell it. The United States can inflict pain and inconvenience on a target, but rarely enough to make it buckle. Economic sanctions hurt the sanctioner as well. It is estimated that in 1995, the United States lost $20 billion of exports, at a cost of 250,000 jobs, to enforce its trade sanctions.[7] We have also not added to the world's love for us.

It is easy to understand why a state, especially a genuinely major economic force such as the United States, might turn to economic sanctions. No one wants to use military force if it can be avoided. Economic sanctions do give people the feeling of doing something, whether or not they have any effect; but they rarely succeed, unless they are universally enforced.

War

The vast majority of international transactions are conducted peacefully, through diplomacy. However, war is a real part of international politics as well. Many important international political outcomes, such as the freeing of Kuwait after its invasion by Iraq in 1990, the unification of South Vietnam and North Vietnam in 1975, and the occupation of Kosovo by the United States and its allies in 1999, have resulted directly from military action. Even when diplomats negotiate peaceably, their states' power—that is, their capacity to wage war or their capacity to manipulate economic outcomes—always lies beneath the negotiations.

War is also not a sometime thing in international politics. Even though most international politics does not involve war directly, there is almost always some warfare going on, somewhere. Since 1939, there has not been a single day that war was not being waged somewhere in the world.

Because war is so damaging to so many people, political scientists have long wrestled with the question of why wars occur. The causes of war appear to be complex:

- *Nationalism* probably is not a major determinant of whether war occurs, because wars were already a common tool of political leaders long before the modern era in which nationalism blossomed. If nationalism is not a cause of war, however, it certainly has added to the brutality of war, along with its companion, racism (the

---

[7]Cited by Paul Magnusson, *BusinessWeek*, 17 November 1997, p. 115.

U.S. Soldiers, Iraq.
© AP/Wide World Photos

other great popular emotion of the modern era). Atrocities come naturally if you think of your enemy as less human than yourself.

- *Transitions* seem to breed war. Change breeds uncertainty in which leaders may imagine either great threats or great opportunities for conquest and expansion. Change also may create unstable state boundaries. One example of change that bred numerous wars was the establishment of new states throughout the Third World after World War II, as former colonies attained national independence. As noted (p. 55), many of these new states had arbitrary boundaries, which might throw together historically hostile peoples. Numerous civil wars followed the establishment of these new states.

   Another period of danger is the break-up of empires, when a former hegemon that has kept order in a region loses its capacity to hold things together. The break-up of the Turkish Empire after World War I is an example. The break-up of the Soviet Union and its system of satellite states in Eastern Europe after 1989 involved dangers of this sort as well.

- *Misperceptions by leaders,* either of their risks or of their opportunities, may spark wars (which might suggest that we should applaud effective spying rather than disapprove of it! It helps to prevent leaders from misreading their situation). *All* of the states that joined initially in the bloody combat of World War I thought they and their allies were so strong that they would win the war in a matter of weeks. They could not have been more wrong. Similarly, Saddam Hussein of Iraq badly miscalculated when he invaded Iran in 1980. He thought the new Islamic government of Iran would be weak and that he could seize territory by invading the country. Due to his miscalculation, Iraq became bogged down in an eight-year war that killed over a million young men.

• *Rich, powerful states* do not seem to make war with each other very often. They have too much to lose in war, and each has too much capacity to damage the other. Similarly, desperately poor states tend not to engage in war at all, because they do not have the capacity to win a war. Most wars involve in-between states that are poor but not destitute; or they may involve a conflict between a powerful state and an in-between state.

• *The most fascinating regularity* that political scientists have explored is the almost universal observation that democracies do not wage war with other democracies, the so-called **democratic peace.** There has never been a case in which two well-established democracies have gone to war, although there have been "gray area" cases in which a democracy warred with a marginally democratic state.

Political scientists debate whether this regularity is due to mere coincidence or really means something, but those who argue that it does mean something note that it could be caused by popular aversion to warfare. In this interpretation, it is ordinary people who bear the costs of war, not leaders. In a democracy, unlike an autocratic system, the people can hold leaders accountable for an unpopular policy, so leaders will try to avoid involvement in war. Therefore, if two state leaders involved in a conflict are democratically accountable to their people, it may be that they will try to resolve the conflict by some means other than war.

The causes of war are multiple and complex. (I have not even gone into the further complication that wars seem to cycle over time with some periods having large numbers of wars and other periods being relatively peaceful.) However, the costs of war are so terrible that working through the complexities to our best understanding of war is one of the most important projects of political science.

Terrorism

Terrorism is perhaps the signature political phenomenon of the twenty-first century. This is true not because of political goals that terrorism has accomplished—in fact, most terrorist movements have not accomplished their goals—but because of the intense focus terrorism has drawn to itself. Every government in the world is concerned with it.

Terrorism is a phenomenon that could have been placed almost anywhere in this book. (You will recall from Chapter 5 that I had the same problem with corruption.) Terrorism is a tactic, and thus may apply to any political arena. It can be part of domestic politics, as in the hideously successful terrorism by which the Ku Klux Klan robbed newly enfranchised African-Americans of their vote in the southern United States in the late nineteenth century. Or, it can be used in civil wars within states, as in the terrorism engineered by the government of Sudan against the population in the secessionist province of Darfur. Or, it can be part of international politics, as in Al Qaeda's attack on the

United States on September 11, 2001. Terrorism can be initiated either by governments or by non-state actors, but it is usually a tactic of the latter—if only because governments usually have other, more promising strategies available to them.

As noted, terrorism could really be addressed anywhere in this book. I have chosen to put it in this chapter because international relations scholars have studied terrorism much more than other political scientists. Most materials available on terrorism deal with its international aspects, civil wars, or failed states.

Terrorism is the use of violent acts against civilians in order to accomplish political goals. Terrorists attempt to accomplish their goals by gaining publicity for their cause, disrupting normal government and infrastructure, and inflicting fear. Terrorism is usually designed to be dramatic and fearsome, including torture, maiming, rape, and indiscriminate bombing.

Terror is especially likely to be used when:

- *Better, alternative tactics are not available.* Terror is a tactic of strategic weakness. It is effective at keeping an issue to the fore, but as we will see below it is difficult for terrorism to actually bring about a desired solution. If other, more promising tactics are available it is not likely that terrorism will arise.

- *The object of the attack can be portrayed as "the other."* Other ethnic groups or religions, an occupying military force, another country—these can be seen by the terrorists' base of support as being alien or "other," and so violence against them will not upset the terrorists' supporters as much as attacks against their own group. Terrorists are usually careful to avoid attacking their own people, because they will quickly lose public support if they do so.

- *The object of attack is widely seen as lacking legitimacy.* It is relatively easy to sustain support of the base group for attacks against an illegitimate central government, a military occupying force, or an ethnic group against whom ancient grievances can be remembered (or invented). In the Bosnian civil war, for instance, Serbs justified atrocities against Moslems by harking back to battles fought five centuries before; this does not necessarily mean that the old grievances were what set off the civil war, but rather that they were brought up as justifications for the atrocities.

- *The government institutes harsh counterterrorism measures after it has been attacked.* Because terrorists usually are found living among the group on whose behalf they started the campaign, harsh counterattacks almost inevitably will injure innocent bystanders and fuel anger that morphs into greater support for the terrorists. For instance, Israel started harsh counterterrorist reprisals against Hamas and Islamic Jihad in the autumn of 2000, including tearing down many Palestinians' houses and assassinating leaders of the groups. Before the Israeli response, no more than a third of Palestinians supported suicide bombings against Israel; but in the months following the response, support for suicide bombing shot up.[8]

- *Paradoxically, though, democracies are easier to attack than autocracies because there are limits to what they can or will do in response.* It is possible to put down

---

[8]Mia Bloom, *Dying to Kill: The Allure of Suicide Terror.* (New York: Columbia University Press, 2005).

terrorism, or at least limit it, if you are willing to be brutal in ways that are probably impossible for democracies. There was little or no terrorism in Saddam Hussein's Iraq, because he was willing to torture and kill opponents on a large scale, drain the marshes across a huge part of the country to deny them hiding places, and so on.

Terrorism is especially effective at bringing an issue forward, particularly an intractable issue that might otherwise lie ignored. Even a relatively small group of people, without great financial resources, can keep a grievance in the news for years if they are willing to resort to dramatic, violent acts. Groups like the Catholics of Northern Ireland, the Palestinians, the Tamil separatists in Sri Lanka, the Basque independence movement in Spain, and Islamic fundamentalists in various Moslem states have been able to keep their demands on the agenda for years or decades. The problem for terrorists is that while they can keep an issue open, their tactic does not help lead them to a satisfactory solution. In fact, by heightening tensions and building mutual grievances, the tactic almost always makes a solution *more* difficult to reach.

Nonetheless, terrorism is a pervasive part of modern politics, especially of international politics. There are many frustrated causes in the world, with no obvious outlets for solution. A tactic that takes relatively low resources (though intense commitment) may engage enough supporters to keep a conflict open for many years.

✦ POWER AND CHOICE IN INTERNATIONAL POLITICS

It is easy to see the "power" side of international politics, but with no central authority to define common goals for the international system, it is not so easy to see that international politics may also involve "choice." Some theorists think that the international system may work toward certain common goals, however, even in the absence of a coordinating authority.

Regime theory, for instance, sees international politics as transcending the power relationships of states. A "regime" is:

> (a set of) principles, norms, rules, and decision-making procedures around which actors' expectations converge in a given issue-area.[9]

In other words, above and beyond the power relationships of states and other international actors, there may emerge a set of values and principles in the international community that modifies the behavior of the members of the community. States may be moved by a shared vision of the common good, not just by narrow interpretations of their individual interests. Since the Second World War, for instance, a basic assumption of the international order, embodied in institutions such as the International Monetary Fund, has been that trade should expand so that all economies may operate more efficiently. This "regime" has not been uncontested; leaders of the Third World have argued that the regime should instead emphasize redistribution of wealth, rather than taking

---

[9]Stephen D. Krasner, ed., *International Regimes* (Ithaca, NY: Cornell University Press, 1983), p. 1; see also Andreas Hasenclever, Peter Mayer, and Volker Rittberger, *Theories of International Regimes* (New York: Cambridge University Press, 1997).

the existing disparities between rich countries and poor countries as a given and striving only for maximal exchange and overall efficiency of the world economy. The point is, though, that there may be a set of values that has had a power of its own and has affected how states act above and beyond the power relationships of those involved.

Other regimes have been identified in areas such as human rights, justice, and protection of the environment.[10]

Proponents of regime theory see it as a way to address common problems in a more hopeful way than my bleak description of the "fiduciary role" might lead us to expect. But critics argue that regimes are froth on the international system, that they are no more than expressions of the power relationships of those involved—that the international regime on trade, for instance, has been what it was because that suited Western and especially United States' interests.

At this point, regime theory, and similar theories based on the idea that international behaviors may stem from a need to address common problems, are important for us because they suggest that even in the anarchy of international politics, politics may be interpreted as more than just the exercise of power. As I have tried to show throughout this book, a proper understanding of politics always requires that we remain simultaneously aware of its two sides. With some of the changes described in this chapter, the bleak picture of traditional international politics may have acquired some cooperative highlights. The growth of interdependence and the entry of more nonstate actors (which softens somewhat the starkness of the fiduciary role) may make international politics in the future a more balanced mix of "power" and "choice."

EXAMPLE

An International Failure: Rwanda

Rwanda is a small, landlocked state in central Africa, about the size of Massachusetts. It is an agricultural country with significant exports of coffee and tea, and with milk production and grain for local consumption. The country is one of the most densely populated in Africa, with over seven hundred people per square mile—a population density slightly greater than that of Massachusetts.

Before Rwanda came into contact with Europeans at the end of the nineteenth century, it was already a fairly well-developed state ruled by a king. The population was ethnically divided between two tribes. The Tutsis were a tribe of cattle herders and warriors. They controlled politics (the king and most warriors were Tutsi), even though they were numerically a distinct minority. The much

---

[10]See, for instance, Helmut Breitmeier, Oran R. Young, and Michael Zurn, *Analyzing International Environmental Regimes.* (Cambridge, MA: MIT Press, 2007).

larger Hutu tribe were land-based farmers, raising crops rather than grazing cattle on the open range. As of the 1956 census, 16 percent of Rwandans were Tutsi, and 83 percent Hutu.

The "tribal" distinction was to some extent physical, with Tutsis taller and longer-faced, but there had been a good deal of intermarriage over the years, and this had blended such physical differences significantly. The operating distinction was in part also an economic one between haves and have-nots. A Hutu could become a Tutsi if he acquired large numbers of cattle, and a Tutsi could become so impoverished that he sank to being a Hutu.

When Rwanda was colonized, first by the Germans and then by the Belgians, the colonizers found a state in which a Tutsi king ruled, but with a good deal of autonomy for localities, many of which were led by Hutus. In setting up a rationalized bureaucracy for tax collection and road-building, the Belgians relied exclusively on the Tutsis to control the population and rewarded them with weapons and power. In so doing, they greatly sharpened the distinction between Tutsi and Hutu and the hierarchical organization of the state. At the same time, by introducing Western ideas of justice and equality, they helped to develop a sense of grievance among the Hutus. When they granted the country independence in 1962, the Belgians left behind a powder keg of ethnic power relationships and resentments.

Even before independence, a brief, bloody civil war in 1959 had led to the overthrow of the monarchy and had given effective political power to the Hutus. Thousands of Tutsis had fled Rwanda at that time. After independence, there were periodic outbursts of ethnic violence. In 1964, approximately twenty thousand Tutsis were killed in massacres by the Hutus. In 1972, the military (dominated by Tutsis) led a massacre of over one hundred thousand Hutus; they concentrated on the better educated, seen as the greatest threat.

Throughout the 1980s, about 250,000 mainly Tutsi refugees lived outside Rwanda in neighboring countries. In the early 1990s, a Tutsi-led rebel force known as the Front Patriotique Rwandais (FPR), based in these refugee groups, began to have significant success against the Hutu-led government, and by 1993, they occupied much of the northern part of the country. The government and the rebels reached a peace accord that called for democratic, multiparty elections, but it was a fragile peace. It was especially ominous that the (now predominantly Hutu) army refused to honor some of the peace directives from the government, even though the government was nominally in charge of the army.

On April 6, 1994, newly elected President Juvénal Habyarimana, who had been actively promoting reconciliation, was assassinated when the plane in which he and the president of neighboring Burundi were passengers was shot down over Rwanda's capital. Immediately, a well-organized campaign of assassinations and massacres began in which Habyarimana's allies (including the prime minister and the president of the Constitutional Court) were murdered, along with other Hutus who favored reconciliation, educated Tutsis, and a number of United Nations personnel. Over the following several weeks, an organized campaign to kill all Tutsis was carried out, in which an estimated five hundred thousand Tutsis—half the total population and including many children—died. The killings were brutal. Some of the tall Tutsis had their feet chopped off "to bring them down to our size."

Meanwhile, the rebel Tutsi force continued to gain ground on the government, although it was too late to save many Tutsis from murder. By July, they effectively controlled the country. Millions of Hutus fled the country to live as refugees in neighboring Zaire. They were kept there by rumors their leaders spread of Tutsi vengeance, even though there was remarkably little evidence of any revenge by the new Tutsi-led government.

A chilling history! Yet the United States and other Western countries did not pay much attention to it, except for brief expressions of horror at moments when the violence periodically erupted at its worst. Rwanda was not of great economic importance, lacked natural resources such as oil, and was not strategically located with regard to shipping lanes or to international conflicts. In the words of Neville Chamberlain at the time that France and Britain acquiesced in Hitler's dismemberment of Czechoslovakia, Rwanda's suffering was "a quarrel in a far-away country between people of whom we know nothing."

The lack of Western attention to the continuing problems of Rwanda was exemplified by the fact that until the horrendous genocide of 1994, the media in the United States consistently showed more concern for the mountain gorillas of Rwanda (which had been filmed in the popular movie *Gorillas in the Mist*) than for the people of that unfortunate country. A keyword search in June 1994 found 1,123 articles combining the keywords *gorilla* and *Rwanda,* but only 138 combining *guerrilla* and *Rwanda.*[11] However, 1993 was a year in which hundreds of Rwandan civilians were killed by both sides, and hundreds of thousands were made homeless. The major coverage of Rwanda that year consisted of stories in the *New York Times, Newsweek, Houston Chronicle,* and Reuters News Service warning that Dian Fossey's camp (featured in the movie) was threatened by the war:

> [The *Houston Chronicle* article] mentioned the war's human toll only in writing that "the hunger and desperation of a million war refugees" had made Rwanda a less "enticing place for visiting scientists to work." Just as tragically, the war had "ruined the eco-tourism trade that made gorilla sightseeing . . . one of Rwanda's leading sources of overseas income."[12]

The Western response even to the 1994 genocide was half-hearted. The French, who had had a continuing relationship with the Hutu government, consistently had the largest Western military presence in the area. Though at times they intervened to protect the Tutsis, it was usually late and sporadic. As late as May, after several hundred thousand had been killed, the French continued to ship arms to the Hutu militias carrying out the organized murders. The strongest French effort eventually came in protecting the Hutu government as it fled the victorious rebels in July.

Britain offered fifty unarmored trucks to aid in helping prevent the slaughter.

The United States was not bathed in glory, either. American diplomats as a matter of stated policy denied the term *genocide* in reference to Rwanda until late in the killings, by which time over a third of Tutsis had been killed. America offered only slow-arriving logistical support to help move troops from other African countries to restore order. In the end, little was done, and order settled on the deathly country without much help from anyone.

After the victory of the Tutsi rebels, a massive exodus of Hutus began. For the next two years, about one-fourth of the population of Rwanda lived in squalid refugee camps on its border, mainly in neighboring Zaire. They were Hutus, afraid to return home because they believed they would be attacked by Tutsi hard-liners in the army. In the meantime, they were often terrorized by the Zairean army—which wanted to force them back to Rwanda to ease the burden of caring for them—and by their own defeated Hutu army, which was trying to prepare a new invasion of Rwanda. The United Nations tried to be helpful by offering humanitarian aid, building camp shelters, and sending observers to check on conditions in Rwanda's prisons. There was little more the United Nations could do. The situation was in the end "resolved" by the descent of Zaire into a chaotic civil war in which thousands of the Hutus, innocent bystanders in Zaire's internal conflict, were killed. The remaining Hutus fled back to Rwanda. They were initially repatriated with relatively little violence. However, the basic ethnic conflict between Tutsis and Hutus remains unresolved.

---

[11]Ken Silverstein, "Guerrillas in the Mist," *Washington Monthly,* September 1994, p. 21.
[12]Ibid., p. 23.

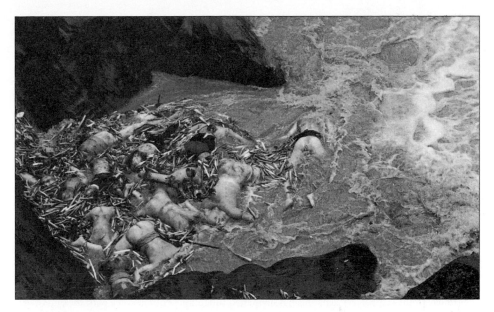

Bodies float at the bottom of a waterfall after a massacre of Hutu refugees in Rwanda.
© AP/Wide World Photos

I titled this "An International Failure," but this may have been unfair. Perhaps there was little the rest of the world could do about the ethnic poison in Rwanda. However, much of the poison was created by the rest of the world during the colonial period. It just does not feel right to throw up our hands at a problem like this. And, history does repeat itself. The continuing massacres and genocide in Darfur over the last several years—unimpeded by any serious international attempt to stop the killing—seem almost to be a rerun of the events in Rwanda.

 # EXAMPLE

The United Nations

 The United Nations was established by the victorious Allies at the end of World War II as an organization to help maintain world peace. It was to do this partly by imposing sanctions against those who broke the peace and partly through programs to remove what were thought to be the causes of war—poverty, suffering, and ignorance. Today, the United Nations has 192 members, nearly all of the world's states.

The decision-making structure of the United Nations was set up by the victorious powers to make them the core of the organization and the guardians of peace. The members of the United Nations are represented in a General Assembly, each with one vote. This is democratic, although it does give undue voting power to tiny countries. However, the victorious Allies added to this General Assembly another body, the Security Council. This body must also agree to any significant action of the United Nations, and each of the World War II victors (the United States, France, Britain, Russia, and China) was made a permanent member of the Security Council. Ten other states rotate on and off the council for terms of two years each. Not only were the victors made permanent members of the Security Council, but each was given an individual veto over its decisions. That is, each of the five permanent members was given the right to veto any significant actions of the UN.

The executive leader of the United Nations is the secretary-general, an individual elected by the General Assembly for a term of five years. The present secretary-general is Ban Ki-moon of South Korea, who was elected in 2007. The secretary-general manages the operations of the UN but works most effectively when persuading rather than pushing. Some secretaries-general have been effective world diplomats; others have been primarily managers of the organization.

This structure might have worked well if the victorious powers had remained united and had operated cooperatively as guardians of world peace. That is what the structure was designed for. Shortly after the establishment of the United Nations, however, the Cold War descended on the world. From then on, either the Soviet Union or the United States was likely to veto any important action of the organization.

Despite this problem, however, the United Nations has developed an important role of peacekeeper in local disputes where the superpowers agreed they wanted to lessen the likelihood of conflict. In the last fifteen years this has happened much more often, since with the end of the Cold War, the likelihood has increased that the five permanent members of the Security Council will find themselves in agreement on issues.

When acting as a peacekeeper, the United Nations organizes a corps of soldiers from states not involved in a conflict who go to the site of the conflict and separate the antagonists. Often this has involved establishment of a demilitarized buffer zone between two territories, which the antagonists agree to keep free of their own troops and which the United Nations peacekeeping force patrols. Over the years, the United Nations has mounted about sixty peacekeeping operations in conflicts such as those between Israel and Lebanon, India and Pakistan, and to monitor agreements in the Darfur province of Sudan. As of 2007, the UN was operating eighteen separate peacekeeping operations around the world; between 1998 and 2007 the number of soldiers involved in UN peacekeeping activities increased by 600 percent.[13]

The nature of the UN's peacekeeping role changed sharply after the end of the Cold War, and the organization is still trying to define the role properly. As long as the world was ordered by the rivalry between the United States and the Soviet Union, the UN filled the useful, but relatively unadventurous, role of monitoring locally negotiated peace agreements. Starting with the breakdown of the Somali state in the early 1990s, however, the UN began to take on a broader mission of entering distressed states and imposing order. This mission failed horribly in Somalia, as local warlords refused to accept the authority of the UN mission, which in turn was badly set up to deal with what became, in effect, a guerrilla war. Next, the UN tried to prevent the bloody ethnic conflict in former Yugoslavia. But all of the "safe havens" it declared, to which ethnic minorities were supposed to be able to flee for security if necessary, simply became traps for those minorities, in which thousands perished when the outgunned UN troops were unable to protect them effectively. By the time of the Rwanda genocide, the UN was so burned by its earlier failures that it dithered in a situation it might have helped. In its current peacekeeping missions, most notably in the Eastern Congo where it is trying to establish peace in the face of insurgent groups, the UN is establishing new, more aggressive rules of engagement for its forces. Rather than just reacting

---

[13]"Call the Blue Helmets," *The Economist*, January 6, 2007, p. 22.

defensively, they are bringing force to those they are trying to control. It is said that the ghost of Rwanda lies heavily on UN peacekeeping forces; they do not want to again stand by guarding a "peace" in which horrible things happen.

Beyond the peacekeeping function, the United Nations operates a wide range of agencies that work to improve the condition of humanity in everything from helping refugees to encouraging trade and development. The scope of this work is large. The United Nations buys half of the world's vaccines for children, protects 30 million refugees in 50 countries, and is the world's largest customer for condoms.[14]

With the end of the Cold War, it at first looked as though the United Nations could take on a more leading role in international affairs, since it would not be stymied by the Soviet-American rivalry. Its peacekeeping roles became more important and more demanding, and in the wake of the Gulf War in the early 1990s the United Nations was asked to take on the massive job of overseeing the regulated sale of oil from Iraq, which was intended to guarantee food and medicines for the beleaguered Iraqi people.

However, the increased visibility of the United Nations soon conflicted with its own creaky bureaucracy, and with major states' unwillingness to cede it a leading role. The oil program with Iraq was plagued by corruption, even involving Kofi Annan's son. The organization developed severe financial problems, primarily because the United States refused to pay its dues for several years. New major powers like Japan, India, Brazil, and Germany began to ask why states like Britain or France should have permanent seats on the Security Council while they did not. And most seriously, the UN underwent a damaging crisis in 2003, when the United States wanted the United Nations to invade Iraq, but France, Germany, and Russia (all permanent members of the Security Council) opposed the action. In the end the United States lost, after a nasty conflict that left the United Nations scarred and the U.S. resentful.

In the wake of all this, and most especially the corruption scandal involving his son and other United Nations officials, Kofi Annan cleaned out a number of senior leaders in the organization and set further reforms on track. Ban Ki-moon has pledged to continue the reform efforts, but it is too early to see how effective he can be.

---

[14]"Pope Kofi's Unruly Flock," *The Economist*, 8 August 1998, p. 19.

✦ A PERSONAL NOTE

Let me close this book with a personal note. We tend, when analyzing politics, to think of it in the abstract and rather dispassionately. We analyze people's actions according to the resources available to them and according to a rational application of those resources to their goals. By and large, this analysis works well. We can usually tell which of two countries will be able to impose its will upon another, what sort of people will turn out to vote in greater numbers at election time, how a change in party finance will affect candidates' strategies, and so on. Sometimes, however, passionate belief can cut through all this. Ideas and ideology can take on a power of their own, which transcends analysis. No political scientists in the early 1960s predicted the tumultuous events of the civil rights movement. Who would have thought that little Vietnam would be able to best the United States in a war? That the democratic opposition would eventually triumph over the Communist Party in Eastern Europe and the Soviet Union?

As a small dog, if it is on its home ground, may be able to send a larger one running away with its tail down, so may the weaker side—even a very weak side—prevail in politics if its supporters believe strongly enough that they are right.

This book has emphasized the analysis of politics, and surely this is important. I hope you will also remember the importance of passion and belief, though. As Marshall McLuhan put it, "Nothing is inevitable as long as one person is aware that it is happening."

KEY TERMS

international politics
global politics
NGOs
IGOs
International Criminal
  Court

United Nations
International Court of
  Justice
fiduciary role
diplomacy
consulates

ambassador
economic sanctions
democratic peace
regime theory
terrorism

FURTHER READING

Bekou, Olympia, and Cryer, Robert, eds. *The International Criminal Court*. Burlington, VT: Ashgate, 2005.

Bloom, Mia. *Dying to Kill : The Allure of Suicide Terror*. New York: Columbia University Press, 2005.

Breitmeier, Helmut, Young, Oran R., and Zurn, Michael. *Analyzing International Environmental Regimes*. Cambridge, MA: MIT Press, 2007.

Doyle, Michael W., and Ambanis, Nicholas. *Making War and Building Peace: United Nations Peace Operations*. Princeton, NJ: Princeton University Press, 2006.

Falk, Richard. *The Declining World Order: America's Imperial Geopolitics*. New York: Routledge, 2004.

Fasulo, Linda. *An Insider's Guide to the UN*. New Haven: Yale University Press, 2003.

Gilpin, Robert. *Global Political Economy: Understanding the International Economic Order*. Princeton: Princeton University Press, 2001.

Goldman, Kjell. "International Relations: An Overview." In *A New Handbook of Political Science,* edited by Robert E. Goodin and Hans-Dieter Klingemann. New York: Oxford University Press, 1997, pp. 401–27.

Hasenclever, Andreas, Mayer, Peter, and Rittberger, Volker. *Theories of International Regimes*. New York: Cambridge University Press, 1997.

Hough, Peter. *Understanding Global Security*. New York: Palgrave Macmillan, 2004.

Howard, Russell D., and Sawyer, Reid L. *Terrorism and Counterterrorism,* 2nd ed. New York: McGraw-Hill, 2006.

Keck, Margaret E., and Sikkink, Kathryn. *Activists Beyond Borders: Advocacy Networks in International Politics*. Ithaca, NY: Cornell University Press, 1998.

Kennedy, Paul. *The Parliament of Man: The Past, Present, and Future of the United Nations.* New York: Random House, 2006.

Keohane, Robert. *After Hegemony: Cooperation and Discord in the World Political Economy.* Princeton: Princeton University Press, 1984.

———, ed. *Neorealism and Its Critics.* New York: Columbia University Press, 1986.

———, and Nye, Joseph S. *Power and Interdependence.* 3rd ed. Glenview, IL: Scott, Foresman, 2001.

Krasner, Stephen D., ed. *International Regimes.* Ithaca, NY: Cornell University Press, 1983.

Ku, Charlotte, and Diehl, Paul F., eds. *International Law: An Anthology.* Boulder, CO: Lynne Rienner Publishers, 1997.

Lutz, James M., and Lutz, Brenda J. *Global Terrorism.* New York: Routledge, 2004.

Mearshimer, John J. *The Tragedy of Great Power Politics.* New York: W. W. Norton, 2001.

Mickolus, Edward F. *Terrorism, 1996–2001: A Chronology.* (2 vols.) Westport, CN: Greenwood Press, 2002.

Murphy, John F. *The United States and the Rule of Law in International Affairs.* New York: Cambridge University Press, 2004.

Nye, Joseph S. *The Paradox of American Power.* New York: Oxford University Press, 2002.

———. *Power in the Global Information Age: From Realism to Globalization.* New York: Routledge, 2004.

———. *Soft Power: The Means to Success in World Politics.* New York: Public Affairs Press, 2005.

Ray, James Lee. *Democracy and International Conflict.* Columbia: University of South Carolina Press, 1995.

Siverson, Randolph M. "A Glass Half-Full? No, But Perhaps a Glass Filling: The Contributions of International Politics Research to Policy." *PS* 33 (March 2000), pp. 59–64.

Stiglitz, Joseph E. *Globalization and Its Discontents.* New York: W. W. Norton, 2002.

Stoessinger, John G. *Why Nations Go to War.* 9th ed. Beverly, MA: Wadsworth, 2004.

Vasquez, John. *The War Puzzle.* New York: Cambridge University Press, 1993.

Vernon, Raymond. *In the Hurricane's Eye: The Troubled Prospects of Multinational Enterprises.* Cambridge: Harvard University Press, 1998.

Waltz, Kenneth. *Theory of International Politics.* Reading, MA: Addison-Wesley, 1979.

Walzer, Michael. *Arguing About War.* New Haven: Yale University Press, 2005.

Weart, Spencer R. *Never at War: Why Democracies Will Not Fight One Another.* New Haven: Yale University Press, 1998.

Zifcak, Spencer, ed. *Globalisation and the Rule of Law.* New York: Routledge, 2005.

---

www WEB SITES OF INTEREST

Counterterrorism Blog
http://www.counterterrorismblog.org

Terrorism Research Center
http://www.terrorism.com

United Nations:
http://www.un.org

European Union delegation to the United States:
http://www.eurunion.org

Foreign Affairs, a journal of international affairs:
http://www.foreignaffairs.org/

International Institute for Strategic Studies:
http://www.iiss.org/

Stockholm International Peace Research Institute:
http://www.sipri.org/

United Nations Environmental Programme page of updates on negotiations in progress for international environmental agreements:
http://www.unep.ch/

Union of International Associations; online Yearbook of International Organizations, plus many links:
http://www.uia.org

APPENDIX
Principles of Political Analysis

There are a number of basic principles of argument and logic that students should learn in an introductory political science course. In part, these should have shown up implicitly in much of the material you have already read and discussed in this course, but it is also helpful to look at them more directly. They are included here not as a tag end or afterthought but because this seems to be the best way to handle them. Some instructors may prefer to use this section at the beginning of a course, some at the end, others at some other point. Locating this discussion in an appendix leaves to the instructor the decision of how to handle it.

FALSIFIABILITY

The most basic principle of political argument is that to be useful, any statement about politics must be **falsifiable.** That is, it must be at least potentially possible that the statement is not true and could therefore be falsified. For example, the statement "two-party systems tend to produce less redistribution of income than multiparty systems" would be falsified if we compared the two-party and multiparty systems of the world and found that there was little difference between the two in the degree of income redistribution they produced. The statement "Ted Kennedy has shown little sympathy for blacks" would be falsified if one produced a long list of statements and actions in which Ted Kennedy demonstrated sympathy for blacks.

On the other hand, some statements about politics are true by definition. "John Kerry lost the 2004 presidential election because most of the voters chose George Bush" is one example. "The poor countries of the world are more backward economically than rich countries" is another. Think about it: How would you go about falsifying either of these statements? They are true by definition.

These statements could not possibly be demonstrated to be false; therefore, they are automatically true. Such a statement does not tell anything about the world that we did not already know before we read the statement. Literally, a statement that is not falsifiable says nothing about the world. Such statements are called **tautologies.**

The two examples given are fairly obvious, and so you might wonder why falsifiability is emphasized here. Surely, mustn't it be obvious when a statement says nothing new? If so, it wouldn't seem to be much of a problem. However, it is not always immediately clear that a statement is a tautology. Consider the following: "A country with a large agricultural sector and a large industrial sector to its economy will tend to have a small service sector." Such a country will not "tend" to have a small service sector; it will *always* have a small one, because this statement is true by definition. To have a large agricultural sector means that a large percentage of the labor force is employed in agriculture; if the country also has a large industrial sector, then another large percentage of the labor force is employed in industry. What's left is the service sector. The percentages employed in different sectors must always sum to 100 percent, so if the first two percentages are large, there cannot be much left for the service sector. Its percentage must by definition be small, and so the statement is a tautology—although to most people it would not be obvious, at first glance, that such was the case.

As you become involved in the analysis of politics, you will be surprised by how often statements about politics turn out, on closer examination, to be true by definition.

We have now cleared the underbrush a bit and know that we are to deal only with statements that are at least potentially falsifiable. Clearly, however, some of these statements will be more interesting than others, and we don't want to waste our time with the uninteresting ones. This leads us to the following question:

WHAT MAKES A STATEMENT INTERESTING?

There are three kinds of statements about politics:

- *Statements of fact:* These state what *is*, they *describe* reality. Examples: "The American president is elected for a four-year term." "There are two major political parties in West Germany." "Chile and Argentina have been engaged in a dispute over boundaries for decades."

- *Statements of value:* These state *how good* something is; they *evaluate* reality. Examples: "The U.S. Constitution provides the best governmental system in the world." "Sales taxes are not as good as income taxes because they are regressive." "A planned economy provides a better life for people than a free-market economy."

- *Explanatory statements:* These state *why* something is as it is; they *analyze* reality. Examples: "The Democratic Party gained seats in the 2006 congressional elections because of the failure of the United States occupation of Iraq." "People whose parents were interested in politics tend to be especially interested in politics themselves." "The sending of unclear diplomatic signals increases the likelihood that war will break out."

All three types of statement are appropriate areas for political investigation and argument. Whatever sort of statement you make, however, you want it to be interesting. A statement will be relatively interesting to the extent that it offers your readers something that (1) is of concern to them and (2) would have been difficult for them to accomplish for themselves. That the statement must be of concern to your readers is obvious and requires no further comment. (Most American readers, for instance, would not be much concerned about the precise arrangements for choosing a king in Sweden, and statements about it would not be especially interesting to them.) However, note the further condition for interest—that the statement should offer your readers something that would have been difficult for them to accomplish for themselves. This is not so obvious.

Consider two descriptive statements about Congress: "Congress has 535 members," and "Three-fourths of the members of Congress have cast a vote at one time or another on direct instructions from a lobbyist." (The second of these is imaginary and, one hopes, false!) These two statements would be of equal *concern* to students of Congress, but the second statement would be more interesting to them because it is something that would have been difficult for them to learn for themselves. They could have learned how many members there are in Congress by a quick glance in any encyclopedia, but it would take a clever investigator, working for a long time, to ascertain the truth of the second statement.

Similarly, "justice is good" is not an interesting statement of value. Presumably, everyone would be able to agree with it without much thought, and so it does not provide us with much that is new. However, the statement "discrimination is good" is a challenging statement, one that goes against the grain. It would not automatically occur to most of your readers and would require a good deal of argument to be rendered plausible for them. Arguing for this statement requires a lot of thought, which you must provide for your readers, and will thus be proportionately more interesting to them.

As a final example, the explanatory statement "Rich countries will tend to have bigger armies than poor countries" is not an interesting explanation of the size of armies, because it is so obvious that coming up with it did not require much thought. "Countries with high unemployment, and therefore cheap labor, will tend to have large armies" is a more interesting explanation of the same thing. A thoroughly obvious, hence uninteresting, explanation is called a **trivial explanation.**

As a general rule, statements of value and explanatory statements require more thought on the part of the writer than descriptive statements, and they are therefore more likely to be interesting statements. Students writing papers are often tempted to write descriptive papers, laying out a set of descriptive statements, because this is easier than justifying statements of value or explanation. You should remember that unless you choose a *challenging* descriptive problem, your work will not be a particularly interesting one. Often you will be given a particular descriptive investigation as an exercise; you might, for instance, be asked to trace the progress of a bill through the legislative process. If so, describe away! If you are asked to "write a term paper about some aspect of the legislative process," however, you will usually be able to write a more interesting paper if you choose a question of value or of explanation.

Causation and Explanation

Let us look a bit more closely at explanation. An explanatory statement necessarily involves the notion of causation. We *explain* a certain thing by saying that another thing *causes* it. For example, we might explain that the U.S. government has difficulty making broad, systematic policy in areas such as energy by blaming it on the separation of powers in the American system. That is, we *explain* the existence of the difficulty by saying that the difficulty is *caused* by the separation of powers. (Presumably this would be because there are many points at which the political power of opponents can be decisive—the presidency, either house of Congress, or the courts. As a result, "difficult" programs are hard to pass.)

In the example, we cannot conceive of any way to explain the American difficulty except to assert one or another possible cause of the difficulty. So to explain is to analyze causes.

What is **causation?** What does it mean to say that one thing causes another? In general, we think that to cause something is to *bring it about,* to bring it forth, to produce it. Turning a key causes my car to start. Russia's opposition to a proposal causes the defeat of the proposal in the United Nations. The increasing electoral advantages of incumbents in U.S. congressional elections have caused an increase in the average seniority of members of Congress. And so on.

We think of causation as working only forward in time. For one thing to produce another thing, the "producer" has to precede the "product" temporally. So it doesn't make sense to think of low turnout in the Sunni areas of Iraq in the 2005 elections as having caused suicide-bomber violence; but it does make sense to think of suicide-bomber violence as one of the causes of the low turnout.

However, temporal precedence is not enough to establish one thing as a cause of another. We do not think of winter as causing spring, for instance, even though we know that "when winter comes, spring can't be far behind." Although the seasons unfold together, we do not think of one season as bringing the other about. Similarly, it is probably true that brunettes tend to be Democrats, since for historical reasons a number of ethnic groups with dark hair—blacks, Native Americans, Chicanos, southern Europeans—have gravitated to the Democratic Party. Although people acquire their hair color long before they give a thought to which party they will support, we do not think of hair color as causing people's party preferences. It is only a coincidence that the two tend to vary together.

Political scientists put a great deal of effort into trying to sort out what things cause the things in which we are interested. Why does the United States have only two major parties? Why are states of the Third World less likely than Western states to be well-established democracies? Why do communist economies not grow more quickly than they do? If we could experiment with politics in a laboratory, as chemists or physicists do in their specialties, we could hold all other possible factors constant; we could allow only the one we wished to examine to vary and then see whether, when it varied, the thing we were trying to explain also varied. For instance, a physicist may place two identical weights on identical wheelchairs on slopes of different angles and measure the effect of the angle of slope on the speed of descent; since nothing else varies, it is clear that only differing angles of slope can be causing differing speeds of descent. If we could manipulate things in this way, we would feel confident in stating that the one thing was causing the other to vary. However, with rare exceptions, we cannot experiment with the things we are examining in political science. We cannot change the electoral system of the United States to see what effect this would have on the number of parties or change states of the Third World to industrial states to see whether their political regimes would change or change command economies to market economies to see whether they would become more productive.

What we *can* do is observe variations and changes as they occur around us and try to figure out which variations or changes actually cause other things to happen. For instance, many states of the Third World, especially in East Asia, are becoming industrialized, so we can watch to see how this changes their politics. The challenge in basing analysis on such changes is that no one thing ever changes in isolation from everything else, in the way a physicist can arrange it in the laboratory. Everything is always changing at once, and we must use our creative sense to try to sort out *which* changes have caused *which* others.

For example, in 1961, France changed its electoral system to one based on a presidency, which should, in principle, tend to bring about a two-party system. Over the years since then, France has indeed seen a coalescence of its party system into five parties, organized in two well-defined blocs. Did the new electoral system bring about the coalescence? At the same time that France was adjusting to its new electoral arrangements, it was also experiencing unprecedented prosperity, which might perhaps have made people less likely to support small radical parties. Also, it was at this time that the popular Charles de Gaulle served as president. He drew a large political party about himself—something he could probably have done no matter what the electoral system was—and that knocked out several smaller parties. What, then, was the effect of the change in electoral arrangements on the number of parties?

Under such circumstances, we cannot be certain of the effects of one thing on another. We can and do use our common sense, asking, for example, what the effects of electoral systems *should* be. And we can look at overall patterns across many cases, asking what has happened after changes of electoral system in other countries. The result is not a firm, indisputable finding but rather something on which to form conclusions and something that can be disputed. There is nothing wrong with this.

HISTORICAL EXPLANATION

A natural affinity between the field of history and what we have been discussing should be apparent to you. Historians follow a series of events as they move forward in time, linking them to one another. This is much like the analysis of causation that political scientists frequently engage in.

There is a difference in emphasis between the two fields, however. Historians are more often concerned to present a single train of events—a biography of Lincoln, a history of negotiations at the Council of Europe, a military history of World War II, and so on—with causal analysis left somewhat implicit. Political scientists, on the other hand, are more likely to look for overall patterns (embodied in theories) and less likely to be concerned with tracing carefully through any single case or train of events.

This is only a difference of degree. Political historians and political scientists are engaged in the same task—to make sense out of the myriad political events occurring around us—and both historians and political scientists do this by *explaining* certain things, showing that they are caused by other things.

Remember from our earlier discussion that it is not enough to show that one thing happened before another. If we are to treat the earlier event as causing the later one, we must also establish some basis for treating it as having brought the other about or having produced it. *This necessity holds as much for the historian as for the political scientist.*

This is an important point for students in political science courses, because as you are assigned research papers to write, a deceptively simple route may appear to be a paper that traces the history of something: a history of the arms race between India and

Pakistan, a biography of Barack Obama, a history of the diplomatic attempts to prevent North Korea from developing nuclear weapons, a description of how the National Security Council developed, a tracing of changes in French fiscal policy after the socialists came to power, and so on. Any of these could make an excellent topic for a paper, but if you do it right, it will be neither easier nor more difficult than any other topic would be. To do the job right is to try to establish causal relationships among the events as they transpire. If, in attempting to write a paper of this sort, you lay out the events—first X happened, then Y, then Z—you will have merely described things. As noted, you will not have an interesting paper. However, if you operate as good historians do—that is, if you try to explain why the train of events occurred as it did—you will have an interesting and not necessarily easily written paper.

A Few Common Pitfalls in Analysis

As you analyze politics, you must think straight. For the most part, common sense will carry you well; and practice and criticism from your readers will help to sharpen your abilities. As an introductory help, you may find it useful to consider three common flaws in analysis that you should watch out for in your own writing and the work of others.

1. Begging the Question. Sometimes writers answer a question with an answer that restates the question. It looks as though it has answered the question, but it has not. It has turned the question into another form and does not produce much progress. This is called **begging the question.**

For example, a person analyzing the victory of North Vietnam in the Vietnam War might state that North Vietnam won because it was more powerful than South Vietnam. This does not really answer the question we want to see addressed; rather, it changes it slightly into the question: Why was North Vietnam more powerful than South Vietnam? Similarly, an analysis of American voting behavior concluding that people vote for candidates they prefer would not seem to have brought us forward. It would leave us with the further question: Why do people prefer certain candidates over others? Questions of value can also be begged. For instance, a paper arguing that socialism is a better system than capitalism because it is more just—unless it expanded on this to show what was meant by "justice"—would leave us with the question: What makes socialism more just than capitalism?

These examples may have seemed rather simple, and you may have wondered why you would need to be cautioned to watch out for a flaw that is so easily avoided. However, begging a question is actually easy to do. Not all instances of it are as obvious as the examples used here. For instance, people often argue about policy on the basis of "natural rights," rights so basic to the nature of humanity that they take priority over all else. The Declaration of Independence appeals to "certain inalienable rights, [among which are] life, liberty, and the pursuit of happiness" and argues that because the king of England had violated these rights, his rule was outlaw; hence, it was proper to rise in revolution against him. At a later period, administrators in Hitler's Germany were charged with the crime of having obeyed and enforced Hitler's laws. This was a crime because the laws themselves were in violation of natural rights. Basic privacy, the right of a woman to control her own body, and the fetus's right to life are other things that have been defended at one time or another as natural rights.

This sort of argument comes readily to us, and we slip easily into it. It is a useful rhetorical device. We should realize, however, when we assert the existence of natural rights, that unless we accompany this assertion with an analysis of human nature, we are begging the question in the following way: "X should be defended because it is a natural right." What makes it a natural right? That it is basic to the nature of a human being. But how do we know what is basic to the nature of a human being?

2. *Circular Argument.* A **circular argument** is one in which a person proves A from B, but we know that B is true only because of A. In other words, B implies A, but we believe B only if we first believe A. The argument goes in a circle and does not offer any new reason to believe either A or B.

Suppose, for example, we argued that political influence of the military is a major cause of the size of defense budgets, but we measured "military influence" by the size of the armed forces. In this case, we would be asserting that military influence is what causes defense budgets to be large, but because our measure of "military influence" is something that is a direct result of the size of defense budgets, finding that the two things tend to rise and fall together would give us no new reason to believe the original statement.

DILBERT: © Scott Adams/Dist. by United Feature Syndicate, Inc. Used by permission.

3. Post Hoc *Explanation.* A **post hoc explanation** is the "Monday-morning quarter-back" of explanation. It consists of taking a set of things that have already happened, showing that one of them plausibly could have resulted from the others and, on the basis of this, asserting that those others are a cause of the thing in question.

For example, many commentators have looked at the sequence of events leading up to World War II and have asserted that it was the appeasement of Britain and France that led Hitler on and resulted in his frantic war of conquest. This is certainly plausible, but it is post hoc.

The danger in post hoc explanations is that for *any* event, there will be some set of things that happened at more or less the same time and that may look like a plausible explanation for it. If those same things happen again in the future, they may or may not produce that same result. It is not that a post hoc explanation is *wrong* but that it leaves us with a greater feeling of certainty than we should have. We confuse the set of events that first suggested an idea to us with verification of the idea. What has suggested that appeasement encourages aggressors? The events leading to World War II. How do we know that it's true? Look at Hitler!

The three problems of argument noted are by no means the only ones you will learn to watch for, but they are three common problems. In the end, these three, and the rest, boil down to a matter of common sense. If you are endowed with some of that, you won't go wrong.

KEY TERMS

falsifiability	causation	circular argument
tautology	begging a question	*post hoc* explanation
trivial explanation		

GLOSSARY

Following each term, the first page on which it is introduced substantively appears in parentheses.

A

agents of socialization (p. 198)   Those who carry out political socialization: parents, schools, media, friendship groups, and so on. The impact of an agent of socialization on one's political knowledge and viewpoints is a function of (a) the agent's relevance to politics, and (b) the agent's credibility.

ambassador (p. 411)   An official charged by his or her state to conduct high-level politics with another state to which he or she is posted.

American conservatism (p. 22)   The rather loose ideology known in the United States as "conservatism." It is really a variant of the more general ideology of liberalism and has relatively little to do with the more general ideology of conservatism; therefore, it has been distinguished in this book by the name *American conservatism.* American conservatism is particularly suspicious of governmental intervention to make people more equal but is often willing to entrust government with power to maintain morality.

American liberalism (p. 22)   The rather loose ideology known in the United States as "liberalism." It is really a variant of the more general ideology of liberalism; therefore, it has been distinguished in this book by the name *American liberalism.* American liberalism is particularly concerned to make people equal, and it is relatively willing to entrust government with power to bring this about; it is also particularly concerned to maintain freedom of expression.

arbitrary action (p. 134)   Action that is taken capriciously. The people affected do not know what to expect before the action and do not learn afterward the grounds on which the action was chosen.

authoritarian democracy (p. 150)   A formal democracy in which, however, through some mix of fraud, intimidation, and control of communications, the same ruler stays in power indefinitely. Though the institutions of democracy are there, the open competition is not. Current examples are Robert Mugabe's rule in Zimbabwe, and Vladimir Putin's in Russia.

authority (pp. 5, 181)   Power based on a general agreement that the holder of the power has the right to issue certain commands and that those commands should be obeyed.

autocracy (p. 161)   A governmental arrangement in which those who hold power did not gain power by any regular constitutional process and are not responsible in their exercise of power to any formal set of rules.

autonomous state (p. 62)   A state in which the government and bureaucracy are relatively insulated from political pressures of groups in the society.

B

begging a question (p. 432)   "Answering" a question (failing to answer it) by offering a rephrasing of it as an answer. Example: "Why did Britain win the Falkland Islands war?" "Because Britain was more successful militarily than Argentina." (This leaves us with the question "Why was Britain more successful militarily than Argentina?" which restates the original.)

"behavioralists" (p. 15)   Political scientists who emphasize statistical analysis and abstract theories seeking out basic, essential regularities across a set of events.

bureaucracy (p. 367)   A way of organizing the public administration that emphasizes professionalism, recruitment, and promotion on the basis of merit, standardization of procedures, and the smooth flow of commands.

C

cabinet (in parliamentary system) (p. 318) The executive portion of a parliamentary government. It consists of ministers, most of whom are usually members of the parliament. Each minister is responsible for the administration of some part of the government's services, such as health or defense. The cabinet leads the parliament, proposing legislation, conducting the country's foreign policy, and so on. It serves at the pleasure of the parliament and can be ousted by a majority vote of no confidence.

case law (p. 380) A legal system emphasizing the independence of the judiciary from the rest of the government. Under case law, the ongoing stream of prior decisions (precedents) becomes an important part of current law. Predominant in Britain and its former colonies.

causation (p. 430) An interpretation of relations between events in which one event "brings about" or produces another event. Example: "Independence of their central banks is a major cause of low inflation for states."

central bank (p. 111) A bank set up by a government to help handle its transactions, to coordinate the policies of private banks, and, above all, to manage interest rates in the economy.

circular argument (p. 433) An argument in which one proves A from B but in which A provides our only evidence that B is true.

civil law (p. 387) The body of law regarding relations between people; cases may include disputes about contracts, suits for damages in injury, divorce, and so on.

civil society (p. 64) That part of society that is organized and active, but neither controlled by the government nor focused on private concerns such as the family or economic activity. In other words, the part of society that is publicly engaged but not controlled by the government. It is the natural counterweight to government in the affairs of the state.

classes (p. 32) In Marx's theory of socialism, groups of people who share the same relationship to the means of production and who therefore develop a distinctive view of themselves and of the world. In his theory, classes were the drivers of social and political change.

coalition (p. 321) A tactical combination of varied groups, constructed so that the groups will in combination be large enough to command power that they can then share among themselves. Frequently applied to parliamentary government, in which 50 percent of the votes in parliament are required to form a cabinet but in which it may be necessary to combine two or more parties to amass 50 percent of the votes.

code law (p. 381) A legal system emphasizing a relative subordination of the judiciary to the rest of the government. Legal interpretation consists primarily of reading and applying codes of legal statute passed by the parliament, rather than looking to the precedent of prior court decisions. Used in various forms in most parts of the world except Britain and its former colonies.

codetermination (p. 123) German system by which corporations are legally required to include workers' representatives on their boards of directors.

committees (legislative) (p. 327) Small group of legislators whose task (usually) is to review carefully a proposed piece of legislation and recommend to the full legislature what action should be taken on it. In many legislatures, bills may be amended by the committee or killed in entirety. Committees may also perform other tasks, such as investigating an area of possible legislation.

communism (p. 34) The more militant branch of socialism. Communists argue that the only way to build a socialist state is by revolution. Therefore, they are sometimes less interested in electoral activity than the democratic socialists. After the 1920s, communists acknowledged the leadership of the Soviet Union in the formulation of their goals and strategies. See also *socialism; democratic socialism.*

"consensus" parliamentarism (p. 329) Parliamentary government in which the adversarial relationship between the cabinet and the opposition parties is reduced through a variety of power-sharing devices, such as allotting control of committees to parties proportionally to their strength, whether or not they are part of the cabinet coalition.

conservatism (p. 27) An ideology positing that the most important goal of politics is to create stable communities based on a hierarchy of power in which leaders and followers have reciprocal responsibilities and obligations. Unlike liberalism, conservatism is not suspicious of power and does not seek to limit the power of the state. Rather, the point of conservatism is that power should be in the hands of a traditional class of rulers. See also *American conservatism*.

constitution (p. 209)   A set of rules by which power is distributed in a political group, such as the state. This usually consists in part of a formal set of rules, but it always contains as well various informal mechanisms, traditions, and understandings by which power is assigned to people.

constitutional law (p. 388)   The body of law regarding the nature of the political process, and whether laws and governmental actions are consistent with the constitution.

constitutional monarch (p. 320; *contrast monarchy*)   A monarch, that is, one who acquires the position of head of state by inheritance, holds it for life, and passes it along to heirs—but with the difference that a *constitutional* monarch serves as head of state in a parliamentary system, and thus serves a symbolic role, not participating in the making of political decisions.

constitutional review (p. 354)   A system under which a judicial or quasi-judicial part of the government can annul acts of other parts of the government if, in its judgment, those acts violate the constitution of the state.

constitutionalism (p. 223)   The doctrine that states' constitutions should be designed fairly, not to give undue advantage to any particular group, and that the government should then be faithful to that constitution. In this way, individuals are protected against arbitrary governmental action.

consulates (p. 411; *contrast ambassador*)   Offices maintained by a state in major cities of another state to deal with individuals' problems regarding trade, immigration, travel, and so forth.

corruption (p. 114)   Improperly performing one's public tasks to receive personal benefits (bribes, etc.).

coup (p. 163)   The forceful deposition of a government by all or a portion of the armed forces and installation of a new military government.

courts (p. 386)   Governmental institutions charged with interpreting the law.

criminal law (p. 387)   The body of law involving charges that persons have disobeyed a law prescribing proper conduct. In criminal law the state brings the case, against an individual defendant who is charged with a crime.

crisis transitions (p. 157)   Transitions from an autocratic to a democratic system that take place in the context of an economic crisis.

D

democracy (p. 149)   A state in which qualified citizens vote at regular intervals to choose, among alternative candidates, the people who will be in charge of setting the state's policies.

democratic peace (p. 415)   The observation that democracies have never, or hardly ever, waged war with other democracies.

democratic socialism (p. 34)   The branch of socialism that supports electoral democracy and holds that the proper way for workers to control society is to win elections. Democratic socialists are also more moderate than communists in the goals they set, being more willing to settle for piecemeal progress rather than holding out for a complete remaking of society. See also *socialism; communism*.

diplomacy (p. 411)   The conduct of relations between states and other global actors other than by war.

dominant-party system (p. 267; *contrast one-party system*)   A political party system in which various parties are allowed to function openly and with reasonable effectiveness but in which a single party nonetheless holds power all the time.

due process (p. 135)   An expectation that certain procedures must always be followed in making a policy and that if they were not, the policy should be void.

E

economic sanctions (p. 412)   A form of nonmilitary coercion in which a state or group of states deliberately withholds normal economic relations with another state to punish it.

effective policy (p. 138)   An effective policy is one that gives the state the greatest benefits at the least cost.

electoral system (p. 235)   A set of rules by which the outcomes of an election (a set of officers elected or whatever) is determined from the distribution of votes cast by the electorate.

empirical theory (p. 15)   A theory describing how things work in the world we observe.

European Union (p. 70)   An organization of twenty-seven Western European states that have set up a rather weak common government and have coordinated many of their economic policies.

externality (p. 144)   A situation in which there are social costs or benefits beyond the individual costs and benefits involved in a transaction.

F

failed state (p. 61)   A geographic entity with no effective central state apparatus, but controlled by various warlords and gangs in loose and fluid relationships with one another.

falsifiability (p. 427)   A property of statements, such that they are in principle capable of being true or false. A statement that is falsifiable is the opposite of a tautology.

fascism (p. 35)   A political movement that appeared in many countries in the 1920s and 1930s. Fascism stressed militaristic pageantry and a strident nationalism as ways of binding the people to a single dramatic dictator. Franco, Mussolini, and Hitler were fascist dictators.

federal state (p. 218)   A state in which the constitution grants to regional governments a legal monopoly over certain political decisions, such as educational policy. Therefore, two different governments will control the same group of people, but with regard to different political questions.

fiduciary role (p. 406)   A role in which one acts as an agent on behalf of someone else's interests. This role often places the agent in problematic positions.

G

global politics (p. 395; *contrast international politics*)   Politics conducted above the level of a state. It is essentially the same thing as international politics but includes the connotation that not only states but also international organizations and nongovernmental organizations are actors in the process.

government (p. 62)   The group of people within the state who have the ultimate authority to act on behalf of the state.

gross domestic product, or GDP (p. 81)   The total value of all goods and services exchanged in a society; that is, the sum of such things as the value of all food sold, the value of all mechanics' work on automobiles, the value of all educational activity, and so on. The higher the GDP, the greater the total amount of economic activity in the society. Per capita GDP divides GDP by the population to measure how economically well-off the average person is.

H

habeas corpus (p. 380)   The right not to be held indefinitely by the police without being formally charged with a crime.

head of state (p. 320)   The executive figure in any state who is the symbolic focus of the state, and represents the state personally. In a presidential system, the head of state also is the leader of political decision making in the state. In a parliamentary system, the two functions are separated, and filled by two different people.

hierarchical command structure (p. 368)   An organization in which there is a single, branching path of power by which a person at the top of the structure issues a command to a set of people at the second tier, each of those in turn passes the command on to a set of people in the next tier, and so on. No commands can move up the structure, and no commands can move laterally across a tier. Bureaucracies are organized hierarchically.

higher civil service (p. 374)   Specialized and executive members of the public administration, corresponding to professionals and managers in the private sector.

hybrid presidential government (p. 353)   A system in which a president with more than ceremonial power coexists with a premier and cabinet who are responsible to a parliament. Executive decision making is shared in some way between the two executives, often with the president having the greater power in defense and foreign policy, while the premier and cabinet have greater power in domestic policies, but the relationship between the two can be quite variable.

I

identity group (p. 38)   A group of people who share an identity that they (and others) think defines them and sets them apart from others.

ideology (p. 20)   A set of ideas that are related and that modify one another; that is, an organized set of ideas about something.

implicit power (p. 5)   Power in which A does what B desires not because of anything B says or does but because (1) A senses that B wants something done and (2) for any of a variety of reasons, A wishes to do what B wants done.

import-substitution industrialization (p. 101) A policy especially followed by many states of the Third World in the 1960s and 1970s whereby the states erected high tariff barriers against imports, hoping to build their domestic industries.

incentive compatibility (p. 213) A situation in which those who make decisions on behalf of society benefit personally when their decisions benefit society. When incentive compatibility is present, society does not need to depend on nobility of character in its officials; it can depend on a more reliable force—their concern for their own self-interest.

inflation (p. 105) A situation in which most prices are rising at the same time and the value of the currency is therefore declining in real terms.

institutional interest group (p. 286) A group that is primarily set up for some purpose other than political activity but becomes politically active to defend its interests in the policy decisions of the state.

interest group (p. 278) An organized group of citizens that has as one of its goals ensuring that the state follows certain policies.

intergovernmental international organization, or IGO (p. 398) An organization set up by a group of states to implement an agreement among the states or to regulate some aspect of their relations.

International Court of Justice (p. 405) The court that hears cases at law between states. It has no power to enforce its ruling.

International Criminal Court (p. 403) An international court that can try any individuals, including heads of state and other officials, for a broad range of crimes, including genocide, "crimes against humanity," war crimes, and the crime of aggression. It is based in the Netherlands.

international politics (p. 395) Politics conducted among states rather than within a single state.

interpretive political scientists (p. 15) Political scientists who emphasize historical, anthropological, and (sometimes) legal methods, and the complex whole that is being studied.

J

justice (p. 132) A situation in which people are treated as they deserve. See *procedural justice* and *substantive justice.*

L

law (p. 379) A collection of rules laid down by the government, binding all members of the state, including members of the government itself. The law includes both criminal law and civil law.

legal systems (p. 379) General, organized sets of legal principles.

legitimacy (p. 183) A belief on the part of large numbers of people in a state that the existing governmental structure and/or the particular persons in office should appropriately wield authority.

liberalism (p. 25) An ideology positing that the most important goal of politics is to help individuals develop their capacities to the fullest. To this end, people should be regulated and aided by governments as little as possible, so that they will learn from the experience of being responsible for their own decisions. Liberalism may be summarized by the slogan, "That government is best which governs least." See also *American liberalism.*

M

manifest power (p. 5) Power based on an observable action by A that causes B to do what A wants.

market mechanism (p. 140) A mechanism whereby social choice results from choices of all members of the collectivity rather than from a decision made by the central governing unit.

military government (p. 163) An autocracy in which military officers rule, perhaps with the help of appointed civilians, but without any sort of auxiliary structure such as a political party.

minority cabinet (p. 330) A cabinet based on a coalition controlling less than a majority of votes in the parliament. It generally governs through an agreement with one or more other parties, which are not part of the cabinet coalition, that they will not vote for motions of no confidence against the cabinet.

mobilization (p. 258) The systematic stimulation of concerted effort by large numbers of people, as in elections or demonstrations. This term is used especially in reference to such stimulation conducted on its own behalf by the government.

monarchy (p. 169) A state in which the power to rule is inherited through descent in a family.

multiparty system (p. 270)   A democratic system in which there are more than two major parties.

N

nation (p. 55)   A large group of people who are bound together and recognize a similarity among themselves because of a common culture; in particular, a common language seems important in creating nationhood. Nations often but not always coincide with the political boundaries of states. The Kurdish language and culture is spread across parts of Turkey, Iraq, and Iran; Irish nationalists and British nationalists are mixed together in Northern Ireland, where they are at each other's throats. There are many similar examples of mismatches between national "boundaries" and the boundaries of states. Such mismatches are a potent source of political turmoil.

nation-state (p. 61)   A term often used to signify today's states; it takes cognizance of the fact that states in the modern era try to develop a sense of nation to coincide with the boundaries of the state, so that emotions of nationalism will lodge on the state as well.

nationalism (p. 59)   Passionate identification with a nation on the part of its citizens.

nationalization of industry (p. 77)   The acquisition of an industrial operation by the government, which then operates it directly as part of the governmental administration.

neocorporatism (p. 294)   A system of government and interest groups in which all interests are organized but—instead of responding to groups' pressures—the government actively involves the groups themselves in the job of governing. This active governmental role distinguishes neocorporatism from pluralism.

neoliberalism (p. 37)   An ideology emphasizing the economic side of liberalism—free markets, free trade, and privatization of industries. The emphasis in neoliberalism, in contrast with liberalism, is more on economic efficiency and economic growth than on the virtues for individuals of being responsible for their own decisions.

nongovernmental international organization, or NGO (p. 398)   A cross-state organization that is not affiliated with or sponsored by governments.

normative theory (p. 16)   A theory that involves making a judgment about the world, not describing how it works.

O

ombudsman (p. 370)   A government official whose primary duty is to seek out citizens' complaints of abuse by public administrators and to negotiate changes in the offending practices.

one-party state (p. 168)   A state in which the government is based on, and in turn supports, a single political party. No other party is allowed to function in other than a token way.

one-party system (p. 266; *contrast* dominant-party system)   A political system in which only a single political party is allowed to be active.

opportunity structure (p. 306)   Aspects of the political situation that offer a social movement (or for that matter, any political group or entrepreneur) advantages and openings. Examples could be the presence of potential allies, the absence of any other political movement in a niche, a breakdown of confidence in an incumbent leader, and so on.

P

pacts (p. 155)   In general, agreements; specifically, with regard to democratization, agreements between the leaders of the new democracy and supporters of the older authoritarian system that soften the change for the latter and help them to accept the democracy.

paradox of voting (p. 245)   The paradox that no one should vote if their only reason for voting is that they wish to help their favored candidate win. The odds that the rest of the voters will produce a tie are incredibly small, and that is the only circumstance in which the person's vote will make any difference to the candidate.

parliamentary government (p. 318)   A democracy in which the executive and legislative functions are merged in one institution, the parliament. The parliament is the state's supreme legislature, but it also appoints a committee (the cabinet) to serve as the political executive for the state.

party identification (pp. 247 and 259)   A personal identification with a political party; not just agreement with its policies or candidates of the moment but an enduring identification with the party itself.

party system (p. 266)   The set of all parties in a state. Political scientists distinguish among such systems primarily by the number and relative size of the parties: for example, two-party systems, multiparty systems, dominant party systems.

per capita GDP; *see also* **PPP per capita GDP (p. 81)**   GDP, that is, gross domestic product, is the sum of all economic transactions in a state. We divide this by the population to obtain per capita GDP, the average amount of economic transactions per person, which is a measure of the average prosperity of the population.

pluralism (p. 293)   A system of government and interest groups in which all interests organize and compete freely, with no one group dominating, and in which the government is open to pressure from the groups so that policy is largely the outcome of groups' competing pressures.

political culture (p. 193)   The attitudes and beliefs held communally by a people, forming the basis for their political behavior.

political economy (p. 120)   A subfield of political science that focuses on ways the state and the economy interact. Political economy is concerned with how the economy affects the state (for example, effects of the economy on elections) and how the state affects the economy (for example, whether independent central banks reduce inflation).

political party (p. 255)   A group of officials or would-be officials who are linked with a sizable group of citizens into an organization; a chief object of this organization is to ensure that its officials attain power or are maintained in power.

political psychology (p. 122)   A subfield of political science that focuses on how individuals, both among political elites and ordinary citizens, make their choices in political decisions. Political psychology draws heavily on the field of psychology for insights and theory.

political science (p. 14)   The academic field that takes as its sole and general task the analysis of politics, especially the politics of the state.

political socialization (p. 198)   The process of learning the facts, assumptions, and attitudes we use in responding to politics. Political socialization occurs most rapidly in childhood and youth but continues throughout life.

politics (p. 1)   The making of common decisions for a group of people through the exercise of power by some members of the group over other members.

***post hoc* explanation (p. 433)**   An explanation tailored to the particular set of events to be explained. (*Post hoc* means "after this.") A danger in this is that mere coincidences may be treated as general relationships in the explanation.

power (p. 4)   The ability of one person to cause another to do what the first wishes, by whatever means. See also *implicit power* and *manifest power.*

PPP per capita GDP; *see also* **per capita GDP (p. 81)**   Straight per capita GDP, expressed in dollars, can be misleading because it depends not only on how much economic activity there has been in the state, but also on the exchange rate between the state's currency and the dollar. PPP per capita GDP corrects for this, putting the per capita GDPs of all states into a comparable unit.

prefect (p. 375)   A civil servant in the central government who oversees local and regional governments and bureaucracies, including elected ones. The prefect in some states has the right to annul acts of local or regional governments, or even to remove them. The office of prefect is a tool for central control of local and regional governments.

presidential government (p. 341)   A democratic system in which the legislature and executive exist independently and are elected independently of each other. The president takes a leading role in forming policy but must have the consent of the legislature if that policy is to be enacted. A presidential system divides power, whereas a parliamentary system unifies it.

privatization (p. 78)   Selling to the public or by some other means transforming to private ownership economic enterprises that were previously owned and managed by the state.

procedural justice (p. 134)   A concept of justice less concerned with fairness of distribution to people than with the procedures by which decisions are reached about them.

progressive taxation (p. 109)   A system of taxes that takes a greater proportion of a person's income if the income is high than if the income is low.

promotional interest group (p. 287)   The "typical" interest group—an organized group of citizens, one of whose primary purposes is to affect the policies of the state.

proportional representation electoral system, or PR (p. 235)   An electoral system in which parties receive a number of seats in the legislature roughly proportional to the number of votes that were cast for them among the electorate.

public administration (p. 363)   The set of people who are not involved directly in the making of major political decisions but who construct and implement the policies that carry out those decisions. Examples are police officers, public health nurses, IRS agents, and public university presidents.

public good (p. 53; *see also* p. 143) Something that benefits all members of the collectivity and that no one can be prevented from using. The basic problem of public goods is that they can allow recipients to be *free riders,* which makes it difficult to accomplish them by voluntary action.

Q

question time (p. 323) A device, originating in the British House of Commons and since imitated in many parliaments, by which cabinet members appear regularly in the parliament to answer questions from members about the administration of their offices. These questions and answers often spark hot debate.

R

rational choice models of politics (p. 121) Models of politics that are based on a core assumption that all who are involved act "rationally"; that is, they make their decisions in order to further certain specific goals. A rational choice model posits what those goals are and then proceeds by deductive logic to demonstrate what political choices a person should make if those are her or his goals.

referendum (pp. 234 and 240) An election in which voters choose directly whether a particular proposal will become law; this contrasts with other kinds of elections in which voters choose among various candidates for a political office.

regime (p. 149) The general form of government of a state, including its constitution and rules of government. A regime generally continues beyond the terms of individual officeholders. A state, in turn, is in principle more enduring than a regime; that is, a state can alter the form of its regime.

regime theory (p. 417) A theory of international relations emphasizing the importance of "regimes," or sets of principles and values that transcend state boundaries and regulate in an informal way areas of policy such as trade, development of the polar regions, and so on.

regional integration (p. 67) A partial merging of the political and economic structures of several states in the same region of the world. The most successful attempt at regional integration to date has been the formation of the European Union.

regressive taxation (p. 109) A system of taxes that takes a greater proportion of a person's income if the income is low than if the income is high.

regulation (p. 141) Direct laying down of rules by the government as to how people may conduct their affairs. This is distinguished from *indirect* governmental direction of choices, as when a government taxes liquor heavily to discourage its use but does not actually make its use illegal. The latter would constitute regulation.

rent (p. 100) *Not* the charge you pay to live in an apartment. In its specialized usage in political economy, *rents* are transfers of money that do not relate to production. Though rents can be good and useful (Social Security is a rent, for instance), they are troubling because (a) many rents are not good and useful (pork barrel projects, for instance), and (b) rents tend to pull money away from investment.

representative bureaucracy (p. 373) The idea that members of the public administration should be similar to the groups they serve in such characteristics as class, race, and gender, so that they will be able to serve them better.

rule of law (p. 223) An assurance that actions of the government are based on general principles that are applied equally to all people. Under the rule of law, governmental actions are not arbitrary, and are not based on personal connections or pay-offs.

S

sectoral interest group (p. 286) A group representing a section of the economy. Examples are trade unions, professional associations, corporations, and trade associations.

selective incentive (p. 284) Benefits that can be given to some people, and denied to others. An organization may offer its members selective incentives in addition to the central purposes of the organization, in order to avoid the problem of free riders. A trade union, for example, may offer its members such added benefits as low-cost package vacations.

Sharia (p. 384) Islamic law, based on a set of rules for moral conduct developed over the first few centuries after the death of Muhammad.

single-member-district plurality electoral system, or SMDP (p. 235) An electoral system in which the state is divided into geographic subdivisions, each subdivision is represented by a single member in the legislature, and the candidate who attains a plurality of votes in that subdivision is the one who fills the seat.

social capital (p. 192)   The interwoven network of associational activities (clubs, churches, civic associations, neighborhoods, etc.) through which people are involved in their communities and build a reservoir of trust and positive expectations about collective action.

social movement (pp. 303–304)   A loosely organized group of people who ordinarily have little power but challenge the state power—usually through disruption and sometimes violently. The object of a social movement is usually an emotional issue, which may range from a very local question such as the location of a new highway all the way up to the constitution or identity of the state.

socialism (p. 32)   An ideology positing that society consists of classes (groups of people similarly placed economically) constantly in conflict. To create a just society in which people are equal, the working class should take over the state and direct all industries.

sovereignty (p. 55)   The legal capacity of a geographic unit to maintain ultimate responsibility for the conduct of its own affairs.

state (pp. 14 and 55)   The basic unit by which people are organized politically; often casually called "country" or "nation." States are militarily independent of each other and are guided by governments that typically regulate the economy, set the laws of the state, and so on. States in the twentieth century tended to be relatively large territories with stable boundaries whose populations are bound together by intimate political ties. In marginal cases such as the European Union, it can be a bit tricky to say exactly whether a unit is or is not a "state." In the United States, *state* also has a second meaning, referring to one of the fifty regional divisions (California, Alaska, Florida, Minnesota, etc.) into which the United States is divided.

state-building (p. 61)   The process of building or reconstructing a state. Because a state is a complex of rules, institutions, and expectations about how collective actions will be performed, state-building is complicated and difficult.

substantive justice (p. 134)   A concept of justice that emphasizes people receiving what they need and deserve, whether on the basis of the contributions they make to common efforts, of their need for the reward, or of at least approximate equality of treatment.

T

tautology (p. 427)   A statement that is logically true and thus cannot be shown false by an examination of evidence. Example: "All brunettes have dark hair."

terrorism (p. 416)   The use of violent acts against civilians in order to accomplish political goals.

theocracy (p. 169)   A state ruled by a set of religious leaders.

theory (p. 15)   A statement linking specific instances to broader principles.

trivial explanation (p. 429)   An explanation that is obvious to the audience and therefore not interesting to them. Example: "Why does John eat so much?" "Because he's hungry."

two-party system (p. 269)   A democratic system in which two parties regularly receive 90 percent or more of votes cast but in which it is rare for either of them to receive more than 55 or 60 percent of the votes. These two parties will replace each other in office fairly frequently.

U

unitary state (p. 218)   A state in which no other governmental body but the central government has any areas of policy that are exclusively under its control. In a unitary state, local and regional governments may potentially be overruled by the central government in any political decision they make.

United Nations (pp. 67 and 421)   An organization of almost all the world's states. The UN provides a forum at which complaints can be aired; it has often helped to cool off conflicts between states; and its specialized committees seek to improve world standards of health, education, and so on.

INDEX

Abacha, General Sani, 69, 165
Abe, Shinzo, 300
Aberbach, Joel D., 373, 377
abortion, 23–24, 291n
Abraham, Henry J. 361, 393
Abramson, Paul R., 252
Abubakar, Atiku, 252
Acre, rubber trappers of, 311–314
action, 145
    arbitrary, 366–367
    collective, 285, 307
    political, 10, 189–190
Adasiewicz, Christopher, 252
Adler, Matthew D., 148
advertisements, public service, 290
administrative courts, 384
AFL-CIO, 302
Africa, 55, 93–94. *See also* apartheid; Nigeria; Rwanda
    bureaucratic culture in, 375–376
    South, 269, 400, 413
African National Congress Party, 269
age, voting and, 249
agents of socialization, 198-200
Ahmadinejad, Mahmoud, 177
AIDS, 93–94, 403–404
al Quaeda, 196–197, 307, 309, 415–416
Aldrich, John H., 252, 275
Alemán, Miguel, 360
Alesina, Alberto, 129
Alexander, Amanda, 316
Alexander, Herbert, 266
Allegretti, Mary, 314
Almond, Gabriel, 18, 178, 191n, 206, 242
Alstott, Anne L., 94
Alt, James, 129
Alter, Karen J., 393
Alvarez, Michael E., 171–172
Amazon, 313
Ambanis, Nicholas, 424
ambassadors, 411
Ambler, Eric, 60-61
amendments, 210, 212
American conservatism, 22–24
American court system, 135n
American Enterprise Institute, 95

American Indian Iroquois Confederation, 208
American Journal of Political Science, 80
American liberalism, 22–24
American political Science Association, 18
American Revolution, 49
Americans for Tax Reform, 309–310
Amin, Idi, 135
Amnesty International, 180
analytic political philosophy, 42
Anderson, Benedict, 60
Anderson, Charles, 131n
Anderson, Perry, 51n
Anderson, Sarah, 102n
Anglin, Douglas, 164
Anglo-saxon case law, 380-381
Anheier, Helmut K., 193n
Animal Farm (Orwell), 268
Annan, Kofi, 423
Annual Review of political Science, 18
apartheid, 269, 400
appeals courts, 358
Appleby, R. Scott, 44
Appleton, Andrew, 297n
apprenticeships, in Germany, 123
APSA Task Force on Inequality and American
    Democracy, 129
Aquinas, St. Thomas, 42–43
arbitrary criminal investigation, 135n
arbitrary policies, 134–136, 366-367
Archambault, Edith, 193n
Arendt, Hannah, 44
Arian, Alan, 267n
Aristotle, 41
Armstrong, Elizabeth, 316
Atlanta, 6–7
Augustine, Saint, 42
Austin, Reginald, 266n
authoritarian democracy, 150, 227
authority, 5, 181–182, 220
    in democracy, 187
    in international politics, 404–406
    legitimacy and, 183
    market mechanisms v. governmental, 140–145
    sovereignty v., 182
    in West Germany, 201–203

1